The
Netherlands

Friesland
(Fryslân)
p207

Northeastern
Netherlands
p225

Haarlem &
North Holland
p111

Amsterdam ✪
p42

Central
Netherlands
p239

Utrecht
p143

Rotterdam &
South Holland
p155

Maastricht &
Southeastern Netherlands
p260

Nicola Williams, Abigail Blasi, Mark Elliott,
Catherine Le Nevez, Virginia Maxwell

Contents

SARAH COGHILL/LONELY PLANET ©

NOORDERMARKT, AMSTERDAM P107

PXL.STORE/SHUTTERSTOCK ©

GROTE KERK VAN ST BAVO, HAARLEM P113

Contents

UNDERSTAND

SURVIVAL GUIDE

COVID-19

We have re-checked every business in this book before publication to ensure that it is still open after the COVID-19 outbreak. However, the economic and social impacts of COVID-19 will continue to be felt long after the outbreak has been contained, and many businesses, services and events referenced in this guide may experience ongoing restrictions. Some businesses may be temporarily closed, have changed their opening hours and services, or require bookings; some unfortunately could have closed permanently. We suggest you check with venues before visiting for the latest information.

SPECIAL FEATURES

Right: Cycling in The Netherlands in autumn (p27).

DENNIS VAN DE WATER/SHUTTERSTOCK ©

WELCOME TO THE

Netherlands

Having family here, the Netherlands has always been a natural port of call for me. Living the high life in Amsterdam, gorging on sand dunes and Van Gogh art in the Hoge Veluwe National Park and two-wheel island-hopping in Friesland are among my highlights. But it's the Dutch life attitude I love most. Fusing an old-fashioned 'great outdoors' simplicity with an insatiable desire to design and innovate for the good of the land, this country has its finger right on the 'live well' pulse.

By Nicola Williams, Writer
For more about our writers, see p352.

The Netherlands

Texel
Artisan producers and outdoor activities abound (p132)

Amsterdam
Explore Golden Age canals (p42)

NORTH
SEA

FRISIAN ISLANDS

East Frisian
Islands

Schiermonnikoog
National Park

NOORD
HOLLAND

FRIESLAND

GRONINGEN

DRENTHE

FLEVOLAND

OVERIJSSEL

Weerribben-
Wieden National
Park

Oostvaardersplassen
Nature Reserve

Wad+denzee

IJsselmeer

Ems

53° N

4° E
5° E
6° E

N 0   50 km
   0   25 miles

Delft
Vermeer's exquisite
home town (p189)

Hoge Veluwe National Park
Discover masterpieces
of nature and art (p258)

Rotterdam
A city-sized gallery
of architecture (p157)

Maastricht
Delve into Roman
history (p261)

GERMANY

BELGIUM

BRUSSELS

GELDERLAND

UTRECHT

NOORD BRABANT

LIMBURG

HOLLAND

ZEELAND

ELEVATION

1500m
1000m
500m
0

Steinfurt
Coesfeld
Enschede
Alhaus
Winterswijk
Groenlo
Aalten
Doetinchem
Zutphen
Apeldoorn
Arnhem
Nijmegen
Emmerich
Kleve
Goch
Dorsten
Gelsenkirchen
Essen
Wuppertal
Solingen
Leverkusen
Cologne
Troisdorf
Wesel
Moers
Duisburg
Düsseldorf
Krefeld
Mönchengladbach
Gelsenkirchen
Düren
Jülich
Geilenkirchen
Aachen
Heerlen
Maastricht
Eupen
Verviers
Liège
Tongeren
Bilzen
Genk
Sittard
Roermond
Maaseik
Weert
Venlo
Venray
Helmond
Cuijk
Oss
's-Hertogenbosch
Eindhoven
Zaltbommel
Tiel
Geldermalsen
Leerdam
Gorinchem
Heusden
Tilburg
Breda
Zundert
Hoogstraten
Turnhout
Mol
Geel
Herentals
Lier
Mechelen
Antwerp
Bergen op Zoom
Roosendaal
Willemstad
Dordrecht
Spijkenisse
Vlaardingen
Delft
Rotterdam
Gouda
Woerden
Utrecht
Zeist
Veenendaal
Ede
Wageningen
Barneveld
Amersfoort
Hilversum
Leiden
Zoetermeer
Den Haag
(The Hague)
Katwijk aan Zee
Hoek van Holland
Oude Tonge
Goes
Kruiningen
Terneuzen
IJzendijke
Vlissingen
Middelburg
Domburg
Renesse
Zierikzee
Schouwen-Duiveland
Noord-Beveland
Zuid-Beveland
Zeebrugge
Bruges
Eeklo
Ghent
Deinze
Oudenaarde
Kortrijk
Roubaix
Mouscron
Tournai
Leuze
Ath
Ronse
Geraardsbergen
Ninove
Aalst
Dendermonde
Lokeren
St-Niklaas
Heist
Sint-Truiden
Tienen
Hannut
Gembloux
Wavre
Nivelles
Halle
Soignies
Leopoldsburg
Bree
Neerpelt
Margraten

The Netherlands' Top Experiences

1 CANAL NAVIGATIONS

Canals ribbon this low-lying land and its magnificent cities such as Haarlem and Leiden and lesser-known gems like Enkhuizen and Hoorn glimmer with webs of waterways that form their lifeblood. Strolling along canal banks and picturesque bridges throughout the day or night provides an ever-changing backdrop. For a more intimate perspective, get out on the water aboard a canal cruise or be your own captain by hiring a rental boat.

Amsterdam

The Dutch capital has more canals than Venice. Amsterdam made its fortune in maritime trade, and the Canal Ring that makes up the city centre was constructed during the city's Golden Age, along with narrow, gabled canal houses tilting over the water. Today it's easy to see why Unesco named the waterways a World Heritage site. p42

Right: Tour boats, Amsterdam

Delft

A jewel-box of medieval and Golden Age architecture and artistic treasures (it's Vermeer's home town and renowned for its delicate blue-and-white pottery), Delft's diminutive streets are woven by exquisite canals. p189

Above: Delft cityscape

Left: Haarlem canal (p113)

Utrecht City

In the engaging city of Utrecht, a spool of tree-shaded canals uniquely have two levels, with former medieval warehouses now housing drinking, dining and other venues that have terrace walkways extending to the water's edge. p144

Above: Traditional houses on the Oudegracht (Old Canal), Utrecht

2 PEDAL POWER

The Netherlands is one of the most bicycle-friendly nations on earth. Not only is the landscape as flat as a classic Dutch pancake but thousands of kilometres of dedicated lanes and paths link virtually every part of the country, allowing you to cycle between enchanting villages, passing cow-filled pastures, creaking traditional windmills and tulips blooming in springtime. Rental outlets are ubiquitous: grab a bike, ring your bell and go.

Waterland

An ideal day trip from Amsterdam, Waterland, as its name suggests, is a watery wonderland that draws together classic Dutch scenery: dykes, canals and lots of emerald-green fields, and is most idyllically explored on two wheels. p119

Below: Monnickendam, Waterland

Nijmegen

Skirt the protected banks of the Waal river from Nijmegen to the German border, and don't miss a visit to the Nationaal Fietsmuseum Velorama, Nijmegen's fascinating collection of vintage bicycles from the golden age of human-powered transport. p252

Above left: Bicycle at the National Fietsmuseum Velorama, Nijmegen.

Scheveningen

Not far from the Netherlands' stately seat of government and third-largest city, Den Haag (known in English as The Hague), at Scheveningen you can leave the crowds behind and ride north or south along the coast past dunes and invigorating wide, windswept beaches. p186

Above right: Cycling among the dunes, Scheveningen.

PLAN YOUR TRIP

3 ISLAND ESCAPES

With so much water around, as well as famously reclaimed land, at times much of the country feels like an island. But there are some proper ones too, which are laced with a mesmerising kaleidoscope of gold-sand beaches, windswept dunes, forest and bird-rich marshland. Hop aboard a ferry (or head along a causeway) and discover a side to the Netherlands that lies beyond many visitors' radars.

Frisian Islands

The Frisian Islands form a natural barrier to the North Sea. The smallest island, Schiermonnikoog, is popular for wadlopen (mudflat walking), while the least visited, Vlieland, is almost entirely natural. p217

Below: Red lighthouse of Schiermonnikoog (p223), Frisian Islands

Texel

Fringed by white-sand beaches, Texel has verdant fields roamed by sheep and cows, with sublime produce including cheese, chocolate and ice cream. p132

Above: Church of Den Hoorn, Texel

Marken

An island fishing port in the Zuiderzee, until 1957, the tiny, traditional village of Marken, while now linked by a causeway, seems as if it's suspended in time. p120

Right: Colourful buildings, Markan.

4 BRUIN CAFÉ CULTURE

KEVIN GEORGE/500PX ©

MYSTOCKVIDEO/SHUTTERSTOCK ©

NATALIA PAKLINA/SHUTTERSTOCK ©

Better experienced than defined, the term *gezelligheid* describes the uniquely Dutch state of conviviality, cosiness, warmth and sense of togetherness. It's a hallmark of the country's famous *bruin cafés* (brown cafes), so named for their aged, tobacco-stained walls from centuries past. These snug, history-steeped pubs are filled with flickering candles and good cheer. Throughout the Netherlands, you'll be quickly drawn into their welcoming atmosphere.

Capital Charm

Amsterdam alone claims around one thousand bruin cafés. Locally loved 't Smalle, in a former jenever (Dutch gin) distillery, lets you dock your boat by its canal-side stone terrace. p99

Above: 't Smalle, Amsterdam

Maastricht Atmosphere

On a cobbled central square in the lively student city of Maastricht, wood-panelled beauty In Den Ouden Vogelstruys pours frothy beers in an atmospheric building dating back to 1730. p267

Delftshaven Delight

Rotterdam's Golden Age remnant, the historic quarter of Deflsthaven, is home to some beautiful bruin cafés such as De Oude Sluis, with a view of Delftshaven's windmill. p175

5 **MASTERFUL ART**

Rembrandt, Vermeer, Hals, Steen, Van Gogh, MC Escher, Mondrian... some of the world's most revered artists hail from the Netherlands, and their exceptional works fill museums and galleries around the country. Alongside the most high-profile art repositories, brimming with masterpieces, there are countless smaller venues to discover, including historic premises where the creators themselves lived and/or worked.

Mauritshuis

Den Haag's Mauritshuis unfurls a who's who of Dutch and Flemish masters: Vermeer's *Girl with a Pearl Earring* and Fabritius' *The Goldfinch* are highlights. Den Haag's Escher in Het Paleis displays Escher's logic-defying creations in a former palace. p181

Above left: Mauritshuis, Den Haag.

Museum De Lakenhal

In a 17th-century cloth guildhall, Leiden's premier museum, the Museum De Lakenhal, exhibits works by luminaries including Rembrandt, who was born in this resplendent city. p195

Top: Museum De Lakenhal

Rijksmuseum

Golden Age riches such as Rembrandt's colossus *The Night Watch* take pride of place at Amsterdam's mighty Rijksmuseum. Its neighbours are the Van Gogh Museum and the Stedelijk Museum, showing Mondrian and De Kooning among its modern stock. p70

Above: *The Night Watch*, Rijksmuseum

6 SAY CHEESE!

Dutch *kaas* (cheese) comes in a vast range of styles and flavours: some finely aged, crumbly and crystallised, others lighter, creamier or laced with aromatic caraway seeds or mustard. Shops across the country stock huge waxy wheels of cheese (tastings are often available), and you can visit towns that inspire notions of cheese more immediately than the photogenic locales that spawned them.

OLEG1824/SHUTTERSTOCK ©

MARC VENEMA/SHUTTERSTOCK ©

Alkmaar

Step back in time at this spectacle of a historic cheese market, which takes place in summer on the main square of Alkmaar, a short distance from Amsterdam. p123

Top: Alkmaar's cheese market

Edam

With drawbridges and cobbled streets, pretty-as-a-picture Edam has a seasonal cheese market that sees farmers transport their prized product by canal boat. p122

Above left: Cheese displayed in Edam.

Gouda

Famed for its cheese produced in the surrounding countryside and traded at its traditional market, Gouda's attractions include a cheese museum. p178

Above right: Wheels of cheese, Gouda.

7 INSPIRED DESIGN

ROCKERSTOOKER/SHUTTERSTOCK ©

BORIS STROUJKO/SHUTTERSTOCK ©

TRAVELLIFESTYLE/SHUTTERSTOCK ©

Eindhoven

Home to electronics pioneer Philips' illuminating museum and a prestigious factory-housed architecture and design institute, the post-industrial city of Eindhoven hosts Dutch Design Week and a dazzling light art festival. p274

Top left: Design Week (p22), Eindhoven.

Rotterdam

Rotterdam's reconstruction after WWII transformed the Netherlands' second-largest city into a veritable open-air gallery of modern and contemporary architecture, featuring landmarks like crazily angled cube houses and inverted-U-shaped Markthal, designed by local firm MVRDV. p157

Left: The Markthal (p166).

Amsterdam

Numerous hybrid spaces across Amsterdam showcase Dutch design. A perfect place to start browsing is Droog, part gallery, part creative hub and part boutique selling one-of-a-kind items. p42

Throughout history, the Dutch have carved out a reputation as innovators, devising ingenious solutions to practical problems that improve quality of life. In fields as diverse as engineering, architecture, furnishings, appliances, homewares, fashion and technology, designers incorporate signature style and wit, invariably with a sustainable focus. Visitors can discover Dutch design across the country at studios, shops and the urban environment.

Need to Know

For more information, see Survival Guide (p321)

Currency
Euro (€)

....

Language
Dutch, English

....

Visas
Generally not required for stays of up to three months. Some nationalities require a Schengen visa.

....

Money
ATMs widely available. Credit cards accepted in most hotels, but not all restaurants, cafes and shops. Non-European credit cards are quite often rejected.

....

Mobile Phones
Local SIM cards can be used in European and Australian phones. Most American smartphones will work.

....

Time
Central European Time (GMT/UTC plus one hour)

When to Go

Texel
GO Apr–Oct

Amsterdam
GO Year-round

Deventer
GO Apr–Oct

Rotterdam
GO Year-round

Maastricht
GO Year-round

Warm to hot summers, mild winters
Warm to hot summers, cold winters

High Season
(Jun–Aug)

➡ Everything is open.

➡ Your best odds of balmy weather to enjoy a *café* terrace or a countryside bike ride.

➡ Crowds fill the famous museums.

➡ Prices peak, book ahead.

Shoulder (Apr &
May, Sep & Oct)

➡ Most sights open.

➡ Few crowds.

➡ Prices are moderate; you'll only need to book popular places in Amsterdam.

➡ Weather can be wet and cold. Bring warm clothes for outdoor *cafés*.

Low Season
(Nov–Mar)

➡ Many sights outside major cities close.

➡ It may just be you and a masterpiece at a famous museum.

➡ Weather can be chilly and/or snowy; biking is only for the hardy.

➡ Deals abound.

Useful Websites

Lonely Planet (www.lonely planet.com/the-netherlands) Destination information, hotel reviews, traveller forum and more.

Netherlands Tourism Board (www.holland.com) Attractions, cultural events and practical info.

Dutch News (www.dutchnews. nl) Daily news from the Netherlands in English.

Holland Cycling Routes (www.hollandcyclingroutes. com) Comprehensive cycling information, including maps, route descriptions, rental and repair outlets.

Dutch Review (https://dutch review.com) Well-written webzine covering Dutch culture, news, food, drink, travel etc.

Expatica (www.expatica.com/ nl) Entertaining guide to life in the Netherlands, with daily news and listings.

Important Numbers

Drop the 0 when dialling an area code from abroad.

Police, Fire, Ambulance	☏112
Netherlands country code	☏31
International access code	☏00

Exchange Rates

Australia	A$1	€0.62
Canada	C$1	€0.67
Japan	¥100	€0.78
New Zealand	NZ$1	€0.59
UK	£1	€1.17
US	US$1	€0.85

For current exchange rates, see www.xe.com.

Daily Costs

Budget: Less than €100

➡ Dorm bed: €22–35

➡ Supermarket and lunchtime meal specials: €15

➡ Bicycle rental: €8–10

Midrange: €100–200

➡ Double room in a midrange hotel: from €100

➡ Dinner in a casual restaurant: €30

➡ Museums and trains: €20

Top end: More than €200

➡ Luxurious hotel double room: from €180

➡ Dinner with drinks in a top restaurant: from €60

➡ First-class trains, tours: €40

Opening Hours

Hours can vary by season and often decrease during the low season.

Banks 9am–4pm Monday to Friday, some Saturday morning

Cafés and Bars Open noon (exact hours vary); most close 1am Sunday to Thursday, 3am Friday and Saturday

General Office Hours 8.30am–5pm Monday to Friday

Museums 10am–5pm daily, some close Monday

Restaurants Lunch 11am–2.30pm, dinner 6–10pm

Shops 10am or noon to 6pm Tuesday to Friday, 10am–5pm Saturday and Sunday, noon or 1pm to 5pm or 6pm Monday (if at all)

Supermarkets 8am–8pm

Arriving in the Netherlands

Schiphol International Airport (Amsterdam) Trains to

Amsterdam Centraal Station cost €4.30 with an OV-chipkaart and take 20 minutes. Taxis to Amsterdam's centre (20 to 25 minutes) have a fixed rate of €39.

Duivendrecht & Sloterdijk bus stations Eurolines buses use Duivendrecht and FlixBus uses Sloterdijk; both have a fast metro or train link to Amsterdam Centraal.

Rotterdam The Hague Airport Bus 33 (€2.50 with an OV-chipkaart) makes the 20-minute run from the airport to Rotterdam Centraal Station every 15 minutes throughout the day; or hop off the bus at the Meijersplein metro station (line E) and continue by metro. Count on €25 for the 10-minute trip by taxi.

Eindhoven Airport Bus 400 and 401 travel up to six times hourly to/from Eindhoven train station (€2.50 with an OV-chipkaart, 25 minutes).

Getting Around

The Netherlands' compact size makes it a breeze to get around.

Bicycle Short- and long-distance bike routes lace the country. All but the smallest train stations have bike-rental shops, as does every town and city.

Train Service is fast, distances short, and trains frequent; buy an OV-chipkaart to get cheaper tickets and use on other forms of public transport too.

Car Good for visiting regions with minimal public transport. Drive on the right.

Bus Only useful for remote villages not serviced by rail.

For much more on **getting around**, see p331

Month by Month

January

The first month of the year is cold and dark but on the bright side, museum queues in major cities are nonexistent and you can thaw out in a cosy *café*.

✴ National Tulip Day

The start of the tulip season is celebrated in mid-January with National Tulip Day. Amsterdam's the Dam fills with around 200,000 tulips, which you take home at the end of the day.

🏃 Elfstedentocht

It hasn't taken place since 1997 but it's the sporting event of the year (p212) everyone waits for with bated breath: ice-skaters race around frozen canals in 11 cities in Friesland, starting and ending in Leeuwarden.

February

It's still cold and the nights are long but if you head south, you'll find the Catholic provinces getting ready for the year's biggest party.

✴ Carnaval

On the weekend before Shrove Tuesday there are celebrations that would do Rio de Janeiro or New Orleans proud, mostly in the Catholic provinces of Noord Brabant, Gelderland and Limburg. Maastricht's party means days of uninhibited drinking, dancing and street music.

☆ Amsterdam International Fashion Week

Amsterdam's fashion scene takes flight biannually during Fashion Week (www.amsterdamfashionweek.nl; February and September), with catwalks, parties, lectures and films around the city. Many events – both free and ticketed – are open to the public.

March

If the weather complies, you can get a jump-start on bulbfield viewing in March, and since the season is still off-peak, you won't have to fight the crowds to enjoy them.

🔒 European Fine Art Foundation Show (TEFAF)

Europe's largest art show (www.tefaf.com) takes place across 10 days in the first half of March in Maastricht. It's your chance to pick up a Monet, or at least do some serious browsing.

✴ Keukenhof Gardens

The largest flowering-bulb show in the world (p200) runs mid-March to mid-May at Lisse in the heart of the Netherlands' bulbfields. Buy tickets in advance.

April

April is all about King's Day in the Netherlands. It's the show-stopping highlight of Amsterdam's jam-packed calendar, but you'll find celebrations taking place all over the country.

✴ King's Day (Koningsdag)

The biggest – and possibly the best – street party in Europe celebrates the monarch on 27 April (26 April if the 27th is a Sunday). In Amsterdam, expect plenty of uproarious boozing, live music and merriment, plus a giant free market.

☆ World Press Photo

An annual show (p81) of stunning and often moving images shot by the best photojournalists on the planet. It's on display at Amsterdam's Nieuwe Kerk from mid-April to mid-July.

May

Alternating rainy and gorgeous weather and plenty of historic events make post–King's Day a perfect time to explore the country. Hope for a balmy weekend to get out and visit the windmills.

☆ Herdenkingsdag & Bevrijdingsdag

On 4 and 5 May the fallen from WWII are honoured on Remembrance Day and Liberation Day in an Amsterdam ceremony followed by live music, debate and a market the following day.

◉ National Windmill Day

On the second Saturday (and Sunday) in May, 600 windmills throughout the country unfurl their sails and welcome the public inside (www.molens.nl). Look for windmills flying a blue pennant.

June

Visitors start flocking in for the summer peak season.

The promise of great weather and very long days draws people outside. It's typically sunny and warm, prime for bicycle rides and drinks on canal-side patios.

☆ Holland Festival

Big-name theatre, dance and opera meet offbeat digital films and experimental music as part of the Netherlands' biggest performing-arts extravaganza (p81). The month-long, high-art/low-art mash-up happens across Amsterdam.

☆ Fashion Festival Arnhem

The modes of the moment take the spotlight with a month of events, exhibits and workshops at locations throughout the nation's fashion capital (www.fashionfestivalarnhem.nl).

◉ Rotterdam Architecture Month

The Netherlands' premier architecture city celebrates its world-class portfolio of striking contemporary buildings with a full month of events (http://rotterdamarchitecturemonth.com), including opening up its hidden rooftops during the weekend-long Rotterdam Rooftop Days.

🚴 Fiets Elfstedentocht

Thankfully not reliant on the weather gods like its ice-skating equivalent, this 11-city race (p212) sees 15,000 cyclists speed 235km around Friesland's 11 main towns and cities.

🏃 Ronde om Texel

The largest catamaran race (p136) in the world is held off Texel; spectators line the

beaches for hours on end watching boats jive back and forth on the sea.

🌟 Oerol

In the latter half of June, this outdoor performance festival (p220) on Terschelling is revered nationwide as a perfect excuse for going to sea.

July

The days are long, the sun is shining, beaches get busy and outdoor *cafés* are mobbed with locals and tourists alike. Nobody wants to be inside.

☆ André Rieu Season

Strauss-influenced extravaganzas (www.andrerieu.com) fill Maastricht's Vrijthof for much of July, and their countless attendees ensure that hotel rooms are at a premium.

☆ North Sea Jazz Festival

In mid-July, Rotterdam hosts the world's largest jazz festival (p163). It attracts around a thousand musicians from around the planet, and vast crowds.

🏃 De Vierdaagse

In mid- to late July, thousands of walkers, both locals and visitors, undertake a four-day, 120km- to 200km-long trek around Nijmegen. (p252)

☆ Zomerfeesten

Around for more than half a century, this massive street party (www.vierdaagsefeesten.nl) lures 1.5 million partygoers to Nijmegen for live music, theatre, performing arts, markets etc.

August

August is a surprisingly pleasant time to visit, with temperatures that are much milder than in many other European hot spots. Many Dutch decamp for holidays elsewhere.

⭐ Pride Amsterdam

The rainbow flag blankets Amsterdam on the first weekend of the month, with oodles of parties and special events. The highlight, the Pride Parade, is the world's only water-borne spectacle of its kind. (p326)

🏃 Sneekweek

Sailing fans flood into small-town Sneek in early August for this festive re-gatta (p215) with fireworks, the largest sailing event on Europe's inland waters.

⭐ Noorderzon

This hugely engaging 11-day arts festival (www.noorderzon.nl), held in mid-August in Groningen, features everything from theatre and music to children's en-tertainers and electronic installations.

⭐ 8 Lowlands

Held in mid-August in Biddinghuizen, Flevoland, this alternative music and cultural megabash has campgrounds for the masses (http://lowlands.nl) to make a three-day party of it.

⭐ Grachtenfestival

Classical musicians pop up in canal-side parks and hidden gardens dur-ing mid-August's 10-day Grachtenfestival (p81). The highlight of the 'Canal Festival' is the free concert on a floating stage in the Prinsengracht.

September

Summer may be technically over but September is one of the best months to visit the Netherlands. There are some superb festivals along with fair weather and fewer crowds.

🏃 Wereldhavendagen

In early September Rot-terdam celebrates the role of its port, Europe's largest (www.wereldhavendagen.nl). There are boatloads of ship tours and fireworks. Festival-goers don retro get-ups for the spin-off de Nacht van de Kaap (Night of the Cape), held in Rot-terdam's former red-light quarter, Katendrecht.

🏃 SUP11

Only the Dutch could come up with a 220km-long tour of Friesland's 11 key towns and cities by stand-up paddleboard. The race (p212) follows the same canal course as January's Elfstedentocht for skaters.

⭐ Nederlands Film Festival

The Dutch film industry may be tiny, but its output is generally top-notch. Find out for yourself at Utrecht city's NFF (www.film festival.nl) in late Septem-ber, culminating in the awarding of the coveted Golden Calf.

October

A kaleidoscope of autumnal hues colours the country's parks and gardens, and while the weather may remain mild, low-season prices kick in and queues thin out.

🏃 Leidens Ontzet

Leiden grinds to a halt on 3 October for Leidens Ontzet, commemorating the day the Spanish-caused starva-tion ended in 1574. Celebra-tions ramp up the night before. (p198)

⭐ Amsterdam Dance Event

An electronic-music cel-ebration (p81) on a massive scale, ADE sees 2200 DJs and artists and more than 300,000 clubbers attending 450 events across the city over five long, sweaty days and nights late in October.

🏃 Dutch Design Week

The southern city of Ein-dhoven's key event is this design expo (www.ddw.nl), a knowledge exchange and showcase for young design-ers. It's held at the Dutch Design Academy in late October.

November

Cultural events and reduced low-season rates make up for the shorter days and chillier nights, while the arrival of Sinterklaas heralds the start of the festive season.

11/11

A wacky prelude to springtime's Real McCoy Carnival, the 11/11 is a huge street party in Maastricht kicking off at 11am on 11 November. (www.sjengkraftkompenei.nl)

☆ Glow

During the second week of November, the home town of Philips, the design hub of Eindhoven, switches on spectacular light installations all over the city during Glow (www.gloweindhoven.nl).

Sinterklaas Intocht

St Nicholas arrives in Amsterdam by boat from Spain for the Sinterklaas Intocht (www.sintinamsterdam.nl) in mid- to late November

and parades on his white horse to the Dam and Leidseplein, to the delight of the city's children.

☆ Le Guess Who?

Four days of alternative music, invariably non-Western and obscure, in Utrecht. Wildly popular among lovers of world music. Buy a four-day pass online in advance. (p148)

☆ International Documentary Film Festival

Ten days in late November are dedicated to screening fascinating true stories from all over the world during this film fest (www.idfa.nl/en) in Amsterdam.

December

Winter magic blankets the Netherlands (as, some years, does snow),

ice-skating rinks set up in open spaces, and the country is a vision of twinkling lights.

Sinterklaas

This long-standing Dutch tradition sees Sinterklaas (St Nicholas) bring children presents and families exchange small gifts on 5 December ahead of religious celebrations for Christmas.

New Year's Eve

In Amsterdam: fireworks displays over the Amstel and elsewhere around town (try Nieuwmarkt). Big stages on the Museumplein host live bands and plentiful beer tents for a giant party. Other cities have impromptu raucous celebrations on main squares.

Itineraries

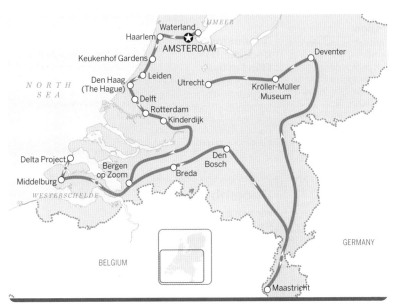

 Southern Sojourn

Catch the Netherlands' most iconic sights on a leisurely spin around the country's south.

Spend the first week in **Amsterdam** and surrounds; enjoy the classic beauty of the **Waterland** region by bicycle.

In the second week, visit Golden Age **Haarlem**, **Keukenhof Gardens** (in season), museum-filled **Leiden**, the Dutch seat of government **Den Haag** and charming **Delft**.

At the start of the third week, hit cutting-edge **Rotterdam**. Ride a waterbus to admire windmills at **Kinderdijk**, then head for Zeeland's restored capital **Middelburg** and the **Delta Project**. Travel through the southern provinces, breaking in **Bergen op Zoom** for the country's oldest surviving city-palace, **Breda** for *café* life and **Den Bosch** for hidden canals. Continue to **Maastricht** for medieval meanderings and great cuisine. Head north to Hanseatic **Deventer**, then west to the **Kröller-Müller Museum** in the Hoge Veluwe National Park. End in historic, cosmopolitan university city **Utrecht**.

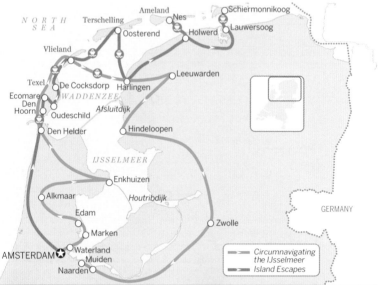

Circumnavigating the IJsselmeer

2 WEEKS

This itinerary focuses on IJsselmeer – the central Netherlands' vast artificial lake.

Spend three days in **Amsterdam** for museums, parks, canal tours and nightlife. Head north along the IJsselmeer coast through the **Waterland** region to the tiny fishing village of **Marken**. Cycle the dykes to **Edam** with its famous, seasonal cheese market (July to August). Stay overnight, then reach **Alkmaar** early to experience its equally riveting, centuries-old cheese market (April to September). Explore the enthralling Zuiderzeemuseum in **Enkhuizen**.

Travel to **Den Helder**, and take a ferry to **Texel**. Spend two days on the island, enjoying the beach and bike exploration, then catch a ferry to **Vlieland**; a seafood lunch here at uber-fashionable *strandpaviljoen* (beach pavilion) Oost is a highlight. From Vlieland, sail aboard a ferry to charming **Harlingen**. From here Friesland's lively capital **Leeuwarden** is a short train journey away, as is the nearby chain of coastal towns, including quaint **Hindeloopen**.

Head to Hanseatic **Zwolle** and also visit the historic fortress towns of **Naarden** and **Muiden**.

Island Escapes

1 WEEK

The low-lying Wadden Islands are strung out like pearls in the Unesco-listed Waddenzee and are perfect for island-hopping. Some ferry links require advance planning.

From **Amsterdam**, head to **Texel**. Bike along the island's western coast from sleepy **Den Hoorn** through dark copses to the **Ecomare** seal and bird refuge. Comb the eastern side, visiting the superb Maritime and Beachcombers Museum in **Oudeschild**.

From **De Cocksdorp** at the northern end of Texel, board the morning ferry to car-free **Vlieland** to explore its nature and hiking trails before catching the boat to **Terschelling**, Friesland's main tourist island. Hole up in peaceful **Oosterend** and cycle the untouched dunes, then hightail it by ferry to **Harlingen**, a pretty little port on the Frisian coast, and on to **Holwerd**, to catch the ferry across to languid **Ameland**. Stay in the whaling port of **Nes**. Return to the mainland and continue east to the port of **Lauwersoog**. From here catch the ferry to the smallest of the Frisian Islands, **Schiermonnikoog**, home to an evocative, windswept national park, before returning to the mainland.

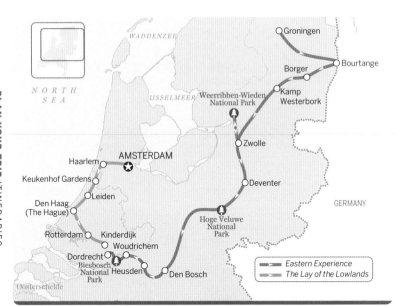

Eastern Experience
2 WEEKS

The Lay of the Lowlands
1 WEEK

The Netherlands' eastern expanse boasts myriad highlights to be discovered.

Begin in **Groningen**, a vibrant city with students, bars, cafes and fine museums. Travel southeast to **Bourtange**, a 17th-century fortified town, then move on to **Borger** and its prehistoric *hunebedden* (stone burial chambers). Make your way to **Kamp Westerbork** to encounter its moving, horrible heritage. Head to **Zwolle**, an unhurried Hanseatic town, and then to the **Weerribben-Wieden National Park**, a unique bog-and-water scape strewn with hiking, biking and canoe-paddling trails.

From Zwolle hop to **Deventer**, one of the Netherlands' most appealing small towns. Explore **Hoge Veluwe National Park** by bike, a natural oasis with a renowned art museum at its green core. Head to **Den Bosch** and visit its terrific Jheronimus Bosch Art Center, then head west to kick back in the fabulous old-world villages of **Heusden** (fortified and moat-ringed) and **Woudrichem** (a citadel village). Get lost in nature at your penultimate stop, **Biesbosch National Park**, before exploring the picturesque streets and canals of **Dordrecht**.

Hit the country's best highlights.

Begin with two days in **Amsterdam**. Visit the big-hitting museums and explore the charming Jordaan neighbourhood by bike. On your second day board a canal boat tour, and stroll through the Red Light District before getting cosy in a brown cafe.

Travel west to beautiful **Haarlem** – stroll the compact historic core, and view masterpieces at the Frans Hals Museum. In tulip season witness the kaleidoscopic colours of the **Keukenhof Gardens**. Spend a day among old-world splendour in **Leiden**. Next, take a day in **Den Haag** and catch the Mauritshuis' exceptional art collection.

Head south to happening **Rotterdam** to tour the harbour and visit the Museum Boijmans van Beuningen, the Maritiem Museum and the architecturally striking food hall, Markthal Rotterdam. The next morning, take a walking tour of the city's incredible contemporary architecture, then hop aboard a waterbus and sail to **Kinderdijk** to explore Unesco-recognised windmills – go local and rent wheels in Rotterdam or Kinderdijk.

Cycling in an Amsterdam park

Plan Your Trip

Cycling in the Netherlands

The Netherlands is the ultimate country to explore by *fiets* (bicycle). Even if it's only a day pedalling along Amsterdam's canals, or a couple of hours rolling past dykes, you'll be rewarded with the sense of freedom (and fun) that only a bicycle can offer.

Best Biking Day Trips

Here are just a few of the endless possibilities:

Amsterdam to Waterland Loop (37km)
One of the country's most picturesque rides.

Amsterdam to Haarlem (50km to 70km return)
A return trip to a great day-trip town that can include a side jaunt to the beach.

Den Haag to Gouda (70km to 80km return)
A classic day trip through lush Dutch countryside to a cute little cheese-famed town.

Rotterdam to Kinderdijk (25km/50km one way/return)
Cycle out to heritage-listed windmills and take a fast ferry back.

Dordrecht to Biesbosch National Park (25km to 50km return)
A trip to a surprisingly natural park that is best appreciated by bike. Explore vast marshlands and see if you can spot a beaver.

Bike Routes

While the Netherlands is webbed with bike routes great and small, one series stands out as the motorway of cycling: the LF routes. Standing for *landelijke fietsroutes* (long-distance routes, also called 'national bike routes') but usually just called LF, this network of routes criss-cross the country and – like motorways – are designed to get you from one locale to another. All are well marked with distinctive green-and-white signs. Most use existing bicycle lanes and rural roads, often beside dykes.

Return visitors can expect to see changes to some LF routes. Work began in 2017 on condensing the original 26 LF routes – comprising close to 4500km – into 12 longer, themed routes. For example, the trio of routes numbered LF21, LF22 and LF23 was combined to form the single, 400km LF Zuiderzee Route around the IJsselmeer. In rural Twente in central Netherlands, the 165km-long 'Tour of Twente' rehashes LF8, LF14 and LF15.

Key LF Routes

➡ LF1 North Sea – Following the Dutch coast from the Belgian border 330km north to Den Helder; it jogs inland briefly near Den Haag and Haarlem. This route links with the LF10 to form one themed 'Dutch Coastal Route'.

➡ LF2 Cities Route – From the Belgian border (it starts in Brussels), this 200km route runs via Dordrecht and Rotterdam to Amsterdam.

➡ LF3 – A marathon 555km-long route that runs north from Maastricht through Nijmegen to Arnhem, then to Zwolle via Deventer and finally to Leeuwarden and the north coast. In winter 2018 sections of this and LF12 joined forces to create a themed, 430km-long 'Maas Cycle Route'.

➡ LF4 Central Netherlands Route – Starts at the coast at Den Haag and runs 300km east through Utrecht and Arnhem to the German border.

➡ LF7 Overland Route – Runs 385km northwest from Maastricht through Den Bosch, Utrecht and Amsterdam to Alkmaar.

Information

Cycling information is copious and widely available. Your biggest challenge will be limiting yourself.

Maps & Books

The best overall maps are the widely available Falk/VVV *Fietskaart met Knooppuntennetwerk* maps (cycling network; www.falk.nl), a series of 22 that blanket the country in 1:50,000 scale. The keys are in English and they are highly detailed and very easy to use. Every bike lane, path and other route is shown, along with distances.

Beyond these maps, there is a bewildering array of regional and specialist bike maps, some as detailed as 1:30,000. Many are only available at the local tourist offices of the region covered.

Websites & Apps

Cycling in the Netherlands (http://holland.cyclingaroundtheworld.nl) Superb English-language site with a vast amount of useful and inspiring information.

Nederland Fietsland (www.nederlandfietsland.nl) Dutch site detailing all the LF routes, bike-rental and repair shops and so on. Includes an indispensable *fietsrouteplanner* (cycling route planner).

Fietsersbond Routeplanner (https://en.routeplanner.fietsersbond.nl) Online route planner powered by the Netherlands' national cycling federation, Fietsersbond; on the road, its smartphone app is indispensable.

Startpagina (http://fiets.startpagina.nl) Dutch site that lists every conceivable website associated with cycling in the Netherlands.

Equipment

Wind and rain are all-too-familiar features of Dutch weather. A lightweight nylon jacket will provide protection, and a breathable variety (Gore-Tex or the like) helps you stay cool and dry. The same thing applies to cycling trousers or shorts.

A standard touring bike is ideal for the Netherlands' flat arena, and for toting a tent and provisions. Gears are useful for riding against the wind, or for tackling a hilly route in Overijssel or Limburg. Other popular items include a frame bag (for a windcheater and lunch pack), water bottles and a handlebar map-holder so you'll always know where you're going. Very few locals wear a helmet, although they're sensible protection, especially for children.

Make sure your set of wheels has a bell: paths can get terribly crowded (at times with blasé pedestrians who don't move) and it becomes a pain if you have to ask to pass every time. Another necessity is a repair kit. Most rental shops will provide one on request. Bike theft is common; you'll want two good locks.

Getting Wheels

Your choices are hiring a bike, buying a bike or using your own. Each has pros and cons.

Hire

Rental shops are available in abundance – every town has at least one. Shops hire out bikes from €8.50 to €12 per day, with discounts by the week. Many have a selection of models, including hugely popular e-bikes (electric bikes). Bikes always come with a lock, often already fitted onto the bike and key-operated, or a chain lock. Some shops require you show a passport or national ID card, and leave a cash or credit-card deposit (usually €25 to €100); many don't require either, though.

Be aware that to brake on a traditional Dutch bicycle, you have to back-pedal. Some bikes have both back-pedal coaster brakes and hand brakes, but many only have the former – to the confusion of many a visitor wholly unaccustomed to braking in such a manner.

In summer it's advisable to reserve ahead, as shops regularly hire out their entire stock, especially in places such as the nearly car-free Frisian Islands where everybody arriving wants a bike.

Countrywide, larger train stations operate their own bicycle-rental shop with secured bike parking. They operate long hours (often 6am to midnight or later) and offer cheap rental (€3.85 per 24 hours). Note, however, that this OV-Fiets (www.ov-fiets.nl) scheme is only available to those with a personal OV-chipkaart (ie people with an address in the Netherlands).

Purchase

Your basic used bicycle (no gears, with coaster brakes, maybe a bit rickety) can be bought for around €100 from bicycle shops or the classified ads. Count on paying €150 or more for a reliable two-wheeler with gears. Good new models start at around €250 on sale. Bike shops are everywhere.

Train Travel

You may bring your bicycle onto any train as long as there is room; a day ticket for

---

BRINGING YOUR OWN BIKE

Flying policies vary by airline, there are no formalities when crossing the border from Belgium or Germany, and ferries usually only have a small bicycle surcharge. See p330 for more information.

Remember, the odds of your bike being stolen are high.

bikes (*dagkaart fiets;* €6.20) is valid in the entire country regardless of the distance involved, but only outside peak periods Monday to Friday, from 9am to 4pm and 6.30pm to 6.30am. There are no restrictions at weekends or during July and August. Travelling with a folding bike is free, providing it is folded and can be considered hand luggage.

Dutch trains often have special carriages for loading two-wheelers – look for the bicycle logos on the side of the carriage.

Security

➡ Be sure you have two good locks. Hardened chain-link or T-hoop varieties are best for attaching the frame and front wheel to a fixed structure (preferably a bike rack).

➡ Some cities have bicycle 'lockers' that can be accessed electronically, but these are rare.

➡ Don't ever leave your bike unlocked, even for an instant. Second-hand bikes are a lucrative trade, and hundreds of thousands are stolen in the Netherlands each year. Even if you report the theft to the police, chances of recovery are virtually nil.

Tours

In most cities you'll find companies offering bike tours of the city. There are multiday trips around the country and many bike-tour operators.

Accommodation

Apart from the recommended camping grounds, there are plenty of nature camp sites along bike paths, often adjoined to a local farm. They tend to be smaller, simpler and cheaper than the regular camping grounds, and many don't allow cars or caravans. The Stichting Natuurkampeerterreinen (Nature Campsites Foundation; www.natuurkampeerterreinen.nl) has 141 locations throughout the Netherlands.

You may also wish to try *Trekkershutten* (www.trekkershutten.nl), basic hikers' huts available at many camping grounds.

Many hostels, B&Bs and hotels throughout the country are well geared to cyclists' needs, offering such things as bike storage and e-bike charge points. Tourist offices can help you track them down.

Suggested Loops
Amsterdam to Waterland

This is an excellent start to your Dutch cycling experience: pretty scenery, cute towns and easy riding on decent bike lanes. The eastern half of **Waterland** is culture-shock material: 20 minutes from central Amsterdam you step centuries back in time into a patchwork of isolated

---

ROAD RULES FOR CYCLISTS

Heavy road and bike traffic can be intimidating, but observe a few basics and soon you'll be freewheeling like a native:

➡ Watch for cars. Cyclists have the right of way, except when vehicles are entering from the right, although not all motorists respect this.

➡ Watch for pedestrians. Tourists wander in and out of bike paths with no idea they're in a dangerous spot.

➡ Use the bicycle lane on the road's right-hand side; white lines and bike symbols mark the spot.

➡ Cycle in the same direction as traffic, and adhere to all traffic lights and signs.

➡ Make sure you signal when turning by putting out your hand.

➡ By law, after dusk you need to use the lights on your bike (front and rear) and have reflectors on both wheels. If your bike does not have lights, you need to use clip-on lights, both front and rear.

➡ It's polite to give a quick ring of your bell as a warning. If someone's about to hit you, a good sharp yell is effective.

➡ Helmets are not required. Most Dutch don't use them, and they don't come standard with a rental.

Amsterdam to Waterland Loop

farming communities and flocks of birds amid ditches, dykes and lakes.

➡ First, take your bike onto the free Buiksloterwegveer ferry behind Amsterdam's Centraal Station across the IJ River.

➡ Continue 1km along the west bank of the Noordhollands Kanaal. Cross the second bridge, continue along the east bank for a few hundred metres and turn right, under the freeway and along Nieuwendammerdijk.

➡ At the end of Nieuwendammerdijk, turn sharply and then continue along Schellingwouderdijk. Follow this under the two major road bridges, when it becomes Durgerdammerdijk, and you're on your way.

➡ The pretty town of **Durgerdam** looks out across the water to IJburg, a major land-reclamation project that will eventually house 45,000 people.

➡ Further north, the dyke road passes several lakes and former sea inlets – low-lying, drained peatlands that were flooded during storms and now form important bird-breeding areas. Colonies include plovers, godwits, bitterns, golden-eyes, snipes, herons and spoonbills. Climb the dyke at one of the viewing points for uninterrupted views to both sides.

➡ The road – now called Uitdammerdijk – passes the town of **Uitdam**, after which you turn left (west) towards **Monnickendam**.

➡ From Monnickendam, return the way you came, but about 1.5km south of town turn right (southwest) towards **Zuiderwoude**. From there, continue to **Broek in Waterland**, a pretty town with old wooden houses.

➡ Cycle along the south bank of the Broekervaart canal towards **Het Schouw** on the Noordhollands Kanaal. Cross the Noordhollands Kanaal (the bridge is slightly to the north); birdwatchers may want to head up the west bank towards Watergang and its bird-breeding areas.

➡ Follow the west bank back down to Amsterdam-Noord. From here it's straight cycling all the way to the ferry to Centraal Station.

Leiden to the Bulbfields

The best time to take this route is mid-March to mid-May when the tulips and daffodils are at their peak and the ribbons of bold colours are astounding. But it's a lovely ride at any time, and especially good in summer when you can stop at the beach for a break on the sand and a refreshing dip in the sea.

Leiden to the Bulbfields Loop

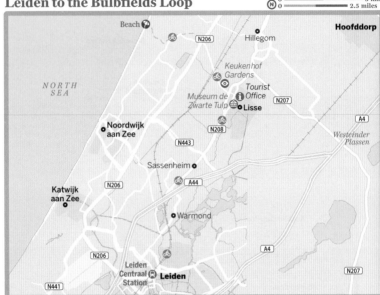

→ Start in **Leiden**, where you can rent a bike at the train station or from one of the vendors in town.

→ Head north from the station following bike lanes and paths along the east side of the train tracks. Stay with the tracks as they curve north. After crossing several bridges (about 3km), you'll see a fair bit of water and the village of **Warmond** to your right.

→ Stay with the rail path *(spoorpad)* and cross under the A44. You'll be at the Rijksstraatweg. Turn right (northeast) and follow the road for 4km as it changes names to Hoofdstraat and reaches the pretty little village of **Sassenheim**. You'll start to see tulips and the bulbfields. Stay on the little road as it passes the churches and you come to the busy N443.

→ Cross the N443. Stay on the good bike paths along Heereweg for almost 4km to the middle of the village of **Lisse**. Here you can visit the Museum de Zwarte Tulp, which has lots of interesting bulb stories.

→ From Lisse, **Keukenhof Gardens** is just 1.25km west.

→ After you've visited the gardens, cross the road to visit stately castle **Kasteel Keukenhof**. Head west for 7.5km to the beach. Start on Delftweg amid bulbfields and stay on the bike lanes as the road crosses N206 (Oosterduinen). The bike route now separates from the road. Stay with the bike route through the sandy landscape.

→ The route curves south; at Langevelderslag, take the parallel path through the dunes. When you cross national bike route LF1, you're at the **beach**.

→ Try some DIY routing to return. Once past the dunes, take little lanes through the bulbfields that take you due south towards Leiden. You'll be dazzled by the colours in spring. Eventually you'll run into a section of your initial route. Then simply retrace your course back to the train station.

Plan Your Trip
Family Travel

The Netherlands is one of Europe's most kid-friendly countries. The famous Dutch tolerance extends to children, and locals are exceptionally welcoming towards them (and their parents). Many attractions are tailored to or specifically designed for younger visitors, and enduring icons such as castles and windmills captivate all ages.

The Netherlands for Kids

Children's needs have been thought of at every turn in the Netherlands.

Eating Out

Children are welcome in all but the most formal restaurants. In fact, the trend towards stylish bistro-style eateries with high ceilings and a slightly raucous atmosphere is all the better for little ones. Everyone is pretty tolerant of any antics children may get up to when dining out. You'll see Dutch families enjoying meals inside and out at cafes, pubs and restaurants, as well as sitting on benches sharing a quick repast from a fish stall, *frites* (French fries) stand or sandwich shop.

Kids' menus are common and often include deep-fried treats that always go down well. You can also ask for high chairs and crayons in many restaurants.

Child-Friendly Facilities

Facilities for changing nappies (diapers) are limited to the big department stores, major museums and train stations, and you'll pay to use them. Breastfeeding is generally OK in public when done discreetly.

Best Regions for Kids

Amsterdam

One of Europe's most kid-friendly cities, with an atmosphere that's cheerfully accommodating to children. In fact, most areas – except the Red Light District, of course – are fair game.

North Holland

Cute old towns, lots of cows, some fun museums and the island of Texel, a huge sandy playground with plenty of cycling trails and easy walks.

Utrecht

Cool canals, castles to bike to and the fantastic 'Dom Under' archaeological adventure trail.

South Holland

The neatest old Dutch cities, a fun amusement park in Den Haag, ubercool things to do in the increasingly happening city of Rotterdam, plus windmills and beaches in Zeeland.

Friesland

The hottest summer spot for Dutch holidaymakers: think fields specked with black and white cows, beautiful islands laced with golden sandy beaches, sailing and water sports galore, kilometres of quiet and scenic cycling paths.

ADMISSION PRICES

There is no rule on how much and from what age children pay – some museums (such as Amsterdam's Rijksmuseum) are free to under 18s, while others only offer free admission to under 17s (Van Gogh Museum or Royal Palace, Amsterdam) or under 12s. The Anne Frank Huis notably is only free to under 9s. In general, children aged four or five get free admission, while those aged five to 17 pay half-price. Some museums offer money-saving family tickets, worth buying once you count two adults and two children or more.

Draw up a list of the museums you plan to visit and check child admission fees carefully before investing in the under 18s version (€32.45) of the Museumkaart – valid for five museum visits in a 31-day period.

On the Road

Most bike-rental shops have trailers for towing younger children, bicycle child seats and kid-sized bikes. Few offer helmets (for any age) so you might want to consider bringing your own.

Trains have 'silent' cars where people can escape noise and everyone (youngsters included) is expected to be quiet. In contrast, other cars can be noisy, including kid-noisy during school holidays in particular.

Children's Highlights

Outdoor Fun

Green spaces, parks, windmills and canals galore add up to plenty of fresh-air fun with the little (and not so little) ones. During winter kids will love the skating rinks and outdoor merriment at the carnivals that spring up in many Dutch cities and towns.

Vondelpark (Map p62; www.hetvondelpark. net; 2 Amstelveenseweg), **Amsterdam** This vast play space, with leafy picnic spots and duck ponds, has cool space-age slides at its western end and a great playground in the centre. (p68)

Westerpark, Amsterdam Kids can splash about in the summer paddling pool. (p68)

Amsterdamse Bos (p83), **Amsterdam** Tykes can feed goats and climb trees in the woods.

Keukenhof Gardens (p200), **Lisse** The millions of flowers might delight kids for a while but they'll really love the huge playground.

Canal Bike (p79), **Amsterdam** Take a unique pedal-powered ride through Amsterdam's beautiful canals.

Canals (p270), **Den Bosch** Most canal towns have short canal-boat tours; those in Den Bosch travel through underground waterways.

Artis Royal Zoo (p56), **Amsterdam** The big cats, fish and planetarium will keep young eyes shining for hours; teenagers and adults will love the beautifully landscaped historical grounds.

Ecomare (p133), **Texel** A nature centre with all sorts of native island animals, and lots of exhibits designed for kids.

Zaanse Schans (p118) Explore windmills north of Haarlem, with gears, pulleys et al.

Watertaxi (p171), **Rotterdam** Sail at speed, beneath bridges and past every other vessel afloat on the Maas River, aboard a nippy black-and-yellow water taxi.

De Zelfpluktuin (p136), **Texel** Kids love picking their own fruit, vegetables and flowers at this family-friendly Texel farm.

Sand & Surf

Beaches Texel and the Frisian Islands have excellent beaches for kids. Much of the west coast is one long beach; Scheveningen near Den Haag is well suited to families.

Horse Riding & Surfing Stables on the island of Texel offer beach rides and surfing for kids.

Windsurfing Amsterdam's newest neighbourhood, IJburg, offers great windsurfing, with rentals available from **Surfcenter IJburg** (www. surfcenterijburg.nl; Berthaanstrakade; windsurfer/wetsuit rental per hour €20/5; ⊙3-9pm Wed & Fri, 11am-6.30pm Sat & Sun Apr-Oct; 26 IJburg).

Mudflats North of Groningen, you can spend a day playing out on the mud. *Wadlopen* (mudflatwalking) lets you head out to sea when the vast tidal areas are clear of water at low tide. It's hours of muddy enjoyment, and you're expected to get dirty.

Kids' Cuisine

Pancakes, *frites,* cheese, ice cream – even adults love fun Dutch food. Every city and town has at least one weekly outdoor market where there are often stalls selling all sorts of tasty items; don't miss the unique holiday treats such as *poffertjes* (tiny Dutch pancakes), served up in winter.

Albert Cuypmarkt (p69), **Amsterdam** For *stroopwafels* (caramel-syrup-filled waffles), fruit smoothies, chocolate, sweets and fresh fruit.

De IJsmaker (p165), **Rotterdam** A trio of ice-cream parlours serving fabulous, Italian-style gelato.

Oudt Leyden (p198), **Leiden** Some of the biggest, best traditional Dutch pancakes around.

Villa Augustus Restaurant (p177), **Dordrecht** Delicious, healthy dishes made from ingredients growing in the organic garden out front; kids can run around alfresco.

Oost (p219), **Vlieland** One of the country's hippest beach restaurants; kids can hone their sandcastle-building while parents feast on seafood.

Vleminckx (p88), **Amsterdam** This hole-in-the-wall is an old *frites* standby; part of the fun is deciding between dozens of sauces.

Friture Reitz (p266), **Maastricht** A favourite for *frites.*

De Haerlemsche Vlaamse (p116), **Haarlem** Local *frites* institution.

IJsboerderij Labora (p137), **Texel** Working dairy farm where you can see the cows that help make your ice cream.

IJs van Co (p259), **Hoge Veluwe National Park** Admire Van Gogh masterpieces in the Kröller-Müller Museum, then pedal to this ice-cream shop to devour the country's finest soft ice cream (and local, syrupy sweet strawberries in season).

Museums

While dragging museum-resistant kids through an exhibition of sombre Dutch Masters' paintings might give parents nightmares, ample museums are accessible, educational and fun.

NEMO Science Museum (p57), **Amsterdam** Tailor-made, kid-focused, hands-on science labs inside; a splashy water feature and amazing views on the roof outside.

Het Scheepvaartmuseum (p56), **Amsterdam** Climb aboard the full-scale, 17th-century replica ship and check out the cannons.

Rijksmuseum (p70), **Amsterdam** Lest the kids be left out of the masterpieces, children get their own audio tour to explore the museum's treasures.

Maastricht Underground (p263), **Maastricht** Explore 2000-year-old tunnels and caves underground. It's spooky and very cool – literally.

Maritiem Museum (p162), **Rotterdam** Bags of hands-on fun (drive a virtual forklift, work out the best locations for wind turbines in the North Sea, take a seafaring safety quiz) at this maritime museum, with historic boats in the neighbouring harbour to scramble on post-museum.

Miffy Museum (p144), **Utrecht** Miffy is one of the most beloved cartoon characters in the Netherlands and you can see a lot of her and other characters at this museum aimed at toddlers.

Natuurcentrum Ameland (p222), **Nes** The seaquarium has more than 200 North Sea species, including barracudas and manta rays.

Fort Kijkduin (p132), **Den Helder** Hilltop fortress with military museum and a subterranean aquarium full of Waddenzee and North Sea marine life.

Markiezenhof (p278), **Bergen op Zoom** Miniature versions of rides from the southern town's famed Carnaval celebration.

Natuurmuseum Fryslân, Leeuwarden (Map p212; ☎058-233 22 44; www.natuurmuseum-fryslan.nl; Schoenmakersperk 2; adult/child €9/6; ☉11am-5pm Tue-Sun Sep-Jun, 10am-5pm Jul & Aug; ♠) A fish-eye stroll round a Friesland canal and a simulated bird flight are among the highlights at this kid-friendly nature museum.

Nederlands Openluchtmuseum (p256), **Arnhem** Like a set from a period film, this village-sized

---

TOP WEBSITES

Holiday Sitters (www.holiday-sitters.com) Professional babysitting service for families visiting Amsterdam, Rotterdam and Den Haag; book directly online, stipulating the spoken language you desire, time slot and duration (from three to 10 hours).

I am Expat (www.iamexpat.nl) Hugely practical website aimed squarely at expats living in the Netherlands, with bags of information for families with children.

Baby Goes 2 (www.babygoes2.com) Why, where, how to travel guide for families.

Top: Efteling theme park (p266)

Bottom: Scheveningen beach (p186)

KARIN REINE/SHUTTERSTOCK ©

open-air museum recreates the Netherlands' past with plenty of hands-on activities.

Amusement Parks

The ultimate kids' attraction.

Efteling (p266), **Kaatsheuvel** This is the most popular amusement park in the Netherlands and it seems every Dutch person of any age has memories of the fun they've had here. Thrill rides, cartoon characters and more. It's in the south near Tilburg.

Madurodam (p184), **Den Haag** See the Netherlands in miniature outdoors at Madurodam; it's what a kid would build with unlimited time and cash.

Waterland Neeltje Jans (p205), **Zeeland** Amid the amazing and vast Delta Project, kid-friendly exhibits tell the story of how the Dutch have battled the sea; there are also seals, a water park and rides.

On Stage

Amsterdams Marionetten Theater (p104) Puts on captivating shows such as Wolfgang Amadeus Mozart's *The Magic Flute*.

Openluchttheater (p104), **Amsterdam** A free theatre in Vondelpark hosting performances most Saturday afternoons in summer.

Planning

For all-round information and advice, check out Lonely Planet's *Travel with Children*.

When to Go

The Netherlands is an all-year-round affair, although families may appreciate the warmer, drier months the most – from Easter to September – when the climate is more conducive to outdoor action, be it on the beach, cycling, sailing or simply frolicking in a city park.

The Dutch festival repertoire is another planning consideration: cold wet February ushers in kid-friendly street parades during carnival season; Sinterklaas brings presents to kids on 5 December; while summer translates as a bonanza of fun festivals and sporting events.

Accommodation

Very few hotels have a 'no kids' rule; those that do are more upmarket addresses mostly in areas of Amsterdam that you wouldn't consider taking children to anyway.

Countrywide, family rooms sleeping four are common and most hotels will happily add an extra bed (for a minimal extra cost) or a baby cot (free of charge) in a double room. New-wave design-driven hostels, with private rooms sleeping up to five or six, are a handy alternative for families with more than two children.

Camping is big with Dutch families, especially on the Frisian Islands and other coastal areas.

Upscale hotels often offer child-minding services.

Regions at a Glance

Amsterdam

Museums
Canals
Entertainment

Magnificent Museums

Amsterdam's world-class museums draw millions of visitors each year. The art collections take pride of place – you can't walk a kilometre without bumping into a Van Gogh, Rembrandt or Mondrian masterpiece.

Golden Age Canals

The gabled houses along Amsterdam's remarkably preserved canals look much as they did during the 17th century, and boats travel the same waterways as they did 400 years ago.

Great Entertainment

Amsterdam's nightlife is legendary. Jazz venues abound and you could easily see a live act every night of the week. The dance-music scene thrives, with big-name DJs spinning at clubs around town. Amsterdam's classical venues put on a full slate of shows. Famously hedonistic diversions include the Red Light District's carnival of vice.

p42

Haarlem & North Holland

Historic Towns
Nature
Activities

Picturesque Towns & Villages

Haarlem evokes the Middle Ages and the Golden Age as you stroll its compact centre, and you half expect to see an old merchant's ship sail into Hoorn's harbour. Smaller and cuter still are places such as Edam and Marken, whose traditions let you observe living history.

Birds & Seals

The largest of the Waddenzee islands, Texel is ringed by wide beaches and national-park-protected dunes. Bird life abounds here; out on the water you'll find colonies of seals.

Adventurous Pursuits

You can kite-surf, hike, sail a boat and more in the region's waters. On land, cycling across the dykes and verdant countryside makes for great days exploring.

p111

Utrecht

Canals
Landmarks
Day Trips

Split-Level Canals

Utrecht feels like Amsterdam without the crowds; its unique two-level canals inset with cavern-bars and hidden restaurants give the city a very special character all of its own.

Historic Icon

For sweeping views climb Utrecht's icon, the soaring Domtoren, and play 'I Spy Amsterdam' on clear days. But to really understand its historic soul, you'll have to go underground, delving into the city's subterranean archaeology with a smart-torch audio-gun at Dom Under.

Castle Capers

The province is dotted with fortifications and pretty castle-towns that make great day trips. Kasteel de Haar is the most spectacular and Doorn's chateau has lots of history, but Amerongen and Wijk bij Duurstede are lower-key delights.

p143

Rotterdam & South Holland

Urban Life
Tulips
Cycling

Urban Renaissance

Rotterdam's urban renaissance includes not only striking new additions to its skyline but also a surge of street art, red-hot restaurant and bar openings, and an ultra-busy festival program.

Blooming Bulbs

Bulbfields fan out around the beautiful city of Leiden and burst into a spectacular display of colour in spring. Keukenhof Gardens puts on dazzling annual displays; the little town of Lisse is home to a tulip museum.

Two-Wheeling

Cycling is as good here as anywhere in the country, whether you're pedalling by Kinderdijk's Unesco-listed windmills, Den Haag's stately palaces and nearby beach Scheveningen, Zeeland's sandy seashore or the medieval buildings gracing Delft's canals.

p155

Friesland

Islands
History
Adventure

Frisian Islands

Off the north coast of the Netherlands, the Waddenzee's rich environment is a Unesco World Heritage site and teems with sea- and bird-life, best appreciated afloat or during a foray onto the mudflats. Even when ferries from the mainland arrive jam-packed, there'll always be an expanse of empty beach with your name on it.

History-Steeped Towns

Harlingen is a fascinating historic port town. Leeuwarden has superb museums covering the province's history and natural history, while Hindeloopen is a gem of an old fishing village.

Boats & Bikes

The Frisian Islands offer endless opportunities for outdoor fun. You can island-hop by boat while exploring by bike, rent a boat yourself to explore the waters, or join a race around the region's 11 towns and cities afloat a stand-up paddleboard.

p207

Northeastern Netherlands

History
Parks
Nightlife

Understanding the Past

Some of the oldest finds in the Netherlands are in its far northeast corner: *hunebedden* (old burial sites) date back 5000 years. The preserved fortress town of Bourtange is a 16th-century time capsule, while Groningen still has echoes of the Golden Age. Much more recent and far more terrible, Kamp Westerbork was used by the Nazis for deporting Jews and others.

Green Lands

Protected zones preserve ancient landscapes that are left to evolve naturally. Explore old farms, forests and heaths on a welter of biking and hiking trails.

Party Time

The ancient university town of Groningen has 20,000 students who ensure there's never a dull moment on its streets or in its *cafés*, cutting-edge bars and pulsating live-music venues.

p225

Central Netherlands

Alluring Towns
Canals
History

Backstreet Explorations

One of the greatest pleasures of the Central Netherlands is wandering the backstreets of its towns and making your own discoveries. Old brick buildings unchanged since Deventer was a Hanseatic trading city delight with carved stone details. Nearby Zwolle offers similar rewards, as does compact little Kampen.

Land & Water

Water courses throughout the centre of the Netherlands. Near the canal-laced rural idyll of Giethoorn, you can follow canals and channels dug over the centuries by peat harvesters and farmers in fascinating Weerribben-Wieden National Park.

WWII Reminders

In and around Nijmegen and Arnhem, monuments and museums recall the fierce battles of WWII and their horrific aftermath.

p239

Maastricht & Southeastern Netherlands

History
Art
Cafés

Roman Relics

The land beneath Maastricht is a honeycomb of tunnels and underground forts dating back through centuries of wars to Roman times. Above ground, almost every era since is represented by a landmark or building in the city's compact and beautiful centre.

Art, Observed

Hieronymus Bosch was a sharp observer of human frailties and his intricate paintings, which are recreated in his namesake city Den Bosch, still ring true today. Maastricht is home to the world's largest annual sales fair of historic art, and artistic treasures fill its museums.

Beer Talk

Café culture brings a special buzz to the bar-filled streets of Breda and Maastricht, while near Tilburg, beer pilgrims converge on Koeningshoeven's monastery-brewery to sample La Trappe's full range of Trappist ales.

p260

On the Road

Amsterdam

Best Places to Eat

➡ Rijks (p94)

➡ D'Vijff Vlieghen (p88)

➡ Ron Gastrobar (p93)

➡ Greetje (p90)

➡ De Kas (p96)

Best Places to Stay

➡ Hoxton Amsterdam (p84)

➡ Sir Albert Hotel (p87)

➡ ClinkNOORD (p87)

Why Go?

Amsterdam works its fairy-tale magic in many ways: via the gabled Golden Age buildings, the glinting boat-filled canals, and especially the cosy, centuries-old *bruin cafés* (pubs), where candles burn low and beers froth high. Art admirers will be hard-pressed to marvel at a more masterpiece-packed city, thanks to rich collections at the Rijks, Van Gogh, Stedelijk and Hermitage museums. Music fans can tune into concert halls booked solid with entertainment from all over the globe. Amsterdam's risqué side, meanwhile, includes the Red Light District and cannabis-selling coffeeshops.

The city is remarkably intimate and accessible, its compact core ripe for rambling. You never know what you'll find among the atmospheric lanes: a hidden garden, an antique-book market, a 17th-century distillery – always worlds within worlds, where nothing ever seems the same twice.

When to Go

➡ Summer is the peak time, when cafe terraces boom and festivals rock almost every weekend. Locals go on holiday in late July and August, so you might find your favourite restaurant closed.

➡ Visitor numbers start to taper in October, and by November off-peak rates begin in earnest. Ice skating, fireplace-warmed cafes and queue-free museums ease the chilly days from December through February.

➡ Crowds start coming back around Easter, and amass in full force around King's Day (27 April), Remembrance Day (4 May) and Liberation Day (5 May).

History

Around 1200, a fishing community known as Aemstelredamme – 'the dam across the Amstel River' – emerged at what is now called the Dam. The town soon grew into a centre for sea trade. Unfettered by high taxes and medieval feudal structures, a society of individualism and capitalism took root. The modern idea of Amsterdam – free, open, progressive – was born.

The city flourished during the 17th century Golden Age. Merchants and artisans flocked in, Rembrandt painted, and city planners built the canals. By the next century though, international wars and trade competition stagnated the local economy.

In 1806 Napoleon's brother Louis became king of Holland. He eventually moved into the city hall on the Dam and transformed it into the Royal Palace. Infrastructure projects such as Centraal Station, the Rijksmuseum and harbour expansion followed later in the 19th century.

WWI and the Great Depression took their toll in the form of food shortages and increasing poverty. WWII brought hardship, hunger and devastation to the local Jewish community during the Nazi occupation. Only one in every 16 of Amsterdam's 90,000 Jews survived the war.

During the 1960s Amsterdam became Europe's 'Magic Centre': hippies smoked dope on the Dam and camped in Vondelpark. In 1972 the first coffeeshop opened, and in 1976 marijuana was decriminalised to free up police resources for combating hard drugs.

By the 1990s the city's economy had shifted to white-collar jobs and a thriving service industry, while gentrification increased. The ethnic make-up had changed too, with non-Dutch nationalities (particularly Moroccans, Surinamese and Turks) comprising more than 45% of the population.

The 21st century has seen Amsterdam become a start-up hub: there are now 1.3 start-ups per 1000 residents. Pioneering projects range from building a canal house and canal bridge by 3D printer to offering networks where residents can trade surplus green energy with each other. Grand urban projects include a 2018-opened metro line and massive artificial suburban islands.

In July 2018 Femke Halsema became Amsterdam's first-ever female mayor and the first from the left-wing Green political party GroenLinks, after it prevailed at the local elections in March that year.

◉ Sights

Amsterdam's Unesco-listed Canal Ring is a sight in itself, and the city is also home to over 60 museums – the world's highest concentration. Several blockbusters conveniently congregate at Museumplein, adjacent to the oasis-like Vondelpark, while other unmissable sights like the Anne Frank Huis are also central. Beyond the Canal Ring, contemporary attractions are opening up in creative areas such as Amsterdam Noord.

◉ Medieval Centre & Red Light District

A handful of museums are tucked in the Medieval Centre, including city-history museum the Amsterdam Museum, along with landmarks like the Royal Palace and charming surprises such as the Begijnhof (p50) courtyard. Racier sights in the Red Light District include sex, prostitution and marijuana museums, contrasting with the 15th-century Nieuwe Kerk (p51) and the Kuan Yin Shrine (p52) Buddhist temple.

★**Royal Palace** PALACE
(Koninklijk Paleis; Map p48; ☑020-522 61 61; www.paleisamsterdam.nl; Dam; adult/child €10/free; ◷10am-5pm; 🚊4/14/24 Dam) Opened as a town hall in 1655, this resplendent building became a palace in the 19th century. The interiors gleam, especially the marble work – at its best in a floor inlaid with maps of the world in the great *burgerzaal* (citizens' hall) at the heart of the building. Pick up a free audioguide at the desk when you enter; it explains everything you see in vivid detail. King Willem-Alexander uses the palace only for ceremonies; check for periodic closures.

★**Amsterdam Museum** MUSEUM
(Map p48; ☑020-523 18 22; www.amsterdammuseum.nl; Gedempte Begijnensloot; adult/child €13.50/free; ◷10am-5pm; 🚊2/11/12 Spui) Entrepreneurship, free thinking, citizenship and creativity are the four cornerstones of the multimedia DNA exhibit at this riveting museum, which splits Amsterdam's history into seven key time periods. Unlike at many of the city's museums, crowds are rare. It's reached via the arcade containing the free Civic Guard Gallery (Map p48; Kalverstraat 92; ◷10am-5pm; 🚊2/11/12 Spui) FREE off Kalverstraat 92.

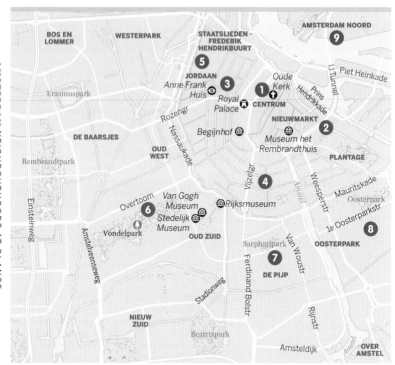

❶ Medieval Centre & Red Light District (p43)

Amsterdam's oldest quarter is remarkably preserved, looking much as it did in its Golden Age heyday. It's the busiest part of town for visitors. While some come to see the Royal Palace and Oude Kerk, others make a beeline for the coffeeshops and Red Light District.

❷ Nieuwmarkt, Plantage & the Eastern Islands (p53)

Buzzing Nieuwmarkt is sewn through with rich seams of history. Here is the Rembrandthuis – the master painter's studio – as well as centuries-old synagogues and the Waterlooplein Flea Market in the old Jewish quarter. Alongside, entering leafy Plantage takes it down a gear, with the sprawling zoo and botanical gardens. It segues into the

Eastern Islands, with a completely different atmosphere involving ex-warehouses turned funkfest bars, and flagship modern Dutch architecture.

❸ Western Canal Ring (p57)

Grand old mansions and tiny, charming speciality shops line the glinting waterways of the Western Canal Ring, one of Amsterdam's most gorgeous areas. Roaming around them can cause days to vanish. But most people come here for a singular reason: to visit Anne Frank's house and see her famous diary.

❹ Southern Canal Ring (p60)

Amsterdam's Southern Canal Ring is a horseshoe-shaped loop of parallel canals. It's home to the nightlife hubs of Leidseplein (p101) and Rembrandtplein, with bars,

where everyone hangs out at some point: stoners, yummy mummies, cyclists, picnickers and sunbathers. Close to the park, the wealth-laden Old South holds the Van Gogh, Stedelijk and Rijksmuseum collections. Head further south still, and there's the lush Amsterdamse Bos (Amsterdam Forest) and the CoBrA Museum. To the north, there's funky Overtoom and the De Hallen food hall and cultural complex.

7 De Pijp (p69)

A hotbed of creativity, village-like De Pijp is home to a diverse mix of labourers, immigrants, intellectuals, sex workers and young urbanites. Marvel at the scene at Amsterdam's largest street market, the colourful Albert Cuypmarkt, and the outstanding eateries and free-spirited *cafés* (pubs) that surround it.

8 Oosterpark & East of the Amstel (p76)

Oost (East) is one of Amsterdam's most culturally diverse neighbourhoods, a melting pot of Moroccan and Turkish enclaves. It's an area that grew up in the 19th century, with grand buildings and wide boulevards. The large English-style Oosterpark was laid out in 1861, while lush Flevopark, further east, dates from when this area was a country retreat. Beyond this is Amsterdam's newest neighbourhood, the IJburg, built across several islands, with the city beach.

clubs and restaurants clustered around large squares. Between these two districts, the canals are lined by some of the city's most elegant houses; the area also encompasses many fine museums, a flower market and waterside restaurants and bars.

5 Jordaan & the West (p65)

A former workers' quarter, the Jordaan teems with cosy pubs, galleries and markets crammed into a grid of tiny lanes. It's short on conventional sights, but it's a wonderfully atmospheric place for an aimless stroll. It abuts the West, industrial badlands that have transformed into an avant-garde cultural hub.

6 Vondelpark & the South (p68)

Vondelpark has a special place in Amsterdam's heart, a lush green egalitarian space

9 Amsterdam Noord (p77)

Amsterdam Noord, across from central Amsterdam, on the other side of the IJ River, encompasses fields, horses and the odd windmill, minutes away from ex-industrial areas, cutting-edge architecture, and hangars turned hipster hang-outs whose walls burst with street art. Long neglected, the area has been reinvented as the city's hippest neighbourhood, where it's great to roam around by bike, and to eat and drink in its out-there venues.

Amsterdam Highlights

① Rijksmuseum
(p70) Plunging into this treasure chest of Vermeers, Rembrandts and other national riches.

② Anne Frank Huis
(p58) Experiencing a young girl's hidden life during WWII.

③ Van Gogh Museum (p74)
Admiring the vivid swirls of a tortured genius.

④ Museum het Rembrandthuis
(p53) Visiting the Golden Age painter's inner sanctum.

⑤ Jordaan (p99)
Feeling *gezelligheid* (a cosy sense of wellbeing) in this atmospheric neighbourhood's lanes and convivial hang-outs like Café Pieper.

⑥ Albert Cuypmarkt (p69)
Trawling the exotic goods at Amsterdam's busiest street market.

⑦ Red Light District (p43)
Observing the evolution of Amsterdam's famous Red Light District as fashion studios, galleries and cafes increasingly move in.

⑧ Vondelpark
(p68) Kicking back amid the ponds, lawns, thickets and paths of this urban oasis.

⑨ Brouwerij 't IJ (p97) Sipping sensational microbrews under an 18th-century windmill.

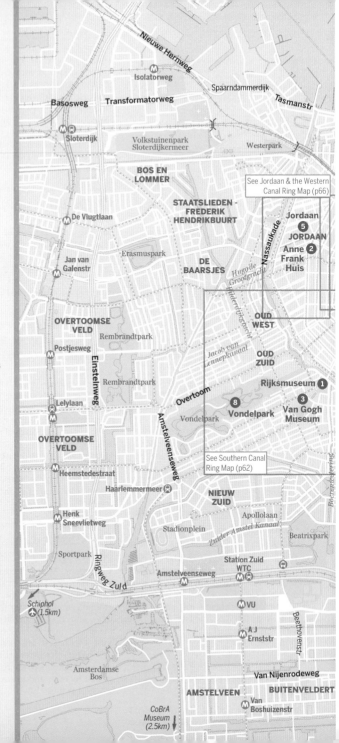

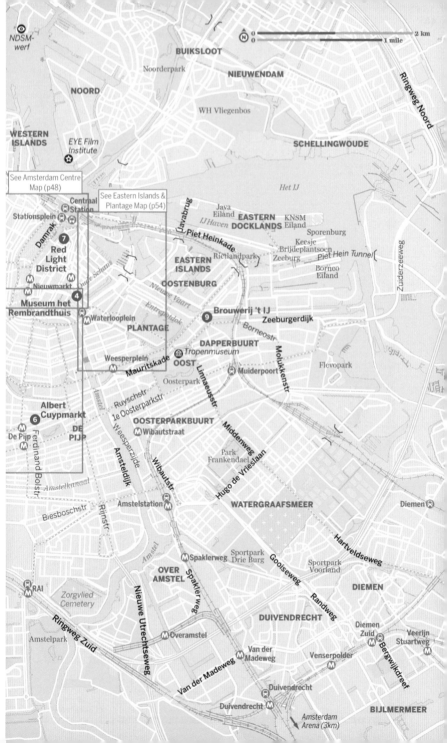

Amsterdam Centre

N

0   200 m
0   0.1 miles

Movies
(500m)

Noordermarkt

Prinsengracht

Prinsenstr

Prinsengr

Keizersgracht

Brouwersgracht

WESTERN
CANAL
RING

Herengracht

Herenstr

Herengr

Bergstr

Herengr

Leliegr
Lauriergr

Torensluis

Haarlemmer
Houttunen

Buiten Brouwerstr

Haarlemmerstr

Herenmarkt

Binnen Vissersstr

Singel

Roomolenstr

Korsjespoortstr

Langestr

Singel

Korte Kolkst

Blauwburgwal

St Nicolaasstr

Mosterdpotst

Beurspassage

59

30
44

20

18

66

29

Haarlemmer
Houttunen

De Bakkerswinkel(1.6km);
North Sea Jazz Club (1.7km)

Westerpark (1.4km/1.6km);

Droogbak

Paleisstr

Gouwenaarsst

Nieuwendijk

Smakstr
Engelsest

Spuistr

Stromarkt

'T Teertkelst

Oude Nieuwstr

Nieuwezijds Voorburgwal

D van Hasseltst
Suikerbakkerst

Nieuwe Nieuwstr

St Geertruidenst

Houseboat Ms Luctor (1km);
Worst Wijncafe (1.6km);
Marius (1.6km)

Open Havenfront

Prins Hendrikkade

Martelaarsgr

Nieuwendijk
Hasselaerstr

Haringpakker-
sst

Karnemelkst

Nieuwezijds Kolkst
Kolk

34

Onze
Lieve
Vrouwest

Mandenmakerst

Oude
Brugst

St Jacobsstr

Piet Heinkade

35

Damrak

24

8

38

Open Havenfront

Centraal
Station
(west side)

Centraal
Station

Orangebike (300m);
Tolhuistuin (400m);
A'DAM Tower (550m);
EYE Film Institute (750m)

IJpleinveer

Het IJ

31

33

Centraal
Station

11 Centraal
Station
(east side)

1 Amsterdam
Visitor Centre

Prins Hendrikkade

Oosterdok

Geldersekade

23

48

67
43

Sint
Olofsst

Nieuwebrugst

Zeedijk

Oudezijds Kolk

65

37

75

Oudezijds Armst

56

Hartje
Hoekst

Lange
Niezel

21

Museum
Ons' Lieve
Heer op
Solder

9
4

Warmoesstr

Oudebrugst

Beursstr

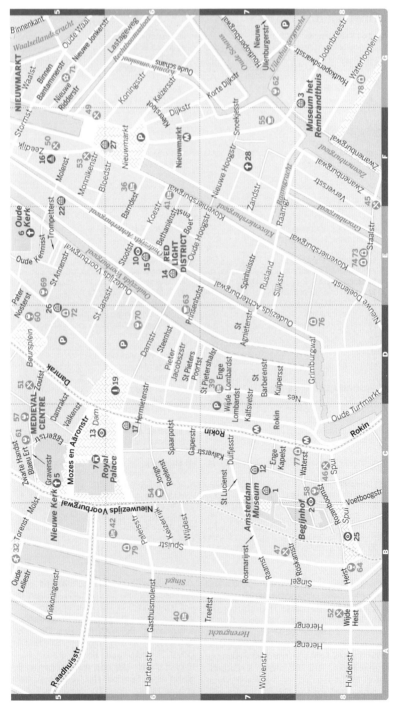

Map labels

5 Binnenkant
Waalseilandsgracht
Oude Waal
Nieuwe Jonkerstr
Lastageweg
Rechtboomssloot
Oude schans
Oude Schans
Houtkopersburgwal
Nieuwe Uilenburgerstr
Uilenburgergracht

NIEUWMARKT
Waalstr
Binnen Bantammerstr
Nieuwe Ridderstr
71

Koningsstr
Keizerstr
Dijkstr
Korte Dijkstr
Houtkopersdwarsstr
Lodenbreestr
Waterplein
62
3 Museum het Rembrandthuis
78

Stormstr
Zeedijk
16 50
Molenstr
Monnikenstr
Bloedstr
53
49
27
Meesloot
Nieuwmarkt
Nieuwmarkt
Nieuwe Hoogstr
Nieuwe Hoogstr
Snoekjesstr
55
28
Zwanenburgwal
Zwanenburgwal
Ververstr
Raamgr
45

6 Oude Kerk
22
Trompetterst
36
Barndest
41
Koestr
Bethaniënstr
Ernst
Kloveniersburgwal
Kloveniersburgwal
Boer
Zandstr
Recamiergracht
Greenburgwal
Staalstr
73 74

Oude Kennisst
St Annenstr
Oudezijds Voorburgwal
Oudezijds Achterburgwal
10
15
14 RED LIGHT DISTRICT
Oude Hoogstr
Spinhuisstr
Rusland
Slijkstr
Kloveniersburgwal
Nieuwe Doelenstr

Pater Nosterst
69
26
60
72
St Jansstr
63
Prinsenhof
St Agnietenstr
Oudezijds Achterburgwal
76
Nieuwe Doelenstr

Beursplein
Damstr
Steenstr
Pieter Jacobszstr
St Pieters Poortst
39
70
Wijde Lombardst
Enge Lombardst
St Barberenstr
Kuiperstr
Nes
Grimburgwal
Oude Turfmarkt

Damrak
19
Hermietenstr
17
Spaarpotst
Gaperstr
Wijde Lombardst
Kalfsvelst
Rokin
77
Waterst
Rokin
Oude Turfmarkt

MEDIEVAL CENTRE
Zoutst
Damkst
Valkenst
13 Dam
Rokin
Enge Kapelst
46
Nes
Spui
Voetboogstr

Zwarte Handst
61 57
51
Blaeu Ert
Eggertst
Gravenstr
54
Jonge Roelenst
St Lucienst
Duifjessteeg
Kalverstr
12
1
58
2
25
Rosmarijnsteeg
Spui

7 Royal Palace
Mozes en Aaronstr
Amsterdam Museum
Begijnhof
Rozenboomst
Spui
64
Heist

Nieuwe Kerk
42
Nieuwezijds Voorburgwal
79
Paleisstr
Keizerstr
Wijdest
Spuistr
St Lucienst
Rosmarijnst
Raamst
47
Singel
Roskamst
Heist

32
Torenst
Molst
Oude Leliestr
40
Treeftst
Singel
Herengr
Herengr
52
Wijde Heist

Driekoningenstr
Gasthuismolenst
Hartenstr
Herengracht
Herengr
Wolvenstr
Huidenstr

Raadhuistr

Amsterdam Centre

★ **Begijnhof**   COURTYARD
(Map p48; www.nicolaas-parochie.nl; ⊙9am-5pm; 🚊2/11/12 Spui) **FREE** Dating from the early 14th century, this enclosed former convent is a surreal oasis of peace, with tiny houses and postage-stamp gardens around a well-kept courtyard off Gedempte Begijnensloot. The Beguines, a Catholic order of unmarried or widowed women who cared for the elderly, lived a reli-gious life without taking monastic vows. The last Beguine died in 1971. Within the *hof* (courtyard) is the charming 1671 **Begijnhof Kapel** (Map p62; www.begijnhofkapel amsterdam.nl; Begijnhof 30; ⊙1-6.30pm Mon, 9am-6.30pm Tue-Fri, 9am-6pm Sat & Sun; 🚊2/11/12 Spui), and the **Engelse Kerk** (English Church; Map p62; www.ercadam.nl; Begijnhof 48; ⊙9am-5pm; 🚊2/11/12 Spui), built around 1392.

Dam SQUARE
(Map p48; 4/14/24 Dam) This square is the very spot where Amsterdam was founded around 1270. Today pigeons, tourists, buskers and the occasional funfair complete with Ferris wheel take over the grounds. It's still a national gathering spot, and if there's a major speech or demonstration it's held here.

Nationaal Monument MONUMENT
(Map p48; Dam; 4/14/24 Dam) The obelisk on the Dam's eastern side was built in 1956 to commemorate WWII's fallen. Fronted by two lions, its pedestal has a number of symbolic statues: four males (war), a woman with child (peace) and men with dogs (resistance). The 12 urns at the rear hold earth from war cemeteries of the 11 provinces and the Dutch East Indies. The war dead are still honoured here at a ceremony every 4 May.

★**Nieuwe Kerk** CHURCH
(New Church; Map p48; 020-626 81 68; www.nieuwekerk.nl; Dam; adult/child €11/free; 10am-6pm; 2/11/12/13/17 Dam) This 15th-century, late-Gothic basilica is only 'new' in relation to the Oude Kerk (Old Church; from 1306). A few monumental items dominate the otherwise spartan interior – a magnificent carved oak chancel, a bronze choir screen, a massive organ and enormous stained-glass windows. It's the site of royal investitures and weddings; the building is otherwise used for art exhibitions and concerts. Opening times and prices can vary depending on what's going on. An audioguide costs €2.

Spui SQUARE
(Map p48; 2/11/12 Spui) Inviting *cafés* (pubs) and high-brow bookshops ring the Spui, a favoured haunt of academics, students and journalists. On Friday (weather permitting) a small book market sets up on the square; on Sunday it's an art market (Map p62; www.artplein-spui.com; Spui; 11am-6.30pm Sun Mar-Dec; 2/11/12 Spui). And just so you know, it's pronounced 'spow' (rhymes with 'now').

Sexmuseum Amsterdam MUSEUM
(Map p48; www.sexmuseumamsterdam.nl; Damrak 18; €5; 9.30am-11.30pm; 2/4/11/12/13/14/17/24/26 Centraal Station) The Sexmuseum is good for a giggle. You'll find replicas of pornographic Pompeian plates, erotic 14th-century Viennese bronzes, some of the world's earliest nude photographs, an automated farting flasher in a trench coat, and a music box that plays 'Edelweiss' and purports to show a couple in flagrante delicto. It's sillier and more fun than other erotic museums in the Red Light District. Minimum age for entry is 16.

Madame Tussauds Amsterdam MUSEUM
(Map p48; www.madametussauds.com/amsterdam; Dam 20; adult/child €24.50/20.50; 9.30am-9.30pm Aug, from 10am Sep-Jul; 4/14/24 Dam) Sure, Madame Tussauds wax museum is overpriced and cheesy, but its focus on local culture makes it fun: 'meet' the Dutch royals, politicians, painters and pop stars, along with global celebs (George Clooney, Barack Obama et al). Kids love it. Buying tickets online will save you a few euro and get you into the fast-track queue. Prepurchasing tickets online for earlier than 11.30am and after 6pm nets further discounts. Hours can vary; check the calendar online.

Centraal Station NOTABLE BUILDING
(Map p48; Stationsplein; 2/4/11/12/13/14/17/24/26 Centraal Station) Beyond being a transport hub, Centraal Station is a sight in itself. The turreted marvel dates from 1889. One of the architects, PJ Cuypers, also designed the Rijksmuseum (p70), and you can see the similarities in the faux-Gothic towers, the fine red brick and the abundant reliefs (for sailing, trade and industry).

★**Oude Kerk** CHURCH
(Old Church; Map p48; 020-625 82 84; www.oudekerk.nl; Oudekerksplein; adult/child €10/free; 10am-6pm Mon-Sat, 1-5:30pm Sun; 4/14/24 Dam) Dating from 1306, the Oude Kerk is Amsterdam's oldest surviving building. It's also an intriguing moral contradiction: a church surrounded by active Red Light District windows. Inside, check out the stunning Vater-Müller organ, the naughty 15th-century carvings on the choir stalls, and famous Amsterdammers' tombstones in the floor (including Rembrandt's wife, Saskia van Uylenburgh). Regular art exhibitions take place in the church; you can also climb the tower (tour €8; 1-7pm Mon-Sat Apr-Oct; 4/14/24 Dam) on a guided tour. Church admission is by credit/debit card only.

★**Museum Ons'**
Lieve Heer op Solder MUSEUM
(Map p48; 020-624 66 04; www.opsolder.nl; Oudezijds Voorburgwal 38; adult/child €11/5.50;

RED LIGHT DISTRICT FACTS & FIGURES

➡ Year prostitution officially legalised in the Netherlands: 2000

➡ Number of sex workers in Amsterdam: approximately 6000, though estimates range between 5000 and 8000

➡ Minimum legal age to work as a sex worker in the Netherlands: 21

➡ Taking photos of the windows is strictly verboten. Your first instinct might be to take a quick snap, but don't do it – out of simple respect, and to avoid having your camera or phone tossed in a canal by the ladies' enforcers.

➡ For their own safety, sex workers' quarters are equipped with a button that, when pressed, activates a light outside. The police or other protectors show up in a hurry.

➡ The red lights of the Red Light District have been around for a long time; even as early as the 1300s, women carrying red lanterns met sailors near the port. Red light is flattering and, especially when used in combination with black light, it makes teeth sparkle.

⊘10am-6pm Mon-Sat, from 1pm Sun; 🚊4/14/24 Dam) Within what looks like an ordinary canal house is an entire Catholic church. Ons' Lieve Heer op Solder (Our Dear Lord in the Attic) was built in the mid-1600s in defiance of the Calvinists. Inside you'll see labyrinthine staircases, rich artworks, period decor and the soaring, two-storey church itself.

Cannabis College   CULTURAL CENTRE
(Map p48; 🖉020-423 44 20; www.cannabis college.com; Oudezijds Achterburgwal 124; ⊘11am-7pm; 🚊4/14/24 Dam) This nonprofit centre offers visitors tips and tricks for having a positive smoking experience and provides the low-down on local cannabis laws. There are educational displays and a library. Staff can provide maps and advice on where to find coffeeshops that sell organic weed and shops that are good for newbies. T-shirts, stickers, postcards and a few other trinkets with the logo are for sale too.

Kuan Yin Shrine   BUDDHIST TEMPLE
(Fo Guang Shan He Hua Temple; Map p48; www. ibps.nl; Zeedijk 106-118; ⊘noon-5pm Tue-Sat, 10am-5pm Sun; Ⓜ Nieuwmarkt) Europe's largest Chinese Imperial–style Buddhist temple, built in 2000, is dedicated to Kuan Yin, the Buddhist goddess of mercy. Enter through the side gates (as is customary; the main gates are reserved for monks and nuns), make a donation, light an incense stick and ponder the thousand eyes and hands of the bodhisattva statue.

The ornate 'mountain gate' refers to the traditional setting of Buddhist monasteries. The middle section set back from the street was designed along principles of feng shui.

Hash, Marijuana & Hemp Museum   MUSEUM
(Map p48; 🖉020-624 89 26; www.hashmuseum. com; Oudezijds Achterburgwal 148; €9; ⊘10am-10pm; 🚊4/14/24 Dam) Simple exhibits here cover dope botany and the relationship between cannabis and religion. Highlights include an impressive pipe collection, an interactive vaporiser and a kiosk where you can create an e-postcard of yourself in a marijuana field. Admission also includes the **Hemp Gallery** (Map p48; www. hashmuseum.com; Oudezijds Achterburgwal 130; incl Hash, Marijuana & Hemp Museum €9; ⊘10am-10pm; 🚊4/14/24 Dam), filled with hemp art and historical items, in a separate building 30m north.

Red Light Secrets   MUSEUM
(Museum of Prostitution; Map p48; 🖉020-846 70 20; www.redlightsecrets.com; Oudezijds Achterburgwal 60h; €12.50; ⊘10am-midnight; 🚊4/14/24 Dam) Inside a former brothel in a 17th-century canal house, this museum fills a gap by showing curious visitors what a Red Light room looks like and answering basic questions about the industry. There's a short film as well as photo opportunities aplenty (ahem, dominatrix room). The venue takes less than an hour to tour. Tickets are €2 cheaper online.

Schreierstoren   HISTORIC BUILDING
(Map p48; www.schreierstoren.nl; Prins Hendrik-kade 95; 🚊2/4/11/12/13/14/17/24/26 Centraal Station) Built around 1480 as part of the city's defences, this tower is where Henry Hudson set sail for the New World in 1609; a plaque outside marks the spot. It's called the 'weeping tower' in lore – as it was where women waved farewell to sailors' ships – but the name actually comes from the word 'sharp' (for the way the corner jutted

into the bay). Step into the VOC Café (Map p54; ☎020-428 82 91; ⏰10am-1am Sun-Thu, to 2.30am Fri & Sat; 🚊2/4/11/12/13/14/17/24/26 Centraal Station) to see inside the tower.

Beurs van Berlage   HISTORIC BUILDING

(Map p48; ☎020-530 41 41, tours 020-620 81 12; www.beursvanberlage.com; Damrak 243; tour €14.50; ⏰tours by reservation; 🚊4/14/24 Dam) Master architect and ardent socialist HP Berlage (1856–1934) built Amsterdam's financial exchange in 1903. He filled the temple of capitalism with decorations that venerate labour, including tile murals of the well-muscled proletariat of the past, present and future. Within two decades trading had outgrown the building and relocated. The building now hosts conferences and art exhibitions. Tours (www.artifex.nu) lasting one hour detail its history and take you up into the bell tower for panoramic views.

Prostitution Information Centre   LIBRARY

(PIC; Map p48; ☎020-420 73 28; www.pic-amsterdam.com; Enge Kerksteeg 3; ⏰noon-5pm Wed-Fri, to 7pm Sat; 🚊4/14/24 Dam) Established by a former sex worker, the PIC provides frank information about the industry to those in the trade, their customers and curious tourists. It has a small on-site shop selling enlightening reading material and souvenirs.

W139   GALLERY

(Map p48; ☎020-622 94 34; www.w139.nl; Warmoesstraat 139; ⏰noon-6pm; 🚊4/14/24 Dam) [FREE] Duck into this contemporary arts centre and ponder the multimedia exhibits, which often have an edgy political angle. Check the website for frequent artist talks.

⊙ Nieuwmarkt, Plantage & the Eastern Islands

Historic buildings and Rembrandt's former home lie close to Nieuwmarkt, while south of this central hub is the vast square of Waterlooplein and the former Jewish quarter, with its stately synagogues containing Joods Historisch Museum (Jewish History Museum). A little to the east are the airy green spaces of Plantage, including parks, the botanical gardens and Amsterdam's lush Artis Royal Zoo.

★ Museum het Rembrandthuis   MUSEUM

(Rembrandt House Museum; Map p48; ☎020-520 04 00; www.rembrandthuis.nl; Jodenbreestraat 4; adult/child €13/4; ⏰10am-6pm; Ⓜ Waterlooplein) Housed in Rembrandt's former home, where the master painter spent his most successful years, painting big commissions such as *The Night Watch* and running the Netherlands' largest painting studio. It wasn't to last, however: his work fell out of fashion, he had some expensive relationship problems and bankruptcy came a-knocking. The inventory drawn up when he had to leave the house is the reason that curators have been able to refurnish the house so faithfully.

★ Joods Historisch Museum   MUSEUM

(Jewish Historical Museum; Map p54; ☎020-531 03 10; www.jck.nl; Nieuwe Amstelstraat 1; adult/child €15/7.50; ⏰11am-5pm; Ⓜ Waterloplein) The Joods Historisch Museum is a beautifully restored complex of four Ashkenazic synagogues from the 17th and 18th centuries. Displays show the rise of Jewish enterprise and its role in the Dutch economy, and the

PUT OUT THE RED LIGHT?

Since 2007 city officials have been reducing the number of Red Light windows in an effort to clean up the Red Light District. They claim it's not about morals but about crime: pimps, traffickers and money launderers have entered the scene and set the neighbourhood on a downward spiral. Opponents point to a growing conservatism and say the government is using crime as an excuse, because it doesn't like Amsterdam's reputation for sin.

As the window tally has decreased, fashion studios, art galleries and trendy cafes have moved in to reclaim the deserted spaces, thanks to a program of low-cost rent and other business incentives. It's called Project 1012, after the area's postal code.

To date, 300 windows remain, down from 482. Scores of sex workers and their supporters have taken to the streets to protest the closures: the concern is that closing the windows simply forces sex workers to relocate to less safe environments. The city is now rethinking its plan to buy back many more of the windows. In the meantime, other initiatives for changing the face of the area include the introduction of festivals such as the Red Light Jazz Festival (www.redlightjazz.com; ⏰early Jun).

Eastern Islands & Plantage

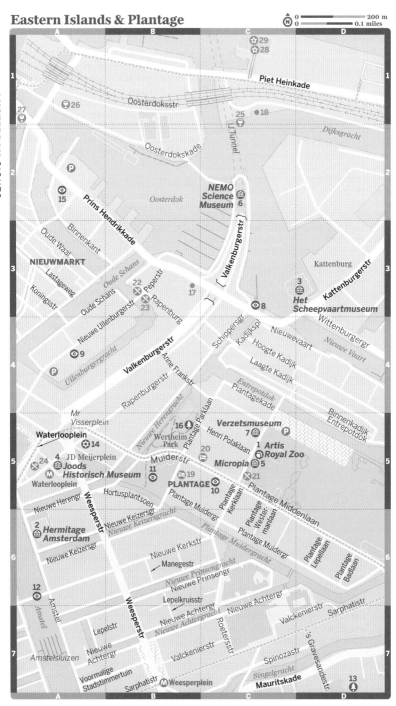

Eastern Islands & Plantage

history of Jews in the Netherlands. An excellent audio tour is included and there's a small children's museum with some activities.

Tickets also include admission to all of the Joods Cultureel Kwartier (Jewish Cultural Quarter) sites, including the Portuguese-Israelite Synagogue and the Hollandsche Schouwburg (p57).

Portuguese-Israelite Synagogue SYNAGOGUE
(Map p54; www.jck.nl; Mr Visserplein 3; adult/child €15/7.50; ⊙10am-5pm Sun-Fri May-Aug, 10am-5pm Sun-Thu, to 4pm Fri Mar, Apr, Sep & Oct, reduced hours Nov-Feb; Ⓜ Waterlooplein) With dizzying wooden barrel-vaulted ceilings, this was the largest synagogue in Europe when it was completed in 1675. It's still in use today, and has no electric light – after dark the candles in the vast chandeliers are lit for services. The large library belonging to the Ets Haim seminary is one of the oldest and most important Jewish book collections in Europe. Outside (near the entrance) stairs lead underground to the treasure chambers to see 16th-century manuscripts and gold-threaded tapestries.

Waag HISTORIC BUILDING
(Map p48; www.indewaag.nl; Nieuwmarkt 4; Ⓜ Nieuwmarkt) The multi-turreted Waag was built as a gate in the city walls in 1488. In 1601 the walls were destroyed so that the city could expand, and the building was turned into Amsterdam's main weigh house, and later a spot for public executions. A bar-restaurant (open 9am to 10.30pm) occupies it today. Out the front, Nieuwmarkt square hosts a variety of events, including a Saturday farmers market and a Sunday antiques market.

Gassan Diamonds FACTORY
(Map p54; www.gassan.com; Nieuwe Uilenburgerstraat 173-175; ⊙9am-5pm; Ⓜ Waterlooplein) FREE See diamond cutters and polishers in action at this workshop. You'll have a one-hour guided tour (no charge), which will prime you on assessing diamonds, then land you up in the shop with a chance to own your own sparklers, at a price.

The factory sits on Uilenburg, one of the rectangular islands reclaimed in the 1580s during a sudden influx of Sephardic Jews from Spain and Portugal. In the 1880s Gassan became the first diamond factory to use steam power.

Zuiderkerk CHURCH
(Map p48; ☑020-308 03 99, tower tours 020-689 25 65; www.zuiderkerkamsterdam.nl; Zuiderkerkhof 72; Ⓜ Nieuwmarkt) Famed Dutch Renaissance architect Hendrick de Keyser built the 'Southern Church' in 1611. This was the first custom-built Protestant church in Amsterdam – still Catholic in design but with no choir. The final church service was held here in 1929. During the 'Hunger Winter' of WWII it served as a morgue.

The interior is now used for private events, but you can contact them

AMSTERDAM IN...

Two Days

Begin with the biggies: visit the masterpieces in the Old South's Rijksmuseum (p70) and neighbouring Van Gogh Museum (p74). In the afternoon, get a dose of Dutch history in the city centre at the Amsterdam Museum (p43), Begijnhof (p50) or Royal Palace (p43) on the Dam (p51). At night venture into the eye-popping Red Light District, or sip beer in a brown cafe such as Hoppe (p97).

Start the next day browsing De Pijp's busy market Albert Cuypmarkt (p69). Cross into the Southern Canal Ring to visit opulent canal houses like the Museum Van Loon (p61) and Museum Willet-Holthuysen (p64) before taking a canal boat tour. At night party at hyperactive, neon-lit Leidseplein.

Four Days

On day three head to the Western Canal Ring's Negen Straatjes (Nine Streets; p107), a noughts-and-crosses board of speciality shops. Nearby, the haunting Anne Frank Huis (p58) is a must. Spend the evening in the Jordaan for a *gezellig* (cosy) dinner and canal-side drinks.

Begin the following day at Museum het Rembrandthuis (p53), then hop over to the Plantage for the Hortus Botanicus, Artis Royal Zoo and organic brewery Brouwerij 't IJ (p97) at the foot of a windmill or take a free ferry to explore Amsterdam Noord's cool former industrial waterfront venues.

about climbing the tower for a sky-high city view at www.westertorenamsterdam.nl.

Scheepvaarthuis   ARCHITECTURE
(Shipping House; Map p54; www.amrathamsterdam.com; Prins Hendrikkade 108; 🚊22/34/35 Prins Hendrikkade) Now the five-star Grand Hotel Amrath, the grand 1916-built Scheepvaarthuis is a neo-Gothic art-deco beauty, the first and finest example of the expressionist Amsterdam School of architecture. The exterior resembles a ship's bow, awash with nautical detailing; look for figures of Neptune, his wife and four females that represent the compass points. Staff are happy for tourists to have a nose around: head up to the 3rd floor to see the Great Hall with its leaded glass designed by Willem Bogtman.

★**Verzetsmuseum**   MUSEUM
(Dutch Resistance Museum; Map p54; 🖉020-620 25 35; www.verzetsmuseum.org; Plantage Kerklaan 61; adult/child €11/6; ⊙10am-5pm Mon-Fri, from 11am Sat & Sun; 🚊14 Plantage Kerklaan) This museum brings the horror of German occupation in WWII vividly alive, using letters, artefacts and personal stories to illuminate local resistance to (but also collaboration with) the Nazis. There's also a section on the Dutch East Indies (now Indonesia) pre- and postwar. Labels are in Dutch and English.

Its **Verzetsmuseum Junior** relates the stories of four Dutch children, putting the Resistance into context for kids.

★**Artis Royal Zoo**   ZOO
(Map p54; 🖉020-523 34 00; www.artis.nl; Plantage Kerklaan 38-40; adult/child €23/19.50, incl Micropia €29.50/25.50; ⊙9am-6pm Mar-Oct, to 5pm Nov-Feb; 🚊14 Artis) A wonderfully leafy expanse, mainland Europe's oldest zoo has a fine range of wildlife, with extensive habitats and room to wander. A lovely stretch runs along the canal looking across to the old Entrepot dock. Habitats include African savannah and tropical rainforest, and there are reptiles, lions, jaguars, elephants, giraffes and lots of primates. There's also an aquarium complex featuring coral reefs, shark tanks and an Amsterdam canal displayed from a fish's point of view, plus a planetarium and kids' petting zoo.

★**Het Scheepvaartmuseum**   MUSEUM
(Maritime Museum; Map p54; 🖉020-523 22 22; www.hetscheepvaartmuseum.nl; Kattenburgerplein 1; adult/child €16/8; ⊙9am-5pm; 🚊22/48 Kattenburgerplein) A waterfront 17th-century admiralty building houses this renovated, state-of-the-art presentation of maritime memorabilia. Highlights include exquisite and imaginatively presented Golden Age maps, fascinating 19th-century photo albums of early voyages and an audiovisual

immersive journey evoking a voyage by ship. Outside, you can clamber over the full-scale replica of the Dutch East India Company's 700-tonne *Amsterdam* – one of the largest ships of the fleet – with its tiny bunks and sailors' hammocks, and the chance to mock-fire its cannons.

★ **NEMO Science Museum** MUSEUM

(Map p54; ☑020-244 01 81; www.nemoscience museum.nl; Oosterdok 2; €16.50, roof terrace free; ☉10am-5.30pm, closed Mon early Sep-early Feb, roof terrace to 9pm Jul & Aug; ☐22/48 Kadijk-splein) Perched atop the entrance to the IJ Tunnel is the unmissable slanted-roof green-copper building, designed by Italian archi-tect Renzo Piano, almost surrounded by water. Its rooftop square has great views and water- and wind-operated hands-on exhibits. Inside, everything is interactive, with three floors of investigative mayhem. Experiment lifting yourself up via a pulley, making bubbles, building structures, divid-ing light into colours, racing your shadow and discovering the teenage mind.

Hortus Botanicus GARDENS

(Botanical Garden; Map p54; ☑020-625 90 21; www.dehortus.nl; Plantage Middenlaan 2a; adult/child €9.50/5; ☉10am-5pm; ☐14 Mr Vis-serplein) A botanical garden since 1638, it bloomed as tropical seeds and plants were brought in by Dutch trading ships. From here, coffee, pineapple, cinnamon and palm-oil plants were distributed through-out the world. The 4000-plus species are kept in wonderful structures, including the colonial-era seed house and a three-cli-mate glasshouse.

Hollandsche Schouwburg MEMORIAL

(National Holocaust Museum; Holland Theatre; Map p54; ☑020-531 03 10; www.jck.nl; Plantage Middenlaan 24; adult/child €15/7.50; ☉11am-5pm; ☐14 Artis) Few theatres have had a history of such highs and lows. It was opened as the Artis Theatre in 1892 and became a hub of cultural life in Amster-dam, staging major dramas and operettas. In WWII the occupying Germans turned it into a Jew-only theatre, and later, horrify-ingly, a detention centre for Jews held for deportation.

Tickets cover admission to all of the Joods Cultureel Kwartier (Jewish Cultural Quarter) sites, including the Joods Histor-isch Museum (p53) and the Portuguese-Israelite Synagogue (p55).

Wertheimpark PARK

(Map p54; Plantage Parklaan; ☉7am-9pm; ☐14 Artis) Adding to the lush greenness of the Plantage area, this park is a brilliant, willow-shaded spot for lazing by the Nieu-we Herengracht. It contains the Auschwitz Memorial, designed by Dutch writer and artist Jan Wolkers: a panel of broken mir-rors installed in the ground reflects the sky, and an inscription reads Nooit Meer (Never Again).

ARCAM ARCHITECTURE

(Stichting Architectuurcentrum Amsterdam; Map p54; ☑020-620 48 78; www.arcam.nl; Prins Hen-drikkade 600; ☉1-5pm Tue-Sat; ☐22/48 Kadijk-splein) FREE The sharply curved Amsterdam Architecture Foundation is a striking water-side building hosting changing architectural exhibitions.

◉ Western Canal Ring

The Anne Frank Huis (p58) is the neigh-bourhood's number-one drawcard, but other engaging museums include the fascinating canal-house museum Het Grachtenhuis (p60). Climbing the striking **Westerkerk bell tower** (Map p66; ☑020-689 25 65; www.westertorenamsterdam.nl; Prin-sengracht 281; tours €8; ☉10am-7.30pm Mon-Sat Apr-Oct; ☐13/17 Westermarkt) rewards with spectacular views over the canals.

Anne Frank Huis MUSEUM

See p58.

Westerkerk CHURCH

(Western Church; Map p66; ☑020-624 77 66; www. westerkerk.nl; Prinsengracht 281; ☉10am-3pm Mon-Sat early May-Oct, 10am-3pm Mon-Fri Nov-ear-ly May; ☐13/17 Westermarkt) The main gather-ing place for Amsterdam's Dutch Reformed community, this church was built for rich Protestants to a 1620 design by Hendrick de Keyser. The nave is the largest in the Neth-erlands and is covered by a wooden barrel vault. The huge main organ dates from 1686, with panels decorated with instruments and biblical scenes. Rembrandt (1606–69), who died bankrupt at nearby Rozengracht, was buried in a pauper's grave somewhere in the church. Its bell tower can be climbed.

Homomonument MONUMENT

(Map p66; www.homomonument.nl; cnr Keizers-gracht & Raadhuisstraat; ☐13/17 Westermarkt) Behind the Westerkerk (p57), this 1987-installed cluster of three 10m by 10m by 10m

TOP SIGHT
ANNE FRANK HUIS

It is one of the 20th century's most compelling stories: a young Jewish girl forced into hiding with her family and their friends to escape deportation by the Nazis. The house they used as a hideaway should be a highlight of any visit to Amsterdam; indeed, it attracts more than one million visitors a year.

Background

Stepping through the bookcase that swings open to reveal the 'Secret Annexe' and going up the steep stairs into the living quarters – where the Frank family lived for more than two years – is to step back into a time that seems both distant and tragically real.

It took the German army just five days to occupy all of the Netherlands, along with Belgium and much of France. And once Hitler's forces had swept across the country, many Jews – like Anne Frank and her family – eventually went into hiding. Anne's diary describes how restrictions were gradually imposed on Dutch Jews: from being forbidden to ride streetcars to being forced to hand over their bicycles and not being allowed to visit Christian friends.

The Franks moved into the upper floors of the specially prepared rear of the building, along with another couple, the Van Pels (called the Van Daans in Anne's diary), and their son, Peter. Four months later Fritz Pfeffer (called Mr Dussel in the diary) joined the household. Here they survived until they were betrayed to the Gestapo in August 1944.

DON'T MISS

➡ Anne's red-plaid diary

➡ Anne's bedroom

➡ WWII newsreels

➡ Peter van Pels' room

➡ Video of Anne's schoolmate Hanneli Goslar

PRACTICALITIES

➡ Map p66

➡ ☏ 020-556 71 05

➡ www.annefrank.org

➡ Prinsengracht 263-267

➡ adult/child €10.50/5

➡ ⏱ 9am-10pm Apr-Oct, 9am-7pm Sun-Fri, to 9pm Sat Nov-Mar

➡ 🚊 13/17 Westermarkt

Ground Floor

The house itself is contained within a modern, square shell that retains the original feel of the building (it was used during WWII as offices and a warehouse). In 2019, the new Westermarkt entrance and extensions to the museum where unveiled. Additions include multilingual news reels of WWII footage narrated using segments of Anne's diary: it inextricably links the rise of Hitler with the Frank family's personal saga.

Offices

View the former offices of Victor Kugler, Otto Frank's business partner; his identity card and the film magazines he bought for Anne are on display. The other office area belonged to Miep Gies, Bep Voskuijl and Johannes Kleiman, two women and a man who worked in the office by day and provided food, clothing, school supplies and other goods – often purchased on the black market or with ration cards – for the eight members of the Secret Annexe. You can see some of their personal documents here.

Secret Annexe

While the lower levels present history with interactive modern technology, the former living quarters of the Frank family in the *achterhuis* (rear house) retain their stark, haunting austerity. It's as if visitors are stepping back into 1942. Notice how windows of the annexe were blacked out to avoid arousing suspicion among people who might see it from surrounding houses (blackouts were common practice to disorient bombers at night).

Take a moment to observe the ingenious set-up of the Secret Annexe as you walk through. You then enter two floors of the dark and airless space where the Franks and their friends observed complete silence during the daytime until they were betrayed, arrested by the Nazis and sent to concentration camps. Otto Frank, Anne's father, was the only survivor.

The Diary

More haunting exhibits and videos await after you return to the front house – including Anne's red-plaid diary itself, sitting alone in its glass case. Watch the video of Anne's old schoolmate Hanneli Goslar, who describes encountering Anne at Bergen-Belsen.

AFTER THE WAR

The Franks were among the last Jews to be deported and Anne died in the Bergen-Belsen concentration camp in March 1945, only weeks before it was liberated. After the war, Otto published Anne's diary, which was found among the litter in the annexe (the furniture had been carted away by the Nazis).

It's compulsory to prepurchase tickets (€0.50 surcharge) via the website, when you must also choose a time slot. While 80% of tickets are released two months ahead, 20% are made available online on the day. You'll need to preprint tickets or show them on your phone.

granite triangles recalls persecution by the Nazis, who forced gay men to wear a pink triangle patch. One of the triangles steps down into the Keizersgracht and is said to represent a jetty from which gay men were sent to the concentration camps. Others interpret the step up from the canal as a symbol of rising hope.

Het Grachtenhuis   MUSEUM
(Canal House; Map p66; ☑020-421 16 56; www.hetgrachtenhuis.nl; Herengracht 386; adult/child €15/7.50; ☉10am-5pm Tue-Sun; 🚊2/11/12 Koningsplein) Learn about the remarkable feat of engineering behind the Canal Ring through this museum's holograms, videos, models, cartoons, scale model of Amsterdam and other innovative exhibits, which explain how the canals and the houses that line them were built. Unlike at most Amsterdam museums, you can't simply wander through: small groups go in together to experience the multimedia exhibits. It takes about 45 minutes, and you'll come out knowing why Amsterdam's houses tilt.

Huis Marseille   MUSEUM
(Map p66; ☑020-531 89 89; www.huismarseille.nl; Keizersgracht 401; adult/child €8/free; ☉11am-6pm Tue-Sun; 🚊2/11/12 Keizersgracht) Large-scale temporary exhibitions from its own collection are staged at this well-curated photography museum, which also hosts travelling shows. Themes might include portraiture, nature or regional photography, and exhibitions are spread out over several floors and in a summer house behind the main house.

French merchant Isaac Focquier built Huis Marseille in 1665, installing a map of the French port Marseille on the facade, and the original structure has remained largely intact. Look out for the 18th-century fountain in the library, and a painting of Apollo, Minerva and the muses in the garden room.

Bijbels Museum   MUSEUM
(Bible Museum; Map p66; ☑020-624 24 36; www.bijbelsmuseum.nl; Herengracht 366-368; adult/child €10/free; ☉10am-5pm Tue-Fri, from 11am Sat & Sun; 🚊2/11/12 Spui) A scale model of the Jewish Tabernacle described in Exodus – built by dedicated minister Leendert Schouten and drawing thousands of visitors even before it was completed in 1851 – is the star attraction at this bible museum. Inside a 1622 canal house, the museum has an extraordinary collection of bibles, including the Netherlands' oldest, a 1477-printed Delft

Bible, and a 1st edition of the 1637 Dutch authorised version. Trees and plants mentioned in the Good Book feature in the garden.

Poezenboot   ANIMAL SANCTUARY
(Cat Boat; Map p48; ☑020-625 87 94; www.depoezenboot.nl; Singel 38; by donation; ☉1-3pm Mon, Tue & Thu-Sat; 🚊2/11/12/13/17 Nieuwezijds Kolk) Cat-lovers may want to check out this quirky boat on the Singel. It was founded in 1966 by an eccentric woman who became legendary for looking after several hundred stray cats at a time. The boat has since been taken over by a foundation and can hold some 50 kitties in proper pens. Some are permanent residents, and the rest are ready to be adopted (after being neutered and implanted with an identifying computer chip, as per Dutch law).

Multatuli Museum   MUSEUM
(Map p48; ☑020-638 19 38; www.multatuli-museum.nl; Korsjespoortsteeg 20; ☉10am-5pm Tue, from noon Wed-Sun; 🚊2/11/12/13/17 Nieuwezijds Kolk) FREE Better known by the pen name Multatuli (Latin for 'I have suffered greatly'), writer Eduard Douwes Dekker is most recognised for *Max Havelaar* (1860), his novel about corrupt colonialists in the Dutch East Indies. This small but fascinating museum-home chronicles his life and work, and shows furniture and artefacts from his period in Indonesia.

◉ Southern Canal Ring

The semicircular grid of the Southern Ring packs in glorious sights particularly evocative of Amsterdam's Golden Age, such as the illustrious art of the Hermitage (p60), the gracious architecture of the Golden Bend (p64), and the canal house museums of Van Loon (p61) and Willet-Holthuysen (p64), plus a scattering of other charming stops, such as the Kattenkabinet (p61).

★Hermitage Amsterdam   MUSEUM
(Map p54; ☑020-530 87 55; www.hermitage.nl; Amstel 51; single exhibitions adult/child €18/free, all exhibitions adult/child €25/free; ☉10am-5pm; Ⓜ Waterlooplein) There have long been links between Russia and the Netherlands – Tsar Peter the Great learned shipbuilding here in 1697 – hence this branch of St Petersburg's State Hermitage Museum. Blockbuster temporary exhibitions show works from the Hermitage's vast treasure trove, while the permanent Portrait Gallery of the Golden Age has formal group portraits of the

DE HALLEN

These red-brick 1902-built tram sheds were formerly used as a squat before being turned into this breathtaking sky-lit space. De Hallen (Map p62; www.dehallen-amsterdam. nl; Bellamyplein 51; ⏰7/17 Ten Katestraat) was stunningly converted in 2014 to create a cultural complex incorporating a food hall (Map p62; www.foodhallen.nl; Hannie Dankbaar Passage 3; dishes €3-20; ⏰11am-11.30pm Sun-Thu, to 1am Fri & Sat; ⏰), a family-friendly brasserie, a library, design shops, such as the Denim City Store (Map p62; ☎020-820 86 14; www.denimcity.org; Hannie Dankbaarpassage 22; ⏰11am-7pm Wed-Fri, 10am-6pm Sat, noon-5pm Sun), a bike seller/repairer (Map p62; ☎020-489 70 29; www.recyclefietsen. nl; Hannie Dankbaar Passage 27; ⏰10am-6pm Tue-Fri, to 5pm Sat), a cinema (Map p62; www. filmhallen.nl; Hannie Dankbaar Passage 12; tickets adult/child from €11/7.50; ⏰10am-midnight) and a hotel (Map p62; ☎020-515 04 53; www.hoteldehallen.com; Bellamyplein 47; d €180-255; ⏰⏰). Regular events held inside include themed weekend markets (such as organic produce or Dutch design); check the website to find out what's happening. A lively daily (except Sunday) street market, Ten Katemarkt (Map p62; www.tenkatemarkt.nl; Ten Kat-estraat; ⏰9am-5pm Mon-Sat), takes place outside.

17th-century Dutch A-list; the Outsider Gallery also has temporary shows. I Amsterdam and Museum cards allow free entrance or a discount, depending on the exhibition.

Bloemenmarkt   MARKET
(Flower Market; Map p62; Singel, btwn Muntplein & Koningsplein; ⏰8.30am-7pm Mon-Sat, to 7.30pm Sun Apr-Oct, 9am-5.30pm Mon-Sat, 11am-5.30pm Sun Nov-Mar; ⏰2/11/12 Koningsplein) Flowers are not treats, but essentials in Amsterdam. Ever since 1860, this famous flower market has been located at the spot where nurserymen and women, having sailed up the Amstel from their smallholdings, would moor their barges to sell their wares directly to customers. No longer floating (it's now perched on piles), the market has plenty of high-kitsch miniature clogs, fridge magnets and wooden tulips; it's also a good place to buy (real) tulips in season and bulbs year-round.

★ Foam   GALLERY
(Fotografiemuseum Amsterdam; Map p62; www. foam.org; Keizersgracht 609; adult/child €11/free; ⏰10am-6pm Sat-Wed, to 9pm Thu & Fri; ⏰24 Keizersgracht) From the outside it looks like a grand canal house, but this is the city's most important photography gallery. Its simple, spacious galleries, some with skylights or large windows for natural light, host four major exhibitions annually, featuring world-renowned photographers such as William Eggleston and Helmut Newton. There's a cafe in the basement.

★ Museum Van Loon   MUSEUM
(Map p62; ☎020-624 52 55; www.museum vanloon.nl; Keizersgracht 672; adult/child €9/5,

free with Museum & I Amsterdam cards; ⏰10am-5pm; ⏰24 Keizersgracht) An insight into noble life in the 19th century, Museum Van Loon is an opulent 1672 residence that was first home to painter Ferdinand Bol and later to the Van Loon family. Important paintings such as *The Marriage of Willem van Loon and Margaretha Bas* by Jan Miense Molenaer and a collection of some 150 portraits of the Van Loons hang inside sumptuous interiors.

Stadsarchief   MUSEUM
(Municipal Archives; Map p62; ☎tour reservations 020-251 15 11; www.amsterdam.nl/stadsarchief; Vijzelstraat 32; ⏰10am-5pm Tue-Fri, from noon Sat & Sun; ⏰24 Keizersgracht) FREE A distinctive striped building dating from 1923, this former bank now houses 23km of shelving storing Amsterdam archives. Fascinating displays of archive gems, such as the 1942 police report on the theft of Anne Frank's bike and a letter from Charles Darwin to Artis Royal Zoo in 1868, can be viewed in the enormous tiled basement vault.

Tours (adult/child €6/free, 1¼ hours) run at 2pm on Saturdays and Sundays. Book.

Kattenkabinet   MUSEUM
(Cat Cabinet; Map p62; ☎020-626 90 40; www. kattenkabinet.nl; Herengracht 497; adult/child €7/free; ⏰10am-5pm Mon-Fri, from noon Sat & Sun; ⏰24 Muntplein) When kitties go to the great sofa in the sky, most doting owners comfort themselves with a photo on the mantel; wealthy financier Bob Meijer founded an entire museum in memory of his red tomcat John Pierpont Morgan III. The collection includes artworks by Tsuguharu Foujita,

Southern Canal Ring

Nassaukade

Singelgracht

Lijnbaansstr
Elandsstr
Hazenstr
Elandsgr

Lijnbaansgr
Lijnbaanstr
Oude Looiersstr

Bilderdijkstr

Da Costagracht

Kinkerstr

Elandsgr

Looiersgr

Jan Hanzenstr

Passeerdersstr

Passeerdersgr

Bellamystr

Kinkerstr

OUD WEST

J V Lennepstr

Passeerderstr

Hasebroekstr

De
Hallen

J V Lennepstr
Nieuwe
Passeerdersstr

Raamplein
Raamstr

Jacob van Lennepkade

Raamstr

Nassaukade

Leidsekade

Leidsegr

Nicolaas Beetsstr

Ten Katestr

Jacob van Lennepkanaal

2e Constantijn Huygensstr

1e Constantijn Huygensstr

Jacob van Lennepstr
Bosboom Toussaintstr

3e Helmersstr

Alberdingk
Thijmstr

2e Helmersstr

Leidsebosje

Marnixstr

Leidseplein

Arie
Biemondstr

1e Helmersstr

Overtoom

Hirschpassage

Max
Euweplein

Jan Pieter Heijestr

Wilhelminastr

Vondelstr
Tesselschadestr

Roemer
Visscherstr

Zandpad

Vondelpark

Overtoom

Anna van den
Vondelstr

Vondelstr

Van Baerlestr

Vossiusstr

Schapenburgerpad

Gerard
Brandtstr

Vondelpark

Pieter Corneliszl Hooftstr

Jan
Luijkenstr

Van de
Veldestr

Paulus Potterstr

Stedelijk
Museum

Van Gogh
Museum

Museumplein

Van Eeghenstr

Jacob Obrechtstr

Willemsparkweg

Van Breestr

Concertgebouwplein

Moreelstr

Koningslaan

Valeriusstr

Cornelis Schuytstr

Bartstr

De Lairessestr

Koninginneweg

Johannes Verhulststr

JJ Viottastr

Nicolaas Maesstr

Frans van Mierisstr

Ruysdaelstr

Heinzestr

De Lairessestr

Reijnier Vinkeleskade

Breitnerstr

Noorder Amstel Kanaal

Apollolaan

Apollolaan

Apollolaan

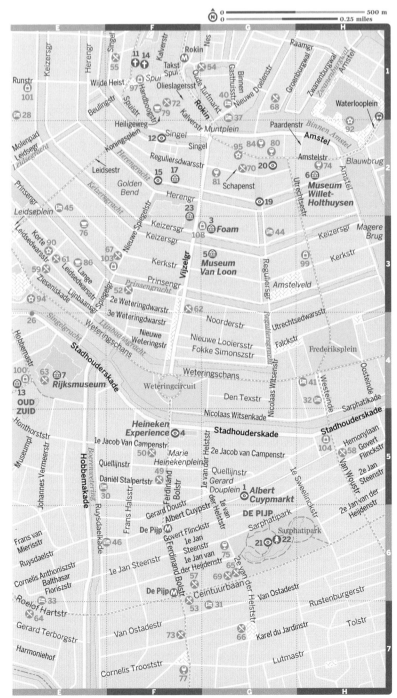

Southern Canal Ring

Théophile Alexandre Steinlen and Amsterdam's chief sculptor, Hildo Krop. A visit here also gives you the opportunity to explore one of the Golden Bend's grand houses; it's the only one open to the public.

★ **Museum Willet-Holthuysen** MUSEUM
(Map p62; ☏ 020-523 17 30; www.willetholthuysen. nl; Herengracht 605; adult/child €10/free; ⊙ 10am-5pm Mon-Fri, from 11am Sat & Sun; ⓐ 4/14 Rembrandtplein) This exquisite canal house was built in 1687 for Amsterdam mayor Jacob Hop, then remodelled in 1739. It's named after Louisa Willet-Holthuysen, who inherited the house from her coal-and-glass-merchant father and lived a lavish, bohemian life here with her husband. She bequeathed the property to the city in 1895. With displays including part of the family's 275-piece Meissen table service, and an immaculate French-style garden, the museum is a fascinating window into the 19th-century world of the super-rich.

Golden Bend ARCHITECTURE
(Gouden Bocht; Map p62; Herengracht, btwn Leidsestraat & Vijzelstraat; ⓐ 2/11/12 Koningsplein) The Golden Bend is Amsterdam's swankiest stretch of property. Its mansions are a monument to the Golden Age, when precious goods swelled in the cellars of homes already stuffed with valuables. The richest Amsterdammers ruled their affairs from here. The earliest mansions date from the 1660s, when the Canal Ring was expanded south. Thanks to some city-hall lobbying, the gables here were built twice as wide as the standard Amsterdam model, and the rear gardens deeper.

Reguliersgracht CANAL
(Map p62; ⓐ 4/14 Rembrandtplein) Crossing Herengracht, Keizersgracht & Prinsengracht canals, this, the prettiest of Amsterdam's waterways, was dug in 1658 to link the Herengracht with the canals further south. The canal is famous for its seven bridges, though if you stand where it crosses Heren-

gracht, you can count 15 bridges in all directions. The houses lining the canal are a decorative feast of gables and adornments. Reguliersgracht was named after an order of monks whose monastery was located nearby.

Where Prinsengracht crosses Reguliersgracht, there is a house with a stork statue above the door – the dwelling once belonged to a midwife.

Magere Brug   BRIDGE
(Skinny Bridge; Map p54; btwn Kerkstraat & Nieuwe Kerkstraat; 🚊4 Prinsengracht) Dating from the 1670s, the nine-arched 'Skinny Bridge' has had several incarnations, first in timber and later in concrete. It has a hand-operated central section that can be raised to let boats through. The bridge is especially pretty at night, when it glows with 1200 tiny lights. It has appeared in several films, including the 1971 James Bond thriller *Diamonds are Forever*. Stand in the middle and feel it sway under the passing traffic.

◉ Jordaan & the West

The area doesn't have any big-hitting sights, but that's not the point. In the Jordaan it's the little things that are appealing – the narrow lanes, the old facades, the funny little shops and taking your time wandering without worrying if you get lost. Likewise in the West, the key attractions are wandering, eating and nightlife (not necessarily in that order).

Noorderkerk   CHURCH
(Northern Church; Map p66; www.noorderkerk.org; Noordermarkt 48; ⊙10.30am-12.30pm Mon & Sat; 🚊3/5 Marnixplein) Near the Prinsengracht's northern end, this imposing Calvinist church was completed in 1623 for the 'common' people in the Jordaan. (The upper classes attended the Westerkerk further south.) It was built in the shape of a broad Greek cross (four arms of equal length) around a central pulpit, giving the entire congregation unimpeded access. Hendrick de Keyser's

Jordaan & the Western Canal Ring

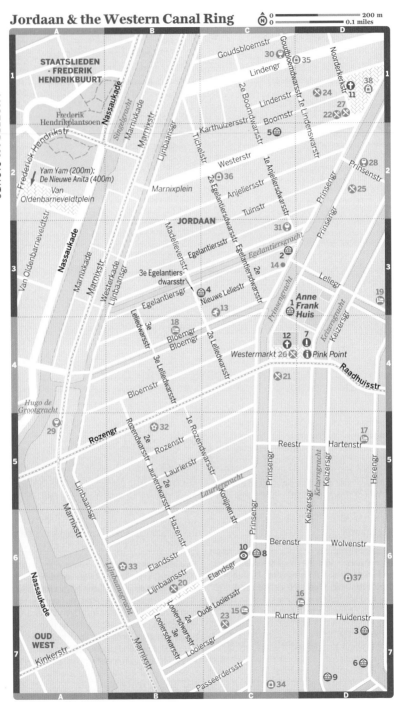

Jordaan & the Western Canal Ring

AMSTERDAM SIGHTS

design, unusual at the time, would become common for Protestant churches throughout the country. It hosts the well-regarded Saturday-afternoon Nooderkerkconcerten (Map p66; 020-620 44 15; www.noorderkerk concerten.nl; tickets from €16; ⊙2pm Sat; 3/5 Marnixplein) concert series.

Houseboat Museum MUSEUM
(Map p66; 020-427 07 50; www.houseboatmuse um.nl; Prinsengracht 296k; adult/child €4.50/3.50; ⊙10am-5pm daily Jul & Aug, Tue-Sun Sep-Dec & Jan-Jun; 13/17 Westermarkt) This quirky museum, a 23m-long sailing barge from 1914, offers a good sense of how *gezellig* life can be on the water. The actual displays are minimal, but you can watch a presentation on houseboats (some pretty and some ghastly) and inspect the sleeping, living, cooking and dining quarters with all the mod cons.

Johnny Jordaanplein SQUARE
(Map p66; cnr Prinsengracht & Elandsgracht; 13/17 Westermarkt) This shady little square is named for Johnny Jordaan (the pseudonym of Johannes Hendricus van Musscher), a popular musician in the mid-1900s who sang the romantic music known as *levenslied* (tears-in-your-beer-style ballads). The

colourfully painted hut – a municipal transformer station – proudly displays one of his song lyrics: *'Amsterdam, wat bent je mooi'* (Amsterdam, how beautiful you are). Behind the hut you'll find Johnny, and members of the Jordaan musical hall of fame, cast in bronze.

Geelvinck Pianola Museum MUSEUM
(Map p66; 020-627 96 24; www.geelvinck.nl; Westerstraat 106; museum adult/child €9/4.50, concert tickets from €12.50; ⊙11am-5pm Fri-Sun year-round, concerts Sep-Jun; 3/5 Marnixplein) This is a very special place, crammed with pianolas from the early 1900s. The museum has around 50, although only a dozen are on display at any given time, as well as some 30,000 music rolls and a player pipe organ. The curator gives an hour-long guided tour and music demonstrations with great zest. Regular concerts are held on the player pianos, featuring anything from Mozart to Fats Waller and rare classical or jazz tunes composed especially for the instrument.

Electric Ladyland MUSEUM
(Map p66; 020-420 37 76; www.electric-lady-land.com; 2e Leliedwarsstraat 5; adult/child €5/ free; ⊙by reservation 2-6pm Wed-Sat; 13/17

WESTERGASFABRIEK

A stone's throw northwest of the Jordaan, the late-19th-century Dutch Renaissance Westergasfabriek (☎020-586 07 10; www.westergasfabriek.nl; Pazzanistraat; 🚊5 Van Limburg Stirumstraat/Van Hallstraat) complex adjacent to the Westerpark green space (Spaarndammerstraat; 🚊3 Haarlemmerplein) was the city's western gasworks until gas production ceased in 1967. The site was heavily polluted and underwent a major clean-up before it re-emerged as a cultural and recreational park, with lush lawns, a long wading pool, cycleways and sports facilities.

The post-industrial buildings now house creative spaces such as advertising agencies and TV production studios, as well as regular festivals and events – including the Sunday Market (www.sundaymarket.nl; ⊘noon-6pm 1st Sun of month), a quality craft and gourmet food event.

Westergasfabriek's slew of dining, drinking and entertainment options includes the following:

Mossel En Gin (☎020-486 58 69; www.mosselengin.nl; Gosschalklaan 12, mains €16.50-17; ⊘kitchen 4-10.30pm Tue-Thu, 2-10.30pm Fri, 1-10.30pm Sat & Sun, bar to midnight Tue-Thu & Sun, to 1am Fri & Sat; 🛜; 🚊21 Van Hallstraat) Gins are used in creative cooking and cocktails.

De Bakkerswinkel (☎020-688 06 32; www.debakkerswinkel.nl; Polonceaukade 1, snacks €4-6, dishes €8-16; ⊘8.30am-5pm Mon-Thu, 8.30am-6pm Fri, 10am-6pm Sat & Sun; 🚊5 Van Limburg Stirumstraat) Split-level cafe inside the gasworks' former regulator's house.

Raïnaraï (☎020-486 71 09; www.rainarai.nl; Polonceaukade 40; mains €19.50-23.50, 2-/3-course menus €32.50/36; ⊘noon-10pm Tue-Sun; 🚊21 Van Hallstraat) Algerian cuisine amid exotic decor.

Westergasterras (www.westergasterras.nl; Klönneplein 4-6; ⊘11am-1am Mon-Thu, 11am-3am Fri, 10am-3am Sat, 10am-1am Sun; 🛜; 🚊5 Van Limburg Stirumstraat) Bar opening to one of Amsterdam's best terraces.

Brouwerij Troost Westergas (☎020-737 10 28; www.brouwerijtroost.nl; Pazzanistraat 27; ⊘4pm-midnight Mon-Thu, 4pm-3am Fri, noon-3am Sat, noon-midnight Sun; 🛜; 🚊5 Van Limburg Stirumstraat) Brewery for hop heads and cool cats.

Pacific Parc (☎020-488 77 78; www.pacificparc.nl; Polonceaukade 23; 🚊5 Van Limburg Stirumstraat) Indie gigs and DJ sets.

Westerunie (☎020-684 84 96; www.westerunie.nl; Klönneplein 6; ⊘hours vary; 🛜; 🚊5 Van Limburg Stirumstraat) Pumpin' post-industrial club.

Westermarkt) The world's first museum of fluorescent art features owner Nick Padalino's psychedelic sculpture work on one side and cases of naturally luminescent rocks and manufactured glowing objects (money, government ID cards etc) on the other. Jimi Hendrix, the Beatles and other trippy artists play on the stereo while Nick lovingly describes each item in the collection. His art gallery–shop is upstairs.

Amsterdam Tulip Museum   MUSEUM
(Map p66; ☎020-421 00 95; www.amsterdamtulip museum.com; Prinsengracht 116; adult/child €5/3; ⊘10am-6pm; 🚊13/17 Westermarkt) Allow around half an hour at the diminutive Amsterdam Tulip Museum, which offers a nifty overview of the history of the country's favourite bloom. Through exhibits, timelines and two short films (in English), you'll learn how Ottoman merchants encountered the flowers in the Himalayan steppes and began commercial production in Turkey, how fortunes were made and lost during Dutch 'Tulipmania' in the 17th century, and how bulbs were used as food during WWII.

☉ Vondelpark & the South

Vondelpark is Amsterdam's green soul, and a few paces away lie the city's greatest museums, all conveniently close together around Museumplein, including the Rijksmuseum, Van Gogh Museum and the Stedelijk Museum. Further south, you can explore the parklands of Amsterdamse Bos, and the Cobra Museum, devoted to the De Stijl art movement. North of Vondelpark, there is the arts and food hall De Hallen, in former tram sheds.

Rijksmuseum MUSEUM
See p70.

Van Gogh Museum MUSEUM
See p74.

★ Stedelijk Museum MUSEUM
(Map p62; 020-573 29 11; www.stedelijk.nl; Museumplein 10; adult/child €17.50/free; 10am-6pm Sat-Thu, to 10pm Fri; 2/3/5/12 Van Baerlestraat) This fabulous museum houses the collection amassed by postwar curator Willem Sandberg. Displays rotate but you'll see an amazing selection featuring works by Picasso, Matisse, Mondrian, Van Gogh, Rothko, De Kooning, Warhol and more, plus an exuberant Karel Appel mural and great temporary exhibitions. The building was originally a bank, built in 1895 to a neo-Renaissance design by AM Weissman, and the modern extension is nicknamed 'the bathtub' for reasons that will be obvious when you see it.

House of Bols MUSEUM
(Map p62; www.houseofbols.com; Paulus Potterstraat 14; admission incl 1 cocktail €16, over 18yr only; 1-6.30pm Sun-Thu, to 9pm Fri & Sat; 2/5/12 Van Baerlestraat) Cheesy but fun: here you undertake an hour's self-guided tour through this *jenever* (Dutch gin) museum. In the 'Hall of Taste' you'll try to differentiate different scents and flavours, while in the 'Distillery Room' you'll learn about the process of extraction. You'll learn loads about the history of gin, and get to try shaking your own cocktail, plus drink a Bols confection of your choice at the end.

Diamond Museum MUSEUM
(Map p62; www.diamantmuseumamsterdam.nl; Paulus Potterstraat 8; adult/child €10/7.50; 9am-5pm; 2/5/12 Rijksmuseum) The extensive bling on display at the small, low-tech Diamond Museum is all clever re-creations. You get a lot of background on the history of the trade and various historic sparkly crowns and jewels. Here you'll learn how Amsterdam was the globe's diamond trade epicentre for many centuries, where local Jews dominated the cutting and polishing business, and how the business moved to Antwerp after WWII following the decimation of the Jewish population here.

Those so inclined can save money by going next door to Coster Diamonds (Map p116; 020-305 55 55; www.costerdiamonds.com; Paulus Potterstraat 2; 9am-5pm) – the company owns the museum and is attached to it – and taking a free workshop tour.

Vondelkerk HISTORIC BUILDING
(Map p62; www.stadsherstel.nl; Vondelstraat 120d; 1/11 1e Constantijn Huygensstraat) Architect Pierre Cuyper built this, his favourite, church between 1870 and 1880. However, it was hampered by lack of funds during construction and damaged by fire in 1904. Slated for demolition in 1978, it was saved by a group of architecture enthusiasts. The interior (a popular wedding venue) is used as offices, and not accessible to the public.

Hollandsche Manege HORSE RIDING
(Map p62; 020-618 09 42; www.dehollandschemanege.nl; Vondelstraat 140; adult/child museum €8/4, private riding lessons per 30/60min €39/64; museum 10am-5pm, riding lessons by reservation; 1/11 1e Constantijn Huygensstraat) The neoclassical Hollandsche Manege is a surprise to discover just outside the Vondelpark. Entering is like stepping back in time, into a grandiose indoor riding school inspired by the famous Spanish Riding School in Vienna. Designed by AL van Gendt and built in 1882, it retains its charming horse-head facade and has a large riding arena inside.

◉ De Pijp

Apart from the Albert Cuypmarkt and the Heineken Experience (p76), sights in De Pijp are few. What's really enjoyable here is wandering through the neighbourhood and soaking up the bohemian atmosphere in the bars, eateries and boutiques.

★ Albert Cuypmarkt MARKET
(Map p62; www.albertcuyp-markt.amsterdam; Albert Cuypstraat, btwn Ferdinand Bolstraat & Van Woustraat; 9.30am-5pm Mon-Sat; 24 Albert Cuypstraat) Some 260 stalls fill the Albert Cuypmarkt, Amsterdam's largest market. Vendors loudly tout their array of gadgets, homewares, and flowers, fruit, vegetables, herbs and spices. Many sell clothes and other goods, too, and they're often cheaper than anywhere else. Snack vendors tempt passers-by with raw-herring sandwiches, *frites* (fries), *poffertjes* (tiny Dutch pancakes dusted with icing sugar) and caramel syrup–filled *stroopwafels*. If you have room after all that, the surrounding area teems with cosy *cafés* (pubs) and restaurants.

TOP SIGHT
RIJKSMUSEUM

The Rijksmuseum is a magnificent repository of art, its restaurant has a Michelin star *and* it's the only museum with a cycle lane through its centre. Beautifully presented, it includes masterpieces by homegrown geniuses, such as Rembrandt, Vermeer and Van Gogh. It was conceived to hold several national and royal collections, which occupy 1.5km of gallery space and 80 rooms.

The Layout

The museum is spread over four levels, from Floor 0 (where the main atrium is) to Floor 3. The collection is huge. You can see the highlights in a couple of hours, but you may want to allocate much longer.

Pick up a floor plan from the information desk by the entrance. Galleries are well marked; each room displays the gallery's number and theme, which is easy to match to the floor plan. The 1st floor is split into two sides by the atrium, with separate access on either side.

Floor 2: 1600–1700

It's best to start your visit on the 2nd floor, which contains the highlights of the collection, with its Golden Age masterpieces, in the Gallery of Honour. It's a bit convoluted to reach, but well signposted.

Johannes (Jan) Vermeer

The next room contains beautiful works by Vermeer, with intimate domestic scenes, glimpses into private life, rendered in almost photographic detail. Check out the dreamy

DON'T MISS

➡ Rembrandt's
The Night Watch

➡ Frans Hals'
The Merry Drinker

➡ Vermeer's
Kitchen Maid

➡ De Hooch's
A Mother's Duty

➡ Delftware pottery

➡ Dollhouses

➡ Michelin-starred restaurant

PRACTICALITIES

➡ National Museum

➡ Map p62

➡ ☎ 020-674 70 00

➡ www.rijksmuseum.nl

➡ Museumstraat 1

➡ adult/child €17.50/free

➡ ⊙ 9am-5pm

➡ 🚊 2/5/12 Rijksmuseum

Kitchen Maid (1660; pictured left). See the holes in the wall? The nail with shadow? In *Woman in Blue Reading a Letter* (1663) Vermeer shows only parts of objects, such as the tables, chairs and map, leaving the viewer to figure out the rest. Pieter de Hooch, Vermeer's contemporary, also depicts everyday life, with subjects such as the intimate quiet of *A Mother Delousing her Child* (1658), also called *A Mother's Duty*.

Jan Steen

Another Jan hangs across the hall from Vermeer. Jan Steen became renowned for painting chaotic households to convey moral teachings, such as *The Merry Family* (1668). None of the drunken adults notice the little boy sneaking a taste of wine, and an inscription translates as 'As the old sing, so shall the young twitter'. Steen's images made quite an impression: in the 18th century the expression 'a Jan Steen household' entered the local lexicon to mean a crazy state of affairs.

Rembrandt

Moving on, you'll reach several wonderful works by Rembrandt, including his resigned, unflinching self-portrait as the Apostle Paul. *The Jewish Bride* (1665), showing a couple's intimate caress, impressed Van Gogh, who declared he would give up a decade of his life just to sit before the painting for a fortnight with only a crust of bread to eat.

Rembrandt's gigantic *The Night Watch* (1642) is the rock star of the Rijksmuseum, with perennial crowds in front of it. The work is titled *Archers under the Command of Captain Frans Banning Cocq*, and *The Night Watch* name was bestowed years later, thanks to a layer of grime that gave the impression it was a nocturnal scene. It's since been restored to its original colours, complete with sunbeams through the windows. It was once larger than today, but was cut down to fit a previous location. Several other huge civic guard paintings surround it.

Delftware & Dollhouses

Intriguing Golden Age swag fills the rooms on either side of the Gallery of Honour. Delftware was the Dutch attempt to reproduce Chinese porcelain in the late 1600s; Gallery 2.22 displays scads of the delicate blue-and-white pottery. Gallery 2.20 is devoted to mind-blowing dollhouses. Merchant's wife Petronella Oortman employed carpenters, glassblowers and silversmiths to make the 700 items inside her dollhouse, using the same materials as they would for full-scale versions.

QUEUES & TICKETS

Entrance queues can be long. Friday, Saturday and Sunday are the busiest days. It's least crowded before 10am and after 3pm. Buy your ticket online to save time. While you still must wait in the outdoor queue, once inside you can proceed straight into the museum (otherwise you must stand in another queue to pay). Museumkaart and I Amsterdam Card holders get the same privilege.

Download the museum's free app (there's free wi-fi at the museum). It either offers a guided tour, or you can select works by number. There's also a family tour available.

AIRPORT MINI-BRANCH

The Rijksmuseum has a free mini-branch at Schiphol airport that hangs eight to 10 stellar Golden Age paintings. It's located after passport control between lounges 2 and 3, and is open from 7am to 8pm daily.

Floor 3: 1900–2000

The uppermost floor has a limited, but interesting, collection. It includes avant-garde, childlike paintings by Karel Appel, Constant Nieuwenhuys and their Co-BrA compadres (a post-WWII movement) and cool furnishings by Dutch designers, such as Gerrit Rietveld and Michel de Klerk. There's also a Nazi chess set, and an unsettling wall of Nias islanders' facial casts, dating from 1910.

Floor 1: 1700–1900

Highlights on Floor 1 include the *Battle of Waterloo,* the Rijksmuseum's largest painting (in Gallery 1.12), taking up almost an entire wall. Three Van Gogh paintings hang in Gallery 1.18. Gallery 1.16 re-creates a gilded, 18th-century canal house room.

Floor 0: 1100–1600

This floor is packed with fascinating curiosities. The Special Collections have sections including magic lanterns, armoury and Dutch status symbols from previous eras, such as musical instruments and silver miniatures. Early gems include works by Dürer, and Charles V's cutlery. The serene Asian Pavilion, a separate structure that's often devoid of crowds, holds first-rate artworks from China, Indonesia, Japan, India, Thailand and Vietnam.

Facade & Gardens

Pierre Cuypers designed the 1885 building. Check out the exterior, which mixes neo-Gothic and Dutch Renaissance styles. The museum's gardens – aka the 'outdoor gallery' – host big-name sculpture exhibitions at least once a year. You can stroll for free amid the roses, hedges, fountains and a cool greenhouse.

RIJKSMUSEUM

Floor 3: 1900–2000

CoBrA Artists

Dutch Designers

Floor 2: 1600–1700

Cupyers Library

The Night Watch

The Jewish Bride

Gallery of Honour

Kitchen Maid, Woman in Blue Reading a Letter & A Mother's Duty

The Merry Family

Dollhouses

The Merry Drinker

Delftware

Great Hall

Floor 1: 1700–1900

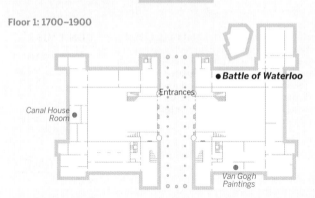

Battle of Waterloo

Entrances

Canal House Room

Van Gogh Paintings

Floor 0: 1100–1600

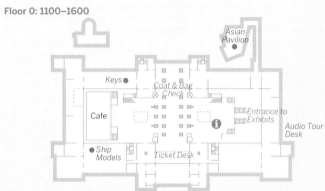

Asian Pavilion

Keys

Coat & Bag Check

Entrance to Exhibits

Cafe

Audio Tour Desk

Ship Models

Ticket Desk

VAN GOGH MUSEUM

This wonderful museum holds the world's largest Van Gogh collection. It's a poignant experience to see the perma-queues outside, then trace the painter's tragic yet breathtakingly productive life. Opened in 1973 to house the collection of Vincent's younger brother, Theo, the museum comprises some 200 paintings and 500 drawings by Vincent and his contemporaries, including Gauguin and Monet.

Museum Set-up & Highlights

In 2015 a swish extension and entrance hall added 800 sq metres of space to the museum, which now spreads over four levels, moving chronologically from Floor 0 (aka the ground floor) to Floor 3. It's still a manageable size; allow a couple of hours or so to browse the galleries. The audioguide is helpful and there's a separate version for children. It's fascinating to see Van Gogh's evolution from his early depictions of sombre countryfolk in the Netherlands to his pulsating, swirling French landscapes. Seminal works to look for:

The Potato Eaters & Skeleton with Burning Cigarette

Van Gogh's earliest works – showing raw, if unrefined, talent – are from his time in the Dutch countryside and in Antwerp between 1883 and 1885. He painted peasant life, exalting their existence in works such as *The Potato Eaters* (1885). The symbolic *Still Life with Bible* (1885), painted after his father's death, shows a burnt-out candle, his Protestant minister father's bible and a much-thumbed smaller book, *La Joi de Vivre,* representing Van Gogh's more secular philosophy. *Skeleton with Burning Cigarette* (1886) – the print all

DON'T MISS

→ *The Potato Eaters*

→ *The Yellow House*

→ *Wheatfield with Crows*

→ *Sunflowers*

→ *Skeleton with Burning Cigarette*

PRACTICALITIES

→ Map p62

→ ☎ 020-570 52 00

→ www.vangoghmuseum.nl

→ Museumplein 6

→ adult/child €18/free, audioguide €5/3

→ ⊙ 9am-7pm Sun-Thu, to 10pm Fri, to 9pm Sat late Jun-Aug, 9am-6pm Sat-Thu, to 10pm Fri Sep-early Nov & Apr-late Jun, 9am-5pm Sat-Thu, to 10pm Fri early Nov-Mar

→ 🚊 2/3/5/12 Van Baerlestraat

the stoners are buying in the gift shop – was painted when Van Gogh was a student at Antwerp's Royal Academy of Fine Arts.

Self-Portraits
In 1886 Van Gogh moved to Paris, where his brother Theo was working as an art dealer. Vincent began to paint multiple self-portraits as a way of improving his portraiture without paying for models, which he was too poor to afford. He met some of the Impressionists, and his palette began to brighten.

Sunflowers & The Yellow House
In 1888 Van Gogh left for Arles in Provence to paint its colourful landscapes and try to achieve his dream of creating an artists' colony in the countryside. *Sunflowers* (1889) and other blossoms that shimmer with intense Mediterranean light are from this period. So is *The Yellow House* (1888), a rendering of the abode Van Gogh rented in Arles. In 1888 Van Gogh sliced off part of his ear during a bout of psychosis.

Wheatfield with Crows
Van Gogh had himself committed to an asylum in Saint-Rémy in 1889. While there his work became ever more extraordinary. His wildly expressive, yet tightly controlled landscapes are based on the surrounding countryside, with its cypress and olive trees. This period includes the sinuous, pulsating *Irises*. In 1890 he went north to Auvers-sur-Oise. One of his last paintings, *Wheatfield with Crows* (1890), is particularly menacing and ominous, and was finished shortly before his suicide, though it wasn't his final work.

Extras
The museum has multiple listening stations for diverse recordings of Van Gogh's letters, mainly to and from his closest brother Theo, who championed his work. The museum has categorised all of Van Gogh's letters online at www.vangoghletters.org.

Other Artists
Thanks to Theo van Gogh's prescient collecting and that of the museum's curators, you'll also see works by Vincent's contemporaries, including Gauguin, Monet and Henri de Toulouse-Lautrec. In addition, paintings by Van Gogh's precursors, such as Jean-François Millet and Gustave Courbet, pepper the galleries, as do works by artists Van Gogh influenced.

Exhibition Wing
influential Dutch architect Gerrit Rietveld designed the museum's main building. Behind it, reaching towards the Museumplein, is a separate wing designed by Kisho Kurokawa and known as 'the Mussel'. It hosts temporary exhibitions by big-name artists.

TICKETS
Prepurchase tickets online and choose a time slot to avoid missing out, as tickets sell out days in advance. Museumkaart holders get free entry but still need to reserve a time slot.

Van Gogh sold only one painting during his lifetime (*Red Vineyard at Arles*). It hangs at Moscow's Pushkin Museum.

FRIDAY NIGHTS
The museum stays open to 10pm on Friday, when it hosts special cultural events and opens a bar downstairs. There's usually live music or a DJ.

The museum's library (Map p62; ☎ 020-570 59 78; Gabriël Metsustraat 8; ☺10am-12.30pm & 1-5pm Mon-Fri; ☒3/5/12 Museumplein) FREE has a wealth of reference material – some 35,000 books and articles – for serious study.

ℹ MUSEUM DISCOUNTS & PASSES

Visitors of various professions, including artists, journalists, museum conservators and teachers, may get discounts at some venues if they show accreditation.

Students regularly get a few euro off museum admission; bring ID. Seniors over 65, and their partners of 60 or older, benefit from reductions on public transport, museum admissions, concerts and more. You may look younger, so bring your passport.

I Amsterdam Card (www.iamsterdam.com; per 24/48/72/96 hours €59/74/87/98) Provides admission to more than 30 museums, a canal cruise, and discounts at shops, entertainment venues and restaurants. Also includes a GVB transit pass. Useful for quick visits to the city. Available at VVV I Amsterdam Visitor Centres and some hotels.

Museumkaart (www.museumkaart.nl; adult/child €59.90/32/45, plus one-time registration €5) Free and discounted entry to some 400 museums all over the country for one year. Purchase it at participating museum ticket counters. You initially receive a temporary card valid for 31 days (maximum five museums); you can then register it online to receive a permanent card sent to a Dutch address, such as your hotel, within three to five working days.

Holland Pass (www.hollandpass.com; three/four/six attractions from €40/55/71.25) Similar to the I Amsterdam Card, but without the rush for usage; you can visit sights over a month. Prices are based on the number of attractions, which you pick from tiers (the most popular/expensive sights are gold tier). Also includes a train ticket from the airport to the city, and a canal cruise. Purchase it online; pick-up locations include Schiphol Airport and the city centre.

Priopass (www.priopass.com) is offered by many hotels. The pass – either a printed piece of paper or an electronic version on your mobile phone – provides fast-track entry to most attractions. It's not a discount card – you pay normal rates for museums and tours. But many visitors like it because it's convenient for queue-skipping, there's no deadline for use (so you don't have to scurry around and see several museums in a day to get your money's worth), and you only end up paying for what you use (ie it's not bundled with transit passes, canal cruises etc). The pass itself is free; you link it to your credit card and get charged as you go along.

★**Heineken Experience**   BREWERY
(Map p62; ☑020-523 94 35; https://tickets.heinekenexperience.com; Stadhouderskade 78; adult/child self-guided tour €21/14.50, VIP guided tour €55, Rock the City ticket €30; ⊙10.30am-7.30pm Mon-Thu, to 9pm Fri-Sun; Ⓜ Vijzelgracht, ⋒24 Ferdinand Bolstraat) On the site of the company's old brewery, Heineken's self-guided 'Experience' provides an entertaining overview of the brewing process, with a multimedia exhibit where you 'become' a beer by getting shaken up, sprayed with water and subjected to heat. Prebooking tickets online saves adults €3 and, crucially, allows you to skip the ticket queues. Guided 2½-hour VIP tours end with a five-beer tasting and cheese pairing. Great-value Rock the City tickets include a 45-minute canal cruise to A'DAM Tower.

Sarphatipark   PARK
(Map p62; Sarphatipark; ⋒3 2e Van der Helststraat) While the Vondelpark is bigger in size and reputation, this tranquil English-style park delivers an equally potent shot of pastoral summertime relaxation, with far fewer crowds. Named after Samuel Sarphati (1813–66), a Jewish doctor, businessman and urban innovator, the grounds incorporate ponds, gently rolling meadows and wooded fringes. In the centre is the 1886-built **Sarphati Memorial** (Map p62), a bombastic temple with a fountain, gargoyles and a bust of the great man himself.

⊙ Oosterpark & East of the Amstel

There are few major sights in the Oost area, but it is home to the fascinating ethnographical Tropenmuseum, as well as lovely nearby Oosterpark and Flevopark, sites of several interesting memorials.

★**Tropenmuseum**   MUSEUM
(Tropics Museum; ☑0880 042 800; www.tropenmuseum.nl; Linnaeusstraat 2; adult/child €15/8; ⊙10am-5pm Tue-Sun; ⋒14/10 Tropenmuseum)

A great arched, galleried space, the Tropenmuseum houses a three-storey collection of artefacts from former colonies, from Indonesian shadow puppets depicting the Dutch, to dioramas of tropical life. It's all presented with insight, imagination and a fair amount of multimedia, and there are great temporary exhibitions. There's a hands-on children's section, great for clambering, a music section (take headphones or buy them there for €1.50), a fine gift shop and a lovely cafe.

Oosterpark   PARK
(Map p54; ☉dawn-dusk; 🚊19 1e Van Swindenstraat) The lush greenery of Oosterpark, with wild parakeets in the trees and herons stalking the large ponds, despite being laid out in English style, has an almost tropical richness in this diverse neighbourhood. It was established in 1891 as a pleasure park for the diamond traders who found their fortunes in the South African mines, and it still has an elegant, rambling feel.

⊙ Amsterdam Noord

The major sights in the Noord are just across the water from the city centre, with the A'DAM Tower offering panoramic views over the city, and the EYE Film Institute showing exhibitions on cinema. Look out also for cutting-edge architecture, including the EYE and Kraanspoor. Seek out the arty enclave of NDSM-werf, with its artist studios, street art and regular IJ Hallen market, and the endearingly pretty dyke houses of Nieuwendammerdijk.

EYE Film Institute   MUSEUM, CINEMA
(📞020-589 14 00; www.eyefilm.nl; IJpromenade 1; adult/child exhibitions €13/3, films €10.50/8; ☉10am-7pm; 🚤Buiksloterweg) At this modernist architectural triumph that seems to balance on its edge on the banks of the IJ (also pronounced 'eye') River, the institute screens movies from the 40,000-title archive in four theatres, sometimes with live music. Exhibitions of costumes, digital art and other cinephile amusements run in conjunction with what's playing. A view-tastic bar-restaurant with a fabulously sunny terrace (when the sun makes an appearance) is a popular hang-out on this side of the river.

★A'DAM Tower   NOTABLE BUILDING
(www.adamtoren.nl; Overhoeksplein 1; lookout adult/child €13.50/7.50, premium adult ticket €19.50, swing €5; ☉lookout 10am-10pm; 🚤Buiksloterweg) The 22-storey A'DAM Tower used to be the Royal Dutch Shell oil company offices, but has been funked up to become Amsterdam's newest big attraction. Take the lift to the rooftop for awe-inspiring views in all directions, with a giant four-person swing that kicks out over the edge for those who have a head for heights (you're well secured and strapped in). There's a swish bar for drinks and light meals and the Moon (📞020-237 63 11; www.restaurantmoon.nl; ☉noon-2pm & 6-9pm; lunch 3-/4-/5-course menu €40/50/60, dinner 5-/6-/7-course menu €60/70/80) revolving restaurant on the 19th floor.

Kunststad   ART STUDIO
(Art City; www.ndsmloods.nl; NDSM-plein; ☉8am-6pm; 🚤NDSM-werf) ⟦FREE⟧ This former shipbuilding warehouse is filled with artists' studios, with some 200 artists working in the NDSM *broedplaats* (breeding ground). It's a big enough space that you can cycle or walk around it, with huge artworks hanging from the ceiling, and structures in the hangar.

★Nieuwendammerdijk   AREA
(🚌32 Buikslotermeerplein) Enchanting chocolate-box prettiness characterises this long, narrow street of wooden Dutch houses, now prime real estate, with hollyhocks nodding beside every porch. Many houses date from the 1500s, and numbers 202 to 204 were where the shipbuilding family De Vries Lentsch lived. Numbers 301 to 309 were once captains' houses.

FOOTBALL FEVER

Amsterdam's Arena (www.johancruijff arena; Arena Blvd 1; 🚇; Ⓜ️Bijlmer ArenA) is a high-tech complex with a retractable roof and seating for 53,748 spectators. Four-times European champion Ajax, the Netherlands' most famous football team, play here. Football games usually take place on Saturday evenings and Sunday afternoons from August to May. The arena is about 7km southeast of central Amsterdam, easily accessible by metro.

Fans can also take a one-hour guided tour of the stadium (adult/child €15/10). There are usually eight tours daily, and you can also book special kids' tours; see the website for the schedule.

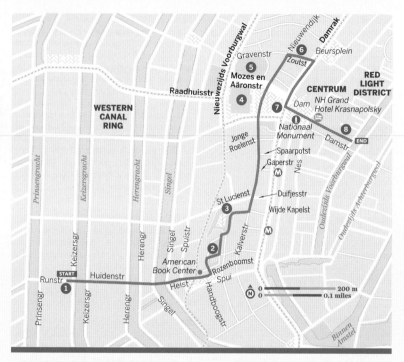

🚶 Walking Tour
Cheese, Gin & Monuments

START DE KAASKAMER
FINISH WYNAND FOCKINK
LENGTH 2KM; 1½ HOURS WITH STOPS

This tour is a hit parade of Amsterdam's favourite food, drinks and historic sights.

The Dutch eat more than 14kg of cheese per person annually, and much of it is sold in **❶ De Kaaskamer** (p106). Wheels of Gouda, Edam and other locally made types are stacked to the rafters. Get a wedge to go.

As you make your way through the Spui, keep an eye out just past the American Book Center for a humble wooden door. Push it open and behold the hidden community known as the **❷ Begijnhof** (p50), surrounding two historic churches and gardens. Cross the courtyard to the other entrance.

From the Begijnhof turn north and walk a short way to the **❸ Civic Guard Gallery** (p43). Paintings of stern folks in ruffled collars stare down from the walls. Cross the gallery and depart through the Amsterdam Museum's courtyard restaurant onto Kalverstraat.

Follow Kalverstraat to the **❹ Royal Palace** (p43), home to King Willem-Alexander and Queen Máxima. The sumptuous interior deserves a look. The palace's neighbour is the **❺ Nieuwe Kerk** (p51), the stage for Dutch investitures. Afterwards, get onto crowded Nieuwendijk, and walk to Zoutsteeg. Swallow any misgivings about eating raw fish and order the famed Dutch herring at **❻ Rob Wigboldus Vishandel** (p88), a three-table shop. Then depart Zoutsteeg onto Damrak.

Cross Damrak to the Nationaal Monument side of the **❼ Dam** (p51) – Amsterdam's birthplace. Wade through the sea of bikes – the urns behind the monument hold earth from East Indies war cemeteries. Follow the street leading behind the NH Grand Hotel Krasnapolsky to **❽ Wynand Fockink** (p97). The Dutch gin-maker's tasting room dates from 1679. The barkeep will pour your drink to the brim, so do like the locals to prevent spillage: lean over it and sip without lifting.

★ NDSM-werf   AREA
(www.ndsm.nl; NDSM-plein; ☻NDSM-werf)
NDSM-werf is a derelict shipyard turned
edgy arts community 15 minutes upriv-
er from the city centre. It wafts a post-
apocalyptic vibe: an old submarine slumps
in the harbour, abandoned trams rust
by the water's edge, and graffiti splashes
across almost every surface. Young creatives hang out at the smattering of cool cafes. Hip businesses like MTV and Red Bull
have their European headquarters here.
The area is also a centre for underground
culture and events, such as the Over het IJ
Festival (p81).

Sexyland   ARTS CENTRE
(www.sexyland.amsterdam; Ms van Riemsdijk-
weg 39; monthly membership €2.50, admission
dependent on event; ☻hours vary; ☻NDSM-
werf) See the neon sign and you'll be for-
given for thinking this is an outpost of
the Red Light District. But Sexyland is a
members' club that has 365 co-owners,
each of whom puts on an annual event.
This can range from ping-pong to
tantric tango, with club nights at weekends; members of the public can attend any
of the activities by buying a month-long
membership.

Kraanspoor   ARCHITECTURE
(☻NDSM-werf) 'Craneway' is an extraordinary piece of architecture, built above a
repurposed (you've guessed it) craneway,
by OTH Architecten in 2007. The glass box
above the stilts of the industrial base looks
almost weightless, and houses offices with
amazing waterfront views.

🏃 Activities

Cycling is by far the most popular activity in
Amsterdam, and a great way to experience
local life. With so many picturesque waterways, boating is also ideal for exploring the
city. Amsterdam's beautiful parks, from the
famous Vondelpark and rambling forest
Amsterdamse Bos to smaller havens like
De Pijp's Sarphatipark, are favourite playgrounds for locals.

Cycling
Fiets (bicycles) outnumber cars in Amsterdam and to roll like a local you'll need a
two-wheeler. Rental shops are everywhere
and cycling maps are available at the tourist
office by Centraal Station.

Boating

★ Rederij Lampedusa   BOATING
(Map p54; www.rederijlampedusa.nl; Dijksgracht
6; 2hr canal tour €19, VIP tours by donation; ☻ca-
nal tours 11am & 1.30pm Sat Jun-Sep, VIP tours Fri
fortnightly Jun-Sep; ☻26 Muziekgebouw) Take a
canal-boat tour or a sunset trip around Amsterdam harbour in former refugee boats,
brought from Lampedusa by Dutch founder
Tuen. The tours are full of heart and offer
a fascinating insight, not only into stories
of contemporary migration, but of how
immigration shaped Amsterdam's history –
especially the canal tour. Both leave from
next to Mediamatic.

Boaty   BOATING
(☎06 2714 9493; www.boaty.nl; Jozef Israëlskade;
boat rental per 3hr/full day from €79/179; ☻9am-
30min before sunset early Mar-Oct; ☻12 Scheld-
estraat) Boaty's location on the peaceful
Amstelkanaal makes it an ideal launching
pad for exploring the waterways before ap-
proaching the crowded city-centre canals.
Rental includes a map outlining suggested
routes; you don't need a boat licence or pri-
or experience. Book ahead online, or phone
for same-day reservations. The season can
run longer or shorter depending on weather
conditions.

Canal Bike   BOATING
(www.stromma.nl; per person per hour €10;
☻10am-6pm late Mar-Oct) These pedal boats
allow you to splash around the canals at
your own speed. Landing stages are by the
Rijksmuseum, Leidseplein and Westerkerk.
Deposit of €20 required. Affiliated with Canal Bus.

Ice Skating
In winter the pond at the Museumplein becomes a popular ice-skating rink, and the
scene looks like the top of a wind-up jewellery box. The rink is free; there's a modest
fee for skate rentals.
  Occasionally the canals freeze over for
skating, but stay away unless you see large
groups of people gliding. The ice can be
weak, especially at the edges and under
bridges.

🚩 Tours

Bicycle Tours
The following companies also rent bikes:

Mike's Bike Tours   CYCLING
(Map p54; ☎020-622 79 70; www.mikesbiketours
amsterdam.com; Prins Hendrikkade 176a; city tours

CANALS OF AMSTERDAM

In Dutch a canal is a *gracht* (pronounced 'khrakht') and the main canals form the central *grachtengordel* (canal ring). These beauties came to life in the early 1600s, after Amsterdam's population grew beyond its medieval walls and city planners put together an ambitious design for expansion. The concentric waterways they built are the same ones you see today.

Amsterdammers have always known that their Canal Ring, built during the Golden Age, is extraordinary. Unesco made it official in 2010, when it listed the waterways as a World Heritage site. Today the city has 165 canals spanned by 1753 bridges – more than any other city in the world.

Starting from the core, the major semicircular canals are the Singel, Herengracht, Keizersgracht and Prinsengracht. An easy way to remember them is that, apart from the singular **Singel** (which originally was a moat that defended Amsterdam's outer limits), these canals are in alphabetical order.

The **Herengracht** is where Amsterdam's wealthiest residents moved once the canals were completed. They built their mansions alongside it (particularly around the Golden Bend), hence its name, which translates to Gentlemen's Canal.

Almost as swanky was the **Keizersgracht** (Emperor's Canal), a nod to Holy Roman Emperor Maximilian I.

The **Prinsengracht** – named after William the Silent, Prince of Orange and the first Dutch royal – was designed as a slightly cheaper canal with smaller residences and warehouses. It also acted as a barrier against the working-class Jordaan beyond.

per adult/child from €28/25, countryside from €32; ☉office 9am-6pm Mar-Oct, from 10am Nov-Feb; 🚊22/48 Prins Hendrikkade) Offers city, countryside and harbour tours, which leave from outside its shop. You can also hire bikes (per 24 hours from €13).

Orangebike CYCLING
(☑06 4684 2083; www.orange-bike.nl; Buiksloterweg 5c; tours €22.50-37.50, hire per hour/day from €5/11; ☉9am-6pm; 🚇Buiksloterweg) Traditional city and countryside tours (including beach and *polder* tours), plus themed options, such as the Architecture and the Snack Tour, sampling *bitterballen* (croquettes) and *jenever*. Minimum participants of four to six, depending on the tour. It also rents bikes, including accessories like child seats and rain ponchos. Located in Amsterdam Noord, it's a five-minute ferry ride from Centraal Station.

Yellow Bike CYCLING
(Map p48; ☑020-620 69 40; www.yellowbike. nl; Nieuwezijds Kolk 29; city tours from €24.50, Waterland tour €34.50; ☉office 9am-6pm; 🚊2/11/12/13/17 Nieuwezijds Kolk) Choose from Yellow Bike's city tours or the longer countryside tour (March to October) through the pretty Waterland district to the north. It also rents bikes (per 24 hours €12).

Boat Tours

Sure they're touristy, but canal cruises are also a delightful way to see the city. Several operators depart from moorings at Centraal Station, Damrak, Rokin and opposite the Rijksmuseum. Costs are similar. To avoid the steamed-up-glass-window effect, look for a boat with an open seating area. On a night tour you'll see the bridges lit up (though these tours usually cost a bit more).

Those Dam Boat Guys (Map p66; ☑06 1885 5219; www.thosedamboatguys.com; tours €25; ☉by reservation Mar-Sep; 🚊13/17 Westermarkt) Small, laid-back local tours.

Canal Bus (☑020-217 05 00; www.stromma. nl; hop-on, hop-off day pass €23, cruises €15-20, pedaloes €8; ☉10am-6pm; 🚲) Handy hop-on, hop-off service.

Blue Boat Company (Map p62; ☑020-679 13 70; www.blueboat.nl; Stadhouderskade 501; 75min tour adult/child €18/8.50; ☉tour half-hourly 10am-6pm Mar-Oct, hourly Nov-Feb; 🚊1/2/5/12 Leidseplein) Day and night-time tours plus various special tours such as a children's pirate-themed tour.

Wetlands Safari (Map p48; ☑06 5355 2669; www.wetlandssafari.nl; incl transport & picnic adult/child €64/35; ☉9.30am Mon-Fri, 10am Sat & Sun early Apr-late Sep; 🚊1/4/11/12/13/14/17/24/26 Centraal Station) OK, so it's not a canal tour, but it is an exceptional five-hour boat trip canoeing through wetlands and past wind-mills and 17th-century villages.

Walking Tours

Hungry Birds
Street Food Tours
WALKING, FOOD
(☎06 1898 6268; www.hungrybirds.nl; day/night tour per person €79/89; ⊙by reservation) Guides take you 'off the eaten track' to chow on Dutch and ethnic specialities. Tours visit around 10 spots over four hours in De Pijp, Utrechtsestraat, Rembrandt-plein and the Spui, from family-run eateries to street vendors. Prices include all food. The meet-up location is given after you make reservations.

Mee in Mokum
WALKING
(Map p48; www.gildeamsterdam.nl; Gedempte Begijnensloot; tours adult/child €10/5; ⊙11am & 2pm Tue-Sun; ☐2/11/12 Spui) Mee in Mokum's walkabouts are led by volunteers of all ages who often have personal anecdotes to add. Tours last between two and three hours and depart from the cafe in the Amsterdam Museum (p43). Reserve at least a day in advance and pay cash on the day.

✳ Festivals & Events

King's Day
CULTURAL
(Koningsdag; ⊙27 Apr) King's Day is a celebration of the House of Orange, with hundreds of thousands of orange-clad locals and visitors filling Amsterdam's streets for drinking and dancing. The city also becomes one big flea market, as people sell off all their unwanted junk.

World Press Photo
CULTURAL
(www.worldpressphoto.org; ⊙mid-Apr–mid-Jul; ☐2/11/12/13/17 Dam) This powerful display of the year's best photojournalism debuts in the Nieuwe Kerk (p51) in mid-April, and stays on display through mid-July.

Herdenkingsdag
CULTURAL
(Remembrance Day; Dam; ⊙4 May; ☐4/14/24 Dam) For the fallen of WWII. King Willem-Alexander lays a wreath on the Dam and the city observes two minutes' silence at 8pm.

Holland Festival
CULTURAL
(www.hollandfestival.nl; ⊙Jun) A month-long, high-art/low-art mash-up, the Holland Festival is the largest performing arts festival in the country. It takes place at venues city-wide, and features everything from theatre, dance and opera to offbeat digital films and experimental music.

Roots Festival
MUSIC
(www.amsterdamroots.nl; ⊙late Jun/early Jul) Late June or early July sees this festival program world music in key venues around town, culminating in the vibrant Roots Open Air all-day fest at the Park Franken-dael (Middenweg; ☐19 Hogeweg).

Over het IJ Festival
CULTURAL
(www.overhetij.nl; ⊙mid-Jul; ☐NDSM-werf) Huge performing-arts events (dance, theatre, music) take place for 10 days around the NDSM-werf (p79) former shipyards in Amsterdam Noord.

Pride Amsterdam
LGBTIQ+
(www.pride.amsterdam; ⊙late Jul-early Aug) Amsterdam flies the rainbow flag. Highlights of this over-the-top fest include the Drag Queen Olympics and a raucous, waterborne Pride Parade (the first Saturday of August).

Grachtenfestival
MUSIC
(Canal Festival; www.grachtenfestival.nl; ⊙mid-Aug) During mid-August's 10-day Grachtenfestival, classical musicians perform in canal-side parks and hidden gardens. Don't miss the free concert on a floating stage in the Prinsengracht.

Amsterdam Dance Event
MUSIC
(ADE; www.amsterdam-dance-event.nl; ⊙mid-Oct) An electronic music extravaganza on a massive scale, ADE sees 2200 DJs and artists and more than 300,000 clubbers attending 450 events at over 120 venues all over the city over five long, sweaty days and nights in mid-October.

🛏 Sleeping

In its typically charming way, Amsterdam has loads of hotels in wild and wonderful spaces: inspired architects have breathed new life into old buildings, from converted schools and industrial lofts to entire rows of canal houses joined at the hip. Many lodgings overlook gorgeous waterways or courtyards. But charm doesn't come cheap, and places fill fast – reserve as far ahead as possible, especially for summer bookings and weekends any time.

Rates and crowds peak during festivals, in summer (June to August) and on weekends at any time of the year. Book *well* ahead if you're travelling then. Prices are lowest from October to April (excluding Christmas, New Year and Easter).

Jeugdherbergen (youth hostels) are popular in Amsterdam. The Netherlands hostel association goes by the name Stay-okay (www.stayokay.com) and is affiliated with Hostelling International (HI; www.hihostels.com). Independent luxury hostels, aka 'poshtels', are starting to pop up around town too.

Any hotel with more than 20 rooms is considered large, and most rooms themselves are on the snug side. You'll see a 'star' plaque on the front of every hotel, indicating its rating according to the Hotelstars Union (www.hotelstars.eu). The stars (from one to five) are determined by the existence of certain facilities, rather than their quality. This means that a two-star hotel may be in better condition than a hotel of higher rank, albeit with fewer facilities.

Properties often include the 6% city hotel tax in quoted rates, but ask before booking. If you're paying by credit card, some hotels add a surcharge of up to 5%.

Lodgings in the centre can be noisy and poor value for money. Western Canal Ring places are near the action but more dignified and quiet. Vondelpark and the Old South offer quality digs that are close to the museums and only a short walk from the action at Leidseplein, but they can slide up the price scale.

🛏 Medieval Centre & Red Light District

St Christopher's at the Winston
HOSTEL, HOTEL €

(Map p48; ☑020-623 13 80; www.st-christophers.co.uk; Warmoesstraat 129; dm/d from €47.80/153; @🛜; 🚊4/14/24 Dam) This place hops 24/7 with rock 'n' roll rooms, a busy nightclub (p97) with live bands nightly, a bar and restaurant, a beer garden and a smoking deck downstairs. En-suite dorms sleep up to eight. Local artists were given free rein on the rooms, with super-edgy (entirely stainless steel) to questionably raunchy results. Rates include breakfast (and earplugs!).

★ Hotel V Nesplein
DESIGN HOTEL €€

(Map p48; ☑020-662 32 33; www.hotelvnesplein.nl; Nes 49; d/ste from €170/260; ❄🛜; Ⓜ Rokin, 🚊4/14/24 Rokin) Vintage and designer furniture fills the public areas and rooms of this hotel, in a fantastic location on theatre-lined Nes. Spacious rooms start at 18 sq metres and have wooden floors, exposed-brick walls and rain showers in the sleek bathrooms (some also have bathtubs). Its industrial-styled restaurant, the Lobby, serves creative modern Dutch cuisine.

Hotel The Exchange
DESIGN HOTEL €€

(Map p48; ☑020-523 00 80; www.hotelthe exchange.com; Damrak 50; d €153-332.50; @🛜; 🚊2/4/11/12/13/14/17/24/26 Centraal Station) Opposite the former stock exchange (hence the hotel's name), these 61 rooms have been dressed 'like models' in eye-popping style by students from the Amsterdam Fashion Institute. Anything goes, from oversized-button-adorned walls to a Marie Antoinette dress tented over the bed. Its one- to five-star rooms range from small and viewless to sprawling sanctums, but all have en-suite bathrooms.

Hotel Résidence Le Coin
APARTMENT €€

(Map p62; ☑020-524 68 00; www.lecoin.nl; Nieuwe Doelenstraat 5; apt €168; 🛜; Ⓜ Rokin, 🚊24 Muntplein) Owned by the University of Amsterdam, Hotel Résidence Le Coin offers 42 small, high-class apartments spread over seven historical buildings, all equipped with designer furniture, wood floors, fast wi-fi and kitchenettes – and all reachable by lift. It's superbly located just a five-minute stroll to pretty Nieuwmarkt.

Hotel Luxer
HOTEL €€

(Map p48; ☑020-330 32 05; www.hotelluxer.nl; Warmoesstraat 11; d from €150; ❄🛜; 🚊2/4/11/12/13/14/17/24/26 Centraal Station) A pleasant surprise, this smart little number offers some of the best value for money in the thick of the Red Light District. Its 47 rooms are small but well equipped (air-con!), and at night the breakfast area becomes a chic little bar. Breakfast costs €9.

★ W Amsterdam
DESIGN HOTEL €€€

(Map p48; ☑020-811 25 00; www.wamsterdam.com; Spuistraat 175; d/ste from €380/567; ❄@🛜🏊; 🚊2/11/12/13/17 Dam) Designer hotel chain W opened its Amsterdam premises in two landmark buildings, the Royal Dutch Post's former telephone exchange and a former bank – part of which now houses Dutch design mega-store X Bank (p105). Its 238 rooms (including connecting family rooms and 28 suites) combine design and vintage elements; there's a state-of-the-art spa, a gym, an amazing rooftop lap pool, restaurants and bars.

Hotel de L'Europe
HOTEL €€€

(Map p62; ☑020-531 17 77; www.deleurope.com; Nieuwe Doelenstraat 2-8; d from €479; ❄@🛜🏊;

AMSTERDAMSE BOS & COBRA MUSEUM

Goats in the forest and wild art reward those who venture southwest of the city to the quiet neighbourhood of Amstelveen, near Schiphol Airport.

The jewel here is Amsterdamse Bos (Amsterdam Forest; ☑ visitor centre 020-545 61 00; www.amsterdamsebos.nl; Bosbaanweg 5; ☉ park 24hr, visitors centre noon-5pm; Ⓜ Van Boshuizenstraat), a vast 2km by 5km tract of lakes, woods and meadows criss-crossed by paths, about a 40-minute bus ride from Centraal Station. Bike rentals (www.amster damsebosfietsverhuur.nl; rental per hour/day €5/10; ☉ 10am-6pm; Ⓜ Van Boshuizenstraat) are available at the main entrance and are vital for park exploration. The Fun Forest (www. funforest.nl; Bosbaanweg 3; adult/child €25/20; ☉ 10am-6pm daily Jul, hours vary other months; ⊡ 170, 172) tree-top climbing park is also by the main gate.

From here head west for 2.5km and you'll come to the open-air theatre (www. bostheater.nl; De Duizendmeterweg 7; ☉ Jun-early Sep; ⊡ 170, 172). It stages classic plays (in Dutch) throughout summer. Nearby at Grote Speelweide you can rent canoes and kay-aks (per hour from €6) and pedal boats (per hour from €10).

About 0.75km south is the park's most delightful attraction. De Ridammerhoeve (www.geitenboerderij.nl; Nieuwe Meerlaan 4; ☉ 10am-5pm daily late Feb-Oct, Wed-Sun Nov-late Feb; ⊡ 170, 172) FREE is an organic, working goat farm where kids can feed bottles of milk to, well, kids (€8 for two bottles). The cafeteria sells goat's-milk ice cream and other dairy products.

The fascinating CoBrA Museum (www.cobra-museum.nl; Sandbergplein 1; adult/child €12/7.50; ☉ 11am-5pm Tue-Sun; Ⓜ Amstelveen Centrum) lies 3km south of the park's main entrance. Formed by artists from Copenhagen, Brussels and Amsterdam after WWII, the CoBrA movement produced semi-abstract works known for their primitive, childlike qualities. The two-storey building holds a trove of boldly coloured, avant-garde paint-ings, ceramics and statues, including many by Karel Appel, the style's most famous practitioner.

☑ 24 Muntplein) Owned by the Heineken fam-ily, Amsterdam's 'other royal palace' blends classical elements (chandeliers, doorkeepers in top hats) with whimsical Dutch design. The 111 rooms are grand, with iPads, ca-nal views, heated floors and white-marble bathtubs. Restaurants include the twin-Michelin-starred Bord'Eau; other highlights are the superb spa, on-site cigar lounge and Freddy's Bar, with brass-topped tables and leather chairs.

art'otel amsterdam   DESIGN HOTEL €€€
(Map p48; ☑ 020-719 72 00; www.artotels.com; Prins Hendrikkade 33; d from €349; ﹡ ☎ ☒; ⊡ 2/4/11/12/13/14/17/24/26 Centraal Station) Located directly opposite Centraal Station, this stylish hotel offers 107 rooms with mod decor and original artworks on the wall. To add to the creative theme, there's an open-to-the-public gallery in the basement. The lobby is a swanky refuge with a fireplace and a library. A beyond-the-norm hot breakfast (and a sumptuous brunch on Sunday) is in-cluded in the rate.

Swim laps, work out at the gym or relax in the sauna at its fitness club.

🛏 Nieuwmarkt, Plantage & the Eastern Islands

Christian Youth Hostel
'The Shelter City'   HOSTEL €
(Map p48; ☑ 020-625 32 30; www.shelterhostel amsterdam.com; Barndesteeg 21; dm €22.90-27.40; @ ☎; Ⓜ Nieuwmarkt) Extremely conven-ient for central Amsterdam, this rambling Christian-run hostel is just outside the Red Light District, but a world away, powered by religious zeal and operating a no-drugs-or-alcohol policy. If you can handle this, the pay-back is spick-and-span single-sex dorms (two to 20 beds), filling, free breakfasts, a quiet cafe and a garden courtyard with bright seat-ing. Towel/padlock rental costs €1/5.

Hotel Hortus   HOTEL €
(Map p54; ☑ 020-625 99 96; www.hotelhortus. com; Plantage Parklaan 8; d with/without shower from €120/110; ℙ ☎; ⊡ 14 Plantage Kerklaan) Facing the botanical garden, this 20-room hotel has spartan, well-worn rooms, but is in a good, leafy, peaceful location, and you can snare some good rates, especially during low season. There's a large common area with a

pool table and several TVs. It has two double rooms with a shower, and two without; all share toilets, but have a safe and a basin.

★ Lloyd Hotel
BOUTIQUE HOTEL €€

(☑ 020-561 36 07; www.lloydhotel.com; Oostelijke Handelskade 34; d/ste from €140/218; @ 🛜; 🚊 26 Rietlandpark) Magnificent waterside Lloyd was a hotel for emigrants from the Netherlands back in 1921, who stayed here before setting sail. Many of the original fixtures remain, alongside contemporary-art installations and design. Rooms range from one to five stars, from budget with a bathroom down the hall to racquetball-court-sized top-end extravaganzas.

Hotel Rembrandt
HOTEL €€

(Map p54; ☑ 020-627 27 14; www.hotelrembrandt. nl; Plantage Middenlaan 17; s/d from €135/150; 🛜; 🚊 14 Plantage Kerklaan) Built for a 19th-century merchant, the Rembrandt Hotel has an impressive red and white facade. Rooms are all different, but are generally light and bright, with colourful curtains or design touches, and prints on the walls. Room 8 has a nearly life-sized mural of *The Night Watch;* one room has a balcony and one a sauna.

Misc EatDrinkSleep
BOUTIQUE HOTEL €€€

(Map p48; ☑ 020-330 62 41; www.misceatdrink sleep.com; Kloveniersburgwal 20; d from €175; ❄️ 🛜; Ⓜ Nieuwmarkt) Steps from Nieuwmarkt square, the Misc has six charming rooms, all decorated differently, from the lanterns and rich canopy of the 'Wonders' room to the fussiness of the 'Baroque'. Three rooms – the stylish 'Afrika', 'Design' and 'Rembrandt' – have canal views (which cost more), and air-conditioning. Rooms with views over the garden have fan only and are smaller, but equally light and bright.

🛏 Western Canal Ring

★ Hotel IX
BOUTIQUE HOTEL €€

(Map p66; ☑ 020-845 84 51; www.hotelixamster dam.com; Hartenstraat 8; d from €180; 🛜; 🚊 13/17 Westermarkt) The only hotel in the delightful Negen Straatjes (p107) shopping district, IX has super-stylish suites (sleeping up to four) named for the area's 'Nine Streets', with black-and-white murals and complimentary minibars. The pick is the Berenstraat suite, with its own roof terrace. Note there's no onsite reception (entry is via digicodes sent prior to arrival), no breakfast and no lift.

★ Hoxton Amsterdam
DESIGN HOTEL €€€

(Map p48; ☑ 020-888 55 55; www.thehoxton. com; Herengracht 255; s/d from €169/209; ❄️ 🛜; 🚊 13/17 Westermarkt) Part of a Europe-based chain known for high style at affordable prices, the Hoxton has 111 rooms – in sizes from 'shoebox' to 'roomy' – splashed through five canal houses. The breakfast snack, speedy wi-fi, free international calls and low-priced canteen items are nice touches. It organises events with city artists and designers, so you get to meet creative locals.

Dylan
BOUTIQUE HOTEL €€€

(Map p66; ☑ 020-530 20 10; www.dylanamsterdam. com; Keizersgracht 384; d/ste from €359/581; ❄️ @ 🛜; 🚊 2/11/12 Spui) Exquisite boutique hotel the Dylan occupies an 18th-century Keizersgracht canal house that is set around a herringbone-paved, topiary-filled inner courtyard. Bespoke furniture such as silverleaf and mother-of-pearl drinks cabinets adorn its 40 individually decorated rooms and suites (some duplex). Its Michelin-starred Restaurant Vinkeles also hosts private chef's tables aboard its boat, the *Muze,* as it cruises the canals.

Andaz Amsterdam
DESIGN HOTEL €€€

(Map p62; ☑ 020-523 12 34; www.hyatt.com; Prinsengracht 587; d/ste from €335/915; @ 🛜; 🚊 2/11/12 Prinsengracht) Visionary Dutch designer Marcel Wanders transformed Amsterdam's former public library into a fantasy of giant gold and silver cutlery, fish murals, Delftware-inspired carpets, library-book pages writ large on the walls and other flights of imagination. The 122 guest rooms and suites have Geneva sound systems, king-size beds, and complimentary snacks and non-alcoholic drinks. Free bikes to use too.

★ 't Hotel
BOUTIQUE HOTEL €€€

(Map p66; ☑ 020-422 27 41; www.thotel.nl; Leliegracht 18; d/f from €145/239; ❄️ 🛜; 🚊 13/17 Westermarkt) Named for Amsterdam's waterways, the eight rooms in this charming 17th-century canal house are individually decorated with black-and-white sketches of old Dutch scenes, printed cushions and shower curtains, and patterned wallpapers by interior-print designer Katarina Stupavska, whose family owns the hotel. Dazzling blue-and-white Delftware designs line the family room, which has a loft sleeping area reached by a ladder.

There's a stair lift but no elevator.

🛏 Southern Canal Ring

⭐ **Cocomama** HOSTEL **€**

(Map p62; ☑020-627 24 54; www.cocomama
hostel.com; Westeinde 18; dm/d from €42/120, minimum 2-night stay; @ 🛜; 🚊4 Stadhouderskade)
Once a high-end brothel, this boutique
hostel's doubles and dorms are light, bright
and decorated with flair, with white walls
and quirky designer Delftware or windmill
themes. Amenities are way above typical
hostel standard, with en-suite bathrooms,
in-room wi-fi, a relaxing back garden, a well-
equipped kitchen, a book exchange and a
super-comfy lounge for movie nights. Breakfast is included.

⭐ **Hotel V Frederiksplein** BOUTIQUE HOTEL **€€**

(Map p62; ☑020-662 32 33; www.hotelvfred
eriksplein.nl; Weteringschans 136; d €99-219; 🛜;
🚊1/4/7/19 Frederiksplein) With soothing, leafy
views over lush Frederiksplein, but a quick
shimmy from the bars and restaurants of
Utrechtsestraat, Hotel V exudes a style that's
well above its price bracket. Its 48 rooms
have cool design cred with touches such as
funky wall stencils and mid-century leather
armchairs.

Hotel Freeland HOTEL **€€**

(Map p62; ☑020-622 75 11; www.hotelfreeland.
com; Marnixstraat 386; s/d from €80/120, s without bathroom from €70; 🛜; 🚊2/5/7/11/12/19
Leidseplein) In a prime canal-side location, the Freeland has 15 simple, nicely
old-fashioned rooms with tiled walls;
each has a floral theme (tulips, roses and
sunflowers). Add in a tasty breakfast and
it pretty much kills the Leidseplein competition. The hotel is gay-friendly and
all-welcoming. Breakfast costs €6.50 per
person.

Seven Bridges BOUTIQUE HOTEL **€€**

(Map p62; ☑020-623 13 29; www.sevenbridges
hotel.nl; Reguliersgracht 31; d €135-280; 🛜; 🚊4
Keizersgracht) Beautifully set on one of Amsterdam's loveliest canals, the Seven Bridges
will immerse you in aristocratic opulence.
Rooms are sumptuously decorated with oriental rugs and polished antiques. The urge
to sightsee may fade once breakfast (€10),
served on fine china, is delivered to your
room.

⭐ **Seven One Seven** BOUTIQUE HOTEL **€€€**

(Map p62; ☑020-427 07 17; www.717hotel.nl; Prinsengracht 717; d from €250; ❇🛜; 🚊2/11/12 Prinsengracht) Looking straight from the pages
of a style magazine, the exquisitely decorated rooms here come with that all-too-rare
luxury: space. It'll be hard to tear yourself
away from these rooms, all of which have
soaring ceilings, vast sofas, striking use of
colour and contemporary-meets-antique
decorations.

🛏 Jordaan & the West

⭐ **Mr Jordaan** DESIGN HOTEL **€€**

(Map p66; ☑020-626 58 01; www.mrjordaan.nl;
Bloemgracht 102; s/d from €107/153; 🛜; 🚊13/17
Westermarkt) Wooden bedheads shaped like a
row of gabled canal houses, lighting made
from plumbing pipes and bedside cacti –
along with vintage fixtures in public spaces
like 1960s TVs, battered suitcases and type-
writers – are just some of the unexpected design elements at this super-cool, refreshingly
irreverent hotel in the heart of the Jordaan.

⭐ **Houseboat Ms Luctor** B&B **€€**

(☑06 2268 9506; www.boatbedandbreakfast.
nl; Westerdok 103; d from €140; 🛜; 🚊48 Bar-
entszplein) 🍃 A brimming organic breakfast
basket is delivered to you each morning at
this metal-hulled, mahogany-panelled 1913
houseboat, moored in a quiet waterway
10 minutes' walk from Centraal Station (five
from the Jordaan). Eco initiatives include
solar power, two bikes to borrow and a canoe for canal explorations. Minimum stay is
two nights.

Amsterdam Wiechmann Hotel HOTEL **€€**

(Map p66; ☑020-626 33 21; www.hotelwiechmann.
nl; Prinsengracht 328-332; s/d from €115/148;
@🛜; 🚊5/7/19 Elandsgracht) Many of the 37
rooms at this family-run hotel in three canal
houses have antique-shop-style furnishings,
while the lobby knick-knacks have been here
since the 1940s. It's in an ace location right
on the pretty Prinsengracht (it's worth paying extra for a canal-facing room), but be
aware that there's no lift and the stairs are
super-steep. Rates include breakfast.

BackStage Hotel HOTEL **€€**

(Map p62; ☑020-624 40 44; www.backstagehotel.
com; Leidsegracht 114; s without bathroom from
€85, d with/without bathroom from €155/125;
🛜; 🚊5/7/19 Leidseplein) Seriously fun, this
music-themed hotel is a favourite among
musicians jamming at nearby Melkweg and
Paradiso, as evidenced by the lobby bar's
band-signature-covered piano and pool table. Gig posters (many signed) line the cor-
ridors, and rooms are done up in neo-retro

AIRPORT ACCOMMODATION

A five-minute walk from the airport terminals, **Citizen M** (☑020-811 70 80; www.citizenm.com; Jan Plezierweg 2; d from €106; ❄@☎; ℞Schiphol) boasts 355 Starship Enterprise–like rooms that are snug, but maximise space to the utmost, with plush wall-to-wall beds, and bathroom pods. Each room includes a lighting control – command central for the lighting (purple, red or white), blinds, flat-screen TV (free on-demand movies), music, temperature and high-pressure rain shower. Some rooms directly overlook the tarmac.

black and white, with music stations and drum-kit overhead lights.

🛏 Vondelpark & the South

Stayokay Amsterdam Vondelpark   HOSTEL €
(Map p62; ☑020-589 89 96; www.stayokay.com; Zandpad 5; dm €27-65, tw from €136; ☎; 🚊1/3/11 1e Constantijn Huygensstraat) Practically in the Vondelpark, this HI-affiliated 536-bed hostel, housed in former university buildings, attracts over 75,000 guests a year, a lively international crowd of backpackers, families and groups. It's the best Stayokay in town, with private rooms and fresh mixed or female-/male-only rooms sleeping from two to nine, sporting lockers, private bathrooms and well-spaced bunks. Breakfast is a cut above most hostels.

Van Gogh Hostel & Hotel   HOSTEL, HOTEL €
(Map p62; ☑020-262 92 00; www.hotelvangogh. nl; Van de Veldestraat 5; dm/s/d from €35/75/129; ❄@☎; 🚊2/3/5/12 Van Baerlestraat) The clue is in the name: this is a few paces from the Van Gogh Museum, and every room has a Van Gogh mural covering the entire wall behind the bedhead. Next door is the more basic hostel, with dorms of six to eight beds, en-suite bathroom and flat-screen TV.

★**Hotel Not Hotel**   DESIGN HOTEL €€
(☑020-820 45 38; www.hotelnothotel.com; Piri Reisplein 34; d with/without bathroom from €139/70; 🚊7/17 Witte de Withstraat) Stay in a work of art at this out-there collection of installations. Sleep inside Amsterdam Tram 965 (in a king-size bed), lounge on a private Spanish villa alfresco terrace, bed down behind a secret bookcase, escape the daily grind in the Crisis

Free Zone framed by Transylvanian-inspired woodcarvings to deter evil spirits, or climb a ladder to a crow's nest.

Owl Hotel   HOTEL €€
(Map p62; ☑020-618 94 84; www.owl-hotel.nl; Roemer Visscherstraat 1; s/d €126/164; ☎; 🚊1/3/11 1e Constantijn Huygensstraat) The owl figurines in the reception of this 34-room hotel have been sent by former guests from all over the world to add to the hotel's collection. Staff are warm and welcoming, and rooms are bright and quiet. The included buffet breakfast is served in a bright, garden-side room.

Hotel Fita   HOTEL €€
(Map p62; ☑020-679 09 76; www.fita.nl; Jan Luijkenstraat 37; s/d from €125/159; ☎; 🚊2/3/5/12 Van Baerlestraat) Family-owned Fita, on a quiet street close to the museums, has 15 rooms with baroque carpeting but otherwise plain decor, nice touches like plants in the rooms, and smart bathrooms; a bountiful free breakfast of eggs, pancakes, cheeses and breads; and a lift. The dynamic young owner keeps the property in mint condition, and service could not be more attentive.

**Conscious Hotel
Museum Square**   BOUTIQUE HOTEL €€
(Map p62; ☑020-820 33 33; www.conscioushotels. com; De Lairessestraat 7; d/f from €135/166; @☎; 🚊3/5/12 Museumplein) 🌿 The most intimate of the Conscious Hotel group, and closest to the major Amsterdam museums, this location has a lush garden terrace, a living plant wall in the lobby and eco- and design-conscious rooms: beds made with 100% natural materials, desks constructed from recycled yoghurt containers, and energy-saving plasma TVs. The organic breakfast costs €15 extra.

★**Pillows Anna
van den Vondel**   BOUTIQUE HOTEL €€€
(Map p62; ☑020-683 30 13; www.pillowshotels. nl; Anna van den Vondelstraat 6; d from €360; ☎; 🚊1/11 Jan Pieter Heijestraat) This grown-up hotel, housed in a row of three grand 19th-century mansions, has rooms with views over the tranquil English garden. Beds are clothed in soft, gleaming white linen, walls are gentle dove-grey, and chairs have a mid-century look and pale-blue crushed-velvet upholstery. Breakfast costs €25.

Conservatorium Hotel   DESIGN HOTEL €€€
(Map p62; ☑020-570 00 00; www.conservatorium hotel.com; Van Baerlestraat 27; d from €472;

✳ 🛜 🛏; 🚋3/5/12 Van Baerlestraat) Opposite the Royal Concertgebouw, this palatial neo-Gothic building was originally a bank, then the city's conservatorium of music. Its most recent incarnation sees it stunningly converted into an eight-storey, 129-room five star with impressive public spaces, especially the huge covered courtyard, where soaring glass and steel connects the 19th-century brickwork and contemporary rooms with neutral hues and designer furnishings.

🏅 De Pijp

★ Sir Albert Hotel
DESIGN HOTEL €€

(Map p62; 🗷020-710 72 58; www.sirhotels. com/albert; Albert Cuypstraat 2-6; d from €159; ✳ @ 🛜; M De Pijp, 🚋3 De Pijp) A 19th-century diamond factory houses this glitzy design hotel. Its 90 creative rooms and suites have high ceilings and large windows, with custom-made linens and Illy espresso machines; iPads are available for use in the Persian-rug-floored study. Energetic staff are helpful and professional. Of the 10 balcony rooms, west-facing 336, 337 and 338 have sunset views over the canal.

Bicycle Hotel Amsterdam
HOTEL €€

(Map p62; 🗷020-679 34 52; www.bicyclehotel.com; Van Ostadestraat 123; d/tr/f from €100/150/160, s/d/tr without bathroom from €30/60/120; @ 🛜; M De Pijp, 🚋3 De Pijp) 🚲 Run by Marjolein and Clemens, this friendly, green-minded hotel has rooms that are comfy and familiar. It also rents bikes (€8 per day April to August; free between September and March) and serves a killer organic breakfast (included in the rate). Look for the bikes mounted on the brick exterior.

Between Art & Kitsch B&B
B&B €€

(Map p62; 🗷020-679 04 85; www.between-art-and-kitsch.com; Ruysdaelkade 75; s/d from €85/100; 🛜; 🚋24 Ferdinand Bolstraat) Mondrian once lived here – that's part of the art – while the kitsch includes the crystal chandelier in the baroque room and a smiling brass Buddha. The art-deco room has gorgeous tile work and views of the Rijksmuseum. Husband-and-wife hosts Ebo and Irene couldn't be friendlier. It's on the 3rd floor, reached by steep stairs (no lift).

Hotel Okura Amsterdam
HOTEL €€€

(🗷020-678 71 11; www.okura.nl; Ferdinand Bolstraat 333; d/ste from €276/335; ✳ @ 🛜 🏊; 🚋12 Cornelis Troostplein) Rare-for-Amsterdam attributes that elevate this business-oriented hotel way above the competition include panoramic city views (particularly from higher-priced north-facing rooms), four Michelin stars on the premises – two at top-floor Ciel Bleu (p95), one at ground-floor Japanese restaurant Yamazato and one at ground-floor teppanyaki restaurant Sazanka – and an amazing health club with an 18m-long jet-stream swimming pool. Bountiful breakfast buffets cost €29.50.

It's locally loved for its social responsibility and donations to the surrounding community.

🏅 Amsterdam Noord

★ ClinkNOORD
HOSTEL €

(🗷020-214 97 30; www.clinkhostels.com; Badhuiskade 3; dm/s/d from €27.30/93/112; ✳ 🛜; ⛴Buiksloterweg) Clink is a designer hostel chain with other branches in London, and here occupies a 1920s laboratory on the IJ riverbank, by the ferry terminal – a free, five-minute ferry ride from Centraal Station (ferries run 24/7). Dorms are done up in minimalist-industrial style, with four to 16 beds and en-suite facilities.

There are female-only dorms available. Join a free walking tour or you can hire bikes to explore on your own.

★ Faralda Crane Hotel
DESIGN HOTEL €€€

(🗷020-760 61 61; www.faralda.com; NDSM-plein 78; ste from €620; ✳ 🛜; ⛴NDSM-werf) What's that imposing industrial crane rising up at NDSM-werf? It's a hotel. The three fantasy-world suites perched at varying heights – Free Spirit, Secret and Mystique – have looks worthy of a drug baron's hideout, with free-standing baths, bold objets d'art and vertiginous views. On the crane's rooftop, you can soak in the heated bubbling outdoor hot tub, with astounding views across to central Amsterdam.

★ Sir Adam
DESIGN HOTEL €€€

(🗷020-215 95 10; www.sirhotels.com; Overhoeksplein 7; d/ste from €224/431; ✳ @ 🛜; ⛴Buiksloterweg) Mammoth, view-framing (from the deluxe rooms) plate-glass windows: tick. Pillow menu: tick. Linen with a 300-thread count: tick. Rainfall shower: tick. Illy coffee-maker: tick. Crosley Cruiser record player: tick. Twenty-four-hour room service: tick. The rooms at Sir Adam have all a self-respecting dude who likes their comforts could want and more.

Eating

Amsterdam's sizzling-hot foodie scene spans classic Dutch snacks to reinvented traditional recipes at contemporary restaurants, on-trend establishments pioneering world-first concepts, a wave of new, ultra-healthy, often vegetarian or vegan eateries, and an increasing focus on wine, cocktail and craft beer pairings. And this multinational city has a cornucopia of cuisines from all over the globe.

Many restaurants, even top-end ones, don't accept credit cards. Or if they do, there's often a 5% surcharge. Conversely, some places accept cards only. Check first.

Phone ahead to make a reservation for eateries in the middle and upper price brackets. Nearly everyone speaks English. Many places offer online booking options.

✗ Medieval Centre & Red Light District

Snack stands and cafes abound for quick, inexpensive dishes, and numerous pubs serve food. Amsterdam's small Chinatown, with pan-Asian restaurants, centres on Zeedijk. Throughout the neighbourhood, however, an increasing number of places offering refined, often highly creative dining are flourishing.

★ Vleminckx   FAST FOOD €
(Map p62; www.vleminckxdesausmeester.nl; Voetboogstraat 33; fries €3-5, sauces €0.70; ⊗noon-7pm Sun & Mon, 11am-7pm Tue, Wed, Fri & Sat, to 8pm Thu; ⓐ2/11/12 Koningsplein) Frying up *frites* (fries) since 1887, Amsterdam's best *friterie* has been based at this hole-in-the-wall takeaway shack near the Spui since 1957. The standard order of perfectly cooked crispy, fluffy *frites* is smothered in mayonnaise, though its 28 sauces also include apple, green pepper, ketchup, peanut, sambal and mustard. Queues almost always stretch down the block, but they move fast.

★ De Laatste Kruimel   CAFE, BAKERY €
(Map p62; ☎020-423 04 99; www.delaatstekruimel.nl; Langebrugsteeg 4; dishes €3-8.50; ⊗8am-8pm Mon-Sat, from 9am Sun; Ⓜ Rokin; ⓐ4/14/24 Rokin) Decorated with vintage finds from the Noordermarkt and wooden pallets upcycled as furniture, and opening to a tiny canal-side terrace, the 'Last Crumb' has glass display cases piled high with pies,

quiches, breads, cakes and lemon-and-poppy-seed scones. Grandmothers, children, couples on dates and just about everyone else crowd in for sweet treats and fantastic organic sandwiches.

★ Gartine   CAFE €
(Map p48; ☎020-320 41 32; www.gartine.nl; Taksteeg 7; dishes €6.50-12, high tea €17.50-25; ⊗10am-6pm Wed-Sat; ✎; Ⓜ Rokin, ⓐ4/14/24 Rokin) ✎ Gartine is magical, from its covert location in an alley off busy Kalverstraat to its mismatched antique tableware and its sublime breakfast pastries, sandwiches and salads (made from produce grown in its garden plot and eggs from its chickens). The sweet-and-savoury high tea, from 2pm to 5pm, is a treat.

Rob Wigboldus Vishandel   SANDWICHES €
(Map p48; Zoutsteeg 6; sandwiches €2-6; ⊗9am-5pm Tue-Sat; ⓐ4/14/24 Dam) A wee three-table oasis in a narrow alleyway just off the touristy Damrak, this fish shop serves excellent herring sandwiches on a choice of crusty white or brown rolls. Other sandwich fillings include smoked eel, Dutch prawns and fried whitefish.

★ D'Vijff Vlieghen   DUTCH €€
(Map p62; ☎020-530 40 60; www.vijffvlieghen.nl; Spuistraat 294-302; mains €19-26; ⊗6-10pm; ⓐ2/11/12 Spui) Spread across five 17th-century canal houses, the 'Five Flies' is a jewel. Old-wood dining rooms overflow with character, featuring Delft-blue tiles and original works by Rembrandt; chairs have copper plates inscribed with the names of famous guests (Walt Disney, Mick Jagger...). Exquisite dishes range from goose breast with apple, sauerkraut and smoked butter to candied haddock with liquorice sauce.

Nam Kee   CANTONESE €€
(Map p48; ☎020-624 34 70; www.namkee.nl; Zeedijk 111-113; mains €12.50-23; ⊗11.30am-10.30pm; Ⓜ Nieuwmarkt) It won't win any design awards, but year in, year out, Nam Kee, serving Cantonese classics, is the most popular Chinese spot in town. The steamed oysters and black-bean sauce are legendary. If you want to avoid the fluorescent-light ambience, try Nam Kee's nearby branch (Map p48; ☎020-639 28 48; www.namkee.net; Geldersekade 117; mains €12.50-23; ⊗4pm-midnight Mon-Fri, 2.30pm-midnight Sat, 2.30-11pm Sun; ✎; Ⓜ Nieuwmarkt) in Nieuwmarkt, which is fancier.

Bird Snackbar
THAI €€

(Map p48; 020-420 62 89; www.thaibird.nl; Zeedijk 77; mains €10-16; 1-10pm Mon-Wed, to 10.30pm Thu-Sun; 2/4/11/12/13/14/17/24/26 Centraal Station) Bird has some of the best Asian food on the Zeedijk – the cooks, wedged in a tiny kitchen, don't skimp on lemongrass, fish sauce or chilli. The resulting curries and basil-laden meat and seafood dishes will knock your socks off. There's a bit more room to spread out in the (slightly pricier) restaurant across the street (No 72).

Haesje Claes
DUTCH €€

(Map p48; 020-624 99 98; www.haesjeclaes. nl; Spuistraat 275; mains €16.25-26.50, 3-course menu €25; noon-10pm; 2/11/12 Spui) Haesje Claes' warm surrounds – with lots of dark wood and antique knick-knacks – make it just the place to sample comforting pea soup and a *stamppot* (potato and vegetable mash) of the day topped with meatballs, sausages and bacon. The fish starter has a great sampling of different Dutch fish.

Hofje van Wijs
CAFE €€

(Map p48; 020-624 04 36; www.wijsenzonen. com; Zeedijk 43; mains €18.50, 2-/3-course menus €23.50/28.50; noon-10pm; 2/4/11/12/13/14/17/24/26 Centraal Station) Two-century-old coffee and tea vendor Wijs & Zonen (the monarch's purveyor) maintains this pretty courtyard restaurant. It serves Dutch stews, fondue and a couple of fish dishes (plus a vegetarian option), along with local beers and *jenevers*.

✗ Nieuwmarkt, Plantage & the Eastern Islands

You've got lots of eating-out choices in Nieuwmarkt, with some gems amid this central Amsterdam hub. Plantage is only a short bike ride away, but a different world in atmosphere. Head to this leafy district for laid-back neighbourhood restaurants. You can expect the spectacular on the Eastern Islands and Eastern Docklands, with many of the best places to dine having fantastic river views.

★ Sterk Staaltje
DELI €

(Map p62; www.sterkstaaltje.com; Staalstraat 12; dishes €4-8; 8.30am-7pm Mon-Fri, 8.30am-6pm Sat, 10am-7pm Sun; 24 Muntplein) With pristine fruit and veg stacked up outside, Sterk Staaltje is worth entering just to breathe in the scent of the foodstuffs, with a fine range of ready-to-eat treats: teriyaki meat-

CHEESE TASTING

Here's your chance to become a *kaas* (cheese) connoisseur. Century-old Dutch cheesemaker Reypenaer (Map p48; 020-320 63 33; www.reypenaer cheese.com; Singel 182; tastings from €16.50; tastings by reservation; 2/11/12/13/17 Dam) offers tastings in a rustic classroom beneath its shop. The hour-long session includes six cheeses – four cow's milk, two goat's milk – from young to old, with wine and port pairings. Expert staff members guide you through them, helping you appreciate the cheeses' look, aroma and taste.

balls, feta and sundried tomato quiche, pumpkin-stuffed wraps, a soup of the day and particularly fantastic sandwiches – roast beef, horseradish and rucola (arugula/ rocket) or marinated chicken with guacamole and sour cream.

★ Tokoman
SURINAMESE €

(Map p54; www.tokoman.nl; Waterlooplein 327; sandwiches €3.75-5.50, dishes €7-13.50; 11.30am-9pm; M Waterlooplein) Queue with the folks getting their Surinamese spice on at Tokoman. It makes a sensational *broodje pom* (a sandwich filled with a tasty mash of chicken and a starchy Surinamese tuber). You'll want the *zuur* (pickled-cabbage relish) and *peper* (chilli) on it, plus a cold can of coconut water to wash it down.

IJsmolen
ICE CREAM €

(Zeeburgerstraat 2; 1/2/4 scoops €1.50/2.75/4.75; noon-9pm; 7 Hoogte Kadijk) Homemade ice cream at this spot near the De Gooyer Windmill comes in Dutch flavours like *stroopwafel* (classic caramel-syrup-filled wafers) and *speculaas* (spicy Christmas biscuits); plus *stracciatella* (vanilla with shredded chocolate) and lemon cheesecake; and pure fruity flavours including mango, mint and watermelon. On hot days it stays open to 10pm. Cash only.

Frenzi
MEDITERRANEAN €€

(Map p48; 020-423 51 12; www.frenzi-restaurant. nl; Zwanenburgwal 232; mains lunch €8-15, dinner €18.50-20.50, tapas €5.50-7; 10am-11pm; 24 Muntplein) Frenzi has lots of atmosphere (scrubbed wood tables, lit with candles) and serves delicious Italian tapas – Manchego cheese and fig compote; marinated sardines;

portobello mushrooms with melted Gorgonzola – but save room for mains like pan-fried cod with fennel mash, pumpkin gnocchi with wilted spinach, and leg of lamb with roast asparagus.

De Plantage
MODERN EUROPEAN €€

(Map p54; ☑ 020-760 68 00; www.caferestaurant deplantage.nl; Plantage Kerklaan 36; mains lunch €7.50-21.50, dinner €17.75-21.50; ⊙ kitchen 9am-10pm Mon-Fri, from 10am Sat & Sun, bar to 1am daily; ☐ 14 Plantage Kerklaan) Huge and graceful, this is an impressive space in a 1870s-built, 1900-expanded former greenhouse decked with blond wood and black chairs, with hothouse views of strutting geese in the grounds of the Artis Royal Zoo (p56). Food is creative and tasty, with dishes like salad with roasted octopus, couscous, fennel, *bacalau* (dried and salted cod), mussels and saffron mayo.

★ Gebr Hartering
DUTCH €€€

(Map p54; ☑ 020-421 06 99; www.gebr-hartering. nl; Peperstraat 10; mains €27.50, 5-/7-course menus €55/80; ⊙ 6-10.30pm; ☐ 22/48 Prins Hendrik-kade) Lined in pale rustic wood, this gem was founded by two food-loving brothers, who offer either à la carte or a multi-course menu that changes daily according to the best seasonal produce available. A meal here is always a delight to linger over, so settle in and enjoy the accompanying wines and canal-side location.

★ Greetje
DUTCH €€€

(Map p54; ☑ 020-779 74 50; www.restaurant greetje.nl; Peperstraat 23-25; mains €23-29; ⊙ 6-10pm Sun-Thu, to 11pm Fri & Sat; ☐ 22/48 Prins Hendrikkade) 🖉 Greetje is Amsterdam's most creative Dutch restaurant, using the best seasonal produce to resurrect and re-create traditional Dutch recipes, like pickled beef, braised veal with apricots and leek *stamppot*, and pork belly with Dutch mustard sauce. Kick off with the Big Beginning (€17), a sampling of hot and cold starters.

✕ Western Canal Ring

The Western Canal Ring may not have the multicultural dining diversity of other parts of town, but bear in mind that the Jordaan neighbourhood is only a hop, skip and jump away. The Negen Straatjes (p107) are filled with cute cafes and small restaurants to match their lovely boutiques.

Pancake Bakery
DUTCH €

(Map p66; ☑ 020-625 13 33; www.pancake.nl; Prinsengracht 191; mains €9-15.65; ⊙ 9am-9.30pm; 🛜 🖉 ♿; ☐ 13/17 Westermarkt) In a restored 17th-century warehouse that once belonged to the Dutch East India Company, this basement restaurant offers a dizzying 77 varieties of pancake, from sweet (like chocolate, banana or peach) to savoury (eg Canadian, topped with bacon, cheese and barbecue sauce, or Norwegian, with smoked salmon, cream cheese and sour cream). Kids' varieties include Pirate, Fireman and Princess pancakes.

Singel 404
CAFE €

(Map p48; Singel 404; dishes €3.50-9; ⊙ 10.30am-6pm; 🖉; ☐ 2/11/12 Spui) It's easy to miss this tucked-away spot, despite its location near the bustling Spui (look for the cobalt-blue awning). The menu is as simple as can be – smoked-salmon sandwiches, pumpkin soup, honey-mint lemonade – but the prices are rock bottom, the portions are generous and the quality is superb. There's a handful of tables inside and out.

Wil Graanstra Friteshuis
FAST FOOD €

(Map p66; Westermarkt 11; frites €2.50-4, sauce €0.50; ⊙ noon-7pm Mon-Sat; ☐ 13/17 Westermarkt) Legions of Amsterdammers swear by the crispy chips at Wil Graanstra Friteshuis. The family-run business has been frying on the square by the Westerkerk since 1956. Most locals top their cones with mayonnaise, though *oorlog* (a peanut sauce–mayo combo), curry sauce and piccalilli (relish) rock the taste buds too.

★ De Belhamel
EUROPEAN €€

(Map p48; ☑ 020-622 10 95; www.belhamel.nl; Brouwersgracht 60; mains €24-26, 3-/4-course menus €35/45; ⊙ noon-4pm & 6-10pm Sun-Thu, 6-10.30pm Fri & Sat; ☐ 18/21/22 Buiten Brouwersstraat) In warm weather the canal-side tables here at the head of the Herengracht are delightful, and the richly wallpapered art-nouveau interior set over two levels provides the perfect backdrop for exquisitely presented dishes such as poached sole with wild-spinach bisque, veal sweetbreads with crispy bacon, onion confit and deep-fried sage, or a half lobster with velvety salmon mayonnaise.

Bistro Bij Ons
DUTCH €€

(Map p66; ☑ 020-627 90 16; www.bistrobijons. nl; Prinsengracht 287; mains €14.50-20; ⊙ 10am-10pm Tue-Sun; ♿; ☐ 13/17 Westermarkt) If you're not in town visiting your Dutch *oma* (grandma), try the honest-to-goodness cooking at this charming retro bistro instead. Classics include *stamppot* with sausage, *raasdonders* (split peas with bacon, onion and pickles) and *poffertjes* (small pancakes with butter and powdered sugar). House-made liqueurs include plum and *drop* (liquorice) varieties.

✖ Southern Canal Ring

Leidseplein has steakhouses cheek by jowl, though there are more interesting gems to be found that are not just about slabs of beef. For more scenic and singular eateries, your best bet is on the nearby side streets or canals.

Rembrandtplein has a somewhat brash feel; for a better meal, walk a few steps to Utrechtsestraat, one of the finest restaurant rows in town.

★ Van Dobben   DUTCH €
(Map p62; ☑020-624 42 00; www.eetsalon vandobben.nl; Korte Reguliersdwarsstraat 5-9; dishes €3-8; ⊙10am-9pm Mon-Wed, to 1am Thu, to 2am Fri & Sat, 10.30am-8pm Sun; 🚊4/14 Rembrandtplein) Open since the 1940s, Van Dobben has a cool diner feel, with white tiles and siren-red walls. Traditional meaty Dutch fare is its forte: low-priced, finely sliced roast-beef sandwiches with mustard are an old-fashioned joy, or try the *pekelvlees* (akin to corned beef) or *halfom* (if you're keen on *pekelvlees* mixed with liver).

Soup en Zo   SOUP €
(Map p62; www.soupenzo.nl; Nieuwe Spiegelstraat 54; soup €5-7; ⊙11am-8pm Mon-Fri, noon-7pm Sat & Sun; ☑; 🚊1/7/19 Spiegelgracht) On a chilly Amsterdam day, you can't beat a steaming cup of soup from this little specialist. Daily choices might include potato with Roquefort; lentil and minced beef, prunes and pumpkin; or spicy spinach and coconut. Takeaway only.

Patisserie Holtkamp   BAKERY €
(Map p62; www.patisserieholtkamp.nl; Vijzelgracht 15; dishes €3-7; ⊙8.30am-6pm Mon-Fri, to 5pm Sat; Ⓜ Vijzelgracht, 🚊24 Vijzelgracht) This is where the Dutch royals stock up on baked goods. It was founded in 1886; the gorgeous art-deco interior was added in 1928 by architect Piet Kramer. There's a lavish fit-for-a-queen spread inside, with delicacies including creamy cakes and its famous *kroketten* (croquettes) with fillings such as

lobster and veal. Its prawn versions are reputably Amsterdam's finest.

★ Buffet van Odette   CAFE €€
(Map p62; ☑020-423 60 34; www.buffet-amsterdam.nl; Prinsengracht 598; mains €9-18.50; ⊙noon-10pm Wed-Mon; 🚊1/7/19 Spiegelgracht) Chow down at Odette's, a white-tiled cafe with an enchanting canal-side location, where delicious dishes are made with great ingredients and a dash of creativity. Try the splendid platter of cured meats and dips, or mains such as ravioli with mature cheese, watercress and tomato, or smoked salmon, lentils and poached egg.

Pantry   DUTCH €€
(Map p62; ☑020-620 09 22; www.thepantry.nl; Leidsekruisstraat 21; mains €13.50-19, 3-course menus €21-30.50; ⊙11am-10.30pm; 🚊2/11/12 Leidseplein) With wood-panelled walls and sepia lighting, this little restaurant is *gezellig* indeed. Tuck into classic Dutch dishes such as *zuurkool stamppot* (sauerkraut and potato mash served with a smoked sausage or meatball) or *hutspot* ('hotchpotch', with stewed beef, carrots and onions).

In de Buurt   INTERNATIONAL €€
(Map p62; www.indebuurt-amsterdam.nl; Lijnbaansgracht 246; mains €12.50-19.50; ⊙kitchen 5pm-midnight, bar to 1am Mon-Thu, to 3am Fri-Sun; 🚊2/11/12 Leidseplein) It may be in the Leidseplein, but In de Buurt keeps it classy, dishing up fantastic mini-burgers with truffle mayo and roasted cherry tomatoes, and serving delicious gin and tonics. It has a canal-side summer terrace and a cosy interior with exposed-brick walls, beams and bottles.

✖ Jordaan & the West

Restaurants in the Jordaan exude the conviviality that is a hallmark of the neighbourhood. Many people gravitate to the eateries along Westerstraat, while the Haarlemmerbuurt offers increasingly trendy options. Or simply wander the narrow backstreets where the next hot spot may be opening up. Self-caterers shouldn't miss the neighbourhood's markets (p107).

Those looking for nouveau scenester eats will strike it rich in the West, particularly in and around Westergasfabriek (p68).

Festina Lente   CAFE €
(Map p66; ☑020-638 14 12; www.cafefestinalente. nl; Looiersgracht 40b; sandwiches €7-8.50, small plates €4.50-7.75; ⊙9am-10.30pm Sun-Thu, from

10am Fri & Sat; 🛉📶; 🚃5/7/19 Elandsgracht) Canal-side neighbourhood hang-out Festina Lente (Latin for 'make haste slowly') typifies Jordaan *gezelligheid*. The wood-panelled, vintage-furnished space is habitually filled with regulars playing board games, reading poetry and snacking on small-portion Mediterranean dishes and big sandwiches.

Boca's
TAPAS €€

(Map p66; 📞020-820 37 27; www.bar-bocas.nl; Westerstraat 30; bar snacks €3-9, platters €20-58.50; ⊘kitchen 9am-9pm Mon & Sat, 10am-9pm Tue-Fri, 11am-9am Sun, bar to 1am Sun-Thu, to 3am Fri & Sat; 🛉; 🚃3/5 Marnixplein) Fronted by a red awning and white-timber facade, this hip little bar is the perfect place for a drink accompanied by bar snacks. Try the mini lasagnes, burgers, bruschetta and steak tartar, or bigger selections on wooden boards: cheese platters, veggie platters, seafood platters, meat platters, sweet platters. If you can't decide, go for Boca's combination platter.

★ Wolf Atelier
GASTRONOMY €€

(📞020-344 64 28; www.wolfatelier.nl; Westerdoksplein 20; mains €24, 4-/5-/15-course menus €42.50/48/75; ⊘noon-5pm & 6-10pm Mon-Sat; 🚃48 Westerdoksdijk) Atop a 1920 railway swing bridge, a glass box with pivoting windows is the showcase for experimental Austrian chef Michael Wolf's wild flavour combinations. Mains might feature sweetbreads with truffle foam, flambéed sea bass with champagne-steamed Zeeland mussels, and deconstructed tonka-bean, chocolate and caramel crumble. The 360-degree views are magical at night; you can linger for a drink until 1am.

★ Balthazar's Keuken
MEDITERRANEAN €€

(Map p66; 📞020-420 21 14; www.balthazars keuken.nl; Elandsgracht 108; 3-course menu €34.50; ⊘6-10.30pm Tue-Sun; 🚃5/7/19 Elandsgracht) In a former blacksmith's forge, with a modern-rustic look and an open kitchen, this is consistently one of Amsterdam's top-rated restaurants. Don't expect a wide-ranging menu: the philosophy is basically 'whatever we have on hand', which might mean wild sea bass with mushroom risotto or confit of rabbit, but it's invariably delectable. Reservations recommended.

Pont 13
INTERNATIONAL €€

(📞020-770 27 22; www.pont13.nl; Haparandadam 50; mains lunch €7-14, dinner €16.50-22.50; ⊘kitchen noon-4pm & 5.30-10pm Tue-Sun, bar noon-midnight Tue-Sun; 🛉; 🚃48 Koivistokade) With sunny decks at either end and a cavernous interior, this vintage 1927 ex-car and passenger ferry once plied the IJ and is now permanently moored in the Western Docklands. Its open kitchen cooks up gastropub-style fare such as lemon- and laurel-marinated sea bass, burgers, rib-eye steaks, and smoked-mackerel and fennel salad.

Koevoet
ITALIAN €€

(Map p66; 📞020-624 08 46; www.koevoet amsterdam.com; Lindenstraat 17; mains €12-25; ⊘5.30-10pm Tue-Sun; 🚃3/5 Marnixplein) The congenial Italian owners of Koevoet took over a former cafe on a quiet side street, left the *gezellig* decor untouched and started cooking up their home-country staples such as handmade ravioli using ingredients imported from Italy's south. Don't miss the signature, drinkable dessert, *sgroppino limone:* sorbet, vodka and Prosecco whisked at your table and poured into a champagne flute.

Yam Yam
ITALIAN €€

(📞020-681 50 97; www.yamyam.nl; Frederik Hendrikstraat 88-90; pizzas €8-14, mains €13.50-17.50; ⊘5.30-10pm Tue-Sun; 🚃3 Hugo de Grootplein) Ask Amsterdammers to name the city's best pizza and many will name-check this hip, contemporary trattoria. The wood-fired oven turns out thin-crust varieties such as salami and fennel seed, and the signature Yam Yam (organic smoked ham, mascarpone and truffle sauce). There are also great pastas and creative desserts such as salted-pecan-caramel tart.

★ Marius
EUROPEAN €€€

(📞020-422 78 80; www.restaurantmarius.nl; Barentszstraat 173; 4-course menu €48; ⊘6.30-10pm Mon-Sat; 🚃3 Zoutkeetsgracht) Foodies swoon over pocket-sized Marius, tucked amid artists' studios in the Western Islands. Chef Kees Elfring shops at local markets, then creates his daily four-course, no-choice menu from what he finds. The result might be grilled prawns with fava-bean purée or beef rib with polenta and ratatouille. Marius also runs the fabulous wine and tapas bar **Worst Wijncafe** (📞020-625 61 67; www.deworst.nl; Barentszstraat 171; tapas €9-17, brunch mains €9-13; ⊘noon-midnight Mon-Sat, 10am-10pm Sun; 🚃3 Zoutkeetsgracht) next door.

✕ Vondelpark & the South

International options abound around Amstelveenseweg and inside De Hallen's Foodhallen (p61). Diverse restaurants also line Overtoom and Jan Pieter Heijestraat.

★ **Braai BBQ Bar**　BARBECUE €
(www.braaiamsterdam.nl; Schinkelhavenkade 1; dishes €6.50-15.50; ⊙4-9.30pm; ⑤1/11/17 Surinameplein) Once a *haringhuis* (herring stand), this tiny place is now a street-food-style barbecue bar, with a great canal-side setting. Braai's speciality is marinated, barbecued ribs (half or full rack) and roasted sausages, but there are veggie options too. Cards are preferred, but it accepts cash. Tables scatter under the trees alongside the water.

Breakfast Club　CAFE €
(Map p62; www.thebreakfastclub.nl; Bellamystraat 2; dishes €4.50-13; ⊙8am-4pm Mon-Fri, to 5pm Sat & Sun; ⑤7/17 Ten Katestraat) If you're hankering for breakfast any time of day, the laid-back Breakfast Club is perfect: Mexican breakfasts with *huevos rancheros* (spicy eggs); English-style, with homemade baked beans, bacon, eggs, mushrooms and sausages; or New York buttermilk pancakes with red fruits and honey butter. There are other tantalising pancake options too, plus cereals, avocado toast and other such First World essentials.

Alchemist Garden　VEGAN €
(☑020-334 33 35; www.alchemistgarden.nl; Overtoom 409; dishes €4-13; ⊙9am-9pm Mon-Sat, from noon Sun; ✍; ⑤1/11 Rhijnvis Feithstraat) 🍃 This bright, high-ceilinged cafe's food may be gluten-, lactose- and glucose-free, but it's tasty, with a health-rich, vitamin-filled organic menu (raw vegetable pies, avocado dumplings and pesto-stuffed portobello mushrooms), plus smoothies, juices and guilt-free treats like raw chocolate cake. Many ingredients are from the owner's own garden. Ask about wild-food foraging walks in the Vondelpark.

★ **Ron Gastrobar**　DUTCH €€
(☑020-496 19 43; www.rongastrobar.nl; Sophialaan 55; dishes €15; ⊙noon-2.30pm & 5.30-10.30pm; ☎; ⑤2 Amsteelveenseweg) Ron Blaauw ran his two-Michelin-star restaurant in these pared-down, spacious designer premises before turning it into a more affordable 'gastrobar' (still Michelin-starred), whereby you get the quality without the formality or

the need to settle down for five courses. He serves around 25 gourmet tapas-style dishes, marrying surprising flavours such as foie gras, raspberry and yoghurt.

Van 't Spit　ROTISSERIE €€
(Map p62; www.vantspit.nl; De Clercqstraat 95; half/whole chicken €11/21; ⊙kitchen 5-10pm, bar to 1am; ⑤13/19 Willem de Zwijgerlaan) At stripped-back Van 't Spit it's all about roast chicken, with piles of wood ready for the rotisserie. Choices are simple – select from a half or whole chicken (there are no other mains), and decide if you want sides (corn on the cob, fries, salad and homemade coleslaw).

l'Entrecôte et les Dames　FRENCH €€
(Map p62; ☑020-679 88 88; www.entrecote-et-les-dames.nl; Van Baerlestraat 47-49; lunch mains €13.50, 2-course dinner menu €24.75; ⊙noon-3pm & 5.30-10pm; ⑤3/5/12 Museumplein) With a double-height wall made from wooden drawers and a wrought-iron balcony, this restaurant has a simple menu of steak or fish: go for the *entrecôte* (premium beef steak), and save room for scrumptious desserts: perhaps chocolate mousse, *tarte au citron* (lemon tart) or *crêpes au Grand Marnier*.

Roc Elements　INTERNATIONAL €€
(Map p62; ☑020-579 17 17; www.heerlijkamsterdam.nl; Roelof Hartstraat 6-8; 2-/3-course lunch menus €12.50/15, 3-/4-course dinner menus €21/24.50; ⊙11.30am-2pm & 6-9pm, closed Jul & Aug; ⑤3/5/12/24 Roelof Hartplein) Students of hospitality and gastronomy – the same ones who run the nearby **College Hotel** (Map p62; ☑020-571 15 11; www.thecollegehotel.com; Roelof Hartstraat 1; d from €227; ✳☎; ⑤3/5/12/24 Roelof Hartplein) – serve contemporary international dishes at this minimalist-chic mod restaurant. The result is white-glove service at an excellent price. Reserve in advance. No credit cards.

★ **Adam**　GASTRONOMY €€€
(☑020-233 98 52; www.restaurantadam.nl; Overtoom 515; mains €25, 3-/4-/5-/6-course menus €37/45/50/60; ⊙6-10.30pm Tue-Sat; ⑤1/11/17 Surinameplein) This seriously gourmet, chic and intimate restaurant serves exquisitely presented fare, such as veal cheek with lentils and bay sauce and *côte de bœuf* (on-the-bone rib steak) for two. Dessert is either a cheese platter or a chef's surprise. Paired wines are available for €7.50 per glass.

★ **Rijks** INTERNATIONAL €€€

(Map p62; 020-674 75 55; www.rijksrestaurant. nl; Rijksmuseum; mains €24-32, 3-/4-course lunch menus €37.50/47.50, 6-course dinner menu €70; 11.30am-3pm & 5-10pm Mon-Sat, 11.30-3pm Sun; 2/5/12 Rijksmuseum) In a beautiful space with huge windows and high ceilings, part of the Rijksmuseum, Rijks was awarded a Michelin star in 2016. Chef Joris Bijdendijk uses locally sourced ingredients, adheres to Slow Food ethics and draws on historic Dutch influences for his creative, highly imaginative cuisine. For lunch or dinner you can choose a set menu or à la carte.

Restaurant Blauw INDONESIAN €€€

(020-675 50 00; www.restaurantblauw.nl; Amstelveenseweg 158; mains €20.50-28, rijsttafel per person €30-33.50; 6-10pm Mon-Wed, 6-10.30pm Thu & Fri, 5-10.30pm Sat, 5-10pm Sun; 2 Amstelveenseweg) Blauw is always busy – reserve ahead. The *New York Times* voted it the 'best Indonesian restaurant in the Netherlands' and legions agree. Highlights include *ikan pesmol* (fried fish with candlenut sauce) and *ayam singgand* (chicken in semi-spicy coconut sauce with turmeric leaf) and mouthwatering Indonesian desserts.

De Pijp

De Pijp's thriving foodie scene is experimental and multicultural yet also quintessentially Dutch. Choices include street-food stalls, salad bars, cheap, filling Surinamese and Asian spots, on-trend addresses like the world's first all-avocado cafe, gastronomic standouts and atmospheric *bruin cafés* serving food.

Brunch is especially good in this neighbourhood, with many cafes specialising in exceptional mid-morning menus. Albert Cuypstraat, Ferdinand Bolstraat and Ceintuurbaan are ideal starting points.

★ **Avocado Show** CAFE €

(Map p62; www.theavocadoshow.com; Daniël Stalpertstraat 61; mains €9.50-15; 9am-5pm; 24 Ferdinand Bolstraat) A world first, this cafe uses avocado in *every* dish, often in ingeniously functional ways (burgers with avocado halves instead of buns, salad 'bowls' made from avocado slices...). Finish with avocado ice cream or sorbet. Avocado cocktails include a spicy Guaco Mary and an avocado daiquiri. It doesn't take reservations, so prepare to queue. Cards only; no cash.

BRUNCH IN DE PIJP

Amsterdam's brunch scene is booming, with much of the deliciousness happening in De Pijp.

Bakers & Roasters (Map p62; www.bakersandroasters.com; 1e Jacob van Campenstraat 54; dishes €7-16; 8.30am-4pm; 24 Ferdinand Bolstraat) Sumptuous brunch dishes served up at Brazilian-Kiwi-owned Bakers & Roasters include banana-nutbread French toast with homemade banana marmalade and crispy bacon; Navajo eggs with pulled pork, avocado, mango salsa and chipotle cream; and a smoked-salmon stack with poached eggs, potato cakes and hollandaise. Wash your choice down with a fiery Bloody Mary. Fantastic pies, cakes and slices, too.

Scandinavian Embassy (Map p62; www.scandinavianembassy.nl; Sarphatipark 34; dishes €5-14; 8am-6pm Mon-Fri, from 9am Sat & Sun; 3 2e Van der Helststraat) Oatmeal porridge with blueberries, honey and coconut, served with goat's-milk yoghurt; salt-cured salmon on Danish rye with sheep's-milk yoghurt; muesli with strawberries; and freshly baked pastries (including cinnamon buns) make this blond-wood-panelled spot a perfect place to start the day – as does its phenomenal coffee, sourced from Scandinavian micro-roasteries (including a refreshing cold brew with tonic water).

CT Coffee & Coconuts (Map p62; www.coffeeandcoconuts.com; Ceintuurbaan 282-284; mains €8-22.50; 8am-11pm; De Pijp, 3/12/24 De Pijp) A 1920s art-deco cinema has been stunningly transformed into this open-plan, triple-level, cathedral-like space (with a giant print of John Lennon at the top). Brunch dishes like coconut, almond and buckwheat pancakes; French-toast brioche with apricots; avocado-slathered toast with dukkah (North African spice-and-nut blend) and lemon dressing; and scrambled eggs on sourdough with crumbled feta are served to 1pm.

Sir Hummus
MIDDLE EASTERN €

(Map p62; www.sirhummus.nl; Van der Helstplein 2; dishes €6.75-12.25; ⊙noon-9pm Wed-Sun; ⚲; ⌂3 2e Van der Helststraat) 🌱 Sir Hummus is the brainchild of three young Israelis whose passion for the chickpea dip led to a London street-market stall and then this hummus-dedicated cafe. Creamy, all-natural, preservative- and additive-free hummus is served with pillowy pita bread and salad; SH also makes fantastic falafels. You can eat in or take away, but arrive early before it sells out.

Geflipt
BURGERS €

(Map p62; www.gefliptburgers.nl; Van Woustraat 15; dishes €9-13; ⊙11.30am-9.30pm Sun-Thu, to 10.30pm Fri & Sat; ⚲; ⌂4 Stadhouderskade) Competition is fierce for the best burgers in this foodie neighbourhood, but Geflipt is a serious contender. In a stripped-back, industrial-chic interior, it serves luscious combinations (like Gasconne beef, bacon, golden cheddar, red-onion compote and fried egg) on brioche buns with sauces cooked daily on the premises from locally sourced ingredients. Bonus points for its Amsterdam-brewed Brouwerij 't IJ beers.

Surya
INDIAN €€

(Map p62; ☎020-676 79 85; www.suryarestaurant.nl; Ceintuurbaan 147; mains €14.50-23; ⊙5-11pm Tue-Sun; ⌂3 2e Van der Helststraat) Indian restaurants can be surprisingly hit and miss in this multicultural city, making classy Surya an invaluable address for fans of Subcontinental cuisine. Menu standouts include a feisty madras, a fire-breathing vindaloo, tandoori tikka dishes and silky tomato-based *paneer makhni* with soft cottage cheese made fresh on the premises each day. Mains come with pappadams, rice and salad.

Volt
MEDITERRANEAN €€

(Map p62; ☎020-471 55 44; www.restaurantvolt.nl; Ferdinand Bolstraat 178; mains lunch €8-15.50, dinner €14.50-20; ⊙kitchen 5.30-10pm, bar 4pm-1am Mon-Thu, 4pm-3am Fri, 11am-3am Sat, 11am-1pm; ⌂12 Cornelis Troostplein) Strung with coloured light bulbs, Volt is a neighbourhood gem for daily changing, market-sourced dishes such as artichoke ravioli with walnuts and rocket (arugula); oxtail with celeriac and potato mousseline; or steak tartare with pickled beetroot. Its bar stays open until late, or head across the street to its *bruin café* (pub) sibling, Gambrinus (Map p62; www.gambrinus.nl; Ferdinand

Bolstraat 180; ⊙11am-1am Sun-Thu, to 3am Fri & Sat; ⚲; ⌂12 Cornelis Troostplein).

Friterie par Hasard
DUTCH €€

(Map p62; www.cafeparhasard.nl; Ceintuurbaan 113-115; mains €10.50-23.50; ⊙noon-10pm Mon-Thu, to 11pm Fri & Sat; ⓂDe Pijp, ⌂3/12/24 De Pijp) Fronted by a red-and-white chequered awning, low-lit Friterie par Hasard is fêted for its *frites* (fries), served with dishes such as ribs in traditional Limburg stew with apple, elderberry and bay-leaf sauce; marinated chicken thighs with satay sauce and pickled cucumber; bavette steak; and beer-battered cod. Its adjacent Frites uit Zuyd (frites small/medium/large €2.50/3/3.50, sauce €0.50-1.50; ⊙2-11pm Mon-Thu, from 1pm Fri-Sun; ⓂDe Pijp, ⌂3/12/24 De Pijp) fries up takeaway *frites*.

★ Graham's Kitchen
GASTRONOMY €€€

(☎020-364 25 60; www.grahamskitchen.amsterdam; Hemonystraat 38; 3-/4-/5-/6-course menus €39/48/57/66; ⊙6-10pm Tue-Sat; ⌂4 Stadhouderskade) A veteran of Michelin-starred kitchens, chef Graham Mee now crafts intricate dishes at his own premises. Multicourse menus (no à la carte) might include a venison and crispy smoked-beetroot *macaron*, cucumber and gin-cured salmon, veal with wasabi and ghost crab, and deconstructed summer-berry crumble with wood-calamint ice cream. Mee personally explains each dish to diners.

★ Ciel Bleu
GASTRONOMY €€€

(☎020-678 74 50; www.okura.nl; Hotel Okura Amsterdam, Ferdinand Bolstraat 333; 6-course menu €185; ⊙6.30-10pm Mon-Sat; ⌂12 Cornelius Troostplein) Mind-blowing, two-Michelin-star creations at this pinnacle of gastronomy change with the seasons; spring, for instance, might see scallops and oysters with vanilla sea salt and gin-and-tonic foam, king crab with salted lemon, beurre blanc ice cream and caviar, or saddle of lamb with star anise. Just as incomparable is the 23rd-floor setting with aerial views north across the city.

🍴 Oosterpark & East of the Amstel

There are some great eating choices – especially ethnic eats and creative cuisine – in Oost: they may take a little more time to reach, but they are well worth the effort.

Wilde Zwijnen DUTCH €€
(☑020-463 30 43; www.wildezwijnen.com; Javaplein 23; mains €20, 3-/4-course menus €31.50/37.50; ⏱6-10pm Mon-Thu, noon-4pm & 6-10pm Fri-Sun, eetbar from 5pm; 🖥; 🚊14 Javaplein) 🍴 The name means 'wild boar' and there's usually game on the menu in season at this modern Dutch restaurant. With pale walls and wood tables, the restaurant has a pared-down, rustic-industrial feel, and serves locally sourced, seasonal dishes with a creative twist. It's more of a meat-eater's paradise, but there's usually a vegetarian choice as well.

★**De Kas** INTERNATIONAL €€€
(☑020-462 45 62; www.restaurantdekas.nl; Park Frankendael, Kamerlingh Onneslaan 3; 3-/4-course lunch menu €32.50/42.50, 5-/6-course dinner menu €52.50/60; ⏱noon-2pm & 6.30-10pm Mon-Fri, 6.30-10pm Sat; 🍴; 🚊19 Hogeweg) 🍴 In a row of stately greenhouses dating to 1926, De Kas has an organic attitude to match its chic glass greenhouse setting – try to visit during a thunderstorm! It grows most of its own herbs and produce right here and the result is incredibly pure flavours with innovative combinations. There's one set menu daily, based on whatever has been freshly harvested. Reserve in advance.

✖ Amsterdam Noord

★**Hotel de Goudfazant** FRENCH €€€
(☑020-636 51 70; www.hoteldegoudfazant.nl; Aambeeldstraat 10h; 3-course menu €32; ⏱kitchen 6-11pm Tue-Sun, bar to 1am Tue-Sun; 🚊34/35 Johan van Hasseltweg, 🚢Zamenhofstraat) With a name taken from lyrics of the Jacques Brel song 'Les Bourgeois', this extraordinary gourmet hipster restaurant spreads through a cavernous former garage, still raw and industrial, and sticks to the theme by having cars parked inside. Rockstar-looking chefs cook up a French-influenced storm in the open kitchen. There is no hotel, FYI, except in name.

🍷 Drinking & Nightlife

Atmospheric *bruin cafés* are Amsterdam's crowning glory. The time-hewn pubs have candle-topped tables and sandy wooden floors, and they induce a cosy vibe that prompts friends to linger and chat for hours over drinks.

Amsterdam's craft-beer scene has exploded in recent years. Alongside long-standing microbreweries are a wave of new ones along with craft-beer specialist bars and/or shops.

Amsterdam's merchants introduced coffee to Europe and it's still the hot drink of choice. Roasteries and microroasteries are springing up around the city, and baristas are increasingly using connoisseur styles of drip coffee.

The city centre has a huge number and variety of boozers. To drink with locals try the Jordaan or De Pijp neighbourhoods.

🍷 Medieval Centre & Red Light District

This area is renowned for its wild pubs and bars as well as its coffeeshops (cannabis cafes), but choices here are surprisingly diverse, taking in genteel *jenever* distillery tasting houses, unchanged-in-decades *bruin cafés,* breweries, and on-trend addresses such as a combined craft-beer bar and barber shop. Zeedijk and Warmoesstraat are the twin hubs of the area's gay scene.

★**Brouwerij De Prael** BREWERY
(Map p48; www.deprael.nl; Oudezijds Armsteeg 26; ⏱noon-midnight Mon-Wed, to 1am Thu-Sat, to 11pm Sun; 🚊4/11/12/13/14/17/24/26 Centraal Station) Sample organic beers (Scotch ale, IPA, barley wine and many more varieties) from the socially minded De Prael brewery (Map p48; ☑020-408 44 70; www.deprael.nl; Oudezijds Voorburgwal 30; tour with 1/4 beers €8.50/17.50; ⏱tours hourly 1-6pm Mon-Fri, 1-5pm Sat, 2-5pm Sun; 🚊2/4/11/12/13/14/17/24/26 Centraal Station), known for employing people with a history of mental illness. Its multilevel tasting room has comfy couches and big wooden tables strewn about. There's often live music. A four-beer tasting flight costs €10.

★**Cut Throat** BAR
(Map p48; ☑06 2534 3769; www.cutthroatbarber.nl; Beursplein 5; ⏱bar 9.30am-1am Mon-Thu, 9.30am-3am Fri & Sat, 11am-1am Sun, barber 11am-8pm Mon-Thu, 11am-7pm Fri, 10am-6pm Sat, noon-6pm Sun; 🖥; 🚊4/14/24 Dam) Beneath 1930s arched brick ceilings, Cut Throat ingeniously combines a men's barbering service (book ahead) with a happening bar serving international craft beers, cocktails including infused G&Ts (such as blueberry and thyme or mandarin and rosemary), 'spiked' milkshakes and coffee from Amsterdam roastery De Wasserette. Brunch stretches to 4pm daily; all-day dishes span fried chicken and waffles, and surf-and-turf burgers.

★**Wynand Fockink**   DISTILLERY
(Map p48; ☎020-639 26 95; www.wynand-fockink.
nl; Pijlsteeg 31; tours €17.50; ⊙tasting tavern
2-9pm daily, tours 3pm, 4.30pm, 6pm & 7.30pm
Sat & Sun; 🚋4/14/24 Dam) Dating from 1679,
this small tasting house in an arcade behind
Grand Hotel Krasnapolsky serves scores of
jenevers and liqueurs. Although there's no
seating, it's an intimate place to knock back
a shot glass or two. At weekends, guides give
45-minute distillery tours (in English) that
are followed by six tastings; reserve online.

Hoppe   BROWN CAFE
(Map p48; www.cafehoppe.com; Spui 18-20;
⊙8am-1am Sun-Thu, to 2am Fri & Sat; 🚋2/11/12
Spui) An Amsterdam institution, Hoppe has
been filling glasses since 1670. Barflies and
raconteurs toss back brews amid the ancient
wood panelling of the *bruin café* at No 18
and the more modern, early-20th-century
pub at No 20. In all but the iciest weather,
the energetic crowd spills out from the dark
interior and onto the Spui.

Tales & Spirits   COCKTAIL BAR
(Map p48; www.talesandspirits.com; Lijnbaans-
steeg 5-7; ⊙5.30pm-1am Tue-Thu & Sun, to 3am Fri
& Sat; 🚋2/11/12/13/17 Nieuwezijds Kolk) Chandeliers glitter beneath wooden beams at
Tales & Spirits, which creates its own house
infusions, syrups and vinegar-based shrubs.
Craft cocktails such as Floats Like a But-
terfly (orange vodka, peach liqueur, saffron
honey and lemon sorbet) and Stings Like
a Bee (Dijon gin, cognac, maple syrup and
soda water) are served in vintage and one-
of-a-kind glasses. Minimum age is 21.

De Drie Fleschjes   DISTILLERY
(Map p48; www.dedriefleschjes.nl; Gravenstraat 18; ⊙2-8.30pm Mon-Sat, 3-7pm Sun;
🚋2/11/12/13/17 Dam) A treasure dating from
1650, with a wall of barrels made by master
shipbuilders, the tasting room of distiller
Bootz specialises in liqueurs, including its
signature almond-flavoured *bitterkoekje*
(Dutch-style macaroon) liqueur, as well
as superb *jenever*. Take a peek at the collection of *kalkoentjes* (small bottles with
hand-painted portraits of former mayors).

Café Belgique   BEER CAFE
(Map p48; www.cafe-belgique.nl; Gravenstraat 2;
⊙3pm-1am Mon-Wed, 1pm-1am Thu & Sun, 1pm-
3am Fri & Sat; 🚋2/11/12/13/17 Dam) Pull up a
stool at the carved wooden bar and choose
from the glinting brass taps. It's all about
Belgian beers here: eight flow from the

spouts, and 50 or so more are available in
bottles. The ambience is quintessentially
gezellig and draws lots of chilled-out locals.
Live music or DJs play some nights.

Proeflokaal de Ooievaar   DISTILLERY
(Map p48; www.proeflokaaldeooievaar.nl; St Olof-
spoort 1; ⊙noon-midnight; 🚋2/4/11/12/13/1
4/17/24/26 Centraal Station) Not much bigger
than a vat of *jenever*, this magnificent little
tasting house has been going strong since
1782. On offer are 14 *jenevers* and liqueurs
(such as Bride's Tears with gold and silver
leaf) from the De Ooievaar distillery, still
located in the Jordaan. Despite appearanc-
es, the house has not subsided but was built
leaning over.

Café de Dokter   BROWN CAFE
(Map p48; www.cafe-de-dokter.nl; Rozenboom-
steeg 4; ⊙4pm-1am Wed-Sat; 🚋2/11/12 Spui)
Candles flicker on the tables, old jazz
records play in the background, and chandeliers and a birdcage hang from the
ceiling at atmospheric Café de Dokter,
which is said to be Amsterdam's smallest
pub. Whiskies and smoked beef sausage
are the specialities. A surgeon opened the
bar in 1798, hence the name. His descend-
ants still run it.

Winston Kingdom   CLUB
(Map p48; www.winston.nl; St Christopher's at the
Winston, Warmoesstraat 131; ⊙9pm-4am Sun-
Thu, to 5am Fri & Sat; 🚋4/14/24 Dam) Even
non-clubbers will love Winston Kingdom
for its indie-alternative music beats, great
DJs and live bands. No matter what's on –
from 'dubstep mayhem' to Thailand-style
full-moon parties – the scene can get pretty
wild in this good-time little space inside St
Christopher's at the Winston (p82).

🖲 **Nieuwmarkt, Plantage
& the Eastern Islands**

★**Brouwerij 't IJ**   BREWERY
(www.brouwerijhetij.nl; Funenkade 7; ⊙brewery
2-8pm, English tour 3.30pm Fri-Sun; 🚋7 Hoogte
Kadijk) 🌿 Can you get more Dutch than
drinking an organic beer beneath the creaking sails of the 1725-built De Gooyer Windmill? This is Amsterdam's leading organic
microbrewery, with delicious standard, seasonal and limited-edition brews; try the fra-
grant, hoppy house brew, Plzeň. Enjoy your
beer in the tiled tasting room, lined by an
amazing bottle collection, or the plane-tree-
shaded terrace.

SkyLounge COCKTAIL BAR
(Map p54; www.skyloungeamsterdam.com; Oosterdoksstraat 4; ⏱11am-1am Sun-Tue, to 2am Wed & Thu, to 3am Fri & Sat; ☎; 🚋2/4/11/12/13/14/17/24/26 Centraal Station) With wow-factor views whatever the weather, this bar offers a 360-degree panorama of Amsterdam from the 11th floor of the DoubleTree Amsterdam Centraal Station hotel – and just gets better when you head out to its vast, sofa-strewn SkyTerrace, with an outdoor bar. To toast the view: a choice of 500 different cocktails. DJs regularly hit the decks.

Hannekes Boom BEER GARDEN
(Map p54; www.hannekesboom.nl; Dijksgracht 4; ⏱10am-1am Sun-Thu, to 3am Fri & Sat; 🚋26 Muziekgebouw) Reachable via a couple of pedestrian/bike bridges from the NEMO Science Museum, this nonchalantly cool, laid-back waterside *café* built from recycled materials has a beer garden that really feels like a garden, with timber benches, picnic tables under the trees and a hipster, arty crowd enjoying sitting out in the sunshine (it comes into its own in summer).

De Sluyswacht BROWN CAFE
(Map p48; www.sluyswacht.nl; Jodenbreestraat 1; ⏱noon-1am Sun-Thu, to 3am Fri & Sat; Ⓜ Waterlooplein, 🚋14 Waterlooplein) Built in 1695 and listing like a ship in a high wind, this tiny black building, out on a limb by the canal, was once a lock-keeper's house on the Oude Schans. Today the canal-side terrace with gorgeous views of the Montelbaanstoren is a charming spot to relax with a Dutch or Belgian beer, and rib-sticking bar snacks like *bitterballen,* chips and toasties.

Western Canal Ring

★**'t Arendsnest** BROWN CAFE
(Map p48; www.arendsnest.nl; Herengracht 90; ⏱noon-midnight Sun-Thu, to 2am Fri & Sat; 🚋2/11/12/13/17 Nieuwezijds Kolk) This gorgeous restyled *bruin café,* with its glowing copper *jenever* boilers behind the bar, only serves Dutch beer – but with over 100 varieties (many from small breweries), including 52 rotating on tap, you'll need to move here to try them all. It also has more than 40 gins, ciders, whiskies and liqueurs, all of which are Dutch too.

Café Tabac BAR
(Map p48; www.cafetabac.eu; Brouwersgracht 101; ⏱noon-1am Mon-Thu, to 3am Fri, 11am-3am Sat, to

1am Sun; ☎; 🚋18/21/22 Buiten Brouwersstraat) Is Café Tabac a *bruin café,* a designer bar, a fantastic place for Indonesian dishes or simply an idyllic place to while away a few blissful hours at the intersection of two of Amsterdam's most stunning canals? The regulars don't seem concerned about definitions but simply enjoy the views and kicking back beneath the beamed ceilings.

Café de Vergulde Gaper BROWN CAFE
(Map p66; www.deverguldegaper.nl; Prinsenstraat 30; ⏱10am-1am Mon, 11am-1am Tue-Thu & Sun, 11am-3am Fri, 10am-3am Sat; ☎; 🚋13/17 Westermarkt) Decorated with old chemists' bottles and vintage posters, this former pharmacy has a canal-side terrace with afternoon sun and occasional live jazz. It's popular with locals, especially for after-work drinks. The name translates to the 'Golden Gaper', for the open-mouthed bust of a Moor traditionally posted at Dutch apothecaries.

Southern Canal Ring

★**Air** CLUB
(Map p62; www.air.nl; Amstelstraat 24; ⏱11.30pm-4am Thu & Sun, 11pm-5am Fri & Sat; 🚋4/14 Rembrandtplein) Big names like Pete Tong cut loose on the awesome sound system at it-club Air, which has interiors – including a tiered dance floor – by Dutch designer Marcel Wanders. Thoughtful touches include lockers and refillable cards that preclude fussing with change at the five bars.

Door 74 COCKTAIL BAR
(Map p62; ☑06 3404 5122; www.door-74.nl; Reguliersdwarsstraat 74; ⏱8pm-3am Sun-Thu, to 4am Fri & Sat; 🚋4/14 Rembrandtplein) You'll need to leave a voice message or, better yet, send a text for a reservation to gain entry to this speakeasy behind an unmarked door. Some of Amsterdam's most amazing cocktails are served in a classy, dark-timbered, Prohibition-era atmosphere beneath pressed-tin ceilings. Themed cocktail lists change regularly. Very cool.

Eijlders BROWN CAFE
(Map p62; www.cafeeijlders.com; Korte Leidsedwarsstraat 47; ⏱4.30pm-1am Mon-Thu, noon-2am Fri & Sat, noon-1am Sun; 🚋2/11/12 Leidseplein) During WWII, this stained-glass-trimmed *bruin café* (traditional Dutch pub) was a meeting place for artists who refused to toe the cultural line imposed by the Nazis, and

LGBTIQ+ AMSTERDAM

Information

Gay Amsterdam (www.gayamsterdam.com) Lists hotels, shops, restaurants and clubs, and provides maps.

Pink Point (Map p66; ☎020-428 10 70; www.facebook.com/pinkpointamsterdam; Wester-markt; ⊙10.30am-6pm; 🚊13/17 Westermarkt) Located behind the Westerkerk, this is part information kiosk, part souvenir shop. It's a good place to pick up gay and lesbian publi-cations, and news about parties, events and social groups.

Entertainment

Amsterdam's gay scene is among the world's largest. Five hubs party hardest: War-moesstraat and Zeedijk in the Red Light District, and Rembrandtplein, Leidse-plein and above all Reguliersdwarsstraat in the Southern Canal Ring.

't Mandje (Map p48; www.cafetmandje.amsterdam; Zeedijk 63; ⊙4pm-1am Tue-Thu, 4pm-3am Fri, 3pm-3am Sat, 3pm-1am Sun; 🚊2/4/11/12/13/14/17/24/26 Centraal Station) Amsterdam's oldest gay bar opened in 1927, then shut in 1982 when the Zeedijk grew too seedy. But its trinket-covered interior was lovingly dusted every week until it reopened in 2008. The devoted bartenders can tell you stories about the bar's brassy lesbian founder Bet van Beeren. It's one of the most *gezellig* places in the centre, gay or straight.

Montmartre (Map p62; www.cafemontmartre.nl; Halvemaansteeg 17; ⊙5pm-3am Sun-Thu, to 4am Fri & Sat; 🚊4/14 Rembrandtplein) A crammed gay bar that's long been a local favourite. It's known for its Dutch music, and patrons sing (or scream) along to record-ings ofDutch ballads and old top-40 hits. There's also a lively programme of karaoke, drag,and '80s and '90s hits.

Festivals

The centrepiece of Pride Amsterdam (p81) celebrations is its waterborne parade with outlandishly decorated boats plying the canals.

the spirit lingers on. It's still an artists' cafe, with waistcoated waiters and a low-key feel by day, but it gets noisier at night, fitting with its Leidseplein surrounds.

De Kroon BAR
(Map p62; www.dekroon.nl; Rembrandtplein 17; ⊙4pm-1am Sun-Thu, 4pm-3am Fri, 3pm-3am Sat; 🚊4/14 Rembrandtplein) Rembrandtplein's renovated *grand café* De Kroon dates from 1898. It has dizzyingly high ceilings, arm-chairs to sink into and glittering chande-liers. There's a long list of cocktails, wine and beers, plus a barbecue-oriented menu of grilled fish and meat. It converts into a club on Friday and Saturday nights.

 Jordaan & the West

⭐'t Smalle BROWN CAFE
(Map p66; www.t-smalle.nl; Egelantiersgracht 12; ⊙10am-1am Sun-Thu, to 2am Fri & Sat; 🚊13/17 Westermarkt) Dating back to 1786 as a *jenev-er* distillery and tasting house, and restored during the 1970s with antique porcelain

beer pumps and lead-framed windows, locals' favourite 't Smalle is one of Amster-dam's most charming *bruin cafés*. Dock your boat right by the pretty stone terrace, which is wonderfully convivial by day and impossibly romantic at night.

⭐Monks Coffee Roasters COFFEE
(www.monkscoffee.nl; Bilderdijkstraat 46; ⊙8am-5pm Tue-Sun; 📶; 🚊3/13/19 Bilderdijkstraat) Monks' phenomenal house blend, prepared with a variety of brewing methods, is hands down Amsterdam's best, but the cafe also serves superb coffee from small-scale spe-cialists such as Amsterdam's Lot Sixty One and White Label Coffee, and Paris' Café Lomi. Its cavernous space is brilliant for brunch (try avocado toast with feta, chilli and lime, or banana bread with mascarpone and caramelised pineapple).

Café Pieper BROWN CAFE
(Map p62; www.cafepieper.com; Prinsengracht 424; ⊙noon-1am Mon, Wed & Thu, 4pm-midnight Tue, noon-2am Fri & Sat, 2-10pm Sun; 🚊2/11/12

TILTED ARCHITECTURE

Yes, Amsterdam's buildings *are* leaning. Some – like De Sluyswacht – have shifted over the centuries, but many canal houses were deliberately constructed to tip forward. Interior staircases were narrow, so owners needed an easy way to move large goods and furniture to the upper floors. The solution: a hoist built into the gable, to lift objects up and in through the windows. The tilt allows loading without bumping into the facade.

Prinsengracht) Small, unassuming and unmistakably old (1665), Café Pieper features stained-glass windows, antique beer mugs hanging from the bar and a working Belgian beer pump (1875). Sip an Amsterdam-brewed Brouwerij 't IJ beer or a terrific cappuccino as you marvel at the claustrophobia of the low-ceilinged bar (people were shorter back in the 17th century – even the Dutch, it seems).

De Kat in de Wijngaert   BROWN CAFE
(Map p66; www.dekatindewijngaert.nl; Lindengracht 160; ⊙10am-1am Sun-Thu, to 3am Fri, 9am-3am Sat; ☐3 Marnixplein) With overwhelming *gezelligheid*, this gorgeous bar is the kind of place where one beer soon turns to several – maybe it's the influence of the arty old-guard locals who hang out here. At least you can soak it all up with what many people vote as the best *tosti* (toasted sandwich) in town.

Cafe Soundgarden   BAR
(Map p66; www.cafesoundgarden.nl; Marnixstraat 164-166; ⊙1pm-1am Mon-Thu, to 3am Fri, 3pm-3am Sat, to 1am Sun; ☐5/13/17/19 Marnixstraat) In this grungy, all-ages dive bar, the 'Old Masters' are the Ramones and Black Sabbath. Somehow a handful of pool tables, 1980s pinball machines, unkempt DJs and lovably surly bartenders add up to an ineffable magic. Bands occasionally make an appearance, and the waterfront terrace scene is more like an impromptu party in someone's backyard.

De Twee Zwaantjes   BROWN CAFE
(Map p66; ☏020-625 27 29; www.cafedetweezwaantjes.nl; Prinsengracht 114; ⊙3pm-1am Sun-Thu, noon-3am Fri & Sat; ☐13/17 Westermarkt) The small, authentic 'Two Swans' is at its hilarious best on weekend nights, when you

can join patrons belting out classics and traditional Dutch tunes in a rollicking, unforgettable cabaret-meets-karaoke evening. The fact that singers are often fuelled by the liquid courage of the Trappist beers on tap only adds to the spirited fun. Don't be afraid to join in.

Vondelpark & the South

★Lot Sixty One   COFFEE
(Map p62; www.lotsixtyonecoffee.com; Kinkerstraat 112; ⊙8am-6pm Mon-Fri, from 9am Sat & Sun; ☐3/7/17 Bilderdijkstraat) ⚑ Look downstairs to the open cellar to see (and better still, smell) fresh coffee beans being roasted at this streetwise spot. Beans are sourced from individual ecofriendly farms; varieties include chocolate-orange Fivr from Brazil, citrussy Kii from Kenya and toffee stonefruit Bombora. All coffees are double shots (unless you specify otherwise); watch Kinkerstraat's passing parade from benches at the front.

★Edel   BAR
(www.edelamsterdam.nl; Postjesweg 1; ⊙10am-1am Sun-Thu, to 3am Fri & Sat; ☐7/17 Witte de Withstraat) Edel on Het Sieraard's waterfront has lots of waterside seating as it's at the sweet spot where two canals cross. Inside and out it's filled with creative types who work in the local buildings. With hipster staff and creative food on offer, its blond-wood interior comes into its own in summer, lit by a canopy of twinkling fairy lights after dark.

Welling   BROWN CAFE
(Map p62; www.cafewelling.nl; Jan Willem Brouwersstraat 32; ⊙4pm-1am; ☐2/3/5/12 Museumplein) Tucked away behind the Concertgebouw (Concert Hall), this wood-panelled lovely is a relaxed spot to sip a frothy, cold *biertje* (glass of beer) and mingle with intellectuals and artists. Don't be surprised if the cafe's friendly cat hops onto your lap. There's often live music, such as by jazz musicians after their gigs at the Concertgebouw.

Butcher's Tears   BREWERY
(www.butchers-tears.com; Karperweg 45; ⊙4-9pm Wed-Sun; ☐24 Haarlemmermeerstation) In-the-know hop heads like to go straight to the source of cult brewsters Butcher's Tears. The brewery's artsy taproom is tucked down an industrial alley, and offers myriad esoteric bottled beers, as well as six brews on tap. Look for Far Out (a saison) and Misery King (a triple-hopped amber ale).

Dutch Drafts   BROWN CAFE
(www.craftanddraft.nl; Overtoom 417; ☺bar
4pm-midnight Mon-Thu, to 2am Fri, 2pm-2am Sat,
2pm-midnight Sun, shop 4-10pm Mon-Fri, 2-10pm
Sat & Sun; ⓐ1/11 Rhijnvis Feithstraat) Craft-
beer fans are spoilt for choice, with no
fewer than 40 beers on tap and a further
100 by the bottle. There are daily draught
offerings, such as Belgian 3 Floyds' Lips of
Faith, American Coronado's Stupid Stout
and Evil Twin's Yang, British Red Willow's
Thoughtless, Swedish Sigtuna's Organic
Ale and Danish Mikkeller's Peter, Pale &
Mary.

🍷 De Pijp

★Brouwerij Troost   BREWERY
(Map p62; ☎020-760 58 20; www.brouwerijtroost.
nl; Cornelis Troostplein 21; ☺4pm-1am Mon-Thu,
to 3am Fri, 2pm-3am Sat, to midnight Sun; ☏;
ⓐ12 Cornelis Troostplein) 🍴 Watch beer being brewed in copper vats behind a glass
wall at this outstanding craft brewery. Its
dozen beers include a summery blonde, a
smoked porter, a strong tripel and a deep-
red Imperial IPA; it also distils cucumber
and juniper gin from its beer, and serves
fantastic bar food, including crispy prawn
tacos and humongous burgers. Book on
weekend evenings.

Boca's   BAR
(Map p62; www.bar-bocas.nl; Sarphatipark 4;
☺noon-1am Mon-Thu, 10am-3am Fri & Sat, 11am-
1am Sun; ☏; ⓐ3 2e Van der Helststraat) Boca's
(inspired by the Italian word for 'mouth') is
the ultimate spot for *borrel* (drinks). Mezzanine seating overlooks the cushion-strewn

interior, but in summer the best seats are
on the terrace facing leafy Sarphatipark. Its
pared-down wine list (seven by-the-glass
choices) goes perfectly with its lavish sharing platters.

🍷 Oosterpark & East of the Amstel

★Canvas   BAR
(www.volkshotel.nl; Wibautstraat 150; ☺7am-1am
Sun-Thu, to 4am Fri & Sat; Ⓜ Wibautstraat) Zoom
up to the Volkshotel's 7th floor (located in
the former *Volkskrant* newspaper office) for
the hotel bar (open to nonguests) with one
of the best views in town. A creative-folk and
hipster magnet, there are few better places
for a beer or cocktail than this slice of urban
cool. On weekend nights, it morphs into a
fresh-beat dance club.

Distilleerderij 't Nieuwe Diep   DISTILLERY
(www.nwediep.nl; Flevopark 13a; ☺3-8pm Tue-Sun
Apr-Oct, to 6pm Nov-Mar; ⓐ3/14 Soembawastraat)
Appearing out of the woods like a *Hansel
and Gretel* cottage, the quaint architecture
and rural setting of this old pumping station
is enchanting and feels like you've escaped
to a magical countryside retreat, though
it's just leafy Flevopark. The little distillery
makes around 100 small-batch *jenevers*,
herbal bitters, liqueurs and fruit distillates
from organic ingredients according to age-
old Dutch recipes.

De Ysbreeker   BROWN CAFE
(www.deysbreeker.nl; Weesperzijde 23; ☺8am-
1am Sun-Thu, to 2am Fri & Sat; ☏; ⓐ3 Wibaut-
straat/Ruyschstraat) This historic but

AMSTERDAM NIGHTLIFE

Nightlife in Amsterdam is undergoing major change. In 2012 the city was the first in the world to appoint a night mayor *(nachtburgemeester)*, to manage and promote its noctur-nal economy and social life.

Its inaugural night mayor, Mirik Milan, established 24-hour club licences for selected venues that provide a contribution to the city's cultural offerings with creative (rather than profit-driven) events, and can also be used during the day. Other criteria for the licences include soundproofing.

New 'Square Hosts' at inner-city nightlife hubs like Leidseplein (Map p62; ⓐ2/5/7/11/12/19 Leidseplein) and Rembrandtplein identify and diffuse issues like exces-sive noise or littering before trouble arises, and ensure the city's residents and clubgoers coexist harmoniously. Infrastructure around nightlife hotspots has also been improved, such as increased lighting on the streets.

The position is jointly funded by city government and the nightlife industry, and has a 20-person advisory council. The initiative has proven so successful that it's been adopted elsewhere – other cities with night mayors now include London, Paris and Zürich.

AMSTERDAM DRINKING & NIGHTLIFE

COFFEESHOPS

First things first: 'café' means 'pub' throughout the Netherlands; a 'coffeeshop' is where one procures marijuana.

While cannabis is not technically legal in the Netherlands, the possession and purchase of small amounts (5g) of 'soft drugs' (ie marijuana, hashish, space cakes and mushroom-based truffles) is allowed, and users won't be prosecuted for smoking or carrying this amount. This means that coffeeshops are actually conducting an illegal business – but this is tolerated to a certain extent.

The government has let individual municipalities decide for themselves whether to enforce the national *wietpas* ('weed pass') law banning tourists from coffeeshops and requiring locals to have ID. While this is in a state of flux in parts of the Netherlands, in tourist-busy Amsterdam, the city has decreed it will conduct business as usual.

Keep in mind the following:

➡ Ask staff for the menu of goods on offer, usually packaged in small bags. You can also buy ready-made joints. Most shops offer rolling papers, pipes or even bongs.

➡ Don't light up anywhere besides a coffeeshop without checking that it's OK to do so.

➡ Alcohol and tobacco products are not permitted in coffeeshops.

➡ Don't ask for hard (illegal) drugs.

➡ Be aware that some local varieties can contain up to 15% tetrahydrocannabinol (THC; the active substance that gets people high), and lead to an intense, long-lasting, unpleasant experience; ask the staff's advice about what and how much to consume and heed it, even if nothing happens after an hour.

Dampkring (Map p62; www.dampkring-coffeeshop-amsterdam.nl; Handboogstraat 29; ☺8am-1am; ☎; ☒2/11/12 Koningsplein) With an interior that resembles a larger-than-life lava lamp, Dampkring is famed for having one of Amsterdam's most comprehensive coffeeshop menus, with details about aroma, taste and effect. Its name references the ring of the earth's atmosphere where smaller items combust.

Abraxas (Map p48; www.abraxas.tv; Jonge Roelensteeg 12; ☺8am-1am; ☎; ☒2/11/12/13/17 Dam) Mellow music, comfy sofas, thick milkshakes and rooms with different energy levels spread across Abraxas' floors (connected by a spindly spiral staircase). The considerate staff make it a great place for coffeeshop newbies (though the fairy-tale artwork can get a bit intense).

Greenhouse (Map p48; www.greenhouse.org; Oudezijds Voorburgwal 191; ☺9am-1am; ☎; ☒4/14/24 Dam) This is one of the most popular coffeeshops in town, with a mostly young, backpacking crowd partaking of the wares. Smokers love the funky music, multicoloured mosaics and high-quality weed and hash. It also serves breakfast, lunch and dinner to suit all levels of the munchies.

Bluebird (Map p48; Sint Antoniesbreestraat 71; ☺9.30am-1am; ☎; Ⓜ Nieuwmarkt) Away from Nieuwmarkt's main cluster of coffeeshops, Bluebird has a less touristy, more local vibe. The multiroom space has beautiful murals and local artists' paintings, a lounge with leather chairs, a nonalcoholic bar and a kitchen serving superior snacks, such as freshly made pancakes. It's especially well known for its hash, including varieties not available elsewhere in Amsterdam.

updated *bruin café* first opened its doors in 1702, and is named after an icebreaker that used to dock in front to break the ice on the river during the winter months (stained-glass windows illustrate the scene). Inside, stylish drinkers hoist beverages in the plush booths and along the marble bar.

🍷 Amsterdam Noord

★**Café de Ceuvel**   BAR

(☎020-229 62 10; www.deceuvel.nl; Korte Papaverweg 4; ☺11am-midnight Tue-Thu & Sun, to 2am Fri & Sat; ☒34/35 Mosp0lein) The inspiring Café de Ceuvel is tucked in a former shipyard in Amsterdam Noord. Designed by architect

Wouter Valkenier and built from recycled materials, this waterside spot is a surprising oasis alongside the canal and built out onto an island. Drinks include homemade ginger lemonade, plus bottled beer from local heroes Oedipus Brewery.

Pllek   BAR
(www.pllek.nl; TT Neveritaweg 59; ⊙9.30am-1am Sun-Thu, to 3am Fri & Sat; ⊛NDSM-werf) Uber-cool Pllek is a Noord magnet, with hip things of all ages streaming over to hang out in its interior made of old shipping containers and lie out on its artificial sandy beach when the weather allows. It's a terrific spot for a waterfront beer or glass of wine.

★ Café Noorderlicht   BAR
(www.noorderlichtcafe.nl; NDSM-plein 102; ⊙11am-midnight Jun-Sep, closed Mon Oct-May; ⊛NDSM-werf) The original Café Noorderlicht was in a boat, which burned down. Safely ensconced in a soaring flag-draped greenhouse, with grassy waterside lawns outside and a mini-stage, it now has a pubgarden-meets-festival vibe. There's a big play area outside, with a tin rocket to climb on, so it's good for families. Food, craft beers and lots of other drinks are on the menu.

☆ Entertainment

Amsterdam supports a flourishing arts scene, with loads of big concert halls, theatres, cinemas, comedy clubs and other performance venues filled on a regular basis. Music fans are superbly catered for here, and there is a fervent subculture for just about every genre, especially jazz, classical, rock and avant-garde beats.

Check out I Amsterdam (www.iamsterdam.com), which lists all sorts of music and cultural goings-on.

★ Concertgebouw   CLASSICAL MUSIC
(Concert Hall; Map p62; ☑020-671 83 45; www.concertgebouw.nl; Concertgebouwplein 10; ⊙box office 1-7pm Mon-Fri, from 10am Sat & Sun; ⊠3/5/12 Museumplein) The Concert Hall was built in 1888 by AL van Gendt, who managed to engineer its near-perfect acoustics. Bernard Haitink, former conductor of the Royal Concertgebouw Orchestra, remarked that the world-famous hall was the orchestra's best instrument. Free half-hour concerts take place Wednesdays at 12.30pm from September to June; arrive early. Try the Last Minute

Ticket Shop (p104) for half-price seats to all other performances.

★ Pathé Tuschinskitheater   CINEMA
(Map p62; www.pathe.nl; Reguliersbreestraat 26-34; ⊙9.30am-12.30am; ⊠4/14 Rembrandtplein) This fantastical cinema, with a facade that's a prime example of the Amsterdam School of architecture, is worth visiting for its sumptuous art-deco interior alone. The *grote zaal* (main auditorium) is the most stunning; it generally screens blockbusters, while the smaller theatres play arthouse and indie films. Visit the interior on an audio tour (€10) when films aren't playing.

Muziekgebouw aan 't IJ   CONCERT VENUE
(Map p54; ☑tickets 020-788 20 00; www.muziekgebouw.nl; Piet Heinkade 1; ⊙box office noon-6pm Mon-Sat, closed mid-Jul-mid-Aug; ⊠26 Muziekgebouw) A dramatic glass-and-steel box on the IJ waterfront, this multidisciplinary performing-arts venue has a state-of-the-art main hall with flexible stage layout and great acoustics. Its jazz stage, Bimhuis (Map p54; ☑020-788 21 88; www.bimhuis.nl; Piet Heinkade 3; ⊠26 Muziekgebouw), is more intimate. Try the Last Minute Ticket Shop for discounts.

Muziektheater   CLASSICAL MUSIC
(Map p62; ☑020-625 54 55; www.operaballet.nl; Waterlooplein 22; ⊙box office noon-6pm Mon-Fri, to 3pm Sat & Sun or until performance Sep-Jul; ⊠Waterlooplein, ⊠14 Waterlooplein) The Muziektheater is home to the Netherlands Opera and the National Ballet, with some spectacular performances. Big-name performers and international dance troupes also take the stage here. Free classical concerts (12.30pm to 1pm) are held most Tuesdays from September to May in its Boekmanzaal.

Tolhuistuin   LIVE PERFORMANCE
(☑020-763 06 50; www.tolhuistuin.nl; IJpromenade 2; ⊛Buiksloterweg) In what was the former Shell workers' canteen for 70 years from 1941, the nifty Tolhuistuin arts centre hosts African dance troupes, grime DJs and much more on its garden stage under twinkling lights, and also houses club nights in its Paradiso nightclub.

Melkweg   LIVE MUSIC
(Milky Way; Map p62; ☑020-531 81 81; www.melkweg.nl; Lijnbaansgracht 234a; ⊠1/2/5/7/11/12/19 Leidseplein) In a former dairy, the nonprofit 'Milky Way' offers a dazzling galaxy of diverse gigs, featuring both DJs and live bands. One night it's electronica,

ℹ️ LAST-MINUTE TICKETS

Not sure how to spend the evening? The **Last Minute Ticket Shop** (www. lastminuteticketshop.nl; ⊘ online ticket sales from 10am on day of performance) sells same-day, half-price tickets for performances including comedy, dance, concerts and even club nights. Events are handily marked 'LNP' (language no problem) if understanding Dutch isn't vital. There's a maximum of two tickets per transaction.

the next reggae or punk, and the next heavy metal. Roots, rock and mellow singer-songwriters all get stage time too. Check out the website for information on its cutting-edge cinema, theatre and multimedia offerings.

Paradiso   LIVE MUSIC
(Map p62; ☑020-622 45 21; www.paradiso.nl; Weteringschans 6; 🕿; 🚊1/2/5/7/11/12/19 Leidseplein) In 1968, a beautiful old church turned into the 'Cosmic Relaxation Center Paradiso'. Today, the vibe is less hippy than funked-up odyssey, with big all-nighters, themed events and indie nights. The smaller hall hosts up-and-coming bands, but there's something special about the Main Hall, where it seems the stained-glass windows might shatter under the force of the fat beats.

Jazz Café Alto   JAZZ
(Map p62; www.jazz-cafe-alto.nl; Korte Leidsedwarsstraat 115; ⊘9pm-3am Sun-Thu, to 4am Fri & Sat; 🚊1/2/5/7/11/12/19 Leidseplein) This is an intimate, atmospheric *bruin café*–style venue for serious jazz and (occasionally) blues. There are live gigs nightly: doors open at 9pm but music starts around 10pm – get here early if you want to snag a seat.

Maloe Melo   BLUES
(Map p66; ☑020-420 45 92; www.maloemelo.com; Lijnbaansgracht 163; ⊘9pm-3am Sun-Thu, to 4am Fri & Sat; 🚊5/7/17/19 Elandsgracht) This is the free-wheeling, fun-loving altar of Amsterdam's tiny blues scene. Music ranges from funk and soul to Texas blues and rockabilly. The cover charge is usually around €5.

Boom Chicago   COMEDY
(Map p66; ☑020-217 04 00; www.boomchicago.nl; Rozengracht 117; 🕿; 🚊5/13/17/19 Marnixstraat) Boom Chicago stages seriously funny improv-style comedy shows in English that

make fun of Dutch culture, American culture and everything that gets in the crosshairs. Edgier shows happen in the smaller upstairs theatre. The on-site bar helps fuel the festivities with buckets of ice and beer.

Amsterdams Marionetten Theater   THEATRE
(Map p48; ☑020-620 80 27; www.marionettentheater.nl; Nieuwe Jonkerstraat 8; adult/child €16/7.50, 90min tour €15; Ⓜ Nieuwmarkt) An enchanting enterprise that seems to exist in another era, this marionette theatre (in a former blacksmith's shop) presents fairy tales or Mozart operas, such as *The Magic Flute,* but kids and adults alike are just as enthralled by the magical stage sets, period costumes and beautiful singing voices that bring the diminutive cast to life.

Openluchttheater   THEATRE
(Open-Air Theatre; Map p62; ☑020-428 33 60; www.openluchttheater.nl; Vondelpark 5a; ⊘ early May-early Sep; 🚊1/3/11 1e Constantijn Huygensstraat) The Vondelpark's marvellous open-air theatre hosts free concerts in summer, with a laid-back, festival feel, as you might expect from Amsterdam's hippiest park. The program includes world music, dance, theatre and more. You can make a reservation (€5 per seat) on the website up to 1½ hours prior to showtime.

Stadsschouwburg   THEATRE
(Map p62; ☑020-624 23 11; www.stadsschouwburgamsterdam.nl; Leidseplein 26; ⊘box office noon-6pm Mon-Sat, 2hr before performance Sun; 🚊1/2/5/7/11/12/19 Leidseplein) When this theatre with the grand balcony arcade was completed in 1894, public criticism of the design was so fierce that the exterior decorations were never completed; architect Jan Springer was so upset, he retired. The horseshoe auditorium seats 1200 spectators and is used for large-scale plays, operettas and festivals. Don't miss the chandeliered splendour of its **Stanislavski** (Map p62; Leidseplein 26, Stadsschouwburg; ⊘10am-1am Sun-Thu, to 3am Fri & Sat; 🕿; 🚊1/2/5/7/11/12/19 Leidseplein) theatre *café*.

Movies   CINEMA
(☑020-638 60 16; www.themovies.nl; Haarlemmerdijk 161; tickets €11; 🚊3 Haarlemmerplein) Amsterdam's oldest cinema, dating from 1912, is a *gezellig* gem screening indie films alongside mainstream flicks. From Sunday to Thursday you can treat yourself to a meal in the restaurant (open 5.30pm to 10pm) or have a pre-film tipple at the inviting *café*.

🔒 Shopping

During the Golden Age, Amsterdam was the world's warehouse, stuffed with riches from the far corners of the earth. The capital's cupboards are still stocked with all kinds of exotica (just look at that red light gear!), but the real pleasure here is finding some odd, tiny shop selling something you wouldn't find anywhere else.

🔒 Medieval Centre & Red Light District

Kalverstraat and its surrounds are filled with high-street chains and get crammed with shoppers, while Damrak is awash with souvenir shops. More esoteric shops, selling everything from Dutch-designed homewares, fashion and art to reconditioned retro games, can be found in the backstreets. The Red Light District is home to a wild assortment of adult and fetish shops, as well as 'smart shops' selling magic truffles.

★ **X Bank**   DESIGN
(Map p48; www.xbank.amsterdam; Spuistraat 172; ☉10am-8pm Mon-Sat, from noon Sun; ☐2/11/12/13/17 Dam) More than just a concept store showcasing Dutch-designed haute couture and ready-to-wear fashion, furniture, art, gadgets and homewares, the 700-sq-metre X Bank – in a former bank that's now part of the striking W Amsterdam (p82) hotel – also hosts exhibitions, workshops, launches and lectures. Interior displays change every month; check the website for upcoming events.

Condomerie Het Gulden Vlies   ADULT
(Map p48; www.condomerie.com; Warmoesstraat 141; ☉11am-9pm Mon & Wed-Sat, to 6pm Tue, 1-6pm Sun; ☐4/14/24 Dam) In the heart of the Red Light District, this brightly lit boutique sells condoms in every imaginable size, colour, flavour and design (horned devils, marijuana leaves, Delftware tiles...), along with lubricants and saucy gifts. Photos aren't allowed inside the shop.

Oudemanhuispoort Book Market   BOOKS
(Map p48; Oudemanhuispoort; ☉11am-4pm Mon-Sat; Ⓜ Rokin, ☐4/14/24 Rokin) Secondhand books weigh down the tables in the atmospheric covered alleyway between Oudezijds Achterburgwal and Kloveniersburgwal, where you'll rub tweed-patched elbows with University of Amsterdam professors thumbing through volumes of Marx, Aristotle et al. Old posters, maps and sheet music are for sale too. Most tomes are in Dutch, though you'll find a few in English mixed in. Cash only.

PGC Hajenius   GIFTS & SOUVENIRS
(Map p48; www.hajenius.com; Rokin 96; ☉noon-6pm Mon, 9.30am-6pm Tue-Sat, noon-5pm Sun; Ⓜ Rokin, ☐4/14/24 Rokin) With its century-old stained glass, gilt trim, Italian marble and soaring leather ceilings, this tobacco emporium is worth checking out even if you're not a cigar connoisseur. Regular customers, including members of the Dutch royal family, have private humidors here. You can sample Cuban and other exotic cigars in the handsome smoking lounge.

Kokopelli   ADULT
(Map p48; www.kokopelli.nl; Warmoesstraat 12; ☉11am-10pm; ☐2/4/11/12/13/14/17/24/26 Centraal Station) Were it not for its trade in 'magic truffles' (similar to the now-outlawed psilocybin mushrooms, aka 'magic mushrooms'), you might swear this large, beautiful space was a fashionable clothing or homewares store. There's a coffee and juice bar and a chill-out lounge area overlooking Damrak.

MAGIC TRUFFLES & SMART SHOPS

Smart shops – which deal in organic uppers and natural hallucinogens – have long been known for selling 'magic' mushrooms. But in 2008 the government banned them after a high-profile incident in which a tourist died. Nearly 200 varieties of fungus then went on the forbidden list – though conspicuously missing was the magic truffle.

Truffles come from a different part of the fungus but they contain the same active ingredients as mushrooms. Truffles are now the smart shops' stock-in-trade. Counter staff advise on the nuances of dosages and possible effects, as if at a pharmacy. Listen to them. Every year, emergency-room nurses have to sit with people on bad trips brought on by consuming more than the recommended amount. Also, it seems obvious, but never buy truffles or other drugs on the street.

it also sells circus supplies, from unicycles to fire hoops to magic tricks.

🅰 Nieuwmarkt, Plantage & the Eastern Islands

Nieuwmarkt has lots of small boutiques and interesting independent shops, selling everything from fetishwear to haberdashery, while there is one of Amsterdam's best flea markets on Waterlooplein, and a cluster of the city's chicest homeware shops on the Eastern Islands.

★**Hôtel Droog**   DESIGN, HOMEWARES
(Map p48; www.droog.com; Staalstraat 7; ⊙9am-7pm; 🚊24 Muntplein) Not a hotel, but a local design house. Droog means 'dry' in Dutch, and these products are full of dry wit. You'll find all kinds of stylish versions of useful things – a chic dish sponge or streamlined hot water bottle – as well as the kind of clothing that should probably by law be worn by a designer or an architect.

Also here is a gallery space, a delightful fairy-tale garden and a high-beamed all-white cafe, overlooked by a tapestry of Rembrandt's *The Night Watch*.

Juggle   TOYS
(Map p48; www.juggle-store.com; Staalstraat 3; ⊙noon-5.30pm Tue-Sat; 🚊24 Muntplein) Wee Juggle puts more than mere balls in the air:

🅰 Western Canal Ring

You could easily spend all of your shopping time in the Negen Straatjes (p107), with its abundance of small, specialist boutiques.

★**Frozen Fountain**   HOMEWARES
(Map p66; www.frozenfountain.com; Prinsengracht 645; ⊙1-6pm Mon, from 10am Tue-Sat, noon-5pm Sun; 🚊2/11/12 Prinsengracht) Frozen Fountain is Amsterdam's best-known showcase of furniture and interior design. Prices are not cheap, but the daring designs are offbeat and very memorable (designer penknives, kitchen gadgets and that birthday gift for the impossible-to-wow friend).

De Kaaskamer   FOOD
(Map p62; www.kaaskamer.nl; Runstraat 7; ⊙noon-6pm Mon, 9am-6pm Tue-Fri, 9am-5pm Sat, noon-5pm Sun; 🚊2/11/12 Spui) The name means 'the cheese room' and De Kaaskamer is indeed stacked to the rafters with Dutch and organic varieties, as well as olives, tapenades, salads and other picnic ingredients. You can try before you buy or pick up a cheese-filled baguette. Vacuum-packing is available to take cheeses home.

🅰 Southern Canal Ring

Whether you're after tulip bulbs, quirky Dutch fashion and design or rare *jenever*, you'll find it on the Southern Canal Ring. The Nieuwe Spiegelstraat (the spine of the Spiegel Quarter) is renowned for its antique stores, bric-a-brac, collectables, tribal and oriental art, and commercial art galleries.

★**Concerto**   MUSIC
(Map p62; www.concerto.amsterdam/en; Utrechtsestraat 52-60; ⊙10am-6pm Mon, Wed, Fri & Sat, to 7pm Thu, noon-6pm Sun; 🚊4 Keizersgracht) This rambling shop is muso heaven, with a fabulous selection of new and secondhand vinyl and CDs encompassing every imaginable genre. There's a sofa-strewn living-room-style cafe and regular live sessions (see the website for details).

Skateboards Amsterdam   SPORTS & OUTDOORS
(Map p62; www.skateboardsamsterdam.nl; Vijzelstraat 77; ⊙1-6pm Sun & Mon, from 11am Tue-Sat;

24 Muntplein) Skater-dude heaven, with everything required for the freewheeling lifestyle: cruisers, longboards, shoes, laces, caps, beanies, bags, backpacks, and clothing including Spitfire and Skate Mental T-shirts and a fantastic selection of band T-shirts.

Eduard Kramer ANTIQUES
(Map p62; www.antique-tileshop.nl; Prinsengracht 807; ⊙11am-6pm Mon, from 10am Tue-Fri, 10am-7pm Sat, 1-6pm Sun; 1/7/19 Spiegelgracht) Specialising in antique blue-and-white Dutch tiles, this engrossing, crammed-to-the-rafters shop is chock-a-block with fascinating antiques, silver candlesticks, crystal decanters, jewellery and pocket watches.

Jordaan & the West

Shops here have an artsy, eclectic, homemade feel. The area around Elandsgracht is the place for antiques and art, as well as speciality shops covering everything from hats to cats. Straddling the Jordaan and Western Canal Ring, the Haarlemmerbuurt, incorporating hip Haarlemmerdijk in the northern Jordaan, teems with trendy food and fashion boutiques. The Jordaan also has some fabulous food and flea markets (p109).

★**Moooi Gallery** DESIGN
(Map p66; ☎020-528 77 60; www.moooi.com; Westerstraat 187; ⊙10am-6pm Tue-Sat; 3/5 Marnixplein) Founded by Marcel Wanders, this gallery-shop features Dutch design at its most over-the-top, from the life-size black horse lamp to the 'blow away vase' (a whimsical twist on the classic Delft vase) .

★**Lindengracht Market** MARKET
(Map p66; www.jordaanmarkten.nl; Lindengracht; ⊙9am-4pm Sat; 3 Nieuwe Willemsstraat) Dating from 1895, Saturday's Lindengracht Market is a wonderfully local affair, with 232 stalls selling bountiful fresh produce, including fish and a magnificent array of cheese, as well as gourmet goods, clothing and homewares. Arrive as early as possible for the best pickings and thinnest crowds.

Noordermarkt MARKET
(Northern Market; Map p66; www.jordaanmarkten. nl; Noordermarkt; ⊙flea market 9am-1pm Mon, farmers market 9am-3pm Sat; 3/5 Marnixplein) A market square since the early 1600s, the plaza in front of the Noorderkerk hosts a couple of lively markets each week. Mon-

day morning's flea market has some amazing bargains, and Saturday morning sees local shoppers flock to the lush boerenmarkt (farmers market), overflowing with organic produce. There's a great selection of cafes surrounding the square, including Winkel (Map p122; www.winkel43. nl; Noordermarkt 43; dishes €4.50-8.50, mains €9-19; ⊙kitchen 7am-10pm Mon & Sat, from 8am Tue-Fri, from 10am Sun, bar to 1am Sun-Thu, to 3am Fri & Sat; 🛜).

Vondelpark & the South

The Old South, south of Vondelpark, is one of Amsterdam's most exclusive areas, with shops to match. Stylish shops line Cornelis Schuytstraat and Willemsparkweg; check www.cornelisschuytstraat.com for new openings. Nearby, ultraluxe shopping avenue PC Hooftstraat teems with designer brands. There are several unusual boutiques as part of the De Hallen complex.

★**Pied à Terre** BOOKS
(Map p62; ☎020-627 44 55; www.piedaterre.nl; Overtoom 135-137; ⊙1-6pm Mon, 10am-6pm Tue, Wed & Sat, 10am-7pm Thu & Fri; 1/3/11 1e Constantijn Huygensstraat) Travel lovers will be in heaven in the galleried, sky-lit interior of Europe's largest travel bookshop. If it's travel or outdoor-related, you can dream over it here.

Bierbaum DRINKS
(Map p62; www.bier-baum.nl; Jan Pieter Heijestraat 148; ⊙2-10pm Sun-Fri, from noon Sat; 1/11 Jan Pieter Heijestraat) Bierbaum offers 250-plus craft beers from over 25 different countries, cold from the fridge, making them perfect to take to the Vondelpark on

---

DON'T MISS

NINE STREETS

In a city packed with countless shopping opportunities, each seemingly more alluring than the last, the Negen Straatjes (Nine Streets; Map p66; www. de9straatjes.nl; 2/11/12 Spui) represent the very densest concentration of consumer pleasures. These nine little streets are indeed small, each just a block long. The shops are tiny too, and many are highly specialised. Eyeglasses? Cheese? Single-edition art books? Each has its own dedicated boutique.

a hot day, as well as four rotating beers on tap that can be bottled to take away cold, too.

Johnny at the Spot FASHION & ACCESSORIES
(Map p62; www.johnnyatthespot.com; Jan Pieter Heijestraat 94; 1-6pm Mon, 11am-6pm Tue, Wed & Sat, 11am-7pm Thu & Fri, 1-5pm Sun; 7/17 Jan Pieter Heijestraat) Cool concept store Johnny at the Spot fills several interconnected buildings with uber-hip men's and women's clothing, shoes and raincoats from all over the globe.

De Pijp

After you've hit the Albert Cuypmarkt (p69), head to the surrounding streets, which are less crowded and are dotted with boutiques and galleries.

 Hutspot DESIGN
(Map p62; www.hutspot.com; Van Woustraat 4; 10am-7pm Mon-Sat, noon-6pm Sun; ; 4 Stadhouderskade) Named after the Dutch dish of boiled and mashed veggies, 'Hotchpotch' was founded with a mission to give young entrepreneurs the chance to sell their work. As a result, this concept store is an inspired mishmash of Dutch-designed furniture, furnishings, art, homewares and clothing as well as various pop-ups.

Information

INTERNET ACCESS

Wi-fi is widespread. For free wi-fi hotspots around the city, check www.wifi-amsterdam.nl.

MEDICAL SERVICES

Onze Lieve Vrouwe Gasthuis (020-599 91 11; www.olvg.nl; Oosterpark 9; 24hr; 1/3 Beukenweg) At Oosterpark, near the Tropenmuseum. It's the closest public hospital to the centre of town.

MONEY

ATMs are easy to find in the centre, though they often have queues. To change money try **GWK Travelex** (020-627 27 31; www.gwktravelex.nl; Stationsplein 13f; 10am-5pm; 2/4/11/12/13/14/17/24/26 Centraal Station) at Centraal Station; there are branches at **Leidseplein** (020-622 14 25; www.gwktravelex.nl; Leidsestraat 103; 9am-9pm; 1/2/5/7/11/12/19 Leidseplein) and **Schiphol International Airport**.

TOURIST INFORMATION

I Amsterdam Visitor Centre (Map p48; 020-702 60 00; www.iamsterdam.com; Stationsplein 10; 9am-5pm; 2/4/11/12/13/14/17/24/26 Centraal Station) Located outside Centraal Station, this office can help with just about anything: it sells the I Amsterdam discount card; theatre and museum tickets; maps; and public-transit passes (the GVB (p109) transport office is attached). Queues can be long; be sure to take a number when you walk in.

I Amsterdam Visitor Centre Schiphol (www.iamsterdam.com; 7am-10pm) Provides maps and discount cards inside Schiphol International Airport (p329) at the Arrivals 2 hall.

Getting There & Away

AIR

Situated 18km southwest of the city centre, Schiphol International Airport (020-653 51 21; www.gwktravelex.nl; 6am-10pm) has ATMs, currency exchanges, tourist information, car hire, train-ticket sales counters, luggage storage, food and free wi-fi. It's linked to the city centre by train.

BICYCLE

It's easy to get to and from Amsterdam by bike, with routes radiating in all directions. Plan routes at www.routeplanner.fietsersbond.nl (there's an English version).

BUS

Buses operated by Eurolines and FlixBus connect Amsterdam with all major European capitals and numerous smaller destinations. Book tickets online.

Eurolines buses use **Duivendrecht station** (Stationsplein 3, Duivendrecht; Duivendrecht), south of the centre, which has an easy metro link to Centraal Station (about a 20-minute trip via metros 50, 53 or 54).

FlixBus (www.flixbus.com) runs to/from **Sloterdijk train station**, west of the centre, linked to Centraal Station by metro number 50 (a six-minute trip).

CAR

If you're arriving by car, it's best to leave your vehicle in a park-and-ride lot near the edge of town. A nominal parking fee (around €8 for the first 24 hours and €1 per day thereafter) also gets you discounted public transport tickets. For more info see www.iamsterdam.com.

TRAIN

Centraal Station (p51) is in the city centre, with easy onward connections. The station has ATMs, currency exchanges, tourist information, restaurants, shops, luggage storage (€7 to €10 per day), and national and international train ticket sales.

Amsterdam is the terminus of the high-speed line south to Rotterdam, Antwerp, Brussels and Paris. Direct Eurostar trains linking Amsterdam (via Brussels and Rotterdam) with London St Pancras launched in 2018, with a London–Amsterdam journey time of three hours 41 minutes. A direct Amsterdam–London service launched in 2019.

TO	PRICE (€)	TIME (MIN)	FREQUENCY (PER HOUR)
Den Haag	11.70	55	2
Haarlem	4.30	15	8
Maastricht	25.30	150	2
Rotterdam	15.40	75	2
Rotterdam (high speed)	17.80	40	5
Schiphol Airport	4.30	15	8
Utrecht	7.60	25	5

🛈 Getting Around

TRAINS

Trains run by NS (www.ns.nl) serve the outer suburbs and, aside from travelling to/from the airport, most visitors to Amsterdam will rarely need to use them unless undertaking trips further afield.

Metro lines, which also serve outer suburbs as well as some inner-city stations, are operated by GVB (p109) and use the same ticketing system (though you must top up OV-chipkaarts at NS machines to use NS trains). If you're travelling between two neighbourhoods served by metro, it can be faster than taking a tram, especially in heavy traffic.

TAXI

➡ Taxis are expensive and not very speedy given Amsterdam's maze of streets.

➡ You don't hail taxis on the road. Instead, find them at stands at Centraal Station, Leidseplein and other busy spots around town. You needn't take the first car in the queue.

➡ Another method is to book a taxi by phone. **Taxicentrale Amsterdam** (TCA; ☎ 020-777 77 77; www.tcataxi.nl) is the most reliable firm.

➡ Fares are meter-based. The meter starts at €2.95, then it's €2.17 per kilometre thereafter. A ride from Leidseplein to the Dam costs about €12; from Centraal Station to Jordaan is €10 to €15.

BICYCLE

Bicycles are more common in Amsterdam than cars (or residents, with an estimated 881,000 bikes) and to roll like a local you'll need a two-wheeler. Rent one from the myriad outlets around town or your accommodation, and the whole city becomes your playground. Cycling is *the* quintessential activity while visiting.

To rent a bike, you'll have to show a passport or European national ID card and leave a credit-card imprint or pay a deposit (usually €50). Prices for basic 'coaster-brake' bikes average €11 per 24-hour period. Bikes with gears and handbrakes cost more. Theft insurance costs around €3 extra per day. Bike locks are typically provided; use them, as theft is rampant. Helmets are generally not available (the Dutch don't wear them). Most cycling tour companies (p79) also rent bikes.

Frederic Rentabike (Map p48; ☎ 020-624 55 09; www.frederic.nl; Binnen Wieringerstraat 23; bike rental per day/week €11/60; ☺9am-5.30pm; 🚊18/21/22 Buiten Brouwersstraat) Frederic rents wheels from its bike shop, which also hosts art exhibitions.

Bike City (Map p66; ☎020-626 37 21; www.bikecity.nl; Bloemgracht 68-70; bike rental per day from €14; ☺9am-5.30pm; 🚊13/17 Westermarkt) These black bikes have no advertising on them, so you can cycle like a local.

Black Bikes (Map p48; ☎0852 737 454; www.black-bikes.com; Nieuwezijds Voorburgwal 146; bike rental per 3/24hr from €6/8.50, electric bikes €24/37.50; ☺8am-8pm Mon-Fri, 9am-7pm Sat & Sun; 🚊2/11/12/13/17 Nieuwezijds Kolk) Black Bikes offers signless city, kids', tandem, cargo and electric bikes at 13 outlets around town, including this one in the centre.

MacBike (Map p48; ☎ 020-624 83 91; www.macbike.nl; De Ruijterkade 34b; bike rental per 3/24hr from €5/9.75; ☺9am-6pm; 🚊2/4/11/12/13/14/17/24/26 Centraal Station) Among the most touristy of the rental companies (the bikes are equipped with big logos), MacBike has several convenient locations (Leidseplein, Waterlooplein, and Overtoom, near Vondelpark, among others) in addition to this Centraal Station branch, and also sells great maps.

BOAT

From late March to early November, the Canal Bus (p80) offers a unique hop-on, hop-off service among its 20 docks around the city and near the big museums.

Free ferries to Amsterdam Noord depart from piers behind Centraal Station.

CAR & MOTORCYCLE

Parking is expensive and scarce. Street parking in the centre costs around €5/55 per hour/day. It's better to use a park-and-ride lot at the edge of town, where rates are as low as €1 per day after 10am. All the big multinational rental companies are in town.

PUBLIC TRANSPORT

The GVB operates the public transport system, a mix of tram, bus, metro and ferry. Pick up tickets, passes and maps at the **GVB Information Office** (www.gvb.nl; Stationsplein

❶ NAVIGATING AMSTERDAM

Amsterdam's concentric canals and similarly named streets make it all too easy to get lost. Some pointers: a *gracht* (canal), such as Egelantiersgracht, is distinct from a *straat* (street) such as Egelantiersstraat. A *dwarsstraat* (cross-street) that intersects a *straat* is often preceded by *eerste, tweede, derde* and *vierde* (first, second, third and fourth; marked 1e, 2e, 3e and 4e on maps). For example Eerste Egelantiersdwarsstraat is the first cross-street of Egelantiersstraat (ie the nearest cross-street to the city centre). Be aware, too, that seemingly continuous streets regularly change name along their length.

10; ⊙7am-9pm Mon-Fri, from 8am Sat & Sun; 🚊2/4/11/12/13/14/17/24/26 Centraal Station) across the tram tracks from Centraal Station.

Tram

➡ Most public transport within the city is by tram. The vehicles are fast, frequent and ubiquitous, operating between 6am and 12.30am.

➡ Tickets are not sold on board. Buy a OV-chipkaart (www.ov-chipkaart.nl; one hour €3) or a day pass (one to seven days €7.50 to €34.50) from the GVB information office.

➡ When you enter *and* exit, wave your card at the machine to 'check in' and 'check out'.

➡ Most tram lines start at Centraal Station and then fan out into the neighbourhoods.

Bus & Metro

➡ Amsterdam's buses and metro (subway) primarily serve outer districts.

➡ The GVB offers unlimited-ride passes for one to seven days (€7.50 to €34.50), valid on trams, some buses and the metro.

➡ Alternatively, buy a disposable OV-chipkaart (www.ov-chipkaart.nl; one hour €3) from the GVB information office (p109).

➡ *Nachtbussen* (night buses) run after other transport stops (from 1am to 6am, every hour). A ticket costs €4.50.

➡ Note that Connexxion buses (which depart from Centraal Station and are useful to reach sights in southern Amsterdam) and the No 397 airport bus are not part of the GVB system. They cost more (around €5).

Travel Passes

➡ Travel passes are handy and provide substantial savings over per-ride ticket purchases.

➡ The GVB offers unlimited-ride passes for one to seven days (€7.50 to €34.50), valid on trams, some buses and the metro.

➡ Passes are available at the GVB information office (p109) and I Amsterdam Visitor Centres (p108), but not on board.

➡ The I Amsterdam Card (www.iamsterdam.com; per 24/48/72/96 hours €59/74/87/98) includes a GVB travel pass in its fee.

➡ A wider-ranging option is the Amsterdam & Region Day Ticket (€18.50), which goes beyond the tram/metro system, adding on night buses, airport buses, Connexxion buses and regional EBS buses that go to towns such as Haarlem, Muiden and Zaanse Schans. The pass is available at the GVB office and at visitor centres.

➡ Another choice is the Amsterdam Travel Ticket (per one/two/three days €16/21/26). It's basically a GVB unlimited-ride pass with an airport train ticket added on. Buy it at the airport (at the NS ticket window) or GVB office.

Haarlem
& North Holland

Best Places to Eat

→ Lucas Rive (p128)

→ Smit Bokkum (p121)

→ Restaurant Mr & Mrs (p116)

→ Restaurant ML (p116)

→ Bij Jef (p138)

Best Places to Stay

→ ML (p115)

→ Fort Resort Beemster (p122)

→ Camp Silver Island Hideaway (p138)

→ Gevangenis Hotel Hoorn (p128)

→ Boutique Hotel Texel (p137)

Why Go?

The quintessentially Dutch province of Noord-Holland (North Holland) wraps around Amsterdam like a crown. Less than 20km west of Amsterdam, but entirely its own city, elegant Haarlem is the region's capital and a charming example of 17th-century grandeur. Canals traverse its centre, while wide, sandy beaches fringe its western edge.

Further afield, smaller centres range from mast-filled Golden Age ports such as Hoorn and Enkhuizen, with architecturally resplendent historic centres, to canal-laced towns and villages like Alkmaar and Edam, famed for their cheese and centuries-old cheese markets. Across the region, bucolic expanses of windswept countryside span extensive *polders* (areas surrounded by dykes where the water can be artificially controlled) to windmill-dotted farmland grazed by cows and sheep, fields of flowers and magnificent dune-scapes, especially on the idyllic island of Texel just a 20-minute ferry ride offshore.

When to Go

→ Easily accessible from Amsterdam, Haarlem's outstanding museums, fabulous bars, cafes, restaurants and great shopping make it a year-round destination.

→ The springtime lambing season in March and April, around Easter, is an especially delightful time to island-hop over to Texel, though it's still too cold for swimming, and not all attractions and activities are yet in full swing.

→ The warmer months of May to September are the prime time to visit smaller towns and villages, which all but hibernate during winter, particularly from November to March, when many sights, activities and attractions close.

Haarlem & North Holland Highlights

1 Frans Hals Museum
(p113) Viewing priceless Dutch Masters in Haarlem.

2 Gestam (p122) Sampling cheeses in the quaint town of Edam.

3 Zuiderzeemuseum
(p129) Learning about hardy seafaring life in the days before the Afsluitdijk (Barrier

Dyke) in the historic port town of Enkhuizen.

4 Texel (p132) Cycling past high sand dunes, deserted beaches, lush forests and green, sheep-filled pastures on this island just off the region's north coast.

5 Muiderslot (p139) Exploring Muiden's mighty

medieval fortress dating from the 13th century.

6 Museum BroekerVeiling
(p126) Experiencing a 'floating auction' in Broek op Langedijk, near Alkmaar.

7 Naarden (p140) Strolling the elegant streets inside the vast star-shaped fortress.

NORTH HOLLAND

Its lively capital, Haarlem, aside, this province has enough historic towns and attractions to fill a week or more of touring.

History

The peninsula now known as Noord-Holland (North Holland) was part of Friesland until the 12th century, when storm floods created the Zuiderzee and isolated West Friesland. By this time the mercantile Counts of Holland ruled the area – or thought they did. One of the early counts, Willem II, became king of the Holy Roman Empire in 1247 but perished in a raid against the West Frisians. His son, Count Floris V, succeeded in taming his defiant subjects 40 years later.

West Friesland was now owned by the county of Holland, a founding member of the Republic of the Seven United Netherlands (1579). North Holland played a key role in the long struggle against Spanish domination, and the town of Alkmaar was the first to throw off the yoke. The era of prosperity known as the Golden Age ensued, and Noord-Holland has a cache of richly ornamented buildings from this period. The fishing and trading ports of Enkhuizen, Hoorn, Medemblik and Edam were at the centre of this boom.

Napoleon invaded in 1795 and split the country in two to break its economic power. Even after Willem I proclaimed himself Sovereign Prince of the United Netherlands in 1813, a divide remained and the provinces of Noord-Holland and Zuid-Holland were established in 1840.

Today North Holland's main business is agriculture, most famously cheese production.

Haarlem

📞 023 / POP 159,556

This classic Dutch city of cobbled streets, historic buildings, grand churches, even grander museums, cosy bars, fine cafes and canals is just a 15-minute train ride from Amsterdam. To its west are the coastal dunes of the Zuid-Kennemerland National Park, and popular beaches of Zandvoort and Bloemendaal aan Zee.

⦿ Sights & Activities

Flanked by historic buildings, restaurants and cafes, the large Grote Markt is Haarlem's beating heart.

★ **Grote Kerk van St Bavo** CHURCH
(www.bavo.nl; Oude Groenmarkt 22; adult/child €2.50/1.25; ⦿10am-5pm Mon-Sat year round, plus from noon Sun Jul & Aug) Topped by a 50m-high steeple, the Gothic Grote Kerk van St Bavo contains some fine Renaissance artworks, but the star attraction is its stunning Müller organ – one of the most magnificent in the world, standing 30m high and with about 5000 pipes, dating from 1738. It was played by Handel and a 10-year-old Mozart. Free organ recitals take place at 8.15pm Tuesday and 4pm Thursday from July to October, and on occasional Sundays at 2.30pm.

★ **Frans Hals Museum – Hof** MUSEUM
(www.franshalsmuseum.nl; Groot Heiligland 62; adult/child incl Frans Hals Museum – Hof €15/free; ⦿11am-5pm Tue-Sat, from noon Sun) A must for anyone interested in the Dutch Masters, this superb museum is located in the poorhouse where Hals spent his final years. The collection focuses on the 17th-century Haarlem School; its pride and joy are eight group portraits of the Civic Guard that reveal Hals' exceptional attention to mood and psychological tone. Other greats represented here include Pieter Bruegel the Younger and Jacob van Ruisdael. Tickets include admission to the modern- and contemporary-art Frans Hals Museum – Hal.

Frans Hals Museum – Hal GALLERY
(📞023-511 57 75; www.franshalsmuseum.nl; Grote Markt 16; adult/child incl Frans Hals Museum – Hof €15/free; ⦿11am-5pm Tue-Sat, from noon Sun) The Frans Hals Museum's modern and contemporary art branch occupies two historic 'halls': the 17th-century Dutch Renaissance Vleeshal, a former meat market and the sole place meat was allowed to be sold in Haarlem from the 17th through to the 19th century, and the neoclassical Verweyhal (fish house). Rotating exhibits span Dutch impressionists and CoBrA artists (an avant-garde group from Copenhagen, Brussels and Amsterdam) to video, installation art and photography by international artists. Tickets include the Frans Hals Museum – Hof.

Corrie ten Boom House HISTORIC BUILDING
(📞023-531 08 23; www.corrietenboom.com; Barteljorisstraat 19; by donation; ⦿10am-3pm Tue-Sat Apr-Oct, 11am-2.30pm Tue-Sat Nov-Mar) Known as 'the hiding place', the Corrie ten Boom House is named for the matriarch of a family who lived in the house during WWII. Using a secret compartment in her bedroom,

Haarlem

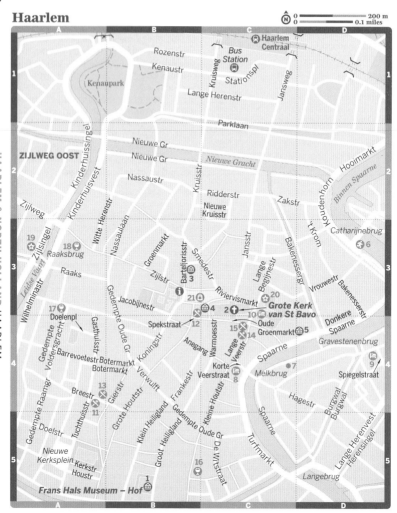

she hid hundreds of Jews and Dutch resistors until they could be spirited to safety. In 1944 the family was betrayed and sent to concentration camps, where three died. Later, Corrie ten Boom toured the world espousing peace. Reserve hour-long tours (English available) at least five days ahead.

Teylers Museum MUSEUM
(☑023-516 09 60; www.teylersmuseum.nl; Spaarne 16; adult/child €13.50/2; ☺10am-5pm Tue-Fri, from 11am Sat & Sun) Dating from 1778, Teylers is the country's oldest continuously operating museum. Its array of whizz-bang inventions

includes an 18th-century electrostatic machine that conjures up visions of mad scientists. A magnificent, sky-lighted Ovale Zaal (Oval Room) displays natural-history specimens in elegant glass cases on two levels.

Free 90-minute guided tours in English and Dutch depart at 2pm on Sundays.

Haarlemmerhout PARK
(www.vriendenhaarlemmerhout.nl; Kleine Houtweg; ☺24hr) Covering 60 hectares, Haarlemmerhout is the Netherlands' oldest public park. It was first mapped in 1539, by which time it was already well established, and was

Haarlem

extensively redesigned in 1760. Planted with beech, horse chestnut, oak, linden, silver maple and plane trees, it's a serene spot for a stroll or picnic. A small petting zoo, playgrounds and a pancake house make it great for kids. Art exhibitions, concerts and festivals take place in the warmer months.

Club Spaarne   BOATING
(📞06 3330 0000; www.clubspaarne.com; Catharijnebrug; boat hire per hour/day from €25/100; ☺11am-9pm Mon-Fri, from 10am Sat & Sun) Explore Haarlem's waterways aboard boats seating four to 12 people. Prices include fuel and life jackets; no boat licence is required.

☞ Tours

Haarlem Canal Tours   BOATING
(📞06 3394 6144; www.haarlemcanaltours.com; opposite Spaarne 17; per person €14; ☺tours 11.30am-5.30pm Apr-Oct) Fun 75-minute tours in vintage open-top boats depart every 90 minutes, passing landmarks including the windmill De Molen Adriaan.

🛏 Sleeping

★Hello I'm Local Boutique Hostel   HOSTEL €
(📞023-844 69 16; www.helloimlocal.com; Spiegelstraat 4; dm €19-42, s/d/tr/q from €84/88.50/128/150; 🛜) In a charming neighbourhood on the edge of the centre, this quirkily named hostel inside a traditional brick Dutch house has 56 beds across 12 rooms, and homey amenities including a kitchen, patio and open fireplace. All rooms

have showers but some share toilet facilities. Upper capsule-like timber bunks are accessed by ladder. Bike hire costs €12.50 per day. Wi-fi is in common areas only.

★ML   DESIGN HOTEL €€
(📞023-512 39 10; www.mlinhaarlem.nl; Klokhuisplein 9; s/d/ste from €105/125/175; ❄🛜) Opened in 2018 in the former printing and die-cast workshop dating from 1703 that once housed the royal printer Johan Enschedé, this stunning property has a monumental metal staircase topped by a stained-glass dome. Its 17 rooms ranging from 30 to 50 sq metres have chandeliers, beamed ceilings and streamlined contemporary decor. Also here are a bistro and Michelin-starred restaurant (p116).

★Brasss Hotel Suites   BOUTIQUE HOTEL €€
(📞023-542 78 04; www.brasss-hotelsuites.nl; Korte Veerstraat 40; ste from €117; ❄🛜) Each of the 10 luxurious suites at this jewel is named after sea creatures (Octopus, Sardine, Langoustine, Mackerel etc) except for Diamonds of the Sea, which comes with its own sauna. All have king-size beds, rain showers and velvety bathrobes. Service surpasses expectations.

🍴 Eating

Native   CAFE, VEGETARIAN €
(www.nativehaarlem.nl; Breestraat 23; dishes €4.50-10; ☺8am-6pm Mon-Sat, from 9.30am Sun; 🛜🍴) 🌿 All-organic dishes are vegetarian and many are vegan and/or gluten-free at this laid-back contemporary cafe on leafy

WORTH A TRIP

GREEN DAY TRIP FROM HAARLEM

Zuid-Kennemerland National Park (www.np-zuidkennemerland.nl) Some 3800 hectares of classic Dutch coastal dunes are being restored in this oasis less than 5km west of Haarlem. Trails snake through hilltop copses of Corsican firs and valleys of low-lying thickets; at the western edge is a massive barrier of thousand-year-old golden sand. Its visitor centre, **De Zandwaaier** (☑023-541 11 23; www.np-zuidkennemerland.nl; Zeeweg 12; ⏲10am-5pm daily Jul & Aug, Tue-Sun Sep-Jun), has nature displays and hires bikes.

Take bus 81 from Haarlem train station (€2.17, 20 minutes, half-hourly) or cycle/drive the N200 towards Bloemendaal aan Zee.

There are car parks at the Koevlak and Parnassia entrances, from where paths lead into the reserve.

Spring sees the dunes sprout desert orchids, the bright rosettes of the century weed and the white-blooming grass of Parnassus. Red foxes, fallow deer and many species of birds are native to the area. Bats slumber in the park's abandoned bunkers before appearing at dusk.

Members of the Dutch Resistance are laid to rest at the **Erebegraafplaats Bloemendaal** (☑023-526 18 69; www.eerebegraafplaatsbloemendaal.eu; Zeeweg 26; ⏲9am-6pm Apr-Oct, to 5pm Nov-Mar) cemetery.

The Vogelmeer lake has a bird observation hut above the south shore. The artificial lake 't Wed teems with bathers in summer. Lookout points, with evocative names such as Hazenberg (Hare Mountain), are scattered throughout. At 50m, the Kopje van Bloemendaal is the highest dune in the country, just outside the eastern border of the park, with views of the sea and Amsterdam.

Breestraat. It doesn't take reservations; stop by for freshly squeezed juices, loose-leaf teas and Amsterdam-roasted White Label Coffee accompanied by pastries (iced cinnamon rolls, fruit tarts), salads, gourmet sandwiches and toasties, and daily specials like pumpkin hummus with flax seed and seaweed crackers.

De Haerlemsche Vlaamse FAST FOOD €
(www.dehaerlemschevlaamse.nl; Spekstraat 3; frites €1.80-4.40; ⏲11am-6.30pm Mon-Wed & Fri, to 9pm Thu, to 6pm Sat, noon-5pm Sun) Line up at this local institution for a cone of crispy, golden fries made from fresh potatoes and one of a dozen sauces, including three kinds of mayonnaise.

Thrill Grill BURGERS €
(☑023-202 40 47; www.thrillgrill.nl; Oude Groenmarkt 26-28; burgers €9.50; ⏲noon-10pm Sun-Wed, to 11pm Thu-Sat; 🛜🚷) Part of an Amsterdam-originated micro-chain set up by former Michelin-starred Dutch TV chef Robert Kranenborg, with four Netherlands locations to date, this central spot overlooking the Grote Kerk van St Bavo serves stellar burgers made from locally sourced beef, chicken, fish and vegetables, with sides such as truffled Parmesan fries. Miniburgers and hot dogs are available for kids.

★**Restaurant Mr & Mrs** BISTRO €€
(☑023-531 59 35; www.restaurantmrandmrs. nl; Lange Veerstraat 4; small plates €11-13, 4-/5-/6-course menu €40/48/56; ⏲5-10pm Tue-Sat) Unexpectedly gastronomic cooking at this tiny restaurant is artfully conceived and presented. Small hot and cold plates designed for sharing might include steak tartar with black truffles, white asparagus with honey-poached egg, mackerel with Dutch shrimp and rose petals, chorizo-stuffed quail with *fregola* (bead-like pasta), and desserts like passion-fruit tart with mint meringue and mango salsa. Definitely book ahead.

Brick EUROPEAN €€
(☑023-551 18 70; www.restaurantbrick.nl; Breestraat 24-26; mains €15.50-21.50; ⏲6-10pm) You can watch Brick's chefs cooking risotto, steaks and gourmet burgers – not only from the street-level dining room but also from the 1st-floor space, which has a glass floor directly above the open kitchen. There are pavement tables out front, but in summer the best seats are on the roof terrace.

★**Restaurant ML** GASTRONOMY €€€
(☑023-512 39 10; www.mlinhaarlem.nl; Klokhuisplein 9; mains €20.50-29.50, 4-/5-/6-/7-course menus €55/65/75/80; ⏲6-9.30pm Tue-Sat) A glass-roofed courtyard and an art-gallery-

style dining room at design hotel ML (p115) are the setting for some of Haarlem's finest dining. Intricate Michelin-starred dishes might include scallops with pea and shallot pesto, langoustine with chicory and apple emulsion, veal and lamb's brain with rosemary fondant, and Texel duck with North Sea crab. Its 12-seat chef's table directly overlooks the kitchen.

At the front of the building, ML's casual bistro, with a 200-seat terrace overlooking Grote Kerk van St Bavo, serves food all day.

Drinking & Nightlife

★ **DeDakkas** ROOFTOP BAR
(www.dedakkas.nl; Parkeergarage de Kamp, 6th fl, De Witstraat; ⏲9am-11pm Tue, Wed & Sun, to midnight Thu-Sat; 📶) From the ground, it looks like any other multistorey car park, but taking the lift to the 6th floor brings you out at this fabulous 2018-opened rooftop with a greenhouse-style glass cafe and timber-decked terrace with sweeping views over Haarlem (you can see Amsterdam on a clear day). Regular events include barbecues, cinema screenings, yoga, DJs and live gigs.

★ **Jopenkerk** BREWERY
(www.jopenkerk.nl; Gedempte Voldersgracht 2; ⏲brewery & cafe 10am-1am, restaurant noon-3pm & 5.30-11pm; 👪) Haarlem's most atmospheric place to drink is this independent brewery inside a stained-glass-windowed 1910 church. Enjoy brews such as citrusy Hopen, fruity Lente Bier and chocolatey Koyt along with Dutch bar snacks – *bitterballen* (meat-filled croquettes) and cheeses – beneath the gleaming copper vats. Or head to the mezzanine for dishes made from locally sourced, seasonal ingredients and Jopenkerk's beers (pairings available).

Uiltje Brewing Co BREWERY
(☎023-844 63 95; www.uiltjecraftbeer.com; Bingerweg 25; ⏲noon-8pm Thu, to 10pm Fri & Sat, to 6pm Sun) At its brewery 4km east of Haarlem's centre, Uiltje has a lively bar area and sunny courtyard where you can try its 10 draught and two cask beers, and an attached bottle shop for stocking up. Regular events include bonfire nights, live music gigs and barbecues. It also runs 40-minute behind-the-scenes tours (English available, per person €12.50 including two beers).

Look out for signature brews like Miss Hooter (IPA), Cry Baby (Berliner Weisse beer), Peat the Scotchman (smoked ale) and the Christmas Tree is on Fire (oatmeal stout).

It's a 10-minute bike ride from central Haarlem; alternatively there's a **city-centre tap room** (www.uiltjecraftbeer.com; Zijlstraat 18; ⏲5-11pm Mon-Wed, noon-midnight Thu, to 2am Fri & Sat, to 10pm Sun).

Entertainment

Philharmonie Haarlem CONCERT VENUE
(☎023-512 12 12; www.theater-haarlem.nl; Lange Begijnestraat 11; ⏲box office 10am-4pm Mon-Fri) Fronted by a striking glass facade, Haarlem's premier concert venue presents a diverse program of classical music (such as the Netherlands' chamber orchestra, the Nederlands Kamerorkest) through to large pop concerts (eg 'shock-rocker' Marilyn Manson).

Patronaat LIVE MUSIC
(☎023-517 58 58; www.patronaat.nl; Zijlsingel 2; ⏲hours vary) Haarlem's top music and dance club attracts bands with banging tunes, from country to punk. Events in this cavernous venue usually start around 9pm.

Shopping

★ **Grote Markt** MARKET
(Grote Markt; ⏲10am-2pm Mon & Sat) Haarlem is at its liveliest during its regular Monday and, especially, Saturday market, when its namesake square fills with stalls selling fresh produce, cheese, preserves, spices, nuts and ready-to-eat Dutch and international snacks, as well as vintage and new clothes, bags, accessories and antiques.

Information

The **tourist office** (VVV; ☎023-531 73 25; www.haarlemmarketing.nl; Grote Markt 2; ⏲9.30am-5.30pm Mon-Fri, to 5pm Sat, noon-4pm Sun Apr-Sep, 1-5.30pm Mon, from 9.30am Tue-Fri, 10am-5pm Sat Oct-Mar) sells discount museum tickets.

Getting There & Around

BICYCLE

Bicycle routes link Haarlem with Amsterdam, 20km east. Given the heavy urbanisation in the area, this is not exactly a pastoral ride; more bucolic routes follow the coast north and south of Haarlem.

BUS

Bus 300 runs between the bus station behind Haarlem's train station and Schiphol airport (50 minutes, every 15 minutes).

WORTH A TRIP

MARKET MADNESS IN BEVERWIJK

Every weekend up to 80,000 bargain hunters flock to the covered De Bazaar Beverwijk (www.debazaar.nl; Montageweg 35, Beverwijk; ⊙ market 9.30am-7pm Sat & Sun, food hall to 9pm), one of Europe's largest ethnic markets with 2000-plus vendors and 69 food stalls. Piled high are Arabian spices, Turkish rugs, garments, handcrafted ornaments and much more. The liveliest of the three biggest halls is the Zwarte Markt, an enormous flea market with a carnival atmosphere.

Parking (per day €5) becomes a problem after 9.30am. Trains run from Amsterdam Centraal (€5.90, 40 minutes, every 30 minutes) and Haarlem (€3.20, 20 minutes, up to four hourly) to Beverwijk, from where it's a 1km walk or three-minute trip aboard bus 76 (every 30 minutes).

TRAIN

Haarlem's 1908 art-nouveau station is served by frequent trains linking Amsterdam and Rotterdam.

TO	PRICE (€)	TIME (MIN)	FREQUENCY (PER HOUR)
Alkmaar	6.90	35	4
Amsterdam	4.30	15	4-8
Den Haag	8.50	40	4
Rotterdam	12.40	60	2-4

Zaanse Schans

☑ 075 / POP 8870

People plan to come to Zaanse Schans for an hour but find they stay for several. On the banks of the Zaan river, this open-air museum of a village is a picturesque place to see windmills in action. While it has a touristy element, the six operating mills are completely authentic and run with enthusiasm and love. Visitors can explore the windmills at their leisure, seeing firsthand the vast moving parts that make these devices a combination of sailing ship and Rube Goldberg contraption (an intricate, deliberately overcomplicated machine designed to perform a simple task).

⊙ Sights & Activities

★ **Zaanse Schans Windmills**   WINDMILLS
(☑ 075-681 00 00; www.dezaanseschans.nl; Kalverringdijk; per windmill adult/child €4.50/2; ⊙ most windmills 9am-5pm Apr-Oct, hours vary Nov-Mar) The working, inhabited village Zaanse Schans functions as a windmill gallery on the Zaan river. Popular with tourists, its mills are completely authentic and operated with enthusiasm and love. You can explore the windmills at your own pace, seeing the vast moving parts firsthand. Individual windmill hours and days vary.

Artists will love the mill with paint pigments for sale – you can see the actual materials used in producing Renaissance masterpieces turned into powders.

The other buildings have been brought here from all over the country to re-create a 17th-century community. There's an early Albert Heijn market, a cheese maker, and a popular clog factory (which has a surprisingly interesting museum) that turns out wooden shoes as if grinding keys. The engaging pewter-smith will explain the story behind dozens of tiny figures while the soft metal sets in the moulds.

Once you've finished exploring the village, take a **boat** (www.voetveerzaandijk.nl; Kalverringdijk; adult/child €1/free; ⊙ on demand 10am-5pm Apr-Sep) across the Zaan river.

Zaans Museum   MUSEUM
(☑ 075-681 00 00; www.zaansmuseum.nl; Schansend 7; adult/child €10/6; ⊙ 9am-5pm Apr-Sep, from 10am Oct-Mar) The impressive Zaans Museum traces windmill history from the very first mills and covers Dutch culture and costume; there's also a painting by Monet, who painted the Zaan region multiple times.

❶ Information

Zaanse Schans Information Desk (☑ 075-681 00 00; www.zaanseschans.nl; ⊙ 9am-5pm Apr-Sep, from 10am Oct-Mar) At the Zaans Museum.

❶ Getting There & Around

BICYCLE

From Amsterdam, a 22km cycling route meanders through farmlands and lakes once it escapes the big smoke.

On the eastern side of the Zaandijk Zaanse Schans train station, **Fietsverhuur Zaanse Schans** (☑ 06 2674 0840; www.zaanseschans bikerent.nl; Stationsstraat, Zaandijk; bike hire per hour €5; ⊙ 9am-6pm Apr-Oct) hires bikes for a spin through Zaanse Schans and surrounding countryside.

BOAT

The **Zaanferry** (☎ 06 3330 0022; www.zaanferry.com; Kalverringdijk; Amsterdam–Zaanse Schans one-way/return per person €10/15; ☻ up to 10 sailings per day) service links Zaanse Schans with De Rijterkade, at the northwestern dock at Amsterdam Centraal Station. Journey time is two hours one way, with four stops en route. Prebook tickets online.

TRAIN

From Amsterdam Centraal Station (€3.20, 18 minutes, four per hour) take the train towards Alkmaar and get off at Zaandijk Zaanse Schans – it's a well-signposted 1.5km walk to Zaanse Schans.

Waterland

Time moves slowly in this rural area that starts just 9km north of Amsterdam. Fields of green are watched by herons standing motionless alongside watery furrows amid surrounding farmland. It's glorious cycling country, with plenty to see, including the picturesque towns of Monnickendam and Marken.

Monnickendam

☎ 0299 / POP 9830

Monnickendam gained its name from the Benedictines, who built a dam here, and traces its roots back to 1356. Since the demise of its fishing industry, it has transformed itself into an upmarket port for yachts and sailors.

The beautiful old fishing trawlers mainly operate pleasure cruises. History still pervades the narrow lanes around the shipyards.

☉ Sights & Activities

Along the main street, Noordeinde, old brick houses tilt at crazy angles as they sink into the soggy ground.

As you stroll the lanes, look for gable stones on buildings – many have a story to tell. The one at Kerkstraat 32 dates to 1620, the one at Kerkstraat 12 tells of the five Jews successfully hidden in the building for the duration of WWII.

The harbour is filled with splendid old *tjalken, botters* and *klippers,* historic boats available for hire (as are skippers if need be); the tourist office (p120) can provide information.

Speeltoren HISTORIC BUILDING

(☎ 0299-652 203; www.despeeltoren.nl; Noordeinde 4; adult/child €4.50/3; ☻ 1-5pm Mon, from 11am Tue-Sun Jul & Aug, Tue-Sun Apr-Jun, Sep & Oct, Sat & Sun Nov-Mar) Monnickendam's trademark building is the 15th-century Speeltoren, an elegant, Italianate clock tower and former town hall. The tower's 17th-century glockenspiel (carillon) – Europe's oldest – performs at 11am and noon on Saturday, when its four mechanical knights prance in the open wooden window twice before retiring. Inside the clock tower, the Museum De Speeltoren covers Waterland's past and present, and allows you to see the amazing old mechanism that powers the clock.

Grote Kerk CHURCH

(Sint Nicolaaskerk; www.grotekerkmonnickendam.nl; De Zarken 2; ☻ 11am-4pm Tue-Sat, from 1pm Sun Apr-Oct, hours vary Nov-Feb) The Gothic Grote Kerk, on the southern outskirts of town, is renowned for its triple nave, tower galleries and a dazzling oak choir screen dating from the 16th century. Its main organ, dating from 1780, is also known as the *zwaluwnestorgel* ('swallow-nest organ') due to its location against the wall of the tower.

🛏 Sleeping & Eating

★ **Posthoorn** BOUTIQUE HOTEL €€

(☎ 0299-654 598; www.posthoorn.eu; Noordeinde 43; s/d/ste from €99/135/159; P 🛜) This beautifully restored building dates to 1697 but the owners suspect it might be older. The 12 romantic rooms blend contemporary and traditional styles, with antique furniture and 17th- and 18th-century paintings of Waterland's landscapes. Kids under eight aren't permitted. The long-standing Michelin-starred restaurant (☎ 0299-654 598; www.posthoorn.eu; Noordeinde 43; mains €33.75-38.50, tasting menus €69-99, with paired wines €111-168; ☻ 6-9.30pm

---

❶ WATERLAND TICKET

If you're planning a day trip by bus north of Amsterdam around the Waterland region, including Monnickendam and Marken, as well as Edam, Volendam and Hoorn, save money by purchasing a Waterland Dagkaart (Waterland Ticket; adult/child €10/2.50). This great-value pass allows a day's unlimited travel on buses 312, 314, 315 and 316. Buy it online at www.ovshop.nl or from tourist offices.

HAARLEM & NORTH HOLLAND WATERLAND

Tue-Sat, noon-2pm & 6-9pm Sun; 🛜) celebrates local produce. Book rooms and courtyard dining in advance on weekends.

Theetuin Overleek   CAFE €
(📞0299-652 735; www.theetuinoverleek.nl; Overleek 6a; dishes €4-10.50, high tea per person €29.50; ⊙10am-5pm Wed-Mon Jul & Aug, Wed-Sun May, Jun & Sep, Sat & Sun Oct) At the water's edge 3km west of town, this seasonally opening wooden teahouse is a charming spot to indulge in high tea (reservations essential), but you can just drop by for light bites like sandwiches and cakes. It also rents electric boats (per two hours €45, day €95) to explore the waterways and can pack picnic lunches (per person €12.50).

🛍 Shopping

Avontuur in Miniatuur   TOYS
(📞0299-652 085; www.avontuurinminiatuur.nl; Noordeinde 76; ⊙10am-5pm Fri & Sat, by appointment Sun-Thu) Dollhouses (and everything you need to furnish, decorate and populate them) are the speciality of this miniature wonderland. When you visit, you may see craftspeople sitting around the shop's large table creating the tiny pieces (many, though not all, are handmade here).

ℹ️ Information

Waterland's small but excellent regional **tourist office** (VVV; 📞0299-820 046; www.vvv-waterland.nl; Zuideinde 2; ⊙10am-5pm Apr-Oct, 11am-2pm Mon-Sat Nov-Mar) can recommend walks, obscure attractions and almost anything fun on the water.

ℹ️ Getting There & Around

Cycling paths follow rural dykes along the IJsselmeer north to Volendam (7km) and Edam (9km). Marken is 8.5km east, while Amsterdam is 15km southwest.

Ber Koning (📞0299-651 267; www.berkonig.nl; Noordeinde 12; per day €12.50; ⊙9am-8pm Tue-Sat Apr-Sep, to 6pm Tue-Fri, to 4pm Sat Oct-Mar) hires bicycles.

Buses 312, 314 and 315 (20 minutes, up to four per hour), covered on the Waterland Ticket (p119), link the centre of Monnickendam to Amsterdam Centraal Station.

Marken

📞0299 / POP 1810

Across Gouwzee Bay lies scenic Marken with a small and determined population. It was an isolated island in the Zuiderzee until 1957

when a causeway linked up with the mainland, effectively turning it into a museumpiece village. However, it still manages to exude a fishing-village vibe (well-used wooden shoes sit outside houses), and the carfree centre helps keep at least some of the crowds at bay.

⊙ Sights

The colourful Kerkbuurt in the village's northeast is the most authentic area, with tarred or painted houses raised on pilings to escape the Zuiderzee floods. The Havenbuurt harbourside area is home to most of the souvenir shops and restaurants.

Marker Museum   MUSEUM
(📞0299-601 904; www.markermuseum.nl; Kerkbuurt 44; adult/child €3/1.50; ⊙10am-5pm Mon-Sat, noon-4pm Sun late Mar–Sep, from 11am Mon-Sat, from noon Sun Oct) A row of eel-smoking houses in the Kerkbuurt area have been converted into the Marker Museum, which delves into Marken's history and includes the re-created interior of a fisher's home, with a wealth of personal odds and ends. It sells a walking-tour brochure (€2), which guides you around the stout wooden structures that line the intricate pattern of lanes.

🛏 Sleeping & Eating

The few restaurants here are at the harbour. Opposite the car park, Marken's supermarket has staples.

Hof Van Marken   HOTEL €€
(📞0299-601 300; www.hofvanmarken.nl; Buurt II 15; s/d from €89/99; 🛜) Marken's only hotel has big beds, fluffy pillows and heavenly duvets. The seven cosy, pastel-hued rooms reflect this region where land and water blend in the mist. Its restaurant serves fresh, stylish takes on local produce and seafood (mains €12.50). Book ahead for both.

ℹ️ Getting There & Away

If you're driving, you'll need to park in the mandatory open-air car park at the village entrance (per car per day €4.50, plus €0.50 per person).

BICYCLE

The 8km ride along the dyke from Monnickendam has moody sea views.

BOAT

The **Marken Express Ferry** (📞0299-363 331; www.markenexpress.nl; Havenbuurt; adult/child one-way €8.50/4.25, return €12.50/6.25, bicycle €1.50/2.50; ⊙10.15am-7.30pm Mar-Sep)

DON'T MISS

THE WORLD'S BIGGEST FLOWER AUCTION

Aalsmeer is home to Bloemenveiling Aalsmeer (www.royalfloraholland.com; Legmeerdijk 313; adult/child €7.50/4.50; ⊙7-11am Mon-Wed & Fri, to 9am Thu), the world's biggest *bloemenveiling* (flower auction), run by vast flower conglomerate Royal FloraHolland. Get to the viewing gallery before 9am to catch the best action as the flower-laden carts go to Dutch auction, with a huge clock showing the starting price. From the starting bell, the hand drops until a deal is struck.

Take bus 357 from Amsterdam Centraal Station to the Hoofdingang stop (45 minutes, frequent, from 4.59am).

Monday is busiest, Thursday quietest.

The one-million-sq-metre space sees some 90 million flowers and two million plants change hands every day of operation. You can take an aromatic self-guided tour on a 3km-long wheelchair-accessible elevated walkway above the frenetic warehouse floor, overlooking the choreography of flower-laden forklifts and trolleys. Along the route, signboards with push-button audio recordings interpret the action; you can also download a free audioguide from the website.

The route passes windows where you can peek into the auction rooms and see blooms being prepped for display as the carts go to auction. More and more transactions are taking place online, so catch it while it's still here.

---

makes the 45-minute crossing from Marken to Volendam every 45 minutes.

BUS

Bus 315 links Marken with Amsterdam (40 minutes, hourly) via Monnickendam (10 minutes); it's covered by the Waterland Ticket (p119).

Volendam

☑0299 / POP 28,490

The former fishing port of Volendam is certainly quaint, with its rows of wooden houses and locals who don traditional dress for church and festive events, but the harbour is awash with kitschy souvenir shops, dress-up-in-Dutch-traditional-costume photo booths, a virtual-reality walk through old Volendam, a huge cheese shop/museum, fish stands, frites stands and rapacious seagulls. On weekends it swarms with visitors.

◉ Sights

Volendams Museum   MUSEUM
(☑0299-369 258; www.volendamsmuseum.nl; Zeestraat 41; adult/child €4/2; ⊙10am-5pm) Local culture is covered at Volendam's history museum with traditional costumes, prints, paintings of harbour scenes and even a cramped ship's sleeping quarters, but this place is really devoted to cigar fans: some 11 million bands are plastered on its walls.

🛏 Sleeping & Eating

A couple of large tourist hotels are located on the waterfront but most people visit as a day trip from Amsterdam, 25km to the southwest.

★Smit Bokkum   SEAFOOD €€
(☑029-936 33 73; www.smitbokkum.nl; Slobbeland 19; mains €15.50-27.50; ⊙10am-9pm Tue-Sun; 🔊) Now run by the sixth generation, Smit Bokkum has been smoking local seafood including eel, sea bass, oysters, mackerel and cockles since 1856. Try its aromatic house specialities at its restaurant, which opens to a sunny harbourside terrace, or reserve ahead for a 20-minute guided smokehouse tour (€4.50, including a tasting). It's 800m southwest of Volendam's main tourist strip.

ℹ Information

Regional accommodation information and cycling maps are available at Volendam's busy **tourist office** (VVV; ☑0299-363 747; www.vvv-volendam.nl; Zeestraat 37; ⊙10am-5pm Mon-Sat, 11am-3pm Sun Apr-Oct, to 4pm Sun Nov-Mar).

ℹ Getting There & Away

Bicycle routes head along the Zuiderzee to Monnickendam, 8km south, and Amsterdam, 23km southwest. Edam is a quick zip 3.5km northwest.

The **Marken Express Ferry** (☑0299-363 331; www.markenexpress.nl; Haven; adult/child one-way €8.50/4.25, return €12.50/6.25, bicycle €1.50/2.50; ⊙9.45am-6.45pm Mar-Sep) makes the 30-minute-long crossing from Volendam to Marken every 45 minutes.

Bus 316 links Volendam to Amsterdam (25 minutes, four per hour) and Edam (10 minutes, four per hour); they're covered by the Waterland Ticket (p119).

Edam

📞 0299 / POP 7380

Once a renowned whaling port – in its 17th-century heyday it had 33 shipyards that built the fleet of legendary admiral Michiel De Ruyter – this scenic little town is another of North Holland's treasures. With its shipping warehouses, quiet cobblestone streets, hand-operated drawbridges and picture-perfect canals, it's enchanting for a stroll.

👁 Sights & Activities

Edams Museum   MUSEUM

(📞 0299-372 644; www.edamsmuseum.nl; museum Damplein 8, annex Damplein 1; adult/child €5/3; ⊙ museum 10am-4.30pm Tue-Sat, from 1pm Sun Apr–late Oct, annex 1-4.30pm Tue-Sun Apr–late Oct) Furnishings, porcelain and silverware spread over three cramped floors of Edam's oldest building, dating from 1540. Its floating cellar is a remarkable pantry that rises and falls with the river's swell to reduce stress on the structure above.

Across the canal in an annex in the 1737 town hall, you'll find more exhibits; among some famous paintings there is an unknown artist's *Tall Girl,* depicting a 9' 3" (2.8m) woman (allegedly the tallest ever).

Gestam   FACTORY

(📞 0299-372 376; www.gestam.com; Voorhaven 127; ⊙ 8.30am-4pm Sat) FREE Sample 30 different cheeses at the wonderful and barely commercial Gestam, a warehouse for regional producers established in 1916.

Grote Kerk   CHURCH

(www.grotekerkedam.nl; Grote Kerkstraat 59; tower €2; ⊙ 1.30-5pm early Apr–late Oct) The 15th-century Grote Kerk bears witness to the vagaries of Dutch weather. Its 32 dazzling stained-glass windows bearing coats of arms and historical scenes were added after 1602, when the church burnt to a cinder after a lightning strike. Its tower can be climbed for views of the town's red rooftops. Check the online agenda for regular concerts.

Kaasmarkt   HISTORIC SITE

(Cheese Market; www.kaasmarktedam.nl; Jan Nieuwenhuizenplein; ⊙ 10.30am-12.30pm Wed Jul–mid-Aug) In the 16th century Willem van Oranje bestowed on Edam the right to hold a Kaasmarkt, which was the town's economic anchor right through to the 1920s. At its peak 250,000 rounds of cheese were sold here every year. Edam's weekly summer cheese market is smaller than the one in Alkmaar (p123) but equally touristy.

Fluisterbootjes   BOATING

(Whisper Boats; 📞 0299-371 664; www.fluisterbootverhuur-edam.nl; VVV, Damplein 1; boat hire per hour €24; ⊙ 9am-5pm Apr–mid-Oct) Glide through Edam's canals in a small electric boat that you pilot yourself. Boats seat up to seven people; no licence is required. Pay and pick up the key from the tourist office .

🛏 Sleeping & Eating

L'Auberge Dam Hotel   BOUTIQUE HOTEL €€

(📞 0299-371 766; www.damhotel.nl; Keizersgracht 1; d/f from €125/175; 🛜 🐾) In the heart of Edam, this art- and antique-filled hotel makes a romantic retreat. Some of its

---

DON'T MISS

UNESCO SPA RETREAT

Built in 1912, **Fort Resort Beemster** (📞 0299-682 200; www.fortresortbeemster.nl; Nekkerweg 24, LC Zuidoostbeemster; d/ste from €155/210; 🅿 🛜 🐾), a former fort and prison 10km west of Edam ,was converted a century later to a stunning spa hotel. Original features include lamps, steel doors and reinforced windows. Some of its 16 rooms are in the gatehouse; those in the fort itself open to patios overlooking the lake. Contemporary Dutch cuisine at its two restaurants is organic.

Spa facilities (generally clothing-free) include Finnish, wood-fired and Himalayan salt-cave saunas, and Turkish steam baths, as well as indoor and outdoor pools.

Rainwater purified from the fort's sand-filled roof is reused in the spa; its waste water is used for underfloor heating.

The fort is part of the Unesco World Heritage–inscribed Stelling van Amsterdam (Defence Line of Amsterdam), a 135km-long ring of fortifications around Amsterdam that takes in 42 forts between 10km and 15km from the city's centre.

11 rooms are on the small side, but that's balanced by huge beds and spiffing contemporary bathrooms. Two family rooms sleep three and four people respectively. Its grand cafe spills on to the main square.

De Fortuna   DUTCH €€
(☏0299-371 671; www.fortuna-edam.nl; Spuistraat 3; mains lunch €6-19.75, dinner €23.50, 3-/4-/5-course menu €36/43.50/49.50; ⊘kitchen noon-3pm & 6-9.30pm mid-Mar–Sep, to 9pm Oct–mid-Mar; 🛜) Amid oil paintings, bay windows and buffed leather seats, this charming restaurant at the De Fortuna (s/d/tr/f from €87.50/107.50/157.50/177.50; 🛜) hotel serves light lunches (gourmet sandwiches on artisan bread, grilled seafood, croquettes and salads). Dinner steps it up with dishes like Waterland beef carpaccio, roast guinea fowl with creamed asparagus, and blackberry crumble with Edam yoghurt ice cream. Tables also fill its waterside terrace.

ℹ️ Information

Tourist office (VVV; ☏0299-315 125; www.vvv-edam.nl; Damplein 1; ⊘10am-5pm Mon-Sat, 10.30am-4.30pm Sun Apr-Oct, noon-4pm Mon, 10am-3pm Tue-Thu, 10am-4pm Fri & Sat Nov-Mar) Inside the splendid 18th-century town hall – part of the Edams Museum (p122).

ℹ️ Getting There & Around

BICYCLE
Cycling routes travel north to Hoorn, southeast to Volendam and west to Waterland. The many IJsselmeer dykes surrounding Edam make for excellent riding.

Ton Tweewielers (☏0299-371 922; www.tontweewielers.nl; Schepenmakersdijk 6; bike/electric-bike hire per day €10/24.50; ⊘8.30am-6pm Mon-Sat, 9.30am-5pm Sun Apr–mid Sep, by appointment mid-Sep–Mar) hires bikes including kids' bikes and tandems, as well as trailers and helmets. Delivery and pick-up can be arranged.

BUS
Buses 312 and 314 link Edam with Amsterdam (35 minutes, six per hour) via Volendam (20 minutes); they're covered on a Waterland Ticket (p119).

Alkmaar

☏072 / POP 107,822
On Friday mornings from April to early September, Alkmaar's canal-ringed centre fills with day trippers eager to catch a glimpse of

DYKE-SIDE BIKE RIDES

Midway between Alkmaar (17km southeast) and Edam (17km west), the village of De Rijp on the N244 is at the south end of several good drives and rides along dykes that give an excellent feel for just how low the land is compared to the waterways coursing between the earthen walls.

The Oostdijk–Westdijk road travels north 6km to the hamlet of Schermerhorn on the N243. Just west, another narrow dyke road runs parallel and meanders past several windmills. Watch out for wandering sheep.

You can hire a bike at Rent a Scooter Alkmaar (☏072-562 85 30; www.ras-alkmaar.nl; Molenbuurt 21; bikes/electric bikes/scooters per 24hr €15/40/55; ⊘9am-5pm Mon-Sat).

the city's famous cheese market. It's a genuine spectacle but even if it's not on, the town is an engaging place to visit any time of year.

The city holds a special place in Dutch hearts as the first town, in 1573, to repel occupying Spanish troops; locals opened the locks and flooded the area with seawater, forcing the perplexed invaders to retreat. The victory won the town weighing rights, which laid the foundation for its cheese market.

👁️ Sights

Waaggebouw   HISTORIC BUILDING
(Weigh House; Waagplein 2; ⊘carillon 6.30pm & 7.30pm Thu, 11am & noon Fri, noon & 1pm Sat mid-Apr–mid-Sep) Built as a chapel in the 14th century, the Waaggebouw was pressed into service as a weigh house two centuries later. This handsome building houses the tourist office (p126) and the Hollands Kaasmuseum (Dutch Cheese Museum; ☏072-562 85 30; www.kaasmuseum.nl; Waagplein 2; adult/child €5/2; ⊘10am-4pm Mon, Thu & Sat, from 9am Fri, 1-3.30pm Sun Feb-Oct, 10am-4pm Sat Nov-Mar) (Dutch Cheese Museum). The mechanical tower carillon springs to life with jousting knights.

Kaasmarkt   MARKET
(Cheese Market; https://kaasmarkt-alkmaar.business.site; Waagplein; ⊘10am-1pm Fri Apr–early Sep) On Friday mornings in season, waxed rounds of kaas (cheese) are ceremoniously

Alkmaar

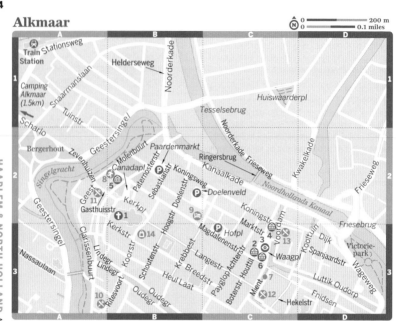

stacked on the main square. Soon, porters appear in colourful cheese-guild hats, and dealers in white smocks insert a hollow rod to extract a cheese sample, and sniff and crumble to check fat and moisture content. Once deals are struck, the porters whisk the cheeses on wooden sledges to the old cheese scale. It's primarily for show but as living relics go it's both fascinating and entertaining.

Stedelijk Museum
MUSEUM

(072-548 97 89; www.stedelijkmuseumalkmaar. nl; Canadaplein 1; adult/child €12/free; ⊙11am-5pm Tue-Sun) The Stedelijk Museum's collection of oil paintings by Dutch Masters, including impressive life-sized portraits of Alkmaar nobles, is alone worth the entry fee. Other works show the city in post–Golden Age decline; sombre scenes of almswomen caring for the poor recall how the church's role grew as trade declined. Modern works on display include Charley Toorop's odd oil painting of the Alkmaar cheese market; her cheese-bearers with grotesque features remain controversial.

Grote Kerk
CHURCH

(072-514 07 07; www.grotekerk-alkmaar.nl; Kerkplein; ⊙11am-5pm Tue-Sun mid-Apr–early Oct, by appointment early Oct–mid-Apr) Alkmaar's Grote Kerk is renowned for its organs. The most famous is the little 'Swallow Organ' (1511) in the north ambulatory. The 17th-century organ built by Jaco van Campen dominates the nave. Organ recitals – which will thrill any fan of 1930s horror movies – take place on Wednesday evenings and at noon on days when the church is open. The pastel stained-glass windows bathe the interior in spring colour.

Nationaal Biermuseum
MUSEUM

(072-511 38 01; www.biermuseum.nl; Houttil 1; adult/child €5/2.50; ⊙10.30am-4.30pm Mon-Sat Jun-Aug, 1-4pm Mon-Sat Sep-May) Housed in the atmospheric old De Boom brewery, the Nationaal Biermuseum has a decent collection of beer-making equipment and wax dummies showing how the suds were made. The video of Dutch beer commercials since the 1950s will have you in stitches. Admission includes a beer (or soft drink) in its sociable bar (p126).

Tours

Grachtenrondvaart Alkmaar
CRUISE

(06 5371 4608; www.rondvaartalkmaar.nl; Mient; adult/child €6/4.50; ⊙hourly 11am-5pm daily May-Sep, Mon-Sat Apr & Oct) Scenic 45-minute canal tours with multilingual commentary depart from Mient, near the Waag. En route you

Alkmaar

pass under 22 bridges, some so low that passengers have to duck to avoid them.

🛏 Sleeping

Alkmaar makes an easy day trip from Amsterdam, 40km to the southeast, but if you want to stay, there are several good hotels in the city centre and more in the surrounding countryside.

Camping Alkmaar CAMPGROUND €
(☏ 072-511 69 24; www.campingalkmaar.nl; Bergerweg 201; campsites €25-30, cabins €50; 🅿 🛜) This year-round campground lies in a pleasant copse convenient to the ring road, 1km northwest of the train station. Tent sites are sheltered; wooden cabins (without bathrooms) sleep two people. There's a kids' playground and ping-pong tables. Take bus 6 to Hogeschool (10 minutes).

Grand Hotel HOTEL €€
(☏ 072-576 09 70; www.grandhotelalkmaar.nl; Gedempte Nieuwesloot 36; d/ste from €100/170; 🛜) A neo-Gothic post office built by Cornelis Hendrik Peters, a student of Pierre Cuypers (who designed Amsterdam's Centraal Station and Rijksmuseum), in 1877 now houses this central hotel. Its 20 rooms have contemporary charcoal-toned decor; some overlook the old town, while others face the courtyard. Higher-priced rooms have minibars, coffee machines and jacuzzis; one has its own sauna.

🍴 Eating

Restaurants surround the Waagplein and Bierkade quay. Away from the cheese-market madness, Koorstraat and Ritesvoort have many excellent bistros and cafes.

De Vlaminck FAST FOOD €
(www.devlaminck.nl; Voordam 2; frites from €2.50; ⊙ 11am-7pm Fri-Wed, to 9.15pm Thu) The hand-cut fries are superb at this storefront counter, as are the 17 different sauces, including peanut, *sambal oelek* (Indonesian chilli sauce), garlic and tomato ketchup. Take your paper cone to the benches in front alongside the canal.

Bistro de 13 Balcken BISTRO €€
(☏ 072-520 00 79; www.13balcken.nl; Zevenhuizen 11; mains lunch €8-18, dinner €21-26; ⊙ 3-9.30pm Mon, Wed & Thu, noon-10pm Fri & Sat, 2-9.30pm Sun; 🛜) Dutch cheeses take centre stage at this corner bistro, both at lunch (on gourmet sandwiches such as goat's cheese with Alkmaar-smoked ham and pickled beetroot) and at dinner (Friesland blue-cheese panna cotta). Don't miss its traditional *spekkoek* (layered spice cake with blackberry sauce and cardamom ice cream) for dessert.

Cafe Restaurant De Buren INTERNATIONAL €€
(☏ 072-512 03 08; www.restaurant-deburen.nl; Mient 37; mains €15.50-28; ⊙ 10am-10pm Mon-Sat, from 11am Sun; 🛜) Outside tables at this vintage cafe/restaurant stretch along the canal and wrap around to the old fish market, while inside, enjoy works by Dutch sculptor Ron Moret. The global menu spans dishes such as coq au vin *blanc* (chicken thighs in white wine) and steak-frites with pepper-cognac sauce to pumpkin ravioli, and smoked spare ribs with corn on the cob.

Abby's EUROPEAN €€
(☏ 072-511 11 11; www.restaurantabbys.nl; Ritesvoort 60; sandwiches €6-10, mains €14.50-27.50; ⊙ 11am-10pm) In the shadow of an old windmill, Abby's has cool jazz inside and cool breezes

WORTH A TRIP

A WATERY DETOUR

The waterlogged area north of Alkmaar was once home to 15,000 tiny, yet productive, farms, each one an island, whose farmers tended their crops by rowboat. At **Museum BroekerVeiling** (Broeker Auction Museum; ☑ 226-313 807; www.broekerveiling.nl; Museumweg 2, Broek op Langedijk; adult/child incl audioguide €17.50/9.25; ⊙ 10am-5pm Jul & Aug, closed Mon Sep-Jun), you can tour the auction house where farmers arrived with boatloads of produce then waited – afloat – inside, until they could paddle through an auction room where wholesale grocery buyers would bid on the produce. Built in 1877, it sits on 1900 piles. Prices include auction-house and museum entry as well as a boat ride.

On its exterior, the museum shows some of the 15,000 islands. Inside, the exhibits on how the farms worked are a combination of high-tech wizardry and old-fashioned mechanised gadgets. It runs 45-minute tours around some of the 200 surviving island plots nearby. On the grounds you can see some of the traditional crops in situ. There's a fine little cafe.

Museum BroekerVeiling is 8.5km northeast of Alkmaar. From Monday to Friday, bus 10 (30 minutes, hourly) runs to the Museumweg stop; on weekends, take bus 9 (30 minutes, hourly) to the Laansloot stop and walk 750m east. A 9km bike route from Alkmaar follows canals and passes through the tiny old village of Sint Pancras.

outside on the terrace. Soups, salads and sandwiches are the mainstays at lunch, but dinner has more adventurous offerings: tournedos (small, round pieces of tenderloin beef) with roast beetroot, asparagus ravioli with shaved fennel and black truffle, and lime-marinated sea bass with citrus pesto.

Drinking & Nightlife

De Boom   BROWN CAFE
(www.proeflokaaldeboom.nl; Houttil 1; ⊙ 2pm-midnight Sun & Mon, from 1pm Tue & Wed, 1pm-2am Thu-Sat) Unchanged since the 1930s, the timber-panelled pub on the ground floor of the Nationaal Biermuseum (p124) lives up to its location. In summer, you can enjoy the fine selection of brews at seats on a moored old canal boat. There's live jazz on the last Thursday of the month.

☆ Entertainment

Theater De Vest   PERFORMING ARTS
(☑ 072-548 98 88; www.theaterdevest.nl; Canadaplein 2; ⊙ box office noon-4pm Mon-Sat, 90min before performance Sun) The centre for Alkmaar's highbrow entertainment, De Vest runs the gamut from traditional plays and puppet shows to avant-garde dance. In summer Canadaplein turns into a stage for the performing-arts festival Zomer op het plein (Summer on the Square).

Shopping

Langestraat is the pedestrianised shopping street with mainstream stores. Laat has a more interesting and diverse collection.

Kaan's Kaashandel   CHEESE
(www.kaanskaas.nl; Koorstraat 11; ⊙ 1-6pm Mon, 9am-6pm Tue-Fri, 8.30am-5pm Sat) Fourth-generation-run Kaan's Kaashandel has a splendid selection of Dutch cheeses, including some 30 varieties of Edam. Cheeses purchased here can be vacuum-packed for free.

ⓘ Information

Tourist Office (VVV; ☑ 072-511 42 84; www.vvvhartvannoordholland.nl; Waagplein 2; ⊙ 10am-5pm Apr-Sep, closed Sun Oct-Mar)

ⓘ Getting There & Away

BICYCLE
Bicycle routes run 40km north to Den Helder alongside bulb fields, 33km south to Haarlem, 45km southeast to Amsterdam and 26km east to Hoorn.

TRAIN
The train station is 1km northwest of the centre.

TO	FARE (€)	TIME (MIN)	FREQUENCY (PER HOUR)
Amsterdam	7.60	35	4
Den Helder	8.10	35	2
Haarlem	6.90	35	4
Hoorn	5.10	25	2

Hoorn

0229 / POP 72,707

With a magnificent horn-shaped harbour, for which it's named, a string of museums and some outstanding restaurants, Hoorn attracts plenty of skippers and weekenders. It was once the capital of West Friesland and, thanks to the presence of the Dutch merchant fleet, a mighty trading city. As a member of the league of Seven Cities, it helped free the country from the Spanish who occupied the town from 1569 to 1573.

Hoorn's most famous son, explorer Willem Schoutens, named South America's storm-lashed southern tip – Cape Horn – after his home town in 1616.

⊙ Sights

A stroll through Hoorn's streets lined by 16th-century buildings is one of the town's greatest draws. The scenic harbour has many stately gabled houses, especially along Veermanskade. Check out the old warehouses on Bierkade, where lager was brought from Germany.

The old quarter begins about 800m southeast of the train station. From the station, walk south along broad Veemarkt to Gedempte Turfhaven, turn right and take the first left on to Grote Noord, the pedestrianised shopping street. At the end is the scenic main square, Rode Steen. The main harbour is 300m further southwest, down a road named West.

Rode Steen SQUARE

Hoorn's heyday as a shipping centre is long gone, but the imposing statue of Jan Peterzoon Coen, founder of the Dutch East India Company, still watches over the Rode Steen (Red Stone or Fortress), the square named for the blood that once flowed from the gallows. On the northeastern side of the square, the Waag, the 17th-century weigh house, has a carved unicorn, the town symbol.

★ Westfries Museum MUSEUM

(0229-280 022; www.wfm.nl; Rode Steen 1; adult/child €9/free; 11am-5pm Mon-Fri, from 1pm Sat & Sun Apr-Sep, closed Mon Oct-Mar) Housed in the former seat of the Staten-College (States' Council), the body that once governed seven towns in Noord-Holland, this absorbing museum has a rich collection of historical paintings – so rich that it was the target of art theft in 2005, when paintings worth €10 million were stolen (five have been recovered, though 19 are still missing, as are 70 pieces of silverware). Fortunately four large group portraits of prominent *schutters* (civic guards) by Jan A Rotius (1624–66) remain.

The building's 1632 wedding-cake facade bears the coat of arms of Oranje-Nassau, the Dutch-German royal dynasty that the Dutch named as rulers when Napoleon left. Its rear courtyard has a number of curious stone tablets from local facades.

Hoofdtoren HISTORIC BUILDING

(Hoofd 2) Overshadowing surrounding historic buildings, the massive defensive gate Hoofdtoren (1532), topped by a tiny belfry, now houses an atmospheric restaurant (p128).

Museum van de Twintigste Eeuw MUSEUM

(Museum of the 20th Century; 0229-214 001; www.museumhoorn.nl; Krententuin 24, Oostereiland; adult/child €9/5; 10am-5pm Mon-Fri, from noon Sat & Sun) In the vast former prison on Oostereiland, south of the Hoofdtoren, this entertaining museum is devoted to household goods and modern inventions. Among the eye-openers are a 1964 Philips mainframe computer – a clunky bookcase-sized unit with a whole 1KB of memory – and a 30-sq-metre scale *maquette* (model) of Hoorn in 1650. Admission includes an audioguide.

🏃 Activities

Museum Stoomtram STEAM TRAIN

(0229-214 862; www.stoomtram.nl; Van Dedemstraat 8; circle ticket adult/child €21/16, bicycle €3.20; daily Apr-Sep, Sat & Sun Oct & Nov) From Hoorn's small train-station-housed museum, steam locomotives puff between Hoorn station and Medemblik (22km, 75 minutes). You can combine train and boat travel on the 'Historic Triangle' (adult/child €26.70/18.50): from Hoorn to Medemblik by steam train, then by boat to Enkhuizen and finally a regular NS train back to Hoorn (20 minutes). Departure times vary, confirm in advance.

☞ Tours

Watertaxi Hoorn CRUISE

(06 4637 4059; www.watertaxihoorn.nl; Oostereiland 21; 1hr tour for up to 4 people €50, water-taxi service per person per stop from €2.50, boat rental per hour €25; by reservation) One-hour tours give you a waterborne perspective of

Hoorn's Golden Age port. The company also rents boats (no licence required) with the option of picnic baskets (per person €15), and operates a water-taxi service around the harbour.

⌹ Sleeping

Bed & Breakfast Grote Noord
B&B €

(☑ 06 2871 9018; www.bedandbreakfastgrote-noord.nl; Grote Noord 3; s/d from €69/79; 🛜) The Rode Steen is just metres from this B&B, in a Dutch East India Company (VOC) merchant's house dating from 1592; rooms are on the 3rd and 4th floors (there's no lift). Both medium and large rooms have exposed 16th-century timbers, and amenities including minibars. Rates drop during the week.

★ Gevangenis Hotel Hoorn
DESIGN HOTEL €€

(☑ 0229-820 246; www.gevangenishotelhoorn.nl; Schuijteskade 5; cell s/d €65/85, standard d/f €95/199; 🛜) Oostereiland's enormous former prison – still with bars on its windows – is now partly occupied by this hip hotel. You can sleep in 11 cells (converted to include a private bathroom) behind the original cell doors, or if that's too unnerving, in 14 standard rooms. Also here is a light-filled, harbour-view brasserie. Parking is across the bridge.

✕ Eating

Wormsbecher
SEAFOOD €

(☑ 0229-214 408; www.wormsbechervis.nl; Wijdebrugsteeg 2; dishes €3-13; ⊙ 11am-6pm) Turquoise tiles front this classic fresh-fish takeaway outlet on the harbour, selling locally loved smoked eel, raw herring, Zuiderzee cockles and bargain-priced seafood salads. There are plenty of picnic spots along the harbour and on Oostereiland.

★ De Hoofdtoren
EUROPEAN €€

(☑ 0229-215 487; www.hoofdtoren.nl; Hoofd 2; mains €15.50-24.50, 3-course dinner menu €32.50; ⊙ noon-10pm) A spiralling red-brick staircase leads up to this exquisite restaurant inside Hoorn's historic Hoofdtoren (p127). In a candlelit bare-boards space, it serves high-end fare – truffle risotto; beef steak with polenta, ruccola *stamppot* (mash) and red-wine jus; sole with sautéed spinach – at good-value prices; reservations are recommended. On the ground floor, its bar has outdoor pavement seating in summer.

★ Lucas Rive
BISTRO €€€

(☑ 0229-213 362; www.lucasrive.nl; Oude Doelenkade 7; mains €28.50-40, 3-/4-/5-/6-course menus €46/52.50/60/67.50; ⊙ 6-10pm Tue, Wed & Sat, noon-2pm & 6-10pm Thu & Fri, 1-3pm & 6-10pm Sun) Chef Lucas Rive took just five months to achieve a Michelin star at this chic, contemporary space on Hoorn's lively harbour front. Book ahead for daily changing menus incorporating dishes such as poached duck liver on smoked duck breast with blood-orange sauce, braised lobster with roast king crab or veal sweetbreads with candied kidneys and mustard jus.

❶ Information

Tourist Office (VVV; ☑ 0229-855 761; www.hallohoorn.nl; Schuijteskade 1, Oostereiland; ⊙ 10am-5pm Mar-Sep, Fri-Sun Oct-Feb) In the old prison on Oostereiland.

❶ Getting There & Around

BICYCLE
Bike routes run 20km south to Edam to join the 25km coastal run to Enkhuizen.

Fietspoint Ruiter (☑ 0229-217 096; Stationplein 1; bike hire per day from €12; ⊙ 4.50am-1am Mon-Thu, to 2.40am Fri & Sat, 7.30am-1am Sun) Hoorn is a popular Amsterdam commuter town and this bike garage/hire outlet at the station operates virtually around the clock.

BUS
The bus station is outside the train station. Bus 135 serves Den Helder (1¼ hours, hourly). Change buses at Den Oever for trips across the IJsselmeer towards Leeuwarden.

Bus 314 serves Edam (35 minutes, four times hourly); it's covered by a Waterland Ticket (p119).

TRAIN

TO	PRICE (€)	TIME (MIN)	FREQUENCY (PER HOUR)
Alkmaar	5.10	25	2
Amsterdam	8.30	35	2
Enkhuizen	4.10	25	2

There's a heritage route to Medemblik and Enkhuizen run by the Museum Stoomtram (p127).

Enkhuizen

☑ 0228 / POP 18,480

The beautifully preserved town of Enkhuizen may be peaceful today but during the Golden Age its strategic harbour sheltered the Dutch merchant fleet. It slipped into relative obscurity in the late 17th century but now possesses one of the largest recreational vessel fleets on the IJsselmeer.

For many travellers, Enkhuizen's biggest drawcard is the indoor/outdoor Zuiderzeemuseum, one of the country's finest.

◉ Sights & Activities

★ Zuiderzeemuseum   MUSEUM
(☑ 0228-351 111; www.zuiderzeemuseum.nl; Wierdijk 12-22; adult/child €16/10; ⏱ Binnenmuseum 10am-5pm year-round, Buitenmuseum 10am-5pm Apr–late Oct) This captivating museum consists of two sections, 300m apart: open-air Buitenmuseum, with more than 130 rebuilt and relocated dwellings and workshops, and indoor Binnenmuseum, devoted to farming, fishing and shipping. Visitors are encouraged to leave their vehicles at a car park (€5) off the N302 at the south edge of town. A ferry (included in admission; every 15 minutes April to October) links the car park with the train station and the Buitenmuseum. Plan to spend half a day here.

Opened in 1983, the Buitenmuseum was assembled from houses, farms and sheds trucked in from around the region to show Zuiderzee life as it was from 1880 to 1932. Every conceivable detail has been thought through, from the fence-top decorations and choice of shrubbery to the entire layout of villages, and the look and feel is certainly authentic. An illustrated guide (in English), included in the ticket price, is an essential companion on your tour.

Inhabitants wear traditional dress, and there are real shops such as a bakery, chemist and sweets shop. Workshops run demonstrations throughout the day. Though varying in character, the displays join seamlessly: lime kilns from Akersloot stand a few metres from Zuidende and its row of Monnickendam houses, originally built outside the dykes. Don't miss the Urk quarter, raised to simulate the island town before the Noordoostpolder was drained. For a special postmark, drop your postcards at the old post office from Den Oever. The Marker Haven is a copy of the harbour built in 1830 on what was then the island of Marken. There's a fun playground at the entrance.

While the grounds are open all year, there are activities here only from April to October.

Occupying a museum complex adjoining the Peperhuis, the indoor Binnenmuseum is in the former home and warehouse of a Dutch shipping merchant. The displays include a fine shipping hall: paintings, prints and other materials tell of the rise and fall of the fishing industry, and the construction of the dykes. Here too are cultural artefacts, such as regional costumes, porcelain, silver and jewellery, that indicate the extent of the country's riches at the time.

Flessenscheepjes Museum   MUSEUM
(Bottleship Museum; www.flessenscheepjesmuseum.nl; Zuiderspui 1; adult/child €4.50/3; ⏱ noon-5pm mid-Feb–Oct & mid-Dec–early Jan, Fri-Mon Nov–mid-Dec & early Jan–mid-Feb) Almost as tiny as the boats in its collection, this enchanting museum contains an astonishing collection of ships in bottles carved by seamen through the ages. There are more than 1000 examples, some up to 750 years old. A film reveals the secret to their construction.

Westerkerk   CHURCH
(www.westerkerkenkhuizen.nl; Westerstraat 138; ⏱ 1.30-5pm Tue-Sat early Jul–early Sep) Along Westerstraat you'll spot the remarkable Westerkerk, a 15th-century Gothic church with a removable wooden belfry. The ornate choir screen and imposing pulpit are worth a look.

Opposite the church is the Weeshuis, a 17th-century orphanage with a sugary, curlicued portal.

🛏 Sleeping

Camping Enkhuizer Zand   CAMPGROUND €
(☑ 0228-317 289; www.campingenkhuizerzand.nl; Kooizandweg 4; campsites €17-27.50; ⏱ Apr-Sep; P 🐾) On the north side of the Zuiderzeemuseum's Buitenmuseum, this popular site is a model of self-sufficiency, with a beautiful white-sand beach, tennis courts, a grocery store and a canteen with wi-fi (though it doesn't extend to all campsites).

★ De Koepoort   BOUTIQUE HOTEL €€
(☑ 0228-314 966; www.hotelldekoepoort.nl; Westerstraat 294; d/tr/f from €104/149/174; P ✳ 🐾) Adjacent to the historic city gate De Koepoort, the western gateway to the town, its namesake hotel has 25 timber-trimmed rooms (some with balconies). Unwind in the lobby lounge with leather armchairs, bar, restaurant using seasonal local produce (breakfast is included in the rate) or on the fabulous rooftop terrace overlooking the gate. There's a handy lift and 24-hour reception.

Family rooms sleep up to four; baby cots are available but must be reserved ahead.

DRAINING THE ZUIDERZEE

The Netherlands' coastline originally extended as far as the sandy beaches of Texel and its Frisian Island companions. The relentless sea, however, never seemed to be in agreement with such borders, and by the end of the 13th century storms had washed seawater over flimsy land barriers and pushed it far inland. The end result was the creation of the Zuiderzee (South Sea).

The ruling Dutch had for centuries dreamed of draining the Zuiderzee to reclaim the huge tracts of valuable farmland. The seafaring folk of the villages lining the sea were of a different opinion, even though the shallow Zuiderzee constantly flooded their homes and businesses, and often took lives with it. A solution needed to be found, and the only way to tame the seas, it seems, was to block them off.

A huge dyke was proposed as early as the mid-17th century, but it wasn't until the late 19th century, when new engineering techniques were developed, that such a dyke could become reality. Engineer Cornelis Lely, who lent his name to Lelystad, was the first to sketch out a retaining barrier. A major flood in 1916 set the plan in motion, and construction began in 1927. Fishers worried about their livelihood, and fears that the Wadden Islands would vanish in the rising seas were voiced, and while the former concerns were legitimate, the latter proved unfounded.

In 1932 the Zuiderzee was ceremoniously sealed off by the Afsluitdijk (Barrier Dyke), an impressive dam (30km long and 90m wide) that links the provinces of North Holland and Friesland. The water level remained relatively steady, but the fishing industry was effectively killed as the basin gradually filled with fresh water from the river IJssel – this is how the IJsselmeer was born. However, vast tracts of land were created and soon turned into arable polders (areas surrounded by dykes where the water can be artificially controlled). A second barrier between Enkhuizen and Lelystad was completed in 1976 – creating the Markermeer – with the idea of ushering in the next phase of land reclamation, but the plan was shelved because of cost and environmental concerns.

For more information on this vast human endeavour, spend some time at Lelystad's Nieuw Land Museum at Batavialand (p141), which details the land reclamation.

🍴 Eating & Drinking

Cafes and restaurants ring the Oude Haven, with more along Venedie and Westerstraat. Supermarkets in the town include a large one on Molenweg.

De Smederij   DUTCH €€
(☑ 0228-314 604; www.restaurantdesmederij. nl; Breedstraat 158; mains €21-25.50, 3-/4-course menu €39.50/44.50; ⊙ 5-10pm Fri-Tue) Cute as a button, this cosy restaurant was once a forge, and is now decorated with beautiful old framed maps. Highly creative seasonal fare might include roast duck breast with wild-boar pâté, rib-eye steak with gingerbread and bock-beer dressing, and samphire-stuffed sea bass with heirloom carrot puree.

De Drie Haringhe   SEAFOOD €€€
(☑ 0288-318 610; www.diedrieharinghe.nl; Dijk 28; mains €23.50-28.50, 4-/5-course menu €39.50/45; ⊙ 5-9pm Wed-Sat, from 11.30am Sun) Inside an old East India Company warehouse, opening to a lovely walled summer garden, this up-market seafood specialist serves seasonally changing Dutch- and French-inspired dishes such as smoked-eel terrine with saffron mayo, smoked salmon and crab cannelloni, and grilled sea bass with green-asparagus risotto. From Wednesday to Saturday, lunch is possible by reservation.

★ De Mastenbar   BAR
(www.demastenbar.nl; Compagnieshaven 3; ⊙ 10am-10pm) Hidden away at the Compagnieshaven marina, local favourite De Masten has a cavernous nautical-themed interior with printed maps on the ceiling, old ship's wheels, compasses and copper lanterns, and a panoramic sun-drenched terrace where you can watch cruise boats and working barges float past. Its kitchen specialises in fresh seafood, Flemish onion soup and tasting plates including wild game.

ℹ️ Information

Opposite the train station, Enkhuizen's **tourist office** (VVV; ☑ 0228-313 164; www.enkhuizen-boeit.nl; Tussen Twee Havens 1; ⊙ 8am-5pm Jul & Aug, from 9am Wed-Sat May-Jun & Sep, 10am-4pm Wed-Fri, 11am-3pm Sat Apr & Oct) sells ferry tickets and has a charging point for electric bikes.

ⓘ Getting There & Around

BICYCLE

Bicycle paths along the Zuiderzee link Enkhuizen with Medemblik, 21km northwest, and Hoorn, 25km southwest. From Enkhuizen, you can also cycle along the Houtribdijk, the long dyke between the IJsselmeer to the north and Markermeer to south, to Lelystad (29km).

Bike Totaal (☑ 0228-325 771; www.biketotaal-bovenkarspel.nl; Westerstraat 25; standard/electric bike per day from €10/25; ☺ 9am-6pm Tue-Sat) hires standard and electric bikes, plus kids' bikes, trailers, panniers and child seats..

BOAT

The **Enkhuizen–Stavoren Ferry** (☑ 0228-326 006; www.veerboot.info; Tussen Twee Havens; adult/child one-way €11.50/7, bicycle €5.30; ☺ 3 daily May-Sep, 2 daily Apr & Oct) plies the IJsselmeer connecting North Holland with Stavoren, Friesland, which is on the train line to Leeuwarden via Sneek; journey time is 80 minutes one way. Boats dock near the tourist office, which sells tickets.

In July and August, **De Zuiderzee** (☑ 06 5360 8813; www.de-zuiderzee.nl; Tussen Twee Havens; adult/child one-way €15/10, return €17.50/12.50, bicycle free; ☺ every 2hr 9am-6pm Mon-Sat Jul & Aug) ferries make the two-hour sailing across the IJsselmeer to Urk.

TRAIN

Direct trains link Enkhuizen with Amsterdam (€11.30, one hour, every 30 minutes) and Hoorn (€4.10, 25 minutes, every 30 minutes).

Medemblik

☑ 0227 / POP 44,275

Peaceful Medemblik is the oldest port on the IJsselmeer. Excavations have shown that it dates from the 7th century, and it later became a member of the Hanseatic League. Parts of the town are especially beautiful, including its busy harbour, old waterfront streets and medieval fortress.

◉ Sights & Activities

Stroll along Kaasmarkt, Torenstraat, Nieuwstraat and the Achterom canal to see richly decorated building facades.

Kasteel Radboud   CASTLE
(☑ 0227-541 960; www.kasteelradboud.nl; Oudevaartsgat 8; adult/child €7/4.50; ☺ 10am-5pm Wed-Sun, hours can vary) Pint-sized Kasteel

Radboud was built by Count Floris V in the 13th century and served as a prison before a 19th-century remodelling by Pierre Cuypers, who designed Amsterdam's Rijksmuseum. The original floor plan has been preserved and the imposing Ridderzaal (Knights' Hall) still looks much as it did in the Middle Ages. Interpretative signs (in English) detail the castle's long history and the count's undoing. It's signposted from the harbour on the eastern side of town. Admission includes an audioguide.

Stoommachine Museum   MUSEUM
(Steam Engine Museum; ☑ 0227-544 732; www.stoommachinemuseum.nl; Oosterdijk 4; adult/child €7.50/5; ☺ 10am-5pm early Jul–Aug, Tue-Sun Mar–early Jul, Sep & Oct) Ever wondered what drove the Industrial Revolution? Part of the answer lies at the Stoommachine Museum, in the old pump station outside Medemblik. Thirty handsome old steam engines from the Netherlands, England and Germany are fired up for demonstrations on various days; check the website for schedules.

The Museum Stoomtram (p127) departs from the old train station for Hoorn. You can also catch a boat to Enkhuizen as part of a triangle tour.

🛏 Sleeping & Eating

Medemblik has B&Bs and campgrounds but accommodation is otherwise limited. There's more choice in Hoorn, 22km south.

Restaurant Meijer's 2.0   DUTCH €€€
(☑ 0228-591 667; www.restaurant-meijers.nl; Oosterhaven 3; mains €19.50-27.50, tasting menus €38-57; ☺ 6-9.30pm Mon, Wed & Thu, noon-4pm & 6-9.30pm Fri, 1-4pm & 6-9.30pm Sat & Sun) Medemblik's finest restaurant takes traditional Dutch cuisine to the next level: dishes such as lobster bisque with shrimp *bitterballen* (croquettes), Waddenzee crab and fennel pie, Middenmeer pork belly with herring caviar, and crossberry-marinated lamb with asparagus panna cotta are as inventive as they are delicious. Oyster-grey-upholstered chairs and fresh flowers fill the dining room; there's a small summer terrace.

ⓘ Getting There & Away

Bicycle trails run south and east along dykes 21km to Enkhuizen.

Bus 239 links Medemblik with Hoorn (30 minutes, every 30 minutes).

Den Helder

📞 0223 / POP 56.308

The Netherlands' main naval base, Den Helder, has a marine museum and a 19th-century fort with a military museum and an aquarium worth checking out before you hop on the ferry to Texel.

◎ Sights

Marine Museum   MUSEUM
(📞0223-657 534; www.marinemuseum.nl; Hoofdgracht 3; adult/child €10/6.50; ⊙10am-5pm Apr-Oct, closed Mon Nov-Mar) In the vast former armoury of the Dutch Royal Navy, which still owns the building today, displays at the Marine Museum cover naval history mainly after 1815, the year the Netherlands became a kingdom. You can explore vessels moored on the docks outside, including a submarine. Also here are the bridge and radar dome of the guided missile destroyer *De Ruyter*, where visitors can experience a simulated crisis situation and learn about 3D radar.

Fort Kijkduin   MUSEUM
(📞 0223-612 366; www.fortkijkduin.nl; Admiraal Verhuellplein 1, Huisduinen; museum & aquarium adult/child €8/6; ⊙10am-5pm Apr-Oct, from 11am Nov-Mar) Built under Napoleon's orders in 1811 to accommodate 1400 soldiers, this hulking hilltop fortress (originally called Fort Morland) now houses a military museum incorporating an armoury, and a fantastic subterranean aquarium with 14 tanks filled with every species of marine life from the Waddenzee and North Sea, one with a walk-through tunnel. Kids love it.

✖ Eating

Kade 60   EUROPEAN €€
(📞0223-682 828; www.kade60.nl; Willemsoord 60; mains lunch €6.50-17.50, dinner €14.50-26.50; ⊙kitchen 11am-10pm Tue-Sun) A former iron foundry now houses this cavernous canalside restaurant near the Marine Museum and ferry terminal. Gourmet sandwiches such as smoked beef, egg and truffle mayo are served at lunch; dinner mains span beetroot-marinated lamb with candied garlic to oven-roasted sea bass with samphire pesto. You can just stop in for a beer, wine or cider.

❶ Getting There & Away

Den Helder is the jumping-off point for car and passenger ferries (p138) to Texel.

BICYCLE

The Noordzee route links Den Helder with Sluis by the Belgian border, passing dunes along the North Sea coast and fields of tulips around Julianadorp, about 9km south of Den Helder.

TRAIN

Direct train services from Den Helder include Alkmaar (€8, 40 minutes, two per hour), Amsterdam (€14.50, 1½ hours, two per hour) and Haarlem (€13.90, 1¼ hours, two per hour).

Texel

📞 0222 / POP 13,643

Sweeping white-sand beaches, wildlife-rich nature reserves, sun-dappled forests and quaint villages are among the highlights of Texel (pronounced *tes*-sel), the largest and most visited of the Wadden Islands.

About 3km north of North Holland's coast, Texel is 25km long and 9km wide. Its typically flat Dutch landscape makes it idyllic for cycling. Sheep are everywhere across the island; the local wool is highly prized and there are numerous dairies producing cheese. During lambing season around Easter, you'll see bouncy lambs all over the island; locals enjoy taking a *Lammetjes Wandeltrocht* (walk to look at the lambs).

With enough diversions to keep you entertained for days on end, Texel is popular with Dutch and German visitors but otherwise little known, making it a wonderful place to explore.

❶ Orientation

Ferries from the mainland dock at **'t Horntje** on the south side of the isle, from where buses head north to Texel's six main villages.

Den Burg The island's modest capital has the most services and is its main shopping destination; 7km north of 't Horntje.

De Koog Texel's beachy tourist heart with a distinctly tacky streak and the island's only hub of boisterous bars; 13km north of 't Horntje.

Den Hoorn A charming village handy to tulip fields and windswept sand dunes; 3.5km northwest of 't Horntje.

Oudeschild Texel's best harbour facilities, an excellent museum and splendid seafood, plus a pirate-themed kids' playground at the north end; 7km northeast of 't Horntje.

Oosterend Quiet hamlet with distinctive architecture; 15km northeast of 't Horntje.

De Cocksdorp At the northern end of the island, this tiny village is a launch pad for the island of Vlieland and the other Frisian Islands; 20km north 't Horntje.

Beaches on the west coast are numbered by the kilometre from south to north.

⊙ Sights

★ Texel Dunes National Park PARK
(Nationaal Park Duinen van Texel; www.npduinenvantexel.nl) The patchwork of dune-scape running along the western coast of the island is a prime reason for visiting Texel. Salt fens and heath alternate with velvety, grass-covered dunes; plants endemic to the habitat include the dainty marsh orchid and orange-berried sea buckthorn. Much of the area is bird sanctuary and accessible only on foot. The visitor centre at Ecomare has schedules and makes reservations for excellent two-hour ranger-led dune walks in English and Dutch (from €7.50), and supplies maps.

De Slufter became a wetland after an attempt at land reclamation failed; when a storm breached the dykes in the early 1900s the area was allowed to flood and a unique ecosystem developed. To the south, De Muy is renowned for its colony of spoonbills that are monitored with great zeal by local naturalists.

A stone's throw from the windswept beach lies the dark, leafy forest of De Dennen, between Den Hoorn and De Koog. Originally planted as a source of lumber, today it has an enchanting network of walking and cycling paths. In spring the forest floor is carpeted with snowdrops that were first planted here in the 1930s.

★ Ecomare WILDLIFE RESERVE
(☎ 0222-317 741; www.ecomare.nl; Ruijslaan 92, De Koog; adult/child €13/9, audioguide €1; ⊙ 9.30am-5pm) 🖈 Initially created as a refuge for sick seals retrieved from the Waddenzee, Ecomare has expanded into an impressive nature centre devoted to the preservation and understanding of Texel's wildlife. It has displays on Texel's development since the last ice age and the islanders' interaction with the sea, as well as large aquariums filled with fish from the Waddenzee and the North Sea (including sharks); outside there are marked nature trails. The highlight is the *zeehonden* ('sea dogs', ie seals) themselves.

Their playful water ballet will delight even the most jaded visitor. Try to catch feeding time at 11.30am or 3.30pm. Feeding of rescued porpoises takes place at 10.30am and 1.30pm; fish feeding is at 2.30pm. Rescued birds are the other main tenants. Look out for its six skeletons of whales stranded in the Waddenzee, including a 15m-long sperm-whale carcass complete with 52 fearsome teeth.

★ Kaap Skil Museum Van Jutters & Zeelui MUSEUM
(Maritime & Beachcombers Museum; ☎ 0222-314 956; www.kaapskil.nl; Heemskerckstraat 9,

---

DON'T MISS

BEACH LIFE

The island offers idyllic swimming, cycling, walking, boating, or just relaxation. Its pristine white beaches, lining the western shore in one unbroken ribbon, are numbered by the kilometre and marked with a *paal* (piling) from south to north.

The currents can be treacherous; lifeguards are on duty in July and August from No 9 northeast of Den Hoorn to No 21 near De Koog.

No matter how crowded the island, with a little hiking you can always find a stretch of deserted sand.

Top beaches include the following.

Paal Uncrowded, and popular with locals and nudists.

Paal 12 Uncrowded, with a sheltered cafe.

Paal 17 Texel's party beach (www.paal17.com) has plenty of day- and night-time activities.

Paal 19 Drinking and dining options abound at this beach (www.paal19.nl).

Paal 20 Right in front of the tourist enclave of De Koog, and rather built up.

Paal 27 A fairly isolated beach popular with nudists.

Paal 31 Near the lighthouse; no swimming due to treacherous rip tides but lots of wind sports.

Paal 33 No swimming, but lots of beach sports and occasional seal-spotting.

Texel

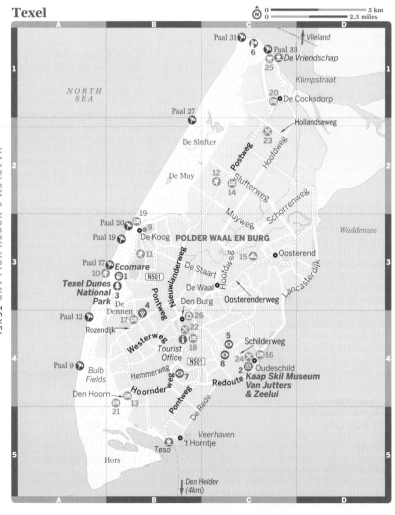

0   5 km
0   2.5 miles

Vlieland

Paal 31
Paal 33
6
De Vriendschap
25
Klimpstraat
20
De Cocksdorp

NORTH SEA

Paal 27
Hollandseweg
De Slufter
23
Hoofdweg
Postweg
12
Slufterweg
De Muy
14
Schorrenweg
Muyweg
Waddenzee
19
Paal 20
9
Paal 19
De Koog
POLDER WAAL EN BURG
11
15
Oosterend
Paal 17
Ecomare
De Staart
Hoofdweg
Lancasterdijk
10
1
N501
Nieuwlanderweg
Texel Dunes
National
Park
De
Dennen
4
De Waal
Den Burg
Oosterenderweg
Paal 12
17
26
Rozendijk
22
5
Westerweg
Tourist
Office
18
Schilderweg
16
Paal 9
Bulb
Fields
Hemmerweg
7
24
8
Oudeschild
2
Kaap Skil Museum
Van Jutters
& Zeelui
Den Hoorn
13
21
Redoute
Hoornderweg
Pontweg
De Rede

Veerhaven
't Horntje
Teso
Hors

Den Helder
(4km)

Oudeschild; adult/child €9/6.50; ⊙10am-5pm Tue-Sat, from noon Sun) A stunning slatted-timber-encased reception building made from recycled materials frames the superb Maritime and Beachcombers Museum. Its extraordinary variety of flotsam and jetsam recovered from sunken ships and the shore is mind-boggling. Demonstrations by rope-makers, fish-smokers and blacksmiths take place in the outdoor section, while the indoor displays cover everything from underwater archaeology to windmill technology.

Reede van Texel, which the museum translates accurately as Texel Roads, has nothing to do with asphalt but rather is a vast and amazingly detailed model of the shipping lanes and ports as they existed in the 17th century.

Eierland Lighthouse   LIGHTHOUSE
(☎0222-317 741; www.vuurtorentexel.nl; Vuurtorenweg 184, De Cocksdorp; €4; ⊙10am-5pm daily Mar-Oct, Wed, Sat & Sun Nov-Feb) Battered by storms and war, Texel's resilient crimson-coloured lighthouse was built in 1864 and stands 35m high. Climb its 153 steps for sweeping views across the islands and shallow waters.

Texel

Activities

Texel has over 140km of well-signposted cycling routes. All roads are suitable for bikes, and you can circumnavigate the island following the dykes in the east and the trails behind the dunes in the west.

Swimming, sailing, kite-surfing, skydiving and horse riding are all popular pursuits.

Kitesurf School Texel   KITESURFING
(☑ 06 1097 1992; www.kitesurftexel.nl; Paal 17; kite-surfer hire per hour from €25, 3hr lesson from €95; ☺ 9am-5pm Apr-Oct) Situated 3km south of De Koog, Kitesurf School Texel offers exhilarating kite-surfing lessons as well as rentals. Participants must be 12 or older.

Tessel Air   SKYDIVING
(☑ 0222-311 464; www.paracentrumtexel.nl; Texel Airport, Postweg 128, De Cocksdorp; 15min scenic flight €37.50, tandem parachute jump €209; ☺ daily Apr-Oct, Sat by request Nov-Mar) Tessel Air offers 15-minute pleasure flights over Texel (minimum two people), and for a bit more cash they'll explore the other Wadden Islands. To really feel the wind in your face, try a tandem parachute jump.

Manege Elzenhof   HORSE RIDING
(☑ 0222-317 469; www.manegeelzenhof.nl; Bosrandweg 252, De Koog; horse ride adult/child per hour €18/9, lesson per 30min €19.50; ☺ 8.30am-5pm May-Oct) One of several horse-riding stables on the island, Manege Elzenhof offers horse and pony rides and lessons on gentle creatures lined up at the troughs with their names inscribed on plaques. Book ahead for beach rides along the shore.

Tours

The still-working fishing harbour at Oudeschild is filled with former large prawn trawlers that found new life as tour boats. Competition is fierce and the best way to choose a boat is to wander along the docks checking out itineraries and offers. Trips around Texel sail close to an endangered seal colony on the sandbanks. Departure times are dependent on tides.

Emmie TX10   CRUISE
(☑ 06 5149 8614; www.garnalenvissenoptexel.nl; Haven 8, Oudeschild; adult/child €12.50/10; ☺ 2hr tours depart 10.30am & 2pm Mon-Sat mid-Mar–Oct, Wed & Sat Nov–mid-Mar) Prawns caught on this fishing trawler's journey on the Waddenzee are prepared fresh for passengers.

Texel 44   CRUISE
(☑ 06 5110 5775; www.tx44.nl; Haven 6, Oudeschild; 2hr tour adult/child €12.50/10; ☺ 2pm Mon, 11am & 2pm Tue-Sat, 12.30pm Sun Apr-Oct)

LOCAL KNOWLEDGE

ISLAND PRODUCE

Across the island you'll find great local produce, from fruit to cheese, chocolate, ice cream, beer and rare-for-the-Netherlands wine. Look out too for Texel-distilled spirits such as gin and whisky at bars and restaurants.

Texelse Bierbrouwerij (☎0222-320 325; www.texels.nl; Schilderweg 214b, Oudeschild; tour adult/child €12.50/5; ⏲tours by appointment, bar 10.30am-7pm Tue-Sun mid-Jul–Aug, to 6pm Tue-Sun Apr–mid-Jul, Sep & Oct, shorter hours Nov-Mar) Tours and tastings take place at Texel's brewery, which also has an on-site bar.

De Kroon van Texel (☎06 5180 8386; www.wijngaarddekroonvantexel.nl; Rozendijk 32, Den Burg; vineyard tour adult/child €9/2.50; ⏲cellar door 10am-5pm May-Sep, vineyard tour 11am Tue & Sat, 2pm Fri May-Sep) Medal-winning winery.

Kaasboerderijk Wezenspyk (☎0222-315 090; www.wezenspyk.nl; Hoondernweg 29, Den Burg; tastings adult/child €5.50/2.75; ⏲9.30am-5pm Tue-Sat, tastings 2pm Tue & Fri, 11am Sat) Taste and buy cheeses produced at this small dairy.

De Zelfpluktuin (☎0222-315 080; www.zelfpluktuin.nl; Middellandseweg 4, Oudeschild; ⏲9.30am-5.30pm Mon-Sat mid-May–Oct) Pick your own fruit, veggies and flowers at this farm.

IJsboerderij Labora Ice cream is the speciality of this working dairy farm.

De Texelse Chocolaterie (☎0222-313 179; www.detexelsechocolaterie.nl; Spinbaan 1a, Den Burg; ⏲11am-5pm Mon, 9am-5.30pm Tue-Sat) Makes chocolates from fresh Texel milk.

De Kade (Haven 9c, Oudeschild; ⏲10am-6pm Jul & Aug, to 5pm Mon-Sat, from noon Sun Mar-Jun, Sep & Oct) A showcase of Texelproducts including cheeses, jams and preserves.

Purpose-built for touring in 1950, the *Texel 44* has a big upper deck for seal spotting and a heated cabin if the weather turns.

Texelstroom CRUISE
(☎06 5179 4992; www.texelstroom.nl; Haven 4, Oudeschild; 3hr tour adult/child €22.50/18; ⏲by reservation mid-Apr–Oct) If you prefer traditional sailing to a powered pleasure craft, take a three-hour tour aboard this beautiful 1906 yacht. It takes up to 12 passengers; under 14s aren't permitted.

Tuk Tuk Express DRIVING
(☎06 2145 2052; www.tuktukexpresstexel.nl; Haven 12, Oudeschild; tuk tuk per day Mon-Fri/Sat-Sun €99/119, buggy per hour/day €50/120; ⏲10am-6pm Apr-Oct, by reservation Nov-Mar) A fun way to spin around the island is behind the wheel of a little three-wheeled, four-seater tuk tuk (Italian Piaggio Calessino convertible, of which only 999 were made). It also hires two-person open buggies.

Jan Plezier TOURS
(☎06 2009 7793; www.janpleziertexel.nl; Nikadel, De Koog; tour adult/child €18/9, horse riding per 3hr €65; ⏲tour 10am & 2pm Mon-Sat Apr-Oct, horse riding by appointment) Scenic three-hour horse-drawn wagon rides follow one of two routes, one primarily along the beach, and one through the forest. Tours depart from the bus stop on Nikadel, De Koog. Experienced horse riders can take a three-hour trek.

Festivals & Events

Ronde om Texel SAILING
(www.roundtexel.com; Paal 17; ⏲early–mid-Jun) The world's largest catamaran race attracts some 600 participants and thousands of spectators along the beaches. It starts and ends at Paal 17, 3km south of De Koog.

Sleeping & Eating

There are more than 45,000 beds on the island, but it's essential to book ahead, especially in July and August. De Koog has by far the most options; hamlets such as Den Hoorn or De Cocksdorp are more peaceful.

The tourist office has a list of B&Bs. Prices drop in the low season (October to April). Texel's campgrounds teem in summer, when many require a week's minimum stay.

Den Burg

Stayokay Texel HOSTEL €
(☎0222-315 441; www.stayokay.com; Haffelderweg 29, Den Burg; dm/d/f from €35.50/78.75/149.50; P📶) Texel's modern HI hostel, 700m south of Den Burg centre, has 240 beds in clean, colourful rooms, and a cafe on-site. You can hire bikes to cycle to the beach 6km away.

Hotel De 14 Sterren   HOTEL €€
(📞0222-322 679; www.14sterren.nl; Smitsweg 4, Den Burg; d/ste from €130/170; 🛜) On the edge of De Dennen forest, charming Hotel De 14 Sterren's 14 rooms are decorated in Mediterranean hues, and most have a terrace or balcony with garden views. Breakfast (included in the rate) is served in your room. Its bistro, De Worsteltent (📞0222-310 288; www.14sterren.nl; Smitsweg 4, Den Burg; mains lunch €6.50-18.50, dinner €15.50-23.50; ⊙noon-8.30pm; 🛜), occupies a rustic barn.

Freya   BISTRO €€
(📞0222-321 686; Gravenstraat 4, Den Burg; 3-course menu €28.50; ⊙6-9pm Tue-Sat) This petite, welcoming restaurant serves a daily changing set menu (no à la carte) of contemporary Dutch cuisine along the lines of smoked duck breast with asparagus, herb-crusted Texel lamb with oven-baked potatoes, and local berries with meringue topped with clouds of whipped Texel cream. Reservations are a must.

Eiland Keuken   DUTCH €€
(📞0222-322 084; www.vincenteilandkeuken.nl; Gravenstraat 7, Den Burg; mains lunch €9-19.50, dinner €15-27.50, tasting menus €42.50-62.50; ⊙noon-10pm Mon & Wed-Sat, from 5.30pm Sun; 🐾) Texel produce forms the backbone of this stylish bistro's quality cooking: Waddenzee oysters with lemon and samphire salsa, smoked-mackerel ceviche, chocolate-dusted Texel lamb with roast Den Burg apples and beetroot mousse, and sea buckthorn and raspberry sorbet with candied blackberries. Kids can dine on half-portions of adult dishes for half price.

🛏 De Cocksdorp

't Anker   HOTEL €€
(📞0222-316 274; www.hotelhetankervantexel.nl; Kikkertstraat 24, De Cocksdorp; s/d from €58/98; 🛜) 🐾 This small, family-run hotel near Roggesloot nature reserve is full of woodsy charm, with eight basic yet comfy rooms behind a solid brick facade, a lush garden and hearty breakfasts featuring homemade bread and island-sourced organic produce. Hot water and electricity is from solar panels. Children aren't permitted.

★ Boutique Hotel Texel   BOUTIQUE HOTEL €€
(📞0222-311 237; www.hoteltexel.nl; Postweg 134, De Cocksdorp; d/f/ste €135/215/225, camping per site from €17.50; ⊙hotel year-round, camping mid-Mar–Oct; 🅿🛜♿) Texel's best hotel has 42 chic rooms in natural charcoal tones and a peaceful camping field out back. Fabulous facilities including an indoor swimming pool, sauna and beauty treatments, and an outstanding restaurant, Gusta (mains €20-24, 3-course dinner menu €29.50; ⊙12.30-3pm & 6-9pm; 🛜) 🐾. Breakfast (included) is a bountiful spread of local produce including cheeses and house-baked treats such as gingerbread. It's 4.5km south of De Cocksdorp, close to Texel's airport.

IJsboerderij Labora   ICE CREAM €
(www.ijsboerderijlabora.nl; Hollandseweg 2, De Cocksdorp; ice cream per scoop €1.35; ⊙11am-8pm May-Aug, noon-5pm mid-Feb–Apr, Sep & Oct) 🐾 At this working dairy farm, you can see the cows being milked (by robots) to make Labora's luscious ice cream. Each day there are 18 flavours, such as strawberry made with strawberries grown on the farm, served in a giant waffle cone and topped with fresh strawberries and handmade strawberry syrup and whipped cream from the cow's milk.

Restaurant Topido   BISTRO €€
(📞0222-316 227; www.topido.nl; Kikkertstraat 21-23, De Cocksdorp; mains €24.50-27.50, 3-course menu €39.50; ⊙5-9pm Tue-Sun) In the heart of the village, casual Topido uses island produce in creative menus: Texel lamb with roast beetroot; sea bass encrusted in locally grown herbs; and local-vegetable strudel. Kids get a three-course menu for €18.50.

Kaap Noord   CAFE
(📞0222-316 340; www.strandpavijoencapnoord.nl; Volharding 4, Paal 33, De Cocksdorp; ⊙10am-midnight Apr-Sep, hours vary Nov-Mar; 🛜) At the island's northern tip, this rustic beach bar has a wind-buffering, glass-walled terrace overlooking the sand and the sea beyond. Its vast timber interior is warmed by a wood-burning stove and sheepskins covering furniture made out of driftwood. Beers include brews by Texelse Bierbrouwerij (p136); it also has Texel-distilled gin and whisky, by-the-glass wines, freshly squeezed juices and homemade lemonade.

Food (salads, sandwiches, steaks, seafood and Dutch pancakes) is served until 8pm.

🛏 Den Hoorn

Texel Yurts   GUESTHOUSE €€
(📞06 3077 1667; www.texelyurts.nl; Rommelpot 19, Den Hoorn; 2-person yurt 3 nights from €370; ⊙Jun-Oct; 🅿) Bed down in a fabric-sided,

timber-beamed yurt warmed by a wood-stove. Hammocks sway in the grounds. There's a minimum stay of three nights. It's 1km south of Den Hoorn.

Bij Jef
BOUTIQUE HOTEL €€€

(☏0222-319 623; www.bijjef.nl; Herenstraat 34, Den Hoorn; d from €245; ⚍) The 12 stylish rooms in this former rectory come with a bath and views of the countryside or the quaint village street. A lavish breakfast (included in the rate) features champagne; the hotel's restaurant has a Michelin star.

★ Bij Jef
EUROPEAN €€€

(☏0222-319 623; www.bijjef.nl; Herenstraat 34, Den Hoorn; mains €55; ⊘6-9pm daily Jul & Aug, Wed-Sun Sep-Jun) The Michelin-starred restaurant of boutique hotel Bij Jef has a constantly changing menu created from local produce, such as Texel suckling lamb, De Westen asparagus and herbs, Den Burg chocolate, De Hoorn cheese, De Cocksdorp strawberries, Waddenzee mackerel and North Sea crab. Try for a garden table.

🛏 De Koog

Strandhotel Noordzee
HOTEL €€

(☏0222-317 365; www.strandhotelnoordzeetexel.nl; Badweg 200, De Koog; s/d from €130/150; 🅿⚍) This is one of Texel's few hotels directly on the sand. Its 10 North Sea–facing rooms (some with waterbeds) have quirky touches such as lamps designed like lighthouses. Balconies extend from some rooms; you can also relax on the large beachside terrace. There's a Finnish sauna on-site. Breakfast is included.

🛏 Oosterend

★ Camp Silver Island Hideaway
CARAVAN PARK €€

(☏0222-318 571; www.campsilver.nl; Eendenkooiweg 2, Oosterend; d from €137.50; ⊘Apr-Oct; 🅿⚍) 🌱 Eight gleaming silver Airstream trailers occupy this glamping paradise 5km northeast of Den Burg. Each one is decked out with designer fabrics and shiny stainless-steel bathrooms; one has a private sauna. Breakfasts (included) are organic; the camp kitchen has a pantry with ingredients, heat-and-eat homemade meals and drinks on an honesty system; there's a geo-dome-housed lounge. Minimum stay is two nights.

🛏 Oudeschild

Design Hotel Texel Suites
DESIGN HOTEL €€€

(☏06 5061 5558; www.texelsuites.com; Haven 8, Oudeschild; ste from €249; ⚍) Inside a historic harbourside brick warehouse, the three panoramic suites here are bigger than many Dutch apartments: two are 90 sq metres (one is a duplex sleeping three), and the third is a whopping 140 sq metres, sleeping four, with a huge gas-powered fireplace. All have kitchenettes; breakfast's included. Seafood caught daily is the speciality of its restaurant, 't Pakhuus (☏0222-313 581; www.pakhuus.com; Haven 8, Oudeschild; mains €24.50-44.50, 3-/5-/6-/7-course menus €36.50/57.50/66.50/74.50; ⊘11am-9pm; ♿).

Vispaleis Rokerij van der Star
SEAFOOD €

(☏0222-312 441; www.vispaleistexel.nl; Heemskerckstraat 15, Oudeschild; dishes €4-11; ⊘8.30am-6pm Mon-Sat) Fresh-from-the-ocean seafood is dished up at this cafe, including garlicky seafood soup and sublime smoked fish. Seating is basic – go for a plastic chair on the terrace.

ℹ Information

Tourist office (VVV; ☏0222-314 741; www.texel.net; Emmalaan 66, Den Burg; ⊘9am-5.30pm Mon-Fri, to 5pm Sat year-round, plus noon-4pm Sun mid-Jul–mid-Aug) Signposted from the ferry terminal; on the southern fringe of Den Burg.

ℹ Getting There & Away

Trains from Amsterdam to Den Helder (€14.70, 75 minutes, every 30 minutes) are met by **Texel Hopper** (☏0222-784 000; www.texelhopper.nl; single/day ticket €3/7.50) buses that whisk you on to the ferry, which the bus also boards.

Teso (☏0222-369 600; www.teso.nl; foot passenger/car return €2.50/37, bicycle incl rider return €5, off-peak car return Tue-Thu €25; ⊘to Texel hourly 6.30am-9.30pm, from Texel hourly 6am-9pm) runs crossings from Den Helder to 't Horntje aboard huge ferries; journey time is 20 minutes. On some summer days there's a service every half-hour – check the timetable online. Services start half-hour to an hour later on Sundays. Car queues can be huge in high season; plan to arrive at the docks at least an hour before departure.

Seasonal passenger ferry **De Vriendschap** (☏06 1352 4734; www.waddenveer.nl; Volharding 2a, Paal 33, De Cocksdorp; adult/child one-way €18.50/12, return €29.50/19.50, bicycle one-way €10; ⊘1 daily May-Sep) runs from Texel's northern tip to car-free Vlieland in the Frisian Islands; one-way journey time is one hour, including transport to Het Posthuys. Due to space constraints, bicycles can only be transported one way, not as a round trip, but you can hire bikes on Vlieland. Book ahead online.

❶ Getting Around

BICYCLE

Touring bikes can be rented at larger towns on Texel from around €10 per day.

At the ferry terminal, **Rijwielverhuur Veerhaven** (✆ 0222-319 588; www.fietsverhuurtexel.nl; Pontweg 2, 't Horntje; standard-bike/electric-bike/scooter hire per day €10.50/21.50/50; ⊙ 8.30am-6pm Apr-Sep, 9am-5pm Oct-Mar) hires standard and electric bikes as well as scooters, kids' bikes, tandems and child seats. There's a free breakdown service. Pick-up and drop-off is possible elsewhere on the island (handy if you're travelling to or from Vlieland in the Frisian Islands).

BUS

Bus 28 run by Texel Hopper operates throughout the year. Buy tickets in advance online, at Den Helder's train station, or at Texel's tourist office or large supermarkets. Alternatively you can use an OV-chipkaart. The route links 't Horntje with Den Burg (seven minutes) and De Koog (another 15 minutes) before returning via the Ecomare wildlife reserve. Buses generally run hourly during daylight (until 10pm in summer).

Texel Hopper also operates minibuses around the rest of the island on demand – reserve at least 30 minutes ahead by phone or online and pay by credit card or give the code of your prepaid bus ticket. An OV-chipkaart is also valid.

TAXI

Taxi Botax (✆ 0222-315 888; www.taxibotax texel.com) takes you between the ferry terminal and any destination on the island, including Den Burg (€14), De Koog (€22.50) and De Cocksdorp (€35). Book in advance.

Muiden

✆ 0294 / POP 6261

An easy jaunt from Amsterdam, Muiden is an unhurried town renowned for its medieval red-brick castle, the Muiderslot. Life otherwise focuses on the busy central lock that funnels scores of pleasure boats out into the IJmeer, a bordering lake that links to the Markermeer and vast IJsselmeer.

◉ Sights

★ Muiderslot ・ CASTLE
(Muiden Castle; ✆ 0294-256 262; www.muiderslot. nl; Herengracht 1; adult/child €15.50/9; ⊙ 10am-5pm Mon-Fri, from noon Sat & Sun Apr-Oct, from

noon Sat & Sun Nov-Mar) Built in 1280 by Count Floris V, son of Willem II, the exceptionally preserved moated fortress Muiderslot is equipped with round towers, a French innovation. The count was a champion of the poor and a French sympathiser, two factors that inevitably spelt trouble; Floris was imprisoned in 1296 and murdered while trying to flee. Today it's the Netherlands' most visited castle. The interior can be seen only on 30-minute guided tours. The I Amsterdam and Museum cards allow free admission.

In the 17th century, historian PC Hooft entertained some of the century's greatest writers, artists and scientists here, a group famously known as the Muiderkring (Muiden Circle). You'll be taken around the castle on the 'Golden Age' tour, seeing precious furnishings, weapons and Gobelin hangings designed to re-create Hooft's era.

Pampus ・ FORT
(www.pampus.nl; adult/child ferry & admission €20/15; ⊙ 10.30am-5pm Tue-Sun May-Oct, 11.30am-4pm Tue-Fri, 10.30am-5pm Sat & Sun Apr) Off the coast of Muiden lies a derelict fort on the island of Pampus. This massive 19th-century bunker was a key member of the Stelling van Amsterdam (Defence Line of Amsterdam), a ring of 42 fortresses that were ultimately rendered useless by aerial warfare. It's now a Unesco World Heritage Site and is great fun to explore. Ferries to Pampus depart from Muiderslot port on a varying schedule in season; the trip takes 25 minutes. You can also take a direct ferry here from the eastern Amsterdam neighbourhood of IJburg.

Once on the island, there is the interactive Pampus Xperience, with audiovisual elements to bring the fort to life. There are also several games for kids.

✖ Eating & Drinking

De Doelen ・ FRENCH €€€
(✆ 0294-263 200; www.restaurantdedoelen.nl; Sluis 1; mains €24.50-29.50; ⊙ noon-2pm & 6-10pm) Prune-stuffed quail, spiced-honey-marinated duck, salt-crusted sea bass, steak-frites with Béarnaise sauce, and grilled lobster with hollandaise sauce, followed by crème brûlée or chocolate profiteroles, are among the French classics served in a romantic, brick-walled dining room hung with impressionist-style paintings or on the tree-shaded terrace overlooking the canal's locks.

Café Ome Ko ・ BROWN CAFE
(www.omekomuiden.nl; Herengracht 71; ⊙ 8am-1am Sun-Wed, to 2am Thu-Sat) With a sunny

canal-side terrace and regular live music in summer, cosy timber-panelled cafe Ome Ko has been the centre of Muiden's social life since 1810; past patrons include Napoleon Bonaparte, who arrived on horseback. Seasonal ciders, local craft beers and *jenevers* are all specialities.

🛈 Getting There & Around

BICYCLE
Bicycle paths link Muiden with Amsterdam to the west and Flevoland to the east.

BOAT
Ferries operated by **Veerdienst** (www.amsterdamtouristferry.com; Krijn Taconiskade 124, IJBurg; adult/child ferry & admission to either Pampus or Muiderslot €20/15; ⏰11am Tue-Sun Apr-Oct) run from the Amsterdam neighbourhood of IJburg (reached from Amsterdam Centraal Station on tram 26 in 20 minutes). Tickets include a tour of either Pampus or Muiderslot. Bicycles travel for free.

BUS
Buses 320, 322 and 327 link Amsterdam's Amstel station (15 minutes, hourly) with Muiden. The castle is then a 1km walk.

Naarden

🗹 035 / POP 17,115

Naarden is a highlight of the Het Gooi woodland area southeast of Amsterdam, thanks to its remarkable fortress, Naarden-Vesting. A military work of art, it has the shape of a 12-pointed star, with arrowheads at each tip, and a double ring of moats. This defence system, one of the best preserved in the country, was built only after the Spanish massacred the inhabitants in the 16th century.

Today the walled town of Naarden-Vesting is an upmarket enclave with fine restaurants, galleries and antique shops.

⦿ Sights

Inside the fortress of Naarden-Vesting, most of the quaint little houses date from 1572, the year the Spaniards razed the place during their colonisation of Noord-Holland. The bloodbath led by Don Frederick of Toledo is commemorated by a stone tablet on the building at Turfpoortstraat 7.

Vestingmuseum   MUSEUM
(Fortress Museum; 🗹035-694 45 59; www.vestingmuseum.nl; Westwalstraat 6; adult/child €9/5; ⊙10.30am-5pm Tue-Sun) The Vestingmuseum brings context to the vast star-shaped fortress, which is the only one in Europe featuring a buffer of two walls and two moats. You can stroll around on the rolling battlements before descending into the cramped casements for insights into a soldier's life here.

Grote Kerk   CHURCH
(www.grotekerknaarden.nl; Markstraat 13; tower adult/child €3/2; ⊙church 10.30am-4.30pm Tue-Sat, from 1.30pm Sun & Mon mid-May–Sep, tower 2-3pm Wed, Sat & Sun mid-May–Sep) It's easy to spot the tall tower of the fort's central Grote Kerk, a Gothic basilica with stunning 16th-century vault paintings of biblical scenes. You can climb the tower's 235 steps for a view of the leafy Gooi and the Vecht river. Organ concerts are held throughout the year – check the agenda for times and varying prices.

Comenius Museum   MUSEUM
(www.comeniusmuseum.nl; Kloosterstraat 33; adult/child €6/free; ⊙noon-5pm Tue-Sun) The 17th-century Czech educational reformer, Jan Amos Komensky (Comenius), is buried in the Waalse Kapel (Walloon Chapel) of the fortress's former monastery. His life and work (he promoted the concepts of universal education for rich and poor) are related next door at the Comenius Museum. Tickets are only available from the tourist office and the Vestingmuseum, not at the Comenius Museum itself.

⇗ Tours

Vestingvaart Naarden   CRUISE
(🗹035-694 11 94; www.vestingvaart.nl; Kooltjesbuurt; adult/child €7/5; ⊙hourly 1-4pm Mon-Fri, 1-5pm Sat & Sun May-Sep, 1-4pm Apr & Oct) One-hour tours on vintage boats explore Naarden-Vesting's moats and some of the reedy natural areas.

🛏 Sleeping & Eating

Naarden has very few places to stay, which book out quickly, but Amsterdam is just 23km northwest.

Passionata   DELI €
(www.passionata-naarden.nl; Marktstraat 31; dishes €3.50-12.50; ⊙10am-6pm Tue-Sat, from noon Sun) This stylish Italian deli is a perfect source for picnic supplies you can take to enjoy out on the town walls. Fantastic sandwiches include fillings such as prosciutto, bresaola, ricotta, Gorgonzola, truffle mayo, sun-dried tomatoes and rucola.

Fine   BRASSERIE €
(🗹035-694 48 68; www.restaurantfine.nl; Marktstraat 66; sharing plates €8.50; ⊙noon-10pm

Wed-Mon) Aptly named, this cosy bar and restaurant has canal-side wicker chairs and wooden tables, plus regular art exhibitions. The monthly changing menu of small plates designed to share is superb and highlights local seafood, such as house-smoked salmon with red-onion mayo, Zuiderzee scallops with asparagus puree, and hoisin-marinated mackerel. You can just stop in for a glass of wine.

ℹ Information

Tourist office (VVV; ☑ 035-694 26 73; www.vvvnaarden.nl; Ruijsdaelplein 6; ⊙10am-5pm Apr-Oct, 11am-4pm Wed-Sun Nov-Mar) Opposite the Utrechtse Poort (Utrecht Gate).

ℹ Getting There & Away

Bicycle routes travel 25km northwest to Amsterdam, via Muiden, 8km from Naarden.

Trains run between Amsterdam Centraal Station and Naarden-Bussum (€4.90, 25 minutes, two per hour). From the station, bus 110 (12 minutes, up to two per hour) runs to the fortress; otherwise it's a pleasant 2km walk north.

FLEVOLAND

Flevoland, the Netherlands' 12th and youngest province, is a masterpiece of Dutch hydroengineering. From 1927 to 1932 an ambitious scheme went ahead to reclaim more than 1400 sq km of land – an idea mooted as far back as the 17th century. The completion of the Afsluitdijk (Barrier Dyke) paved the way for the creation of Flevoland. Ringed dykes were erected, allowing water to be pumped out at a snail-like pace. Once part of Overijssel province, Noordoostpolder was inaugurated in 1942, followed by Southeastern Flevoland (1957) and Southwestern Flevoland (1968). The first residential rights were granted to workers who helped in reclamation and to farmers, especially those from Zeeland, who lost everything in the great flood of 1953.

Flevoland's uninspiring main hubs – Almere, Lelystad and Emmeloord – are laid out in unrelieved grid patterns; highlights here are the old fishing villages Urk and Schokland, and Lelystad's maritime- and aviation-focused museums.

Urk

☑ 0527 / POP 20,421

Until 1939, Urk was a proud little island that was home to a sizeable fishing fleet and was an important signal post for ships passing into the North Sea. It reluctantly joined the mainland when the surrounding Noordoost-polder was pumped dry.

Although now cut off from the North Sea, Urk is still a centre of the seafood industry, with dozens of historic fishing boats moored around the harbour. The town is divided

---

WORTH A TRIP

A FAMILY DAY OUT

Flevoland's sprawling capital, Lelystad, squirrels away two engaging museums for kids and adults alike.

Batavialand (☑ 0320-261 409; www.batavialand.nl; Oostvaardersdijk 1-13; adult/child €14/7.50, combination ticket with Luchtvaart Themapark Aviodrome €22.50/16.50; ⊙10am-5pm Mon-Sat, from 11am Sun) Batavialand's centrepiece is a replica of a 17th-century Dutch merchant frigate, the *Batavia*, which took 10 years to reconstruct. The original was a 17th-century *Titanic* – big, expensive and supposedly unsinkable. True to comparison, the *Batavia*, filled to the brim with cannon and goods for the colonies, went down in 1629 on its maiden voyage off the west coast of Australia. The replica, however, redeemed its predecessor in 2000 by sailing around the Pacific.

Luchtvaart Themapark Aviodrome (☑ 0320-289 842; www.aviodrome.nl; Pelikaanweg 50; adult/child €16.95/14.95, combination ticket with Batavialand €22.50/16.50; ⊙10am-5pm Tue-Sun, daily during school holidays) Fronted by a reception area designed like an airport check-in counter, this hugely engaging museum has 70 historic aircraft on display, including a replica of the Wright Brothers' 1902 Flyer, Baron von Richthofen's WWI triplane, a Spitfire and a KLM 747. You can also play air-traffic controller in a re-created flight tower or watch aviation films in the mega-cinema. It's at Lelystad Airport, 8km southeast of the train station; take bus 148 (15 minutes, two hourly).

WORTH A TRIP

THE FORMER ISLAND OF SCHOKLAND

Schokland's islanders eked out an existence for hundreds of years on a long, narrow strip of land in the Zuiderzee. By the mid-19th century the clock had run out: fish prices plummeted and vicious storms were eroding the island away. The plucky locals hung on, despite the appalling living conditions, prompting Willem III to order their removal in 1859. Schokland was eventually swallowed up by the Noordoostpolder in the 20th century. The Schokland Museum (📞 0527-760 630; www.museumschokland.nl; Middelbuurt 3, Schokland; adult/child €7.50/5; ⊙ 11am-5pm Jul & Aug, closed Mon Sep-Jun) affords glimpses into this tortured past.

Displays, including a film in English, detail the history of the island, now a Unesco World Heritage Site. Views from the lower path hint at just how big the waves were at the prow-shaped barrier, constructed from tall wooden pilings. Ironically, since the area was drained the foundations have begun to dry out. Schokland is sinking but no longer into the sea.

The museum is 14km east of Urk; there's no public transport, so you'll need your own wheels. Once here, you can follow a 10km walking route around the old island.

into *wijken* (districts); Wijk 1 takes in the central harbour, Wijk 2 the eastern side of the harbour, and Wijk 3 the town centre and western shore.

◉ Sights

Vuurtoren van Urk LIGHTHOUSE
(Wijk 3; €2.50; ⊙ 10am-4pm Jul & Aug) Urk's 18.5m-high lighthouse was built in 1845, replacing a small stone tower where a coal fire guided ships into port. Climb 295 steps to the top for views of the town and the IJsselmeer.

Museum het Oude Raadhuis MUSEUM
(📞 0527-683 262; www.museumopurk.nl; Wijk 2; adult/child €4.75/2.60; ⊙ 10am-5pm Mon-Fri, to 4pm Sat Apr-Oct, to 4pm Mon-Sat Nov-Mar) Urk's former town hall now contains a small museum covering the history of the one-time island through traditional clothing, model ships, re-creations of fishers' cottages and local artworks.

Kerkje aan de Zee CHURCH
(Prinshendrikstraat 1; ⊙ 10am-5pm Mon-Sat, noon-4pm Sun Apr-Sep) The supports of the village church are made entirely out of masts of VOC (Dutch East India Company) ships that brought back exotic goods from the East Indies. Inside are ship models and, at times, haunting recitals by the choir.

Vissersmonument MONUMENT
(Fishers' Monument; Wijk 3) Opposite the church by the water's edge is the Vissersmonument, a lonely statue of a woman in a billowing dress gazing seaward where her loved ones were lost. Marble tablets around the perimeter list the Urk seafarers who never returned, with new names still being added.

🛏 Sleeping & Eating

Urk has no hotels, though there are a handful of B&Bs; the tourist office has a list. Otherwise, Kampen (30km southeast) and Zwolle, 45km southeast, make good bases.

The harbour is the focal point of Urk's dining scene, with everything from takeaway stalls to high-end seafood restaurants.

De Boet SEAFOOD €€€
(📞 0527-688 736; www.restaurantdeboet.nl; Wijk 1; 3-/4-/5-course menus €39.50/49.50/57.50; ⊙ noon-2pm & 5.30-9.30pm Tue-Fri, 5.30-10pm Sat) Urk's finest restaurant serves multicourse menus (no à la carte) using seafood landed daily by the fishing fleet out front. Sole with *jenever*-steamed cockles and oysters with herring roe and smoked eel are typical offerings.

ℹ Information

Tourist Office (VVV; 📞 0527-684 040; www.touristinfourk.nl; Wijk 2; ⊙ 10am-5pm Mon-Fri, to 4pm Sat Apr-Oct, to 4pm Mon-Sat Nov-Mar) Just north of the harbour.

ℹ Getting There & Away

Bus 141 runs between Urk and Kampen (50 minutes, two per hour Monday to Saturday), which has the nearest train station, and Zwolle (1¼ hours, four per hour Monday to Saturday).

Cycle routes run 30km southeast to Lelystad and 45km southeast to Zwolle, a scenic ride passing dykes, rivers and Schokland.

In July and August, **De Zuiderzee** (📞 06 5360 8813; www.de-zuiderzee.nl; Handelskade; adult/child one-way €15/10, return €17.50/12.50, bicycle free; ⊙ every 2hr 9am-6pm Mon-Sat Jul & Aug) ferries make the two-hour sailing across the IJsselmeer to Enkhuizen.

Utrecht

Best Places to Eat

→ Blauw (p150)

→ Heron (p150)

→ Jackie Brown (p154)

→ Kasteel Amerongen (p151)

→ Gys (p150)

→ Corazon Coffee (p154)

Best Places to Stay

→ Mother Goose Hotel (p149)

→ Eye Hotel (p149)

→ Mary K Hotel (p149)

→ Hotel de Tabaksplant (p154)

→ Strowis Hostel (p148)

Why Go?

Don't underrate the petite province of Utrecht. Its famous namesake city – with its throngs of students, tree-lined canals and medieval quarter – deserves the limelight. No set piece, it has a plethora of hip, fun bars and cafes. Those with calmer tastes can visit more than a dozen museums big and small. Or wander the back streets and revel in reminders of the 17th century.

And this is no mere city-state. By bike you can explore evocative castles such as the splendid Kasteel de Haar on Utrecht's doorstep. To the east stretches the Randstad's largest park, the Utrechtse Heuvelrug, studded with more magnificent estates. Amersfoort, birthplace of abstract artist Piet Mondrian, is a major city in its own right, the centre radiating plenty of medieval character.

When to Go

→ Utrecht is a university city, so, apart from festivals, live-music options reduce in July and August, outside term time.

→ April and October are ideal times for bike rides around the province.

→ Autumn is the time for bock beer events, a big film festival and Utrecht's eclectic Guess Who?

UTRECHT CITY

 030 / POP 345,100

It's hard not to fall in love with Utrecht, one of the Netherlands' oldest urban centres and for centuries its religious heart. Now a vibrant university city, the compact medieval core radiates out from the iconic 15th-century Domtoren, ringed by a loop of very pretty tree-lined canals. Their central sections have distinctive double-level sides inset with what were once medieval warehouses – many now forming fascinating venues to eat, drink, dance or sleep, with terrace-walkways that extend right to the waterside. The brilliant cafe culture goes well beyond the canals – Utrecht's vibrant concert schedules are a big draw and, if the budget stretches, it's worth luxuriating in one of numerous historic mansions that have been turned into indulgent boutique hotels.

◉ Sights

There's plenty to see around Domplein, the heart of the city in a space where a cathedral should be. Nearby, focus on strolling the old (11th-century) and new (14th-century) canals, Oudegracht and Nieuwegracht. A third canal, the Singel, surrounds the ancient core.

Scene of many a wedding photo, the bend in the Oudegracht is illuminated by lamplight in the evening; hundreds sit at outside cafes here by day. South of this point, the canal and pretty streets are quieter, stretching 1km to the southern tip of the old town.

A tips-based three-hour 'free' walking tour starts outside Domtoren on Saturdays (noon) and Sundays (2pm).

★ **Domtoren**   HISTORIC BUILDING

(Cathedral Tower; www.domtoren.nl; Domplein 9; tower tour adult/student/child €9/7.50/5; ⊙11am-5pm Tue-Sat, noon-4pm Sun) Utrecht's most striking medieval landmark, this 112m tower is worth the 465-step climb for unbeatable city views: on a clear day you can see Amsterdam. Visits are by guided tour only, departing at least hourly on the hour. Buy tickets at the tourist office (p152) across the square or prebook online (advisable in summer). The tower was originally part of a splendid 14th-/15th-century cathedral complex whose nave was blown down by a freak hurricane in 1674.

It was never rebuilt, which has left the tower disconnected from the remnant transept and chancel of the Domkerk. Where the nave should be is now the open square of Domplein.

Domkerk   CATHEDRAL

(www.domkerk.nl; Achter de Dom 1; €2.50 donation; ⊙11am-3.30pm or longer Mon-Sat, 12.30-4pm Sun) The cathedral's eastern end survived the 1674 hurricane and now forms a curiously truncated – if still impressive – place of prayer.

★ **Dom Under**   ARCHAEOLOGICAL SITE

(www.domunder.nl; Domplein 4; adult/child €12.50/10; ⊙tours hourly 11.30am-4.30pm Tue-Fri, from 10.30am Sat & Sun) Talented volunteer guides and fascinating educational films with CGI effects set the historical scene. Then it's your turn to become an amateur archaeologist as you're let loose in the subterranean half-dark beneath Domplein with your finger on the trigger of a smart-torch audio-gun. Finding clue-targets, you unravel the meaning of rubble-strata and the odd pottery piece, identifying relics of Utrecht's original Roman *castrum* and its early churches.

If you can show a ticket for the Domtoren you get a 20% discount on Dom Under and vice versa.

Centraal Museum   MUSEUM

(⊇030-236 23 53; www.centraalmuseum.nl; Agnietenstraat 1; adult/student/child €13.50/5.50/free; ⊙11am-5pm Tue-Sun) More than half the museum's 10 gallery-rooms feature temporary exhibitions (so check the schedules). Meanwhile the core collection takes a thought-provoking if disorientating thematic hop through Utrecht's 2000-year history using the lens of design and counterpointed art.

Highlights include surrealist delights by 'Dutch Dali' Johannes Moesman and others, plus the conceptual play-off between the city's contrasting architectural heritages, notably the Gothic intricacy of the Domtoren versus the functionalism of Rietveld furniture (which features extensively). The garden cafe is a pleasant oasis accessible without ticket. Admission for adults includes the Miffy Museum (p144) across the road, though since that's only really for toddlers (and might require prebooking), the gesture isn't especially generous.

Miffy Museum   MUSEUM

(Nijntje Museum; ⊇030-236 23 62; www.nijntje museum.nl; Agnietenstraat 2; adult/child €3.50/8.50; ⊙10am-5pm Tue-Sun; ⊕) Designed to delight young children, this bold, touch-everything play-museum celebrates beloved cartoon rabbit Miffy plus other related characters designed by local artist Dick Bruna. Online reservations advised.

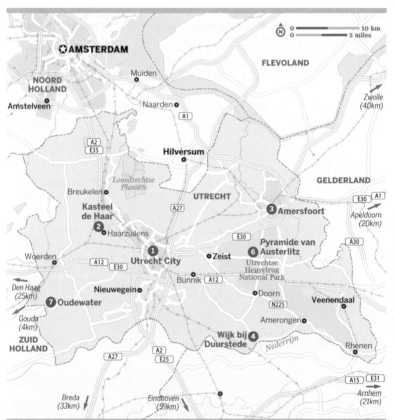

Utrecht Province Highlights

1 Domtoren (p144)
Seeing clear to Amsterdam from the tower of Utrecht's 'missing' cathedral, whose foundations also make for fascinating guided explorations.

2 Kasteel de Haar (p151) Combining medieval atmosphere with what was, in the late 19th century, the epitome of technologically advanced interiors, all in one moated, neo-Gothic castle.

3 Amersfoort (p153)
Getting into the mind of abstract artist Piet Mondrian, then strolling the pretty central streets and canal-sides.

4 Wijk bij Duurstede (p153) Exploring one of the region's quaintest small towns and making a waterside excursion to Amerongen.

5 Utrecht Canals (p149) Paddling a kayak,

piloting a motorboat or just ambling beside the restaurant-hugged double-levelled banks of Utrecht's waterways.

6 Pyramide van Austerlitz (p152) Stumbling upon a monolith-topped pyramid in the middle of a forest, then learning why French soldiers built it.

7 Oudewater (p154)
Checking your weight in witchiness.

★ **Rietveld-Schröderhuis**   HISTORIC BUILDING
(☑ reservations 030-236 23 10; www.rietveld schroderhuis.nl; Prins Hendriklaan 50; €16.50; ⊙ hourly tours 11am-4pm Tue-Sun, to 8pm some Fri; 🖳8) Years ahead of its time, this small but

uniquely conceived house was built in 1924 by celebrated Utrecht designer Gerrit Rietveld. He'd be amazed to find that it's now a Unesco-recognised monument. Visiting feels like walking into a 3D Piet Mondrian

Utrecht City

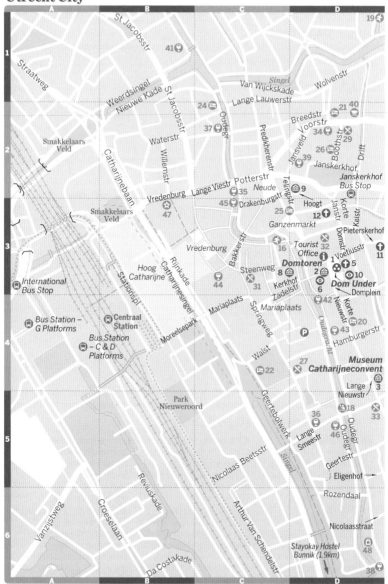

abstract, and things get especially interesting when the walls start to move. To see a contextualising video, arrive 20 minutes before your tour time.

Book as far ahead as possible: space constraints limit tours to a maximum of 12 visitors per hour. The ticket is also valid for the Centraal Museum (p144), which displays many of Rietveld's trademark chairs. If you start the day at the Centraal Museum they'll give you a map and lend you a bicycle for the 1.8km ride, but you need to return it by 4.45pm. By bus take route 8 to de Hoogstraat from central stops Neude or Janskerkhof.

Christianity, in fact – housed in a Gothic former convent and an 18th-century canal-side house. Marvel at the many beautiful illuminated manuscripts, look for the odd Rembrandt and enjoy the wide-ranging scope of the impressive special exhibitions.

Pieterskerk CHURCH
(Pieterskerkhof 3; ⊘ noon-4pm Sat Sep-Jun, 11am-5pm Tue-Sat Jul & Aug) His body has gone, but the 1054 sarcophagus of Utrecht's Prince-Bishop Bernold still lies in the crypt of the 1048 Pieterskerk. That's one of four Utrecht chapels he founded and is now the city's oldest extant church.

Universiteitsmuseum MUSEUM
(☑ 030-253 80 08; www.museum.uu.nl; Lange Nieuwstraat 106; adult/child €8/4.50; ⊘ 10am-5pm) Utrecht University's work is highlighted through exhibitions on current research plus past glories evoked through a late-19th-century classroom, historic dentistry tools and models of medical maladies.

Spoorweg Museum MUSEUM
(Railway Museum; ☑ 030-230 62 06; www.spoorwegmuseum.nl; Maliebaanstation; €17.50; ⊘ 10am-5pm Tue-Sun) Entered through a gloriously restored 1874 station with magnificent art-nouveau chandeliers, the national railway museum offers countless historic locos, a vast collection of model trains and a range of rides and interactive experiences for railway fans of all ages. The superb eye for detail even extends as far as the antique-style toilets. Don't miss De Vuurproef, a Harry Potter meets Willy Wonka experience that morphs from a history of railways into an award-winning simulator ride.

Sonnenborgh Museum & Observatory MUSEUM
(☑ 030-820 14 20; www.sonnenborgh.nl; Zonnenburg 2; adult/child €7.50/4.50; ⊘ 11am-5pm Tue-Fri, from 1pm Sun) The Sonnenborgh is actually two museums in one: upstairs has an exhibit on the history of astronomy in an 1850 building that was once among the foremost astronomical research sites on earth. Below are the foundations of the much older city-wall bastions on which it was constructed.

★ **Museum Catharijneconvent** MUSEUM
(☑ 030-231 38 35; www.catharijneconvent.nl; Lange Nieuwestraat 38; adult/senior/student/child €14/12.50/7/7; ⊘ 10am-5pm Tue-Fri, from 11am Sat & Sun) Museum Catharijneconvent has the finest collection of medieval religious art in the Netherlands – virtually the history of

Museum Speelklok MUSEUM
(☑ 030-231 27 89; www.museumspeelklok.nl; Steenweg 6; adult/child €13/7; ⊘ 10am-5pm Tue-Sun Sep-Jun, daily Jul-Aug) Within an old church, discover a colourful collection of self-playing organs, musical boxes and assorted mechanised noise-makers dating

Utrecht City

from the 18th century onwards. Hourly tours demonstrate them with gusto. Save money with a joint ticket to Domtoren (p144) (adult/child €17/9.50). Children over 12 pay adult rates.

Tickets also let you access the restoration workshop in Flora's Hof (p150), but only at 2pm on the first Wednesday of each month.

Museum voor het Kruideniersbedrijf MUSEUM
(Grocer's Museum; ☑ 030-231 66 28; www.krui deniersmuseum.nl; Hoogt 6; ⊙ 12.30-4.30pm Tue-Sat) **FREE** Tucked into a narrow lane is this charming replica of an old grocery store, where apron-costumed people sell sweets and tea by weight from decorative containers.

The blocks of white liquorice candy are, by old Dutch tradition, used to add flavour to hot milk.

Sint-Willibrod-Kerk CHURCH
(www.kerkenkijken.nl; Minrebroederstraat 19; ⊙ 1-5pm Tue-Sat) Easily missed, this 1877 neo-Gothic church has a gorgeously colourful interior with splendid stained glass, pattern-painted columns.

★ Festivals & Events

★ Le Guess Who? MUSIC
(www.leguesswho.nl; 4-day pass €117.50; ⊙ Nov) Four-day festival of alternative music, often non-Western and obscure, held at various venues around Utrecht.

⎚ Sleeping

Utrecht is rapidly expanding its collection of enticing boutique hotels in restored historic buildings. There are also a few options for sleeping in a canal-side cavern room, notably through Hotel 26. Backpackers can choose from at least four central hostels.

★ Strowis Hostel HOSTEL €
(☑ 030-238 02 80; www.strowis.nl; Boothstraat 8; dm €22-28, s/d €72.50/82.50, s/d/tr without bathroom €62.50/72.50/95; @ ⓢ) Utrecht's most

appealing hostel occupies a high-ceilinged 17th-century building; the dorms don't feel overly cramped even in the 16-bunk room. In the basement, luggage lockers (free with €10 deposit) are good-sized and some incorporate a charger plug. The appealing cafe-lounge area opens on to a quirky rear garden. The small but well-equipped kitchen closes at 10.30pm.

★ Eye Hotel   BOUTIQUE HOTEL €€
(✆030-303 63 03; www.eyehotel.nl; Wijde Begijnstraat 1; small/standard r from €110/145; �)) This fabulous 36-room boutique hotel has beautifully modernised a fine old mansion that became the Netherlands' first eye clinic in 1858 – hence all the ocular references and optician art photos. It has bright white decor, sculpted bowl-sinks and bedside tables shaped like mini school desks.

★ Mother Goose Hotel   HERITAGE HOTEL €€
(✆030-303 63 00; www.mothergoosehotel.com; Ganzenmarkt 26; r €120-250; ☜) Sensitively restored from what was originally a fortified 13th-century mansion, this 23-room boutique hotel retains many salvaged historic details and time-stressed artefacts into rooms full of contemporary comforts. The chatty, intelligent local staff add a very personal touch, and the reception is wonderfully homely – you might even find a handwritten welcome postcard on your bed.

★ Mary K Hotel   HOTEL €€
(✆030-230 48 88; www.marykhotel.com; Oudegracht 25; d from €107; ☜) ✈ A bevy of Utrecht designers and artists decorated the 10 rooms at this ideally situated 18th-century canal house. Rooms come in four basic sizes (cosy, medium, large and XL). No two are alike. All make use of historical features, and you might find a timber beam running through your bathroom or a stuffed animal snoozing in the rafters.

Grand Hotel Karel V   HOTEL €€
(✆030-233 75 55; www.karelv.nl; Geertebolwerk 1; r from €167.50; P✹@☜) Utrecht's only five-star hotel started life as a 14th-century monastery and hosted visiting knights and sovereigns, including Holy Roman Emperor Charles (Karel) V in 1543. It was rebuilt as a grand military hospital in 1823. Today, the high-quality hotel rooms, complete with canopy beds, are split between the Napoleon-classical main building ('Empire rooms') and the 2007 'Roman Wing'.

Hotel 26   APARTMENT €€€
(✆030-303 63 06; www.hotel26.nl; Nieuwgracht; r €116-245) Not a hotel at all but half a dozen canal-side cavern-rooms that have been converted into guest rooms. Check in via the Court Hotel (✆030-233 00 33; www.courthotel. nl; Korte Nieuwstraat 14; standard/cavern r from €100/140; ☜).

UTRECHT UTRECHT CITY

DON'T MISS

UTRECHT AFLOAT

At least hourly, Schuttevaer (✆030-272 01 11; www.schuttevaer.com; Oudegracht a/d Werf 85; adult/child €11.95/8.50; ☉11am-5pm) runs fixed-departure canal tours, but there are many alternatives for getting afloat. Locals often bring friends and a picnic then jump aboard an electric-powered open-top boat. Renting one for eight people or less, the cheapest deals are usually SMS-activated boats from Greenjoy (✆085-401 95 55; www.greenjoy.nl; opposite Wittevrouwensingel 57; 2hr rental €50-90; ☉9am-10pm). However Sloep Delen (✆030-711 62 00; www.sloepdelen.nl; Hooghiemstraplein; 2hr off-peak/peak €60/120, deposit €150) provides somewhat bigger boats (up to 12 people) and usually has someone at their departure dock to help if you can't work out how to pilot the craft. Both companies require advance online bookings, prices often dropping to half on weekdays for departures before 4pm. Several outfits including Lekkerbootje (www. lekkerbootjevaren.nl) and Sloephuren (www.sloephurenutrecht.nl) offer piloted vessel charters, which can include catering. Much simpler options include kayaks (kano) from Kanoverhuurutrecht (✆030-633 22 36; www.kanoverhuurutrecht.nl; Oudegracht a/d Werf 275; single/double kayak per hour €6/12, per day €14/28; ☉1-8pm Mon, from 10am Tue-Sun) or pedalos – known as canal-bikes (www.stromma.nl; opposite Oudegracht 167; 90min per adult/child €9.50/4.75, deposit €20; ☉10am-6pm daily Jul & Aug, Wed-Sun Apr-Jun & Sep-Oct) - rented on Oudegracht's lower level in front of the municipal library.

LOCAL KNOWLEDGE

GREEN ESCAPES

For a moment of calm head to an Utrecht garden. Behind the Universiteitsmuseum (p147), De Oude Hortus (free with a museum ticket, €2.50 without) is a wonderfully peaceful and ancient botanical garden sheltering trees and plants collected by the Dutch during their world exploits.

Pandhof (Kloosterhof; www.pandhofvandedom.nl; Domplein; ⊙10am-4pm Mon-Fri, noon-5pm Sat & Sun) Between the Domkirk and Academiegebouw, a gateway leads through to this charming little formal garden ringed by 15th-century Gothic cloisters.

Flora's Hof (Servetstraat 1; ⊙9am-5pm) This petite walled garden, tucked behind the Steven Sterk bookshop, makes a peaceful retreat from which to stare up and observe the Domtoren (p144).

Utrechtse Heuvelrug National Park (www.np-utrechtseheuvelrug.nl) Cycling and hiking is ideal in this 65km green arc east of Utrecht city. The national park has the Netherlands' second-largest sweep of wildlife-rich forest but also incorporates meadows and high dunes, patchworked with areas of human habitation.

🍴 Eating

Utrecht's dining range is astonishing. Wharfside restaurants on the Oudegracht, along with terrace places along narrow, bustling Dreiharingstraat, are appealing, although often tourist-centred, with a global selection of cuisines on offer. Increasingly fashionable student-oriented Voorstraat has bargain takeaway, oriental and snack foods, plus tempting fine-dining options. There's more on the street's eastern extension, Biltstraat. Cheap pizza places compete on Nobelstraat.

Kimmade VIETNAMESE €
(☑030-737 09 93; www.kimmade.nl; Mariastraat 2; baguettes €3.95, dishes €5.95-8.50; ⊙noon-10pm Mon-Sat, 1-8pm Sun) This four-table hole in the wall is the least glamorous of numerous buzzing street-terrace cafe-restaurants on Mariastraat but the great-value Vietnamese street-food-style dishes mean it's ever popular.

Gys CAFE €
(☑030-259 17 88; www.gysutrecht.nl; Voorstraat 77; lunch/dinner mains from €7.50/10; ⊙10am-9.30pm; 🔊🍴) 🌿 Everything's organic at this bright and airy bistro, which positively exudes aromas of healthy living, yet feels invitingly spacious, with low-wattage ball lamps, botanical prints and plants in flowerpots on the walls. Most but not everything is vegetarian, vegan and/or gluten-free.

★Heron EUROPEAN €€
(☑030-230 22 29; www.heronrestaurant.nl; Schalkwijkstraat 26-28; 1-/2-/3-/4-/5- courses €22/33/35/40/45; ⊙5.30-9.30pm Tue-Sat) This adorable 'petit restaurant' presents expectant diners with a list of cryptic clues to a dinner that's brimming with imaginative flavours and is eminently seasonal. Expect 100% locally sourced fare including forage plants collected by the forester owner. Six lucky guests get to sit right at the central cooking counter watching every move of the expert chefs.

★Blauw INDONESIAN €€
(☑030-234 24 63; www.restaurantblauw.nl; Springweg 64; veg/meat/fish mains from €20.50/24.50/27, rijsttafel €30/33.50/33.50; ⊙6-10pm Mon-Fri, from 5pm Sat & Sun) Blauw is *the* place for perfectly cooked Indonesian food; indeed it's hard to imagine better, even in Jakarta. Perfectly blended flavours, right down to the amuse-bouche of home-made sambal, leave diners swooning with delight.

Loetje Utrecht DUTCH €€
(☑030-231 50 40; www.utrecht.loetje.nl; Oudkerkhof 29; mains €8.50-24, sandwiches €4.75-8.75; ⊙10am-10.30pm) The growing Loetje chain prides itself on its tenderloin steak (from €18.25) but also has more specifically Dutch options such as meatballs on farmer's bread, seasonal asparagus, and *kapucijners,* a huge bowl of soft brown peas served with onions, gherkin, piccalilli and fried bacon. The stylish Utrecht branch gives the feeling of a grand cafe given a Dutch-modernist makeover.

Concours EUROPEAN €€€
(☑030-223 11 58; www.restaurantconcours.nl; Biltstraat 23; 3-/4-/5-/6-course dinner €34.50/42/50/58; ⊙5.30-10.30pm Mon-Sat) Intimate and decoratively sparse, Concours is a great choice for a gourmet meal. It's romantic without being stuffy, comparatively affordable

and dishes are presented with great aplomb. There's no choice – just put yourself in the hands of celebrated chef Alex Zeelenberg for the day's menu based on fresh, locally sourced produce.

For Masterchef wannabes, private cooking workshops can be arranged on Sundays, and there are themed monthly masterclasses.

Syr MIDDLE EASTERN €€€
(📞030-233 11 04; www.restaurantsyr.nl; Lange Nieuwstraat 71; 3-/4-/5-course dinner €32.50/37.50/42.50; ⏰5-10pm daily & 11.30am-4pm Sat & Sun) In an unfussy, effortlessly relaxed cafe atmosphere, Syr serves reliably delicious Middle Eastern food with a European fusion twist, cooked and served by refugees who have escaped Syria's tragic civil war.

🍷 Drinking & Nightlife

Utrecht has many marvels for beer fans, and anyone will delight in the atmospheric cafes that dot the Oudegracht canal-side. In sunshine, Ganzenmarkt becomes a popular locals' spot for beer-and-sandwich lunches and Tolsteegbrug bustles at sunset. At night Neude and Janskerkhof come alive, the latter with dancing later. Rougher pubs on Nobelstraat draw in students.

★Olivier BROWN CAFE
(https://utrecht.cafe-olivier.be; Achter Clarenburg 6a; ⏰11am-midnight Sun-Wed, 10am-2am Thu-Sat) Located unpromisingly beside the ugly Hoog Catharijne building is this blessed beer heaven, an astonishingly slick yet super-characterful reworking of a large former church, complete with organ.

★Kafé België BAR
(www.kafebelgie.nl; Oudegracht 196; ⏰11am-3am Tue-Sat, from 1pm Sun & Mon) This merrily rough-edged bar's 20 Benelux brews on tap supplement uncountable scores of other brews by the bottle.

't Oude Pothuys BROWN CAFE
(www.pothuys.nl; Oudegracht 279; ⏰noon-1am or later) On a summer day you can drink or dine right at the canal-side facing the brick arched Smeebrug bridge. This cosy pub-restaurant's real draw is the free nightly live music in its whitewashed double-barrelled medieval cellar. Concerts rarely start before 11pm (10pm quieter evenings).

Heen en Weer BAR
(Oudegracht 13; ⏰10.30am-10pm Mon-Wed, to 1am Thu-Sat, to 8pm Sun) For the perfect perch choose the corner table in this 1702 house with views straight down the canal to a double-arch bridge. Or in warm weather sit on the triangle of terrace tucked between street and upper canal-side.

ACU BAR
(www.acu.nl; Voorstraat 71; ⏰from 6pm Tue-Thu & Sat, 8pm-4am Fri, 2-11pm Sun) A political reference point in Utrecht, ACU combines bar, music venue, lecture hall and more. Argue about whether Trotsky was too conservative while chomping organic vegan food by the inimitable Kitchen Punx (6pm to 9pm Tuesday to Thursday plus Saturday).

Cafe DeRat PUB
(📞030-231 95 13; www.cafederat.nl; Lange Smeestraat 37; ⏰2pm-late; 🛜) This cosy, board-floored corner pub has a lot of soul and a

UTRECHT UTRECHT CITY

CASTLE CAPERS

Grandiose castles lie within easy half-day-trip distance of Utrecht city, easily navigable by bicycle, bus or your own four wheels.

Kasteel de Haar (📞030-677 85 15; www.kasteeldehaar.nl; Kasteellaan 1, Haarzuilens; adult/child tour €16/10, gardens only €5/3.50; ⏰park 9am-5pm, castle 11am-5pm, tours hourly to 4pm) The nation's biggest moated castle is a remarkable feast of Gothic spires, turrets and portcullis gates. It has a glorious chapel, and is surrounded by a large English landscaped garden with broad paths, statues and canal-like stretches of pond.

Kasteel Amerongen (📞0343-563 766; www.kasteelamerongen.nl; Drostestraat 20, Amerongen; adult/child €12/6, gardens only €4; ⏰11am-5pm Tue-Sun Apr-Oct, 11.30am-4pm Thu-Sun Nov-Mar; 🚌50) Kasteel Amerongen is a moated, rectilinear castle-mansion whose sumptuous salons can be perused by joining an hourly guided tour (in Dutch). If you just want to look at the rather austere frontage you can stroll down to the very impressive Bentinck cafe-restaurant. Bus 50 takes 65 minutes from Utrecht (€5.15) and 15 minutes from Doorn (€2.20).

WORTH A TRIP

PYRAMIDE VAN AUSTERLITZ

One of the oddest rural landmarks south of Amersfoort is **Pyramide van Austerlitz** (www.pyramidevanausterlitz.nl; Zeisterweg 98, N224; climb €3; ⊕ info centre noon-4pm Easter-Oct, pyramid-climb 11am-5pm Tue-Sun Easter-Oct, Sun only Nov-Easter), a 36m-high pyramid-shaped hill that was originally built in 1804 to keep some 18,000 French troops out of bored mischief. Topped by a monolith, it was restored in 2004–5. In the car park, an information centre screens a fascinating free film giving eight minutes of historical context. Walk 400m through woodlands to see the pyramid itself. Viewing is free; climbing it requires a ticket.

remarkable ability to source rare beers from little-known brewers. This includes a whole menu of Lambics (sour, spontaneously fermented beers).

De Bastaard   PUB
(www.debastaard.nl; Jansveld 17; ⊕4pm-2am) This unpretentious, jazz-toned bar serves a full range of La Trappe Dutch Trappist beers that you can sip while dining cheaply on takeaway – it has no kitchen so you're welcome to bring your own food.

De Ontdekking   COFFEE
(Voorstraat 110; coffee €2.25-3.45, breakfast €5-11; ⊕8am-6pm Mon-Fri, from 9am Sat & Sun) Travel magazines in various languages adorn this stripped old house on a canal-facing street-corner, but the big draw is excellent coffee, breakfasts and high tea.

Cafe Kalff   GAY & LESBIAN
(⊘030-231 09 19; www.cafekalff.nl; Oude Gracht 47; ⊕4pm-1am Tue-Fri, from 3pm Sat & Sun) 'Go where you're celebrated, not where you're tolerated' declares this narrow canal-facing pub, which is a focus of LGBTIQ+ social life.

Ekko   CLUB
(⊘030-231 74 57; www.ekko.nl; Bemuurde Weerd WZ3) This cultural innovator has a nose for new trends so it's always worth checking out what it's doing, from club nights to concerts. All payments are PinPay.

Bas/s   CLUB
(www.clubbasis.nl; Oudegracht a/d Werf 97; cover €8-13; ⊕11pm-6am Fri & Sat) Predominantly techno music in a reverberant canal-side

cavern with stark, concrete-industrial decor. Check the website for events and online discounts. No cash accepted, pay by card.

☆ Entertainment

Utrecht is blessed with many cinemas, theatres and a particularly dazzling series of five concert halls at **TivoliVredenburg** (⊘030-231 45 44; www.tivolivredenburg.nl; Vredenburgkade 11).

Many hostels and hotels provide the weekly **UitLoper** listings sheet and the free bimonthly what's-on brochure, **MagUtrecht** (www.magutrecht.com). Visit www.duic.nl/uitgaan for a daily 'going out' suggestion.

🛍 Shopping

It's hard to avoid the vast Hoog Catharijne mall – you're almost forced to transit through it between the train station and city centre. There are mainstream shops on Vredenburg and Steenweg but more interesting choices down Voorstraat and especially along the southern end of Oudegracht.

★ De Bierverteller   ALCOHOL
(⊘030-737 13 06; www.debierverteller.nl; Twijnstraat 47; ⊕11am-7pm Tue-Fri, 10am-6pm Sat, noon-6pm Sun) Obliging, knowledgeable staff can help you make sense of over 700 varieties of beer. Every month or so there are tasting sessions – sign up online. Or just give in to temptation and buy a case of the marvellous Zuster Agatha from Muifel Brouwerij.

★ HetFotoAtelier   PHOTOGRAPHY
(⊘030-243 49 98; www.hetfotoatelier.nl; Lange Nieuwstraat 86; ⊕2-7pm Wed-Sat) If you love pre-digital, black-and-white photography, this specialist shop-gallery will probably be your highlight in Utrecht.

ℹ Information

Tourist Office (VVV; ⊘030-236 00 04; www.visit-utrecht.com; Domplein 9; ⊕11.45am-5pm Mon, 10am-5pm Tue-Sat, noon-5pm Sun) Has plentiful brochures and sells Domtoren (p144) tickets. Some hostels and hotels offer the excellent *Use-it* map-guide, full of useful locals' tips.

ℹ Getting There & Away

Utrecht is a public transport hub, but if driving, be aware that the very limited street parking is payable almost 24/7.

BICYCLE
National bike route **LF9** runs north through farmlands for 23km to a junction with **LF23**,

which covers both Muiden and Flevoland. To the south it runs through rich farmlands towards Breda. Marathon route **LF7** passes through Utrecht on its 350km route from Alkmaar to Maastricht; Amsterdam is about 50km north-west. **LF4** runs east 80km to Arnhem.

Regional buses can depart from two main areas, both on the west side of Utrecht CS. Breda-bound bus 401 (€11.95, 75 minutes, hourly) uses the **G Platforms** (Jaarbeursplein) opposite the World Trade Centre building. Most other useful services, including bus 107 to Gouda via Oudewater, use the **C & D Platforms** (Jaarbeurszijde) accessed by escalators descending from the west station concourse. For bus 50 to Doorn and Amerongen it's generally easier to board at the central **Janskerkhof bus stop** (Nobelstraat; 🚌 50).

For information on bus and tram routes, visit the **U-OV Service Winkel** (www.u-ov.info; ☉ 6.30am-7pm Mon-Fri, 7am-5.30pm Sat, 10am-5pm Sun) in the train station.

International buses use an awkward-to-find **bus stop** (Westplein) just north of the NH Hotels tower, beyond the G Platforms and tram station (northwest of the train station).

TRAIN

Utrecht CS (Centraal Station) is the national rail hub. Useful direct services include the following.
Amsterdam Centraal (€7.60, 27 minutes, four per hour)
Den Haag (€11.20, 40 minutes, twice/four times per hour weekdays/weekends)
Groningen (€24.90, 1hr 55 minutes, hourly)
Maastricht (€23.90, two hours, twice hourly)
Schiphol Airport (€8.80, 32 mins, four per hour)
Rotterdam (€10.50, 37 minutes, at least three hourly)

There are **left-luggage lockers** (Utrecht Centraal; small/large locker from €6/9; ☉ 24hr) at the station, although they're hard to find. Find them above Burger King, entered from the northern passage, or by walking through Bistro Centraal and along the upper station balcony until you're over platforms 18/19. Coming from town, don't go through the ticket barriers.

AMERSFOORT

🔲 033 / POP 154,700

Delightful Amersfoort grew exceedingly rich from beer, wool and tobacco in the 16th century and retains an egg-shaped old-town core that's full of striking merchants' houses, small canals and a trio of historical gateways. Evocative for random strolling, it's also a hot spot for art and great dining.

◉ Sights

Much of Amersfoort's appeal comes from wandering the lanes, squares and canal-sides of the old town, which retains more than 300 pre-18th-century buildings.

Onze Lieve Vrouwe Toren   HISTORIC BUILDING
(www.olvkerk.nl; Lieve Vrouwekerkhof; adult/child €5/4; ☉ tours hourly noon-5pm Tue-Sun Jul & Aug, 2pm daily rest of year) This 15th-century Gothic tower is Amersfoort's defining architectural icon. It's the only surviving component of a church that was otherwise destroyed by an unfortunate gunpowder blast in 1787.

★Mondriaanhuis   MUSEUM
(www.mondriaanhuis.nl; Kortegracht 11; adult/child €8/free; ☉ 11am-5pm Tue-Sun) This small but absorbing museum honours the life and work of the famous De Stijl artist Piet Mondrian (1872–1944) in the house where he was born.

A five-minute film imaginatively traces his artistic evolution from realist landscapes through impressionism to the abstract lines and primary colours which became his hallmark after moving to Paris in 1911.

Kade Museum   GALLERY
(🔲 033-422 50 30; www.kunsthalkade.nl; Eemplein 77; adult/child €10/free; ☉ 11am-5pm Tue-Sun) This boldly designed gallery hosts large-scale temporary exhibitions devoted to contemporary visual artists or themes.

🛏 Sleeping & Eating

There's a superb choice of dining options dotted throughout the old-town area,

WORTH A TRIP

WIJK BIJ DUURSTEDE

The delightful canal-ringed antique core of Wijk includes a street of cafes and galleries (Peperstraat) behind the distinctive church (on Markt) and a very romantic castle, shattered into two remnant towers. Though the castle is private and used as a wedding venue, its semiwild wooded park is freely accessible to visitors.

Wijk is accessible by bus 41 from Utrecht Centraal (€4.30, 35 minutes) or bus 56 from Amersfoort via Doorn. To find the old centre, walk down Zandweg beside the Gouden Leeuw hotel-restaurant and cross the canal bridge.

WITCHERY IN OUDEWATER

Stepping onto the 'witch-weighing' scales is the main attraction of the little **Heksen-waag** (www.heksenwaag.nl; Leeuweringerstraat 2; adult/child €6/3; ⊙11am-5pm Tue-Sun Apr-Oct & Mon Jul-Sep, Fri-Sun Nov-Mar), or Witches' Weighing House in the town of Oudewater, a 40-minute ride from Utrecht on bus 107. During the horrific witch hunts of the 16th century, close to a million women all over Europe were executed – burnt, drowned or otherwise tortured to death – on suspicion of being witches. Weighing was one of the more common methods of determining witchery: a woman who was too light for the size of her frame was 'obviously a witch because hags like that have no soul'! A woman who weighed the 'proper' amount was too heavy to ride a broom and thus was not a witch.

notably along Krommestraat, which has options in all price ranges, from bakery-cafes to one of the Netherlands' more-affordable Michelin-starred restaurants, Bloks.

UTRECHT AMERSFOORT

★**Hotel de Tabaksplant**　　HOTEL €
(☏033-472 97 97; www.tabaksplant.nl; Coninckstraat 15; s/tw/ste from €85/95/140, without bathroom tw/tr €67/75; ⊙8am-11pm) Three historic buildings, including a pre-1623 tobacco merchant's house, have been combined to create a 25-room hotel with very obliging service and an understated sense of style.

Corazon Coffee　　CAFE €
(www.coffeecorazon.nl; Krommestraat 18; lunch dishes €5.95-13.95; ⊙10am-6pm; 🖥) Put away iPads or computers in this people-friendly cafe – digital devices are discouraged but there's a free book exchange and close-packed tables to encourage conversation. Many of the sandwiches and lunch plates are vegan, or you can savour one of the 16 types of pure Arabica coffee, 30 teas, lassis or smoothies.

Jackie Brown　　FUSION €€
(www.jackiebrown.nl; Hof 23; lunches €7-11, dinner dishes €6-8; ⊙11.30pm-late) Black walls with low-wattage lamps and a crowned mural of Notorious B.I.G. give Jackie Brown a self-consciously 'urban' vibe, but the tapas-sized portions of Euro-Asian fusion food tend towards gourmet in both presentation and quality.

🍷 Drinking & Nightlife

Hof and Lieve Vrouwekerkhof both teem with cafes and pubs, with later-night options on Groenmarkt. Shop at **Hop** (www.facebook.com/bierwinkelhop; Achter Het Oude Stadhuis 2; ⊙noon-6pm Wed-Fri, to 5pm Sat, 1-5pm Sun) for an excellent selection of takeaway beers.

Drie Ringen Bierbrouwerij　　MICROBREWERY
(www.dedrieringen.nl; Kleine Spui 18; beers €3.95; ⊙2-7.30pm Tue-Thu, from 1pm Fri-Sun) Near

the Koppelpoort, this much-heralded microbrewery takes its name from a 17th-century predecessor and serves seven of its 11 sturdy beer varieties on tap.

ⓘ Information

Tourist Office (VVV; ☏per call €0.50 0900-112 23 64; www.vvvamersfoort.nl; Breestraat 1; ⊙11am-5.30pm Mon, 10am-17.30pm, Tue-Fri; 10am-4pm, Sat; 11am-4pm, Sun; closed Sun Nov-Mar) Organises walking tours and has cycling maps. It's on the corner of the main square, across from the Onze Lieve Vrouwe Toren.

ⓘ Getting There & Around

BICYCLE

Utrecht is 23km southwest on a beautiful ride through forests and farms on national bike route **LF9**, which runs north 23km to meet **LF23**; both continue into Flevoland.

Fietsboot Eemlijn (☏06 5194 2279; www.eemlijn.nl; Grote Kapel; adult/child per sector €2/free, bike €1; ⊙daily mid-Jun–mid-Sep, four days weekly mid-Apr–mid-Jun & mid-Sep–mid-Oct) Amersfoort's 'bike boat' plies the Gelderse valley taking 3½ hours to either Huizen or Spakenburg on the Eemmeer. It departs at 10am from a jetty just 200m northwest of Koppelpoort; return trips start at 2pm. Outbound/return stops are Soest (10.45am/5pm), Baarn (11.30am/4.15pm) and Eemdijk (12.30pm/3.15pm). From any stop it's pleasant to cycle back through the woods.

City-centre **Rijwielhandel van Hoeijen** (☏033-461 37 73; www.van-hoeijen.nl; Krommestraat 61; 7-gear/electric bikes per day €10/20; ⊙1-6pm Mon, from 9am Tue-Fri, 9am-5pm Sat) rents bikes by the calendar day, so overnight hires cost double.

TRAIN

Amersfoort's train station is a 500m walk west of the centre. Useful destinations include Amsterdam (€8.60, 35 to 50 minutes), Deventer (€10.80, 35 minutes, three hourly) and Utrecht (€4.60, 13 to 20 minutes, up to six hourly).

Rotterdam & South Holland

Best Places to Eat

➡ Fouquet (p187)

➡ In den Doofpot (p199)

➡ Villa Augustus
Restaurant (p177)

➡ Fenix Food Factory (p168)

➡ AJÍ (p167)

Best Places to Stay

➡ Hotel The Roosevelt (p203)

➡ Ex Libris (p198)

➡ Hotel Indigo (p186)

➡ Citizen M (p163)

➡ De Luthiers (p176)

Why Go?

It's the contrasts that make South Holland and Zeeland such compelling destinations. One day, you're in the ongoing architectural experiment that is Rotterdam, marvelling at its ever-growing portfolio of cutting-edge buildings. The next day you might be in Delft, where the historic town centre is so well-preserved that you'll feel as if you've been transported back to Holland's 17th-century Golden Age. And the contrasts aren't confined to building stock: Den Haag has a sophisticated urban charm, enchanting visitors with its art, fine dining and cultural scene; Zeeland has a dramatic back-of-beyond feel, with a sparsely populated and windswept landscape; and Gouda plays to every Dutch stereotype, with wheels of its famous yellow cheese and traditionally garbed locals ever-present. The bottom line for travellers is that there's something for everyone here, whether it be windmills or wine bars, tulips or tasting menus.

When to Go

➡ Rotterdam's museums, shopping, restaurants, bars and nightlife – as well as its excellent public-transport network – mean you can ignore the weather while indoors, and comfortably visit year-round.

➡ Spring brings an explosion of colour to the glorious tulip-filled gardens at Keukenhof, encouraging visitors into a photographic frenzy. The gardens are open for just eight weeks a year and are well worth scheduling a trip around.

➡ Between spring and autumn, you'll find many more attractions open throughout the region than in the winter months, and greater odds of enjoying a balmy canal stroll or a beach swim.

➡ July and August is festival season, with events on streets, in parks and by the beach.

N

| 0 | 20 km |
| 0 | 10 miles |

Alkmaar
(18km)

Hoorn
(23km)

AMSTERDAM

Haarlem A9 A10

Sneek
(110km)

Keukenhof
Gardens
2

Amstelveen

Lisse

Aalsmeer

Zwolle
(87km)

Noordwijk aan Zee

NORTH
SEA

Katwijk aan Zee A44

A4

E35

Leiden 6

A2

Alphen aan den Rijn

Scheveningen

Utrecht

Den Haag 3 E19

A12 E30

Monster

A12

7 **Gouda**

Hoek van Holland

4 **Delft**

A13

E25

A20

A27

1

Rotterdam

Arnhem
(64km)

A15

5 **Kinderdijk**

**ZUID-
HOLLAND**

A15

Gorinchem

Dordrecht

A29

A16

Biesbosch
National
Park

A59

Renesse
Haamstede
Westenschouwen

Schouwen-
Duiveland

Willemstad E19

A261

Nijmegen
(55km)

Waterland
Neeltje Jans

Delta
Project

Zierikzee

A4 A59

Sint
Philipsland

N57

Domburg

Noord-
Beveland

Tholen

A17

Breda E312

Tilburg

Veere

Walcheren

Goes

Bergen
op Zoom

Roosendaal

Middelburg

Zuid-
Beveland A58

Vlissingen

Kruiningen E312

Perkpolder A4

Turnhout

Zeeuws-
Vlaanderen

IJzendijk

ZEELAND

BELGIUM

Venlo
(51km)

Westerschelde

Oosterschelde

Antwerp

Rotterdam & South Holland Highlights

1 Rotterdam (right)
Exploring cutting-edge
architecture, art and the
vibrant cafe culture on offer in
'the city that's never finished'.

2 Keukenhof Gardens
(p200) Tiptoeing through
flowering tulips at this
sensational seasonal
attraction.

3 Mauritshuis (p181) Being
bewitched by Vermeer's *Girl
with a Pearl Earring* in Den
Haag.

4 Nieuwe Kerk (p189)
Climbing the spiralling steps
inside the tower for views over
Delft's medieval townscape.

5 Kinderdijk (p170) Walking
or cycling alongside creaking
windmills and windswept dykes.

6 Rijksmuseums Leiden
(p194) Immersing yourself
in the collections of the
Volkenkunde, Boerhaave and
Van Oudheden museums.

7 Sint Janskerk (p178)
Marvelling at the immense size
and magnificent stained-glass
windows in Gouda's 16th-
century cathedral.

SOUTH HOLLAND

Home to two of the country's major cities – Rotterdam and Den Haag – and to many of its prettiest and most historic towns, Zuid-Holland (South Holland) is popular with domestic and international tourists alike. Along with the provinces of Noord-Holland (North Holland) and Utrecht, it is part of the Randstad, the economic and population heart of the Netherlands. Known for its architecture, museums, sandy beaches and bird-filled national parks, it is a region that richly rewards those who visit.

Rotterdam

010 / POP 629,606

Innovation is the mantra in the Netherlands' second metropolis and Europe's largest port, and locals embrace it with an enthusiasm that makes a visit here exhilarating. Tourist arrivals in Rotterdam are increasing every year and it's clear to everyone what the main attraction is: world-class architecture and urban design. Combine this with top museums, a proliferation of art, enticing cafe culture and a slew of waterways bursting with local life – locals zipping across a slew of graceful designer bridges, grabbing a watertaxi, sauntering along picturesque inner-city canals – and Rotterdam's metropolitan charm becomes irresistible.

Split by the vast Nieuwe Maas shipping channel, Rotterdam is crossed by a series of tunnels and bridges, notably the dramatic Erasmusbrug – the swooping white cable-stayed bridge dubbed de Zwaan (the Swan). On the north side of the water, the city centre is easily strolled.

History

Rotterdam has come a long way since its establishment as a fishing village: from being one of the bases of the Dutch East India Company, the world's first multinational corporation, to developing into Europe's busiest shipping port, and being a global leader in the fields of contemporary architecture and urban design.

Rotterdam's history as a major port dates to the 16th century. In 1572 Spaniards being pursued by the rebel Sea Beggars were given shelter in the harbour. They rewarded this generosity by pillaging the town. Rotterdam soon joined the revolution.

Astride the Netherlands' major southern rivers, Rotterdam is ideally situated to service trading ships. Large canals first constructed in the 1800s and improved ever since link the port with the Rhine River and other major waterways.

On 14 May 1940 the invading Germans issued an ultimatum to the Dutch government: surrender or cities such as Rotterdam will be destroyed. The government capitulated; however, the bombers were already airborne and the raid was carried out anyway.

Rather than rebuild in historical style, skyscrapers and groundbreaking architectural statements give Rotterdam an evolving skyline unlike any other in the Netherlands.

◉ Sights

With so many memorable buildings and landmarks, Rotterdam is easy to navigate. The city centre is also a lot smaller than it seems for such a bustling metropolis – you might never need to use the efficient public-transport system of metros, buses and trams. The ultimate way to see the city and visit its sights is by bike.

★ Museum Boijmans van Beuningen
MUSEUM

(www.boijmans.nl; Museumpark 18-20; adult/student/child under 19 €17.50/8.75/free; ⊙11am-5pm Tue-Sun; Ⓜ Eendrachtsplein, 🚊 Museumpark, Eendrachtsplein) In early 2019 the museum closed for major renovations, expected to take seven years, but other museums will exhibit part of its collection during this period. The roll-call of artists represented in the collection of Rotterdam's pre-eminent fine-arts museum is stellar and spans multiple periods and movements: Rubens, Rembrandt, Monet, Degas, Van Gogh, Picasso, Miró, Bacon and many other luminaries are represented. Highlights include Jan van Eyck's *The Three Marys at the Tomb* (1425–35), Hieronymus Bosch's *The Pedlar* (c1500) and Pieter Brueghel the Elder's *Tower of Babel* (c1568).

Kunsthal
GALLERY

(☏ 010-440 03 00; www.kunsthal.nl; Westzeedijk 341; adult/student/child €14/7/free; ⊙10am-5pm Tue-Sat, 11am-5pm Sun; 🚊 Kievitslaan) This dynamic cultural institution in Rotterdam's main museum enclave is known for its constantly changing and inevitably thought-provoking exhibition program. There are always at least three exhibitions to visit – rom painting to photography, fashion to graphic design – and these are spread across the architecturally notable multifloored building,

Rotterdam Central

500 m
0.25 miles

BLIJDORP

BLIJDORP

Bergselaan

Beaemertstr

Stadhoudersweg

Statensingel

Statenweg

Schepenstr

Walenburgerweg

Spoorsingel

Eudokiaplein

Belgraweg

Noordsingel

Agniesestr

Banierstr

Jacob Catsstraat

Noordmolenstr

Woelwijkstr

Tollensstr

AGNISEBUURT

Heer Bokelweg

Raampoortstr

Vijverhofstraat

Provenierssr

PROVENIERSWIJK

Schepenstr

Conradstr

Tourist Information Desk

Centraal Station

Schiekade

Stationsplein

Weena

Karel Doormanstr

Centraal

Karel Weena Zuid

Kruisstr

Kruiskade

Stadhuis

Stadhuispl

Mauritsweg

Westersingel

West Kruiskade

Gouvernestr

OUDE WESTEN

Hennegouwerlaan

1e Middellandstr

Beukelsdijk

Jacobusstr

Binnenwegpl

Lijnbaan

Mauritsstr

Van Oldenbarneveltstr

Aert van Nesstr

Schouwburgplein

Korte Lijnbaan

Kruisstr

Coolsingel

Meent

Beursplein

Tourist Office

Bulgersteyn

Nieuwstr

Blaak

Posthoornstr

Hoogstr

Markthal

Steigersgracht

Westewagenstr

Hoogstr

Haagseveer

Pompenburg

Goudsesingel

Meent

Coolsingel

Binnenwegpl

Lijnbaan

Zaagmolenkade

Admiraal de Ruyterweg

Zaagmolenstr

Linker Rotterkade

Zwaanshals

Crooswijksesingel

Goudse Rijweg

RUBROEK

Boezemweg

Jonker Fraansstraat

Pannekoekstr

Mariniersweg

Hoogstr

Oostzeedijk

Oostpl

Oudehaven

Geldersekade

Blaak

Hurricadiat

Boompjes

Maasboulevard

De Rotte

Van Nelle Fabriek (1.3km)

17
48
52
15
40 22
51 27
6
49
35
47
39
57 34
43
46
58
50
11 21
28
56 2
18
5
33
14
53
45

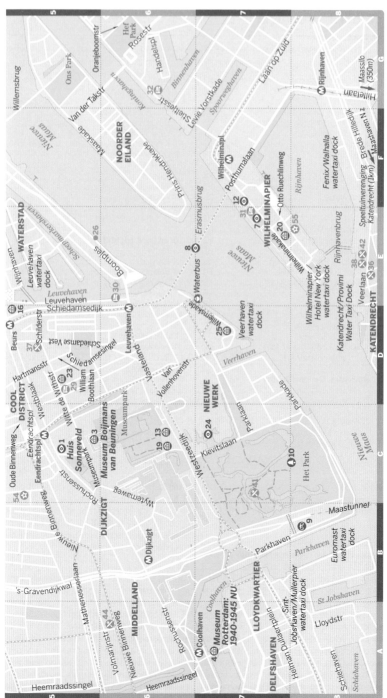

Rotterdam Central

which abuts a dyke embankment and was designed in 1988–89 by Rem Koolhaas and Fuminori Hoshino from local firm OMA.

Witte de With Centre for Contemporary Art MUSEUM
(☏010-411 01 44; www.wdw.nl; Witte de Withstraat 50; adult/student & child under 18 €6/3, free entry Fri 6-9pm, combination ticket with TENT €9/4.50; ◎11am-6pm Tue-Thu, Sat & Sun, to 9pm Fri; Ⓜ Eendrachtsplein, ⧉ Museumpark) Sharing a premises with TENT (www.tentrotterdam. nl; adult/student & child under 18 €5/2.50, free entry Fri 6-9pm), this gallery has its finger on the pulse of breaking developments in contemporary art worldwide. Its experimental exhibitions, installations and events have a laser-sharp social and political focus, and

often launch up-and-coming talent. It closes between exhibitions while new works are being set up, so check ahead to be sure it's open. In 2018, the gallery announced that it was considering a name change, but no final decision had been made.

Museum Rotterdam MUSEUM
(☏010-217 67 50; www.museumrotterdam. nl; Rodezand 26; adult/student/child 4-17 €7.50/3.75/2.50, free 1st Sat of the month; ◎10am-5pm Tue-Sat, 11am-5pm Sun; Ⓜ Stadhuis, ⧉ Stadhuis) The attractive Timmerhuis building designed by Rotterdam-based Rem Koolhaas is a classy location for this museum profiling the city's past, present and future. There are three main exhibits – an engaging 'History of the City' exhibit on the

ground floor with plenty of artefacts and scale models of the city in 1694, 1940 and now; a multimedia space focusing on the stories of local residents; and an upstairs space for temporary exhibitions – as well as a small kids' play area.

★ **Van Nelle Fabriek** NOTABLE BUILDING
(Van Nelle Factory; www.vannellefabriek.com; Van Nelleweg 1, Spaanse Polder; ☐ 38 & B9 from Centraal Station) Designed and built between 1925 and 1931, this modernist World Heritage–listed factory northwest of the city centre is an icon of 20th-century industrial architecture. Often described as a 'glass palace' (it's largely constructed of steel and glass), it functioned as a state-of-the-art coffee, tea and tobacco factory until the 1990s and now houses creative industries. Though closed to the public, the factory sometimes offers guided tours on weekends at 1pm (adult/child under 13 €8.50/5); check the factory website for details. Urban Guides (p162) also runs one-hour guided tours (per person €15) at noon on most Saturdays and Sundays (book ahead).

★ **Museum Rotterdam: 1940-1945 NU** MUSEUM
(War & Resistance Museum; www.40-45nu.nl; Coolhaven 375; adult/child 4-17 €7.50/2.50; ☉ 10am-5pm Sat, 11am-5pm Sun; Ⓜ Coolhaven) Good things often come in small packages, and so it is with this small but excellent museum sheltered under a bridge on the Coolhaven. An eight-minute immersive multimedia experience outlines the terror and destruction caused by the bombing of Rotterdam on 14 May 1940, when 54 German aircraft dropped 1300 bombs on the city over a 13-minute period. Artefact-driven displays focus on all aspects of the wartime experience, interspersing tales of optimism and bravery among many sad stories.

Nederlands Fotomuseum MUSEUM
(☏ 010-203 04 05; www.nederlandsfotomuseum.nl; Wilhelminakade 332, Wilhelminapier; adult/student 18-25/child under 18 €12/6/free; ☉ 11am-5pm Tue-Sun; Ⓜ Wilhelminaplein) This national institution has a collection of over five million photos, and its upstairs gallery highlights curated selections from this incredible resource. The work of major Dutch photographers such as Ed van der Elsken, Aart Klein and Cas Oorthuys often features. The ground-floor galleries host temporary exhibitions of the work of big-name photogra-

phers from the Netherlands and around the world.

Euromast VIEWPOINT
(www.euromast.nl; Parkhaven 20; adult/child €9.75/6.25; ☉ 9.30am-11pm Apr-Sep, 10am-11pm Oct-Mar; ⛴ Euromast/Erasmus MC) Designed by HA Maaskant as a landmark and built between 1958 and 1960, the 185m-high Euromast offers unparalleled 360-degree views of Rotterdam from its 100m-high observation deck, or from its rotating glass Euroscoop elevator, which goes right to the top of the mast.

It's also possible to enjoy a drink or meal at the cocktail bar/brasserie underneath the observation deck, or overnight in two hotel suites on the observation deck (including breakfast from €385). Thrill seekers can sign up for weekend abseiling and ziplining up and down the tower (€55 each, May to September, bookings essential).

Het Park PARK
(⛴ ; ⛴ Euromast/Erasmus MC) Landscaped in English-garden style, this park was established in 1852 and is much loved by locals, who come here to jog, picnic, barbecue, cycle, kick around footballs and enjoy a coffee, drink or meal at charming Parqiet (p165), a cafe with deck-chair seating on the lawn..

🏃 **Activities**

The major activity here is cycling and there's an extensive network of bike paths, including a 28km route along the north and south banks of the Nieuwe Maas. Organised tours tend to concentrate on the city's architecture, but the tourist office (p169) can organise private tours on alternative themes on request.

👉 **Tours**

★ **De Rotterdam Tours** ARCHITECTURE
(www.derotterdamtours.nl) Led by experts, these tours are a great choice for architecture buffs. Offerings include a one-hour tour

ℹ **CENT SAVER**

The Rotterdam Welcome Card (per adult 1/2/3 days €12/17/21) gives discounts of up to 25% on museum and attraction admission charges, as well as free public transport on RET metro, tram and bus services. Purchase it at Rotterdam's tourist offices.

DON'T MISS

FAMILY FAVOURITES

Wereldmuseum (World Museum; www.wereldmuseum.nl; Willemskade 25; 🚊 Willemskade) Inside the 19th-century Royal Yacht Club building, this ethnographic museum celebrates multiculturalism. Check out the interactive Superstreet exhibition (for kids aged six and older) or pick up an Animal Bingo card at the front desk and try to find all of the animals as you explore the exhibitions.

Maritiem Museum Rotterdam (Maritime Museum; 🕿 010-413 26 80; www.maritiem museum.nl; Leuvehaven 1; adult/student & child over 4 €12.50/9; ⊘10am-5pm Tue-Sat, 11am-5pm Sun; 👪; Ⓜ Beurs, 🚊 Beurs) Children adore this museum overlooking Leuvehaven, whose permanent exhibits are emphatically kid-focused. The best of these is the 'Offshore Experience', which investigates day-to-day operations on North Sea oil and gas platforms and includes nine interactive activities. Older kids can test their dexterity with crane simulators, take safety quizzes, steer ships with a joystick and more. Little ones will get more out of the 'Professor Splash' play activity. Adults can engage with temporary exhibitions, which deal with all things maritime.

Tickets include entry to the museum's collection of historic vessels and cranes moored in the Leuvehaven; all are in working order and many can be boarded (open until 4pm).

Natural History Museum (Het Natuurhistorisch; 🕿 010-436 42 22; www.hetnatuur historisch.nl; Westzeedijk 345; adult/student & child 5-15 €7/3.50; ⊘11am-5pm Tue-Sun; 👪; 🚊 Kievitslaan) Geared predominantly towards children, the collection at this small museum focuses on delivering facts in a fun way. The 'Uitslovers' exhibit profiles the biggest, most unique and most unusual animals, while the 'Biodiversity' exhibit delivers loads of information about animal and plant species. There are also plenty of bones and fossils to look at, including the assembled skeleton of a huge Asian elephant called Ramon.

Speeltuinvereniging Katendrecht (www.svkatendrecht.nl; Staalstraat 91, Katendrecht; membership €20, adult/child day pass €1/0.50; ⊘10am-6pm Mon-Fri, noon-5pm Sat & Sun Apr-Oct, 11am-5pm Mon-Fri Nov-Mar; 👪; 🚌 77) Families with children adore this huge, well-designed playground located near the SS Rotterdam, which has equipment for both toddlers and older children. Take bus 77 from the Rijnhaven metro stop.

of the Markthal and Cube Houses (€15.95), a 2½-hour 'Tour of Titans' visiting De Rotterdam building, Markthal and Cube Houses (€29.95 including a watertaxi ride), and a 2½-hour 'Turbo Tour' visiting De Rotterdam, Centraal Station, the Timmerhuis and the Markthal (€29.95).

Urban Guides   WALKING
(🕿 010-433 22 31; www.urbanguides.nl; Schiekade 205; boat tour adult/child under 12 €17/free; ⊘office 10am-6pm Mon-Sat, noon-5pm Sun; Ⓜ Stadhuis, 🚊 Pompenburg, Weena, Stadhuis) Based in the Schieblock (www.schieblock.com; Schiekade189; 🚊🚊 Weena, Pompenburg), this group of passionate Rotterdammers offers a selection of architecture-focused outings, including a one-hour boat tour on weekends at 3pm (May to October only) and a two-hour bike tour on occasional Saturdays (€5 + €10 bike hire). It also offers a guided tour of the Van Nelle Fabriek (p161) and rents bikes (per day €10).

S'dam Gin Tour   FOOD & DRINK
(www.sdam.nl/zien-doen/tours-tickets/info/gintour-sdam; €34.95; ⊘2.30-5pm Sat) This 2.5km walking tour of Schiedam's historic distillers' district visits the *waag* (weighing house) with its scales that once weighed juniper berries used in *jenever*-making, and passes warehouses and other buildings associated with the industry. It also includes a stop at the National Jenevermuseum Schiedam, where various Schiedam gins are tasted. Book via the website.

Whisper Boat   BOATING
(www.sdam.nl/rondvaarten/info/vertrek-tijden; Lange Haven 99, Schiedam; adult/child 4-12 €6.50/3.50; ⊘11.45am, 1.30pm & 3pm Tue-Sun mid-Apr–mid-Oct; Ⓜ Schiedam Centrum or Parkweg) Departing from near the historic *vismarkt* (fishmarket), these canal tours on a *fluisterboot* (whisper boat) pass warehouses, distilleries and windmills on their lei-

surely progression. Purchase tickets at the tourist office.

 Festivals & Events

Rotterdam Architecture Month DESIGN
(http://rotterdamarchitecturemonth.com/; ⊙Jun) This annual festival offers guided architecture walking and cycling tours (some in English), site visits, exhibitions and workshops.

Rotterdam Bluegrass Festival MUSIC
(www.bluegrassfestival.nl; Pijnackerplein; ⊙late Jun; ⊚Benthuizerstaat) **FREE** High-profile musicians from the Netherlands and overseas entertain an enthusiastic crowd at Pijnackerplein Park in the city's hip Noord neighbourhood.

Metropolis Festival MUSIC
(www.metropolisfestival.nl; ⊙early Jul; Ⓜ Zuidplein) **FREE** One of the largest events held in the city, this one-day festival held in the Zuiderpark features up-and-coming bands from around the world. Crowds can number more than 35,000.

★**North Sea Jazz Festival** MUSIC
(www.northseajazz.nl; ⊙mid-Jul) One of the world's most-respected jazz events sees hundreds of musicians perform. A free 'North Sea Round Town' festival in the weeks preceding the festival proper sees a variety of jazz acts performing in public spaces and concert halls around the city.

Pleinbioscoop Rotterdam FILM
(http://pleinbioscooprotterdam.nl/; Museumpark; ⊙Aug; Ⓜ Eendrachtsplein, ⊚Museumpark or Vasteland) The biggest outdoor cinema in Europe sets up in Museumpark for most of August.

🛏 Sleeping

Accommodation options are limited, and while the range of choices is slowly expanding, it can still sometimes be hard to find a room. Book well in advance, especially if you are travelling here between April and September, the city's high season. Centrum is the most convenient option.

★**King Kong Hostel** HOSTEL €
(☎010-818 87 78; www.kingkonghostel.com; Witte de Withstraat 74; dm €19-26, d €75-105; ☎; Ⓜ Beurs, ⊚Museumpark) There's plenty to like about this hip hostel in Rotterdam's major party precinct. Female and mixed-sex dorms sleep between four and 18, with bunks, under-bed lockers and plenty of power points.

Shared bathrooms are modern and clean. Facilities include a laundry (per load wash and dry €8), a luggage room, a communal kitchen, bike storage, a chill space and a ground-floor cafe.

Stadsvilla Mout Hotel BOUTIQUE HOTEL €
(☎010-200 44 99; www.stadsvillamout.nl; Lange Haven 71, Schiedam; small d €74-89, ste €94-129; ✳☎; Ⓜ Schiedam Centrum or Parkweg) This hotel in an 18th-century canal mansion offers stylish, good-sized suites with kitchenette (breakfast hamper available, per person €12.50). There are also a few standard and family rooms. Parking costs €12.

★**Citizen M** BOUTIQUE HOTEL €€
(☎010-810 81 00; www.citizenm.com; Gelderse Plein 50; r from €66; Ⓟ@☎; Ⓜ Blaak, ⊚Blaak) A new-generation hostel for travellers who have progressed past dorms and shared bathrooms but want to recreate the casual conviviality of backpacker joints, Citizen M is as welcoming as it is well located. Capsule-like rooms are comfortable enough, with Smart TVs offering channels and free movies. The first-floor bar, cafe and lounge are super-stylish spaces where you can relax or work.

★**Urban Residences** APARTMENT €€
(☎010-414 32 99; www.urbanresidences.com; Hennekijnstraat 104; studio €95-150, 2-bedroom apt €220-280; Ⓟ✳☎; Ⓜ Beurs) You'll get a real taste of inner-city Rotterdam life when staying at these sleek apartments in the centre of town. Scattered over 15 floors of a recently constructed high-rise building, there are 76 generously sized apartments – many with impressive views. The Alessi interior fitouts have a sternly minimalist decor but are very comfortable, offering couches, dining tables and well-equipped kitchens.

ALL THAT JAZZ

The Dutch jazz scene has produced some mainstream artists in recent years. Among some gifted young chanteuses are Fleurine, Ilse Huizinga and the Suriname-born Denise Jannah, who records for Blue Note and is recognised as the country's best jazz singer. Jannah's repertoire consists of American standards with elements of Surinamese music.

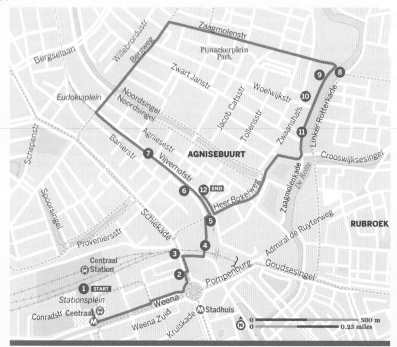

Walking Tour
Northeast Rotterdam

START CENTRAAL STATION
FINISH CENTRUM
LENGTH 4.4KM

This wander through the streets northeast of ❶ **Centraal Station** (p166) gives a taste of life in one of Rotterdam's most multicultural neighbourhoods. Start in the forecourt of the station, heading east to the huge roundabout at Hofplein and then to the rooftop of the ❷ **Schieblock** (p162) to visit one of Europe's largest largest harvestable rooftop gardens, perhaps having a drink or snack in the rooftop's hip ❸ **Op Het Dak** (p165) cafe. Continue across the ❹ **Luchtsingel** (Air Canal; Ⓜ Stadhuis 🚊 Heer Bokelweg), a wooden pedestrian bridge designed by local studio ZUS and funded by a crowdsourcing campaign, and make your way to ❺ **Station Hofplein**, a retail and eating development in a former railway station. Continue north along Vijverhofstraat, home to the ❻ **Hofbogen**, an arched concrete railway viaduct that now

houses shops, cafes and studio spaces. Stop for a coffee at the city's best coffee roastery, ❼ **Man Met Bril** (p167), and then turn right (northeast) into Bergweg, continuing until you reach Zaagmolenstraat. Head east until you reach ❽ **De Rotte Canal**, and turn right to explore one of Noord's most popular cafe strips, where you can enjoy a healthy and tasty lunch at ❾ **Bertmans** (Cafe; 📞 010-844 88 60; https://bertmans.nl; Zaagmolenkade 15; breakfast dishes €7-13, lunch mains €12-16, dinner mains €14-22; ☺ 8.45am-10pm Mon-Fri, 9.30am-5.50pm Sat & Sun; 🛜 🖊 🚊 Zwaanshals), a craft beer at ❿ **Brouwerij Noordt** (Brewery; 📞 010-223 05 66; www.brouwerijnoordt.nl; Zaagmolenkade 46; ☺ taproom 3-7pm Wed-Fri, 2-6pm Sat-Sun; 🚊 Zwaanshals) or a decadent high tea at ⓫ **Lof der Zoetheid** (Cafe; 📞 010-265 00 70; http://lofderzoetheid.com; Noordplein 1; afternoon tea €25; ☺ 10am-5pm Mon & Wed-Fri, to 5.30pm Sat & Sun; 🚊 Zwaanshals). From here, it's an easy walk into Centrum, perhaps detouring for a drink at one of Rotterdam's popular ⓬ **micro-breweries** (p167).

Pincoffs
BOUTIQUE HOTEL €€

(☎010-297 45 00; www.hotelpincoffs.nl; Stieltjesstraat 34, Feijenoord; s €125-145, d €145-175, ste €175-275; P❄@🛜; MWilhelminaplein) 🍃 A clever re-use of a former customs house built in 1879, Pincoffs is Rotterdam's only truly boutique hotel. Blending recycled and vintage art and furniture with 21st-century style, it's an excellent, albeit slightly out-of-the-action, choice. In winter, a wood-burning fireplace blazes in the elegant bar; in summer, the terrace restaurant attracts river breezes. Breakfast costs €18; parking €16.

nhow
HOTEL €€

(☎010 206 7600; www.nhow-rotterdam.com; Wilhelminakade 137, Wilhelminapier; standard r €99-129, premium r €114-184, ste €225-255; P❄🛜🅿; MWilhelminaplein) The 248 rooms in this hotel (pronounced 'now') are as sleek and minimalist as the Rem Koolhaas tower in which they reside. The best are those in the 'Premium Skyline' category, which are spacious and have huge windows overlooking the Maas. Facilities include a 7th-floor cocktail bar with terrace, a restaurant and a gym. Breakfast costs €20; parking €25.

Mainport
DESIGN HOTEL €€€

(☎010-217 57 57; www.mainporthotel.com; Leuvehaven 77; r from €150, ste from €450; P❄@🛜🅿; MLeuvenhaven, 🚃Leuvenhaven) Locations don't come better than the Mainport, spectacularly set on the harbour a heartbeat from the city's action. Plush rooms are subtly themed to reflect far-flung locations. Rooms have huge beds, work desks and tea/coffee facilities; suites have a sauna and/or jacuzzi. There's also a small indoor pool, a sauna and gym (free), and a spa (charged) with hammam.

🍴 Eating

Forget fine dining – Rotterdammers don't like formality and fuss, and are at their happiest when enjoying fresh, seasonally driven, cafe-style food. The city is replete with informal restaurants and also has two great food markets – the Markthal and Fenix Food Factory – that have eateries alongside produce stalls.

De IJsmaker
ICE CREAM €

(☎010-341 84 19; http://deijsmaker.nl/; Witte de Withstraat 7a; per scoop €1.30-1.80; ⊗11am-11pm Mon-Sat, from noon Sun; MBeurs, 🚃Museumpark) Fresh flavours reign supreme at this artisanal ice cream parlour on Witte de Withstraat and only quality produce is used – the simply spectacular pistachio is made with nuts from Bronte in Sicily and the seductive vanilla is made with beans sourced in Madagascar.

Tante Nel
FAST FOOD €

(www.tante-nel.com; Pannekoekstraat 53a; fries €2.50-8.75; ⊗noon-10pm Mon-Sat, to 9pm Sun; 🚃Meent) Differing from traditional *frites* (fries) stands in a number of crucial ways, Tante Nel has pleasant street-side seating where its many and varied regulars settle in to enjoy treats such as hand-cut, expertly cooked fries with truffle mayonnaise or *patat stoofvlees* (fries topped with a rich meat stew), washed down with a gin and tonic, beer or milkshake.

⭐Urban Espresso Bar
CAFE €

(UEB West; ☎010-477 01 88; www.urbanespressobar.nl; Nieuwe Binnenwag 263; sandwiches €5-6, mains €7-9; ⊗9am-6pm Mon-Sat, 10am-6pm Sun; 🛜🅿; 🚃Claes de Vrieselaan) Could this be Rotterdam's best cafe? The coffee here is definitely a cut above most of its competitors (Giraffe beans, expert baristas), as is the food (artisan breads and pastries, house-baked cakes, global flavours, organic ingredients). We can highly recommend the *tosties* (toasted sandwiches), soups and burgers, and we always enjoy chatting with fellow customers at the communal table. Cash only.

Parqiet
CAFE €

(☎06 5100 1606; www.parqiet.nl; Baden Powelllaan 20; breakfast dishes €5-9, sandwiches €6-9; ⊗9am-6pm; 🛜🅿; 🚃Euromast/Erasmus MC) The wild flowers in Kilner jars, terrace seating and striped deckchairs on the front lawn all contribute to the charm of this cafe in a former coach house in Het Park (p161). Dishes are light and fresh, with plenty of vegetarian options, and baristas get the best out of the Marzocco espresso machine using freshly roasted Man Met Bril beans.

Op Het Dak
CAFE €

(www.ophetdak.com; Schiekade 189, 7th fl; breakfast dishes €8-13, lunch dishes €8-14; ⊗8.30am-5pm Tue-Sat, from 9am Sun; 🅿; 🚃Weena, Pompenburg) 🍃 Perched on top of the Schieblock office building, Op Het Dak ('On the Roof') is a pavilion with indoor, deck and garden seating amidst one of Europe's largest harvestable rooftop gardens. Healthy breakfast

DON'T MISS

ARCHITECTURE HIGHLIGHTS

Rotterdam is a vast open-air museum of modern and contemporary architecture, with myriad important and eye-popping buildings. There are many triumphs, including some magnificent buildings by architecture firms OMA and MVRDV, and also a fair number of magnificent failures (the Innport Hotel and the Shipping and Transport College immediately come to mind). One thing that they all have in common is a willingness to innovate and experiment with built form.

Markthal (Market Hall; https://markthal.klepierre.nl/; Nieuwstraat; ⊙10am-8pm Mon-Thu & Sat, to 9pm Fri, noon-6pm Sun; ⓂBlaak, 🚊Blaak) One of the city's signature buildings, this extraordinary inverted-U-shaped market hall was designed by local architecture firm MVRDV and opened for business in 2014. It comprises highly sought-after glass-walled apartments arcing over a 40m-high market hall with a striking fruit- and vegetable-muralled ceiling.

Centraal Station (www.ns.nl/stationsinformatie/rtd/rotterdam-centraal; Stationsplein 1; Ⓜ Centraal Station, 🚊Centraal) The most used – and quite possibly best loved – building in Rotterdam, Centraal Station was designed by Benthem Crouwel, MVSA and West 8. Built between 1999 and 2013, it features a dramatically angled passenger hall with a pointed stainless-steel-clad roof that almost punches into the sky.

De Rotterdam (www.derotterdam.nl; Wilhelminakade 177, Wilhelminapier; Ⓜ Wilhelminaplein) Designed by OMA, whose star architect Rem Koolhaas is a Pritzker-winning local hero, this 'vertical city' with its three interconnected towers was completed in 2013 and is the city's most acclaimed contemporary building.

Van Nelle Fabriek (p161) Designed and built between 1925 and 1931, this modernist World Heritage–listed factory northwest of the city centre is an icon of 20th-century industrial architecture.

Overblaak Development (Blaakse Bos; Blaak Woods; Overblaak; ⓂBlaak, 🚊Blaak) Designed by Amsterdam-based architect Piet Blom and built between 1978 and 1984, this mind-bending development facing the Markthal is marked by its pencil-shaped tower and 'forest' of 38 cube-shaped apartments on hexagonal pylons. This vibrantly coloured, crazily tilting apartment block is one of the city's most recognisable structures. One apartment, the **Kijk-Kubus Museumwoning** (Cube House Museum; 📞 010-414 22 85; www.kubuswoning.nl; Overblaak 70; adult/student/child under 11 €3/2/1.50; ⊙10am-6pm), is open to the public.

Huis Sonneveld (Sonneveld House; www.huissonneveld.nl; Jongkindstraat 25; adult/student/child under 18 €10/6.50/free; ⊙10am-5pm Tue-Sat; Ⓜ Eendrachtsplein, 🚊Museumpark) When company director Albertus Sonneveld decided to commission an architect to design a contemporary home for his family, the obvious choice was Leendert Van der Vlugt, who had designed the magnificent Van Nelle factory. Working with Johannes Brinkman, Van der Vlugt designed a streamlined, state-of-the-art building that was hailed an outstanding example of Dutch Functionalism as soon as its construction was completed in 1933.

KPN Telecom Headquarters (Toren op Zud; Wilhelminakade 123, Wilhelminapier; Ⓜ Wilhelminaplein) Designed by celebrated architect Renzo Piano and opened in 2000, the bizarre KPN Telecom headquarters building leans at a sharp angle, seemingly resting on a long pole.

Bijenkorf Department Store (p169) Legendary Bauhaus architect Marcel Breuer worked with Amsterdam-based architect Abraham Elzas on the design of this department store, which opened in 1957. Clad in distinctive hexagonal travertine panels, it features a monumental sculpture by Russian Constructivist Naum Gabo on its Coolsingel facade.

For more coverage of the city's architectural highlights, purchase a copy of *Rotterdam Architecture City* by Paul Groenendijk and Piet Vollaard, which is available in both Dutch- and English-language versions. Rotterdam Tourist Information offices also stock a handy 'Rotterdam, City of Architecture' brochure that lists significant buildings and includes a map.

and lunch dishes are often made with the herbs, vegetables, fruit and honey grown here – veggie and vegan choices are the rule rather than the exception.

★ AJi INTERNATIONAL €€

(☎010-767 01 69; www.restaurantaji.nl; Pannekoekstraat 40a; snacks €5-24, small plates €16-24; ☺noon-2pm & 5-10pm Tue & Wed, noon-11pm Wed-Sat; ⓜMeent) Good-quality Asian food is hard to source in Rotterdam, so we were thrilled to discover this chic bistro serving dishes inspired by Asia and the Mediterranean. Build a meal with a few small plates, or just pop in for drinks and a platter of oysters or Spanish cured meats. There are good wines by the glass and bottle, too.

Pierre FRENCH €€

(☎010-842 37 57; https://pierre.nl/; Pannekoekstraat 38a; mains €8-25; ☺10am-10pm; 🛜🍴; ⓜMeent) Like many locals, we love visiting Pierre at all times of the day. At breakfast, the croissants are buttery; at lunch the baguettes have delectable fillings; and at dinner, classic brasserie dishes (beef bourguignon, duck confit, steak frites) can be ordered as small or large plates. Staff are friendly, street-side tables are sunny and the wine list is excellent. *Formidable!*

★ CEO Baas van Het Vlees STEAK €€€

(☎010-290 94 54; www.ceobaasvanhetvlees.nl; Sumatraweg 1-3, Katendrecht; mains €21-39; ☺5-11pm Tue-Sat; ⓜRijnhaven) Meat lovers should be sure to book a table at Rotterdam's best steakhouse. Working in their open kitchen, chefs cook spectacular cuts of beef to order. We love the fact that half portions of steak and delicious desserts are offered, and have rarely been so impressed by a wine list (by both glass and bottle). Truly excellent.

🍸 Drinking & Nightlife

Locals are equally enamoured of coffee and beer, and can often be convinced to enjoy an expertly made cocktail, too. There's no lack of cafes, cocktail bars, microbreweries and pubs – many with outdoor seating for summer – and these are scattered across a variety of neighbourhoods. Witte de Withstraat is the main bar street.

★ Man Met Bril COFFEE

(www.manmetbrilkoffie.nl; Vijverhofstraat 70; breakfast deal €6.66; ☺8am-5pm Mon-Fri, 9pm-6pm Sat & Sun; 🛜; ⓕSchiekade, Walenburgerweg)

Rotterdam's first artisan coffee roastery (there are now 12), Man Met Bril sources direct-trade, 90% organic beans from across the globe and then roasts them in this hip space under a railway viaduct north of Centraal Station. The on-site cafe offers expertly prepared brews, cakes and sandwiches. Arrive before 10am to take advantage of the generous and dirt-cheap breakfast deal.

★ Biergarten BEER GARDEN

(☎010-233 05 56; www.biergartenrotterdam.nl; Schiestraat 18; ☺noon-midnight or later; ⓜCentraal Station) A sun-bleached labyrinth of wooden tables, brightly painted stairs, exotic foliage and low-slung festoon lighting, the Biergarten throngs with thirsty locals enjoying ice-cold pilsner, homemade lemonade and a tempting selection of barbecued meats. On Fridays, DJs preside over the always-inclusive action.

★ Verward WINE BAR

(☎06 50 67 04 95; www.verward.nl; Hoogstraat 69a; ☺2-11pm Thu-Mon; ⓜBlaak, ⓕBurg Van Walsumweg, Kipstraat) Beer is a more common tipple than wine in Rotterdam, so many bars here have less-than-stellar selections of wine by the glass or bottle. That's not the case at this friendly wine bar, where sommelier Ward De Zeeuw pours an interesting selection of Old World wines. Sit at the large wooden bar or outside to enjoy a glass or two.

Cheese and charcuterie platters served

Suicide Club COCKTAIL BAR

(☎010-846 87 97; www.thesuicideclub.nl; Stationsplein 45, 8th fl; ☺4pm-2am Sun, Wed & Thu, 4pm-5am Fri & Sat; ⓜRotterdam Centraal, ⓕCentraal) Situated on the top floor of the iconic and monolithic Groothandelsgebouw building, this rooftop bar is where the beau monde comes to mingle. Expect cushioned cabanas, cutting-edge DJs (Friday and Saturday) and can't-stop-talking-about-them views. Try the Bamboo Chute (vodka, gin, lemon, coconut, pandan and cinnamon).

Aloha BAR

(☎010-210 81 70; www.alohabar.nl; Maasboulevard 100; ☺noon-11pm Sun-Thu, noon-1am Fri & Sat; ⓜOostplein) 🌿 Sustainable, innovative and funky as anything, this bar-cafe in the former Tropicana baths has a large terrace boasting views across the Nieuwe Maas river. Operated by Blue City collective, a group of environmental entrepreneurs,

MARKET DINING

Almost everything in **Fenix Food Factory** (www.fenixfoodfactory.nl; Veerlaan 19d, Katendrecht; ⊙10am-7pm Tue-Thu, to 8pm Fri, to 6pm Sat, noon-6pm Sun, individual stall hrs vary; 🚗 🚭; Ⓜ Rijnhaven), a vast former warehouse, is made locally and sold by entrepreneurs making their mark on the food scene. They include Booij Kaasmakers (cheese, milk, yoghurt, eggs), Cider Cider, Jordy's Bakery (bread and baked goods), Stielman Koffiebranders (coffee roasters), Stroop Rotterdam (*stroopwafels*), Kaapse Brouwers (craft brewery), Firma Bijten (meat) and De Westlandse Tuin (fruit and veggies).

There's plenty of seating at which to enjoy a meal sourced at on-site eateries, which include Meneer Tanger (Moroccan mezes) and **The Kaapse Kitchen** (www.kaapse brouwers.nl; Veerlaan 19d, Katendrecht; price varies; ⊙4-10pm Mon-Fri, from noon Sat & Sun; Ⓜ Rijnhaven). Firma Bijten also fires up a daily barbecue. Popular eatery **Posse** (🎫010-737 18 15; www.posse.nl; Veerlaan 19a, Katendrecht; mains €17-25; ⊙noon-8.45pm Mon, Thu & Fri, 11am-8.45pm Sat, 11am-6pm Sun; Ⓜ Rijnhaven) is in an adjoining building.

The market is easy to access from Wilhelminapier, via the Rijnhaven pedestrian bridge.

---

it's a fabulous spot for summer lunches (sandwiches €6 to €9, snacks €5 to €13) or a drink accompanied by the house speciality, mushroom *bitterballen* (deep-fried croquettes).

Very few cafes have sustainability credentials as strong: Aloha has its own bee colony for honey, grows its own veggies (including the mushrooms, which are grown in the basement on used coffee grounds instead of soil), composts waste whenever possible, filters its own water, makes leather out of overripe fruit (huh?) and melts down plastic to make signage. Needless to say, there are plenty of vegetarian and vegan choices on the menu.

In summer, you'll need to BYO sunscreen, as there isn't much shade. Give it a miss in the cooler months.

Bokaal
BAR

(🎫010-720 08 98; www.bokaalrotterdam.nl; Nieuwemarkt 11; ⊙11am-1am Sun-Thu, to 2am Fri & Sat; 🚉Meent) In a *bokaal* (trophy) location at the heart of the enclave around pedestrian Nieuwmarkt and Pannekoekstraat, Bokaal has an indoor bar and a huge all-day sun terrace that heaves with people on summer nights. Beer (craft and Trappist) is its speciality, with nine on tap, and more than 80 in bottles. There's a food menu, but many take advantage of on-site foodtrucks.

Maassilo
CLUB

(🎫010-476 24 52; www.maassilo.com; Maashaven Zuidzijde 1-2; ⊙hrs vary; Ⓜ Maashaven) With exposed pipes, graffiti-scrawled concrete pillars and metal railings, this former grain store from the early 20th century is now

Rotterdam's biggest club. Depending on the night, expect DJs to pump out everything from thumping tech-house to bass-heavy Soca music. Check the online agenda for event details.

☆ Entertainment

Music dominates the city's entertainment programs, with plenty of festivals and venues on offer. Many live-music venues resist being confined to one genre, programming everything from jazz to rock, reggae to R&B. After parties during the world-famous North Sea Jazz Festival (p163) in July are held in venues across the city and are renowned for their impromptu performances.

★ Bird Jazz Club
LIVE MUSIC

(http://bird-rotterdam.nl; Raampoortstraat 24-28, Station Hofplein; ⊙5.30pm-1am Tue-Thu, to 4am Fri & Sat) Named for American jazz saxophonist Charlie 'Bird' Parker; Bird is the city's temple to jazz but also programs soul, hip-hop, funk and electronica; check the online agenda to see who's playing and prepurchase tickets. Its excellent restaurant serves wood-fired pizzas and small plates; the kitchen closes at 9.30pm. The club hosts after-parties during the North Sea Jazz Festival.

De Doelen
CLASSICAL MUSIC

(🎫010-217 17 17; www.dedoelen.nl; Schouwburgplein 50; ⊙ticket office 2-6pm Mon-Fri; Ⓜ Centraal, 🚉Kruisplein) Home venue of the renowned Rotterdam Philharmonic Orchestra, this sumptuous 1950s concert hall seating 2200 is also renowned for its jazz and world-music concerts.

Annabel LIVE MUSIC

(📱06 28 28 94 91 (WhatsApp only); www.annabel.
nu; Schiestraat 20; ⏰8pm-1am Thu, 8pm-2am Fri &
Sat; Ⓜ️Stadhuis, 🚇Weena, Pompenburg) Hosting
bands from all genres, Annabel is a choice
midsized live-music venue that also hosts
regular dance nights. Acts range from hip-
hop to pop to electronica.

KINO CINEMA

(📱010-268 11 60; www.kinorotterdam.nl; Gouvern-
estraat 129-133; ⏰10am-1am Sun-Thu, to 2am Fri
& Sat; 🚇Bloemkwekersstraat) Since the ribbon
was cut in 1909, this legendary Rotterdam
cinema has had bit-part roles as a music
venue, a theatre and even as a hospital. Renovated in 2016, when it reopened as KINO,
it now houses four cinemas, a bar and a
restaurant. The film selection tends to veer
towards the daring.

🛍️ Shopping

Shopping isn't a major preoccupation here.
Global chains have outlets in Lijnbaan
(Ⓜ️Stadhuis, Beurs, 🚇Stadhuis, Beurs) and in the
Beurstraverse (aka the 'Koopgoot', or 'Shopping Gutter'), a semi-subterranean shopping arcade that intersects Lijnbaan and
crosses under Coolsingel. Also in this area
is upmarket Bijenkorf Department Store
(Coolsingel 105; Ⓜ️Beurs, 🚇Beurs). Boutiques
can be found on and around Meent, as well
as Nieuwemarkt, Pannekoekstraat, Witte de
Withstraat, OudeBinnenweg and Nieuwe
Binnenweg.

★De Groene Passage MARKET

(http://degroenepassage.nl/; Mariniersweg 9;
⏰8am-8pm Mon-Fri, to 6pm Sat; 🚇Meent) An
emporium of eco-conscious and sustainable products, this indoor market hosts
small businesses selling food, soaps, clothing, homewares, furniture and textiles. If
you want to join a tai chi, yoga or Pilates
class, or perhaps consult a naturopath, this
is the place to come. On Saturdays, organic
food stalls sometimes set up on the street
outside.

★Groos FASHION & ACCESSORIES

(📱010-0413 33 44; http://groos.nl; Achterklooster
13; ⏰10am-6pm Tue-Sat, noon-5pm Sun; 🚇Kip-
straat) Its name is revived local slang for
'pride', and this concept store in the Het In-
dustriegebouw creative industries building
is clearly proud of the products it stocks,
which are conceived, designed and produced in Rotterdam. These include fashion,
jewellery, homewares, artworks, books, stationery, music and edibles.

Blaak Markt MARKET

(⏰9am-5pm Tue & Sat; Ⓜ️Blaak, 🚇Blaak) This
huge street market sprawls across its namesake square east of the Markthal. Stalls sell
all manner of food, gadgets, clothes, snacks
and much more.

ℹ️ Information

Tourist Office (📱010-790 01 85; www.rotter
dam.info; Coolsingel 114; ⏰9.30am-6pm; 📶;
Ⓜ️Beurs) Main tourist office.

Tourist Office (www.rotterdam.info; Stationsplein 21, Centraal Station; ⏰9am-5.30pm
Sun-Wed, 9am-8pm Thu-Sat mid-Aug–early Jul,
9am-7pm early Jul–mid-Aug) Centraal Station
branch.

ℹ️ Getting There & Away

AIR
The Netherlands' huge international airport,
Schiphol (p329), is roughly equidistant by
high-speed train to Rotterdam and Amsterdam

ℹ️ LGBTIQ+ ROTTERDAM

There is a thriving LGBTIQ+ scene in Rotterdam. The biggest event of the year is Rotterdam Pride, (https://rotterdam-pride.com/en; ⏰late Sep) a three-day festival in late
September. This includes a Pride walk, parties, seminars and other events. There are also
usually LGBTIQ+ events on King's Day (27 April).

Many bars and clubs are found in the 'gay triangle' of the city, which is edged by
Churchillplein, Westblaak, Mauritsweg and van Oldebarneveldtstraat, near the Eendrachtsplein metro station.

In summer, the LantarenVenster (📱010-277 22 77; www.lantarenvenster.nl; Otto Reuch-
linweg 996, Wilhelminapier; adult/student €9.50/8; ⏰11.30am-1am Mon-Thu, 11.30am-2am Fri
& Sat, 10am-midnight Sun; Ⓜ️Wilhelminaplein) arthouse cinema presents a Gay & Lesbian
Summer Film Festival, with LGBTIQ+ films shown every Tuesday night.

Gay Rotterdam (www.gayrotterdam.nl/en) is a useful resource.

ROTTERDAM & SOUTH HOLLAND ROTTERDAM

ROTTERDAM DAY TRIP: KINDERDIJK

Unesco World Heritage site **Kinderdijk** (☑ 078-691 28 30; www.kinderdijk.com; Nederwaard 1; ⊙ site 24hr, museums & visitor centre 9am-5.30pm; ⊠ Kinderdijk) **FREE** is a beautiful landscape of empty marshes and waterways above which 19 historic windmills (some brick, some timber) rise like sentinels. The mills are kept in operating condition and some still function as residences. In summer, tall reeds line the two canals, lily pads float on the water and bird calls break the silence. It's a wonderful – and quintessentially Dutch – landscape to wander through.

A pumping station has been repurposed as a visitor centre and a dual pedestrian and bicycle path between the canals. Two of the windmills – the 17th-century Nederwaard and Blokweer mills – function as museums, offering an insight into the past lives of miller families. A video about the *polder* and its windmills screens in the 19th-century Wisboom pumping station. The walk or ride along the length of the site and back is an easy 5.7km. Entry is free, but you'll need to purchase a ticket (adult/child €8/5.50, €1 cheaper online) to enter the two windmill museums and the visitor centre. There are also optional cruises along the canal (adult/child €5.50/3).

The name Kinderdijk is said to derive from the horrible St Elizabeth's Day Flood of 1421, when a storm and flood washed a *kind* (child) in a crib up onto the dyke. Since that time, this part of the country has been a focus of Dutch efforts to claim land from the water. Several of the most important types of windmill are found here, including hollow post mills and rotating cap mills. The latter are among the highest in the country as they were built to better catch the wind.

Getting There & Away

Despite its proximity, there are no viable bus or train services from Rotterdam.

Bicycle Kinderdijk is close to Rotterdam (16km) and Dordrecht (11km).

Ferry The fastest and most enjoyable way to visit is on **Waterbus** (www.waterbus.nl; ⊙ adult/child €4/2) fast ferry 202 from Rotterdam Erasmusbrug (adult/child €4/2, 30 minutes, eight daily) or Dordrecht Merwekade (adult/child €4/2, 30 minutes, frequent). Bikes are carried for free. Direct ferries operate from May to October only; between November and April you'll need to take a waterbus to Ridderkerk (adult/child €4/2, 30 minutes, frequent) and another to Kinderijk (adult/child €1.70, 10 minutes, frequent). The ferry dock is 250m from the Kinderdijk entrance.

Rebus (☑ 06 55 82 64 63; www.rebus-info.nl; adult/child under 12 €17.50/12.50; ⊙ noon Tue-Sun Apr-Oct; Ⓜ Leuvehaven) runs four-hour boat tours from Rotterdam that allow a fairly quick visit to the mills.

(around 20 to 30 minutes each). Rotterdam The Hague Airport (p329), serving more than 40 European destinations, is less than 6km northwest of Rotterdam.

BICYCLE

National bike routes between Amsterdam and Belgium and between Den Haag and Breda pass through Rotterdam. Although the city seems large, 15 minutes of fast pedalling has you out in the country.

Bikes travel for free on Waterbus services between Rotterdam, Kinderdijk and Dordrecht.

BOAT

Waterbus (www.waterbus.nl; Willemskade) fast ferries travel between Rotterdam, Kinderdijk and Dordrecht; services vary with the seasons.

Boats leave from Willemskade near the Erasmusbrug.

TRAIN

Rotterdam's main station is Rotterdam Centraal (CS); trains heading south often stop at Blaak Station after Centraal.

There are frequent high-speed Thalys trains to/from Brussels (1¼ hours), as well as NS Intercity direct services (two hours). Thalys also travels to/from Paris Nord (2½ hours). Eurostar trains linking Amsterdam with Brussels stop here; passengers can change to a London-bound service at Brussels. The full Rotterdam–Paris journey time is around four hours.

Major domestic services on state-owned Nederlandse Spoorwegen (NS; www.ns.nl):

TO	PRICE (€)	TIME (MIN)	FREQUENCY (PER HR)
Amsterdam (Intercity/ Sprinter)	15.40	75	4
Amsterdam (Intercity Direct)	17.80	40	4
Breda	9.50	25	5
Schiphol (Intercity)	12.40	50	2
Schiphol (Intercity Direct)	14.80	25	4
Utrecht	10.50	40	4

ℹ Getting Around

TO/FROM THE AIRPORT
RET bus 33 makes the 20-minute run from the airport to Rotterdam Centraal Station every 15 minutes between 5.40am and midnight (€3.50).

It's also possible to take this bus to Meijersplein metro station, from where you can take Line E to Rotterdam; one two-hour ticket (€3.50) will cover both legs of your trip.

A taxi takes 10 minutes to get to the centre and costs around €25.

BICYCLE
Zwann Bikes (☑ 010-412 62 20; www.czwaan. nl; Weena 703-707; per day standard/electric bike €12.50/17.50; ⊙7.30am-7.30pm Mon-Fri, 9am-7.30pm Sat & Sun) Rents bikes from a location close to Centraal Station.

BOAT
Fast black and yellow **watertaxis** (☑ 010-403 03 03; www.watertaxirotterdam.nl; around €30 per 15min) are the Ferraris of the Nieuwe Maas. Tickets are charged by zone according to distance travelled, and cost between €4.50 and €10 per passenger; children under 13 travel half price. See the website for dock locations and zone information.

PUBLIC TRANSPORT
Rotterdam's tram, bus and metro services are provided by **RET** (www.ret.nl). Most converge near Rotterdam Centraal Station. The **RET information booth** (www.ret.nl; Stationsplein 20, Centraal Station; ⊙7am-10pm Mon-Fri, 9.30am-5.30pm Sat & Sun) sells tickets and is located in the main entrance hall at Centraal Station. There are other information booths in the major metro stations.

A rechargeable two-hour ticket purchased from a bus driver or tram conductor costs €3.50 and a Tourist Day Pass (€13.50) covers unlimited travel by day on trams, buses, the metro and Waterbus services. Ticket inspections are common.

Delfshaven & Schiedam

Just 3km southwest of Rotterdam city centre, the historic enclave of Delfshaven – once the official seaport for the city of Delft – survived the war and is filled with pretty-as-a picture canals and gabled houses dating from the Golden Age. West again is charming Schiedam, known for its historic *jenever* (traditional Dutch gin) distilleries. Delfshaven is easily reached by foot, bike, metro or trams 4 or 8; Schiedam is served by metro.

◉ Sights & Activities

Oude of Pelgrimvaderskerk CHURCH
(Pilgrim Fathers Church; ☑010-477 41 56; www. oudeofpelgrimvaderskerk.nl; Aelbrechtskolk 22,

ROTTERDAM & SOUTH HOLLAND DELFSHAVEN & SCHIEDAM

GET PEDALLING

There are a number of popular cycling routes in and around the city, including the following:

Roaming Rotterdam (10 km, map available at the tourist office) Passes iconic architecture and other city highlights.

Rondje Katendrecht (15 km; https://rotterdam.info/bezoekers-informatie/rondje-rotterdam/) Follows a route along the quays and through Rijnhaven and Maashaven ports; also offers optional extra trips to Katendrecht, the Wilhelminapier and Noordereiland.

Nieuwe Maasparcours (28 km; www.rotterdam.nl/vrije-tijd/nieuwe-maasparcours) Divided into seven sections stretched along the north and south banks of the Nieuwe Maas, ranging from 3.5km to 5km. Download details online or pick up a brochure outlining the route at the tourist office.

1. Kinderdijk (p171)
A beautiful landscape of empty marshes and waterways dotted with historic windmills.

2. Van Nelle Fabriek (p161), Rotterdam
Designed and constructed between 1925 and 1931, this modernist World Heritage–listed factory is an icon of 20th-century industrial architecture.

3. Keukenhof Gardens (p200), Lisse
The world's largest bulb-flower garden, this green space attracts around 1.4 million visitors during its eight-week season.

Delfshaven; ⊘noon-6pm Sat & every 2nd Fri; 🚇Delfshaven) The Pilgrims (p195) prayed for the last time at this church before leaving the Netherlands for America aboard the *Speedwell* on 1 August 1620. They could barely keep the leaky boat afloat and, in England, eventually transferred to the *Mayflower* – the rest is history. The building dates from 1417, but was extensively rebuilt in the late 16th century. Inside is an 1890 outbuilding housing a memorial to the Pilgrims.

National
Jenevermuseum Schiedam — MUSEUM

(National Jenever Museum; 📞010-246 96 76; www.jenevermuseum.nl; Lange Haven 74; adult/child 13-17/child under 13 incl entrance to Branderij €8.50/8/free, combined ticket with Korenmolen de Walvisch €12/11.50/free; ⊘11am-5pm Tue-Sun; Ⓜ Schiedam Centrum or Parkweg) Housed in an 18th-century distillery, this museum is dedicated to the industry that Schiedam is best known for: production of the traditional Dutch gin known as *jenever*. In 1850, when the industry was at its height, there were hundreds of businesses distilling malt wine and adding juniper to produce this liquor, which was shipped all over the world. The distillery's huge bins, cooling vessels and copper distilling kettles are still here, as are a number of upstairs exhibits about *jenever*-making.

Korenmolen de Walvisch — WINDMILL

(📞010-246 95 06; www.molendewalvisch.nl; Westvest 229, Schiedam; adult/child 13-17/child under 13 €7.50/7/free, combined ticket with National Jenevermuseum Schiedam €12/11.50/free; ⊘11am-5pm Tue-Sun; 🚻; Ⓜ Schiedam Centrum or Parkweg) One of the highest windmills in the world, the 'Mill of the Whale' dates from 1794 and was rebuilt in 1996 after a fire. Built to grind malt for the gin industry, it now functions as a museum, with exhibits explaining the milling process and a video presentation about the Netherlands' 1200 windmills (a third of which still work). A downstairs shop sells flours milled at De Vrijheid mill, the only one of Schiedam's seven historic mills still functioning.

✖ Eating & Drinking

Restaurant Frits — MODERN EUROPEAN €€

(📞010-477 30 25; www.facebook.com/restaurant-frits/; Piet Heynsplein 25, Delfshaven; 8-course menu €40; ⊘6-10pm Thu-Sun; 🚇Delfshaven) Inside a pretty Delfshaven canal house,

Delfshaven ⓝ

with an intimate split-level, dark-timber interior, Frits serves an astounding-value eight-course surprise menu using ingredients from its own kitchen garden. Although there's no choice on the night (and no à la carte), chef Robbert van Gammeren skilfully adapts to dietary requirements (gluten-free, vegetarian, allergies) with advance notice. Reservations are essential.

Stadsbrouwerij De Pelgrim — BREWERY

(📞010-477 11 89; www.pelgrimbier.nl; Aelbrechtskolk 12, Delfshaven; ⊘noon-midnight Wed-Sat, to 10pm Sun; 🚇Delfshaven) The sight of bubbling copper vats and the heady scent of hops greets you at this vintage brewery abutting the Oude Kerk. Here you can take a voyage through its wonderful seasonal and standard beers such as the popular Mayflower Tripel in the bar, canal-side terrace or courtyard. A tasting flight of five beers costs €5.

De Oude Sluis BROWN CAFE

(☎010-477 30 68; www.cafedeoudesluis.nl; Havenstraat 7, Delfshaven; ☉noon-1am Mon-Thu, noon-2am Fri, 2pm-2am Sat, 2pm-1am Sun; 🚋Delfshaven) The view up the canal from the terrace tables stretches as far as Delfshaven's windmill at this *bruin café*, which has been a popular neighbourhood spot since 1912. There's occasional live music and a good choice of beer on tap and by bottle.

❶ Getting There & Away

DELFSHAVEN

Tram Line 4 (direction Marconiplein) travels from Rotterdam Centraal; alight at the Delfshaven stop.

Metro Lines A, B and C; Delfshaven stop.

Dordrecht

🖉 078 / POP 118,899

Unlike other historic towns in South Holland, daily life in Dordrecht isn't dictated by the demands of tourism, making it a relaxing and rewarding destination to explore. The town's strategic trading position (precipitating a boom in the wine trade) and its status as the oldest Dutch city (having been granted a town charter in 1220), ensured that it was one of the most powerful Dutch regions until the mid- to late-16th century, and many well-preserved buildings dating from this time remain. There are a number of museums to visit, an array of excellent restaurants to dine in and plenty of opportunities for outdoors adventures in the vast and watery expanse of nearby Biesbosch National Park.

◉ Sights & Activities

Most sights are on or near the three old canals – the Nieuwehaven, the Wolwevershaven and the Wijnhaven.

Grote Kerk CHURCH

(☎078-614 46 60; www.grotekerk-dordrecht.nl; Lange Geldersekade 2; tower adult/child €1/0.50; ☉10.30am-4.30pm Tue-Sat, noon-4pm Sun Apr-Oct, 2-4pm Tue, Thu & Sat Nov–mid-Dec) **FREE** The massive tower of the 14th- to 15th-century Grote Kerk was originally meant to have reached much higher toward the heavens, but it took on a lean during its 150-year-plus construction. You can climb to the top – 275 steps – to enjoy excellent views of the town. Inside the church are a grand marble pulpit with carved wooden canopy, finely carved 16th-century choir stalls and a few stained-glass windows.

Dordrechts Museum MUSEUM

(☎078-770 52 17; www.dordrechtsmuseum.nl; Museumstraat 40; adult/child €12/free, combined ticket with Museum Simon van Gijn €15/free; ☉11am-5pm Tue-Sun) Celebrating Dordrecht's artistic heritage, this fine-art museum has two floors filled with canvases depicting the landscape in this part of the Netherlands, as well as detailed portraits of local luminaries. The highlights are works by Aelbert Cuyp (1620–91) and Jan van Goyen (1596–1656). Van Goyen was one of the first Dutch painters to capture the interplay of light on landscapes – look for his *View of Dordrecht* – while Cuyp is known for his many works painted in and around the town.

Distilleerderij Rutte DISTILLERY

(☎078-613 44 67; www.rutte.com; Vriesestraat 130; 25-/90-minute tastings €5/15, jenever-making workshop €34; ☉shop 9am-5pm Mon-Fri, 9.30am-5pm Sat) Learn about the local *jenever* at this

ROTTERDAM & SOUTH HOLLAND DORDRECHT

WORTH A TRIP

SLOT LOEVESTEIN

Located near the tiny, beautiful little walled town of Woudrichem, **Slot Loevestein** (☎018-344 71 71; www.slotloevestein.nl; Loevestein 1, Poederoijen; adult/child 4-18 €13.50/9; ☉11am-5pm daily Jul & Aug, 11am-5pm Tue-Sun May-Sep, 11am-5pm Sat & Sun Mar, Apr & Oct, 11am-4pm Sat & Sun Nov-Feb) is an evocative 14th-century keep that has functioned as a prison, residence and toll castle. These days it hosts tourists and various cultural events. Note that tickets can be purchased with cash only.

The castle is difficult to access via public transport. From the Gorinchem train station, it's a 1.6km walk to the harbour at Binnenstad, from where you can take a **water ferry** (☎018-365 93 14; www.riveer.nl; day pass €3) or a **watertaxi** (☎06 22 55 82 33) to the castle. Check the website for the ferry timetable; you'll need to book the water taxi in advance.

Dordrecht

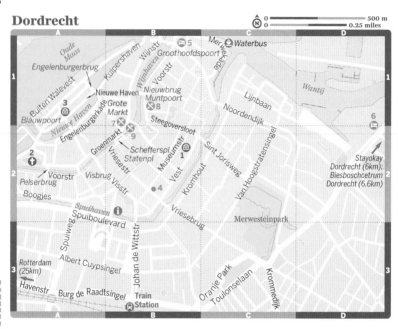

Dordrecht

distillery, which has been concocting its aromatic firewater since 1872. Better yet, book in for a tour and tasting, or a three-hour workshop to learn how to make it yourself. The distillery's shop also sells bottles of its prized spirits.

Advance bookings are necessary for the 90-minute tour, but not for the 25-minute 'mini' tour and tasting, which runs at 3pm and 4pm every Friday and Saturday.

🛏 Sleeping

★ De Luthiers   B&B €
(☏ 078-631 33 90; www.deluthiers.nl; Voorstraat 13; r €90-95; P 🛜) Above a luthiers' atelier (a place where string instruments are built and repaired), this B&B has two cosy rooms

tucked up in the attic under sloping timber eaves. Both have a small equipped kitchenette and squeaky-clean bathroom. Breakfast is served in the room. An on-site music room has a grand piano and children's play nook. Great value.

Villa Augustus   BOUTIQUE HOTEL €€
(☏ 078-639 31 11; www.villa-augustus.nl; Oranjelaan 7; d €125-155, f/ste €155/210; P 🛜) This converted 1882 water tower surrounded by gardens is an ode to the ingenuity of Dutch design. Inside, 20 individually designed rooms are decorated with art and recycled furniture; the family rooms are in sheds next to the garden and are nowhere near as atmospheric.

À la carte breakfasts are enjoyed in an on-site restaurant, which overlooks a large kitchen garden and orchard. The popularity of the restaurant means that the surrounds can lack tranquillity. Private boat rental is available.

Eating & Drinking

Scheffersplein, a large central square built over a canal, is ringed by cafes with umbrella-shaded terraces that are great people-watching spots in summer. Cafes serving good coffee and snacks are strangely hard to find; the most impressive is set in the garden of the Museum Simon van Gijn (☑078-770 87 08; www.huisvangijn.nl; Nieuwe Haven 29; adult/child under 19 €10/free, combined ticket with Dordrechts Museum €15/free; ⊙11am-5pm Tue-Sun). There are a number of welcoming wine bars on Wijnstraat and Voorstraat.

★ Villa Augustus
Restaurant   MODERN EUROPEAN €€
(☑078-639 31 11; www.villa-augustus.nl; Oranjelaan 7; sandwiches €9-10, afternoon tea €20, pizzas €8-14, mains €17-38; ⊙7am-10.45pm; 🛜🅿) ✔ Chefs here make the most of the harvest from the large attached kitchen garden and orchard, supplemented by what is in season at the local markets. Produce is largely organic, and always fresh. You'll dine in the former pumping station of the historic water tower housing hotel Villa Augustus, a bustling space with a vast open kitchen and pizza oven.

Magazijn   INTERNATIONAL €€
(☑078-890 27 80; www.magazijndordrecht.nl; Voorstraat 180; small plates €4-10, large plates €15-18; ⊙10am-midnight Wed-Thu & Sun-Mon, to 1am Fri & Sat; 🛜🅿🍴) As hip as Dordrecht gets, this hybrid bar, cafe and restaurant shares an airy and historic space with an art gallery at the rear and a music shop with lots of vinyl on offer upstairs. The dishes emerging from the semi-open kitchen are cafe-style and global in nature, with vegan and vegetarian choices. There's even a kids play area and a rear garden courtyard.

Bistro Twee 33   EUROPEAN €€
(☑078-740 00 04; www.bistrotwee33.nl; Wijnstraat 233; mains €17-26; ⊙4-10pm Tue-Fri, 2-10pm Sat & Sun) In fact, there's nothing twee about this modern bistro and wine bar, which features a warm colour scheme, pendant lights,

wine-lined shelves and an open bar and kitchen. The menu eschews fuss, concentrating on house-made charcuterie, oysters and French bistro classics (*bavette,* steak tartare, savoury tarts). Wine is a passion; international selections are available by the glass and bottle.

Strada del Vino   ITALIAN €€
(☑078-740 00 01; www.stradadelvino.nl; Wijnstraat 170; pizzas & pastas €8-19; ⊙5-11.30pm Sun-Thu, to midnight Fri & Sat; 🅿🍴) Green, red and white flags flying outside make it clear that this place is proudly Italian. Dominated by a large pizza oven at the rear, it's popular with families, local chefs (it's one of the few places in town to open on Mondays) and pretty well everyone else in town. Pizzas, pastas and espresso are all authentically and deliciously *Italiano.*

🔒 Shopping

The northern stretch of Voorstraat is the best street for browsing.

★ Wereldwijven   TEXTILES
(☑078-613 63 07; www.wereldwijven.info; Voorstraat 178; ⊙9am-5pm Mon-Sat) A shop associated with a social enterprise, Wereldwijven (Worldpeople) trains migrant women in sewing and embroidery, giving them a potential income-generating skill, teaching them Dutch and offering networking opportunities and cultural connection at the same time. The enterprise funds itself by selling their work – the cushions, clothes, toys and other items lining the shop shelves are lovely.

ℹ Information

Dordrecht's vast **tourist office** (VVV Dordrecht; ☑ 078-632 24 40; www.vvvdordrecht.nl; Spuiboulevard 99; ⊙10am-6pm Mon, 9am-6pm Tue-Fri, 10am-5pm Sat) is located midway between the train station and the town centre.

ℹ Getting There & Away

Local buses leave from the interchange to your right as you exit the train station.

BICYCLE
Bike paths go to Rotterdam, 27km to the north, running through pleasant countryside that includes Kinderdijk. Biesbosch National Park is just a 10km ride east by a number of good routes.

Bike Total Zwaan (☑ 078-635 6830; www.czwaan.nl; Stationsplein 10; standard/electric bike hire per day €12/17.50; ☺ 4.30am-1.30am Mon-Fri, 6.30am-1.30am Sat, 7am-1.30am Sun) Located in the *fietsenstalling* (bike garage) next to the train station.

BOAT

The **Waterbus** (☑ 0800 023 25 45; www.water bus.nl; one-way adult/child 4-11 €6/4) fast ferry service links Dordrecht with Rotterdam. From May to October there are also services travelling via Kinderdijk.

TRAIN

From the train station, it's a 700m walk north to Dordrecht's centre. Regular services:

TO	PRICE (€)	TIME (MIN)	FREQUENCY (PER HR)
Amsterdam	18	30	1 or 2
Breda	6.10	25	3
Rotterdam	4.40	20	4

Gouda

☑ 0182 / POP 71,189

Gouda's association with cheese has made it famous – the town's namesake export is among the Netherlands' best known, and busloads of tourists descend on the town every Thursday in spring and summer to watch the pantomime-style *kaasstad* (cheese market) in front of the historic *waag* (weighing house). Non-cheesy attractions (and we mean that in both senses of the word) include magnificent Sint Janskerk, home to the largest cache of in-situ 16th-century stained glass in the world, and an excellent city museum. All are located in the town's compact canal-ringed historic centre, which is a mere five-minute walk from the train station.

◉ Sights

The main sights are within a 10-minute walk of the trapezoidal Markt, but it pays to wander off down little side streets such as Achter de Kerk and Lage Gouwe, which pass quiet canals and seem untouched by the centuries.

★ **Sint Janskerk**   CHURCH
(Church of St John's; ☑ 0182-512 684; www.sintjan. com; Achter de Kerk 2; adult/student & child 13-18 €7/3.50; ☺ 9am-5pm Mon-Sat Mar-Oct, 10am-4pm Mon-Sat Nov-Feb) Impressive for both its size and its magnificent stained-glass windows, Sint Janskerk had chequered begin-

nings: previous incarnations of the building burned down with ungodly regularity every 100 years or so from 1361 until the mid-16th century, when the current structure was completed. At 123m it is the longest church in the country. A free audioguide in English gives loads of information about the 72 windows, which together form the largest cache of in-situ 16th-century stained glass in the world.

The windows created by Dirck Crabeth, his brother Wouter, and Lambert van Noort in the mid-16th century are particularly impressive. Their works, which are numbered, include highlights such as window No 6 (John the Baptist; the folks on either side paid for the window), No 22 (Jesus purifies the temple; note the look on the face of the moneychanger) and 25 (the relief of Leiden in 1574, at the height of the Dutch War of Independence led by William of Orange). The oldest windows in the church are above the choir, and depict Jesus and the 12 apostles.

Museum Gouda   MUSEUM
(☑ 0182-33 10 00; www.museumgouda.nl; Achter de Kerk 14; adult/child 5-17 €10/4; ☺ 11am-5pm Tue-Sun) Housed in a medieval hospital building, the town's major museum has a collection of artefacts and artworks related to Gouda and surrounding areas. There's plenty of *Gouds plateel* (glazed earthenware pottery), a collection of paintings by artists of the 19th-century Barbizon and Hague schools, a scale model of 1562 Gouda and a ghoulish basement section on local torture in the Middle Ages. The museum also hosts travelling and temporary exhibitions. There are entrances on both Achter de Kerk and Oosthaven.

Goudse Waag   HISTORIC BUILDING
(Gouda Weighing House) This former cheese-weighing house was built in 1668. Check out the reliefs carved into the side showing the cheese being weighed. Today it houses a tourist information desk and the **Kaaswaag** (Cheese Museum; ☑ 0182-529 996; www.goudsewaag.nl; Markt 35; adult/child under 12 €4.50/free; ☺ noon-5pm Fri-Wed, 10am-5pm Thu mid-Mar–Oct, 10am-3pm Wed-Sun Nov–mid-Dec & mid-Jan–mid-Mar), a museum that follows the history of the cheese trade in the Netherlands.

Gouda Kaasstad   MARKET
(Gouda Cheese Market; www.goudakaasstad.nl; Markt; ☺ 10am-12.30pm Thu early Apr–late Aug) **FREE** This staged cheese market on the

Gouda

Markt draws plenty of local and international-al day trippers, as do the stalls selling other dairy goods and souvenirs. A few locals dress up in costume and pose for photos. It's all – dare we say it – terribly cheesy.

🏃 Activities

A good circle ride traverses what's billed as the *Groene Hart* (Green Heart) of the region. It begins just south of the centre and runs 42km through the canal-laced farmlands south of Gouda. Called the Krimpenerwaard Route after the region it covers, it includes stops at dairies where cheese is made. Pick up the free brochure from the tourist office (p180), which also sells detailed maps.

Download handy walking-tour maps and information at http://www.xplregouda.nl

Reederij de IJsel   BOATING
(☑ 06 8370 5193; www.reederijdeijsel.nl; Oosthaven 12; adult/child 3-12 €10/5; ☉ 1.30pm & 3.30pm

Thu & Sat mid-Apr–mid-Oct; ⚓) Barges take passengers on 90-minute boat cruises around Gouda's canals and waterways.

🛏 Sleeping & Eating

The fact that Gouda is commonly perceived as a day-trip destination is underscored by the town's lack of decent accommodation options – you are best off overnighting elsewhere.

The eponymous cheese isn't the only Dutch culinary signature to originate here – the much-loved *siroopwafel* (crispy biscuits formed by two wafers jammed together with caramel syrup) is a local creation, and can be tasted straight off the production line at Kamphuisen Siroopwafels (☑ 0182-634 965; www.siroopwafelfabriek.nl; Markt 69; tour €9.95; ☉ 10am-6pm) on the Markt. Specialty cheese shops are scattered across town, but there's a lack of good eateries serving treats, cheesy or otherwise.

David's Gelato   ICE CREAM €
(☑ 06-28 55 85 59; www.davidsgelato.nl; Lange Tiendeweg 23; per scoop €1.50; ☉ 10am-10pm Tue-Sat, from noon Mon & Sun; ⚓) The young entrepreneur who owns this ice-cream parlour was the subject of Mirjam Van Veelen's 2017 documentary *Chill: The Road to David's Gelato,* the story of his Mediterranean pilgrimage to learn all about running a successful gelateria. Fruity and creamy flavours join

WORTH A TRIP

THE GREAT OUTDOORS: BIESBOSCH NATIONAL PARK

Created when a large tract of polder land was submerged in the St Elizabeth flood of 1421, 7100-hectare wetland Biesbosch National Park (http://np-debiesbosch.nl/; 🖳 Hollandse Biesbosch) is Europe's largest freshwater tidal zone in Europe and one of the Netherlands' largest expanses of natural landscape. Preserving landscape and animal habitats on both banks of the Nieuwe Merwede River, east and south of Dordrecht, it is home to beavers (reintroduced to the Brabant area of the park in 1988), deer and voles, along with scores of birds. Three visitor centres, designated hiking routes and a large network of rivers, creeks and islands to explore by canoe make it a popular choice for those seeking outdoors adventure.

Of the three park visitors centres, Biesboschcentrum Dordrecht (☎ 078-770 53 53; www.biesboschcentrumdordrecht.nl/; Baanhoekweg 53, Dordrecht; ⊙ 9am-5pm Tue-Sun Apr-Jun & Sep-Oct, 9am-5pm daily Jul & Aug, 10am-4pm Tue-Sun Nov-Mar; 🖳 Hollandse Biesbosch) near Dordrecht is the easiest to access. It offers guided boat and walking tours as well as boat and canoe rental (April to October only). Changing exhibits highlight its flora, fauna and natural features.

To get here on public transport, take a waterbus (year round) or bus (summer only). Waterbus service 23 travels from Merwekade to Hollandse Biesbosch (adult/child €4/2, 12 minutes); there are no weekend sailings October to April. From the waterbus stop, it's then an 800m signed walk to the centre. In summer, bus 801 travels between Dordrecht railway station and the centre (€3.50).

sorbets and frozen yoghurts in the display case, and are loved by locals and tourists alike.

Kamphuisen   DUTCH €€
(☎ 0182-514 163; www.kamphuisen.com; Hoge Gouwe 19; mains €17-23, 3-course dinner menu €27; ⊙ 5pm-midnight, kitchen to 10pm; 🖉) This classic *bruin café* has a wooden floor and bar whose worn patina pay testament to decades of drinking action. Outside, there are tables under the eaves of the old fish market. The bar menu offers dishes inspired by regions as diverse as Italy, Australia and the Middle East. Book for dinner.

Brunel   BISTRO €€
(☎ 0182-518 979; http://restaurantbrunel.nl; Hoge Grouwe 23; mains €19-21, set menus €27-30; ⊙ 5-9.30pm Tue-Sat; 🖉) Regional produce is utilised well here, ensuring that the modern French and Italian dishes devised by the chef are always fresh and tasty. In summer, dine along the canal in the old colonnaded fish market.

🛍 Shopping

The most interesting shopping strip is Lange Groenendaal, which has boutiques, concept stores and an organic grocery.

't Kaaswinkeltje   FOOD
(☎ 182 51 42 69; www.kaaswinkeltje.com; Lange Tiendeweg 30; ⊙ 8.30am-6pm Mon-Fri, 8am-5pm Sat) The most alluring (and aromatic) of Gouda's many cheese shops, this place next to the canal is full of tasty unpasturised farmer's cheese from local producers.

ℹ Information

Tourist Office (VVV Gouda; ☎ 0182-589 110; www.welkomingouda.nl; Waag, Markt 35; ⊙ 10am-5pm daily Apr-Oct, 10am-3pm Wed-Sun Nov-Mar)

ℹ Getting There & Around

BICYCLE
Bike routes link Gouda with Amsterdam and Rotterdam.

Oldenburger (☎ 0182-516 111; www.oldenburger.nl; Burgemeester Jamesplein 2; stand-ard/electric bike-rental per day €12.50/20; ⊙ 6am-12.15am Mon-Fri, from 7am Sat, from 9am Sun) rents bikes.

BUS
The bus interchange is immediately to the left as you exit the train station on the Centrum side. Bus 107 runs to Oudewater (€2.90, 25 minutes, twice hourly) and continues to Utrecht (€6.10, 55 minutes). There are reduced services on Sundays.

TRAIN

Gouda's train station is close to the city centre. Regular services:

TO	PRICE (€)	TIME (MIN)	FREQUENCY (PER HR)
Amsterdam	11.50	55	4
Den Haag	5.70	20	8
Rotterdam	5.10	20	6
Utrecht	6.40	20	8

Den Haag (The Hague)

📞 070 / POP 519,988

There's a lot more to Den Haag than immediately meets the eye. The popular perception of the Netherlands' third-largest city is of a stately, regal place populated with bureaucrats and businesspeople. While this is true to some extent, there is so much more: the city's cultural scene – anchored by the presence of the world-renowned Mauritshuis museum and Nederlands Dans Theater (and about to be boosted by the opening of the Spuiplein cultural precinct) – is one of the most exciting in the country; its culinary scene is replete with contemporary restaurants; and its entertainment scene has moved far past the embassy cocktail parties that once predominated, making the party precinct of Grote Markt and the much-loved Paard live-music venue essential stops for every visitor. Easy to explore on foot or by tram, this is a city that amply rewards those who stay for a few days.

History

Officially known as 's-Gravenhage (the Count's Hedge), Den Haag is the Dutch seat of government and home to the royal family. Prior to 1806, it was the Dutch capital; however, that year Louis Bonaparte installed his government in Amsterdam. Eight years later, when the French had been ousted, the government returned to Den Haag but the title of capital remained with Amsterdam.

In the 20th century Den Haag became the home of several international legal entities, including the UN's International Court of Justice.

◉ Sights

★ **Mauritshuis**   MUSEUM

(Royal Picture Gallery; 📞 070-302 34 56; www. mauritshuis.nl; Plein 29; adult/student/child under 19 €15.50/12.50/free; ⊙1-6pm Mon, 10am-6pm Tue, Wed & Fri-Sun, 10am-8pm Thu; 🚊 Centrum) Offering a wonderful introduction to Dutch and Flemish art, this splendid museum is set in a 17th-century mansion built for wealthy sugar trader Johan Maurits. It became a museum housing the Royal Picture Collection in 1822, and acquired a swish modern wing in 2012–14. The 800-strong collection of paintings focuses on works created between the 15th and 18th centuries. It includes masterpieces such as Vermeer's *Girl with a Pearl Earring* (c1665) and Rembrandt's intriguing *The Anatomy Lesson of Dr Nicolaes Tulp* (1632).

The list of artists represented in the collection is formidable: in addition to works by Vermeer and Rembrandt, there are multiple pieces by Anthony van Dyke, Rubens, Jan Brueghel I, Hans Holbein II, Hals and Steen. Don't miss Van der Weyden's *The Lamentation of Christ* (c1460–64), Fabritius' *The Goldfinch* (1654) and Vermeer's *View of Delft* (c1660–61), the most famous cityscape of the Dutch Golden Age.

Audiotour hire costs €3.50, but there is also a free multimedia smart tour downloadable through the Apple Store and Google Play. The cafe and gift shop in the new wing are both very good.

Your ticket includes entry to Galerij Prins Willem V (p183).

Binnenhof   PALACE

(🚊 Centrum) Home to both houses of the Dutch government, this complex of buildings next to the Hofvijver (Court Pond; 🚊 Centrum) is arranged around a central courtyard that was once used for executions. Its splendid ceremonial Ridderzaal (Knights Hall) dates back to the 13th century. The 17th-century North Wing is still home to the Upper House, but the Lower House meets in a chamber in the modern eastern part of the complex. Visitor organisation ProDemos (📞 070-757 02 00; www.prodemos.nl; Hofweg 1; Ridderzaal tour €5.50, Ridderzaal, House of Representatives & Senate tour €11; ⊙office 10am-5pm Mon-Sat, tours by reservation; 🚊 Kneuterdijk, Centrum) conducts guided tours.

Museum de Gevangenpoort   MUSEUM

(Museum of Prison Gate; 📞 070-346 08 61; www. gevangenpoort.nl; Buitenhof 33; adult/child under 13 €10/6, combination ticket with Galerij Prins Willem V adult €12.50/6; ⊙10am-5pm Tue-Fri, from noon Sat & Sun, last tour 3.45pm; 🚊 Kneuterdijk) A surviving remnant of the 13th-century

Den Haag (The Hague) Central

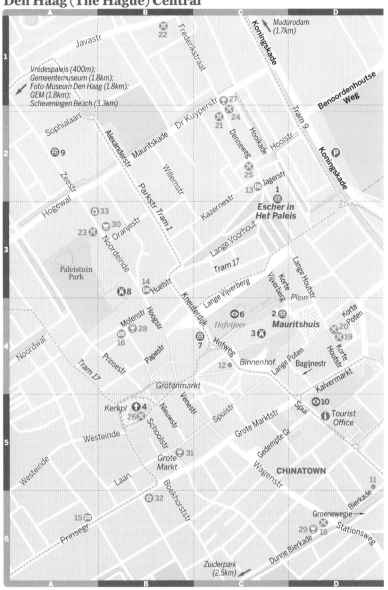

city fortifications, the Gevangenpoort functioned as a prison from 1428 to 1825. Guided tours (30 minutes) run hourly on weekdays and every half-hour on weekends, evoking what life would have been like for both prisoners and their gaolers. Tours are not suitable for young children, as some guides take a ghoulish delight in describing the incarceration and torture of miscreants in vivid detail. English-language tours are offered at 2.15pm on Saturdays and Sundays.

dijk) Sharing an entrance with the Gevangenpoort, this was the first public museum in the Netherlands when it opened in 1774 as a showcase of William V's art collection. It closed after many of its works were 'acquired' by the occupying French in 1794 and didn't reopen in the same location until 2010. Today, the fully restored gallery houses 150 old masters from the Mauritshuis collection (Steen, Rubens, Potter et al) hung cheek-by-jowl in the style of the late 18th century.

Grote Kerk   CHURCH
(070-302 86 30; www.grotekerkdenhaag.nl; Rond de Grote Kerk 12; adult/child under 12 €2/free; 11am-5pm Tue-Sat, 2-5pm Sun late May–Sep; Grote Markt) Dating from 1450, the Great Church has a fine pulpit that was constructed in the following century. If you're here outside its limited visitor season (note that openings can be unreliable), you can take in concerts and organ recitals – check its on-line agenda for dates.

The neighbouring Oude Raadhuis (Old Town Hall; 1565) is a splendid example of Dutch Renaissance architecture.

★ Escher in Het Paleis   MUSEUM
(070-427 77 30; www.escherinhetpaleis.nl; Lange Voorhout 74; adult/student/child 7-15/child under 7 €9.50/8.50/6.50/free; 11am-5pm Tue-Sun; Korte Voorhout) Once home to members of the Dutch royal family, the 18th-century Lange Voorhout Palace now houses a collection of the work of Dutch graphic artist MC Escher (1898–1972). The permanent exhibition features notes, letters, photos and plenty of woodcuts and lithographs from various points of his career, including everything from the early realism to the later phantasmagoria. All are fascinating exercises in the blending of different perspectives, and the conjunction of mathematical rules and artistic subject matter.

Gemeentemuseum   MUSEUM
(Municipal Museum; 070-338 11 11; www.gemeentemuseum.nl; Stadhouderslaan 41; adult/child €15/free, combination ticket with Foto-Museum Den Haag and GEM €19/free; 10am-5pm Tue-Sun; Gemeentemuseum/Museon) Known predominantly for its De Stijl exhibit, this museum is housed in an unusual art-deco building designed by HP Berlage. It opened in 1935. The De Stijl exhibit suffers from an overemphasis on unremarkable pre–De Stijl paintings by Piet Mondrian, but the major drawcard, his unfinished *Victory Boogie Woogie* (1942–44),

Galerij Prins Willem V   GALLERY
(www.mauritshuis.nl; Buitenhof 33; adult/child under 19 €5/free, combined ticket with Mauritshuis adult/child under 19 €15.50/free, combined ticket with Museum de Gevangenpoort adult/child under 13 €12.50/6; noon-5pm Tue-Sun; Kneuter-

Den Haag (The Hague) Central

is an undoubted masterpiece. Upstairs, the 'Discover the Modern' exhibit includes Egon Schiele's exquisite *Portrait of Edith* (1915) among early-20th-century works by Van Gogh, Picasso, Kandinsky and others.

Fotomuseum Den Haag MUSEUM
(☑ 070-338 11 44; www.fotomuseumdenhaag.nl; Stadhouderslaan 43; incl GEM entry adult/child €8/free, combination ticket with Gemeentemuseum €19/free; ☉ 11am-6pm Tue-Sun; ☒ Gemeentemuseum/Museon) Adjoining the Gemeentemuseum (p183) and sharing a building with **GEM** (☑ 070-338 11 11; www.gem-online.nl; ☉ 11am-6pm Tue-Sun), Den Haag's excellent photography museum mounts several major exhibitions a year. The ground-floor cafe overlooks the ornamental lake in front of the Gemeentemuseum and is a popular meeting spot in this part of town.

Madurodam AMUSEMENT PARK
(☑ 070-416 24 00; www.madurodam.nl; George Maduroplein 1; weekday/weekend admission €16.50/17.50, family ticket €52.50, child under 3 free; ☉ 9am-8pm mid-Mar–Aug, 9am-7pm Sep & Oct, 11am-5pm Nov–mid-Mar; ☒ ; ☒ Madurodam) A miniaturised Netherlands, this theme park sports 1:25 scale versions of Schiphol, Amsterdam, windmills and tulips, Rotterdam harbour, the Delta dykes and more.

It's an enlightening example of the Dutch tendency to put their world under a microscope. Kids love it.

Panorama Mesdag GALLERY
(☑ 070-310 66 65; www.panorama-mesdag.com; Zeestraat 65; adult/student/child 4-11 €10/8.50/5; ☉ 10am-5pm Mon-Sat, 11am-5pm Sun; ☒ Mauritskade) Home to the *Panorama* (1881), an immense, 14m-high, 360-degree painting of the sea, dunes and fishing village of Scheveningen, this museum is one of Den Haag's most unusual cultural attractions. The work, which is 120m in circumference, was created by Hendrik Willem Mesdag (1831–1915), a member of the Impressionist-influenced Hague School of painters. Viewed from an upper platform, it gives the illusion that the viewer is high on a dune looking at the scene.

Mesdag's creation is the oldest 19th-century panorama still displayed in its (purpose-built) original location. He, his artist wife Sientje Mesdag–Van Houten (1834–1909) and three other painters worked on mobile scaffolding to create the scene on 18 large pieces of canvas that had been sewn together. Using panoramic photographs as a base reference, the extremely realistic depiction of Scheveningen was lit by natural light from concealed skylights and wowed the public when it opened as a tourist attraction in August 1881. A downstairs gallery gives background on the panorama's creation.

Haagse Toren
VIEWPOINT

(📞070-305 10 00; www.haagsetoren.nl; Rijswijkseplein 786; admission €9; ⏱observation deck noon-10pm; 🚊Rijswijkseplein) A glass elevator whisks you up in just 40 seconds to the observation deck on the 42nd floor (135m) of this tower; there's also a less-dizzying option of riding a windowless lift. On a clear day, panoramas from the indoor viewing areas and outdoor balcony extend as far as Rotterdam, Leiden and Hoek van Holland. Tickets include a beer, house wine or soft drink in the Sky Bar (after 6pm, this offer stretches to a cocktail).

Vredespaleis
HISTORIC SITE

(Peace Palace; 📞070-302 42 42; www.vredespaleis.nl; Carnegieplein 2; visitor-centre admission free, tours adult/child under 9 €11/free; ⏱visitor centre 10am-5pm Tue-Sun Apr-Oct, 11am-4pm Tue-Sun Nov-Mar; 🚊Vredespaleis) Home to the UN's Permanent Court of Arbitration and International Court of Justice, the Peace Palace is housed in a grand 1913 building donated by American steelmaker Andrew Carnegie. Its visitor centre has multimedia exhibits detailing the history of both the building and the organisations within; these are enjoyed in a free 30-minute audioguide tour. Hour-long guided afternoon tours of the palace in Dutch and English are offered on weekends; these should be booked ahead on the website.

Twenty places on each tour are kept for walk-in visitors on the day – turn up at 10am if you are keen to score one. A passport or an EU identity card or driving licence must be shown on entry.

Tours

De Ooievaart
BOATING

(📞070-445 18 69; www.rondvaartdenhaag.nl; Bierkade 18b; adult/child €12/8; ⏱daily Jul & Aug, Tue-Sun Apr-Jun & Sep; 🚊Bierkade) Offers 90-minute boat tours, taking in Den Haag's most interesting sights at canal level. Departure times vary; confirm in advance.

🛏 Sleeping

Den Haag hosts all the major international chains but there are also some interesting smaller hotels. Numerous beachfront possibilities crowd Scheveningen; none are particularly alluring. Accommodation prices in the city are highest on weekdays during the Dutch parliamentary year (see www.houseofrepresentatives.nl for dates) and when the UN's Permanent Court of Arbitration and International Court of Justice sit.

KingKool
HOSTEL €

(📞70 215 8339; www.kingkool.nl; Prinsegracht 51; dm €21-31, d with shared bathroom €55, d €69-76; 📶; 🚊Brouwersgracht) Close to Paard (p188) and the Grote Markt party precinct, this is Den Haag's backpacker central. The ground-floor bar is a popular gathering spot and the mixed dorms (sleeping eight to 12, some on three-tier bunks) are made cheerful with street-art-style murals; those on the first floor are best. Shared bathrooms are barracks-like but clean, with plenty of hot water.

Most dorms have lockers, but no reading lights or dedicated power points; the exception is the battery-hen-like 'Dorm Deluxe', in which each bed has a curtain, power point and reading light. Private rooms are simple but comfortable. There's a communal kitchen, but no laundry. The entire hostel is hot in summer.

Stayokay Den Haag
HOSTEL €

(📞070-315 78 88; www.stayokay.com; Scheepmakerstraat 27; dm €19-35, s €43-75, d €49-85, tr €93-125; @📶; 🚊Rijswijkseplein, 🚉Den Haag HS) 🖋 Located southeast of the city centre, this HI-affiliated hostel has 4- to 8-bed single-sex ensuite dorms. Each dorm bed has a power point and reading light; lockers (€2 for 24 hours) are available at reception. Private rooms are frill-free. Facilities include a laundry, a bar with pool table and a sunny terrace next to the canal. Breakfast (included) and dinner buffet (€8.50 to €14.50) are served in the cafeteria.

Bike hire costs €10 per day; towel hire €3.50.

Hotel Sebel
HOTEL €

(📞070-345 92 00; www.hotelsebel.nl; Prins Hendrikplein 20; s/d from €65/75; 📶; 🚊Elandstraat, Van Speijkstraat) Sebel is a good-value 33-room hotel that spreads out across three proud art-nouveau corner buildings. The cheapest rooms are minuscule but others have balconies and studios have kitchenettes. Breakfast costs €12.50.

Paleis Hotel
BOUTIQUE HOTEL €€

(📞070-362 46 21; www.paleishotel.nl; Molenstraat 26; d from €89; 📶❄📶📶; 🚊Kneuterdijk) Located near the Noordeinde palace, this hotel

DON'T MISS

URBAN BEACH LIFE

The long beach at Scheveningen, pronounced – if possible – as s'CHay-fuh-ningen, attracts nine million visitors per year. It's heavily developed, with numerous cafes elbowing each other for space on tiers of promenades by the beach.

This beach won't be to everyone's taste, but you might just find pleasure in the carnival atmosphere, or the waves themselves. Aloha Surf (🖉 070-322 71 71; www.alohasurf. nl; Strand Noord 2b, Scheveningen; surfboard/SUP rental 1st hr/subsequent 30 min €10/2.50; ⊙ 8.30am-sunset; 🚌 Vuurbaakstraat) rents boards and wetsuits and runs lessons.

Better yet, you can escape to wide-open beaches and nature with just a bit of effort, especially to the south, where the hype tapers off as you pass the harbour.

Most Den Haag streets heading west reach Scheveningen, 4km away, or take trams 1 or 11 from Hollands Spoor station (HS).

has 20 attractive but slightly worn rooms. Standards are smallish with cramped bathrooms; those in the superior category are more spacious and the executive rooms are even larger, but overlook a busy and potentially noisy courtyard restaurant. There's a guest lounge and an airy breakfast room (breakfast €18.50).

⭐ **Hotel Indigo**   BOUTIQUE HOTEL €€€
(🖉 070-209 90 00; www.hotelindigo.com; Noordeinde 33; standard r €160-230, superior r €220-290; 🗪; 🚌 Kneuterdijk) A clever transformation of the former 1884 De Nederlandsche Bank headquarters, the Indigo is located on fashionable Noordeinde. Its 63 good-sized rooms are stylish, with smart furnishings and amenities – those in the attic have bags of character. Start the day with breakfast in the ground-floor cafe (included in room rate) and finish with a cocktail in the basement speakeasy.

Hotel Des Indes   HISTORIC HOTEL €€€
(🖉 070-361 23 45; www.hoteldesindesthe-hague.com; Lange Voorhout 54-56; s/d/ste from €155/169/469; 🅿 ❄ 🗪; 🚌 Korte Voorhout) Built as a residence in 1858 and functioning as a luxury hotel since 1881, this is Den Haag's most upmarket accommodation choice. Your check-in will be efficient and the hotel's location couldn't be better, but some of the rooms on the lower floors lack natural light, and public areas – particularly the bar area – are in need of refurbishment.

✖ Eating

Den Haag's gastronomic scene is top-notch, with quality matched by the variety you'd expect in an international city. The cobbled streets and canals off Denneweg continually host adventurous new openings.

For cheap eats, head to Chinatown.

Bloem   CAFE €
(🖉 070-737 0589; www.bloemdenhaag.nl; Korte Houtstraat 6; sandwiches €6.50-7.50, cakes €3.50, high tea per person €20.50; ⊙ 11am-4pm Tue, to 6pm Wed-Sun; 🚌 Kalvermarkt-Stadhuis) The rear salon in this cute cafe has a granny-style decor, replete with petit-point creations, knick-knacks and a floral carpet. It's a popular spot for afternoon high tea, and serves cakes, quiche and sandwiches at other times.

Walter Benedict   BISTRO €€
(🖉 070-785 3745; www.walterbenedict.nl; Denneweg 69a; breakfast dishes €3.50-11, lunch dishes €8-18, dinner mains €16-25; ⊙ 9am-11pm; 🗪; 🚌 Dr Kuyperstraat) All-day breakfasts (including a €5 coffee, juice and croissant deal) are on offer at this self-styled cafe-bistro, alongside lunch choices including soup, burgers and salads. Dinner is a mainly meaty affair – the steak served with smoked-garlic gravy and potatoes pan-fried in duck fat is renowned.

Het Heden   CAFE €€
(🖉 070-346 46 64; https://hetheden.nl/; Noordeinde; sandwiches & piadini €5-10, high tea €20, dinner mains €18-24; ⊙ 11am-10pm Tue-Sat, to 5pm Sun; 🗪; 🚌 Mauritskade) The main draw here is the sunny rear garden, which is a lovely spot in which to enjoy a sandwich or *piadina* (Italian flatbread) lunch, a generous high tea or a simple dinner. The building, with its ornate brick exterior and stained-glass windows, dates from the 19th century and is one of the prettiest on Noordeinde.

Zebedeüs   CAFE €€
(🖉 070-346 83 93; www.zebedeus.nl; Rond de Grote Kerk 8; sandwiches €7-9, pastas €10, dinner mains €21-24; ⊙ 11am-9.30pm; 🗪; 🚌 Gravenstraat or Grote Markt) 🌿 Abutting the walls of the Grote Kerk, Zebedeüs serves open sand-

wiches, toasties, pastas and soup all day, and a limited menu of more elaborate mains at night. Much of the produce is organic. Cold-pressed veggie juices and freshly squeezed fruit juices are offered alongside coffee and alcohol. In fine weather, the best seats are at the chestnut-tree-shaded tables outside.

★ **De Basiliek**   INTERNATIONAL €€

(📞 070-360 61 44; www.debasiliek.nl; Korte Houtstraat 4a; mains €18-24, 3-course menu €37.50-42.50; ⊘ noon-4pm & 6-10pm Mon-Fri, 6-10pm Sat; 📶 🍴; 🚇 Kalvermarkt-Stadhuis) Moody lighting, comfortable seating and unobtrusive service set the scene for enjoyable meals at this classy choice. The menu is predominantly Italian and French, with a few Indian and Middle Eastern dishes thrown in as wildcards. The food is fresh and full of flavour, made with top-notch produce, and the stellar wine includes loads of by-the-glass options. Great coffee, too.

Basaal   MEDITERRANEAN €€

(📞 070-427 68 88; www.restaurantbasaal.nl; Dunne Bierkade 3; mains €21-24, set menus €37-60; ⊘ 6-10pm Tue-Sat; 🚇 Bierkade) Neighbourhood bistros are rarely as stylish as this one, and few have locations as pretty. Overlooking the canal, with waterside seating in summer, it offers well-priced modern Mediterranean fare and a similarly focused wine list. Chef Bas Oonk uses regional seasonal produce to create meat and fish dishes bursting with flavour; his three-course Bib-Gourmand menu (€36.50) is a steal.

Oogst   MEDITERRANEAN €€

(📞 070-360 92 24; www.restaurantoogst.nl; Denneweg 10b; small plates €9, 4-course single-plate menu €30; ⊘ noon-2pm & 6-10pm Tue-Sat; 🍴; 🚇 Malieveld, Dr Kuyperstraat) Classy is the appropriate descriptor for this small restaurant on Den Haag's prime foodie stretch, and it applies to everything from the interior (brocade-covered banquettes, fine napery, delicate glassware) to the food menu (small, beautifully presented plates). The chef utilises super-fresh produce to create dishes that are both delicious and easy on the wallet.

Dekxels   INTERNATIONAL €€

(📞 070-365 97 88; www.dekxels.nl; Denneweg 130; 4-course small-plate menu from €31.50; ⊘ 5.30-11pm; 🍴; 🚇 Dr Kuyperstraat) A member of Den Haag's ever-growing coterie of bistros with menus dominated by small plates rather than main courses, Dekxels concentrates on Asian dishes but also draws on Italy

for inspiration. Flavours are good, though presentation is overly fussy. The well-priced wine list trawls the globe.

Oker   INTERNATIONAL €€

(📞 070-364 54 53; www.restaurantoker.nl; Denneweg 71; small plates €9-15; ⊘ 11.30am-10pm Sun-Wed, to 11pm Thu-Sat; 📶; 🚇 Kuyperstraat) Take your taste buds on a journey around the globe at perennially popular Oker. The menu of small plates draws on Italian, Japanese, Thai, French, Chinese and Lebanese cuisine for inspiration, and the list of wines by the glass is equally diverse. During 'oyster happy hour' (Saturday and Sunday between 3pm and 6pm) a plate of a dozen Fines de Claire oysters costs €15.

★ **Fouquet**   DUTCH €€€

(📞 070-360 62 73; www.fouquet.nl; Javastraat 31a; mains €25-28, 3-course menus €30-38; ⊘ 6-9.30pm Mon-Sat; 🍴; 🚇) The three-course 'market fresh' menu at this elegant restaurant is an excellent and bargain-priced introduction to Sebastiaan de Bruijn's seasonally inspired French-Mediterranean fare. The menu changes daily, responding to what is fresh in the local markets, and is prepared with love and great expertise. Presentation, service and the wine list are all equally impressive.

🍸 Drinking & Nightlife

Be it cafes, wine bars, speakeasies or pubs, Den Haag has plenty of places where you can wet your whistle. The main cafe strips are Denneweg and Noordeinde. The most popular pub and bar enclave is Grote Markt.

★ **Lola Bikes & Coffee**   CAFE

(www.facebook.com/LolaBikesandCoffee/; Noordeinde 91; ⊘ 8am-6pm Tue-Sun; 🚇 Mauritskade) The owners and staff at this cafe are passionate cyclists, and operate a workshop in the rear where they repair racing bikes in between serving excellent coffee and cake to a host of regulars. Sit in the rear garden or relax in the shabby-chic front space. It's the home base of the Lola Cycling Club, which welcomes new members.

Café De Oude Mol   BROWN CAFE

(📞 070-345 16 23; www.facebook.com/DeOudeMol/; Oude Molstraat 61; ⊘ 5pm-1am Sun-Wed, to 2am Thu-Sat) Pass through the ivy-covered door of Café de Oude Mol and you'll find this intimate, earthy pub that sums up the Dutch quality of *gezelligheid* (conviviality, cosiness). Live rock music takes to the stage

ROTTERDAM & SOUTH HOLLAND DEN HAAG (THE HAGUE)

on Mondays. Food is available from Wednesday to Saturday.

De Paas
PUB

(☑070-360 00 19; www.depaas.nl; Dunne Bierkade 16a; ☻3pm-1am Sun-Thu, 3pm-1.30am Fri & Sun Apr-Nov, from 4pm Dec-Mar; ☎) A highly atmospheric old bar with a huge selection of Dutch, Belgian and other international beers, De Paas has 13 beers on tap, including unusual seasonal brews. In summer, head to its floating terrace aboard a canal boat.

Bouzy
WINE BAR

(☑070-780 35 63; www.bouzywineandfood.nl; Denneweg 83; ☻3-11pm; ☒Dr Kuyperstraat) On buzzing Denneweg, this sun-drenched corner bar has a wine list concentrating on European tipples but flirts with the New World, too; there are dozens of bubbly varieties. Food choices include charcuterie and cheese platters, *flammkuchen* (Alsatian-style pizza) and the ubiquitous *bitterballen* (croquettes).

VaVoom!
COCKTAIL BAR

(☑070-346 75 06; www.gmdh.nl/vavoom/; Grote Markt 29; ☻1pm-1am Mon-Wed & Sun, to 1.30am Thu-Sat) Rum-based cocktails are the draw at this tiki bar in the city's major party precinct. An impressive 85 rums are available, and are used in knock-'em-dead concoctions such as the Jungle Jetsetter (Malibu rum, Maraschino cherry liqueur, lime and pineapple juice).

☆ Entertainment

Most performances by Nederlands Dans Theater (www.ndt.nl; ☒Statenlaan), National Theatre (www.hnt.nl), Koninklijk Conservatorium (Royal Conservatory; www.koncon. nl) and Residentie Orkest (Philharmonic Orchestra; www.residentieorkest.nl) are currently staged at the Zuiderstrandtheatre (South Beach Theatre; ☑070-880 03 33; www. zuiderstrandtheater.nl; Houtrustweg 505, Vissershaven; ☒Statenlaan).

In summer, free concerts are often staged in the Zuiderpark southwest of the city centre. The city's best venue for contemporary live music is Paard (p188).

★ Paard
LIVE MUSIC

(☑070-750 34 34; www.paard.nl; Prinsegracht 12; ☻hrs vary; ☒Grote Markt) Call it a club, a temple to live music or just a great place to hang out, Paard is a Den Haag institution. The program of live music is eclectic – everything from jazz to metal, blues,

roots, reggae and soul – and festivals staged here include the Mondriaan Jazz Festival in October. Check the website for the program.

Shopping

Den Haag has plenty of tempting shopping options, with several great areas for browsing. Grote Marktstraat is, fittingly enough, where you'll find the major department stores and chains. Hoogstraat, Noordeinde, Huelstraat and Prinsestraat are lined with boutiques and galleries. Denneweg is celebrated not only for its restaurants and bars but also its offbeat boutiques.

Mauritshuis Gift Shop
GIFTS & SOUVENIRS

(Plein 29; ☻1-6pm Mon, 10am-6pm Tue, Wed & Fri-Sun, 10am-8pm Thu; ☒Centrum) Classy souvenirs inspired by works in the museum collection, postcards, posters, books and more are on offer at the excellent gift shop in the Mauritshuis (p181).

Frenken
CLOTHING

(www.frenkenfashion.com; Noordeinde 113a; ☻noon-9pm Thu, 10am-6pm Fri, 11am-6pm Sat; ☒Mauritskade) Saint Martins–trained Eric Frenken was the head designer of women's wear at Viktor & Rolf before launching his own equally quirky label. His beautifully tailored ready-to-wear pieces are sold at this sleek boutique on one of the city's most alluring shopping strips.

ⓘ Information

Tourist Office (VVV; ☑070-361 88 60; www. denhaag.com; Spui 68; ☻noon-6pm Mon, 10am-6pm Tue-Fri, 10am-5pm Sat, noon-5pm Sun; ☎; ☒Kalvermarkt-Stadhuis) On the ground floor of the public library in the landmark **Stadhuis** (Town Hall; Spui 70; ☻7am-7pm Mon-Wed & Fri, 7am-9.30pm Thu, 9.30am-5pm Sat).

ⓘ Getting There & Away

BICYCLE

A coastal national bike route runs just inland of Scheveningen. Leiden can be reached by going some 20km north and heading inland. There's also a route running southeast 11km to Delft.

Rijwielshop Centraal (☑070-383 00 39; www. rijwielshopcentraal.nl; Lekstraat 21-25; bike rental per day €10; ☻8am-6pm Mon-Fri, 10am-5pm Sat; ☒Centraal, ☒Den Haag Centraal) At Centraal Station; rents bikes.

Rijwielshop Hollands Spoor (☑070-389 08 30; www.rijwielshop-hollands-spoor.nl; Stationsplein 29; bike rental per day €7.50; ☻5am-

ROTTERDAM & SOUTH HOLLAND DEN HAAG (THE HAGUE)

2am Mon-Fri, 6am-2am Sat & Sun; 🚲 HS/
Stationsplein, 🚉 Hollands Spoor) At Holland
Spoor station; rents bikes almost around the
clock.

BUS

Eurolines long-distance buses and regional
buses depart from the bus & tram station above
the tracks at Centraal Station.

TRAIN

Den Haag has two main train stations.

Centraal Station (CS) – a terminus – is on the
eastern edge of the centre. The city's main train
station, it is also a hub for local trams and buses.

Hollands Spoor Train Station (HS) – a 1.5km
walk southwest of Centraal Station and on the
main railway line between Amsterdam and
Rotterdam.

Den Haag's Centraal Station is also linked to
Rotterdam by metro line E (€4.90, 30 minutes).

Regular services:

TO	PRICE (€)	TIME (MIN)	FREQUENCY (PER HR)
Amsterdam	11.70	55	2 (CS), 2 (HS)
Delft	2.50	5-20	6 (CS), 6 (HS)
Leiden	3.50	15	7 (CS), 4 (HS)
Rotterdam	4.70	20-35	6 (CS), 6 (HS)
Schiphol	8.20	30	5 (CS), 2 (HS)

ⓘ Getting Around

Most tram routes converge on Centraal Station
(CS), at the tram and bus station above the
tracks and on the western side. A number of
routes also serve Hollands Spoor station (HS),
including the jack-of-all-trades tram 1, which
starts in Scheveningen and runs all the way to
Delft, passing through the centre of Den Haag
along the way. Tram 11 also links Scheveningen
with Den Haag HS. The last tram runs in either
direction at about 1.30am. One-hour tickets can
be purchased with cash on lines 1, 6, 12 and 16.

One-hour bus and tram tickets cost €3.50
(cheaper on an OV chipkaart). Tram and bus
operator HTM (www.htm.net) also sells a highly
useful day pass for adult/child 4-12 €6.50/1.50.
Note that night buses are not covered by this.

Delft

🚲 015 / POP 101,034

An amalgam of austere medieval magnif-
icence and Golden Age glory, Delft's exquisite town centre is a hugely popular Dutch
day-trip destination, awash with visitors

strolling its narrow, canal-lined streets and
central Markt. The centre is time capsule–
like, having changed little since Golden Age
artist Johannes Vermeer, who was born in
Delft and lived his whole life here, painted
his famous *View of Delft* in 1660–61.

Founded around 1100, the town grew rich
from weaving and trade in the 13th and 14th
centuries. In the 15th century a canal was
dug to the Maas river, connecting it with
the small port of Delfshaven and increasing
trade. In the 17th century, artisans started to
produce Delftware, the distinctive blue-and-
white pottery originally duplicated from
Chinese porcelain. Delftware continues to
be produced today, and the town also has a
thriving university that is renowned for its
architecture faculty.

◎ Sights & Activities

Delft is best seen on foot: almost all the
interesting sights lie within a 1km radius
of the vast Markt. Much of the town dates
from the 17th century and is remarkably
well preserved.

★ **Vermeer Centrum Delft**   MUSEUM
(🚲 015-213 85 88; www.vermeerdelft.nl; Voldersgracht 21; adult/student/child 12-17 €9/7/5;
⊙ 10am-5pm) Johannes Vermeer was born
in Delft in 1632 and lived here until his
death in 1675, aged only 43. Sadly, none of
his works remain in Delft, making it hard
for the town to make the most of its connection to the great painter. Hence this centre,
where reproductions of his works are exhibited, a short film about his life is screened
and displays about 17th-century painting
techniques and materials give context.

Markt   SQUARE
One of the largest historic market squares
in Europe, the rectangular Markt was first
paved in the late 15th century. It is edged by
the **Stadhuis** (Town Hall; Markt), Nieuwe Kerk,
cafes, boutiques and souvenir shops. A market is held here on Thursdays.

★ **Nieuwe Kerk**   CHURCH
(New Church; 🚲 015-212 30 25; https://oudeen-
nieuwekerkdelft.nl/; Markt 80; adult/child 6-11 incl
Oude Kerk €5/1, Nieuwe Kerk tower additional €4/2;
⊙ 9am-6pm Mon-Sat Apr-Oct, 11am-4pm Mon-Fri,
10am-5pm Sat Nov-Jan, 10am-5pm Mon-Sat Feb
& Mar) Construction of Delft's Nieuwe Kerk
began in 1381; it was finally completed in
1655. The church has been the final resting
place of almost every member of the House

ROTTERDAM & SOUTH HOLLAND DELFT

Delft

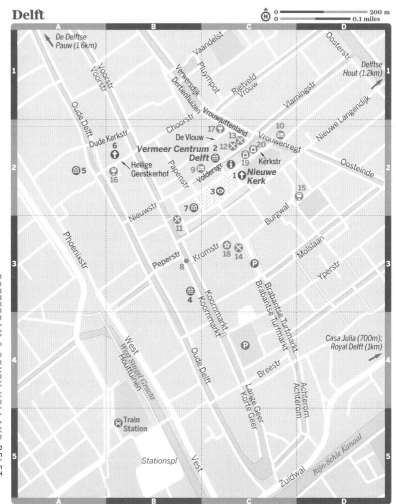

0 — 200 m
0 — 0.1 miles

of Orange since 1584, including William of Orange (William the Silent), who lies in an over-the-top marble mausoleum designed by Hendrick de Keyser. Children under five are not permitted to climb the 109m-high tower, whose 376 narrow, spiralling steps lead to panoramic views.

Oude Kerk   CHURCH
(Old Church; ☑015-212 30 15; https://oude ennieuwekerkdelft.nl/; Heilige Geestkerkhof 25; adult/child 6-11 incl Nieuwe Kerk €5/1, Nieuwe Kerk tower additional €4/2; ☺9am-6pm Mon-Sat Apr-Oct, 11am-4pm Mon-Fri, 10am-5pm Sat Nov-Jan, 10am-5pm Mon-Sat Feb & Mar) Founded

c1246, the Oude Kerk is a surreal sight: its 75m-high tower, which was erected c1350, leans nearly 2m from the vertical due to subsidence caused by its canal location, hence its nickname Scheve Jan ('Leaning Jan'). The older section features an austere barrel vault; the newer northern transept has a Gothic vaulted ceiling. One of the tombs inside the church is that of painter Johannes Vermeer (p193).

Museum Prinsenhof Delft   MUSEUM
(☑015-260 23 58; http://prinsenhof-delft.nl; St Agathaplein 1; adult/child 13-18/child 4-12 €12/6/3; ☺11am-5pm Apr-Aug, closed Mon Sep-Mar)

Delft

William of Orange (William the Silent) was assassinated in this former convent in 1584 (the bullet hole in the wall is preserved), becoming the world's first political leader to be murdered by a handgun. Now a labyrinthine museum, it includes a room about the history of the House of Orange, an exhibit about Delft and innovation and a dedicated exhibit titled 'Delftware: The Making of a Global Brand'. An audiotour of the building costs €1.

Museum Paul Tetar van Elven   MUSEUM
(☑015-212 42 06; www.tetar.nl; Koornmarkt 67; adult/student & child €5/free; ⊙1-5pm Tue-Sun) Off the usual tourist radar, this museum is the former studio and home of 19th-century Dutch artist Paul Tetar van Elven, who lived and worked here from 1864 until 1894, and bequeathed it to the town. The museum features his reproductions of notable paintings (this was his speciality), along with antique furniture, oriental porcelain and Delftware that he collected. The evocative interior retains its original furnishings and lived-in feel.

Tours

Canal Boat Tour   BOATING
(www.rondvaartdelft.nl; adult/child €8.50/4; ⊙hourly 11am-5pm Apr-Oct) Float through Delft's canal-scapes on a 45-minute boat tour departing from Koornmarkt 113.

🛏 Sleeping

Delft's attractions, walkable size and central train station make it a great base for exploring Zuid-Holland. Its popularity and the presence of the university means that accommodation is heavily booked and rates at many places shoot up at weekends and during holiday periods; reserve well ahead.

Delftse Hout   CAMPGROUND €
(☑015-213 00 40; www.delftsehout.nl; Korftlaan 5; camp sites €30-38, cabins from €63; ⊙Apr-Dec; P 🛜 🏊) This well-equipped, year-round campground is just 1.5km northeast of town. Its on-site restaurant operates from April to September. Take bus 61 or 64 (€2.50) from the bus station or use the campground's shuttle. It has 160 sites and is a 15-minute walk from the Markt.

Hostel Delft   HOSTEL €
(☑06 16 49 66 21; www.hosteldelft.nl; 1st fl, Voldersgracht 17; ⊙dm €22.50-26.50, private r per person €25-27; 🛜) In the heart of the old town, this small and well-maintained hostel is a great choice. Three dorms sleeping between four and 16 have private bathrooms, as do three large family or group rooms. Each bed has a power point, reading light and small locker. There's a well-equipped communal kitchen, a comfortable lounge and TV room, and roof terraces. No breakfast.

Casa Julia   B&B €€
(☑015-256 76 12; www.casajulia.nl; Maerten Trompstraat 33; r/ste/f from €70/115/135; 🛜) Close to the university, this boutique B&B in a 1920s building is the most stylish and comfortable accommodation in Delft, offering 24 rooms with smart TV, work desk and tea set-up. Most are small, so opt for a 'comfort'

DON'T MISS

CHINA SHOPPING

Delft's eponymous blue-and-white china is ubiquitous throughout town. Given that the process was first developed in China, it's ironic that the mass of fake Delftware sold in tourist shops also comes from that part of the world.

The real stuff is produced in fairly small quantities at a few factories in and around Delft. There are four places where you can actually see the artists at work.

Royal Delft (Koninklijke Porceleyne Fles; ☎ 015-760 0800; www.royaldelft.com; Rotterdamseweg 196; adult/child 13-18/child under 13 €13.50/8.50/free; ⊙ 9am-5pm Mar-Oct, 9am-5pm Mon-Sat, noon-5pm Sun Nov-Feb) The most famous of the Delft potteries, and also the one with the slickest tourist offering. Entry tickets include a multi-language audio tour that includes a painting demonstration, a visit to the company museum and a peek into the production area. Visitors can also attend a painting workshop (€29 to €39; book ahead). Unsurprisingly, all tours end in the factory's gift shop.

De Delftse Pauw (The Delft Peacock; ☎ 015-212 49 20; www.delftpottery.com; Delftweg 133, Vrijenban; ⊙ 9am-4.30pm mid-Mar–Oct, 9am-4.30pm Mon-Fri, 11am-1pm Sat & Sun Nov–mid-Mar) `FREE` Another well-known and historic pottery, 'The Delft Peacock' offers regular, free, short guided tours explaining how its products are manufactured. There are also weekday tile-painting workshops (€35) for which you will need to book in advance.

De Candelaer (☎ 015-213 18 48; www.candelaer.nl; Kerkstraat 13a; ⊙ 9.30am-5.30pm Mon-Fri, to 5pm Sat May-Sep, shorter hrs Oct-Mar) There are usually a few artists painting Delftware at this small, centrally located producer and shop.

De Blauwe Tulp (☎ 015-214 80 92; www.bluetulip.nl; Kerkstraat 12; ⊙ 9.30am-5.30pm Mon-Sat) Though it doesn't make its own pottery, this shop off the Markt does do its own painting. Artists double as shop assistants, and are always happy to explain the production process.

option if possible. There's also a suite with kitchenette and two family rooms sleeping four. Breakfast costs €15.

Hotel de Emauspoort HOTEL €€
(☎ 015-219 02 19; http://emauspoort.nl; Vrouwenregt 9-11; s €115, d €125-170, gypsy caravan d €125, apt €150; ☏) This friendly little hotel near the Markt has 28 old-fashioned but neat rooms, as well as an apartment with kitchenette and two quaint gypsy caravans (each with bathrooms) in the courtyard. A bountiful buffet breakfast is included in the room rate.

 Eating

YS Van Jans ICE CREAM
(☎ 015-820 09 70; www.jansdelft.nl/ijs; Brabantse Turfmarkt 87; per scoop €1.25; ⊙ 10am-5.30pm Mon & Sun, 9am-5.30pm Tue-Fri, 8.30am-5.30pm Sat, reduced hrs winter; ☏) Enjoying the artisanal ice cream and sorbet sold at this parlour is a popular pastime when promenading through the town centre. The rich chocolate, salted caramel and yoghurt, honey and walnut flavours are particularly *lekker* (yummy).

★**Kek** CAFE €
(☎ 015-750 32 53; http://kekdelft.nl/; Voldersgracht 27; breakfast dishes €4-10, sandwiches €6-10; ⊙ 8.30am-6pm; ☏) ☏ The baskets of organic fruit and vegetables at the front of this stylish cafe are a good indicator of what's on the menu – freshly squeezed juices, fruit smoothies and a tempting array of cakes, muffins, tarts and sandwiches made with local seasonal produce (no-sugar, vegan and gluten-free options available). Other draws include all-day breakfasts and coffee made using Giraffe beans.

Puro Cucina CAFE €
(☎ 015-820 03 90; www.purocucina.nl; Voldersgracht 28; breakfast dishes €6-10, lunch dishes €5-14; ⊙ 9am-6pm Wed-Mon) Describing itself as a cooking studio, this hybrid cafe and cooking school has a sleek modern interior arranged around an open kitchen. The menu offers breakfast favourites (pancakes with ricotta and honey, granola with yoghurt and fruit), simple but tasty lunch dishes (pasta dish of the day, salads) and homemade cake with coffee at all times of the day.

De Waag   CAFE €€

(☏015-213 03 93; www.de-waag.nl; Markt 11; sandwiches €4-10, cafe mains €15-20, restaurant mains €24; ⊙kitchen 11am-10pm Sun & Mon, 10am-10pm Tue-Sat; 🛈🍴) With a sprawling terrace behind the Stadhuis (town hall) and atmospheric eating and drinking spaces inside its historic premises, De Waag is a perfect spot for a post-sightseeing beer. The food is quite good, too – enjoy one of the globally inspired dishes in the upmarket restaurant on the first floor (dinner only) or you could opt for a more casual meal downstairs.

 Drinking & Nightlife

Most of the drinking and partying action unfolds at the pubs on the Beestenmarkt or at renowned student hang-out De Oude Jan.

De Oude Jan   BROWN CAFE

(☏015-214 53 63; www.oudejan.nl; Heilige Geestkerkhof 4; ⊙10am-1am Mon, to 4am Tue-Thu & Sun, to 3am Fri & Sat Easter-Oct, opens noon Nov-Easter; 🛈) Opposite the Oude Kerk, this is one of Delft's most popular hangouts. It's known for student-friendly hours and occasional performances by live bands, who take to the umbrella-shaded courtyard's outdoor stage.

Food is served during the day (toasties €3 to €4, burgers €13).

Café-Brasserie Belvédère   BEER GARDEN

(☏015-212 32 97; www.bbcbelvedere.nl; Beestenmarkt 8; ⊙11am-1am Mon-Thu, 11am-2am Fri, 10am-2am Sat, noon-1am Sun) Belgian beer is the popular choice here, enjoyed in great quantities at a sea of tables in the leafy Beestenmarkt. There are more than 10 beers on tap, and pub-style grub including mussels.

Doerak   PUB

(☏06 45 69 49 28; www.cafedoerak.nl; Vrouwjuttenland 17; ⊙3pm-1am Mon-Thu, 3pm-2am Fri, noon-2am Sat, 1pm-1am Sun) Canal-side and pavement seating are popular perches at this friendly drinking den, but regulars tend to claim seats at the long indoor bar before ordering their tipples from a huge array of craft and Trappist beers, 12 of which are on tap.

 Entertainment

Bebop Jazzcafé   LIVE MUSIC

(☏015-213 52 10; www.facebook.com/Jazzcafe Bebop/; Kromstraat 33; ⊙8pm-1am Mon, 4pm-1am Tue-Thu, 4pm-2am Fri, 3pm-2am Sat, 4pm-1am Sun)

VERMEER'S DELFT

Johannes Vermeer (1632–75), one of the greatest of the Dutch Masters, lived his entire life in Delft, fathering 11 children and leaving behind fewer than 40 paintings (the actual number is disputed as the authorship of some canvasses attributed to him has been called into question by modern-day Vermeer experts). Vermeer's works have rich and meticulous colouring and he captured light as few other painters have ever managed to do. His subjects were drawn from everyday life in Delft, his interiors depicting domestic scenes and his portraits – the most famous of which is the *Girl with a Pearl Earring* (1665) – were both fond and remarkably lifelike.

Vermeer's best-known exterior work, the c1660–61 *View of Delft* brilliantly captures the play of light and shadow of a partly cloudy day. Visit the location where he painted it, across the canal at Hooikade, southeast of the train station. Unfortunately, none of Vermeer's works remain in Delft, although the Vermeer Centrum Delft (p189) gives a good introduction to his life and work, and the tourist office sells a 'Vermeer Trail' walking tour brochure (€2.50). Both *Girl with a Pearl Earring* and *View of Delft* can be seen at the Mauritshuis (p181) in Den Haag, while arguably his most famous painting, *The Milkmaid*, resides in Amsterdam's Rijksmuseum (p70) alongside *Woman in Blue Reading a Letter* (1663–64) amongst other works.

Vermeer's life is something of an enigma, but his fame as a painter has long been acknowledged. The 2003 film *Girl with a Pearl Earring* (based on Tracy Chevalier's novel) speculated on his relationship with the eponymous girl. The following year, a work long thought to be a forgery was finally confirmed as authentic – *Young Woman Seated at the Virginals* was the first Vermeer to be auctioned in more than 80 years, selling to an anonymous buyer for €24 million.

The excellent website www.essentialvermeer.com has exhaustive details on the painter and his works, including where the paintings are exhibited at any given time.

Live jazz plays every Sunday at this *bruin café*, which has a dark indoor space and a summer-only beer garden. There are jam sessions on Tuesdays, live bebop on Wednesdays and jazz on some Sunday afternoons. Check the Facebook feed for the program of events.

🛈 Information

Tourist Information Point (☎ 015-215 40 51; www.delft.com; Kerkstraat 3; ☺10am-4pm Sun & Mon, 10am-5pm Tue-Sat Apr-Oct, 11am-3pm Sun & Mon, 10am-4pm Tue-Sat Oct-Mar) Sells useful walking-tour brochures and also offers guided walking tours of the town.

🛈 Getting There & Around

Den Haag is linked to Delft by tram 1 (€3.50, 30 minutes, frequent).

BICYCLE

There are bike trails from Den Haag (11km northwest) and Rotterdam (28km southeast).

Delft By Cycle (☎ 06 24 34 26 10; https://delftbycycle.nl/en/; Phoenixstraat 112; per day €15; ☺9am-5pm) rents bikes.

TRAIN

Regular services from Delft:

TO	PRICE (€)	TIME (MIN)	FREQUENCY (PER HOUR)
Amsterdam	13.20–15.60	60	8
Den Haag	2.50	15	10
Rotterdam	3.40	15	10

Leiden

☎ 071 / POP 122,561

Vibrant Leiden is one of the Netherlands' great cities. Woven with canals lined by beautiful 17th-century buildings, its cache of museums, all within walking distance of each other, are a major draw, as is wandering the picturesque canals and soaking up the nightlife, fuelled by a nearly 27,000-strong student population.

Leiden is renowned for being Rembrandt's birthplace, the home of the Netherlands' oldest and most prestigious university (Einstein was a regular professor), and the place in which the Pilgrims raised money to lease the leaky *Speedwell*, which took them on the first leg of their journey to the New World in 1620.

History

Leiden's university – the Netherlands' oldest – was a gift from Willem the Silent in 1575 for withstanding two Spanish sieges in 1573 and 1574. It was a terrible time, ending when the Sea Beggars arrived and repelled the invaders. According to lore, the retreating Spanish legged it so quickly that they abandoned a kettle of *hutspot* (hotchpotch, stew) – today it's still a staple of Dutch menus in restaurants and in homes.

Decades later, Protestants fleeing persecution elsewhere in the Low Countries, France and England arrived in Leiden to a somewhat warmer welcome. Most notable was the group led by John Robinson, which would sail to America and into history as the pilgrims aboard the *Mayflower*.

Wealth from the linen industry buttressed Leiden's growing prosperity, and during the 17th century the town produced several brilliant artists, most famously Rembrandt van Rijn – better known by his first name alone. Rembrandt was born in Leiden in 1606 and remained here for 26 years before achieving fame in Amsterdam.

⊙ Sights

As you walk five minutes southeast from Centraal Station, the city's traditional character unfolds, especially around the Pieterskerk and south. Leiden's district of historic waterways is worth at least a full day of wandering.

⭐**Rijksmuseum van Oudheden**   MUSEUM
(National Museum of Antiquities; ☎ 071-516 31 63; www.rmo.nl; Rapenburg 28; adult/student/child 5-17 €12.50/6/4; ☺10am-5pm Tue-Sun) Home to the Rijksmuseum's collection of Greek, Etruscan, Roman and Egyptian artefacts, this museum is best known for its Egyptian halls, which include the reconstructed Temple of Taffeh, a gift from Anwar Sadat to the Netherlands for helping to save ancient Egyptian monuments from flood. Other Egyptian exhibits include mastabas from Saqqara and a room of mummy cases. First-floor galleries are replete with Greek, Etruscan and Roman statuary and vases, as well as treasures from the ancient Near East.

⭐**Museum Volkenkunde**   MUSEUM
(National Museum of Ethnology; www.volkenkunde.nl; Steenstraat 1; adult/student/child 4-18 €14/8/6; ☺10am-5pm Tue-Sun) Cultural achievements by civilisations worldwide are on show at this splendid museum, which has a collection of

more than 300,000 artefacts from across the globe. Permanent galleries are dedicated to the cultures of Africa; the Arctic and North America; Asia; Central and South America; China; Indonesia; Japan and Korea; and Oceania. Highlights include the atmospherically lit Buddha Room next to the Japan and Korea section and the 'Mountain of the Immortals' carving in the China section. Temporary exhibitions are also impressive.

Museum De Lakenhal   MUSEUM
(www.lakenhal.nl; Oude Singel 28-32; adult/child €12.50/free; ⊙10am-5pm Tue-Sun) Leiden's foremost museum reopened in 2019 following a three-year renovation. Its 1640-built premises (a former cloth warehouse) again displays its exceptional permanent art and history collection. Adjoining it, a striking new building hosts temporary exhibitions. The museum's masterpieces include *The Spectacles Pedlar* by the city's native son Rembrandt, *The Astronomer* by Gerrit Dou (Rembrandt's first student), *Playing Couple* by Jan Steen, and *The Last Judgement* by Lucas van Leyden. Hour-long guided tours in English at 2pm on Sundays are free.

De Valk   MUSEUM
(The Falcon; ☑ 071-5165353; https://molenmuseum devalk.nl/en; 2e Binnenvestgracht 1; adult/child 6-15 €4/2; ⊙10am-5pm Tue-Sat, 1-5pm Sun) Leiden's landmark tower windmill – built in 1743 and now a museum – is considered one of the best examples of its kind. Its arms still occasionally rotate, but the last grain was ground here in 1965. Upstairs, an audiovisual presentation imparts plenty of information about windmills in the Netherlands.

★**Rijksmuseum Boerhaave**   MUSEUM
(☑ 071-751 99 99; www.rijksmuseumboerhaave. nl; Lange St Agnietenstraat 10; adult/student/ child 4-17 €12.50/7.50/5; ⊙10am-5pm Tue-Sun) Named in honour of physician, botanist, chemist and University of Leiden teacher Herman Boerhaave (1668–1738), this impressive museum of science and medicine has exhibits profiling major discoveries in science in the Netherlands, and the doctors and scientists behind them. The museum is housed in a 15th-century convent that later became the first academic hospital in Northern Europe, and a multimedia introduction is presented in a recreated anatomical theatre. Teenagers will enjoy the opportunities for hands-on interaction in the Waterland exhibit.

Hortus Botanicus Leiden   GARDENS
(☑ 071-527 51 44; www.hortusleiden.nl; Rapenburg 73; adult/university student/child 4-12 €7.50/2/3;

THE PILGRIMS IN LEIDEN

In 1608 a group of Calvinist Protestants split from the Anglican church and left persecution in Nottinghamshire, England, for a journey that would span decades and thousands of miles. Travelling first to Amsterdam under the leadership of John Robinson, they encountered theological clashes with local Dutch Protestants.

In Leiden they found a more liberal atmosphere, thanks to the university and some like-minded Calvinists who already lived there. They also found company with refugees who had escaped from persecution elsewhere. However, the group's past was to catch up with them. In 1618 James I of England announced that he would assume control over the Calvinists living in Leiden. In addition, the local Dutch were becoming less tolerant of religious splinter groups.

The first group of English left Leiden in 1620 for Delfshaven in what is now Rotterdam, where they bought the *Speedwell* with the intention of sailing to the New World. Unfortunately, the leaky *Speedwell* didn't live up to its name; after several attempts to cross the Atlantic, the group gave up and, against their better judgement, sailed into Southampton in England. After repairs to their ship and a thwarted attempt to restart their journey, the group joined the much more seaworthy *Mayflower* in Dartmouth and sailed, as it were, into history as the Pilgrims.

This legendary voyage was actually just one of many involving the Leiden group. It wasn't until 1630 that most had made their way to the American colonies founded in what is today New England. Some 1000 people made the voyages, including a number of Dutch who were considered oddballs for their unusual beliefs.

In Leiden today, traces of the Pilgrims are elusive. The best place to start is the Leiden American Pilgrim Museum (p197).

ROTTERDAM & SOUTH HOLLAND LEIDEN

Leiden

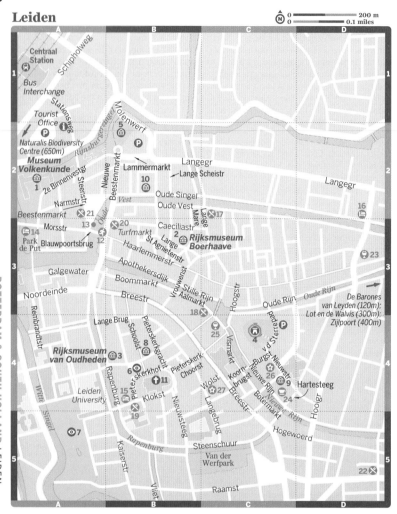

⊗10am-6pm daily Apr-Oct, to 9pm Wed July & Aug, 10am-4pm Tue-Sun Nov-Mar) Founded by the University of Leiden in 1590, this is one of Europe's oldest botanical gardens (the oldest was created in Padua, Italy, in 1545). The majority of its botanical collections have come from South-East and East Asia, and its stated mission is to maintain a living plant collection for research, education, public interest and enjoyment. Built structures include an 18th-century orangery and a tropical glasshouse constructed in 1938; more recent additions include a winter garden and Chinese herb garden.

Naturalis Biodiversity Centre   MUSEUM
(www.naturalis.nl; Darwinweg 2; adult/child €12/9; ⊗10am-5pm) This museum houses the first T-Rex skeleton in Europe. Its sections span botany, geology, entomology (insects), invertebrates, vertebrates and palaeontology (fossils and more) collected by Dutch explorers, archaeologists and scientists all over the globe.

Burcht van Leiden   CASTLE, PARK
(⊗sunrise-sunset; 🚹) FREE This 11th-century citadel on a *motte* (raised earthwork) surrendered its protective function as the city grew around it and subsequently fell into disrepair. Now a shell, it has been trans-

Leiden

formed into a park commanding views over the town's rooftops.

Pieterskerk CHURCH
(071-512 43 19; www.pieterskerk.com; Kloksteeg 16; adult/child under 12 €4/free; ⊙11am-6pm) Crowned by its huge steeple, this now de-consecrated church is often under restoration – a good thing, as it has been prone to collapse since it was built in 1121. Its most distinctive feature is an unusual marble and stone floor. Museumkaarts are not accepted.

The precinct includes the gabled Latin School (Lokhorststraat 16), which – before it became a commercial building – was attended by a pupil named Rembrandt from 1616 to 1620. Across the plaza, look for the Gravensteen (Pieterskerkhof 6), which dates from the 13th century and was once a prison. The gallery facing the plaza was where judges watched executions.

Leiden American Pilgrim Museum MUSEUM
(071-512 24 13; www.leidenamericanpilgrim museum.org; Beschuitsteeg 9; adult/child under 7 €5/free; ⊙1-5pm Thu-Sat) This museum is a fascinating restoration of a one-room house occupied around 1610 by the soon-to-be Pilgrims (p195). The house itself dates from 1365–70 (check out the original 14th-century floor tiles), but the furnishings are from the Pilgrims' period. Curator Jeremy Bangs is an author who has written extensively on the Pilgrims and has a vast knowledge of their Leiden links.

🏃 Activities

Bootjes en Broodjes BOATING
(⌨06 22 61 05 52; www.bootjesenbroodjes.nl; Blauwpoortsbrug 1; 2hr electric-boat rental €75, canal tours adult/child €10/6; ⊙10am-7pm Apr-Oct, 11am-5pm Nov-Mar; ⊛) As the name ('Boats and Bread Rolls') implies, you can buy sandwiches here to take on your voyage (these must be ordered in advance). Rent a quiet electric boat (no boat licence required) or join a 50-minute guided tour. Private tours are also available on request.

👉 Tours

Rederij Rembrandt BOATING
(⌨071-513 49 38; www.rederij-rembrandt.nl; Blauwpoortshaven 5; adult/child 4-12/child under 4 €10/6.50/2.50; ⊙10.30am-4pm) Leisurely one-hour canal-boat tours taken in the channel around the old-town centre, accompanied by multilingual commentary (including English).

🎉 Festivals & Events

Leidse Lakenfeesten CULTURAL
(Leiden Cloth Festival; www.lakenfeesten.nl; ⊙Jun) Held around the last weekend in June, this four-day festival includes street performances, dragon-boat races and an art exhibition. It incorporates the 'Leiden Culinair' and 'Leiden Bierfest' festivals. The event celebrates the history of the city's cloth industry, now sadly obsolete.

Leidens Ontzet CULTURAL

(3 October Festival; https://3october.nl/; ⊘3 or 4 Oct) Leiden grinds to a halt for Leidens Ontzet, commemorating the day the Spanish-caused starvation ended in 1574. The revelry is undiminished more than four centuries later, and there is much eating of the ceremonial *hutspot* (stew), herring and white bread. Beer-fuelled celebrations kick off the night before. If the 3rd falls on a Sunday, the celebration is postponed until the 4th.

🛏 Sleeping

Budget accommodation is hard to come by in Leiden as most sleeping options are of the boutique variety. Book well in advance if you want to stay in town during Leidens Ontzet (p198).

⭐ Ex Libris B&B €€

(☎071-240 86 36; www.hotelexlibris.com; Kloksteeg 4; r €120-200; ✳🛜) There are plenty of boutique B&Bs in the Netherlands, but few are as stylish, comfortable and welcoming as this one. Occupying a former bookshop and adjoining house near the Pieterskerk, it offers five quiet rooms accessed via steep stairs; these have coffee/tea set-up and a smart TV. The chic downstairs breakfast room offers a €17 cafe-style repast (smoothies, granola, eggs, pancakes, toasties).

D'Oude Morsch BOUTIQUE HOTEL €€

(☎071-569 00 90; www.hoteldeoudemorsch.nl; Park de Put 1; r €94-180; 🅿🛜) Sharing a canal bank with De Put windmill, this hotel occupies the 1870 watchhouse of a former army barracks. A great deal of thought has gone into the building's transformation, and the resulting 18 rooms are comfortable and stylish; some have unusual bathroom set-ups. Breakfast (€14.50) is enjoyed in the ground-floor bar/cafe, which has both indoor and canal-side seating.

Huys van Leyden BOUTIQUE HOTEL €€

(☎071-260 07 00; www.boutiquehotelsvanleyden.nl; Oude Singel 212; s/d from €100/110; 🅿🛜) Steeped in history, this hotel in two 1611 canal houses has seven attractive rooms (ask for number 4, which is large and has a canal view) and a grand dining salon where breakfast (€15.50), high tea (€22.50) and dinner (mains €18 to €20) are served. Facilities include a sauna and a jacuzzi. Parking costs €15 per day.

Eating

Leiden is one of the country's foodie hubs. There's a profusion of excellent restaurants serving modern European cuisine; opt for a set menu featuring seasonal produce – they're both delicious and well priced. The main cluster of fine-dining establishments is on Kloksteeg, in the shadow of Pieterskerk. In summer, most eateries offer some form of outdoor seating, often overlooking a canal.

Dapp Frietwinkel FAST FOOD €

(www.frietwinkel.nl/leiden/; Aalmarkt 14; fries €2.70-4; ⊘11.30am-7pm Wed & Sun, to 9pm Thu-Sat; 🖋) 🍴 If you're going to indulge in a paper twist of French fries, it's best to opt for ones like those served at this branch of a national chain, which are made with organic potato and topped with rich organic mayonnaise (vegan version available), curry sauce or ketchup.

Oudt Leyden CRÊPES €

(☎071-513 31 44; www.oudtleyden.nl; Steenstraat 49; pancakes €7-16; ⊘11.30am-9.30pm; 🖋🧒) The giant Dutch-style pancakes here make kids and adults alike go wide-eyed. Whether you're after something savoury (marinated salmon, sour cream and capers), sweet (apple, ginger and powdered sugar) or simply adventurous (ginger and bacon), this welcoming place hits the spot every time.

Vishandel Atlantic SEAFOOD €

(☎071-513 73 31; www.vishandelatlantic.nl; Levendaal 118; herring per piece €1.75, fish & chips €8.50-12.50; ⊘10am-8pm Tue-Fri, 10.30am-late Sat, 11.30am-9pm Sun) Two Turkish brothers opened this fish stand in 1989 and their attention to quality has propelled them to the Netherlands' top ranks of seafood vendors. Their raw herring rates 10 out of 10 in contests where 5.5 is considered a good score. You can also try all types of smoked fish as well as dishes including fish and chips.

Brasserie de Engelenbak DUTCH €€

(☎071-512 54 40; www.deengelenbak.nl; Lange Mare 38; sandwiches €9, salads €11, dinner mains €17-23; ⊘from 5pm Tue, from 11am Wed-Sun) In the shadow of the 17th-century Marekerk, this elegant bistro serves a seasonally changing menu of fresh fare that takes its cues from across the continent. Local organic produce features in many of the dishes. Tables outside enjoy views of the passing crowds. Its adjoining *café* (pub) serves snacks until midnight.

Dartel EUROPEAN **€€**
(☑071-512 40 12; http://restaurantdartel.nl/; Kloksteeg 13; 2-/3-/4-course lunch menu €29/39/45, 3-/4-/5-/6-course dinner menu €39/47/57/67; ☺noon-2pm & 6-10pm Mon-Fri, 6-10pm Sat; ☑) A small menu of dishes making the most of local seasonal produce draws locals and food-focused visitors to this restaurant in the shadow of the Pieterskerk. The restaurant has its own greenhouse where fruit and vegetables are grown, and chef Norbert van Dartel incorporates the harvest into his menus in creative ways.

Lot en de Walvis INTERNATIONAL **€€**
(☑071-763 03 83; www.lotendewalvis.nl; Haven 1; breakfast €7-9, sandwiches €9-10, burgers €15-17; ☺9am-10pm Mon-Fri, to 1am Sat & Sun) The name means 'little things mean a lot', but it's not the little things that makes this cafe in the handsome 1889 De Volharding warehouse a Leiden hots pot – rather, it's the excellent food, friendly staff and sun-drenched terrace at the water's edge. Book in advance for the hugely popular buffet 'recovery' breakfast (€15) on Sundays from 9am to noon.

⭐**In den Doofpot** EUROPEAN **€€€**
(☑071-512 24 34; www.indendoofpot.nl; Turfmarkt 9; mains €30, 3-/4-course lunch menu €39/45, 4-/5-/6-course dinner menu €55/65/75; ☺12.30-3pm & 5.30-10pm Mon-Fri, 5.30-10pm Sat) Given the sky-high calibre of chef Patrick Brugman's food, In den Doofpot's prices are a veritable steal. This is extremely assured and creative cooking, as good to look at as it is to eat. Vegetarian menus are available on request, as are expert wine pairings by the glass (€8 per course). Highly recommended.

🍸 **Drinking & Nightlife**

This is a university town, so there are loads of cafes, bars and pubs to choose from. There are concentrations on and around Nieuwe Rijn, Breestraat, Aalmarkt and the Haven area.

⭐**Borgman & Borman** CAFE
(☑071-566 55 37; www.borgmanborgman.nl; Nieuwe Rijn 41; ☺9am-5pm Mon, 8am-6pm Tue-Sat,10.30am-5pm Sun; 🖥) The Giesen roaster in the window signals that this hip cafe is serious about its coffee, and once you've ordered you'll find that the baristas de-

liver on this promise. There's also a small menu of breakfast dishes, sandwiches (€5 to €7) and toasties. Service is friendly and the music on the sound system is excellent – not a '70s or '80s pop song to be heard. Cash only.

Bad Habits International Pub PUB
(☑071-512 23 07; www.badhabitsleiden.nl; Pelikaanstraat 64; ☺noon-1am Sun-Wed, to 2am Thu-Sat) We all have them, so why not celebrate your bad habits at this popular student pub – beer and burgers definitely qualify and there's a good choice of both on offer. In summer, patrons spill out onto the front square. Regular events include live-music acts, jam sessions, *Game of Thrones* nights and live football on big-screen TVs.

Waag BAR
(☑071-740 03 00; https://waagleiden.nl/; Aalmarkt 21; sandwiches €6-11, dinner mains €15-22; ☺from 10am Sat-Wed, from 9am Thu & Fri) Leiden's historic *waag* (weigh station) is now home to one of the town's most popular eating and drinking spots, a bustling place attracting locals of every age. In the morning, canal-side tables and the rear conservatory are sunny spots for a coffee; at night, the vaulted main room with its tables and golden-lit marble bar attracts drinkers and diners alike.

On Friday and Saturday nights, the place morphs into the Waag een Borrel club, with plenty of action at the bar and on the impromptu dance floor between 10pm and 3am.

⭐ **Entertainment**

De Twee Spieghels LIVE MUSIC
(www.detweespieghels.nl; Nieuwstraat 11; ☺4pm-1am Mon-Thu, 4pm-2am Fri, 2pm-2am Sat, 3-11pm Sun) Live jazz takes to the stage at this intimate wine bar at least four nights a week; check the agenda to see what's coming up. Concerts are free.

Dranklokkal de WW LIVE MUSIC
(www.deww.nl; Wolsteeg 36; ☺2pm-2am Sun-Wed, to 3am Thu, to 4am Fri & Sat) On Friday and Saturday nights, live rock in this bar can expand to an impromptu stage in the alley, with crowds trailing up to the main street. On other nights DJs play. Though the emphasis is on the music, there's a great beer selection. Cash only.

🔒 Shopping

Haarlemmerstraat is home to all the mainstream chain stores. Big department stores spill across to Breestraat. Look for more interesting shops on side streets such as Vrouwenstraat and in the lanes around Pieterskerk.

The town's market days are Wednesday and Saturday. Street stalls line Botermarkt, Vismarkt, Aalmarkt and Nieuwe Rijn.

ℹ Information

Tourist Office (☑ 071-516 60 00; www.visitleiden.nl; Stationsweg 26; ☺7am-7pm Mon-Fri, 10am-4pm Sat, 11am-3pm Sun; 🛜) Extremely helpful office near the train station.

ℹ Getting There & Around

Regional and local buses leave from the bus interchange in front of Centraal Station.

BICYCLE

Head west from the station on bike paths along Geversstraat and then via Rijnsburg for 10km to the beach at Katwijk. There you can pick up a route heading to Haarlem, 34km north. Head south 20km along the shore to reach Scheveningen and Den Haag.

Oldenburger (☑ 071-760 05 66; www.oldenburgerfietsspecialist.nl; Stationsplein; standard/electric bike per day €12.50/20; ☺7am-7pm Mon-Fri, 10am-6pm Sat & Sun) rents bikes.

TRAIN

Leiden's train station is 400m northwest of the centre. Regular services:

TO	PRICE (€)	TIME (MIN)	FREQUENCY (PER HR)
Amsterdam	9.10	35	6
Den Haag	3.50	15	6
Rotterdam	7.40	35	4
Schiphol Airport	5.90	15-25	8

Lisse

☑ 0252 / POP 22,606

Once a rural retreat for wealthy city merchants, Lisse changed in the 19th century when its manor houses surrounded by formal gardens and forests were sold and their land was given over to what this pocket of South Holland is best known for: the cultivation of bulb flowers. Today, flowers and the tourists they attract are the town's major industry, and the main attraction, the Keukenhof Gardens, hosts over a million annual visitors during the short season when its gloriously colourful tulip fields come into bloom. Though there are few reasons to visit at other times of the year, a trip here in spring (preferably April) will be one of the highlights of your time in the Netherlands.

⊙ Sights & Activities

This is the very heart of the Netherlands' tulip-growing land. In spring you may be lucky enough to fly over the brightly coloured fields as you fly into Schiphol. It's definitely worth getting a bike and riding around the town and the countryside during the tulip season.

★**Keukenhof Gardens**   GARDENS
(☑ 0252-465 555; www.keukenhof.nl; Stationsweg 166; ☺8am-7.30pm mid-Mar–mid-May; 🚼) The 32-hectare Keukenhof is the world's largest bulb-flower garden, with over seven million bulbs and a total of 800 varieties of tulips. It attracts around 1.5 million visitors during its eight-week season, when its fields and planted displays of multicoloured tulips, daffodils and hyacinths are in bloom. You can hire bikes outside the gardens (per day €15), or take a cruise from Keukenhof's windmill to view the floral kaleidoscope. Online tickets are slightly cheaper. It's 1km west of Lisse.

Special Keukenhof Express buses run from destinations including Europaplein at RAI in Amsterdam's south during the season; combination tickets including transport are available.

Kasteel Keukenhof   CASTLE
(☑0252-465 555; www.kasteelkeukenhof.nl; Keukenhof 1; ☺garden 8.30am-7.30pm Apr-Sep, to 5pm Oct-Mar) **FREE** This grand castle across the road from Keukenhof Gardens was built in 1641 by VOC (Dutch East India Company) commander Adriaan Muertenszoon Block and sits on more than 80 hectares of woodland, meadows and flowering gardens. The castle itself was closed for renovation during research and no completion date was available; check the website for details.

Museum de Zwarte Tulp   MUSEUM
(Museum of the Black Tulip; ☑ 0252-417 900; www.museumdezwartetulp.nl; Heereweg 219; adult/child 5-18 €7.50/3.50; ☺10am-5pm Tue-Sun Mar-Aug, 1-5pm Tue-Sun Sep-Feb) The small Museum de Zwarte Tulp displays everything you

might want to know about bulbs, including why there's no such thing as a black tulip, a mythical bloom that helped drive Tulipmania in 1636. It shares a building with the tourist office.

🛏️ Sleeping & Eating

Few people overnight in Lisse, instead visiting on day trips. There are a few options in town, and many more in nearby Leiden.

De Vier Seizoenen B&B €
(📞0252-418 023; http://rdvs.nl; Heereweg 224; d from €80; 🛜) Lisse's best options for eating and sleeping are conveniently in the same building. Upstairs are four small rooms in chocolate-box tones with sloped ceilings and natural-stone bathrooms. A breakfast hamper (per person €12) is enjoyed in your room or on the roof terrace. Downstairs, the excellent restaurant (🍴sandwiches €8-12, lunch mains €20, dinner mains €20-29; ⏰noon-2.30pm Mon-Sat Apr-Sep, 5.30-9.30pm Wed-Mon year-round) serves contemporary French cuisine. Wisteria drapes the courtyard garden in spring.

Den Ouden Heere INTERNATIONAL €€
(📞0252-418 660; www.denoudenheere.nl; Heereweg 207; mains €16-28; ⏰5pm-1am Mon-Thu, to 3am Fri & Sat) Set over two floors with a buzzing pavement terrace facing Lisse's main square, this bistro and cocktail bar is a popular spot for dinner or late-night drinks. The globally influenced menu includes everything from Asian-style fish dishes to steaks cooked in a Big Green Egg (ceramic charcoal barbecue cooker). There's not much joy for vegetarians, though.

ℹ️ Information

Tourist Office (📞0252-417 900; www.vvvlisse.nl; Heereweg 219; ⏰10am-5pm Tue-Sun Mar-Aug, 1-5pm Tue-Sun Sep-Feb) Inside the Museum de Zwarte Tulp (p200), Lisse's tourist office can supply options for bulb-field touring.

ℹ️ Getting There & Away

Lisse is an easy bike ride from both Leiden and Haarlem.

Bus 361 serves Amsterdam's Schiphol Airport (€5, 45 minutes, four hourly). Bus 50 serves Haarlem (€4.90, 55 minutes, four hourly) and Leiden (€4.60, 40 minutes, four hourly); alight at Nassaustraat and walk approximately 2km west to reach the gardens and Kasteel Keukenhof.

In season, special buses link Keukenhof with Schiphol Airport and Leiden's Centraal Station; combination tickets covering entry and transport are usually available.

ZEELAND

The province of Zeeland (Sealand) incorporates a clutch of islands and peninsulas – Schouwen-Duiveland, Tholen, Sint Philipsland, Noord-Beveland, Walcheren and Zuid-Beveland – that nestle in the middle of a vast delta through which many of Europe's rivers drain; it also incorporates Zeeuws-Vlaanderen, a strip of land bordering the Belgian region of Flanders. As you survey the calm, flat landscape, consider that for centuries the resilient Zeelanders have been battling the North Sea waters, devising and implementing ingenious methods of water management, including the huge Delta Project.

Friendly Middelburg is the provincial capital, and the closest thing Zeeland has to a city. Most visitors head to this part of the country to laze on one of the sandy beaches along the North Sea coast (the regional population increases fourfold during high summer). Others visit this place of tenuous land and omnipresent water just to see the sheer size and admire the engineering genius of the Delta Project's dykes and barriers. Either way, they invariably leave happy and rested.

ℹ️ Getting There & Away

Middelburg is easily reached by train, but for most other towns you'll need to rely on the bus network. **Connexxion/Interliner** (📞0900 266 63 99; www.connexxion.nl; ⏰8am-7pm Mon-Sat) bus 395 makes a one-hour journey every hour between Rotterdam's Zuidplein metro station and Zierikzee (€10, one hour), where you can transfer to buses for other Zeeland destinations.

Middelburg
📞 0118 / POP 47,873

Wandering alongside Middelburg's majestic harbour, across its Markt and through its winding cobbled streets, you'd never guess that in 1940, German bombers destroyed much of the town's historic centre. Unlike the similarly devastated Rotterdam, Zeeland's capital was recreated rather than redesigned, and retains a historic flavour. The

Middelburg

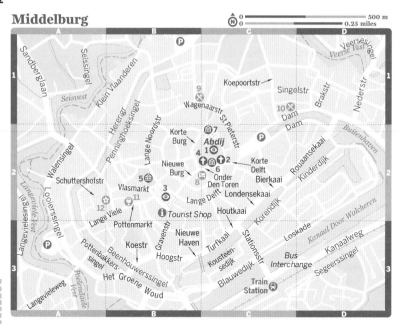

Middelburg

fortifications built by the Sea Beggars in 1595 can still be traced in the pattern of the main canals encircling the old town, and the central Markt remains the pulsing heart of the town that it has been since it was built in 1575, especially during the Thursday street market.

◉ Sights & Activities

This pretty town is eminently suitable for walking, with snaking alleyways leading in and away from the Markt.

The area around the elongated Damplein (east of the Abdij) preserves many 18th-century houses, some of which have been turned into interesting shops and cafes.

Ninety-minute walking tours of the city centre (adult/child under 12 €7.50/free) run daily at 1.30pm; get tickets at the Tourist Shop (p203).

★ **Abdij**   HISTORIC SITE
(Middelburg Abbey; Abbey of Our Lady; Onder den Toren; ⊘ churches 10.30am-5pm Mon-Fri Easter-Oct, also 1.30-5pm Sat & Sun Jul-Sep) **FREE** Dating from the 12th century, this huge abbey complex houses the regional government as well as two churches: the **Koorkerk** (⊘ 10.30am-5pm Mon-Fri Easter-Oct, also 1.30-5pm Sat & Sun Jul-Sep) **FREE** (built for the clergy) and **Nieuwe Kerk** (for parishioners). These were largely rebuilt in the 16th century after a fire ravaged the complex. The churches are joined by a central choir called the **Wandelkerk**. The **Muntplein**, a cloister with a tiny herb

garden at its centre, is located behind the Wandelkerk, as is a vast rear courtyard, the Abdijplein.

The former monk's dormitories now house the Zeeuws Museum.

Zeeuws Museum   MUSEUM
(📞0118-653 000; www.zeeuwsmuseum.nl; Abdijplein; adult/child under 19 €9.50/free; ⏰11am-5pm Tue-Sun) Housed in the former monks' dormitories of the abbey complex, this museum is divided into three permanent sections: one concentrating on fashion; another on the history, culture and landscape of Zeeland; and the third presenting a themed assortment of items from the museum's collection arranged as a jam-packed *Wanderkamer* (Chamber of Wonder). The last is a hit with children and adults alike. There is also one floor devoted to temporary exhibitions. The on-site cafe is a good lunch spot.

Stadhuis   HISTORIC BUILDING
(Town Hall; 📞0118-675 452; tours adult/child under 12 €5.50/free; ⏰tours 11.30am) Dominating the Markt, the town hall certainly grabs the eye. It's ornately beautiful, and displays a pastiche of styles: the Gothic side facing the Markt is from the mid-1400s; the more classical portion on Lange Noordstraat dates from the 1600s.

Inside there are several sumptuous ceremonial rooms that boast treasures such as the ubiquitous Belgian tapestries. Visits to the building are by one-hour guided tours, which are offered most days. These visit the mayor's room, the aldermen's room, the city council room and the court of justice; purchase tickets at the Tourist Shop.

Lange Jan Tower   CHURCH
(Long John Tower; 📞0118-471 010; www.langejanmiddelburg.nl; Onder den Toren; €4; ⏰11am-4.45pm Jul & Aug) This 91m tower is topped with a gilded imperial crown, a tribute to Holy Roman Emperor Maximilian I. Climb the 200-odd steps to enjoy views over town.

🛏 Sleeping & Eating

Though it's a tourism hub, most visitors head to Middelburg for day trips rather than overnight stays. This means that there is a limited range of accommodation options. The best of these is undoubtedly Hotel The Roosevelt (📞0118-436 360; www.hoteltheroosevelt.com; Nieuwe Burg 42; d €119-

199, ste €169-330; ❋🛈), which is one of the country's best boutique hotels.

★Vliegendt Hert   EUROPEAN €€
(📞0118-236 046; www.vliegendthert.nl; Dam 61; mains €13-16, snacks €3-22; ⏰from 3pm Wed-Sun, kitchen from 5.30pm) The world needs more wine bars like this super-stylish conversion of a 16th-century mansion. The eating and drinking action occurs behind a wine shop stocked with a world-class selection of European and New World bottles. Choose a bottle to enjoy with a meal or snack in the rear wine bar/restaurant (corkage €10), or choose from 60 wines offered by the glass.

The *borrelkaart* (snack menu) includes French and Italian charcuterie and cheese; the small but delicious dinner menu features fish and meat dishes. You can also opt for a wine tasting accompanied by *borrel hapjes* (snacks).

Restaurant De Eetkamer   DUTCH €€€
(📞0118-635 676; www.eetkamermiddelburg.nl; Wagenaarstraat 13-15; mains €26-30, 3-/4-/5-/6-course menu €40/50/60/68; ⏰noon-2pm, 5.30-9.30pm Tue-Sat) The modern French cuisine served at this classy restaurant highlights seasonal, local produce and the resulting plates are a joy to both behold and eat.

🍸 Drinking & Nightlife

Contemporary coffee culture has made its presence felt in recent times, and there are a number of hip cafes on or near the Markt. There are also a number of excellent wine bars. Nightlife centres around the town's arthouse cinema and the popular De Spot (📞0118-633 229; http://despotmiddelburg.nl; Beddewijkstraat 15; ⏰10pm-4am Thu-Sat, hrs vary) live-music venue.

De Zaak   BROWN CAFE
(📞0118-853 200; www.dezaakmiddelburg.nl; Pottenmarkt 24; ⏰10am-8pm Mon & Tue, 10am-6pm Wed, 10am-2am Thu-Sat, noon-8pm Sun) De Zaak's rustic interior with hefty beams and wine barrels makes it a cosy spot in the cooler months, but it's best in warm weather when the front terrace spills onto Pottenmarkt and turns into a giant street party.

ℹ Information

There's no official VVV tourist office in Middelburg but the **tourist shop** (📞0118-674 300; www.uitinmiddelburg.nl; Markt 51; ⏰11am-6pm Mon, 9.30am-6pm Tue-Wed & Fri, 9.30am-9pm

Thu, 9.30am-5.30pm Sat, plus 1-5pm 1st Sun of month; ☎) counter inside De Drvkkery bookshop does an excellent job.

❶ Getting There & Away

Regional buses stop along Kanaalweg close to the train station.

BICYCLE

A bike route heads east to Breda (140km) via the fertile countryside and offers detours to charming villages such as Goes (36km).

TRAIN

Middelburg's station is 300m southeast of the centre. Regular services:

TO	PRICE (€)	TIME (MIN)	FREQUENCY (PER HR)
Amsterdam	25.30	155	2
Roosendaal	12.50	55	2
Rotterdam	20.10	100	2

Veere

☑ 0118 / POP 1500

Here, you'll feel like you're in a Vermeer painting: rich Gothic-style houses abound, a testament to the wealth brought into the town through its role as a staple port for the Scottish wool trade between the late 17th and late 18th centuries. In recent times, the town turned to tourism when its access to the sea on the Veerse Meer (Veere Lake) was closed as part of the Delta Project. It now has a busy yacht harbour.

Veere's late-Gothic-style **Stadhuis** (Town Hall; ☑ 0118-555 444; Markt 5), built in the late 15th century, houses a tower stuffed with bells – 48 at last count – and the **tourist office** (VVV; ☑ 0118-435 858; www.vvvzeeland.nl; Markt 5; ◷10am-5pm; ☎). Staff can advise on boat rentals and bike routes.

🛏 Sleeping & Eating

Accommodation options in town are limited to B&Bs and one boutique hotel.

De Werf   BISTRO €€€

(☑ 0118-502 105; www.dewerf.nl; Bastion 2; sandwiches €9-11, dinner mains €25-29; ◷11.30am-9pm; ☑) De Werf's menu has a Mediterranean slant, but its overall package is international, with sleek surrounds, an outdoor terrace overlooking the yacht harbour and a buzzy ambience. The friendly staff welcome children, who can order from a dedicated menu of kiddie favourites.

❶ Getting There & Away

Bicycle Veere is an easy ride from Middelburg (8km).

Bus Bus 584 (€2.20, 20 minutes) travels between Veere and Middelburg every hour.

Domburg

☑ 0118

Although Domburg is a low-key seaside town, it's still jammed-packed in summer due to its lovely beach. To escape the crowds, head south along the tall dunes. You can keep going past the golf course for a good 4km.

The tourist office can steer you to one of many bike-rental shops and provides maps of the popular 35km Mantelingen bicycle route, which begins and ends at Domburg. It takes in beaches, countryside and atmospheric villages such as Veere.

🛏 Sleeping & Eating

Stayokay Domburg   HOSTEL €

(☑ 0118-581 254; www.stayokay.com; Duinvlietweg 8; dm €24-32, d €63-85; ◷Apr-Oct; 🅿 ☎) Domburg's HI-affiliated hostel is set in a 13th-century castle 2km east of the town and 1km from the beach. Its mixed-sex dorm beds and private rooms are understandably popular; reserve well in advance. Bus 52 from Middelburg stops along the N287 near the entrance (Kasteel Westhove stop). Prices include breakfast in one of the two terrace cafes; parking costs €6.

★ Het Badpaviljoen   SEAFOOD €€€

(☑ 0118-582 405; www.hetbadpaviljoen.nl; Badhuisweg 21; lunch dishes €8-28, dinner mains €18-48; ◷11am-11pm, reduced hrs winter; 🅿 ☑ 🎡) Perched on the grassy dunes of Domburg, this legendary restaurant is housed in a majestic 19th-century bathhouse with a huge terrace. Indulge in splendidly prepared seafood dishes, steaks and pastas in the restaurant or enjoy drinks and Dutch bar snacks outside while savouring the seashore views. The colouring books and crayons are appreciated by both children and their parents.

❶ Information

Domburg's seasonal **tourist office** (VVV Domburg; ☑ 0118-583 484; www.vvvzeeland. nl; Schuitvlotstraat 32; ◷9.30am-5.30pm Mon-Sat, 11am-3pm Sun late Mar-Sep) is near the entrance to town, just past the windmill.

THE DELTA PROJECT

Begun in 1958, the Delta Project consumed billions of guilders, millions of labour hours and untold volumes of concrete and rock before it was finally completed in 2010. The goal was to avoid a repeat of the catastrophic floods of 1953, when a huge storm surge rushed up the Delta estuaries of Zeeland and broke through inland dykes. This caused a serial failure of dykes throughout the region, and much of the province was flooded.

The original idea was to block up the estuaries and create one vast freshwater network. But by the 1960s this kind of sweeping transformation was unacceptable to the Dutch public, who had become more environmentally aware. So the Oosterschelde was left open to the sea tides, and 3km of movable barriers were constructed that could be lowered ahead of a possible storm surge. The barriers, between Noord Beveland and Schouwen-Duiveland, are the most dramatic part of the Delta Project and the focus of Deltapark Neeltje Jans (below), which has displays detailing the enormous efforts to complete the barrier.

The project raised and strengthened the region's dykes and added a movable barrier at Rotterdam harbour, the last part to be completed. Public opinion later shifted, but large areas of water had already been dammed and made into freshwater lakes. At Veerse Meer the fishing industry has vanished and been replaced by tourists and sailing boats.

The impact of the Delta Project is still being felt. At Biesbosch National Park the reduction of tides is killing reeds that have grown for centuries. But those who recall the 1953 floods will trade some reeds for their farms any day.

Although the enormous project was eventually completed in 2010, work is ongoing to strengthen and heighten portions to deal with rising water levels due to climate change.

ⓘ Getting There & Away

Bicycle The area is laced with ideal bike paths along dykes and through the green countryside. Purchase a 'Bike Hub' map at one of Zeeland's tourist offices and start exploring; local bike rental outfits are listed at www. vvvzeeland.nl. Middelburg is about 13km via various routes.

Bus Bus 52 (€3.30, 30 minutes) travels between Domburg and Middelburg every hour.

Waterland Neeltje Jans

Travelling the N57, you are on the front lines of the Dutch war with the sea as you traverse the massive developments of the Delta Project, a succession of huge dykes and dams designed to prevent floods. Possibly the most impressive stretch is between Noord Beveland and Schouwen-Duiveland, to the north. The long causeway built atop the massive movable inlets is designed to allow the sea tides in and out of the Oosterschelde. This storm-surge barrier, more than 3km long and spanning three inlets and two artificial islands, took 10 years to build, beginning in 1976.

Around the midway point between Noord Beveland and Schouwen-Duiveland

on the N57, the Delta Project's former visitor centre has morphed into a theme park, Deltapark Neeltje Jans (☑ 0111-655 655; www.neeltjejans.nl; Neeltje Jans; adult/child 4-11/child 2-3 €23/17.50/8.50, 1hr boat trip extra €4; ☉ 10am-6pm late Jul–mid-Aug, to 5pm Apr-Jun & Sep-Oct; Ⓟ 🚻), complete with a mermaid mascot. Attractions include a 3D film about the devastating flood of 31 January 1953, a seal pool, a tropical salt-water aquarium, and a water park including a water slide, water playground and hurricane simulator. A boat trip takes you out onto the Oosterschelde for a panoramic view of the barriers and beyond.

The island has a long beach at the southern end, which is hugely popular with windsurfers.

The entire region has coastal sections that are part of the National Park Oosterschelde (www.np-oosterschelde.nl; ☉ 24hr) FREE; there are interesting displays in the unmanned information point across the N57 from Deltapark.

Bus 133 follows the N57 and stops at Deltapark on its run from Middelburg train station (€4.40, 40 minutes, every 30 minutes to two hours) or Zierikzee (€5.30, 40 minutes).

ROTTERDAM & SOUTH HOLLAND WATERLAND NEELTJE JANS

Schouwen-Duiveland

POP 33,821

The middle 'finger' of the Delta, this compact island of dunes is a sleepy, sparsely populated area for most of the year but comes to life in high summer, when it is inundated with tourists from the Netherlands and Germany. Drawn by the North Sea beaches and holiday ambience, many of these visitors have vacation properties near the village of Renesse on the island's west coast. The island's main settlement, Zierikzee (pop 11,017), is where most services can be accessed. The streets surrounding its historic Oude Haven (Old Harbour) are home to many historic buildings and are well worth a wander. The VVV website (www.vvvzeeland. nl) is a good resource.

◉ Sights & Activities

Zierikzee   VILLAGE

The largest village in Schouwen-Duiveland, Zierikzee was settled in the Middle Ages and retains a number of buildings dating from this time, including De Dikke Toren – the tower of the former Sint Lievensmonstertoren church, which burned down in the early 19th century. Other historic structures include Sint Lievensmonstertoren's replacement, the Nieuwe Kerk, constructed between 1835 and 1848, and the 16th-century Stadhuis (town hall). Wandering around the historic centre and enjoying a drink or meal at the harbour are popular activities.

Westerschouwen   VILLAGE

Located at the tip of Schouwen-Duiveland, next to the village of Burgh-Haamstede, this small settlement once had a thriving herring industry but its harbour silted up in the 16th century and many of its residents moved to Zierikzee. These days, the local economy relies on summer tourism, with the village's dune-backed sandy beaches the main attraction. Outdoor enthusiasts also head here to explore the 330-hectare Boswachterij Westerschouwen (Westerschouwen Forest) by bicycle, foot and horseback.

❶ Information

There are VVV tourist offices in **Zierikzee** (VVV; ☑ 0111-410 940; www.vvvzeeland.nl; Nieuwe Haven 7, Zierikzee; ☺10am-5pm Mon-Sat Jul-Aug), **Renesse** (☑ 0111-463 446; www.vvvzeeland. nl; Roelandsweg 3b, Renesse; ☺9am-5pm mid-May–mid-Sep) and **Haamstede** (VVV; ☑ 0111-450 524; www.vvvzeeland.nl; Ring 32, Haamstede; ☺10am-5pm Mon-Sat Jul & Aug); all are open in the summer months only.

❶ Getting There & Away

Bus The island's bus hub is Zierikzee; the bus stop is north of the town centre, a five-minute walk across the canal along Grachtweg. Bus 133 travels to Renesse (€3.20, 30 minutes) and then along the N57 over the Delta Works to Middelburg (€8.60, 50 minutes), stopping at many villages en route. Connexxion/Interliner bus 395 makes a one-hour journey every hour to/from Rotterdam's Zuidplein metro station (€10, one hour).

Bike The best mode of transit here. Routes abound, including one running north and south along the coast and over the various parts of the Delta Project.

Friesland (Fryslân)

Best Places to Eat

➡ Oost (p219)

➡ Restaurant 't Golfje (p219)

➡ Proefverlof (p212)

➡ De Bessenschuur (p220)

➡ Restaurant By Ús (p212)

➡ Pure Vida (p221)

Best Places to Stay

➡ Hotel Nobel (p223)

➡ Alibi Hostel (p211)

➡ Hotel Post Plaza (p211)

➡ De Eilanden (p214)

➡ Sier aan Zee (p222)

Why Go?

This unspoilt northerly province is the spot to take your foot off the pedal and go slow, Friesian-style, amid raw coastal nature and a profusion of namesake black-and-white cows.

Frieslanders are a staunchly self-reliant bunch, with their own language proudly emblazoned on road signs. Here they didn't just have to build dykes to protect their land; they had to build the land as well. Their unique mudflats, laced into the Waddenzee (Wadden Sea), are on Unesco's world treasures list, and the slender islands across this body of water are the country's hottest summertime destination, with forest, dunes and beaches threaded with cycling paths.

Piercing the province's centre is its beguiling, canal-ringed capital Leeuwarden, a European City of Culture in 2018 with a dynamic vibe to match. Elsewhere, craggy fishing villages and port towns such as Hindeloopen and Harlingen charm with 16th-century architecture and a contagious, laid-back pace unchanged for centuries.

When to Go

➡ Summer is the obvious time to visit. Water sports, such as sailing on the IJsselmeer, are at their peak and offshore islands have the most to offer.

➡ For festival lovers, late June is the time to hit Terschelling for its anything-goes Oerol festival. Enthusiastic sailors can party at the world's largest inland-water regatta in Sneek in August.

➡ Off-season has its own charm in old towns like Leeuwarden and Harlingen where moody canal-scapes, riveting museums and edgy cultural happenings enthral.

➡ In winter, if conditions are just right – deep frozen, that is – the entire nation pauses for the province-spanning ice-skating race Elfstedentocht.

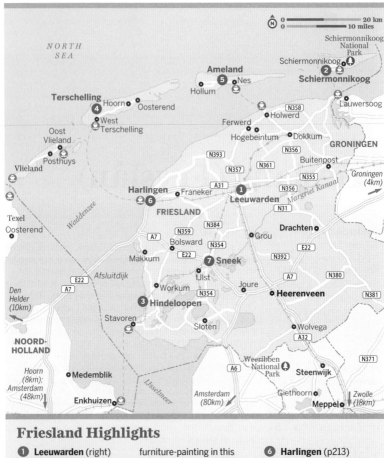

Friesland Highlights

1 Leeuwarden (right)
Exploring the provincial
capital's excellent museums
and creative culinary scene.

2 Schiermonnikoog
(p223) Communing with
nature on 'Grey Monk Island',
a national park teeming with
bird life and serenity.

3 Hindeloopen (p216)
Travelling back in time to
the Dutch Golden Age and
learning about traditional

furniture-painting in this
picture-postcard coastal
town.

4 Terschelling (p219)
Dancing all night and
catching performances by
day during the top-billing
Dutch festival Oerol.

5 Ameland (p222)
Losing all track of time on
this island idyll, home to a
picture-book lighthouse and
endless untouched nature.

6 Harlingen (p213)
Watching boaters navigate
old canals, and feasting on
local herring, mackerel,
eels and the nail-sized
Dutch prawns fresh off
the boats.

7 Sneek (p215) Donning
your sailor's hat – or stand-
up paddle – on Frisian lakes
and rivers in this premier
water-sports town.

History

Having dredged their home out of the Waddenzee armload by armload, the Frisians are
no strangers to struggling with their natural
environment.

Farming, fishing and shipbuilding have
been the area's principal activities for centuries, and made Friesland one of the wealthiest regions in the Netherlands in the pre-
republic era. The Frisians became integrated further into Dutch society – not entirely

willingly – in 1932 when the Afsluitdijk (Barrier Dyke) opened, closing the Zuiderzee. This provided better links to Amsterdam and the south but was devastating for small fishing villages, who suddenly found themselves sitting beside a lake.

ℹ Getting There & Around

The capital, Leeuwarden, is easily reached by train from the south; trains can be caught from there to the coastal towns of the southwest, the port of Harlingen in the west and Groningen in the east. Note that the branch lines are run by Arriva, so if you're using an OV-chipkaart you must scan it separately from an NS train journey. For example, if you ride an NS train from Amsterdam to Sneek, at Leeuwarden you need to scan off on an NS machine, then scan on again on an Arriva machine for the branch line to Sneek.

The rest of the province requires more patience, but can be reached by bus or, in the case of the islands, by ferry; various day passes are available.

Cycle paths crisscross Friesland. National bike route LF3 bisects the province north and south through Leeuwarden; LF10 cuts across Waddenzee on the Afsluitdijk (30km) from Noord Holland and takes in the north Frisian coast and all the ferry ports; while LF22 covers the southern coast before heading inland towards Zwolle.

LEEUWARDEN (LJOUWERT)

📞 058 / POP 107,600

An unexpected combination of style, gritty back alleys, cafe-lined canals and urban renewal, Friesland's capital is well worth a visit. Its superb trinity of museums and inventive cultural projects left over from a fabulous year as European Capital of Culture in 2018 are fascinating to explore. A continuous flow of cyclists ride happily along the broad paths that flank the city's canals, whose tunnels are atmospherically illuminated purple at night. Stick around and sample some of the northern hospitality, easily found in Leeuwarden's many bars and cafes throbbing with fun-loving Liwwadders (as people from Leeuwarden are officially known).

◉ Sights

Most of Leeuwarden's sights are concentrated within a leisurely 10-minute walk of Nieuwestad, Zaailand, the central square otherwise known as Wilhelminaplein, is the cultural centre of town: the Fries Museum

occupies a landmark building at one end. Fun and free weekend city tours with A Guide to Leeuwarden (www.aguidetoleeuwarden.nl) **FREE** take you around the key sights.

Look for historic ships of all kinds moored along the canals; the tourist office (p213) has information on canal cruises and gondola tours.

★ Keramiek Museum Princessehof   MUSEUM

(Princessehof Ceramic Museum; 📞058-294 89 58; www.princessehof.nl; Grote Kerkstraat 11; adult/child €12.50/free; ⊙11am-5pm Tue-Sun) Pottery lovers will adore the Netherlands ceramics museum. Here you'll find the largest collection of tiles on the planet, an unparalleled selection of Delftware and works from around the globe – the Japanese, Chinese and Vietnamese sections are superbly displayed. Watch for top-billing temporary art exhibitions too.

It's all atmospherically housed in Princessehof, the 17th-century mansion where the world-famous Dutch graphic artist MC Escher (1898–1972) was born and lived until 1903 when his family moved to Arnhem. Look out for street art around town celebrating the artist's mathematically inspired lithographs, prints and cut-outs.

Fries Museum   MUSEUM

(📞058-255 55 00; www.friesmuseum.nl; Wilhelminaplein 92; adult/child €13/6.50; ⊙10am-5pm Tue-Sun Sep-Jun, 10am-5pm Jul & Aug) The provincial museum occupies an imposing glass-fronted building sporting a striking wood-and-steel roof that projects out over Wilhelminaplein. The three levels are divided into a series of galleries. A good place to start is the Ferhaal fan Fryslân gallery (1st floor), an overview of the province with representative objects from the collection.

Oldehove   LANDMARK

(📞058-233 23 50; www.oldehove.eu; Oldehoofsterkerkhof; adult/child €3.50/1.50; ⊙1-5pm mid-Apr–Sep) At the northwest corner of the historic core stands the notoriously off-kilter Oldehove – Friesland's rival to the Leaning Tower of Pisa. Things went wrong shortly after the tower was started in 1529 and it never regained its proper posture, nor its intended height. Ride the lift up its 39 lopsided metres to enjoy a bird's-eye view of the vast square below, polka-dotted with engraved slabs of stone recalling the cemetery that was here until 1833.

Leeuwarden

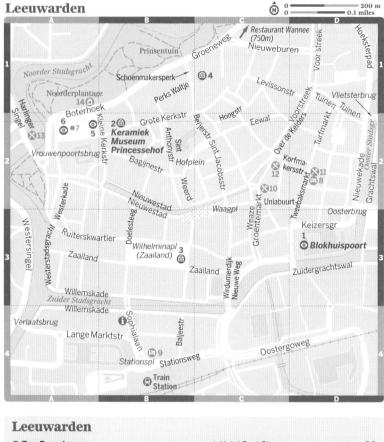

Leeuwarden

Obe Paviljoen CULTURAL CENTRE
(Heer Ivostraatje 1; ⊙ hours vary) Named after the local Frisian poet Obe Postma (1868–1963), this contemporary wood-and-glass pavilion is razor-sharp in both architectural design and the cultural exhibitions it hosts. Its wave-shaped roof doubles as a public grandstand with a great view of historic square Oldehoofsterkerkhof and the lop-sided Oldehove (p209) tower.

★ Blokhuispoort   CULTURAL CENTRE
(☑ 06-1117 2362; www.blokhuispoort.frl; Blokhuisplein 40; adult/child €10/free; ⊙ 9am-5pm Mon-Thu, 9am-11pm Fri, noon-5pm Sat, guided tours 2pm & 4pm Sat) No single sight evokes the undercurrent of explosive creativity pulsating through the Frisian capital quite like this 19th-century prison-turned-cultural centre. Dozens of entrepreneurial start-ups and young businesses now occupy the old cells; artist workshops, tattoo parlours, artisan boutiques and a designer hostel fill cell block H; while trendsetting Proefverlof (p212) is the hippest place in town for a canal-side bite or drink. Guided tours, led by a former prison guide complete with uniform, kick off from the latter.

🛏 Sleeping

★ Alibi Hostel   HOSTEL €
(☑ 06 1207 7449; https://alibihostel.nl; Blokhuisplein 40; dm €23.50-25, d with bathroom €72.70-77.50, d without bathroom €50-55; @ 🛜) The novelty factor is high at this snazzy designer hostel in the town's old prison Blokhuispoort. There are 63 beds in all, split between one huge 17-bed dorm (mixed, with triple bunk-bed-styled pods) and various four-bed cells and doubles, with shared or private bathroom.

★ Hotel Post Plaza   BOUTIQUE HOTEL €€
(☑ 058-215 93 17; www.post-plaza.nl; Tweebaksmarkt 27; d €92-310; ✳@🛜) A line of black bicycles stands outside the smartest hotel in town, an urban-chic spot inside the 19th-century post office and a neighbouring old bank. Wooden parquet floors, rich fabrics, the odd ancient beamed ceiling and eye-catching lighting are a beautiful blend of old and new. Family rooms sleep four, and one of the two suites has its own fireplace.

A glass tunnel connects the main hotel building with its wildly popular Grand Café, pretty much the perfect spot to eat or drink any time of day.

Oranje Hotel   HOTEL €€
(☑ 058-212 62 41; www.oranjehotelleeuwarden.com; Stationsweg 4; d from €125; ✳@🛜) Directly opposite the train station, this business hotel is the city's historic hotel address. In the biz for 130-odd years, it exudes a timeless elegance with its large windows fronting its bustling ground-floor brasserie, classical interiors and clean-cut rooms in gold and Bordeaux hues. Rear rooms enjoy a peaceful, leafy outlook. Park your bike in the hotel garage. Breakfast €20.

🍴 Eating & Drinking

Leeuwarden has a bevy of restaurants run by creative chefs as well as a generous stack of student-friendly sandwich bars and take-away eateries.

Broodje Bewust   SANDWICHES €
(☑ 058-203 00 20; www.broodjebewust-leeuwarden.nl; Groentemarkt 1; sandwiches €5.50-8; ⊙ 8am-5.30pm Mon-Fri, 9am-5.30pm Sat; 🖉) Join cent-smart locals at this student-busy sandwich shop for a light lunch overlooking the canal. Everything is organic, and the vast sandwich menu has lots of vegan and vegetarian options as well as creative fish, meat, cheese and egg choices. Salads, savoury tarts, burgers and quiches too.

Stek   CAFE €
(☑ 058-203 73 37; www.stekleeuwarden.nl; Harlinger Singel 2; breakfast €5.95-11.95, bowls & salads €7.95-12.95; ⊙ 9am-6pm Tue & Wed, 9am-8.30pm Thu-Sat, 11am-6pm Sun & Mon; 🛜) With a wooden decking terrace right above the water, views of canal action – yachts sailing past beneath the neighbouring bridge that rises to let them through – are impossibly romantic at this fashionable cafe, inside the old bridge guardhouse. A health-driven menu featuring fruit bowls, detox juices and smoothies, wraps, creative salads and burgers only adds to the enchanting ensemble.

SPEAKING FRISIAN
....

Frisians speak Frisian, which is actually closer (in some ways) to German and Old English than to Dutch; there's an old saying that goes 'As milk is to cheese, are English and Frise'. The majority of Frisians are, however, perfectly conversant in mainstream Dutch.

A ruling in 2002 officially altered the spelling of the province's name from the Dutch 'Friesland' to 'Fryslân', the local version of the name. Likewise, town names are generally presented in two versions, so Leeuwarden is also called 'Ljouwert', Sneek, the region's second city, 'Snits', and Hindeloopen is 'Hylpen'. To ingratiate yourself with the locals try uttering the following phrase: *'Fryslân boppe!'* (Friesland rules!).

FRIESLAND (FRYSLÂN) LEEUWARDEN (LJOUWERT)

DON'T MISS

THE GREAT DUTCH RACE(S)

Skating and the Dutch culture are interwoven and no event better symbolises this than the **Elfstedentocht** (Eleven Cities Tour; www.elfstedentocht.nl). Begun officially in 1909, although it had been held for hundreds of years before that, the race is 200km long, starting and finishing in Leeuwarden and passing through 11 Frisian towns: Sneek, IJlst, Sloten, Stavoren, Hindeloopen, Workum, Bolsward, Harlingen, Franeker and Dokkum.

The record time for completing the race is six hours and 47 minutes, set in 1985 (record-setter Evert van Benthem won again in 1986, making him a living legend). While it is a marathon, what makes the race a truly special event is that it can only be held in years when it's cold enough for all the canals to freeze totally; this has only happened 15 times since 1909. The last time was in 1997.

The infamous Elfstedentocht has inspired other races, thankfully not reliant on the weather: the 235km-long cycling race **Fiets Elfstedentocht** (www.fietselfstedentocht.frl; ☉ Whit Monday) sees 15,000 cyclists gather in small town Bolsward on Whit Monday for a biking tour of Friesland's traditional 11 cities. **SUP11** (https://sup11citytour.com; ☉ Sep) is a five-day stand-up paddle race along the same canals as the ice-skaters' Elfstedentocht.

★**Proefverlof** INTERNATIONAL €€
(☑058-302 00 30; www.proefverlof.frl; Blokhuisplein 40; mains lunch €7.50-12.50, dinner €13.50-21; ☉11am-11pm; 🛜) Cocktail quaffing does not get cooler than afloat the giant pink inflatable flamingo moored alongside the wooden decking terrace of Proefverlof, the hottest hybrid spot in town for drinking and dining with the A-lister crowd. The menu boasts everything from Frisian wild goose, pea risotto and oysters to crispy fried octopus, steaks, meal-sized salads and tempting finger foods.

Coffee comes with a bite-sized *Fryske dúmkes* (a traditional Frisian almond or hazelnut and aniseed cookie). Solo diners keen to meet other travellers or newbies-in-town can reserve a spot on the 'inmate table'. Find Proefverlof in the town's old 19th-century prison (p211).

Grand Café INTERNATIONAL €€
(☑058-215 93 17; www.post-plaza.nl; Tweebaksmarkt 25-27; mains €16.50-28.50; ☉7am-11pm; 🛜) Aptly named, this contemporary eatery is grand in every sense. Its building, a redbrick post office from 1903, is glorious inside and out. Dining covers everything from an 'anti-hangover' breakfast fry-up to afternoon tea with *Fryske sûkerbôle* (Frisian sugar loaf), gourmet *jenever* (Dutch gin) pairings and seafood platters to share. Watch for cocktail soirées with live music and lazy Sunday tunes.

The cafe also has its own coffee roastery and serves excellent, cold-brew mocktails and speciality coffees. Ample plugs for laptops, too.

Restaurant Wannee DUTCH €€
(☑058-303 08 00; www.restaurantwannee. nl; Rengerslaan 8; 1/3/4 dishes €7.50/15/20; ☉7am-9pm Mon-Fri Jul & Aug, 7am-9pm Mon-Fri, 8am-9pm Sat & Sun Sep-Jun; 🛜) Dining doesn't get more grassroots Frisian than at this contemporary restaurant run by students from the local hotel-management school. Begin with a fantastic Frisian Mojito (aka Flying Dutchman rum and local Beerenburg – a herb-infused *jenever*), followed by an exceptional-value feast featuring bags of local produce. Extra kudos for the miniature veg patch in the restaurant's middle and tasty pre-dinner succession of inventive amuse-bouches.

Dining is all-day, delicious wine pairings are suggested for each course, and in keeping with the 'New Dutch cuisine' philosophy, the meat or fish element plays second fiddle to the dominant vegetable components.

★**Restaurant By Ús** DUTCH €€€
(☑058-215 86 63; www.restaurantby-us.nl; Over de Kelders 24; 3-/4-/5-course menu €40/50/58; ☉6-9pm Wed-Sun; ☑) Organic local foods are celebrated at Michiel and Lilian's candlelit bistro with a funky wood-and-leather-meets-street-art interior. Frisian-inspired dishes stand out on a seasonally changing surprise menu – pick how many courses you desire, state if you're vegetarian and leave the rest up to the chef. There's also an excellent wine list, while faux furs and a wood-burning stove add winter warmth.

Entertainment

Podium Asteriks   LIVE MUSIC
(http://podiumasteriks.nl; Blokhuisplein 40; €7.50-12.50; ☺Sep-Jun) The stage in the city to catch upcoming Frisian and Dutch bands, with concerts kicking off most Fridays at 8pm. Find it in Leeuwarden's former prison (p211).

Shopping

Mooch the length of Kleine Kerkstraat and Tuinen to uncover some of Leeuwarden's more original shops and boutiques. For traditional blue-and-white ceramics, hit the museum shop at Keramiek Museum Princessehof (p209).

Afûk   BOOKS
(☑058-234 30 79; http://afuk.frl; Boterhoek 3; ☺9.30am-5.30pm Mon-Fri 10.30am-5pm Sat) For an excellent selection of books about Friesland, including a couple of translations of Frisian poets and novelists, duck into this Frisian bookshop and cultural centre.

It is run by Lan fan taal (https://lanfantaal.com), a cultural organisation that promotes both Frisian and new experiences in diverse languages. When exiting the bookshop, look for the giant exclamation mark – made up of hundreds of social-media posts from Friesland in dozens of different languages – emblazoned on the side of the building.

ⓘ Information

Tourist Office (VVV; ☑ 058-234 75 50; www.vvvleeuwarden.nl; Sophialaan 4; ☺11am-5pm Mon, 9.30am-5pm Tue-Fri, 10am-4pm Sat, noon-3pm Sun)

ⓘ Getting There & Away

Leeuwarden is at the end of the main train line from the south; it's also the hub for local services in Friesland, with westward branch lines to Harlingen (via Franeker), Stavoren (via Sneek) and Groningen by Arriva. Find lockers in the station foyer.

TO	PRICE (€)	TIME (MIN)	FREQUENCY (PER HR)
Groningen	10	45	3
Utrecht	24.10	120	2
Zwolle	12.40	60	3

Buses are to the left as you exit the train station. Leeuwarden is about 110km north of Kampen (near Zwolle) on national bike route LF3.

WADDENZEE COAST

Between the capital and the picturesque harbour of Harlingen is an intensively farmed area highlighted by one significant town, Franeker, an ancient centre of learning. North of Harlingen, a high dyke parallels the mudflats of the Waddenzee, linking a series of remote villages of stoic farmers whose squat brick houses overlook vast crop fields.

Harlingen

☑ 0517 / POP 15,822

Of all the old Frisian ports, only Harlingen has kept its link to the sea. It still plays an important role for shipping in the area, and is the busy launchpad for year-round ferries to the islands of Terschelling and Vlieland.

Harlingen retains a semblance of its architectural history: much of its attractive centre is a preserved zone of quaint 16th- and 18th-century canal-side houses fronted by tiny, neat-as-a-pin gardens with bench for canal-gazing and beds of brightly coloured hollyhocks. The carillon at the *stadhuis* (town hall) can be heard all over town when it chimes the hour and half-hour with its pretty melody, just as it has always done since the mid-18th century.

⊙ Sights & Activities

Harlingen is best enjoyed on foot. Stroll along the canals, many with drawbridges that rise with rhythmic regularity, especially yacht-

---

LOCAL KNOWLEDGE

DE TOBBEDANSER

Across from the ferry port, this bronze statue (Oude Ringmuur) encircled by a wooden bench is a lovely spot to sit and contemplate the pretty waterside views. Sculpted by Bert Kiewiet (1918–2008), the statue harks back to Harlingen's wool-manufacturing days. Fabric was washed in large tubs of water with one's feet, hence the local nickname for people from Harlingen – *Tobbedansers* ('tub dancers').

WORTH A TRIP

FRANEKER (FRJENTSJER)

About 6km east of Harlingen, the quaint town of Franeker squirrels away the world's oldest working planetarium. A well-preserved town centre clearly designed with casual summertime ambling in mind rounds off a half-day visit here. The town was once a big player in education, until Napoleon closed its university down in 1810.

The **Eise Eisinga Planetarium** (☑ 0517-393 070; www.planetarium-friesland.nl; Eise Eisingastraat 3; adult/child €5.25/4.50; ⊙ 10am-5pm Tue-Sat, 11am-5pm Sun year-round, 11am-5pm Mon Apr-Oct) is named after its builder, an 18th-century wool comber with a serious sideline in cosmic mathematics and astrology. Between 1774 and 1781, he built the planetarium himself in the living room of his canal-side home to illustrate how the heavens actually worked. It's startling to contemplate how Eisinga could have devised a mechanical timing system built to a viewable working scale that could encompass and illustrate so many different variables of time and motion.

An Arriva train stops in Franeker (from Leeuwarden; €4, 16 minutes, two hourly), 500m from the centre.

---

filled **Zuiderhaven** and **Noorderhaven**. The latter has been a place for ocean-going boats to dock since the 16th century. It is lined with houses from the rich era of trading. For a terrific view of the bustling harbour and church-spire-laced old town, spiral up the metal staircase to the upper deck of the bright-white, art-deco-style **lighthouse**.

Museum Hannemahuis Harlingen   MUSEUM
(☑ 0517-413 658; www.hannemahuis.nl; Voorstraat 56; adult/child €5/2.50; ⊙ noon-5pm Tue-Sun) Housed in the 18th-century mansion of a prominent Harlingen family, this museum deals primarily with the town's maritime heritage, in particular its role in the whaling industry, which brought so much wealth to Friesland in the 1700s. Other exhibits cover such other noble pursuits as silver crafting and *jenever* distilling.

🛏 Sleeping

't Heerenlogement   HOTEL €
(☑ 0517-415 846; www.heerenlogement.nl; Franekereind 23; s/d/tr/q €70.50/92/126/144; P) This 300-year-old relic has been zealously preserved by its owners, down to the period wallpaper in some of the uniquely designed rooms, all of which project a definite decades-old vibe. The hotel's canal-side location is unbeatable though: think flower-adorned terrace in the evening sun and a neighbouring English garden rising along ancient ramparts.

De Eilanden   BOUTIQUE HOTEL €€
(☑ 0517-210 002; Noorderhaven 24; d €95-120) For hard-core charm, check into this gorgeous, canal-side boutique hotel in a toy-like

vintage townhouse with caramel brickwork and sunflower-yellow paintwork. Stylish parquet, patterned wallpapers and rich fabrics adorn the contemporary rooms; those on the top floor enjoy centuries-old beams and sterling sea views (one even has a roof terrace). Check-in and breakfast are handled by neighbouring Hotel Zeezicht.

Hotel Zeezicht   HOTEL €€
(☑ 0517-412 536; www.hotelzeezicht.nl; Zuiderhaven 1; d €115; 🕾) There is no finer name than 'Zeezicht' (sea view) for this waterfront hotel, grandly placed across the water from the ferry port and vintage lighthouse. Several rooms, some with the added bonus of balcony, have sea view, and the hotel's terrace bar is the last word in local chic for a sundowner. Rates include breakfast.

🍴 Eating

Voorstraat and its western continuation, Grote Bredeplaats, are lined with casual places to eat and drink, with tables spilling atmospherically onto the street in warm weather. Fish and oysters from the North and Wadden Seas are the obvious local specialities.

★ De Tjotter   SEAFOOD €€
(☑ 0517-414 691; www.detjotter.nl; St Jacobstraat 1-3; menus €26.50-39.50, mains €20-26.50; ⊙ noon-10pm Wed-Sat, 1-10pm Sun-Tue) Herring, mackerel, cod, eel and shoals of tiny Dutch prawns come straight off the boats at Harlingen's premier seafood address. If you can't decide, opt for the five-fish taster plate served with fries, salad and a delicious caper sauce or luxuriate in a lavish four-course

shellfish and crustacean menu. Dine casually at the bar, waterside, or in the formal restaurant.

Nooitgedagt   INTERNATIONAL €€

(📞 0517-434 211; www.eetcafenooitgedagt.nl; Grote Bredeplaats 35; mains €17-21.50; ⊙ 11.30am-10pm) With its name roughly translating as 'Something you'd never think of', you can expect a unique experience at this stylish cafe in a wine warehouse from 1647. Interior design mixes urban white tiling with weathered wood tables, sunflower-yellow bar stools, jazz music and a hipster beach-shack vibe. Creative cuisine travels the world: fish curry, spare ribs and Waddenzee oysters, etc.

ⓘ Information

Tourist Information (📞 0517-430 207; www. harlingen-friesland.nl; Grote Bredeplaats 12; ⊙ 10am-5pm Mon-Sat, noon-4pm Sun)

ⓘ Getting There & Away

Harlingen is connected to Leeuwarden (€5.49, 22 minutes) by two Arriva trains hourly. There are stations south of the centre and by the harbour (Harlingen Haven), 300m from the ferry terminal. Year-round ferries serve Vlieland (90 minutes) and Terschelling (45 or 90 minutes); ticket offices open 7.30am to 8.10pm daily.

The ferry port is on national bike route LF10, which runs 8km south on the coast to the Afsluitdijk and the crossing to North Holland; going northeast, it passes the ferry ports to Ameland and Schiermonnikoog islands.

SOUTHWESTERN FRIESLAND

The lake-studded region southwest of Leeuwarden is a magnet for sailors, windsurfers and other water-sport aficionados. Since being hemmed in by the Afsluitdijk, the coastal villages of Hindeloopen and Stavoren are sleepier places with echoes of their seagoing past. The latter port is the embarkation point for ferries to Noord-Holland.

Sneek (Snits)

📞 0515 / POP 33,855

As the saying goes, 'All Frisians know how to sail, and all Frisians know how to fish'. This is certainly true of the residents of Sneek, but then again, they have no choice in the matter: Frisian lakes and rivers are linked to the IJsselmeer and decorate the land not unlike the spots on the local dairy cows. If you've got a hankering to get out under sail, this is the place.

◉ Sights & Activities

Fries Scheepvaart Museum   MUSEUM

(📞 0515-414 057; www.friesscheepvaartmuseum. nl; Kleinzand 16; adult/child €7.50/3; ⊙ 10am-5pm Mon-Sat, noon-5pm Sun) Sneek has been a nexus of Frisian waterways for centuries, and this museum elegantly illustrates many aspects of shipping and seafaring in the province. Pride of place is given to models of the *skûtsjes* and *koffs* that figured so largely in inland and overseas trade.

JFT Watersport   BOATING

(📞 0515-443 867; www.jft-watersport.nl; Hendrik Bulthuisweg 16; rentals per day €50-200) This family-run business rents a large range of sailboats, both open boats and vessels with sleeping facilities. Stand-up paddle boards (per hour/four hours/day €10/25/35) are its other big draw and it rents wetsuits too (€5); book in advance online.

✱✲ Festivals & Events

Sneekweek   SPORTS

(www.sneekweek.nl; ⊙ early Aug) No time is more festive in Sneek than the annual sailing festival in early August, the largest sailing event on Europe's inland waters. A regatta with fireworks opens the fest, which involves lots of racing activity, a market and frivolity in the streets.

🛏 Sleeping & Eating

Accommodation is limited; many day-trip it here from Leeuwarden.

Stadslogement King-Size   B&B €

(📞 0515-487 605; www.stadslogementkingsize. nl; Prins Hendrikkade 20; d €70-90; ❋ 🛜) Five stylishly contemporary rooms are available in this historic building from 1898, the very spot where the Netherlands' famous extra-strong King peppermints were first made in 1902. Luxurious rooms are equipped with a kettle and sophisticated lighting, and a spiral staircase twists up to two loft rooms. Breakfast, 100% organic and delivered to your room, costs €10.

Note that the B&B has no reception; guests dial various telephone numbers to open the automatic-opening front door and bedrooms.

THE ORIGINAL GIN

No drink is more traditional to seafaring Sneek than Beerenburg, a local herb-infused gin originally drunk by sailors to warm their cockles at sea and stave off illness. Since 1864 it has been distilled at **Weduwe Joustra** (☑ 0515-412 912; www.weduwejoustra.nl; Kleinzand 32; ☺ 9am-6pm Mon-Fri, to 5pm Sat), an enchanting vintage liquor shop run by the fifth generation, with a museum and tasting room up top and a distillery out back.

A secret mix of herbs – including bay leaves, juniper berries, thistle, gentian root, sandalwood, sweet carrot root and orange peel – are thrown into huge vats with *jenever* (Dutch gin) and left to macerate for a minimum of four weeks to produce the aromatic spirit, with a not-to-be-scoffed-at alcoholic strength of 32%. The shop also sells ceramic bottles of Beerenburg FS and Beerenburg FSOB, both with a fiery 38% alcoholic content and aged for three and five years respectively in oak barrels to create the perfect after-dinner Frisian digestif.

Call ahead to reserve a one-hour guided tour (adult/child €5/free), with tastings.

Royaal Belegd   SANDWICHES €
(☑ 0515-750 503; www.royaalbelegd.nl; Lemmerweg 4; sandwiches €3.95-6.50; ☺ 9am-5pm Tue-Fri, 10am-5pm Sat & Sun) 'Fair trade, homemade and good food' is the holy grail for chefs at this fun corner cafe. Bar seating in front of big windows provides ringside views of Sneek's iconic Watergate, and creatively stuffed *broodjes* (sandwiches), served on a choice of various nut and grain breads, make the perfect light lunch. Breakfast and excellent specialist coffee too.

ℹ Information

Tourist Office (VVV; ☑ 0515-750 678; www.vvvzuidwestfriesland.nl; Kleinzand 16; ☺ 10am-5pm Mon-Fri, noon-5pm Sat)

ℹ Getting There & Around

From the train station to the centre of town is a five-minute walk along Stationsstraat. Arriva trains on the Leeuwarden–Stavoren line cost €4.68 (22 minutes, two per hour).

Profile Rodenburg (☑ 0515-413 096; www.profiledefietsspecialist.nl; Lemmerweg 13-15; ☺ 9am-6pm Tue-Fri, to 5pm Sat), 150m west of the Waterpoort, rents bikes.

Hindeloopen (Hylpen)

☑ 0514 / POP 920

Huddled up against the banks of the IJsselmeer, Hindeloopen has been set apart from the rest of Friesland for centuries. As you approach across the flat Frisian countryside, the sudden appearance of a forest of yacht masts marks the town in the distance.

In the 16th and 17th centuries, trade ships from Amsterdam dropped anchor at this Zuiderzee harbour on their way to England and Scandinavia, boosting its prosperity and connecting it with the outside world. The exuberant beauty and charm of the Dutch Golden Age lives on today in Hindeloopen's narrow streets, flower-bedecked canals, multitude of bridges (16 to be exact) and handful of highly skilled cabinet makers who continue to craft exotically painted oak furniture by hand as their ancestors have done for generations.

◉ Sights & Activities

The grassy dyke ringing the town, specked with grazing sheep in summer, is invigorating walking terrain and rewards with sweeping views of the IJsselmeer. To the south, the windblown coast is popular with kite-surfers.

Museum Hindeloopen   MUSEUM
(☑ 0514-521 420; www.museumhindeloopen.nl; Dijkweg 1; adult/child €6/4; ☺ 11am-5pm Mon-Sat, 1.30-5pm Sun Apr-Oct) Displays in this small museum, inside the former town hall (1683) next to the church, focus on the town's seafaring history and traditional crafts, in particular the fine art of 16th- and 17th-century furniture painting for which Hindeloopen is renowned. A couple of rooms feature blue-and-white Frisian ceramic wall tiles and life-sized recreations of people in traditional dress in 1740.

**Het Eerste Friese
Schaatsmuseum**   MUSEUM
(Frisian Skating Museum; ☑ 0514-521 683; www.schaatsmuseum.nl/home; Kleine Weide 1-3; adult/child €3/2; ☺ 10am-6pm Mon-Sat, 1-5pm Sun) In extraordinarily cold winters Hindeloopen is one of the key towns on the route of the

Elfstedentocht (p212) race. This icy spectacle and ice skating in general are the museum's focus. Displays covering skating through the centuries are enthralling, as is the history of the competition.

Eating & Drinking

Feasting on local oysters and dark and nutty *Fries roggebrood* (Frisian rye bread) is a rite of passage. The sprinkling of restaurants overlooking the old harbour all serve these local specialities alongside shoals of fresh fish.

De Hinde   DUTCH €€
(📞 0514-523 868; www.dehinde.nl; 't Oost 4; lunch mains €6-12.50, dinner mains €12-29.50, 3-course dinner menu €37; ⊙ 11am-9pm Thu-Tue) The terrace across from a vintage lifeboat shed is the main draw at this harbour-side restaurant, run by the same family for three generations. Limited lunchtime dining (noon to 4pm) includes pea soup, herring salad and *Fries roggebrood* topped with fresh sheep's cheese. Dinner involves delicious fishy dishes like local oysters, IJsselmeer smoked eel and pike-perch.

Above its restaurant, De Hinde has a couple of stylish rooms with sea view to rent.

De Drie Harinkjes   DUTCH €€
(📞 0514-522 222; www.de3harinkjes.nl; Buren 39; mains €19-22.50; ⊙ 5-9pm Mon, Tue & Fri, 4-9pm Sat, noon-9pm Sun) On nippier days, kick back at this fish restaurant inside a historic garage at the old harbour. Its 1st-floor dining room and roof terrace dish up exhilarating views of the IJsselmeer and sun sinking into the horizon at sunset. Fish specialities include whole plaice baked in butter, and cod in a mustard sauce, alongside a tasty choice of grilled meats.

De Foeke   CAFE
(📞 06 4257 6330; www.defoeke.com; Nieuwstad 49; ⊙ garden 10am-variable Wed-Sun, club 10pm-late Sat May-Sep) Tucked away at the end of the harbour, this home-from-home *terras* is a peaceful spot to chill out on the grass overlooking a tiny canal fringed with other equally flowery back gardens. Romantic sofas for two, made from old wooden pallets, sit on the water's edge, and snacks are served.

Between May and September, Saturday night ushers in all-night Club De Foeke dance parties (admission €2); doors open at 10pm.

Shopping

★ **Roosje Hindeloopen**   ARTS & CRAFTS
(📞 0514-521 251; https://roosjehindeloopen.com; Nieuwstad 44; ⊙ 8.30am-12.30pm & 1.30-5pm Mon-Sat) A mooch around the workshop and boutique of Hindeloopen's oldest furniture maker is a highlight. Founded in 1894, the family business is run today by Bertus and his two sons, Johan and Titus, who craft exquisite folding tables, chests and traditional ice sledges evocative of the highly ornate pieces wealthy seafaring commodores decorated their homes with in the 17th century.

Their custom-made, handmade pieces – decorated with a profusion of flowers, birds, swirling motifs, Greek mythology scenes et al, all painstakingly painted by hand in oil – are exported all over the world and cost thousands of euro. Their shop squats inside a sea captain's house dating to 1656, complete with original hand-painted wall panels and murals in the upstairs office; ask nicely and Titus might just let you have a peek.

Information

The small but helpful tourist information point inside the Museum Hindeloopen (p216) has lists of hotels and B&Bs in town and sells a handy booklet (€1.50) detailing a fascinating walking tour around town.

Getting There & Away

The tiny train station – no more than a single platform amid fields – is a scenic 2km walk from town; otherwise, cross your fingers and hope your train coincides with bus 102 or shuttle-bus Opstapper (€4, hourly) linking the station and town museum. Arriva trains run hourly to/from Leeuwarden (€8.25, 45 minutes) via Sneek (€4.70, 20 minutes) and onward to Stavoren, where you can catch a ferry to Enkhuizen in Noord-Holland.

By bike, it's 27km from Sneek to Hindeloopen via IJlst, where a pair of wind-driven sawmills attest to that idyllic town's former timber industry, and the lake-studded region west of Oudega. From Hindeloopen you can pick up the coastal national bike route LF22 north to Harlingen or south to Stavoren.

FRISIAN ISLANDS

The crescent of islands over Friesland – Vlieland, Terschelling, Ameland and Schiermonnikoog – form a unique natural entity and a distinct Dutch region. A natural

ℹ️ ISLAND ACCOMMODATION

With the huge influx of tourists in the summertime (populations routinely multiply tenfold on warm weekends) it can get crowded, so try to make arrangements in advance. Among the myriad accommodation options are hotels, B&Bs and cottages, and there are plenty of camp sites.

barrier between the Frisian coast and the North Sea, they hem in the mudflats of the Waddenzee, a Unesco World Heritage site since 2009 and a hot spot for *wadlopen* (mudflat walking) with professional guides. Villages, *polders* and salt marshes fringe the islands along their Waddenzee shores, while swaths of beach and dunes lace the seaward side. Inland, expect ample forest and heath crisscrossed with hiking and cycling trails.

Populated for at least a thousand years, the remote islands have frequently fallen victim to the whims of nature as the sea washed towns off the map and shifting sands altered the terrain. Challenging as it was to live off the land, inhabitants turned to fishing and whaling for their livelihoods. Since WWII, tourism has been the mainstay.

ℹ️ Getting There & Away

Frequent ferries link the islands with the mainland. There are surcharges for taking cars or bicycles, and only residents may take their cars to Vlieland and Schiermonnikoog. All the Frisian Islands have decent bus service as well as bike-rental shops with e-bikes and regular bikes right by the ferry docks.

Check deals carefully online; when sailing to Terschelling or Vlieland, for example, **Rederij Doeksen** (📞 0889 000 888, 06 1332 6406; www.rederij-doeksen.nl) offers a brilliant-value day ticket with all-day bike rental upon arrival.

Vlieland

📞 0562 / POP 1145

Historically the most isolated of the islands, and the least visited, Vlieland is a windswept and wild place, but this is part of its charm. The ferry arrives at the sole town, Oost Vlieland, at the east end of the island and ringed by forest. It's where you'll find all hotels, restaurants and services. The west end of the island is a sandy wasteland at the mercy of the sea, parts of which are used by the military.

💿 Sights & Activities

Most of the island's 72 sq km lies waiting to be explored by bike or on foot, including 18km of beaches. Cycling around Vlieland can be exhilarating; there are many unsealed tracks that confident off-roaders can tackle. The tourist office (p219) provides English-language self-guided nature walks and bike rides.

Museum Tromp's Huys MUSEUM
(📞 0562-451 600; www.trompshuys.nl; Dorpsstraat 99; adult/child €4/2.50; ⏰ 2-5pm Tue-Thu & Sat, 10am-1pm Fri) Journey back in time to island life in the early 20th century at this tiny house-museum, inside the oldest building on Vlieland, dating to 1575. The Norwegian landscape painter Betzy Akersloot-Berg (1850–1922) lived and worked here from 1896, painting the island and its seascapes endless times. Several of her works hang in the museum, alongside antique ship models, maps, silver and other exhibits typical of an early-20th-century Vlieland home.

Vlieland Outdoor Center KAYAKING
(📞 06 5146 0152; www.vlielandoutdoorcenter. nl) Pretty much anything outdoors is what this activity centre does: it rents rafts and kayaks, kite-surfs (two hours with instructor €70) and stand-up paddle boards (€12.50/ hour), and offers lessons. It also organises beach golf, beach tennis and outdoorcooking workshops (three hours €72), during which you forage in the mudflats for cockles et al, then return to base camp and cook them. Find the centre on the sands, west of Badweg.

De Noordwester
Information Centre OUTDOORS
(📞 0562-451 700; www.denoordwester.nl; Dorpsstraat 150; ⏰ 10am-5pm Mon-Fri, 2-5pm Sat, noon-5pm Sun Jun-Sep, hours vary rest of year) Join a hiking or birdwatching group here. It also offers daily boat tours around the island that include a bit of *wadlopen*.

🍴 Eating & Drinking

Dozens of cafes and restaurants, all with a steak-seafood-bit-of-pasta menu and summertime terraces, cluster on main street Dorpsstraat. On the same street, shop for beach picnics at Vlieland's two small supermarkets at No 38 and No 108, and for fresh bread and cakes at the village bakery at No 100.

Leut Koffiebar & Logies CAFE **€**

(☎0562-853 791; www.leutvlieland.nl; Dorpsstraat 118; salads & sandwiches €5.25-11.95; ⊙9am-6pm; 🛜) With a pretty terrace beneath trees, this caramel-brick townhouse is the fashionable spot on the main street for a chai latte, smoothie or freshly infused herbal tea. Breakfast translates as ample yoghurt and fruit bowls; delicious salads and wraps are served for lunch between 11.30am and 5pm; and high tea involves copious amounts of island cranberries and *slagroom* (whipped cream).

Should you fall hopelessly in love with the fantastic coffee, healthy food and Scandinavian design–inspired interior, Leut has three chic hotel rooms (d from €100) with shared kitchenette above.

★ **Oost** SEAFOOD **€€**

(☎06 1007 8585; https://oostvlie.nl; Fortweg 20, Strand Fortweg Vlieland; mains €9.95-15; ⊙10am-10pm Apr-Sep) There is no more fashionable *Strandpaviljoen* (beach pavilion) on the island than the utterly fabulous Oost, a contemporary shoebox hidden between sand dunes and a dreamy swath of fine golden sand. Fish and shellfish from the North and Wadden Seas – with a creative fusion touch and baked in a charcoal oven – is what it does best.

The lunch special, *Schelpen in het Zand* ('mussels in sand'), aka a herb-laced bowl of mussels and spiced breadcrumbs with bread and seaweed butter, is outstanding, as is the homemade beef burger with wakame seaweed and wasabi mayo. Between meals, there are sardine platters, herrings, cockles and fishy spring rolls to nibble on. Dinner, served from 6pm, is a four-course affair strictly by reservation.

ⓘ Information

Tourist Office (VVV; ☎0562-451 111; www.vlieland.net; Havenweg 10; ⊙9am-5pm Mon-Fri, 10am-5pm Sat, 10am-noon & 4-5pm Sun)

ⓘ Getting There & Away

Rederij Doeksen (p218) runs regular ferries from Harlingen to Vlieland (adult/child return €26.66/13.26) that take 90 minutes. Departures are typically at 8.30am or 9am, 2pm and 7pm, but schedules change each season. A fast service (€39.36/26.42) takes 45 minutes direct and 90 minutes via Terschelling. Check for good-value seasonal deals: in 2018 the ferry firm was offering a day ticket for €25, or €29 including all-day bike rental or bus travel on the island.

In summer **De Vriendschap** (☎022-231 64 51; http://waddenveer.nl; adult/child day return €29.50/19.50, bike €10; ⊙May-Sep) connects Vlieland to Texel island, a 30-minute trip over the shallow waters. Day trips (adult/child €29.50/19.50) depart from Het Posthuys in the centre, where passengers hop aboard the **Vliehors Express** (☎06 2182 0842; www.vliehorsexpres.nl; Dorpsstraat 74; adult/child €16.50/11) for a 12km drive to the Vliehors harbour on the west end of Vlieland, from where boats sail to Texel. One-way journeys (€18.50/12) are also possible if you want to stay on Texel.

ⓘ Getting Around

Jan van Vlieland (☎0562-451 509; www.janvanvlieland.nl; Havenweg 7; ⊙9am-9pm Jul & Aug, 9am-6pm Apr-Jun & Sep, shorter hours rest of year) rents bikes/e-bikes (€8/20 per day) opposite the ferry landing; tandems, kids' bikes and trailers are also available. A bus wanders the few roads of Oost-Vlieland.

Terschelling

☎0562 / POP 4720

Terschelling is the largest of the Frisian Islands; it's also the most developed and most visited. A string of villages line up between

ⓘ ISLAND HOPPING

In summer, daily ferries connect the islands of Texel, Vlieland and Terschelling without the need to return to the mainland.

But if you've got the time, a more adventurous alternative connects all the islands to Noord-Holland. The (☎020-261 46 28; www.eilandhopper.nl; ⊙Jul & Aug) runs a pair of graceful century-old clippers: the *Avontuur* sails between Amsterdam and Terschelling (via Enkhuizen and Stavoren), and the *Willem Jacob* between Texel and Schiermonnikoog, visiting all the islands en route. Trips range from several days (with accommodation and meals on board), to a one-day trip (€55 per person) or overnight (€70) typically departing from Terschelling at 6pm and docking on Ameland the following morning at 11am. Check schedules and book online.

polder and dunes along its 30km expanse. West-Terschelling, with the ferry port at the island's west end, and neighbouring Midsland are the largest villages, peppered with souvenir shops, cafes and restaurants. The eastern end of the island is a wild and isolated place. Overall, there are 250km of walking and cycling trails.

◉ Sights & Activities

The tourist office (p221) is the starting point for a huge range of organised trips, activities and workshops including mudflat walking, seal-watching, birdwatching and nature walks with a forest ranger.

Bunker Museum   MUSEUM
(Stellung Tiger; ☑0562-850 732; http://bunker sterschelling.nl; Tigerpad 5, West-Terschelling; adult/child €5/free, guided tour €8; ⊙10am-5pm Tue-Fri, noon-5pm Sat, 11am-4pm Sun) Hidden in woods east of West-Terschelling is an extraordinary subterranean network of 85 bunkers used as a military radar station during WWII. Construction work began in 1941 and continued until 1944. Visits include a small exhibition about the station and a couple of bunkers displaying helmets, glass bottles, bullet cartridges, sketchpads and all sorts belonging to the 200 German soldiers stationed at Stellung Tiger and other radar stations along the Atlantic Wall. Guided tours include the actual transmission room.

**Terschelling Museum
't Behouden Huys**   MUSEUM
(☑0562-442 389; www.behouden-huys.nl; Commandeurstraat 30, West-Terschelling; adult/child €5/2; ⊙11am-5pm Mon-Fri, 1-5pm Sat & Sun Apr-Oct, 1-5pm Wed, Sat & Sun Nov-Mar) Good for a rainy day, this small museum covers traditional Terschelling life and maritime history. It's named after the cabin on the Novaya Zemlya archipelago where native son Willem Barentsz and his crew had to hibernate after getting locked in by ice during an exploratory expedition of the Polar Sea in 1596; there's a reconstructed version of their shelter.

De Boschplaat   PARK
An extensive natural reserve at the eastern end of the island, De Boschplaat was a separate island until 1880, when the channel between the two silted up. Trails criss-cross a zone of high grassy dunes teeming with migratory birds.

✵ Festivals & Events

Oerol   CULTURAL
(www.oerol.nl; adult/child €30/7.50, pre-sale €25/5; ⊙late Jun) The annual Oerol outdoor performance festival is revered nationally as a perfect excuse for going to sea. It started years ago with farmers letting their cows run loose one day each year (hence the name *oerol,* which means 'all over'). It's a wild, arty party, piercing the otherwise unflappable northern facade for 10 days in the latter half of June.

Think theatre, music and street entertainment galore, with stages springing up at impromptu venues all over the island, including on beaches and in sand dunes and pine forests.

⌨ Sleeping

From camp site to hostel and luxurious hotel, all budgets are covered on this large island. The villages of West-Terschelling and Midsland are the main accommodation bases.

Stayokay Terschelling   HOSTEL €
(☑0562-442 338; www.stayokay.com/terschelling; 't Land 2, West-Terschelling; dm from €26.50, d/tr/q €120/136/160; ⊙reception 9am-5pm; 🛜) This branch of the nationwide chain stands on a bluff overlooking the harbour, 1.5km east of the lighthouse in West-Terschelling. Sea views from the canteen, terrace and many rooms are second to none and the location is remote enough to feel adventurous. Bus 121 stops nearby (Dellewal stop) or follow the coastal cycling track northeast. BYO towel or rent one for €3.50.

't Wapen van Terschelling   HOTEL €
(☑0562-448 801; www.twapenvanterschelling. nl; Oosterburen 25, Midsland; s without bathroom €40, d with/without bathroom €99/69; 🛜) Slapbang on the main boutique- and cafe-clad street in Midsland, 6km east of the ferry, this long-standing inn is above a welcoming brown cafe with renowned beer selection and mesmerising vintage memorabilia (street signs, musical instruments, figurines, cooking utensils etc). Its 24 rooms are well maintained and carpeted, some with shared bathroom and others with balcony. Rates include breakfast.

✗ Eating & Drinking

De Bessenschuur   CAFE €
(☑0562-448 800; www.terschellingercranberry. nl; Badweg West 1, West-Terschelling; cakes €4-7; ⊙11am-5pm) Once a storage shed for the

SOMETHING FISHY IN THE KITCHEN

Island native Flang offers unique culinary tours and workshops at Kookstudio Flang in de Pan (☑0562-850 134; www.flangindepan.nl; Dorpsstraat 25), his kitchen-studio in Hoorn, including a two-hour *wadlopen* excursion on the Waddenzee (April to October; adult/ child €20/12.50) to collect oysters, periwinkles and seaweed for a meal he'll then teach you to prepare. Winter workshops include scavenging for peas and preparing traditional pea soup (€19.50/16.50, including lunch).

Serious fish lovers will adore the hike to a traditional *takkenfuik* on the mudflats to learn how fish is traditionally caught, followed by a lesson in fish preparation and a meal (€67). Flang also has a couple of B&B rooms to rent above his kitchen-studio.

copious cranberry harvest in this part of the island, this pretty forest cottage with red-and-white-striped canopies now serves various berry-based drinks, pastries and puddings. It makes an ideal stop on a bike ride to or from the beach in West ann Zee (2.3km further north).

A traditional fruit of the island for centuries, wild cranberries pepper the sand dunes, and cranberry heather – a blaze of pink-purple during the flowering period in late May and early June – carpets the wet dune valleys. The harvest usually takes place from early September until November. A small museum on the 1st floor of Bessenschuur includes black-and-white photos of the cranberry harvest over the centuries.

★ **Pure Vida**   INTERNATIONAL €€
(☑ 06 1185 5457; www.puravidaterschelling.nl; Oosterburen 36, Midsland; toasts & sandwiches €6.95-8.95, mains €14.50, small/large bowls €10.50/16.50; ⊘kitchen 10am-10pm, bar 10am-midnight; ☎) This hipster organic food bar hits the sweet spot, whether for a smoothie to kickstart your day (try spinach, ginger, yuzu and almond milk), a cocktail or a full-blown meal. Lunch on lavishly topped toasts, sandwiches, salads and burgers (lamb, fish or seaweed). Dinner (from 5.30pm) also features world-fusion bowls bursting with raw fish, nuts, Chinese cabbage and all sorts.

De Walvis   SEAFOOD €€
(www.walvis.org; Groene Strand 1, West-Terschelling; mains €15-25; ⊘10.30am-8.30pm Thu-Tue, bar 10am-11pm Feb-Dec) At the foot of the western dunes is the Whale, a low-lying wooden beach pavilion on a grassy dune with vast terrace overlooking the shifting panorama of the Waddenzee. Apart from the catch of the day, the kitchen cooks up a hearty bouillabaisse (fish stew) and French Limousin beef. Between meals, order the cranberry tart with whipped cream.

★ **Restaurant 't Golfje**   DUTCH €€€
(☑0562-448 105, 06 2060 8796; www.restaurant-tgolfje.nl; Heereweg 22a, Midsland; 4- to 7-course menus €42.50-62.50; ⊘6-9pm Wed-Sun, closed 2 weeks Jul) Terschelling born-and-bred chef extraordinaire Helga Stobbe woos gourmets at her small cottage restaurant on the northern fringe of Midsland village with a succession of small courses, featuring local fish, shellfish and unexpected combos inspired by her travels. Fantastic wine pairings are suggested for each course: pick the number of courses, remembering multicourse menus don't include cheese/dessert (€11/8.50).

De Ouwe Smitte   COFFEE
(☑ 0562-448 069; www.deouwesmidte.nl; Oosterburen 37, Midsland; ⊘10am-5pm Mon-Sat) Thanks to the Dutch love for serious coffee, the island has its very own bean roaster with a tantalising cafe, tearoom and boutique on Midsland's main street. Choose from French press, cold drip, filter, espresso and a ravishing choice of flavoured cappuccinos and lattes: the Black Pearl with raw chocolate and chilli pepper is sensational.

Specialist teas, artisan Dutch chocolate, homemade cranberry fudge, and scones with whipped cream are among the irresistible sweet treats served.

❶ Information

Tourist Office (VVV; ☑ 0562-443 000; www. vvvterschelling.nl/en; Willem Barentszkade 19a, West-Terschelling; ⊘9.30am-4pm Mon-Fri, 10am-3pm Sat, 11am-2pm Sun May-Sep, shorter hours rest of year)

❶ Getting There & Away

Rederij Doeksen (p218) runs regular ferries from Harlingen to Terschelling (adult/child return €26.66/13.26, bicycle €15), a two-hour journey. There are generally three departures daily, with up to five on summer weekends. A fast service (adult/child return €39.36/26.42) takes 45 minutes and usually goes three times daily.

In summer, there are two fast ferries per day to nearby Vlieland (30 minutes) midweek. Check current schedules online.

Keep an eye out for good-value seasonal deals: in 2018 a day ticket to either island cost €25, or €29 including all-day bike rental or bus travel.

❶ Getting Around

Hourly buses (€2) run the length of the main road. On the main street in West-Terschelling, **Rijwielverhuur Tijs Knop** (☑ 0562-442 052; www.tijsknop.nl; Torenstraat 10/12, West-Ter-schelling; 3-/7-speed bike per day €6.50/8.50; ☺ 9am-6pm) is one of several bike-rental outlets on the island. It also transports your luggage to your accommodation.

Ameland

☑ 0519 / POP 3591

Of the Frisian Island quartet, Ameland strikes the best balance. Its four peaceful villages – Buren, Nes, Ballum and Hollum – are less developed than those on Terschelling, but they provide enough social structure for most visitors. Although Mother Nature doesn't rule the roost as on Schiermonnikoog or Vlieland, it still retains generous swaths of untouched natural splendour. All in all, Ameland is an idyll that's just right.

Just 8km from the Frisian mainland, Ameland is a quick ferry ride, and some even choose to walk it (p234), but only when accompanied by a trained guide. Its history may be the strangest of the four isles: it was an independent 'lordship' for almost three centuries until the ruling family died off in 1708. It is actually comprised of three islands that were fused together in the 19th century.

◉ Sights & Activities

Of the villages, the 18th-century former whaling port of Nes is the busiest and cut-est, its streets lined with tidy brick houses. Hollum, the most western village, has wind-swept dunes within an easy walk, and is in sight of a famous red-and-white lighthouse with expansive views.

The eastern third of the island is given over to a combination of wetlands and dunes, with not a settlement in sight.

Just 25km from end to end, Ameland is easily tackled by pedal power. Bicycle paths cover the entire island and include a 27km

packed sand track that runs almost the full length of the northern shore just south of protective sand dunes.

Lighthouse   LIGHTHOUSE
(Oranjeweg 57, Hollum; adult/child €5/3.75; ☺ 1-5pm Mon, 10am-5pm Tue, 10am-5pm & 7-9pm Wed-Sun Mar-Oct, shorter hours rest of year) Ameland's iconic red-and-white banded lighthouse stands 55m tall on the island's west side. The only lighthouse in the island chain that is open to the public, the cast-iron structure can be climbed (236 steps) for expansive views over the entire island and across the Waddenzee. Exhibits on the way up explain the history of the lighthouse, and you can listen to digital stories by lighthouse keepers.

To get here from the village of Hollum (1km east), cycle west along the Badweg, then follow the undulating sandy path through the Hollumerbosch, a pine forest.

Natuurcentrum Ameland   MUSEUM
(Ameland Nature Centre; ☑ 0519-542 737; www.amelandermusea.eu; Strandweg 38, Nes; adult/child €6.75/4.75; ☺ 10am-5pm Mon-Fri, 11am-5pm Sat & Sun Mar-Nov, shorter hours rest of year) Just north of Nes village, this centre features an excellent seaquarium in which a number of North Sea species swim around, including manta rays, barracuda and eels. Get shore-to-shore views from the adjacent observation tower and take a 2.2km nature loop walk to Nesserbos forest. The centre offers tours, including *wadlopen*, beach walks and net-fishing excursions.

🛏 Sleeping

Camping Middelpôlle   CAMPGROUND €
(☑ 06 2386 8480; Het Westerpad 3, Nes; camp site €6.50, plus adult/child €5/3.50; ☺ Apr-Sep) Peace, perfect peace, between sand dunes and forest is the lure of this nature-friendly camp site, with 40 tent pitches and dozens of wild rabbits roaming about on grassy knolls between trees. There is no electricity and the beach is an easy 15-minute walk away. Campers who like their creature comforts can rent one of three fully equipped Quonset tents with kitchen.

Sier aan Zee   HOSTEL €
(☑ 0519-555 353; http://sieraanzee.nl; Oranjeweg 59, Hollum; s/d/tr/q €55/65/82.50/110; 🛜) Peter and Ruth are the creatives behind this buzzing hostel in Hollum, built as a convalescent home for German soldiers during WWII. The atmosphere is decidedly summer camp,

with families making the most of the basic but well-kept rooms, organised children's activities and undulating sand dunes on the doorstep. Find the hostel 200m past the lighthouse; bus 130 stops here.

Hotel De Jong HOTEL **€**
(☎0519-542 016; www.hoteldejong.nl; Reeweg 29, Nes; s/d €74.20/89; 🛜) Standing at Ameland's crossroads, this friendly inn is buzzing in high season, when you can lounge at a terrace table and observe the comings and goings from the ferry pier, 1km south. Its 12 rooms mix crisp white walls and bed linens with pale-wood parquet and the odd seascape painting. Seafood stew and herbed eel are tasty hits in the cafe.

⭐**Hotel Nobel** DESIGN HOTEL **€€**
(☎0519-554 157; www.hotelnobel.nl; Gerrit Kosterweg 16, Ballum; d from €160; ❋ @ 🛜) The perfect designer sleeping-eating hybrid, luxurious Hotel Nobel sports 19 chic rooms with a dazzling white palette and fashion-photography wall murals in a converted farmhouse. Two romantic suites languish in their very own deconsecrated, red-brick chapel in the leafy green grounds, and the adjoining brown cafe is the very spot where Ameland's famous Nobeltje liqueur was created in 1902.

🍴 Eating & Drinking

⭐**Sunset** BAR
(☎06 2070 3648 0519-554 280; www.thesunset. nl; Oranjeweg 61, Hollum; ⊙10am-11pm Mon, Tue, Thu & Fri, 9am-11pm Wed, noon-11pm Sat & Sun) Not far from the picture-book lighthouse (p222) in Hollum is this sizzling beach club on the sand. Lounge here with islanders in the know over a G&T and cocktail and the finest sunset views on the island. Paired with a plate of freshly shucked oysters, you can't go wrong.

All-day dining is equally fabulous. The kitchen cooks up creative fish, pulled-pork and felafel sandwiches (€12) alongside soups, toasties and burgers for lunch. Come dusk, tuck into spicy tuna sushi, smoked mackerel with green-tea noodles or simply the catch of the day fresh from the North Sea.

ℹ️ Information

The island's main **tourist office** (VVV; ☎0519-546 546; www.vvvameland.nl; Bureweg 2, Nes; ⊙9am-5pm Mon-Fri, 10am-3.30pm Sat) is in Nes, a seven-minute walk or one bus stop from the ferry terminal.

ℹ️ Getting There & Away

Wagenborg (☎0900 9238, from abroad 088-103 10 00; www.wpd.nl) operates ferries between Nes and the large ferry port at Holwerd on the mainland. The ferries run almost every two hours (adult/child return €15.10/8.35, car with driver/bicycle €22.90/9.50, 45 minutes) all year from 9am to 8pm, and hourly on Friday and Saturday from July to August.

To reach the Holwerd ferry terminal from Leeuwarden, take Arriva bus 66 (€5, 40 minutes, hourly). By bike, it's 26km via the LF3b.

Taxis and a small network of public buses that serve the island's four towns meet the ferries. Single bus tickets cost €1.50/2 with/without an OV-chipkaart and a day pass allowing unlimited bus travel is €5. **Kiewiet Fietsverhuur** (☎0519-542 130; www.fietsenopameland.nl; Oude Steiger 1, Nes; 3-/7-gear bike per day €8/9; ⊙8am-7pm Mon-Thu, 9am-9pm Fri, 8.30am-7pm Sat & Sun), with a branch just up from the ferry dock, rents Gazelle seven-speed bikes.

Schiermonnikoog

☎0519 / POP 947

The smallest, most serene of the Frisian Islands, Schiermonnikoog is the place to get away from it all. The sheer isolation as you explore its modest 16km length, 4km width and 18km of beaches can be intoxicating – but then, the entire island bar its only town is protected as a national park. Its name means 'grey monk island', a reference to the 15th-century clerics who once lived here.

⊙ Sights & Activities

Schiermonnikoog is great for cycling and is also a popular destination for *wadlopers* ('mud-walkers') from the mainland. By night the island, almost entirely free of light pollution, rewards stargazers with stunning celestial vistas.

Schiermonnikoog National Park NATIONAL PARK
(☎0519-531 641; www.np-schiermonnikoog.nl; Torenstreek 20; ⊙visitor centre 10am-noon & 1.30-5pm Mon-Sat, 1.30-5pm Sun) The entire island, except for its single town and surrounding *polder*, was designated the Netherlands' first national park in 1989. It's easy to lose yourself exploring its 54 sq km of beaches, dunes, salt marshes and woods. Those who desire a bit more organisation to their wanderings can join a variety of tours; for information and bookings pop into the Bezoekerscentrum Schiermonnikoog (park visitor

FRIESLAND (FRYSLÂN) SCHIERMONNIKOOG

OFF THE BEATEN TRACK

LAUWERSMEER: SHALLOWS & SEALS

Nature lovers are in paradise in tiny Lauwersmeer National Park (☑ 06 5123 0923; www.np-lauwersmeer.nl/doen-zien/activiteitencentrum; De Rug 1, Lauwersoog; ⊙ visitor centre 11am-5pm Tue-Sun) which protects the man-made watery shallows of Lauwersmeer, split between Friesland and the neighbouring province of Groningen. The lake was formed in 1969 when the dyke between the Lauwerszee, formed by a flood in 1280, and the Waddenzee was closed. Keen-eyed ornithologists can spot the rare sea eagle, white-tailed eagle and dozens of migratory birds in the shallows, while wild geese and Konik horses inhabit the surrounding grasslands.

Fishing remains the traditional industry in Zoutkamp, a tiny fishing village where fishers' houses are painted a rainbow of colours and eels are still smoked in its quay-side *rokerij* (eel smokehouse). From the port village of Lauwersoog, ferries sail to the national-park island of Schiermonnikoog. A 1.5km-long nature trail at the visitor centre here provides a good introduction to the park; book guided nature walks and birdwatching expeditions with a park ranger.

In 2020 Pieterburen Seal Sanctuary opened in Lauwersoog. Designed by Danish architect Dorte Mandrup, the contemporary glass building is constructed on stilts above the water and features exhibitions on the Waddenzee ecosystem, a research centre, a cafe and rooftop seal pools where the once-endemic grey seal can be observed.

centre), located in an old power station at the foot of the white lighthouse in town.

To survey the surroundings, head for the Wassermann, the remains of a German bunker atop high wooded dunes north of town. For birders, bitterns may be spotted among the reeds of the Westerplas, a lake just west of town, while salt marshes are populated by herring gulls, terns and spoonbills.

🛏 Sleeping & Eating

Schiermonnikoog has few hotels or B&Bs, but plenty of bungalows and apartments. Camping is not allowed in the national park. The tourist office has a list of farmstays, sometimes with rooms to rent, where you can pitch your tent, help feed the calves and feast on fresh farm milk and yoghurt for breakfast.

Hotel van der Werff   HOTEL €€
(☑ 0519-531 306; www.hotelvanderwerff.nl; Reeweg 2; s/d/tr €57.50/115/172.50; 🛜) Parts of this historic grand hotel date back 200 years. Its 57 modern, comfortable rooms have dark period furniture, Bordeaux carpets and the odd vintage print on the wall. Some rooms have balcony with view, and suites are well suited to families. The hotel's cafe terrace is *the* spot for a lazy breakfast, and its own vintage bus meets ferries.

Ambrosijn   DUTCH €€€
(☑ 0519-720 261; www.ambrosijn.nl; Langestreek 13; 3- to 6-course menus €32.50-65, mains €26.50; ⊙ noon-4.30pm & 5.30-8.30pm Mon-Sat) Named after the wild apples that grow on Schier-

monnikoog, Ambrosijn ('Ambrosia') is an ode to seasonal island produce, lovingly crafted into exquisite dishes by owner/chef Co Huijbrechts. Gourmets should order the tasting menu, a succession of surprise dishes. No meal is complete without a scoop of Ambrosijn's Friesian-milk ice cream – elderflower, buckthorn or island honey depending on the month.

The restaurant has three luxurious suites above and also has its own ice-cream parlour (open April to October).

❶ Information

The **tourist office** (☑ 0519-531 233; www. vvvschiermonnikoog.nl; Reeweg 5; ⊙ 9.30am-5pm Mon-Sat) is in the middle of town, and a grocery store, ATM, pharmacy, bicycle-repair shop and other services are all in a tight knot in town.

❶ Getting There & Away

Wagenborg (☑ 0900 9238; www.wpd.nl; adult/child return €15.30/8.55, bicycle €9.50) runs large ferries between Schiermonnikoog and the port of Lauwersoog in Groningen province. Ferries make the 45-minute voyage up to five times daily between 6.30am and 6.30pm. Hotel and public buses (return €3.50) meet all incoming ferries at the port, 3km from the town of Schiermonnikoog. There is a bicycle-rental facility at the port. Non-residents are not allowed to bring cars onto the island.

Bus 50 makes the one-hour run to Lauwersoog almost hourly from Leeuwarden (€8). From Groningen, bus 163 takes about the same time to reach the ferry port.

Northeastern Netherlands

Best Places to Eat

➡ Bistro Vive La Vie (p232)

➡ 't Zielhoes (p235)

➡ Roezemoes (p231)

➡ Bistro 't Gerecht (p232)

➡ Wadapartja (p232)

➡ Villa Tapas (p238)

Best Places to Stay

➡ Hotel Miss Blanche (p230)

➡ The Student Hotel (p230)

➡ Prinsenhof Groningen (p231)

Why Go?

Few travellers venture to this far corner of the Netherlands, but those who don't go are missing out on the country's rural heart, a place where traditions are kept alive and prehistoric relics dot the landscape. The Netherlands' best-known walking trail, the Pieterspad, legs it from here, from Pieterburen 490km south to Maastricht.

Provincial capital Groningen is a buzzing, youthful city. Museums, restaurants, bars, theatres, canals, festivals – it's the north's cultural point of reference and a fine base for exploring.

On the coast, try the strangely intriguing pastime of *wadlopen* (mudflat-walking). Or head to Bourtange, on the eastern border with Germany; its hefty defences are just as forbidding now as they were in the 16th century. South, Drenthe is a great garden with shifting tableaus of sheep pastures, stream-cut peat bogs, marshlands and fascinating *hunebedden* (neolithic burial chambers), often accessible only by bike or on foot.

When to Go

➡ Summer is best. The long days provide a surfeit of light that fades ever so slowly into dusk, cafe terraces overflow with high spirits well into the night, and beach frolickers hit the sand on Groningen's urban riverside beach.

➡ August is festival month in the happening city of Groningen: think arts, music and fireworks on 28 August to celebrate the defeat of invading troops led by the Bishop of Munster in 1672.

➡ May to October is the season for mudflat-walking with a *wadlopen* guide along the Wadden coast.

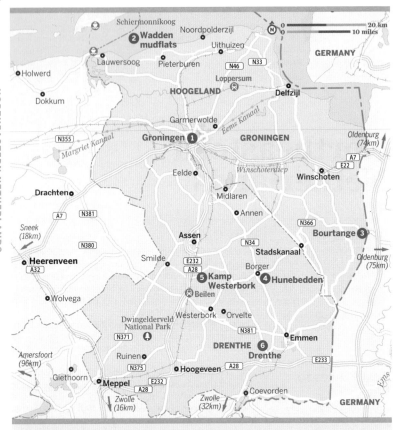

Northeastern Netherlands Highlights

1 Groningen (right)
Experiencing northern culture at its best in this vibrant student city packed with interesting museums, elegant churches, atmospheric cafes and edgy bars.

2 Hoogeland (p235)
Donning a pair of welly boots and stomping out a muddy trail across the Wadden Sea's tidal mudflats

with an experienced guide; night walks are particularly magical.

3 Bourtange (p236)
Walking the 16th-century fortified ramparts of this remote fortress town.

4 Hunebedden (p237)
Wondering at the mighty prehistoric stone dolmens scattered like pieces of Lego across the rural landscape.

5 Kamp Westerbork
(p237) Pondering the traumatic past of WWII in a Nazi transit camp.

6 Drenthe (p236)
Grabbing two wheels and getting lost in the rural byways, peat fields, mystical dolmen formations and remote national parks busting with fauna and flora in this largely forgotten part of the Netherlands.

GRONINGEN PROVINCE

Tucked away in the country's far northeastern corner, this overtly agricultural province is a treasure trove of pleasant surprises. At its heart lies capital, Groningen, a handsome 14th-century Hanseatic city that has

lost none of its charm over the centuries and turns heads today with its prestigious university, contemporary food scene, edgy nightlife and innovative pulse.

To the south, right by the country's border with Germany, stands one of the

Netherlands' best-preserved fortifications. North of Groningen is Menkemaborg, an authentic manor house, beyond which flat countryside spills out towards the Wadden Sea. The mudflats in end-of-the-earth Hoogeland provide mountains of exciting thrills and spills for *wadlopers* (mudflat hikers) in welly boots who flock here to pick their way across at low tide.

Groningen

📞 050 / POP 202,567

Looking at a map of the Netherlands, Groningen seems a long way from anywhere – but this vibrant, youthful city is among the country's most progressive urban metropolises, with a 40,000-strong student population injecting bags of creative zest into its buzzing cafe culture, hedonistic nightlife and rampant cultural scene.

Groningen was already an independent city-state and key trading centre by the late Middle Ages; the iconic Martinitoren stands as a reminder of this Golden Age, miraculously surviving fierce fighting here late in WWII before Groningen's liberation on 17 April 1945. Groningen's highly regarded university dates to 1614, and its refreshingly car-free centre is a result of zealous town planning in the 1970s that saw the city controversially get rid of motorised traffic from its old town. Dozens of Dutch cities followed suit, but it is pioneering Groningen that remains one of the country's most brilliant cycling cities.

◉ Sights

The old centre is compact and entirely ringed by canals. Just southwest of the main Grote Markt is Vismarkt, a more intimate and attractive square. To the north, in the rapidly upcoming Ebbingekwartier neighbourhood, lies the city beach.

★ **Groninger Museum**   MUSEUM
(📞050-366 65 55; www.groningermuseum.nl; Museumeiland 1; adult/child €15/free; ⊙10am-5pm Tue-Sun) Those arriving by train can't help but notice the Groninger Museum. Occupying three islands in the ring canal in front of the station, the museum is, at the very least, a striking structure that will draw an opinion from any observer. Within is a scintillating mix of international artworks from throughout the ages.

The wildly eclectic architecture was the brainchild of Alessandro Mendini, who invited three of his fellow architects to each tackle a section. This explains why, to many, the museum has little consistency and appears thrown together on a whim. Inside, things are quite different: bright, pastel colours add life to the exhibition halls, and natural light seeps in from all angles.

The Mendini Pavilion, a picture of deconstruction, holds temporary exhibitions; like the curatorial direction, they are a wonderfully eccentric mix.

Martinikerk   CHURCH
(📞050-311 12 77; www.martinikerk.nl; Martinikerkhof 3; ⊙11am-5pm Mon-Sat May-Sep, also 2-5pm Sun Jul & Aug) **FREE** This huge 16th-century church commands the northeast corner of Grote Markt. The iconic church and its tower, Martinitoren (p229), are among the few remnants of the Golden Age to survive fierce fighting late in WWII before Groningen's liberation. The large square on which it stands, framed with historic houses, was used until 1837 as a graveyard.

★ **Noordelijk Scheepvaartmuseum**   MUSEUM
(Northern Shipping Museum; 📞050-312 22 02; www.noordelijkscheepvaartmuseum.nl; Brugstraat 24-26; adult/child €7.50/4; ⊙10am-5pm Tue-Sat, 1-5pm Sun) This engaging tour of the lives of seamen and their ships unfolds through the set of buildings that once made up a 16th-century distillery. Going through the labyrinth of 18 rooms is a navigational feat in itself. Highlights include an intricately carved replica of the church at Paramaribo – the capital of former Dutch colony Suriname – in a bottle (Room 3) and detailed models demonstrating just how the many local shipyards operated throughout the centuries (Room 8).

Grote Markt   SQUARE
The main square holds some gems, of which the Town Hall (Stadhuis; Grote Markt), dating from 1810, is the most dazzling. The string of cafes along the south side are perpetually buzzing. A 1950s melange that sprang up on the east side following wartime devastation opened in 2019 as the aptly named Nieuwe Markt (New Market).

★ **Nieuwe Markt**   SQUARE
This dynamic city's most ambitious redevelopment project to date, the gleaming 'New

Groningen

28

17

Boterdiep

18

Noorderbinnensingel

Noorder
plantsoen

26

Ebbingebrug

Spilsluizen NZ

Turfsingel

Maagdenbrug

Turfsingel

Kattenhage

Hofstr

9

Kijk in 't Jatbrug

Lopendediep NZ

Lopendediep ZZ

Boteringebrug

Spilsluizen ZZ

Hardewikerstr

12

Oude Ebbingestr

Kleine
Butjesstr

Jacobijner-

St Walburgstr

16

Noorderhaven NZ

Muurstr

Oude Boteringestr

Butjesstr

str

Martinikerkhof

Werfstr

Noorderhaven

Noorderhaven ZZ

Hoekstr

Visserstr

Oude Kijk in 't Jatstr

19

15

Weeshuisstr

Kreupelstr

8   7

Visserbrug

Rechten en
Letteren

De Laan

Uurwerkersgang

Kleine
Kromme
Elleboog

30

4

Broerstr

Stalstr

Poststr

Grote Markt

5

2

Nieuwe
Markt

Westerbinnensingel

Hoge der A

Lage der A

Turftorenstr

27

35

Grote
Kromme
Elleboog

Zwanestr

Guldenstr

10   6

Tussen Beide
Markten

Herestr

32

22

Oosterstr

Gelkingestr

Westersingel

13

Lutkenieuwstr

A-Kerkstr

Stoeldraaiersstr

Vismarkt

Citycamp
Stadspark
(2.2km)

A-Brug

25

Brugstr

A-Kerkhof NZ

Korenbeurs

Pelsterstr

A-Str

Bakkers Rijge

Noordelijk
Scheepvaartmuseum

Schuitemakersstr

Reitemakersrijge

Munnekeholm

Torenstr

A-Kerkhof ZZ

21

Schoolholm

34

Folkingestr

Haddingestr

Klein
Pelsterstr

Caroliweg

Herestr

24

Nieuwstad

Eeldersingel

Museumbrug

Sluiskade

Ganzevoortsingel

Praediniussingel

Stationsstr

Gedempte Zuiderdiep

Coehoorn

Ubbo Emmiussingel

Ruiter Str

Herepl

Zuiderhaven

Emmapl

Ubbo Emmiussingel

Emmasingel

Emmabrug

Ubbo Emmiussingel

1

Groninger
Museum

Stationsweg

11

Train Station

Market' square is slated to become an A-lister hub for alfresco lounging when it finally takes shape in 2019. Its eastern side will be hemmed by the pyramidical hulk of the Forum Cultural Centre (p231), and several cafe terraces, including trendy Het Concerthuis (p233), will fringe its southern side.

For foodies, the main lure will be Merck (old Dutch for 'market'), a state-of-the-art food hall with 24 kitchen stalls, a coffee roastery, rooftop terrace and distillery by cocktail king Mr Mofongo (p232). In 2020 luxury hotel, four-star WestCord Market Hotel Groningen, opened on the square, complete with bakery, bar, restaurant and terrace.

Martinitoren
TOWER

(adult/child €3/2; ⏱ 11am-5pm Mon-Sat Apr-Oct, also 11am-4pm Sun Jul & Aug, noon-4pm Mon-Sat Nov-Mar) A climb up 251 steep and spiralling stone steps to the summit of this elegant, 96m-tall medieval tower (1482) rewards with grand views – and worrisome proximity to its giant bells, which ring every 15 minutes most days. Buy admission tokens at the tourist office (p234) across the street.

From the top terrace, another 54 steps wind up to the carillonneur's cabin where, twice a week, at noon on Tuesday and 11am on Saturday, the city's carillonneur (a professor at the university) performs a mesmerising one-hour concert. The current carillon was cast in 1662–63 and comprises 52 bells. Year-round, watch for occasional concerts on public holidays and during festivals.

Academiegebouw
UNIVERSITY

(Academy Building; Broerstraat 5) The stunning, Dutch Renaissance Academiegebouw is the main building of the university, with a breathtaking, richly decorated exterior from 1909.

Prinsentuin
GARDENS

(Prince's Garden; Turfsingel; ⏱ 10am-6pm Apr-Oct, 10am-4.30pm Nov-Mar) **FREE** Take a breather at the serene gardens of Prinsenhof, a 15th-century mansion-turned–luxury hotel with peaceful Renaissance-style gardens fragranced with roses and an abundance of herbs. Don't miss the sundial.

☞ Tours

Canal Tours
BOATING

(☎ 050-312 83 79; www.rondvaartbedrijfkool.nl; Stationsweg 1012; adult/child €12.50/7) Tours of the city's largest canals take approximately

Groningen

Top Experiences
1 Groninger Museum C7
2 Nieuwe Markt D4
3 Noordelijk Scheepvaartmuseum B5

Sights
4 Academiegebouw C3
5 Forum Cultural Centre D3
6 Grote Markt D4
7 Martinikerk D3
8 Martinitoren D3
9 Prinsentuin D2
10 Town Hall D4

Activities, Courses & Tours
11 Canal Tours D7

Sleeping
12 Auberge Corps de Garde C3
13 Hotel Miss Blanche B4
14 Martini Hotel E5
15 NH Hotel de Ville C3
16 Prinsenhof Groningen D3
17 Simplon Jongerenhotel C1
18 The Student Hotel C1

Eating
19 Bistro 't Gerecht C3
20 Bistro Vive La Vie E5
21 Eeterie de Globe B5
22 Gustatio D4
23 Roezemoes E5
24 Wadapartja D5

Drinking & Nightlife
25 Café de Sigaar B5
26 Café de Toeter C2
27 De Pintelier B4
28 Dot D1
29 Het Concerthuis E4
30 Mr Mofongo C3

Entertainment
31 De Oosterpoort F6
32 Grand Theatre D4
33 Vera E5

Shopping
34 Folk Concept Store C5
35 Holtbar B4
36 Kaashandel van der Ley E5

one hour and leave from out front of the train station between one and six times daily, depending on the season.

Sleeping

★ **The Student Hotel** DESIGN HOTEL €
(050-206 91 61; www.thestudenthotel.com; Boterdiep 9; d from €79;) With the slogan 'Everybody should like everybody' printed on its facade, the Student Hotel could not provide a warmer or more playful welcome. Bananas hang from the ceiling in the bright open-plan lobby; deck chairs beg guests to lounge alfresco; and there's a library, table football, patio garden, rooftop pool, communal kitchen, trendy bar called the Pool and laptop-friendly work spaces.

There's a gym and designer VanMoof bike rental too. Find the hotel in the upcoming Ebbinge neighbourhood, north of the old town. Breakfast €14.

Simplon Jongerenhotel HOSTEL €
(050-313 52 21; www.simplonjongerenhotel.nl; Boterdiep 73-2; dm/s/d/tr/q Sun-Wed, €18/36/45/86.50/116, Thu-Sat €20/40/64/90/122;) Housed in an early-20th-century brick structure that served as a cannery, and more famously the Simplon raincoat factory, this is a creatively designed hostel that is affably operated by staff being trained to re-enter the workforce. It also features fine cafe **Eetcafé 73-2** (mains €11) with several toothsome, reasonably priced vegetarian options. Count an extra €5.50 per person for breakfast.

Martini Hotel HOTEL €
(050-312 99 19; www.martinihotel.nl; Gedempte Zuiderdiep 8; s €69-89, d €74-109, tr €104-129, q 109-129;) The city's oldest hotel has been in the business since 1871, with vintage fittings and fixtures to prove it – check out the glass-walled elevator, majestic bar and restaurant **Weeva** cooking up old-world Groningen specialities like feisty *Groningen bloedworst* (black pudding). Rooms feel dated but are excellent value. The lavish breakfast buffet costs an extra €12.50 per person.

★ **Hotel Miss Blanche** BOUTIQUE HOTEL €€
(050-820 09 66; www.hotelmissblanche.nl; Hoge der A 4; d from €109;) Youthful and chic in equal measure, canal-side Miss Blanche is one sassy chick when it comes to stylish sleeping. Each of the 46 suites – scattered across a handful of nearby historic buildings – are individually designed, many with romantic canal view. Decor is quietly contemporary, with eye-catching art works. Some

superior suites and apartments, sleeping up to six, have kitchenette and dining area.

NH Hotel de Ville HOTEL €€

(☎050-318 1222; www.nh-hotels.com/hotel/nh-groningen-hotel-de-ville; Oude Boteringestraat 43-45; d low/high season from €115/212; ✳@🛜) With its stunning part-period, part-contemporary interiors and central location on one of Groningen's trendiest streets, this four-star hotel is always full. A beautiful, breakfast-perfect garden surrounds the red-brick townhouse. Rooms have tea- and coffee-making facilities, and the hotel has a fantastic bar and lounge with fireplace. Bike rental per day €5.

Auberge Corps de Garde HOTEL €€

(☎050-314 54 37; www.corpsdegarde.nl; Oude Boteringestraat 74; s €85, d €145; ✳🛜) Originally the town guard's quarters, the 17th-century building sports carved animal heads above the door. The 19 rooms are a mix of vintage and contemporary styles. 'Historic rooms' feature ancient wooden beams that may delight or imperil, depending on your height.

★ Prinsenhof Groningen HISTORIC HOTEL €€€

(☎050-317 65 50; www.prinsenhof-groningen.nl; Martinikerkhof 23; d from €164; P🛜) A fabulous rebirth of a medieval monastery, 16th-century residence of the Nassau viceroys *(de stadhouders),* military hospital and TV station, this luxurious hotel oozes history from every burnt-red brick. Each of the 34 rooms is different, with some overlooking the romantic Prinsentuin gardens (p229) or imposing Martinitoren (p229). Find the Grand Café within the original chapel (1436), complete with stained glass and huge windows.

✗ Eating

Eetcafés (pubs where you can get a meal) dominate the culinary landscape in Groningen, a reflection perhaps of its budget-minded student body. A colourful array of cafes, bistros and craft-coffee shops line busy eat-street Oude Kijk in 't Jatstraat. A state-of-the-art food hall with 24 kitchen stalls opened on Nieuwe Markt (p227) in 2020.

Eeterie de Globe DUTCH €

(☎050-318 22 26; www.eeteriedeglobe.nl; A-kerkhof ZZ 22; 2-course menus €6.50-9; ⊗noon-3pm & 5-8pm Mon-Fri, 5-8pm Sat; 🍴) Such a deal: soup or appetizer plus a hearty plate of veggies, fish or meat with sides for under €10. No wonder the large, bright dining hall is much patronised by students and other cent-pinchers. The menu changes daily and always includes a vegetarian option; check the website for the week's offerings.

★ Roezemoes DUTCH €€

(☎050-314 88 54; www.eetcafe-roezemoes.nl; Gedempte Zuiderdiep 15; stew €12.50, 3-stew tasting €14.50; ⊗noon-11pm Mon, 11am-11pm Tue, Wed & Sun, 11am-midnight Thu, 11am-2am Fri & Sat) A timeless address since 1996 for traditional Dutch cuisine, this brown cafe cooks up heart-warming *stamppotten* (stews) comprising homemade meatballs, smoked sausage or vegetarian 'meat' ball alongside other ingredients such as tasty kale and bacon or endive with walnuts and cheese. The other house speciality is *Groninger Rijsttafel* – no rice, but plenty of bacon and onions with pickles and apple sauce.

DON'T MISS

THE FORUM

Bombed to smithereens during WWII, the entire zone east of the Grote Markt is undergoing a dramatic renaissance. The eyesore 1950s melange that sprang up on the east side following the wartime devastation has been demolished to make way for the centrepiece Forum (www.groningerforum.nl). Impossible to miss due to its gargantuan trapezoidal form, this 45m-tall contemporary structure with a zigzag hollow section in the middle is clad in the same Wachenzelles dolomite stone as the nearby Martinitoren and has become Groningen's premier cultural centre since it's unveiling at the end of 2019. It houses the tourist office (p234),Storyworld, the city library, auditoriums, five cinemas, exhibit spaces and subterranean car and bike parks. Films are screened beneath the stars on its rooftop terrace, open to anyone who simply wants to scale its 10 storeys and marvel at the terrific city panorama from the top. A cafe on the ground floor sport sa vast pavement terrace on the city's newest square and A-lister people-watching hub, Nieuwe Markt (p227).

WORTH A TRIP

FIGURATIVE ART TRIP

Museum De Buitenplaats (☑050-309 58 18; www.museumdebuitenplaats.nl; Hoofdweg 76, Eelde; adult/child €10/free; ☉11am-5pm Tue-Sun) In Eelde, 5km south of Groningen, this space is devoted to figurative art from around Europe. The main organic structure, which blends into its natural surroundings, features paintings from some of the Netherlands' more progressive 20th-century artists, such as Wout Muller, Henk Helmantel, Herman Gordijn and Matthijs Röling. Fascinating temporary exhibitions complement the permanent collection.

The exquisite gardens present an immaculate kaleidoscope of perfectly clipped yew trees and holly bushes, geometric flowerbeds, ornate rose gardens, apple orchards and climbing vines interspersed with a wonderful collection of sculptures. There is a sun-bathed cafe, and in summer, poetry readings, storytelling and concerts are performed most Sundays on the open-air stage here.

From Groningen, take bus 52 (€4, 28 minutes, every half-hour); otherwise there's a cycle route along the west side of Paterswolder Meer.

Wadapartja INTERNATIONAL €€

(☑06 3903 4837; www.wadapartja.nl; Gedempte Zuiderdiep 39-41; mains lunch €5.50-9.75, dinner €13.95-16.50; ☉9am-6pm Tue, 9am-10pm Wed-Fri, 10am-10pm Sat, 11am-6pm Sun & Mon) *Wadapartja* means 'How very special!' in Groningen – perfectly apt given the funky spirit of this zany curiosity shop–cafe with sun-drenched pavement terrace (in summer customers can sit with their feet in a paddling pool of water). The menu covers all appetites: breakfasts includes Moroccan stew, bacon and eggs, and homemade banana bread dunked in orange-blossom syrup.

Lunch features several vegan and vegetarian options, and a gin-and-tonic cheesecake that is impossible to resist.

Gustatio ITALIAN €€

(☑050-313 64 00; http://gustatiogroningen.nl/; Oosterstraat 3; mains €11-17; ☉noon-9.30pm Tue & Wed, to 10.30pm Thu-Sat, 1-9.30pm Sun & Mon) Creative fresh pasta dishes are the order of the day at this appealing trattoria with vivacious Roman-in-Groningen Valerio Pizzonia running the show. Be it salmon lasagne, blacker-than-coal squid ink gnocchi with peas or artichoke-stuffed ravioli with lamb ragu, everything is deliciously homemade.

For die-hard pasta traditionalists, one page of the menu is dedicated to classic recipes immortalised in stone in the Italian *cucina*.

★ Bistro Vive La Vie BISTRO €€€

(☑050-850 39 70; www.vivelaviegroningen.nl; Oosterstraat 39; 4-/5-/6-/7-course tasting menu €39/46/55/59; ☉6-9.30pm Tue-Sat) Among Groningen's most sophisticated dining choices is this smart little bistro with sharp black facade and old-world beamed ceiling.

Chef Jeroen Sportel works with local seasonal products to create his inventive tasting menus with a distinctly French accent (the name of the restaurant translates as 'Live the Life').

Bistro 't Gerecht BISTRO €€€

(☑050-318 12 22; www.bistrohetgerecht.nl; Oude Boteringestraat 43; mains €24-32, menu €36.50; ☉6-10pm Mon-Sat) Modern European fare is cooked up at this stylish bistro on one of Groningen's most lively streets. Savour creative combos such as mackerel with radish, monkfish in a leek and white-wine sauce or beer tartare spiced with oysters, celeriac, fennel and tarragon. End with fresh mango served with coconut cream, lychee sorbet and biscuit crumble. Reservations recommended.

🍷 Drinking & Nightlife

Groningen's student nightlife centres on Poelestraat and its adjoining streets. If there's a hint of good weather, these places are jam-packed. Away from the crowds, Grote Kromme Elleboog is a quaint, old-world lane with a couple of lovely cafes.

★ Mr Mofongo BAR

(☑050-314 42 66; www.mofongo.nl; Oude Boteringestraat 26; ☉11am-3am) Drinking spaces don't get cooler than Mr Mofongo. Think student-hip cafe with buzzing pavement terrace on the ground floor, and cocktail bar with sensational 'wall' of 56 homemade spirits tapped by a robotic arm, craft distillery, and wine bar on the 1st. Don't miss the traditional *jenever* (Dutch gin) and stunning liqueurs, vodkas and gins made from ginger, thyme, and all sorts.

In the equally hi-tech wine bar, rotating shelves ensure glasses remain dust-free and potted herbs get their fair share of sunlight and water. A robotic arm retrieves bottles from the cellar and even pours out the wine.

The bar is named after an explorer the globetrotting owner (an underwater photographer) met at the Santa Lucia lagoon in Cuba after diving with bull sharks

★ **Café de Sigaar**   CAFE
(☑050-311 23 99; http://cafedesigaar.nl/; Hoge der A 2; ☺noon-9pm Mon, 10am-11pm Tue & Wed, 10am-midnight Thu-Sat, 11am-9pm Sun) With traditional, plum-painted facade overlooking the Hoge der A canal, this stylish cafe is the last word in canal-side chic. Its summertime terrace – one of the few to be truly on the water's edge – gets packed when the sun shines. Tables lounge by trees, near a contemporary bronze sculpture of a frog sprouting out of the stone-paved quayside.

Inside, bespoke stained glass and oil paintings by Groningen artist Olga Wiese (b 1944) create a fashionable bohemian vibe.

★ **Het Concerthuis**   BAR
(☑050-230 42 50; www.hetconcerthuis.nl; Poelestraat 30; ☺10am-3am Fri & Sat, to 1am Sun-Wed, to 2am Thu; 🛜) The hip go-to address at any time, the Concert House is a hybrid cafe, bar, and DJ and live-music space with pavement terrace overlooking one of the city's busiest people-watching squares. Saggy vintage sofas, patterned ginger rugs and recycled-wooden-pallet shelving create an instant distressed look inside, while its Sunday Brakke Brunch ('Hangover Brunch', €13.80) is a hot weekend date.

★ **De Pintelier**   BAR
(☑050-318 51 00; www.depintelier.nl; Kleine Kromme Elleboog 9; ☺3pm-2am Sun-Wed, 3pm-3am Thu-Sat) Step back to the 1920s at this cosy Belgian bar where the selection of beer and *jenever* reads like an encyclopaedia. Its long wooden bar and thicket of candlelit tables are timeless. Catch a breeze in the courtyard, always packed out with students and laptops.

Café de Toeter   CRAFT BEER
(☑050-312 44 99; www.cafedetoeter.nl; Turfsingel 6; ☺7pm-3am Mon & Tue, 4pm-3am Wed, Thu & Sun, 3pm-3am Fri & Sat) A student favourite that never seems to lose its appeal, this vintage bar is known for its fantastic choice of bottled beers (more than 160 types) and malt whisky (choose from a mind-boggling

350 varieties). But the real show-stopper is the craft beer brewed in its very own Rockin 'Ludina brewery, aboard a barge moored in front of the canal-side bar.

☆ **Entertainment**

Vera   LIVE MUSIC
(☑050-313 46 81; www.vera-groningen.nl; Oosterstraat 44) To see the next big rock act, head to this club where four concerts and a movie night are held every week. U2 played to 30-odd people in the early 1980s, and Nirvana later gave a performance to a crowd of about 60 before going supernova. Buy tickets in advance online.

De Oosterpoort   LIVE MUSIC
(☑050-368 03 68; www.de-oosterpoort.nl; Trompsingel 27; 🛜) De Oosterpoort is the place to catch big-name musical acts passing through town. Jazz and classical concerts are the mainstay of its monthly program.

Grand Theatre   PERFORMING ARTS
(☑06 4360 0093; www.grandtheatregroningen.nl; Grote Markt 35) Restored to its original grandeur, this circa 1929 art deco–style venue stages a varied program of classical music, dance and children's theatre.

🔒 **Shopping**

Markets are held on Grote Markt and Vismarkt Tuesday, Friday and Saturday. Chain stores line up along Herestraat; explore Folkingestraat for quirkier options. Galleries and trendy concept stores abound on the west side, especially on Visserstraat and Oude Kijk in 't Jatstraat.

LOCAL KNOWLEDGE

URBAN BEACH PARTY

Yet another trendy hang-out zone confirming Groningen's creative, innovative spirit, Dot (☑050-211 25 14; www.dotgroningen.nl; Vrydemalaan 2; ☺11am-11pm) is a spacious and airy cafe-bar with St-Tropez-style summer terrace next to its sandy city beach in the increasingly happening Ebbingekwartier. There are DJ sets and live concerts in summer and film screenings are held in the 2nd-floor domed cinema. Simply head for the building resembling a giant white ball.

Buy cinema tickets (€6) and tickets for weekend dance parties, Sunday jazz and other events in advance online.

DON'T MISS

EXPLORING THE MUDFLATS

When the tide retreats across the Waddenzee, locals and visitors alike attack the mudflats with abandon, marching, and inevitably sinking, into the sloppy mess. Known as *wadlopen* (mudflat-walking), it's an exercise in minimalism, forcing you to concentrate on the little things as you march towards the featureless horizon.

The mud stretches all the way to the Frisian Islands offshore, and treks over to Schiermonnikoog and Ameland are popular. Because of the treacherous tides, and the fact that some walkers can become muddled and lose their way, *wadlopen* can only be undertaken on a guided tour. Proponents say that it is strenuous but enlivening; the unchanging vista of mud and sky has an almost meditative quality. The call of birds and the chance to focus on little details, such as the small crabs and cockles underfoot, puts one in touch with nature.

The centre for *wadlopen* is in Pieterburen, on the coast north of Groningen, where several groups of trained guides are based, including the following:

Wadloopcentrum (☑0595-528 300; www.wadlopen.com; Hoofdstraat 76, Pieterburen; ☺May-Oct)

Dijkstra Wadlooptochten (☑0595-528 345; www.wadloop-dijkstra.nl; Hoofdstraat 118, Pieterburen; ☺10am-9pm)

Wadlopers.nl (☑0595-528 689; www.wadlopers.nl; Wierhuisterweg 63, Pieterburen)

Guided walks have set rates and take place between May and October. Options range from a short 5km saunter across the mudflats (€11, three hours) to a more challenging 20km hike to Schiermonnikoog (€35, five hours); the latter, with its national park, is the most popular destination. Ticket prices include the ferry ride back from the islands.

It's essential to book around a month in advance. You'll be told what clothes to bring depending on the time of year. Note that you need rubber boots or hi-top sneakers for the trek.

★**Holtbar** CONCEPT STORE
(☑050-851 72 22; www.holtbar.nl; Oude Kijk in 't Jatstraat 20; ☺10am-6pm Mon-Sat) With its organic coffee bar, homemade cakes and impeccable choice of Dutch brands, this small concept store is worth lingering in. Among its designer homewares, jewellery and stationery, look for plant-filled lamps by Spruitje Amsterdam, accessories aimed at globetrotting women by Anna+Nina and handmade jewellery pieces by Riverstones.

Kaashandel van der Ley CHEESE
(☑050-312 93 31; www.kaasvanderleij.nl; Oosterstraat 61-63; ☺9am-6pm Tue-Fri, 9am-5pm Sat) In business since 1934, this cheesemonger sells the finest cheese from the Netherlands – more than 300 types – and around the world. Look for local organic varieties and some of the rare aged numbers that the Dutch never export. Deli items and a large array of olives ensure a perfect picnic.

Local cheeses to taste include some fabulous *boerenkaas* ('farmer cheese') made with unpasteurised milk in small quantities on surrounding farms.

Folk Concept Store ARTS & CRAFTS
(www.folk-store.nl; Folkingestraat 17; ☺1-6pm Mon, 11am-6pm Tue-Fri, 10am-6pm Sat) Browse an enchanting and eclectic mix of clothing, organic snack bars, vanity bags, homewares, jewellery and arts and crafts at this ecofriendly, folk concept store. It's the ingenious creation of two Groningen artists – a carpenter and a jewellery designer – who source all their products locally.

ⓘ Information

Tourist Office (VVV; ☑050-313 97 41; www.toerisme.groningen.nl; Grote Markt 29; ☺noon-6pm Mon, 9.30am-6pm Tue-Fri, 10am-5pm Sat, 10am-4pm Sun)

ⓘ Getting There & Away

The regional bus station is to the right as you exit the train station.

BICYCLE

Pick up wheels at student prices at **Bikes in Groningen** (☑06 2451 5546; www.facebook.com/BikesInGroningen/; Sint Jansstraat 25; ☺11am-6pm Mon-Fri, noon-5pm Sat). In the city centre, watch for patrolling bike stewards in Bordeaux-coloured T-shirts who won't hesitate to remove badly-parked bikes and re-park them nearby in neat strict lines in allowed parking zones.

National bike route **LF9** runs south all the way to Utrecht (about 200km) and beyond. It's been designed to follow what would be the Dutch coastline if there were no dykes. **LF14** heads 48km northwest to Lauwersoog, where you can get the ferry to Schiermonnikoog.

TRAIN

The grand 1896 train station, restored to its original glory, is worth seeing even if you're not catching a train. Lockers can be found on platform 2b and there is a good range of services. Two branch lines by Arriva cover the north of the province.

Sample train fares and schedules:

TO	FARE (€)	TIM (MIN)	FREQUENCY (PER HR)
Leeuwarden	11.17	40	3
Utrecht	25.90	120	1
Zwolle	19	60	4

Hoogeland

North from Groningen to the coast, stoic centuries-old churches, windmills and dykes built to protect the land from rising waters dot the flat countryside known as Hoogeland (literally 'highland'). They are a lasting testament to the pious, hardscrabble people who eked out lives in the muddy, sandy soil here, and much-loved today by intrepid *wadlopers* who come here to hike across the muddy flats and bogs. The tiny village of Pieterburen is the main jumping-off point for guided forays into the mud.

◉ Sights & Activities

Noordpolderzijl   HARBOUR

The tiniest harbour in the Netherlands is 29km north of Groningen and 4.5km northwest of the village of Usquert. Its desolate beauty is striking and is best appreciated from the mudflats. Used until recently by shrimpers from Usquert (the nearest train station), the harbour now serves mainly as a takeoff point for *wadlopers*. To reach it from Usquert, cycle or drive by car between flat fields with huge clouds on the horizon.

The old inn that once served the sluice gate, 't Zielhoes (☎0595-423 058; www.zielhoes.nl; Zijlweg 4, Usquert; sandwiches €3-7.50, mains €10.50-12.50; ⊙10am-6pm Tue-Fri, 10am-7pm Sat & Sun), is still in operation and its *waddentaart*, a rum-infused fruit pie, alone is well worth the trip.

Zeehondencreche
Pieterburen   WILDLIFE RESERVE

(Seal Creche; ☎0595-52 65 26; www.zeehondencentrum.nl; Hoofdstraat 94a, Pieterburen; adult/child €9.50/6; ⊙10am-5pm) Devoted to the rescue and rehabilitation of sick and injured seals, this centre houses 20 to 30 sea mammals, which can be seen lounging and swimming in various pools. The centre also leads seal-watching cruises on the Waddenzee, departing from Lauwersoog, and is the starting point for guided mudflat-walking hikes. Check schedules and make reservations on the website for both.

FRACKING OUT

After a farmer discovered natural gas deposits near the town of Slochteren in 1959, Groningen province began major drilling, fuelling the country's growth. But the rapid extraction of this mineral from what is Europe's largest natural gas field (and the world's 10th largest) has, over the years, triggered a series of small earthquakes around the village of Loppersum. Protests in Groningen by an anti-fracking movement, formed by residents angry about the damage inflicted to their homes and public buildings, finally prompted the government to reduce drilling in 2014 (from a peak of 54 billion cubic metres in 2013) and pay compensation totalling €1.2 billion over a period of five years to locals affected. In 2016 gas extraction was limited further still from 27 to 24 billion cubic metres a year.

A major quake in January 2018 – measuring 3.4 on the Richter scale, with its epicentre in the village of Zeerijp near Loppersum but felt as far as Groningen city – has hopefully resolved the matter once and for all. The government confirmed that it will aim to reduce gas production at the Groningen field by 12 billion cubic metres a year, with the hope of ending drilling completely by 2022. Currently some 40% of the country's energy comes from gas.

Back in the 1970s, seeing how pollution and tourism were taking their toll on the local seal colonies, Lenie 't Hart, a resident of the small coastal town of Pieterburen, began caring for the creatures in her backyard. From this small start arose this centre, which has released hundreds of seals back into the wild since then.

Menkemaborg   HISTORIC BUILDING

(☑0595-431 970; www.menkemaborg.nl; Menkemaweg 2, Uithuizen; adult/child €7.50/3.50; ☺10am-5pm Tue-Sun Mar-Sep, to 4pm Oct-Dec) Some 25km northeast of Groningen, in the town of Uithuizen, is one of the Netherlands' most authentic manor houses. Originally a fortified castle dating from the 14th century, Menkemaborg received its present gentrified appearance – a moated estate of three houses surrounded by lavishly landscaped gardens – early in the 18th century, and it has barely been altered since. Inside, the rooms retain all the pomp and ceremony of 18th-century aristocratic life, complete with carved-oak mantelpieces, stately beds and fine china.

The gardens surrounding the mansion have been painstakingly restored to their symmetrical design of 1705 and replanted with herbs and flowers from the original plans.

❶ Getting There & Away

This remote coastal region is best accessed by car or bicycle, with bike route **LF10** passing right through Menkemaborg.

By train from Groningen, you can get as far as Usquert (€6.60, 30 minutes) or Loppersum (€6.60, 25 minutes). To get to Pieterburen, 12km west of Usquert, take a train from Groningen to Winsum (€3.75, 15 minutes), then bus 68 (20 minutes).

Bourtange

☑0599 / POP 430

The reconstructed fortress of Bourtange holds an isolated spot in the extreme southeast of the province, 7km east of the sleepy community of Vlagtwedde. Remote as it is, the surrounding countryside and wetlands are worth exploring and are ideal for tackling by bike or canoe.

◉ Sights & Activities

Bourtange Fortress   FORTRESS

(☑0599-354 600; www.bourtange.nl; Willem Lodewijkstraat 33; adult/child/family €8.50/4.50/22; ☺9.15am-5pm Mon-Fri, 10am-5pm Sat & Sun Apr-Oct, 11am-4pm Sat & Sun Feb-Mar & Nov-Dec) One of the best-preserved fortifications in the country stands at tiny Bourtange near the German border. With its flooded moats, solid defences and quaint houses protected from all sides, it is a sight to behold, taking you back to a time when rogue armies wandered the land and villagers built walls to keep them at bay.

De Sikkepit   CANOEING

(☑0599-354 748; www.sikkepit.nl; Bisschopsweg 15; per hr 1-/2-/3-person canoe €8/12.50/15.50, rowing/electric boat €13/17.50; ☺Apr-Nov) To view Bourtange from a different perspective, rent a canoe, rowing boat or electric 'whisper boat' from De Sikkepit on the Fortress Farm to paddle, punt or cruise along the fortress canals and Natte Horizon, a lake south of the fortress town. Ask for a map marked up with various itineraries before setting off.

❶ Getting There & Away

From Groningen, 60km west, the trip by train and bus takes about two hours and costs €11.40. Catch a train east to Winschoten, then bus 14 south to Vlagtwedde, then bus 11 for Bourtange. Check schedules on transport info website www.9292.nl.

If touring by bike, you can combine Bourtange with visits to the *hunebedden* in Drenthe, some 40km southwest, for a multiday ride.

DRENTHE PROVINCE

If ever there was a forgotten corner of the Netherlands, this is it. With no sea access or major city to call its own (postwar project Emmen is the largest), Drenthe is as Vincent van Gogh described in 1883: "Here is peace." His paintings of the peat collectors in the province's southeast bear him out.

Peace is exactly why this mostly rural region deserves some of your time. There's a growing collection of national parks, plus you get to explore the mysterious *hunebedden* (dolmens), dotted liberally along the Hondsrug, an elevated fringe along the province's eastern portion.

Assen

☑0592 / POP 67,600

As pretty as a picture with its mellow, canalside cycling paths and grandiose art museum, small-town Assen is the place to take

OFF THE BEATEN TRACK

TRACKING DOWN PREHISTORY

People have been enjoying the quiet in Drenthe since as early as 3000 BC, when prehistoric tribes lived here amid the bogs and peat. These early residents began cultivating the land and created what is arguably the most interesting aspect of Drenthe today, the *hunebedden*.

Hunebedden, which predate Stonehenge, are prehistoric burial chambers constructed with boulders, some of which weigh up to 25,000kg. It is thought the stones arrived in the Netherlands via glaciers from Sweden some 200,000 years ago. Little is known about the builders of the *hunebedden*, who buried their dead along with their personal items and tools, under the monolithic stones. Fifty-two of these impressive groupings of sombre grey stones can be seen in Drenthe and two in Groningen.

The impressive Hunebedden Centrum (☑0599-23 63 74; www.hunebedcentrum.nl; Bronnegerstraat 12, Borger; adult/child €9.50/5.25; ⊙10am-5pm Mon-Fri, 11am-5pm Sat & Sun) is the logical place to start a tour. It's in Borger, a little town 17km northwest of Emmen. The website www.hunebedden.nl is also a good source of info.

The centre has many displays relating to the stones as well as excavated artefacts, and the largest *hunebed* is located just outside its doors. Most are clumped around the villages of Klijndijk, Odoorn, Annen and Midlaren, which are strung out along the N34, a picturesque road linking Emmen and Groningen.

It's best to explore the *hunebedden* with your own transport; pick up a map and one of several themed cycling itineraries (6km to 53km) from the Hunebedden Centrum and look out for the pictograph signs. Borger is 25km southeast of Assen on national bike route LF14.

your foot off the pedal and slow right down. It also serves as an excellent base for rural explorations of the nearby national parks, *hunebedden* and Kamp Westerbork. Once a year in June hundreds of leather-clad bikers incongruously descend upon the sleepy town during the annual TT motorbike fest.

Assen tourist office is an excellent source of cycling and hiking maps of the region and info on the national parks.

◉ Sights

Drents Museum MUSEUM
(☑0592-377 773; www.drentsmuseum.nl; Brink 1; adult/child €15/free, garden free; ⊙11am-5pm Tue-Sun, garden 11am-5pm Apr-Oct, to 4pm Nov-Mar) Painting and applied arts from the late 19th century and early 20th century, and contemporary realism, are the main focus of the art collection at the town museum, at home in a magnificent red-brick mansion built in 1882 for the town governor. Enter via the 18th-century coachhouse, looking up to admire the rooftop statue of a heroic Drenthe warrior, clad in animal skin and wielding a spear and hammer. Temporary exhibitions fill the museum's dazzling-white contemporary wing.

Kamp Westerbork HISTORIC SITE
(☑0593-59 26 00; www.kampwesterbork.nl; Oosthalen 8, Hooghalen; adult/child €8.75/4; ⊙10am-

5pm Mon-Fri, 11am-5pm Sat & Sun Feb-Dec) Of the 107,000 Jews living in the Netherlands before WWII, all but 5000 were deported by the Nazis to concentration and death camps in central and eastern Europe. Their fateful journey began at Kamp Westerbork, a Nazi transit camp in a forest 10km south of Assen, near Hooghalen village. An excellent on-site museum traces the history of the holocaust in the Netherlands, and photo blow-ups mark the locations of Nazi-era features such as the punishment building and workshops where internees worked as virtual slaves.

Kamp Westerbork, ironically, was built by the Dutch government in 1939 to house German Jews fleeing the Nazis. From 1942 the Germans used it as a transit point for those being sent to death camps, including Anne Frank.

The camp itself is a 2km walk through a forest from the museum (or a €2 bus ride). There is little to see here today: after the war the Dutch government used the barracks for South Moluccan refugees, and then had them demolished. Listening to voice recordings of inmates recounting life at the camp (taken from recovered diaries), it is not hard to imagine the distress and horror of the detainees.

Of several monuments standing here, perhaps the most moving is at the roll-call

OFF THE BEATEN TRACK

RENDEZVOUS WITH NATURE

Dwingelderveld National Park
(☑0522-472 951; www.nationaalpark-dwin
gelderveld.nl; Benderez 22, Ruinen;
⊙10am-5pm daily Apr-Sep, 10am-5pm
Wed-Sun Oct-Mar) preserves 3700 hectares of the largest wet heathland in
Europe. More than 60km of hiking paths
and 40km of cycling paths wander amid
the bogs, meadows and forest. It's a
starkly beautiful place and very popular
on summer weekends. The **visitor
centre** is at the southwest corner of
the park outside Ruinen, 7km west of
the A28 on the N375. Pick up hiking and
cycling maps here before setting off to
explore.

site in the centre of the camp, with 102,000
stones set upon a map of the Netherlands.

The camp is 7km north of Westerbork
town (and 7km south of Assen). There is no
direct public transport to the site.

By train, use the station at Beilen on the
Zwolle–Assen train line (at least two trains
per hour), then take bus 22 to Hooghalen,
from where it's a 25-minute walk east. By
bike, head south from Assen via the rural
knooppunten 9-8-33-31-58 cycle route.

Drentsche Aa National Landscape   AREA
(www.drentscheaa.nl) Drentsche Aa National
Landscape takes in a varied 10,000 hectares
of ancient farms, deep woods and straggly
heath that bursts into purple bloom in late
summer. Cycling through this bell-shaped
area just northeast of Assen is sublime, and
there are maps posted at each *knooppunt*
(numbered marker) to guide you around.

National bike route LF14 goes right down
the middle.

Several *hunebedden* (dolmens) can be
spotted just north of Gasteren, in the centre
of the park, and beside a medieval church at
Rolde to the south.

🛏 Sleeping & Eating

Assen's handful of hotels are geared more towards a business clientele. The tourist office
has a list of cosier, more intimate B&Bs in
and around town.

Villa Tapas   TAPAS €€
(☑0592-202 123; www.villatapas.nl; Vaart NZ 2;
bottomless tapas Mon-Thu €19.50, Fri-Sun €23.50;
⊙4.30-10pm; 🛜) With a sun-drenched pavement terrace overlooking the canal and a
fixed-price, eat-as-much-as-you-can tapas
deal, this contemporary eat/drink hybrid
can do little wrong. Inside, designer chairs
lounge beneath a dazzling glass canopy roof
strung with lanterns, and orders are taken
via your own pictorial tablet menu. Kids
aged three to 11 years pay, amusingly, €1.50
for each year of their life.

ⓘ Information

Tourist Office (☑0592-24 37 88; www.
drenthe.nl; Marktstraat 8; ⊙noon-6pm Mon,
9.30am-6pm Tue-Fri, 9.30am-5pm Sat, 1-5pm
Sun)

ⓘ Getting There & Away

Frequent trains connect Assen with both Groningen (€5.70, 20 minutes) and Zwolle (€18, 60
minutes).

A **shop** (☑030-751 51 55; Stationsplein 5c; per
hr €7.50) to the left of the station rents 3-speed
bikes (€50 deposit). National bike route **LF14**
runs south 34km from Groningen and on to
Emmen (about 40km southeast).

Central Netherlands

Best Places to Eat

➡ Cèpes (p259)

➡ De Zilte Zeemeermin (p257)

➡ Fresca (p254)

➡ De Hemel (p254)

➡ Fooddock (p242)

Best Places to Stay

➡ Hotel de Serrenberg (p258)

➡ Lucy Cube (p241)

➡ Boutique Hotel Straelman (p254)

➡ Hotel Credible (p253)

➡ De Librije (p245)

Why Go?

The 'forgotten' provinces of the central Netherlands, Overijssel and Gelderland, combine historic trade centres of abundant cultural wealth with natural beauty. Hoge Veluwe National Park, containing the Kröller-Müller Museum (with one of the world's finest Van Gogh collections), should star in any Dutch itinerary.

Deventer, Zwolle and Kampen are centuries-old towns, filled with atmospheric buildings that recall their heritage as members of the Hanseatic League. Nijmegen has a waterfront vibe, masses of students and an annual march that now takes the form of a week-long party. On the other side of history, there are many WWII memorials and locations to contemplate around Arnhem.

Cut through by the Waal and IJssel rivers and their tributaries, this region also offers splendid cycling routes, particularly along the marshy banks of the Waal east of Nijmegen and the IJssel delta north of Kampen, a remote protected are laced with silvery channels.

When to Go

➡ Rural Netherlands is at its best in summer when the fields are verdant, the waters are swimmable and the nights are long. Meandering the myriad bike lanes and hiking trails this time of year is a joy. Activities are at their peak and you can canoe and kayak for hours on end.

➡ Most canoe-rental outfits have seasonal openings (April to September/October).

➡ Thousands of walkers descend upon Nijmegen in July for the walking fest De Vierdaagse. Book accommodation well in advance.

➡ Wandering the streets and squares of towns and cities is an atmospheric pleasure almost any time of year.

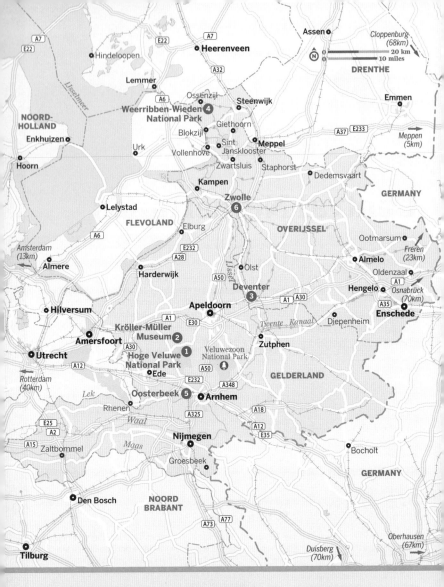

Central Netherlands Highlights

❶ Hoge Veluwe National Park (p258) Grabbing a free white bike and pedalling through forest, sand dune and pea-green parkland.

❷ Kröller-Müller Museum (p258) Admiring the world's second-largest collection of works by Vincent Van Gogh.

❸ Deventer (p241) Uncovering sumptuous medieval architecture in the backstreets of this Hanseatic city and head-turning new innovations in its old harbour.

❹ Weerribben-Wieden National Park (p249) Exploring Overijssel's mysterious wetlands by bike, boat or on foot.

❺ Oosterbeek (p257) Unravelling the country's harrowing, war-torn past at the Airborne Museum Hartenstein and nearby war cemetery.

❻ Zwolle (p243) Scaling the 'Peppermill' church tower for a bird's-eye view of this ancient city's star-shaped walls, canal and fountain-pierced squares.

OVERIJSSEL

With the majestic IJssel River forming much of its western border, it's not surprising that this small province in Central Netherlands is called Overijsse or 'Across the IJssel'. In the east, next door to Germany, the lay of the land is refreshingly hilly, while more 'flat and soggy' sums up the former coastline – now landlocked by Flevoland's Noordoostpolder – in the west.

To explore this rural neck of the woods, anchor yourself in the picture-postcard Hanseatic town of Deventer or provincial capital Zwolle. Mooching north, the sweat and tears of peat workers crafted the largely unsung, serene beauty of the Weerribben-Wieden National Park. Making your way through this wetland to the Venetian-style village of Giethoorn in an old-fashioned rowing boat is a highlight. The eastern region of Twente, anchored by university town Enschede, is a secret among local lovers of the remote wild.

Deventer

☑ 0570 / POP 98,510

Deventer surprises. It's at its best on a beautiful August night, with a wander among the Hanseatic ghosts along the twisting old-town streets searching out the odd detail in the ancient facades. What looks like a crack in the wall is really a tiny passage to the IJssel. Then there's the Havenkwartier, a once-thriving, now-derelict harbour area where young creatives are turning heads with funky new hotels and eating spaces.

Deventer was already a bustling mercantile port by AD 800, and it maintained its prosperous trading ties for centuries – evidence of which you'll see everywhere in its sumptuously detailed old buildings.

◎ Sights & Activities

The Brink is the main square and hub of Deventer cafe life. Moving east from the vast elongated square, the bohemian Bergkwartier bristles with beautiful, restored Hansa-era buildings.

The banks of the IJssel River are a scenic place for cycling. A 32km round-trip follows the riverbank north to Olst, where you can take a ferry across and return along the other side to Deventer. You can do the same thing going south to Zutphen, a 47km loop.

★ Museum de Waag   HISTORIC BUILDING
(☑0570-693 780; http://museumdewaag.nl/; Brink 56; adult/child €9/2.50; ◷11am-5pm Tue-

Sun) At home in one of the country's oldest weighing houses (1528), this evocative museum in the middle of the Brink explores local history. During Deventer's heyday in the 14th and 15th centuries, merchants and traders brought their wares here to be weighed and sized before selling them at one of the town's five annual fairs, held on the huge city square.

★ Grote of Lebuïnuskerk   CHURCH
(☑0570-612 548; www.pkn-deventer.nl; Grote Kerkhof 38; tower €2.50; ◷church 11am-5pm Apr-Nov, to 4pm Dec-Mar, tower 1-4pm Sat plus Mon-Fri during school holidays Apr-Oct) The city's main church is named after the English cleric who founded it in 738; the present Gothic structure dates from the late 15th century. Its many wall paintings, whitewashed by Protestant mobs in 1580, were later restored and patient observers can discern scenes of the Last Judgment, among others. Scale the church tower for panoramic city and IJssel River views.

⊨ Sleeping

Camping De Worp   CAMPGROUND €
(☑0570-613 601; www.stadscamping.eu; Worp 12; camp sites €6, plus €5/3/2.50 per adult/child/car; ◷Apr-Oct; ☞) This small, intimate and leafy camp site is a lovely spot to pitch up and enjoy elegant views of the Hanseatic town on the opposite river bank. The jetty for the passenger ferry into town, a five-minute voyage, is a five-minute walk away, and an abundance of cycling paths lace the green surrounds.

Hotel de Leeuw   HOTEL €
(☑0570-610 290; www.hoteldeleeuw.nl; Nieuwstraat 25; s/d from €79/89; @☞) A sweet place to stay, not just because it has a bakery museum and old candy store. Every comfort you can think of is provided, down to the weather forecasts at breakfast (which you can take in the courtyard). The simple rooms are comfy and many have kitchenettes. Rates include breakfast.

★ Lucy Cube   DESIGN HOTEL €€
(☑06 4123 8068; http://elucy.nl/; Scheepvaartstraat; d week days/weekend €165/200; ☞) One of a trio of micro-hotels in the increasingly happening Havenkwartier, Lucy Cube is a designer hotel with just one room – situated above the ground in an old grain hopper, on the water's edge in the old harbour district. The sharp, all-white interior includes bathroom, fridge stocked with welcome beer and wine, a glass ceiling for romantic stargazing and a rooftop terrace.

Deventer

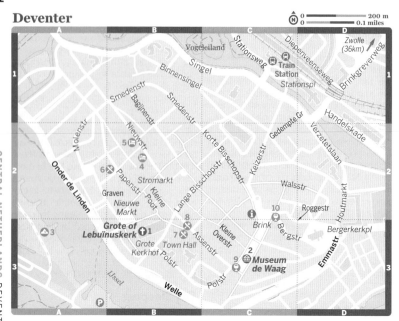

Deventer

◎ Top Experiences

🛏 Sleeping

🍴 Eating

🍷 Drinking & Nightlife

Hotel Gilde　　　　　　　　HOTEL €€
(☑0570-641 846; www.hotelgilde.nl; Nieuwstraat 41; s €69-89, d €99-129, tr €124-153; 🛜) Once a convent, this 37-room hotel is a stunning celebration of 17th-century architecture. Inside, the lavish attention to trimmings and frills only goes as far as the public areas: spartan rooms ensure one does not forget the austerity of former tenants. Rates include a generous breakfast buffet, served in the 1st-floor breakfast room or beneath trees in an atmospheric courtyard garden.

✖ Eating

Brood van Joop　　　　　SANDWICHES €
(☑06 3377 6827; www.facebook.com/brood vanjoop/; Grote Poot 12; sandwiches €6-7, salads €9.95; ☺8.30am-5.30pm Tue-Fri, to 5pm Sat) 'Ambachtelijk brood' (artisanal, handmade bread), organic to boot, is the alluring promise of this modern eatery. There's bar seating inside and a twinset of simple benches in front for alfresco munching with perfect people-watching views over a pretty backstreet square. Pick from a delectable choice of fresh salads, homemade soups and open sandwiches with a fabulous array of creative toppings.

★ Fooddock　　　　　　　FOOD HALL €
(http://en.fooddock.nl/; Zuiderzeestraat 2; meals €5-10; ☺noon-9pm Wed, Thu & Sun, noon-11pm Fri & Sat) For something different, head east to the old harbour or Havenkwartier where an old industrial silo has been transformed into a funky food hall with a dozen-odd food stalls and rustic bench seating around shared wooden tables. Pick from ramen bowls; fried tofu poke bowls; pulled bar-

becue pork; spicy tuna *temaki* (sushi hand roll); crispy tempura; frozen yoghurt and smoothies; sweet waffles with various killer-calorie toppings. Cash only.

Bouwkunde BISTRO **€€**
(✆0570-614 075; www.theaterbouwkunde.nl; Klooster 4; 2-/3-/4-course menu €29.50/34.50/43; ✆6-9pm Tue-Sat) Chef Pieter van de Pavoordt adds a French accent to local organic ingredients and sommelier Heleen Boom chooses the right wines at this polished eatery below a small theatre. Dishes include exquisitely tender *confit de canard* (preserved duck) and tarte Tatin with a white-chocolate mousse and Grand Marnier-laced sabayon. End with a trio of unpasteurised French cheeses.

Summertime dining spills into a peaceful, herringbone-brick-paved courtyard with secret garden beyond. Book ahead.

Jackie's INTERNATIONAL **€€**
(✆0570-616 666; www.jackiesnyc.com; Grote Poot 19; mains €16.50-32.50, 5-course menu €55; ✆5-11.30pm; 🛜) It might not quite be 'New York cuisine' as its strapline suggests, but the international kitchen at this trendy eatery is top-notch and the alfresco terrace, absolutely sublime. The menu mixes a surprise five-course feast with creative dishes like Peking duck pancakes, pork-belly slices with peanut and coriander, oysters, caviar, burgers, juicy Black Angus steaks and seasonal oysters.

🍸 Drinking & Nightlife

De Hip BAR
(✆0570-745 091; www.dehip.nl; Brink 21; ✆Tue-Sat noon-late, Sun hours vary, shop 10am-6pm) Cafe, bar, cultural centre, concert venue, theatre, exhibition space and hip shop rolled into one, De Hip is Deventer's after-dark hot spot. Its canteen cooks up a daily cheap-eat dish (€12.50); its late-night, alternative undercover jam sessions lure a huge crowd; and Sunday afternoon is the time to boogie. Check its website or Facebook page for the week's events. Reservations recommended.

De Heks BROWN CAFE
(✆0570-613 412; www.deheks.nl; Brink 63; ✆2pm-2am Sun-Thu, to 3am Fri & Sat) At least 25 brews are on tap and another 100-odd in bottles at this veteran *bierencafé* (beer bar) where a jolly mix of students and well-worn regulars rub shoulders at the bar or, in warm weather, on the picturesque pavement ter-

race on Deventer's ancient market square. House beers Witte Maan ('White Moon') and blonde bitter De Pyromaan ('the Pyromaniac') come highly recommended.

ℹ️ Information

Tourist Office (✆0570-710 120; www.deventer.info; Brink 89; ✆11am-5pm Mon, 10am-5pm Tue-Sat)

ℹ️ Getting There & Around

The bus station is located to the right as you leave the train station.

BICYCLE
National bike route LF3 runs 36km north through farmlands to Zwolle. Going southwest, it runs 55km to Arnhem and the gateway to Hoge Veluwe National Park, mostly following wide river banks and dykes.

TRAIN
Deventer sits at the junction of two train lines. At the train station find luggage lockers on platform 3.

TO	PRICE (€)	TIME (MIN)	FREQUENCY (PER HR)
Amsterdam	17.60	75	2
Arnhem	8.60	30	2
Nijmegen	11.90	50	2
Zwolle	6.30	24	2

Zwolle

 038 / POP 125.806

Ringed by a star-shaped canal and ancient city walls, medieval Zwolle is often a case of love at first sight. Within the ancient city, quaint cobbled lanes lead to lively fountain-pierced squares framed by cafe pavement terraces, independent boutiques, contemporary works of art and hipster coffee shops. Summer ushers in weekend markets, festivals, cocktails on the beach and mellow paddling in a canoe or kayak along the lily-pad-speckled canal.

In the 14th and 15th centuries Zwolle garnered wealth as the main trading port for the Hanseatic League and became a cultural centre of some repute. It remains the capital of Overijssel province and is an easy day trip from Kampen or Deventer.

👁 Sights & Activities

Standing on Oude Vismarkt, you have a good view of two key monuments. The

Zwolle

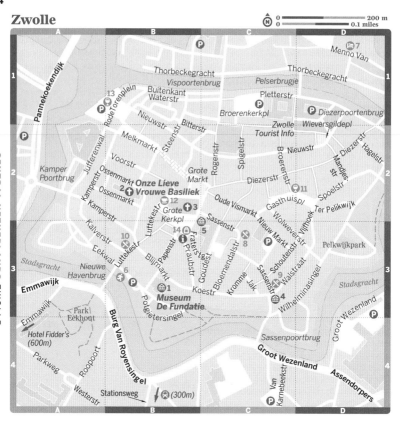

Zwolle

Grote Kerk (☎038-421 25 12; www.academiehuis.nl/grote-kerk/; Grote Markt 18; ⊙11am-5pm Tue-Sat) is grand but was much grander before lightning knocked down the tower. Much of what's left is from the 15th century. Next door, the **Town Hall** (Stadhuis; Lübeckplein 2) has a typically Dutch old part (15th century) and a typically oddball (1976) new part.

★ **Onze Lieve Vrouwe Basiliek** CHURCH
(Peperbus; www.peperbus-zwolle.nl; Ossenmarkt 10; tower entry adult/child €2.50/1; ⊙1.30-4.30pm

Mon, 11am-4.30pm Tue-Sat) People from Zwolle say they know they're home when they see the iconic Onze Lieve Vrouwetoren (also known as the *Peperbus*, or Peppermill), a huge basilica built between 1394 and 1452 to dominate the skyline. From atop its 75m-tall tower (234 steps!) you can appreciate a panorama of the city and the Museum De Fundatie's strange rooftop appendage.

★ **Museum De Fundatie**   MUSEUM

(📞0572-38 81 88; www.museumdefundatie.nl; Blijmarkt 20; adult/child €12.50/free; ⊙11am-5pm Tue-Sun) Housed in a neoclassical courthouse by the canal, Zwolle's acclaimed art museum stages large-scale temporary exhibits by contemporary figures. The small permanent exhibit traces the trajectory of modern art through representative pieces (another part is exhibited at Nijenhuis Castle, 17km southeast). The surreal additions to the rooftop – a gold bird and a snail-shaped slug of a cocoon that sparkles silver in the sunlight – are impossible to miss.

Sassenpoort   HISTORIC BUILDING

(Sassen Gate; 📞038-203 84 56; www.sassenpoort-zwolle.nl; Sassenstraat 53; ⊙11am-5pm Wed & Sat) The 15th-century Sassenpoort, built in 1409 at the southern end of Sassenstraat, is one of the remaining town gates and must surely be one of the country's fanciest, with its twinset of crenellated towers topped with witch-hat turrets and central, neo-Gothic clock tower.

Hiawatha Actief   BOATING

(📞0529-43 60 66; www.hiawatha-actief.nl; Potgietersingel; ⊙11am-6pm daily Jul & Aug, 1-6pm Wed & Fri, noon-6pm Sat & Sun Apr-Jun & Sep) Down by the water, next to the Nieuwe Havenbrug ('New Bridge'), rent a canoe (per two hours €15), electric boat (per hour €35) or stand-up paddle board (per 1½ hours €11.50) to explore the town's star-shaped canal. The icing on the cake is lunching aboard an ingenious 'donut', a bright-orange rubber ring boat for up to 10 people with electric motor and barbecue (per 2½ hours €175).

🛏 Sleeping

Hotel Fidder's   HOTEL €€

(📞421 83 95; www.hotelfidder.nl; Koningin Wilhelminastraat 6; d from €110; 🛜) Three late-19th-century homes have been combined into one grand 23-room family-run hotel. Inside, antiques abound; guests can linger in the library with piano and fire-

place; and some of the elegant rooms have ornate four-poster beds, hot tub or their own private infra-red sauna. In-room coffee- and tea-making facilities are standard across the house. Dining in the restaurant (mains €18) is strictly organic.

★ **De Librije**   DESIGN HOTEL €€€

(The Library; 📞038-421 20 83; www.librije.com; Spinhuisplein 1; d €310; P ❄ 🛜) The bold creation of Zwolle restaurateurs Jonnie and Thérèse Boer, Zwolle's most luxurious hotel occupies the former prison (1739), retaining charming reminders like the original window bars and cell doors. Nineteen lavishly decorated rooms come with iPads, Bang & Olufsen sound system and butler service.

Dining in the courtyard restaurant (mains/menus from €45/170) is a gastronomic, triple Michelin-starred treat bursting with top-quality regional products.

Eating

Lots & More   EUROPEAN €

(📞06 508 983 68; www.lotsandmorezwolle.nl; Sassenstraat 49; small/medium/large bowls from €3.95/4.95/6.50, salads €10; ⊙9.30am-6pm Tue-Fri, 9.30am-5pm Sat, noon-5pm Sun) All-day brunch is the speciality of this appealing lifestyle cafe, footsteps from the Sassenpoort and waterfront beyond. Yoghurt and smoothie bowls come in small, medium or large sizes and include some wonderfully creative combos, as do the sweet- and savoury-topped waffles. Best up is the mix-and-match yoghurt and salad menu, allowing foodies to put together their very own bespoke brunch.

LOCAL KNOWLEDGE

FOLLOW THE LINE

Walking from the train station into the old town, you might well notice a curious blue-and-white striped line snaking its way along the pavement. This is, in fact, part of a contemporary art installation called *Portal* (2015) by Dutch-Israeli sculptor Ram Katzir (b 1969) and Hertog Nadler (Dutch artist duo and couple Chaja Hertog and Nir Nadler). The art route holds various sculptures and artworks, including a bronze 3D map of the city crafted like a wax city seal in the pavement on Burg Van Royensingel and an audioscope trumpeting out music next to the Nieuwe Havenbrug.

DON'T MISS

LIFE'S A BEACH

Two huge potted palm trees herald the entrance to **Stads Strand Zwolle** (☑ 038-760 01 01; www.stadsstrand-zwolle. nl; Rodetorenplein; ⊙ 11am-11pm May-Sep), a pop-up beach bar, inside an industrial container by the canal. Striped deckchairs lounge on golden sand by the water's edge and there's baby-blue and soft-grey blankets to wrap up in on chillier evenings. Cocktails and beer are the drinks de rigueur and there are tasty beach bites to keep the munchies at bay. Think burgers, frozen yoghurt, surf and turf, fish and chips, bruschetta and salads. On Friday evenings, stand-up paddle enthusiasts gather on the beach for a dusk paddle; boards can be rented (per 1½ hours €11).

Blue Sakura   JAPANESE €€
(☑ 038-333 53 33; www.bluesakura.nl; Bethlehemkerkplein 35; lunch/dinner €18.50/26.50; ⊙ 1-10pm Mon, noon-10pm Tue & Wed, noon-12.30am Thu-Sun,) When you tire of Dutch or European cuisine, head to this Japanese and sushi grill, which pulls in the crowds with its bottomless 'all-you-can-eat-in-2½-hours' menu and absolutely breathtaking location inside the monumental Gothic church (1309) of the Bethlehem Augustinian Monastery. Stained-glass windows, the altar and noble family tombs all remain firmly intact, making dining here a surreal experience.

Poppe   DUTCH €€
(☑ 038-421 30 50; www.poppezwolle.nl; Luttekestraat 66; mains €18.50-28.50, 3-/4-/5-course menu €33.50/39.50/46.50; ⊙ noon-3pm Tue-Fri, 5pm-midnight daily) Find this elegant restaurant tucked behind a part-black, part-red brick facade in a former blacksmith's shop. A steady stream of superb seasonal dishes – springtime asparagus, summertime mussels and autumnal wild duck with pear compote – comes out of its open kitchen, and dining spills onto the pavement terrace in front in warm weather.

🍷 Drinking & Nightlife

★ **Dogtails**   COCKTAIL BAR
(☑ 038 853 17 09; www.dogtails.nl; Gasthuisplein 13; ⊙ noon-11pm Wed & Sun, noon-midnight Thu, noon-1am Fri & Sat) 'Fancy hotdogs and original cocktails' is the driver of this uber-hip bar and eatery on fashionable Gasthuisplein. All of othe craft cocktails (€7.50 to €10) are listed by pre-*drooglegging* (prohibition), post-*drooglegging* and *drooglegging* era, and include stunning creations like Blood & Sand and Bees Knees No 5. Order a dog (€6 to €8.50), served on a wooden platter, to match.

Espressobar Maling   COFFEE
(www.facebook.com/malingzwolle/; Luttekestraat 28; ⊙ 8.30am-6.30pm Mon-Sat, 10am-5.30pm Sun) Be it a cortado, mug of filter coffee, macchiato or creamy flat white, this pocket-sized espresso bar is the spot in Zwolle for specialist coffee. The baristas clearly know their stuff, working mainly with carefully selected beans by innovative Dutch coffee roaster Keen. The small pavement terrace, with 'sofas' and tables crafted from up-cycled pallets, enjoys five-star people-watching views over Grote Kerkplein.

ℹ️ Information

Zwolle does not have a tourist office as such, rather an **info point** (☑ 038-421 88 15; www. visitzwolle.com; Grote Kerkplein 13; ⊙ 10am-5pm Mon-Sat) with helpful staff and accommodation and sightseeing information, located inside the city's historic sweet shop **Zwolle Balletjeshuis** (☑ 038-421 88 15; www.zwolse-balletjes.nl; Grote Kerkplein 13; ⊙ 10am-5pm Mon-Sat).

ℹ️ Getting There & Around

BICYCLE

The OV-fiets bicycle shop (rental €3.85 per 24 hours with a OV-chipkaart travel pass) is to the left as you exit station.

Historic Urk in Noord-Holland is 50km northwest on national bike route LF15, a scenic ride of dykes and rivers. Deventer is 36km south on LF3, and there are a lot of optional routes along the IJssel.

TRAIN

Zwolle is a transfer point with good connections. At the train station, find left-luggage lockers (small/large €3.85/5.70 per 24 hours) on platform 14.

TO	PRICE (€)	TIME (MIN)	FREQUENCY (PER HR)
Deventer	6.30	24	2
Groningen	18	60	4
Leeuwarden	16.60	60	2
Utrecht	15.60	60	4

Kampen

📍 038 / POP 53,063

Picturesque Kampen, a former Hanseatic city, is 15km west of Zwolle. Its historic centre is one of the country's best preserved, boasting numerous medieval monuments, including houses, gates and towers. The closing of the Zuiderzee ended Kampen's status as an important port, and the long economic decline that followed kept modernisation down and old buildings up.

One of the town's most distinctive features is its glittering drawbridge, graced with golden wheels and a pedestrian platform to observe at close quarters the middle section of the bridge rise up to allow large boats to pass.

◉ Sights

Sightseeing in Kampen is as much about meandering its web of medieval streets, laid out in a linear fashion parallel to the IJssel, and lapping up the historic vibe as it is about visiting museums.

★ Nieuwe Toren   HISTORIC BUILDING

(New Tower; Oudestraat; €3; ⊙10am-5pm Thu late-Jul-Aug) This landmark tower, built purely as a show of wealth in the 17th century, stands tall (albeit it with an incredible lean) on main street Oudestraat. Its carillon (1659–62), originally strung with 30 bells but now counting 48, is played by the city carilloneur on market days (Monday and Saturday) and at 7.30pm on Friday in summer. The neoclassical tower can only be climbed on five Thursdays in summer, during Kampen's

annual *Kamper Ui(t) dagen* (Kampen Days; www.kamper-uitdagen.nl) festival.

Kamper Kogge   SHIP

(📍038-331 05 15; www.kamperkogge.nl; Havenweg 7; ⊙variable) Nicknamed the Black Lady of Kampen, the *Kampe Kogge* is an impressive reconstruction (using medieval materials and techniques) of a 14th-century cog – a ship used to transport salt, wood, grain, herrings, wine, amber etc during the glory days of the Hanseatic League. Its mast towers 22.4m tall, and a mind-boggling 10,000 hand-forged cog nails were used to keep the magnificent oak ship together. A reconstructed medieval fisherman's cottage, carpentry workshop and smithy complete the interesting ensemble.

Stedelijk Museum   MUSEUM

(📍038-331 73 61; www.stedelijkemuseakampen.nl; Oudestraat 133; adult/child €5.50/free; ⊙10am-5pm Tue-Sat, 1-5pm Sun) The city museum occupies the old and new town halls, the former a late Gothic masterpiece adorned with sculpted figures. The top-floor exhibit is devoted to water and its crucial role in the town's development; below it hang full-length, life-sized portraits of all the members of the House of Orange. Temporary exhibitions fill the ground floor.

🛏 Sleeping & Eating

Hotel van Dijk   HOTEL €

(📍038-331 49 25; www.hotelvandijk.nl; IJsselkade 30-31; s/d/tr/q €60/90/125/145; 🛜) The welcome could not be warmer at this overwhelmingly friendly, three-star hotel facing the river. Cyclists are well catered for with a locked bicycle room, not to mention the

---

LOCAL KNOWLEDGE

THE KAMPEN COW

There's good reason why a contemporary bronze sculpture (1980) of a frolicking cow stands in front of the Nieuwe Toren (above) and, more bizarrely, why a life-sized plastic cow is strung by a rope from the top of the same-said tower for five weeks in July and August during Kampen's summer festival, Kamper Ui(t) dagen (above). The cows evoke an old legend born out of ancient rivalry between towns in the region. It was said that people from Kampen not only spoke their own dialect (known as Kampers) but were a tad silly to boot, hence the tale of the hanging cow: one day the top of the Nieuwe Toren collapsed, prompting grass to sprout from its crown. Upon spotting the lush green grass, a local farmer tied a rope around the neck of one of his cows and hoisted it up the tower – only for the cow to die before arrival at the top. Neither farmer nor local townsfolk could understand why, apparently. To this day, each year, Kampen's summertime festival opens with a life-sized plastic cow being merrily hoisted up to the top of the landmark tower.

THE HANSEATIC LEAGUE

The powerful trading community known as the Hanseatic League was organised in the mid-13th century and its member towns quickly grew rich through the import and export of goods that included grain, ore, honey, textiles, timber and flax. The league was not a government as such, but it did defend its ships from attack and it entered into monopolistic trading agreements with other groups, such as the Swedes. It achieved its powerful trading position through bribery, boycotts and other underhand methods. The Hanseatic League members did work hard to prevent war among their partners, for the simple reason that conflict was bad for business.

Seven Dutch cities along the IJssel River were prosperous members: Hasselt, Zwolle, Kampen, Hattem, Deventer, Zutphen and Doesburg. It's ironic that the Hanseatic League's demise is mostly attributable to the Dutch. The traders of Amsterdam knew a good thing when they saw it and during the 15th century essentially beat the league at its own game, outmuscling it in market after market.

enthusiastic itinerary recommendations and tips from Irma, who runs the hotel with husband Herman. Decor is 1980s style, the 18 rooms are all different, and the breakfast buffet (included in rates) is a true feast.

March to late summer, the homemade strawberry jam and fresh strawberries from a local farm are heaven on earth (ask Irma for the address, should you fancy combining a bike ride with strawberry picking on the farm). The hotel can arrange bike rental.

Boetiek Hotel Kampen   BOUTIQUE HOTEL €
(☑ 038-888 87 37; www.hotelkampen.nl; IJsselkade 20; s/d/ste from €85/97.50/125; 🛜) Expect a B&B vibe at this contemporary riverside retreat, at home in a vintage taupe-and-green brick house with decorative ceramic tiling and sweeping river views. Each of its 10 rooms and apartment are different, with partly open-plan bathrooms, fantastic rain showers and beautiful fabrics. Guests share an espresso machine, and breakfast (included in rates) is served in the designer salon or bijou backyard.

Banketbakkerij Smit   CAFE €
(Oudestraat 148; cakes from €2; ⊗9am-6pm Mon-Fri, to 5pm Sat) Irresistible house specialities at this old-world cafe and tea room include *vulkoek* (almond paste enrobed in a spicy cinnamon and nutmeg biscuit), *Kamper slof* (a rich, walnut and caramel biscuit-cake) and the lurid pink *vanillestang* (vanilla slice) – all perfect when taken with a cup of coffee or tea.

Restaurant de Bottermarck   DUTCH €€€
(☑ 038-331 95 42; www.debottermarck.nl; Broederstraat 23; mains €25-35; ⊗noon-9pm Tue-Fri, 5-9pm Sat, by reservation only Mon, also Sun May-Aug & two wks Mar) With an enchanting terrace overlooking quaint Bottermarkt, top-end dining here is a summertime highlight. Cuisine is bistro style with a French accent, and bursts with local seasonal produce, often organic: think springtime asparagus with ham in a parsley and butter sauce or scallops in a vegetable and nut cream, followed by Champagne-laced turbot or duck breast with shiitake mushrooms.

❶ Information

Tourist Office (De Van Heutszkazerne; ☑ 038-202 23 66; www.ontdekdeijsseldelta.nl; Oudestraat 216; ⊗10am-4pm Tue-Sat) Guided walking tours and ample info for DIY urban explorers.

❶ Getting There & Around

BICYCLE

Rent wheels locally from **Fietsverhuurkampen. nl** (☑ 038-333 71 10; www.fietsverhuurkampen. nl; IJsseldijk 37; per day from €8.75; ⊗9am-8pm Mon-Sat).

Kampen is a hub of national bike routes: LF15, which heads northwest to Urk and east to Zwolle (18km); LF23, which follows the old coast below Flevoland and goes 130km west to Amsterdam; LF22, which also follows the old coast north and west to Friesland; and LF3, which runs south via Zwolle to Arnhem.

To get to the Weerribben-Wieden National Park, 21km north, pick up national bike routes LF3 or LF22.

TRAIN

Kampen has two stations: one just across the IJssel for the local run from Zwolle (€3.50, 10 minutes, two per hour), and another 2km south, Kampen-Zuid, on the direct line to Amsterdam (€16.70, 70 minutes) via Lelystad. Bus No 74 shuttles between the two stations.

Weerribben-Wieden National Park

A serene and mysterious landscape of canals, ponds and lakes, the Weerribben-Wieden National Park is the largest freshwater wetland in northwestern Europe. Its swampy 10,000 hectares contain centuries-old peatlands, bogs, reed beds dotted with different orchid varieties, forest and a treasure trove of wildlife. Warblers, bitterns, western marsh harriers and purple herons all nest here, much to the joy of birdwatchers who flock here to absorb the park's rich array of species – from a traditional punt or along one of the park's many scenic cycling and hiking trails.

The villages of Sint Jansklooster and Venice-like Giethoorn are key bases from which to explore.

Giethoorn

0521 / POP 2620

Giethoorn – a highlight of Weerribben-Wieden National Park – is a town with no streets, only canals, walking paths and bike trails. Contrary to most Dutch geography, this 'Dutch Venice' is built on water crossed by a few bits of land. Farmers even used to move their cows around in row boats filled with hay. Hugely popular in summer, at other times it has an almost mystical charm as you wander its idiosyncratic waterways.

When the tourist hordes get too thick (the site has become a must-visit for Asian tour groups), head to the northern part of the village, which is quieter and quainter.

🏃 Activities

Boating is by far the most fun way of navigating the park's waterways. Giethoorn is the main spot for boat rental in the national park, with kayaks and canoes, rowing boats, traditional punt and blissfully silent electric boats matching every taste and energy level. Eco Waterliner (☑ 0527-20 56 60; www.visitweerribbenwieden.com/Fietsen/EcoWaterLiner; Beulakerpad 1, Sint Jansklooster; day pass adult/child/bike €10/5/6; ☉ 10am-5pm May-Sep) allows you to combine a cruise with a bike ride.

Several peaceful cycling trails criss-cross the national park, the silence only broken by the calls, clucks, coos and splashes of birds, fish, frogs, otters, beavers and eels. Rent wheels at De Gele Lis (The Yellow Iris; ☑ 0561-477 442; www.degelelis.nl; Hoogeweg 27a, Ossenzijl; ☉ 10am-5pm Apr-Oct) in Ossenzijl, then follow the LF22a south to Blokzijl for a wonderfully serene journey along the Kalenberg River, traversing numerous wooden bridges over side canals en route.

🛏 Sleeping & Eating

★ The Black Sheep Hostel   HOSTEL €
(☑ 06 8009 0614; http://hostelgiethoorn.com; Zuiderpad 19; dm from €29; @ 🕏) Dazzling, up-to-the-minute white dorms with pine bunk beds and the odd splash of sunflower-yellow become a minor detail when one considers the pretty flower-bedecked garden with hammock et al, the canal-side location, the designer breakfast room and the traditional thatched roof at this stunning cottage on

CENTRAL NETHERLANDS WEERRIBBEN-WIEDEN NATIONAL PARK

WORTH A TRIP

A TRIP FIT FOR A KING

A dazzling palace 3.5km north of downtown Apeldoorn, Paleis Het Loo (☑ 055-577 24 00; www.paleishetloo.nl; Amersfoortweg 1; adult/child €7/2.50; ☉ 10am-5pm Tue-Sun) was built in 1685 for William III, and Queen Wilhelmina lived here until 1962. Its furnished interior – the royal bed chambers, the collection of regal paintings, the lavish dining room from 1686 – is closed for extension work costing €123.2 million. But the splendid stables (1907–09) and coach house, magnificent 17th-century gardens with their symmetrically planted flowerbeds and allusive statuary, and palace rooftop offering a bird's eye view of the entire estate all remain open.

Beyond the palace gardens sprawls Palace Park, an immense, beautifully landscaped section of the estate where the Oranges promenaded at leisure (entry until 3.30pm). Follow the Orange Trail to uncover the key features of the park, including the royal boathouse and various romantic pavilions. Lunch afterwards in one of two on-site restaurants serving Dutch and European fare, or picnic.

From Apeldoorn train station take bus No 10 to the Tuinmanslaan stop (€4, 15 minutes), a five-minute walk from Palais Het Loog.

Giethoorn's main canal. Chinese-Indonesian Jimmi and Dutch Gea are the savvy pair behind the family-run hostel.

❶ Information

De Wieden Visitor Centre (Bezoekerscentrum De Wieden; ☑0527-24 66 44; www.natuur monumenten.nl/natuurgebieden/de-wieden; Beulakerpad 1, Sint Jansklooster; ⊙noon-5pm Mon, 10am-5pm Tue-Sun Jun-Sep, 10am-5pm Tue-Sun Apr, May & Oct, noon-4pm Wed, Sat & Sun Nov-Mar) Sint Jansklooster.

Outside Centre Weerribben (Buitencentrum Weerribben; ☑0561-477 272; www.np-weer ribbenwieden.nl; Hoogeweg 27, Ossenzijl; ⊙10am-5pm Apr-Oct) Ossenzijl.

Tourist Office (VVV; ☑0521-360 112; http:// touristinformationgiethoorn.nl; Eendracht-splein 1; ⊙10am-5pm Mon-Sat) Giethoorn.

❶ Getting There & Around

Bus 70 serves Giethoorn on its route between Steenwijk (18 minutes) and Zwolle (one hour). Service is hourly.

Twente

POP 627,000

Twente forms a distinct region on the southeastern fringe of Overijssel, straddling the German border. Populated by local Twentenaren or 'Tukkers', this is the most urban part of Overijssel province: university town Enschede is bolstered by a dynamic 26,000-strong student population, notable industrial heritage (textiles and brewing) and two alluring art museums.

Yet, like a vast garden, rural Twente is also known for its bucolic landscape of rolling hills and meadows, peat bogs and marshes, flowering heather fields and golden-sand river beaches protected by a nature reserve. Peaceful walking and cycling paths spider-web across this old-world landscape, past fourth-generation farmsteads and a scant sprinkling of villages where time seemingly stands still. Ootmarsum, with a Gothic church and surfeit of touristy galleries and craft shops, is the medieval showpiece.

◉ Sights

Rijksmuseum Twenthe   MUSEUM
(☑053-435 86 75; www.rijksmuseumtwenthe.nl; Lasondersingel 129-131, Enschede; adult/child €12.50/free; ⊙11am-5pm Tue-Sun) Only a fraction of the 9000-piece art collection of Twente's fine arts museum is exhibited at any one time at this attractive villa, arranged in two wings around a central courtyard. The purpose-built museum was created by textile manufacturer Jan Bernard van Heek and his brother – both passionate art collectors – in 1930 and its collection spans every movement of Western art from the Middle Ages to present. Its medieval sculptures, reliquaries and manuscripts are particularly impressive.

De Museumfabriek   MUSEUM
(The Factory Museum; ☑053-201 20 99; www. demuseumfabriek.nl; Het Rozendaal 11, Enschede; adult/child €8.50/7.50, family €25; ⊙11am-5pm Tue-Sun) Designed to pique and inspire curious minds of all ages, this unusual gallery mixes history-related exhibits with applied arts, local traditional crafts, natural history, science and technology. Highlights of its permanent collection include a 3.6m-tall skeleton of a mammoth, a life-sized reproduction of a traditional thatched-roof *lös hoes* (one-room homestead shared by both a family and its livestock) and various pioneering aircraft from the 1920s. The final room showcases several 19th-century weaving looms that make an absolute din when in action.

Monument
vuurwerkramp Enschede   MONUMENT
(Enschede Fireworks Monument; Tollensstraat 7523, Lasonderbleek Park) This unusual monument in a grassy park in front of De Museumfabriek remembers the 23 people who died and thousands injured following a fatal explosion in a firework factory here on 13 May 2000. The black-granite outlines of house foundations embedded in grass evokes the some 400 surrounding homes (and nearby Grolsch brewery) damaged by the explosion and subsequently demolished. The entire Roombeek district, north of Enschede's historic old town, has since been rebuilt.

Grolsch Brewery   BREWERY
(☑053-483 33 33; www.royalgrolsch.com; Brouwerslaan 1, Enschede; adult/child 12-18yr €15/12.50; ⊙9.30am-noon, 1.30-4pm & 7-9.30pm Wed & Thu, 9.30am-noon & 1.30-4pm Fri) One of the world's most famous beers, easily recognisable by its iconic swing-top Pilsner bottle, has been brewed in Enschede since 1895. Guided tours last 2½ hours and take visitors through everything from the beer's history to production, bottling, branding and tasting. Its blonde De Klok beer is a nod to the original brewery

OFF THE BEATEN TRACK

LOVELY LUTTERZAND

In Twente's far eastern realm, snug on the German border, spectacular sand drifts rise up along the banks of the Dinkel River to meet aromatic juniper bushes, pine forests and flat moorland beyond to form **Lutterzand** (www.lutterzand.nl), a protected, 750-hectare nature reserve. The tiny hamlet of **De Lutte** is the starting point for a 35km circular cycling trail into the Lutterzand (closed when river water levels are too high) and walkers can enjoy five marked trails (3km to 7km long).

Pick up maps and information at the Tourist Information Point inside the **Paviljoen Lutterzand** (☎0541-551 386; www.lutterzand.nl; Lutterzandweg 12, De Lutte; sandwiches €5.20-8.50, pancakes €5.80-9.50, mains €15-22.50; ⏲10am-8pm Tue-Sat, 10.30am-8pm Sun Apr-Oct, 11am-8pm Wed-Sun Nov-Mar) in De Lutte.

near Groenlo where the beer was first brewed in 1615. De Klok merged with De Enschedesche Bierbrouwerij in 1922 to become the Grolsch brewery.

Above the brewery, the **Grolsch Living History** (free admission) displays Grolsch memorabilia collected by a passionate Groslch fan for the last 25-odd years.

The Grolsch brewery was based in the industrial Roombeek district, north of the historic centre, until 2000 when it was severely damaged by an explosion in a neighbouring fireworks factory. Its state-of-the-art brewery (2004) lies on the far-eastern outskirts of town near Boekelo. From Enschede train and bus station take bus No 506 (€4, 15 minutes) to the Usselerhofweg stop, a 10-minute walk away.

Sleeping & Eating

Het Meuleman CAMPGROUND €
(☎0541-551 289; www.camping-meuleman.nl; Lutterzandweg 16, De Lutte; camp site €29-45, 2-person hikers' cabin €50, 6-person cottage from €250; ⏲Apr-Oct;) Sprawled across seven hectares, partly protected by the Lutterzand nature reserve, this old-school campsite is a sweet invitation to get lost in nature. Be it fishing or swimming in the pond, hiking, biking, canoeing along the Dinkel or chilling on the sandy beach, life on this 113-pitch estate is blissfully peaceful. Fully equipped cottages are available, as are hikers' huts with fireplace, hot plate and fridge.

Facilities include restaurant, well-used mini-golf course, boules pitch, volleyball court and treetop climbing trail. It also rents bikes.

Twentsche Foodhall FOOD HALL €
(Performance Factory; ☎053-203 23 12; www.twentschefoodhal.nl; Hoge Bothofstraat 39a, Enschede; mains €5-15; ⏲4-10pm Thu & Fri, noon-10pm Sat, noon-9pm Sun) Enschede's sustainable food hall is the hipster spot for everything from a Twente sandwich stuffed with *bakworst* (oven-baked slices of liver sausage) to spicier Indian or Bolivian fare, Surinamese soul food, vegan raw food or Texan ribs. Kitchen stalls are strictly artisan, must be headed by a local chef and can only work with produce sourced from within 40km of Enschede.

Find it inside the Performance Factory, aka the former Polaroid camera factory building.

Information

Enschede Tourist Office (Enschede Promotie; ☎053-480 19 70; www.uitinenschede.nl; Langestraat 41, Enschede; ⏲8.30am-5.30pm Mon-Fri)

Getting There & Around

BICYCLE

National bike routes LF14, LF15 and LF8 pass through Twente's enticing kaleidoscope of farmland, peat fields and gentle hills, but this could change when the three routes are set to be replaced by a new eastern Holland itinerary. Check www.hollandcyclingroutes.com for updates.

TRAIN

Enschede is the main entry point by train, with daily connections to Zwolle (€13.44, one hour), Deventer (€12.30, 45 minutes) and Utrecht (€22.30, 1¾ hours), from where connecting trains continue to Amsterdam, Groningen and elsewhere in the country.

GELDERLAND

The largest Dutch province, Gelderland embraces a lush green landscape of vast heathlands, forests, corn fields and meandering dykes. During WWII, its capital, Arnhem, was heavily bombed and its river bridges destroyed during the disastrous Operation Market Garden, but the town has since risen from the ashes to become a sparky, modern place with appealing museums and parks.

To the north lies the serene Hoge Veluwe National Park, home to one the country's best art museums and sculpture parks, and a myriad of nature-rich cycling and walking trails. In the south of the province, practically within spitting distance of the border with Germany, big city Nijmegen on the banks of the Waal River honours its distant Roman origins and buzzes with creative energy thanks to its notable student population.

Nijmegen

📞 024 / POP 170,681

From Roman camp to Catholic university town of 13,000 students, Nijmegen is a vibrant place to spend a couple of days. This is the oldest town in the Netherlands, with a compact medieval centre yet all the urban cool of a big city. Historic cafes, specialist craft-coffee shops and a decent smattering of museums and monuments lace its streets that stagger gently from the 16th-century Lower Town by the banks of the Waal River to the older Upper Town. In summer, Dutch party lovers pour into town for its annual four-day hiking fest and Zomerfeesten music festival.

◎ Sights

Grote Markt   SQUARE

Thankfully, Nijmegen's sweeping market square was among the few parts of the old town to survive WWII. Open-air markets are still held here each week on Saturday and Monday, while ornate Dutch Renaissance De Waagh (Weigh House; Grote Markt) – built in 1612 – is now a popular cafe. In the middle of the square is the statue of a repentant Mariken van Nieumeghen, a maiden from late medieval Dutch literature who was seduced by Moenen ('the devil') and spent seven years living in sin.

Sint Stevenskerk   CHURCH

(📞 024-360 47 10; www.stevenskerk.nl; Sint Stevenskerkhof 62; tower adult/child €4/2; ⊙ church 10.30am-5pm Mon-Sat, noon-5pm Sun Apr-Oct, tower 11am-1pm Mon, 2-4pm Wed, Sat & Sun Apr-

Oct, weekend only Nov & Dec) From Grote Markt duck beneath the ornate Gothic Kerkboog (1542; Church Arch) – originally with cattle grid and pit beneath to prevent pigs from the market place escaping into the churchyard – to uncover this iconic church. It was built between the 13th and 15th centuries, but heavily bombed during WWII. Subsequent reconstruction of its classic reformist interior saw no expense spared with the whitewash or chandeliers. A hike up the 183 steps in the tower rewards with a marvellous city panorama.

Valkhofpark   PARK

Perched in a commanding position over the Waal River, the Valkhof is a lovely park and the site of a ruined palace begun by Charlemagne in the 8th century and continued by Emperor Frederick Barbarossa from 1155 (see it in better days in the Jan van Goyen painting at the museum across the way). All of it bar two side chapels was destroyed in 1796: admire the 16-sided Sint Nicolaaskapel, a rare example of Byzantine architecture in the Netherlands, and the ruined Sint Maartenskapel.

Museum het Valkhof   MUSEUM

(📞 024-360 88 05; www.museumhetvalkhof.nl; Kelfkensbos 59; adult/child €11/5.50; ⊙ 11am-5pm Tue-Sun) Changing temporary exhibitions form a substantial part of this regional history museum, at home in a striking glass shoebox-style building by Valkhof Park. Among the museum's rich collection of first-rate Roman artefacts is a column fragment from Nijmegen's Roman foundation, a replica of which doubles as a sundial on the square in front of the museum.

★ Nationaal Fietsmuseum Velorama   MUSEUM

(National Cycling Museum; 📞 024-322 58 51; www.velorama.nl; Waalkade 107; adult/child €5/3; ⊙ 10am-5pm Mon-Sat, 11am-5pm Sun) Down by the riverfront is this museum with more than 250 bicycles: everything from 19th-century wooden contraptions and hand-propelled bikes to an entire room devoted to penny farthings, plus more modern machines. It's a must-see for anyone who has marvelled at the Dutch affinity for two-wheelers.

Festivals & Events

★ De Vierdaagse   CULTURAL

(Four Days Marches; www.4daagse.nl; ⊙ mid-late Jul) Nijmegen's big event is the annual four-

Nijmegen

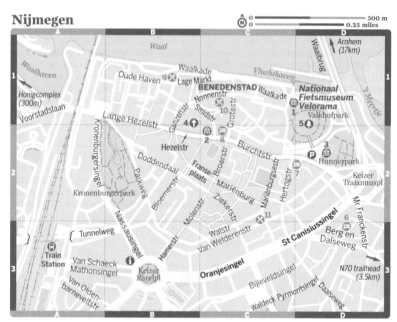

day, 120km- to 200km-long hike, around since 1909. Thousands walk a minimum of 30km a day. Routes vary according to gender and age. Completing the walk is considered a national honour and comes with a medal. Many suffer debilitating blisters, while thousands more endure horrific hangovers, as the Wandelvierdaagse is the city's excuse for a weeklong party.

Sleeping

★ Hotel Credible   DESIGN HOTEL €
(☑ 322 04 98; www.in-credible.nl; Hertogstraat 1; s/d €55/75; ☜) Fun and vintage chic are buzzwords at this achingly cool hotel, in a townhouse painted every colour of the rainbow, across the street from Valkhofpark. Eighteen bright-white rooms across three floors feature naked light fixtures, books to read and inspirational slogans ('Why stop dreaming when you wake up?').

DJs spin strictly vinyl every Saturday in the ground-floor bar, an address in itself serving excellent specialist coffee and all-day breakfast and lunch (mains €5.50 to €12.50) packed with hipster superfoods. Kudos for the faux fire flickering on the screen of a vintage TV set, sofa seating, shelves of books to browse and buzzing pavement terrace.

Hotel Karel
HOTEL €

(☑024-360 30 00; www.hotelkarel.nl; Grote Markt 38-40; s €50-59, d €75-85; ⛢) With its eye-catching cream-and-red brick facade and twinset of jazzy orange parasols on the Grote Markt, this long-standing hotel remains thoroughly up to the minute. Its buoyant ground-floor bistro with a creative mix-and-match menu doubles as reception, and its triple and quad rooms make it a solid family bet. Count €9.50 for breakfast.

★Boutique Hotel Straelman
BOUTIQUE HOTEL €€

(☑024-388 80 00; www.boutique-hotel-straelman.nl; Straalmanstraat 28; d from €100; ⛢) Owner Tanja Seegers is the design talent behind this chic, five-room boutique hotel in an elegant 19th-century townhouse with breakfast room opening onto a beautiful garden and patio. Each room is unique and named after a luxurious product – caviar, truffle, champagne and so forth – and rates include a sensational homemade breakfast. Guests seeking romance and intimacy won't be disappointed.

✕ Eating

★Fresca
INTERNATIONAL €

(☑024-324 02 78; https://frescanijmegen.nl/; Van Broeckhuysenstraat 16; breakfast €3.50-8.50, sandwiches & salads €7-10, high tea €21.50; ⊙10am-6pm; ⛢) With a pretty terrace overlooking a tree-shaded square and an all-day menu bursting with fresh homemade salads, super-food bowls and imaginative cakes, Fresca attracts a savvy local crowd. Bread is organic with a gluten-free option, and the seasonal-veg frittata or cinnamon- and cashew-nut laced couscous are excellent vegetarian options.

Serious speciality coffee by Brinks roasters (with soya, oat or coconut milk options), flavoured iced lattes (spiced pumpkin or hazelnut latte anyone?), a daily smoothie, fresh juices and a killer 'guilty pleasure freak shake' (salted caramel chocolate with whipped cream, caramel fudge, mocha beans and marshmallows) all make Fresca an A-lister drinking hub too.

De Firma
TAPAS €€

(☑024-322 60 40; https://defirmanijmegen.nl/; Lage Markt 47; shared dishes €7-10, menu €30; ⊙5pm-midnight) Given its near-water location on a 16th-century street in the so-called 'lower town', De Firma's appealing beachy vibe is appropriate. Vintage, sea-blue floor tiling and all-white tables and chairs create a trendy nautical vibe, and the shared tapas-style dishes cater to all moods and tastes with their colourful world influences.

Drinking & Nightlife

Down Town
CAFE

(www.downtownnmgn.nl; Kannenmarkt 16; ⊙8.30am-5pm Wed-Sun) Duck behind the weigh-house (p252) on Grote Markt to uncover this hipster coffee shop, at home in a picture-postcard townhouse with pretty olive-green facade and wicker bistro chairs lined up on its lively pavement terrace in front. Hipsters pile into its bright white interior for specialist coffee by Nijmegen craft-roaster Blommers, avocado toast, pancake stacks and the finest brunch in town.

Café In De Blauwe Hand
BROWN CAFE

(Blue Hand; ☑024-323 20 66; https://indeblauwehand.nl/; Achter de Hoofdwacht 3; ⊙3pm-

---

DON'T MISS

NIJMEGEN'S CREATIVE GOURMET HUB

A monumental, red-brick building with tranquil tree-shaded courtyard, **Commanderie van St Jan** (Franseplaats 1) is an epicurean delight. It boasts a brewery in its basement, a couple of restaurants and bistro-bar **De Hemel** (Heaven; ☑024-333 30 94; https://restaurantdehemel.nl; Franseplaats 1, Commanderie van St Jan; sandwiches €4.50-9.75, salads €12.50-19.75, high tea €18.95, dinner menu €34.75; ⊙noon-6pm Mon, to midnight Tue-Thu, to 1am Fri & Sat, 11am-1am Sun) on the ground floor, an artisan coffee roaster on the 1st floor and a cooking school on the 2nd. It was built in 1196 as a shelter for pilgrims and was adopted by the monastical Order of St John in the 13th century.

Monks brewed beer here, and subsequent centuries saw the building used as a school, church and student digs. Watch for cuppings and workshops by baristas at coffee roaster **Holy Beans** (www.holybeans.nl) and fascinating cookery workshops focusing on antiquarian dishes at **Eeet Verleden** (www.eetverleden.nl)

midnight Mon & Tue, 3pm-1am Wed & Thu, 3pm-2am Fri, 1pm-2am Sat, 2pm-midnight Sun) Occupying a corner of the Grote Markt is this inviting spot, as evidenced by its motto: 'A frosty mug of rich beer gives you warmth, joy and sweet pleasure.' One of the city's most historic cafes, it derives its name from its 17th-century customers – workers at a nearby dye shop – who would pop in for a jar, hands stained blue with indigo.

ℹ️ Information

Tourist Office (VVV; ☎ 0900 112 23 44; www.visitnijmegen.com; Keizer Karelplein 32h; ⊙ 9.30am-5.30pm Tue-Sat)

ℹ️ Getting There & Around

Regional and local buses depart from the bus station neighbouring the north side of the train station.

BICYCLE

Rent bikes at **Rijwielshop** (☎ 024-322 96 18; Stationsplein 7; bike/tandem or e-bike rental per day €7.50/17.50; ⊙ 5.20am-3.10am Fri & Sat, 7am-midnight Sun, 5.20am-5am Mon & Tue, 5am-1am Wed & Thu) at the train station or in town at **Nijmegen Actief** (☎ 06 2783 4974; http://nijmegenactief.nl; Waalkade 113; bike/e-bike per day €9/20; ⊙ 10am-5pm).

Arnhem is 40km along the sinuous riverside course of national bike route LF3. Den Bosch is about 70km southwest along the equally curvy LF12.

TRAIN

At the train station, find left-luggage lockers on platform 1A.

TO	PRICE (€)	TIME (MIN)	FREQUENCY (PER HR)
Amsterdam	19.20	85	2
Arnhem	4.30	13-18	8
Den Bosch	8.30	28-42	4

Groesbeek

☑ 024 / POP 11,388

Of particular interest to WWII veterans and their families, the small town of Groesbeek, 10km south of Nijmegen, is known for its informative National Liberation Museum 1944–45 (National Bevrijdingsmuseum; ☎ 024-397 44 04; www.bevrijdingsmuseum.nl; Wylerbaan 4; adult/child €10/5.50, family €25; ⊙ 10am-5pm Mon-Sat, noon-5pm Sun) and nearby Canadian War Cemetery (www.cwgc.org; ⊙ 24hrs) FREE, 2km north, where 2598 known and 20 unknown

soldiers – predominantly Canadian, with a few British, Australian, Polish and Belgian too – who fell here during Operation Market Garden now rest in peace. Visiting both can be an emotional experience, best done as a half-day trip from nearby Nijmegen.

ℹ️ Getting There & Away

Take bus No 5 (€4, 20 minutes, every 15 minutes) from Nijmegen train station to the 'Oude Molen' stop in Groesbeek, a 300m-walk from the museum. Bus No 562 (€4, 20 minutes, every 15 minutes) stops in front of the cemetery.

By bike from Nijmegen take the **LF3b** south to knooppunt 33 (junction 33) – steep climb – then turn east to point 88, a 13km ride.

Arnhem

☑ 026 / POP 156,600

Tracking down key locations in the catastrophic Battle of Arnhem, fought here on both banks of the Nederrijn River in September 1944, remains the big reason for many visitors to explore Arnhem. With its centre all but levelled during WWII, Arnhem has rebuilt itself as a prosperous town with fine museums, some beautiful parks and a thriving fashion industry born out of its fashion and design institute ArtEZ. The country's premiere fashion expo is held here each year in June.

⊙ Sights & Activities

Sightseeing in Arnhem is spread between the old town, ringed with medieval city walls until the 19th century, when they were mostly destroyed (Sabelspoort is the only original gate to remain); the riverfront with the town's iconic 'bridge too far' evoking WWII; and the city's leafy northern suburbs with a string of attractive parks.

John Frostbrug   HISTORIC SITE
(John Frost Bridge) The modern and busy replacement for the infamous 'bridge too far' may not look too dramatic, but its symbolic value is immense. This would have been the last of the 14 bridges over the Rhine that British paratroops had to cross during WWII's infamous Operation Market Garden.

Airborne at the Bridge   MUSEUM
(☎ 026-333 77 10; www.airbornemuseum.nl; Rijnkade 150; ⊙ 10am-5pm) FREE There is no finer view of Arnhem's iconic John Frost bridge than from this small riverside museum with glass lookout tower. A six-minute

film in the basement introduces the story of the Battle of Arnhem, and exhibits on the ground floor evoke the battle through the eyes of three soldiers – a Dutchman, an Englishman and a German – who fought.

Eusebiuskerk   CHURCH
(St Eusebius Church; ☏026-443 50 68; http://eusebius.nl; Kerkplein 1; adult/child church €2.50/1.50, tower €7.50/5; ☺10am-5pm Mon-Sat, noon-5pm Sun Apr-Oct, 11am-4pm Mon-Sat, noon-4pm Sun Nov & Dec, 11am-4pm Tue-Sat, noon-4pm Jan-Mar) Awe-inspiring and gigantic, this late-Gothic church is well worth a mooch, if only to ride the lift up its 73m-tall spire to gawp at Europe's biggest carillon (featuring 54 bells) and the magnificent city panorama that unfolds from the glass balconies at the top.

Nederlands Openluchtmuseum   MUSEUM
(Netherlands Open Air Museum; ☏026-357 61 11; www.openluchtmuseum.nl; Hoeferlaan 4; adult/child €19/16; ☺10am-5pm Apr-Oct) The village-sized open-air museum, 7km north of the train station, showcases a nationwide collection of buildings and artefacts, with everything from farmhouses and stagecoaches to working windmills. Volunteers in period costumes demonstrate traditional skills like spinning and weaving flax, milling flour, forging iron with the blacksmith, farmhouse cooking and even brewing (yes, the museum has its own brewery). Buy cheaper tickets (€17.50/14.50) in advance online.

To get here, take bus 3 (direction Burgers Zoo Openl.Museum) from the train station to the Peter van Anrooylaan stop (€2, 17 minutes) then walk some five minutes, or bus No 8 (direction Velp Ziekenhuis) to the Openluchtmuseum Oost stop (€2, 10 minutes).

🛏 Sleeping & Eating

Stayokay Arnhem   HOSTEL €
(☏026-442 01 14; www.stayokay.com/arnhem; Diepenbrocklaan 27; dm €27, d/tr from €53/79.50; ☎) Perched on a wooded hill 2km north of town, Arnhem's hostel is inconvenient for the centre, but that much closer to De Hoge Veluwe National Park. Its English-styled pub is open till midnight. From the train station ride bus 3 (direction Burgers Zoo Openl.Museum) for 10 minutes (€2) to the Ziekenhuis Rijnstate (hospital) stop. Rates include breakfast.

★**Hotel Modez**   BOUTIQUE HOTEL €€
(☏026-442 09 93; www.hotelmodez.com; Elly Lamakerplantsoen 4; s/d from €106/119; P ☎) Beside a delightful square in the heart of Arnhem's

---

A BRIDGE TOO FAR: OPERATION MARKET GARDEN

The battle they called Operation Market Garden, famously featured in the epic war film *A Bridge too Far* (1977), was devised by British General Bernard Montgomery to end WWII in Europe by Christmas 1944. Despite advisers warning that the entire operation was likely to fail, Montgomery pushed on. He had often groused that the Americans under General George Patton were getting all the headlines in their charge across France. The plan was for British forces in Belgium to make a huge push along a narrow corridor to Arnhem in the Netherlands, where they would cut off large numbers of German troops from being able to return to Germany, thereby allowing the British to dash east to Berlin and end the war.

Everything went wrong. The British paratroops were only given two days' rations and the forces from the south had to cross 14 bridges, all of which had to remain traversable and lightly defended for the plan to work. The southern forces encountered some of the German army's most hardened troops and the bridges weren't all completely intact. This, in effect, stranded the Arnhem paratroops. They held out there and in neighbouring Oosterbeek for eight days without reinforcements. The survivors, a mere 2163, retreated under darkness. More than 17,000 other British troops were killed.

The results of the debacle were devastating for the Dutch: Arnhem and other towns were destroyed and hundreds of civilians killed. The Dutch resistance, thinking that liberation was at hand, came out of hiding to fight the Germans. But without the anticipated Allied forces supporting them, hundreds were captured and killed.

Finally, Montgomery abandoned the country. The winter of 1944–45 came to be known as the 'Winter of Hunger', with starvation rife as no food could be imported from Allied-held Belgium.

HALF-DAY FORAY: OOSTERBEEK

An old upscale suburb 5km west of downtown Arnhem, Oosterbeek retains a distinctly bourgeois atmosphere with its leafy-green parks and elegant villas harking back to the 19th century when the wealthy had country homes built here. It was the scene of heavy combat during Operation Market Garden in September 1944, and its war museum is an essential port of call on any WWII trail.

Inside a 19th-century, primrose-yellow mansion used by both the British and the Germans as HQ during Operation Market Garden, the much-visited Airborne Museum Hartenstein (☏ 026-333 77 10; www.airbornemuseum.nl; Utrechtseweg 232; adult/child €10/6; ☉ 10am-5pm Mon-Sat, noon-5pm Sun) does a good job of laying out this disastrous mission and putting it into context. A bunker running beneath the cafe terrace is the atmospheric venue for the Airborne Experience, a dramatic, subterranean maze simulating a night scene from the Battle of Arnhem (17–26 September 1944) using B&W footage from the 1946 film *Theirs is the Glory.*

Nearby, row upon row of white gravestones of 1691 Allied troops, mostly British, killed during Operation Market Garden in September 1944 are buried in Oosterbeek's war cemetery (☏ 01628-507 200; Van Limburg Stirumweg 6861; ☉ 24hrs), 500m east of Oosterbeek train station; follow the signs.

Post-museum, rejuvenate weary spirits with a meal-sized club sandwich, creative salad or staple *bitterballen* at Klein Hartenstein (☏ 026-334 21 21; www.kleinhartenstein. nl; Utrechtseweg 226; mains €7.75-13.50; ☉ 10.30am-11pm, kitchen 11.30am-9pm; ☎ ♿), an attractive cream-stone villa (1779) next to the war museum with summer garden overlooking the village green.

From Arnhem train station, take bus 352 directly to the museum (€4, 10 minutes, every 30 minutes) or bus No 1 from Velverplein to the A Weeninklaan stop (€4, 10 minutes), a five-minute walk from the museum. Local trains on the line between Arnhem and Utrecht stop at Oosterbeek (from Arnhem €2.30, three minutes, every 30 minutes). By bike, take the LF4b west, skirting the railroad tracks much of the way.

fashion district, this boutique hotel has 20 rooms, individually decorated by a leading fashion designer. Depending on your taste, you can fall asleep counting buttons on the ceiling, surround yourself in knitted furnishings and fittings, sleep between gold walls or spend the night deciphering a floor-to-ceiling patchwork of QR codes.

★ **De Zilte Zeemeermin** SEAFOOD €
(The Silent Mermaid; ☏ 026-379 48 16; www.de ziltezeemeermin.nl; Steenstraat 83a; small plates from €5; ☉ bar 4-10pm Thu-Sat, shop 9am-10pm Tue-Sat) *Hollandse Nieuwe* or soused herrings (lightly brined, raw, young herrings), herring sandwiches, *gerookte meervalfilet* (smoked catfish fillet), oven-baked clams and freshly shucked oysters served with a variety of tantalising sauces are among the specialities served at this wildly popular fish bar.

★ **Caspar** EUROPEAN €€
(☏ 026-840 35 24; www.caspararnhem.nl; Elly Lamakerplantsoen 2; mains €9.40-18.60; ☉ 9.30-1am Sun-Wed, to 2am Thu-Sat; ☎) Modern Dutch and European cuisine is served alfresco beneath trees or in a designer interior with leather-seat bar stools and inviting sofa corner.

MeeM INTERNATIONAL €€
(☏ 06 2376 0851; http://meemetenendrinken. nl; Coehoornstraat 8; burgers €13-16; ☉ 4-11pm Thu-Mon, kitchen from 5.30pm; ☎) Grab a pew at this casual eatery by the train station serving up gourmet salads, burgers and hotdogs. Star of the show is the Bucketlist Burger (€40), a feast of a multi-burger to share that stacks up a mind-boggling 50cm in height.

🍺 Drinking

★ **'t Taphuys** BAR
(☏ 026-202 02 58; www.taphuysarnhem.nl; Jansplein 56; ☉ 11am-1am Sun-Thu, 11am-3am Fri & Sat; ☎) Make a beeline for this huge beer bar with 100 beers and 80 wines on tap in the former post office, a magnificent red-brick building on Arnhem's buzziest old-town square. Buy a tap card (deposit €2), charge it up with cash and then serve yourself whichever brew or vintage takes your fancy.

❶ Information

Tourist Office (☎ 0900 112 23 44; www.visit arnhem.com; Stationsplein 13; ◷ 9.30am-5.30pm Mon-Fri, to 5pm Sat) In the train station.

❶ Getting There & Around

Regional buses leave from in front (south) of the train station.

BICYCLE

The train station has a below-ground bike rental shop on the left as you exit, with 7-speed Batavuses (€7.50 per day, plus €50 cash deposit). National bike route LF3 runs 55km northeast to Deventer; Nijmegen is a twisting 40km south.

Train

At Arnhem's train station, find luggage lockers (per 24 hours small/large €3.85/5.70) opposite the public toilets on the ground floor.

TO	PRICE (€)	TIME (MIN)	FREQUENCY (PER HR)
Amsterdam	16.90	60	2
Deventer	8.60	35	2
Nijmegen	4.30	12-18	8

Hoge Veluwe National Park

The marshlands, lizard-laced heathlands, swaths of ancient pine, oak and beech forests alive with woodpeckers and red deer, and dramatic open-drift sands would be reason enough to visit this 5500-hectare national park (www.hogeveluwe.nl; adult/child €9.50/4.75, with museum €19/9.50; ◷ 8am-10pm Jun & Jul, 8am-9pm May & Aug, 8am-8pm Apr, 9am-8pm Sep, 9am-7pm Oct, 9am-6pm Nov-Mar), the largest in the Netherlands. But its Van Gogh art museum and sensational sculpture park dotted with contemporary art pieces make it simply unmissable.

There are myriad bike paths and 42km of hiking trails, with two routes signposted by *paddenstoelen* (mushroom markers). At the north edge, **Jachthuis Sint Hubert** (☎ 0800 8353 628; www.hogeveluwe.nl; Apeldoornseweg 258, Hoenderloo; 45-minute guided tour adult/child €4/2, excluding park admission; ◷ tours every half-hour between 11.30am and 4pm) is the lakeside country residence built for the Kröller-Müllers and named after the patron saint of hunting.

Visitors – by foot, bike or car – pay an admission fee to enter the national park at one of three entrances: Schaarsbergen (south), Hoenderloo (east) and Otterlo (west, the busiest of the three). Buy tickets online or from ticket offices at entrances; the latter sell invaluable park maps (€2.50) too.

◉ Sights & Activities

★**Kröller-Müller Museum** — MUSEUM
(☎ 0318-591 241; www.krollermuller.nl; Houtkampweg 6, Otterlo; incl park admission adult/child €19/9.50; ◷ museum 10am-5pm Tue-Sun, sculpture garden to 4.30pm) Nestled between trees, this striking museum has works by some of the greatest painters of several centuries, from Bruyn the Elder to Picasso. Its Van Gogh collection rivals that of the artist's namesake museum in Amsterdam: the world's second-largest, it includes the dark *Weavers* (1884), *The Potato Eaters* (1884) and *Place du Forum* (1888), painted in southern France, among many more. Impressionists include Renoir, Sisley, Monet and Manet.

Then there's the sensational sculpture garden in the museum grounds, with 160-odd alfresco works by Rodin, Moore and others peppering its 25 hectares of pea-green lawns, pristine flower beds and shady alleys.

Count on 3km from the park entrance in Otterlo, 4km from the Hoenderloo entrance and 10km from the Schaarsbergen one by bike to the museum.

🛏 Sleeping & Eating

De Houtkamp — B&B €
(☎ 0318-591 706; www.dehoutkamp.nl; Houtkampweg 7, Otterlo; s/d €45/65; ☏) With three doubles in a 1930s farmhouse and a self-catering cottage sleeping six to 10 guests, this picture-postcard farm near the Otterlo entrance to De Hoge Veluwe makes the perfect overnighter for national-park exploring. Breakfast in warm weather is alfresco beneath trees.

★**Hotel de Serrenberg** — DESIGN HOTEL €€
(☎ 0318-591 228; www.sterrenberg.nl; Houtkampweg 1, Otterlo; d €170; ❊ @ ☏ ☷) Urban chic meets natural beauty at this stunning countryside hotel, a five-minute bike ride (600m) from the Otterlo entrance of the Hoge Veluwe National Park. Forty-four rooms offer every comfort, and the wellness centre boasts a pool, a sauna, a steam room and an utterly divine tepidarium.

★ **Cèpes**   EUROPEAN

(☎ 0318-591 228; http://cepes.nl/en/; Houtkamp-weg 1, Otterlo; lunch mains €13.50-18, dinner mains €24-28; ⊘ noon-4pm & 5.30-8.30pm; 🛜) With a parasol-shaded terrace overlooking flowery gardens and grassy fields beyond, this on-trend contemporary address is particularly delightful in warm weather. Chef Robert Hartelman sources his fresh, organic produce from local farms and cheese dairies, to stunning effect.

ℹ Information

Ticket offices at park entrances sell park maps (€2.50) marked up with cycling and walking itineraries (2.6km to 9.2km). They also organise stacks of fascinating guided visits in the park: birdwatching at dawn, meditation workshops, themed nature walks etc. Tickets (€10 to €23) must be reserved in advance.

The **Hoge Veluwe National Park Visitors Centre** (Bezoekerscentrum & Museonder; ☎ 0800 8353 628; www.hogeveluwe.nl; Hout-kampweg 9c, Otterlo; ⊘ 9.30am-6pm Apr-Oct, to 5pm Nov-Mar) has information on the park's nature, culture and history. It likewise takes bookings for guided visits. In 2019 it opened in a new state-of-the-art building.

ℹ Getting There & Away

BICYCLE

The park is easily reached from any direction: national bike route LF4 through Arnhem is the closest major route, and there are 40km of cycling paths within the park.

Rent wheels at **Geerts Tweewielers** (☎ 0318-595 404; www.geerts-tweewielers.nl; Dorpsstraat 2c, Otterlo; bike/e-bike per day

ICE-CREAM HEAVEN

Discover gourmet artistry at **Ijs van Co** (☎ 055-378 1502; www.ijsvanco.nl; Krimweg 33d, Hoenderloo; cones €0.70-2, tubs €0.90-8, toppings €0.50-2; ⊘ noon-8pm), a humble ice-cream parlour in Hoenderloo, a 10-minute stroll from the park entrance. It has been making its smooth, soft and creamy vanilla ice-cream since 1938 and is a local legend, as the line outside the shop attests. To get here by bike from the park entrance, follow signs for *knooppunt* 12.

€9/22; ⊘ 8.30am-6pm Mon-Sat) in Otterlo village or use the park's famous free white bicycles (complete with toddler seat), available at entrances. In high season arrive before noon on Sunday to ensure you snag one of the 1800 available bikes.

BUS

From Arnhem train station, take bus 9 (€4, 25 minutes, every half-hour) to the Schaarsbergen entrance (stop: Koningsweg) or bus 105 (direction Barneveld) to Otterlo (€4, 30 minutes, every half-hour). From Apeldoorn train station in the north, bus 108 travels to Hoenderloo (€4, 25 minutes, hourly). Within the park, bus 106 (€4, 10 minutes) links the Hoenderloo and Otterlo entrances, stopping en route at the Kröller-Müller Museum en route.

CAR & MOTORCYCLE

Motorists can park in huge car parks at all three entrance to the park (€4.40) or pay €6.75 to drive into the park; find car parks at the visitors centre and Kröller-Müller Museum.

Maastricht & Southeastern Netherlands

Best Places to Eat

➡ Restaurant Hemingway (p278)

➡ Dames Pellens (p278)

➡ Dit (p271)

➡ Witloof (p266)

➡ De Burgerij (p276)

Best Places to Stay

➡ Kruisherenhotel (p265)

➡ Sense Hotel (p271)

➡ Bliss Hotel (p277)

➡ Hostel Roots (p275)

➡ Hotel Nassau (p277)

➡ Hotel Restaurant Parkzicht (p268)

Why Go?

Things are different below the rivers: the provinces of Noord Brabant and Limburg have a character that's more Catholic, more relaxed, and in the case of southern Limburg, hillier than elsewhere in the Netherlands. Among the obvious southern influences are a preference for good beer and food, as embodied in the concept *Bourgondisch:* eating and drinking with a verve worthy of the epicurean inhabitants of France's Burgundy.

Maastricht's medieval ramparts, delicate brick towers, polyglot inhabitants and its role in brokering the Eurozone all suggest a closer kinship with Europe than with a Dutch town. And the hilly terrain to the east makes for panoramic (if strenuous) cycling and hiking.

Noord Brabant is a discordant combination of historically evocative towns like Den Bosch and Breda, and post-industrial urban centres like Tilburg and Eindhoven which are forging new identities as havens of design, culture and technology, within cycling distance of tranquil landscapes.

When to Go

➡ Warming the chill of February or early March, carnivals in this area are the Netherlands' most uninhibited, celebrated with special gusto in Bergen op Zoom and Maastricht.

➡ The wonderful cafe-terrace scene comes alive from late spring to early autumn, especially in Breda and Maastricht.

➡ Late spring to early autumn is also ideal for cycling the Noord Brabant riverbanks or walking in the verdant hills around Valkenburg, though avoid July and August when tourism overload can reduce the latter's charm.

➡ May sees major jazz festivals in Breda and Den Bosch.

Maastricht & Southeastern Netherlands Highlights

1 Maastricht (below) Thrilling in the good life and going bonkers at the annual Carnaval.

2 Jheronimus Bosch Art Center (p269) Decoding the myriad messages in the works of the artist with whom Den Bosch is inextricably associated.

3 Philips Museum (p274) Mixing nostalgia with tech-design artistry at this brilliant museum

that celebrates Eindhoven's trademark international brand.

4 Breda (p276) Drinking your way around the superb beer-bars of this vibrant party town, crowned by a beautiful Gothic church tower.

5 Heusden (p270) Getting off the beaten track in this charm-filled former citadel-village.

6 Efteling (p266) Delighting the whole family with a trip to one of Europe's foremost theme parks.

7 Koningshoeven (p275) Tasting Dutch Trappist treasures in the abbey where they're brewed, just outside Tilburg.

8 Den Bosch's Canals (p270) Gliding beneath street level on the mysterious subterranean waterways.

MAASTRICHT

♪ 043 / POP 122,500

Lively and energetic, Maastricht has Roman history, a maze of tunnel-caves and historical buildings aplenty, plus a Burgundian sophis-

tication to its dining, a bacchanalian delight to its drinking culture, and a student-friendly street-life out of all proportion to its size. The people are irreverent, shrugging off the shackles of Dutch restraint while speaking a dialect

Maastricht

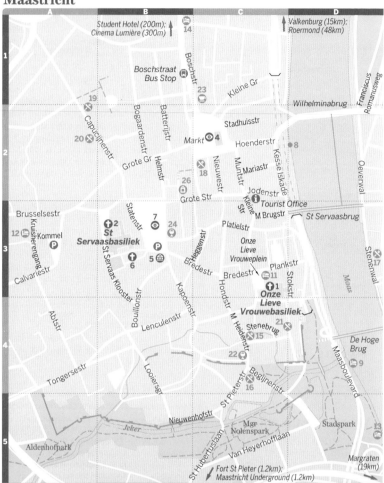

('Mestreechs') that baffles Hollanders. No visit to the Netherlands is complete without a visit.

◉ Sights & Activities

Far more than the sum of its 'sights', Maastricht's greatest charm is randomly exploring the compact area of narrow, cafe-filled streets on both sides of the pedestrianised Sint Servaasbrug, notably between the three main squares, Vrijthof, Markt (p267) and Onze Lieve Vrowplein, plus in the ramparts area directly south. For a hike, climb the green Sint Pietersberg plateau or join a Maastricht Underground tour to burrow

into one of the world's most complex mazes that lies beneath.

★ **St Servaasbasiliek** CHURCH
(www.sintservaas.nl; Keizer Karelplein 3; adult/child €4.50/3; ◉10am-5pm Mon-Sat, from 12.30pm Sun) Built above and around the shrine of St Servaas (Servatius), the first bishop of Maastricht, the basilica presents an architectural pastiche whose earliest sections date from 1000AD. Its beautiful curved brick apse and towers dominate the Vrijthof. Tickets include access to the cloister garden and the four-room treasury whose star attractions

with few passing points) can feel rather claustrophobic.

Museum Aan Het Vrijthof   MUSEUM

(☏ 043-321 13 27; www.museumaanhetvrijthof. nl; Vrijthof 18; adult/teenager/child €9/4.50/free; ◷ 10am-5.30pm Tue-Sun) Exhibitions in this small museum change every few months but even if the current subject doesn't interest you it's worth popping your head inside.

The grand cafe, accessible without entry ticket, straddles a skylit courtyard incorporating the stone loggia of a building known as the Spaans Gouvernement. It was here that Holy Roman Emperor Charles V would stay when visiting Maastricht 500 years ago.

★ Onze Lieve Vrouwebasiliek   CHURCH

(☏ 043-321 38 54; www.sterre-der-zee.nl; Onze Lieve Vrouweplein 9; treasury adult/child €3/1; ◷ 8.30am-5pm, treasury 11am-4pm) Dominating an intimate cafe-filled square, this millennium-old basilica-church is a fabulous example of Mosan architecture, made 'extra authentic' through 1886–1916 restorations led by Pierre Cuypens (of Rijksmuseum fame). Still a deeply spiritual place, you'll usually come in past pilgrims kneeling at the candle-filled medieval shrine to 'Maria Star of the Sea' and will need to adjust slowly to the brooding darkness of the interior, with its gigantic Romanesque pillars.

Bonnefantenmuseum   GALLERY

(☏ 043-329 01 90; www.bonnefanten.nl; Ave Cèramique 250; adult/child €12.50/free; ◷ 11am-5pm Tue-Sun) Maastricht's star gallery has an excellent collection of early European painting and sculpture on the 1st floor, but is best known for contemporary art, with works by Limburg artists displayed upstairs and accessed via a dramatic sweep of stairs. There are regularly changing exhibitions.

Maastricht Underground   CAVE

(☏ 043-321 21 21; www.maastrichtunderground.nl; Luikerweg 71; cave tour adult/child €6.25/5, combination tour €9.95/6.95; ◷ see website) Maastricht Underground runs spooky, amusing and fascinating tours into sections of the vast tunnel network beneath St-Pietersberg massif. Departures run on a constantly shifting schedule, with up to five tours daily in summer, very few off season – check the website.

Fort St Pieter   FORTRESS

(☏ 043-325 21 21; www.maastrichtunderground. nl; Luikerweg 71; fort tour adult/child €6.75/5.30,

are St Servaas's gilded bust and 11th-century sarcophagus.

St Janskerk   CHURCH

(Vrijthof 24; tower adult/child €2.50/1.50; ◷ 11am-4pm Mon-Sat) This attractive 17th-century Gothic church has a soaring if relatively unadorned interior and a 43m limestone tower whose deep red hue was originally achieved with coats of ox blood (now just paint). Climbing the tower reveals wide views, well explained by explanatory panels that make for a great introduction to Maastricht, but the narrow spiral stairs (around 260 of them

MAASTRICHT & SOUTHEASTERN NETHERLANDS MAASTRICHT

Maastricht

combination tour €10.40/8; ⊙5 tours daily, in English at 12.30pm) Set within a deep-cut dry moat, this hefty five-sided brick fort once formed the city's southern defence and is linked to a network of underground tunnels. Dating from 1701, it is sturdily striking more than beautiful and best viewed from the footpaths that loop around it for fine city panoramas.

The restored interior can be seen on guided tours which can be combined with North Cave tunnel tours. Purchase tickets at the Chalet Bergrust restaurant overlooking the (payable) car park.

It's a 2km walk south of Maastricht, or take bus No 7 and get off at 'Mergelweg'. Three nature walks begin from here, each marked by colour-coded posts. The fort is also the southernmost point of the Pieterpad, one of the Netherlands' most popular long-distance hikes, extending 492km to Pietersburen in Groningen province.

☞ Tours

Stiphout Cruises
BOATING
(☎043-351 53 00; www.stiphout.nl; Maaspromenade 58; adult/child from €10/5.75; ⊙daily Apr-Oct, Sat & Sun Nov-Dec) Stiphout runs hourly pleasure cruises on the Maas (11am to 5pm), with some departures allowing you to break the journey at Slavante Jetty. These are timed such that you can walk up from Slavante to the Zonneberg Cave meeting point in time for scheduled tours...and back again afterwards if you don't dawdle.

 Festivals & Events

★ Carnaval
CARNIVAL
(www.carnavalinmaastricht.nl; ⊙Feb or Mar) *Everything* stops for Carnaval. Since November, Maastricht has been preparing. The partying and carousing finally begins the Friday before Shrove Tuesday and lasts until the last person collapses sometime on Wednesday.

⫿ Sleeping

Stayokay Maastricht
HOSTEL €
(☎043-750 17 90; www.stayokay.com/maastricht; Maasboulevard 101; dm €21-41, d €53-96; @🌐) Much of the main floor of this excellent hostel is a cafe-bar which spills out on to a wide terrace overlooking the Maas. Prices rise dramatically at weekends and peak holiday periods. HI members save €2.50.

Botel Maastricht
HOTEL €
(☎043-321 90 23; www.botelmaastricht.nl; Maasboulevard 95; dm €35, s/d with bathroom €63/70, without bathroom €57/64) This centrally moored boat has 34 basic, inexpensive cabins which are very compact with beds that won't suit the tall. Doubles ensure that couples get very intimate, many featuring tiny but well-equipped bathrooms.

Trash Deluxe
B&B €€
(☎043-852 55 00; www.trashdeluxe.nl; Boschstraat 55; d €82-145, f €130-225; 🌐) 🖉 Recycled rubber conveyor belts, industrial lighting, packing crates etc create a unique, ultra-stylish atmosphere in eight artist-designed rooms

spread across two historic buildings near the Markt. Big/light breakfasts cost €6/13.50 extra. Though calling itself a hotel, there's no real reception so don't lose your access code when booking.

★ **Student Hotel** HOTEL €€
(☑ 043-711 22 35; www.thestudenthotel.com; Sphinxcour 9a; r €80-130) 'Sit down...or dance with us' suggests the colourful, open-plan reception in this light-suffused, 140-room hotel that oozes industrial-chic in a brilliantly repurposed factory that once made ceramic toilet bowls. While hip and very contemporary, you certainly don't have to be a student to stay here, and the rooms are fully equipped.

Hotel Derlon HISTORIC HOTEL €€
(☑ 043-321 67 70; www.derlon.com; Onze Lieve Vrouwplein 6; r midweek/weekend €150/200) Calling archaeologists! Certainly the venerable 1870 Derlon has a perfect old-city location and 48 freshly renovated rooms, but what really makes it unique is the subterranean breakfast space with tables ranged around an entirely unexpected attraction – the unearthed remnants of a Roman piazza plus showcases of other found treasures accompanied by explanatory notes.

Designhotel DESIGN HOTEL €€
(☑ 043-328 25 25; www.designhotelmaastricht.com; Stationsstraat 40; r €89-220; ❄ @ 🛜) With its own in-house artist, this calm, professional design hotel has a lobby with '70s retro vibe and a respected brasserie oozing comfortable contemporary modernism. The 105 rooms come in varying sizes and styles, all with kettle and coffee machine and usually parquet wooden floors. Breakfast costs €15 per person.

★ **Kruisherenhotel** BOUTIQUE HOTEL €€€
(☑ 043-329 20 20; www.kruisherenhotel.nl; Kruisherengang 19-23; r weekday/weekend from €195/279; ❄ @ 🛜) This prize-winning design statement is housed inside the former Crutched Friar monastery complex, dating from 1483. Modern touches, such as moulded furniture and padded walls, accent the historical surroundings. Each of the 60 sumptuous rooms is unique. Some have murals and artwork, others are in the rafters of the old church. Breakfast is suitably heavenly.

🍴 Eating

Maastricht has many excellent dining places. It's worth browsing the eastern end of Tongersestraat, the little streets around the

MAASTRICHT & SOUTHEASTERN NETHERLANDS MAASTRICHT

LOCAL KNOWLEDGE

DARK AT THE END OF THE TUNNEL

Overlooking Maastricht from the south, the raised tableland of Sint Pietersberg is a great area for hiking, guarded by a hefty brick fortress. But even more intriguing is the phenomenal labyrinth of quarry-tunnels beneath, an amazing feat of mostly pre-industrial engineering. Marlstone and limestone have been laboriously hand-cut here since Roman times, and at one stage, there were 20,000 separate underground passages stretching past the Belgian border, with a total length of some 230km. They offered refuge in times of war, a smuggling route in pre-EU days, and a section was long used as a secret NATO command base (NAVO-hoofdkwartier; www.limburgs-landschap.nl; Cannerberg; ⊙ see website). Over a third of the maze remains intact and there are several ways to visit, always by guided tour: getting lost here would likely be fatal. Walking through the tunnels is an eerie experience and you'll feel a deep chill if you're not suitably dressed; it's 11°C year-round with 95% humidity.

The most frequent tours visit the North Caves, where guides focus particularly on the tunnels' role in Napoleonic French history. Although not always accessible, ask the guide and you just might be able to visit the extraordinary vault where 750 paintings were stored for safe-keeping by Nazi occupiers during WWII. These included Rembrandt's *The Night Watch,* kept rolled in a tapestry and transported here in a coffin. Check tour times through Maastricht Underground (p263) and consider prebooking at busy periods. North tour departures are from the Fort St Pieter ticket booth. Use the same website for details of less frequent tours to the taller, equally intriguing Zonneberg Caves (Grotten Zonneberg; Slavante 1) decorated with generations of charcoal drawings, from ancient Roman stick figures to wartime depictions of movie stars. Visits start behind the Buitengoed Slavante cafe some 3km south of town (free parking).

WORTH A TRIP

THE DUTCH RIVAL TO DISNEYLAND

Is **Efteling** (www.efteling.nl; Europalaan 1; €38, parking €10; ⊙10am or 11am-6pm Sep-Jun, to 8pm Jul & Aug; ⓟ300, 301) Europe's greatest theme park? The Dutch certainly think so. Their rival to Disneyland pulls in more than four million visitors annually and offers a great selection of enchanting fairy-tale themed entertainment, talking trees and water shows but also some of the craziest rollercoasters you're likely to ride, including the 360-degree screamer 'Baron', and in-the-dark sensory-overload 'Vogel Kock'.

Efteling is near the unassuming town of Kaatsheuvel. Buses 300 and 301 stop at Efteling between Tilburg (€3, 20 minutes) and Den Bosch (€4.90, 40 minutes), running several times an hour.

Vrijthof and Rechtstraat, just east of the river. Onze Lieve Vrouweplein is excellent for a warm-weather cafe interlude, and several characterful mini-restaurants line the lane running directly south from there – a good place on Monday evenings, when most other places close.

★ Bisschopsmolen
BAKERY €

(www.bisschopsmolen.nl; Stenebrug 3; vlaai €2.40, baguette sandwiches €6; ⊙9am-6pm Tue-Sat, 10am-5pm Sun) A working 7th-century waterwheel powers a vintage flour mill that supplies its adjoining bakery with the spelt that is used to bake its 100% spelt loaves and *vlaai* (seasonal fruit pies). You can dine on-site at the cafe, and, if it's not busy, self-tour the mill and see how flour has been made for aeons.

Friture Reitz
FAST FOOD €

(www.reitz.nl; Markt 75; small/large frites €3/3.50, sauce €0.75-1; ⊙11am-7pm Tue-Sun) Join the takeaway queue at this iconic snack bar, which has been turning Limburg potatoes into scrumptious double-fried *frites* since 1909.

Marres Kitchen
MEDITERRANEAN €€

(☑06-1333 3583; www.marres.org; Capucijnenstraat 98; mains €18-24; ⊙noon-5pm & 6-10pm Tue-Sun) Adjunct to a gallery for contemporary art, dishes span the Mediterranean spectrum, with a fair variety of meat-free options especially among the beautifully crafted Middle

Eastern mezes. The semiwild garden is an appealing part of the atmosphere, tucked quietly away off a noncommercial minor street.

★ Witloof
BELGIAN €€

(☑043-323 35 38; www.witloof.nl; Sint Bernardusstraat12; mains €17.50-21.50, 2-/3-course dinner €27/33; ⊙5.30-9.30pm Wed-Sun) A decade after hitting the *New York Times'* list of world's trendiest restaurant concepts, Witloof still cuts the mustard with top-quality Belgian traditional food, an astounding beer-cellar (do take a look!) and a tongue-in-cheek humour with decor worthy of a 21st-century Magritte.

Café Sjiek
DUTCH €€

(☑043-321 01 58; www.cafesjiek.nl; St Pieterstraat 13; mains €13.50-26; ⊙kitchen 5-11pm Mon-Wed, from noon Thu-Sun, bar to 2am; ☎) This cosy spot is a great place to try traditional *zuurvlees* (sour stew) made with horsemeat and served with apple sauce. But there are also fresh fish dishes and cafe-classics like stroganoff, steaks, chicken and chips and quiche. It doesn't take reservations and is always busy, but you can eat at the bar.

Kantine De Brandweer
FUSION €€

(☑043-852 22 29; www.debrandweer.com; Capucijnenstraat 21; mains €17-24; ⊙10am-6pm Mon, to 10.30pm Tue-Sun) The vibe is friendly and casual in this former firehouse turned hip dining hall and activity centre. Sit at amply spaced formica tables beside a long book-lined counter and watch the young chefs work their wizardry on an adventurous melange of cuisines.

Eetcafé Ceramique
DUTCH €€

(☑043-325 20 97; www.eetcafeceramique.nl; Rechtstraat 78; mains €17-25; ⊙5.30-10pm) A local dining favourite for decades, Ceramique's relaxed, unfussy interior is always buzzy and low-lit by candles in paper bags. The wide-ranging menu mixes traditional home cooking with international dishes and flavours, with a large proportion of vegan or vegetarian choices: try the chicory-rhubarb lasagne with lime-vodka sauce. Reservations are wise.

🍷 Drinking & Nightlife

Maastricht has a thriving bar scene and most cafes serve food. The east side of the Vrijthof harbours numerous options, while Onze Lieve Vrouweplein and nearby lanes are arguably cosier on terrace-warm afternoons. Three cafes have enviable river facing terrace-perches beside the east end of St Servaasbrug. The Coffeelovers chain's most audacious barista joint is within the Boekhandel Dominicanen.

★ **In Den Ouden Vogelstruys** BROWN CAFE
(www.vogelstruys.nl; Vrijthof 15; ⊙9.30am-late) Right on a sunny Vrijthof corner, this classic brown bar features swords, medals and portraits of 1950s patrons on the dark panelled walls. Seven draft beers include two Trappists (La Trappe Blond and Westmalle Dubbel) and carefully selected bottled offerings like local unfiltered Klinker III (8.5%) and Jopen's prize-winning Mooie Nel IPA (aka 'Northsea', 6.5%).

Café de Pieter BROWN CAFE
(www.cafedepieter.nl; Sint Pieterstraat 22; ⊙noon-2am Tue-Sun, from 3pm Mon) Small, wonderfully authentic brown bar with higgledy-piggledy art, terrace seating beside a rampart wall and tap beers including Valkenburg-brewed Leeuw IPA and Tongerlo. Somehow it crams in a stage for Wednesday open-mic nights, jazz-flavoured bands at weekends and a DJ some Fridays.

De Gouveneur CAFE
(☎043-852 11 25; www.degouverneurmaastricht. nl; Boschstraat 105a; ⊙10am-late) Sit on a perfectly located market-edge terrace and peruse the 'bible' listing 270 varieties (16 on tap) in this veritable museum of beer. Classic Belgian food is available including cones of excellent *frites*.

Zondag CAFE
(www.cafezondag.nl; Wycker Brugstraat 42; sandwiches €6-8; ⊙10am-2am Sun-Thu, to 3am Fri & Sat) Hitting the perfect note between hipster coffee house, cosy lunch spot and in-the-know drinking hole, Zondag draws a smart youthful set day and night behind an old storefront with original tile floors.

☆ Entertainment

★ **Cinema Lumière** CINEMA
(☎043-321 40 80; www.lumiere.nl; Bassin 88) Great for offbeat and classic films but also worth visiting for its former powerstation setting, tempting waterside bar-terrace and quirky, post-ndustrial restaurant.

🔒 Shopping

The **Markt** is the scene of several markets, general on Wednesdays: fish on Fridays and *brocante* (ie used everything) on Saturdays

and Sundays. There's also a Thursday afternoon organic market (Stationstraat; ⊙1.30-6.30pm Thu).

Boekhandel Dominicanen BOOKS
(☎043-321 08 25; Dominicanenkerkstraat 1; ⊙10am-6pm Mon, from 9am Tue-Sat, from noon Sun; 🛜) A cathedral of books – literally. Don't miss the relaxed coffee-house area that takes the place of the altar.

ℹ Information

Tourist Office (VVV; ☎043-325 21 21; www. vvvmaastricht.nl; Kleine Straat 1; ⊙10am-6pm Mon, 11am-5pm Sat & Sun) In the 15th-century Dinghuis (old courthouse); cycling tours offered.

ℹ Getting There & Around

BICYCLE
Aon de Stasie (Stationsplein; ⊙7am-10pm Mon-Sat, 9am-9pm Sun), to the left as you exit the station, rents city bikes (from €5/10 per day without/with hand-brakes) and mountain bikes (from €20).

BUS
For Valkenburg buses 8 and 4 (€2.85, 30 minutes) pick up at **Boschstraat**, Mosae Forum and from the uncovered **bus-station area** (Parallelweg) outside the train station on the northwest side. **Bus 350** (Parallelweg) from here drives four times hourly via the US war graves at **Margraten** (€2.60, 20 minutes) and the celebrated brewery at **Gulpen** to Aachen (Germany, single/day-return €6/8.50, 65 minutes).

TRAIN
Click your OV-chipkaart on the yellow posts for NS trains including twice-hourly services to Amsterdam (€25.30, 2½ hours), Den Bosch (€20.40, 85 minutes) and Utrecht (€23.90, two hours). Use blue posts for Arriva trains to Valkenburg (€3, 12 minutes) and Roermond (€9.50, 45 minutes).

For Brussels, Paris and Cologne use the hourly Belgian Railways service to Hasselt (95 minutes) and change in Liège (€6.80, 33 minutes). Though planned for many years, construction of the far-faster direct Maastricht–Hasselt fast-tram has yet to begin.

Valkenburg

☎043 / POP 16,400
An easy 12km hop from Maastricht, little Valkenburg is an overgrown village that's been a popular local tourist destination for at least a century. Overlooked by the fragmentary ruins

of an ancient castle (Valkenburg Castle; ☑043-820 00 40; www.kasteelvalkenburg.nl; Grendelplein; adult/child €6.50/4.50, with tunnels €12/9; ☺10am-5.30pm Mar-Oct, to 4pm Nov-Dec, limited opening Jan & Feb), the cafe-filled town centre has many historic elements and a series of mini-bridges spanning the small twin rivers, but the overall effect is more of holiday honeypot than quaint getaway. A replica of Roman catacombs (☑043-601 25 54; www.katakomben.nl; Plenkerstraat 55; adult/child €9.75/6.25; ☺11am, 1pm & 3pm Tue-Sun) installed in an old limestone mine are by architect Pierre Cuypers of Rijksmuseum fame. Hiking and biking abounds in the gently hilly terrain to the east and southeast; Drielandenpunt (the convergence of the Netherlands, Belgium and Germany) is on the highest hill in the country (323m).

❶ Getting There & Away

Arriva trains to Maastricht (€3.30, four hourly) take eight to 15 minutes. Buses 4 (twice hourly) or 8 (hourly) take 20 to 30 minutes.

Roermond

☑047 / POP 57,300

The principal town of central Limburg, Roermond stands alongside the Maas, here skirted by a string of yacht harbours and artificial lakes fitted out for recreation. WWII and a 1992 earthquake did much damage but the bustling centre retains some older architecture, including two ancient if much restored churches, each on its own square with plenty of terrace cafes. The highlights of the 13th-century Munsterkerk (www.roermondparochiecluster.nl; Munsterplein; ☺2-5pm Apr-Oct, Sat only Nov-Mar) are the twin effigies on its central tomb. The light-suffused Sint-Christoffelkathedral (St Christopher's Cathedral; www.roermondparochiecluster.nl; Grote Kerkstraat 29; ☺2-5pm Mon-Fri, from 1pm Sat & Sun) has a tower that was painstakingly reconstructed having been blown to smithereens by retreating Germans in the last days of WWII. Roermond also has a gigantic outlet mall.

Roemond is famed as the home town of master architect Pierre Cuypens (1827–1921), the design talent behind Amsterdam's Centraal Station and Rijksmuseum. His former home and workshop (☑047-535 91 02; www.cuypershuisroermond.nl; Pierre Cuypersstraat 1; adult/child €6/4; ☺11am-4.30pm Tue-Sun) offers fascinating insights to the processes he used.

Should you decide to stay overnight, genteel Hotel Restaurant Parkzicht (☑047-531 74 54; www.parkzichtroermond.nl; Parklaan 8; d/ste €84/104; ☺restaurant 5-9pm; ✳🛜; 🛏61), around 1km southeast of the centre, is a gem of an old-world cafe and family restaurant cooking up good-value Italian.

❶ Getting There & Away

Roermond is on the intercity line linking Amsterdam, Utrecht, Den Bosch, Eindhoven (€9.80, 30 minutes) and Maastricht (€8.80, 30 minutes). Be careful to select the Arriva click-in post if using the slower Stoptrein to Maastricht (€9.50, 45 minutes) or the twice-hourly service to Nijmegen via Venlo (€5.20, 20 minutes).

NOORD BRABANT

Wedged between Zeeland and Limburg, the Netherlands' largest province shares a long border with Belgium, and is culturally linked to its southern neighbour. Don't be surprised to encounter Catholic shrines at crossroads and some of the Netherlands' more interesting villages. Cafe culture is lively, superb Brabantine beers include the Netherlands' only Trappist brews, and city calendars are studded with festivals. Richly historic towns like Breda and Den Bosch bear remnants of ancient canals and ramparts, while postindustrial younger siblings Eindhoven and Tilburg revel in contemporary culture. Home to Vincent van Gogh (who hailed from Zundert, south of Breda), Noord Brabant gives its artists pride of place in great museums. And the rural landscapes, river valleys and woods that inspired them are all easily accessed via a superb cycling network.

Den Bosch

☑073 / POP 153,000

Den Bosch ('the Forest') is the commonly used short form of 's-Hertogenbosch (Duke's Forest), though the trees have long gone and it's now the capital of Noord Brabant. It's best known as the birthplace of 15th-century painter Jheronimus van Aken, who later took his surname from the town and is remembered worldwide under the name Hieronymus (or Jeroen) Bosch for his surreal hell-scenes. As well as sights linked to him, the city also has a remarkable statue-festooned church, many attractive old streets, a great cafe-dining scene and some unique tunnel canals. The area was

Den Bosch

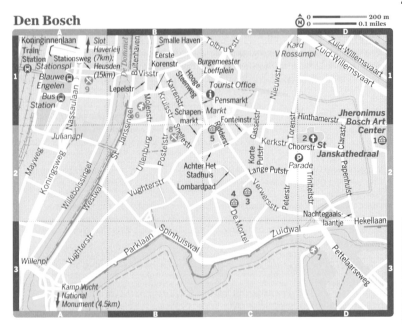

N 0 — 200 m
0 — 0.1 miles

hotly contested during the Eighty Years' War, and you can still see where lines of fortifications followed the shape of the canals.

◉ Sights

You can see the city in one large looping walk or by hopping on and off the free Blauwe Engelen (www.gastvrij-shertogenbosch.nl; Stationplein; ⊙10am-5pm Tue-Sat, noon-4pm Sun) **FREE** minibus.

★ St Janskathedraal
CHURCH

(✆073-681 49 33; www.sint-jan.nl; Choorstraat 1; tower adult/child €5/2.50; ⊙8.30am-5pm, tower tours 11am, 1pm & 3pm Tue-Sun Apr-Oct) One of the finest churches in the Netherlands, this cathedral took from 1336 to 1550 to complete. The interior has late-Gothic stained-glass windows, an organ case from the 17th century and a much-revered statue of the Madonna which, in May, is the focus of pilgrimages. Take the opportunity to climb the 73m tower, with its carillon and great views.

Stadhuis
HISTORIC BUILDING

(Markt) At the southern edge of Den Bosch's vast, triangular market square, the spired town hall was given its classical baroque appearance in 1670.

Den Bosch

◉ Top Experiences
1 Jheronimus Bosch Art Center D2
2 St Janskathedraal D2

◉ Sights
3 Design Museum Den Bosch C2
4 Noordbrabants Museum C2
5 Stadhuis C2

◉ Activities, Courses & Tours
6 Binnendieze B1
7 Bossche Broek D3

◉ Sleeping
Sense Hotel .... (see 1)

◉ Eating
8 Dit B2
9 Jan de Groot A1

★ Jheronimus Bosch Art Center
MUSEUM

(✆073-612 68 90; www.jheronimusbosch-art center.nl; Jeroen Boschplein 2; adult/child €7/3.50; ⊙11am-5.30pm Tue-Sun, from noon Sat & Sun Apr-Oct, to 5pm Tue-Sun Nov-Mar) Housed in the grand, century-old St Jacob's Church, this remarkable museum has reproductions of all 29 known Bosch paintings, brought to life by an explanatory free booklet. Atmosphere is

WORTH A TRIP

VILLAGE ENCOUNTERS

A trio of photogenic villages provide ample waterfront charm, vintage soul and surprise quirk for curious travellers keen to really sink their teeth into unexplored Noord Brabant.

Heusden (www.hbtheusden.nl) Picture-postcard little Heusden features antique tile-roofed houses, post-mills, minibridge and lovely inner yacht-harbour all wrapped in a fortified river-moat still retaining triangular ravelins (island-bastions).

Its hotel and loveable B&Bs are often used by families heading for Efteling (p266; 16km southwest), but Heusden richly warrants a visit in its own right. Take bus 135 from Den Bosch (€3.40, 25 minutes) or better still stop here while cycling between Den Bosch and Woudrichem.

Woudrichem (Woerekum; www.woudrichem.nl) Ringed by grassy medieval rampart-banks, the charming citadel-village of Woudrichem became famed as the set for popular TV drama Dokter Tinus. Its small harbour is filled with old-world fishing boats, the relatively intact central square (Hoogstraat) is lined with 17th-century houses, and there are a couple of floating restaurants. An 'on call' mini-ferry (€1.40 each way) takes pedestrians across the creek from the yacht marina to Kasteel Loevesteen, a 14th-century moated castle that's also an upmarket B&B.

Cyclists can reach nearby Gorinchem using a different ferry, beside whose dock parks a fish-seller's van selling delicious, locally caught perch (*baars*) which they'll fry up to order.

Baarle-Nassau (toerismebaarle.com) Together Baarle Nassau (NL) and Baarle Hertog (B) form an extraordinary geopolitical quirk divided by the world's messiest border jigsaw: 22 miniature exclaves of Belgium lie within the Netherlands, and a further half-dozen Dutch pockets lie within these. Visit the tourist office for an exhibition explaining the background then stroll the (otherwise ordinary) streets, noticing studs and crosses marked on roadways and pavements denoting the eccentric frontier line.

added by dangling 3D sculptures, an astronomical clock and a basement re-creation of the artist's studio.

A lift takes you past temporary exhibits to a fine 5th-floor viewpoint. On the way down again, do stop in the organ loft to see a Monty Pythonesque interpretive video.

Noordbrabants Museum `MUSEUM`
(☑ 073-687 78 77; www.hetnoordbrabantsmuseum. nl; Verwersstraat 41; adult/child €12/free; ⊙ 11am-5pm Tue-Sun) Housed in the 18th-century former governor's residence, this modern museum uses art and several immersive experiences to give interesting if sometimes confusingly disconnected overviews of Brabant's convoluted history.

Much more space is allocated to galleries of major, regularly changing art exhibitions, and there are always some elements from the excellent core collection featuring Brabantine artists from 1500 to the present.

Ten rather dark canvases by Vincent Van Gogh are much touted but more exciting are the underrated canvases of local impressionist Jan Sluiters (1881–1957).

Design Museum Den Bosch `MUSEUM`
(Stedelijk Museum; www.designmuseum.nl; De Mortel 4; adult/child €7/free; ⊙ 11am-5pm Tue-Sun) Opened in 2014 and rebranded in 2018, the museum's two large halls offer changing, interactive exhibitions focusing especially on ceramics and jewellery but also taking fascinating glances at the design concepts that underpin contemporary society.

🏃 Activities

★ Binnendieze `BOATING`
(www.dagjedenbosch.com; Molenstraat 15a; adult/child €8/4; ⊙ tours 10am-5.20pm Tue-Sun, from 2pm Mon Apr-Oct) Many canal tours in Den Bosch are partially subterranean adventures. Of several options, the most popular depart three times hourly from Molenstraat for 50-minute loops. Commentary is generally in Dutch but with a brochure in English. The manoeuvring through narrow spaces and low gaps is memorable in any language.

Bossche Broek `CYCLING`
(Sterrebosweg) Immediately across the Dommel River from the centre of Den Bosch, the

urban landscape gives way to open mead-owland in this 202 hectare nature reserve. It's laced with hiking and cycling trails and offers attractive views back towards the city skyline and ramparts.

🛏 Sleeping & Eating

★ **Sense Hotel**   BOUTIQUE HOTEL **€€**
(Stadshotel Jeroen; ☑ 073-610 35 56; www.stads hoteljeroenbosch.nl; Jeroen Boschplein 6; s/d/ste from €108.10/146.20/181.20; 🛜) Right next to the Jheronimus Bosch Art Center (p269), this charming little hotel has four rooms and three suites, each with its own spe-cial decor. Breakfast (€17.50) is served in a suave restaurant which is frequently cited as one of Den Bosch's top gourmet dining spots.

Jan de Groot   BAKERY **€**
(www.bosschebollen.nl; Stationsweg 24; Bossche bol €2.25; ☺ 8am-6pm Mon-Fri, to 5pm Sat) With its pink-and-white love-heart decor, this otherwise unassuming patisserie-cafe is *the* place to try the local speciality *Bossche bol* (Den Bosch ball), an overgrown profiterole the size of a grapefruit, filled with sweetened cream and coated in rich chocolate.

★ **Dit**   BISTRO **€**
(www.eetbar-dit.nl; Snellestraat 24; snacks €6-12; ☺ noon-9pm Mon, from 10am Tue-Sun) Fun and funky, Dit ('This') is a total delight for drinks, snacks or offbeat meals, some of them im-aginative flights of fancy, including goat's-cheese eclairs with caramelised hazelnuts – a delicious work of art.

Peruse the comedy-photo menu-booklet at bright-yellow benches facing the little bar with its plastic flamingo, Madonna and pin-ball machine. Or catch the lunchtime rays on a small square of street terrace.

ⓘ Information

Tourist Office (☑ 073-612 71 70; www.bezo-ekdenbosch.nl; Markt 77; ☺ 1-5pm Mon, from 10am Tue-Sat)

ⓘ Getting There & Around

BICYCLE

National bike route **LF12** heads due west through lush countryside some 70km to Dordre-cht via the north side of Biesbosch National Park (p180). **LF12** goes northeast 70km to Nijmegen along a twisting river route.

Bicycles are available to hire from **Fiets RataPlan** (Stationsplein; back-pedal/3-gear bikes per day €8.50/10; ☺ 5am-1.25am Mon-Fri, from 7.15am Sat & Sun), the cycle garage beneath the train station (enter via the tunnel west of the Golden Dragon roundabout). If you want electric bikes or more gears try **Kemps Bike Totaal** (☑ 073-613 76 86; www.kemps biketotaal.nl/services/fietsverhuur; Koren-brugstraat 12; bike per day/week €9.50/47.50; ☺ 9am-5pm Tue-Sat), which has seven-speed city bikes.

BUS

The **bus station** (Stationsplein) is directly south of the train station. Bus 300 and 301 head for Tilburg via Efteling, and 156 is for Eindhoven.

TRAIN

The train station is north of the bus station and 600m east of the Markt. Lockers are on the concourse over the tracks.

TO	PRICE (€)	TIME (MIN)	FREQUENCY (PER HR)
Amsterdam	15.50	60	2
Breda	8.30	35	4
Maastricht	20.40	90	2
Nijmegen	8.30	27-42	4
Utrecht	9.10	30	4

MAASTRICHT & SOUTHEASTERN NETHERLANDS DEN BOSCH

DON'T MISS

VILLAGE-HOPPING BY BIKE

For a great 40km cycling trip along the Maas – with much of the route atop dykes – head northeast out of Den Bosch to Heusden (p270), one of the Netherlands' prettiest small towns. It's surrounded by well-preserved grassy ravelins and moats, and blessed with three windmills, a cafe-dotted square and a charming little harbour. From there, continue to lesser-known but equally lovely Woudrichem (p270), with historic boats in its inner harbour, 17th-century houses on Hoogstraat and a mini-ferry taking pedestrians across to a moated castle on request. From just outside Woudrichem's city wall, a slightly bigger ferry carries cyclists across the river to Gorinchem, where you can put the bike on the return train to Den Bosch (one hour including a change in Geldermalsen).

MATYAS REHAK/SHUTTERSTOCK ©

1. Canal tour (p270), Den Bosch

There are several canal tour options in Den Bosch, many of which are partially subterranean adventures.

2. Philips Museum (p274), Eindhoven

This fascinating museum tells the story of the light-bulb maker turned multinational electronics firm.

3. St Servaasbasiliek (p262), Maastricht

The earliest sections of this beautiful basilica date from 1000AD.

4. Heusden (p270)

This picturesque village boasts antique tile-roofed houses, postmills, a minibridge and a beautiful inner yacht-harbour.

LOCAL KNOWLEDGE

DETOUR TO THORN

If you're driving between Maastricht and Eindhoven, the very pretty historic village of Thorn (www.vvvmiddenlimburg.nl; parking €2.50; 🖭73) makes a delightful short detour. Once the smallest principality of the Holy Roman Empire, it was the domain of *vorstendom* – rich independent women who wanted to live free of men.

Almost every building apart from the fine church (now a museum) has been painted white since the 1790s, when the then French rulers decided to tax homeowners by the size of their windows. Many chose to reduce their window sizes but needed to paint over the changes to hide differences in the additional brickwork. Or so the story goes.

An appealing way to visit Thorn (pronounced *To*-ren) on weekends (April to September) or daily in July and August, is by the Cascade Boat from Wessem, a small town on the E25 north of Maasbracht. The boat makes three trips a day also linking to gently attractive Stevensweert.

Eindhoven

📝 040 / POP 227,800

If you find yourself in the Netherlands' fifth-biggest city it's probably for an international budget flight or to watch a football match at PSV's Philips Stadium. But Eindhoven is also a vibrant centre for creative design and post-industrial reinvention. OK, so visually the townscape has all the charm of Minsk on a bad hair day, but before rushing on, do at least consider visiting the fascinating Philips Museum, which tells the story of the global electronics company that essentially created modern Eindhoven. There's also a highly thought-provoking modern-art gallery and a UFO-shaped quirk of 1960s architecture.

◉ Sights & Activities

★ **Philips Museum**   MUSEUM
(www.philips-museum.com; Emmasingel 31; adult/child €9/4.50, tour €5; ⊙ 11am-5pm Tue-Sun) From Keith Richards' tape-recorder to a wide-screen projector that once won an Oscar, this engaging museum tells the extraordinary story of the light-bulb maker turned multinational electronics company who invented the CD and shaped a century of development in Eindhoven.

Van Abbemuseum   GALLERY
(📝 040-238 10 00; www.vanabbemuseum.nl; Bilderdijklaan 10; adult/child €12/free, free from 3pm Tue; ⊙ 11am-5pm Tue-Sun; 🖭1) This superb modern-art gallery uses elements of its rich collection (including originals by Picasso, Braque and Kandinsky) along with plenty of contemporary material to ask probing questions about the nature of art, its changing role and the space that contains it. The building itself is

a dramatic architectural statement, the original castle-style 1936 gallery conjoined with a multilevel 2003 grey-stone addition that incorporates a weir of the Dommel river. The waterside cafe is worth a linger too.

Area 51   SPORTS
(📝 040-234 10 60; www.area51skatepark.nl; Klokgebouw 51, Strijp-S; skater/spectator €6/free; ⊙ 4-10pm Mon, 3-11pm Tue-Fri, 11am-1am Sat, noon-8pm Sun) Skaters know this world-class indoor skatepark for its MU-bowl and long practice runs. Non-skaters can gawp for free at their tricks and somersaults from the bar and other view areas.

🛏 Sleeping & Eating

Within the centre, the De Bergen area (www.debergeneindhoven.nl) is ideal for hunting out accessible but original dining options, notably along Bergstraat, which also has a brilliantly stocked beer shop. Alternatively, find several design-character choices hidden away in post-industrial Strijp-S.

Blue Collar Hotel   HOTEL, HOSTEL **€**
(📝 040-780 33 34; www.bluecollarhotel.nl; Klokgebouw 10; dm/d/q/ste from €29.50/69/135/149) Big, glowering murals of Lemmy and Beethoven stare each other out across the rock-attitude bar which doubles as reception for this unusual ho(s)tel. Located in one of the repurposed Strijp-S factory buildings, rooms and well-planned cubicle-dorms ooze design style with a conscious nod to the area's industrial heritage. Breakfast is €10.

❶ Getting There & Around

AIR

Eindhoven Airport (p329), 6km west of the centre, is a hub for budget airlines Ryanair, WizzAir and Transavia. Destinations include London Stansted, Dublin and many Mediterranean and Eastern European cities.

Airexpress (www.airexpressbus.com; P2 parking area, Eindhoven Airport) buses run to Eindhoven Airport from Amsterdam (€22.50, 1¾ hours) via Utrecht (ring-road stop) and Den Bosch (€8.50, 30 minutes). From central Eindhoven, buses 400 and 401 run to the airport from the north side of the train station (with/ without OV-card €2.50/3.50, 25 minutes).

BICYCLE
Via national bike route LF7, Eindhoven to Den Bosch is a day's cycle ride.

TRAIN
Handy connections from Eindhoven Centraal are as follows.

Amsterdam (€19.50, 80 minutes)
Breda (€10.80, 40 minutes)
Maastricht (€17, one hour)
Schiphol Airport (€20.10, 1½ hours)
Tilburg (€7.30, 22 minutes)
Utrecht (€14.50, 50 minutes)

'Sprinter' local trains from Tilburg and Den Bosch allow you to alight directly at Eindhoven Strijp-S station, a five-minute walk from Blue Collar Hotel.

Tilburg

📞 013 / POP 215,600

'Jug city' Tilburg could never be described as pretty, but dig a little and you'll find a lot of spirit, superb beer and an impressive attempt at regeneration. An award-winning textiles museum remembers Tilburg's proud industrial heritage, the once-derelict Spoorzone northeast of the station is now a crucible of creativity (www.spoorzone013.nl) and the Dwaalgebied's few streets of 19th-century brick houses are dotted with delightful eateries and a cool hostel. A joyful carnival, huge annual street fair and substantial student presence keep Tilburg

humming. And in the contrastingly contemplative leafy confines of Koenigshoeven Abbey, monks brew what were (until 2012) the Netherlands' only Trappist beers.

◉ Sights

De Pont Museum MUSEUM
(📞 013-543 83 00; www.depont.nl; Wilhelminapark 1; adult/child €10/free, free 5-8pm Thu; ⊙11am-5pm Tue-Sun) With regularly changing exhibitions, this expansive contemporary art space occupies the site of a former wool-spinning factory. Even if the museum is closed, it's worth the 1km walk northwest from Tilburg Centraal to watch Anish Kapoor's Skymirror outside the entrance, turning little passing clouds into works of art.

Textile Museum MUSEUM
(Textielmuseum; 📞 013-536 74 75; www.textielmuseum.nl; Goirkestraat 96; adult/student/teen/child €12/5.50/3.50/free; ⊙10am-5pm Tue-Fri, from noon Sat & Sun; 🚌5) Winner of the Netherlands' 2017 'museum of the year' award, this innovative place celebrates, and continues the production of, original textiles – an industry that was Tilburg's economic mainstay for at least a century. It's within a historic mill building 1.5km north of Tilburg Centraal.

You can admire early-20th-century spinning and weaving technology and watch working new machines creating cutting-edge art designs for fabrics that are sold in the popular museum shop.

🛏️ Sleeping & Eating

★**Hostel Roots** HOSTEL €
(📞 0652-308 518; www.hostelroots.nl; Stationsstraat 41; dm/d from €21/65; @🛜) Friendly, stylish and handily close to Tilburg station, Roots has given a former 19th-century bank building a design-aware makeover to create one of the Netherlands' best hostels. Comfortable, super-sturdy bunks come with personal lamp and plenty of power points.

NON-BELGIAN TRAPPIST BEER

Brewed at **La Trappe Brewery** (📞013-572 26 50; www.latrappe.nl; Eindhovenseweg 3, Koeningshoeven; ⊙kitchen noon-5pm, shop to 6pm Tue-Sun, 1.30-5pm Mon, reduced hours Nov-Mar, tours 1pm Tue & Thu, 11.30am Sat) in the leafy surroundings of Koeningshoeven Monastery on the outskirts of Tilburg, La Trappe was, until 2012, the world's only non-Belgian Trappist beer. The monastery's *proeflokaal* (tasting room) is a modern, neo-traditional thatch-sided cafe offering excellent lunches as well as nine varieties to try. For a boisterously humorous 90-minute brewery tour (in English, €12) it's worth booking ahead online.

MOVING HOUSE?

Hasselt Rotonde is an unprepossessing traffic circle at the northwest corner of Tilburg's Ringbaan inner ring-road. But if you sit and watch awhile it might seem as though the small house within the roundabout has shifted location. You're not dreaming. In the space of 53 minutes this life-sized Draaiend Huis (Ringbaan; ▣ 300, 301) makes a full circle on a system of underground rails, all in the name of art.

Breakfast is €8.50. The private rooms are bright and some have a balcony.

★ **De Burgerij**   EUROPEAN €€
(www.deburgerij.nl; Nordstraat 87; mains €9.95-25.50; ☺10am-midnight) In the expanded living room of a Tilburg townhouse, this lovable restaurant offers modern Burgundian food with a touch of old Dutch or, in their words, everything from kale to caviar. So you can order a *stamppot* that's as near gourmet as mashed potato allows, to delicate French-influenced nouveau cuisine. Or a steak.

❶ Getting There & Away

Four hourly trains stop at Tilburg Centraal between Breda (€4.60, 12 to 18 minutes) and Den Bosch (€4.70, 15 minutes).

The uncovered **bus station** (Burgemeester Brokclaan) area is a two-minute walk west of the station's north exit. Useful hourly services include 411 to Koningshoeven Monastery (alight at the second Koningshoeven stop), 300 to Den Bosch via Efteling and 132 to Breda via Baarle Nassau.

Breda

📕076 / POP 183,600
Viewed from beside the Hoge Brug, Breda is as pretty as a picture: the Gothic church tower rises majestically above the fine old houses (now bars) of Vismarktstraat, while boats and the sturdy (if inaccessible) bastion-gates of Breda Castle reflect in the calm water of a canal junction. Beyond lies a small old-town area and a pretty park that backs on to the charming Begijnhof, but the real delight of a visit to Breda is to dive into its vibrant cafe scene, especially during the citywide jazz-fest in early May.

◉ Sights & Activities

On sunny days, canoes (per person €10) and motor launches (per person €15) are available for two-hour rentals at the northern end of Haven.

With a bicycle, there are appealing rides south of the city, taking riders through the Mastbos forest and along the pretty Mark riverside. Given a couple of hours you could take in the old market square of Ginneken, pass the pretty moated Bouvigne Castle and cross the invisible Belgian border to Meersel-Dreef with its Lourdes-like Catholic grotto.

★ **Grote Kerk**   CHURCH
(www.grotekerkbreda.nl; Kerkplein 2; optional audioguide €3; ☺10am-5pm Mon-Sat, from 1pm Sun) Finished in 1509, the ornate tower-spire of this soaring Gothic church is one of the Netherlands' most beautiful. At 97m it still forms the iconic focus of old Breda and can be climbed on Saturdays (plus summer Thursdays) as part of a guided tour (€5) that starts from inside the church at 1pm, no booking required.

Stedelijk Museum Breda   MUSEUM
(MOTI; 📞076-529 99 00; www.stedelijkmuseumbreda.nl; Boschstraat 22; adult/child €12/6; ☺10am-5pm Tue-Sun) Breda's main museum tells the city's remarkable history through paintings and artefacts, but to make sense of it you'll need to request the explanatory booklet and read as much as you peruse. The order can be confusing, and attempting such a task in just two of the museum's six galleries can feel overly ambitious. The rest of the space features regularly changing exhibitions, typically imaginative and focused on the manipulation of visual images.

Begijnhof   HISTORIC SITE
(www.begijnhofbreda.nl; Catharinastraat 29; ☺noon-5pm Tue-Sun) FREE Delightfully calm and pretty, if a little grander than many of the better-known beguinages of Belgium and Holland, these almshouses for unmarried or widowed women (*begijnen*) were moved to their present location in 1535. Traditional herb gardens are surrounded by two-storey pale-brick houses, the upper stories and St Catherine's Chapel being 19th-century additions.

✪ Festivals & Events

Breda Jazz Festival   MUSIC
(www.bredajazzfestival.nl; ☺May) For four days starting from Ascension Day, the Nether-

Breda

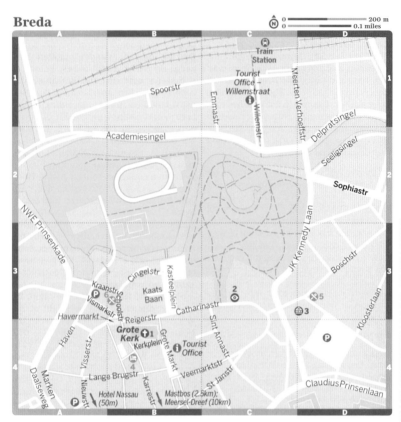

lands' best-established jazz-fest fills well over a dozen outdoor public spaces with over 100 free performances, plus there are many other payable but bargain-value indoor concerts.

🛏 Sleeping & Eating

⭐ **Bliss Hotel**   BOUTIQUE HOTEL €€€
(☑ 076-533 59 80; www.blisshotel.nl; Torenstraat 9; r €200-320; ⊘ reception 7am-10pm; ✳ 🕿) A glass of bubbles welcomes guests to the very personal, high-service Hotel Bliss, where each of the nine suites is individually designed, typically with strong colours (or all-white in two), working fireplaces and old-world style furniture that create a very classic feel (tripod lamps, bookcases etc).

⭐ **Hotel Nassau**   HERITAGE HOTEL €€€
(☑ 076-888 49 21; www.hotelnassaubreda.nl; Nieuwstraat 23; r €124-199, ste €200-249; ✳ @ 🕿) Shoehorning a sparklingly modern 94-room

Breda

◉ **Top Experiences**

◉ **Sights**

🛏 **Sleeping**

🍴 **Eating**

hotel into three historic houses creates quite a maze, enlivened by naughty-nun photo artwork (a little heretical for some tastes). However, with a breakfast area in a large stone chapel and a few rooms incorporating original beam-work (202, 203 plus executive room 213), the Nassau is a great choice for both comfort and originality.

★ **Den Boerenstamppot** DUTCH €
(☑076-514 01 62; www.facebook.com/denboeren stamppot; Schoolstraat 3-5; 1/3-course dinner €7/10; ⊗4-7.30pm Mon-Sat) Joyously life-affirming proprietors Fred and Marloes van Weerd have been serving up good old homestyle Dutch dinners here for 45 years. The classic meal is a vast plate of *stamppot* (potato mashed with veg of the day) topped with your choice of meatballs, *stofvlees* (beef stew), chicken, sausage, cutlet etc. For just €10 total you can add soup or starter and dessert.

★ **Dames Pellens** FRENCH €€€
(☑076-887 69 29; www.damespellens.nl; Boschstraat 24; mains €19-25, 3/4/5/6 courses €34.50/44.50/53.50/62.50; ⊗4pm-midnight Tue & Wed, from noon Thu-Sat, to 10pm Sun) This cosy wine bar has a superb selection of well-priced, well-chosen wines, but the biggest draw is the food. Any evening you can have salads, coq au vin or the meal of the day. But Thursday to Sunday things turn gourmet with superb, somewhat experimental 'chef-special' fine dining of up to six courses. Advance bookings advisable.

ⓘ Information

There are currently two helpful tourist offices, though they may be combined in the future:

Central branch (VVV; ☑ 076-522 89 24; www. vvvbreda.nl; Grote Markt 38; ⊗10.30am-5.30pm Wed-Fri, to 5pm Sat; ☏)

Willemstraat (☑toll number 0900-522 24 44; Willemstraat 17-19; ⊗1-5pm Mon, from 10am Tue-Fri, to 2.30pm Sat)

ⓘ Getting There & Around

BICYCLE

National bike route LF11 starts here and runs northwest 110km to Den Haag via Dordrecht and Rotterdam. LF9 runs via Utrecht all the way to the north coast, and LF13 runs via Breda straight east from Middelburg to the German border.

To rent city bicycles, **Fiestenstalling Oude Vest** (Oude Vest 25; bicycle per day €5, deposit €50; ⊗7am-midnight Mon-Wed, to 3.30am Thu-Sat, 11am-1am Sun) has cheap prices and long opening hours, but if you want gears and handbrakes go to **De Klein Fietsen** (☑076-532 48 70; www.dekleinfietsen.nl; Markendaalsweg 38; bicycle per 24hr €7.50; ⊗9am-6pm). Bus 6 drives past Bouvinge Castle.

TRAIN

Useful train connections include Rotterdam (€9.50, 21 to 31 minutes), Den Bosch (€8.30, 35 minutes) and Eindhoven (€10.80, 40 minutes).

Bergen op Zoom
☑0164 / POP 66,200

One of the Netherlands' forgotten little gems, Bergen op Zoom is best known as a base for exploring the Brabantse Wal countryside. There are also more than 800 listed buildings in town, including the superb **Markiezenhof** (☑0164-277 077; www. markiezenhof.nl; Steenbergsestraat 8; downstairs free, upstairs adult/child €6.50/3; ⊗11am-5pm Tue-Sun), considered the Netherlands' oldest surviving city palace and one of its top 25 monuments. The **tourist office** (www. vvvbrabantsewal.nl; Steenbergsestraat 6; ⊗1-5pm Mon, from 10am Tue-Sat, from 11am Sun) is inside.

One of the nation's most joyous carnivals, Krabbegat's three days of festivities feature a wide range of characters, most memorably De Peperbus – the bell tower of Sint-Gertrudiskerk anthropomorphically 'dressed up' with face and robes.

Should you fancy staying the night, indulge in dinner and an overnight at the longest continuously running hotel in the Netherlands, **De Draak** (☑0164-252 050; www.hoteldedraak.nl; Grote Markt 38; d €79-139, ste €99-199; P❋☏). A highly impressive Prosecco-fuelled breakfast buffet is served in an antique map-ceilinged hall, and its **Restaurant Hemingway** (☑0164-252 050; www. restauranthemingway.nl; Grote Markt 36; lunch/ dinner mains €12.95/27.50, 3-/4-/5-/6-course dinner menus €37/45/62.50/75; ⊗12.30-2.30pm Jun-Sep & 6-9pm year-round) is one of the region's finest purveyors of modern, locally sourced Dutch food. Its *drakenei* ('dragon egg') dessert is famed far and wide.

ⓘ Getting There & Away

Bergen is on the Amsterdam–Dordrecht–Vlissingen line, one stop (10 minutes) west of Roosendaal, where you change for Breda (€7.30, 30 minutes total), Tilburg (€10.80, 50 minutes) or Antwerp (Belgium, 80 minutes). The latter journey costs €17 from Antwerp, €12 with a ticket bought in Bergen, but is cheapest if you go first from Bergen to Roosendal (with/ without OV-chipkaart €3.20/4.20) then pay the Roosendaal–Antwerp section (€6.80, debit card only, 48 minutes) using the Belgian Railways ticket machine beside the Kiosk shop at Roosendaal station.

Understand the Netherlands

History

Given how peaceful the Netherlands seems now, it's hard to believe the high drama of its history. Greed, lust and war are prominent in the Dutch story, along with pirates and high-sea adventures. It's the story of land much invaded, whether by armies on land or from the sea. Yet through it all, a society has emerged that has a core belief in human rights, tolerance and perhaps most surprising given the vicissitudes of its existence, consensus.

Invaders

The first invaders to take note of the locals in today's Netherlands were the Romans, who, under Julius Caesar, conquered a wide region along the Rijn (Rhine) and its tributaries by 59 BC. Celtic and Germanic tribes initially bowed to Caesar's rule and Utrecht became a main outpost of the empire.

As Roman power began to fade, the Franks, a German tribe to the east, began to muscle in. By the end of the 8th century, the Franks had completed their conquest of the Low Countries and began converting the local populace to Christianity, using force whenever necessary. Charlemagne, the first in a long line of Holy Roman emperors, was by far the most successful Frankish king. He built a palace at Nijmegen, but the empire fell apart after his death in 814.

For the next 200 years, Vikings sailed up Dutch rivers to loot and pillage. Local rulers developed their own fortified towns and made up their own government and laws.

Over time, the local lords, who were nominally bound to a German king, began to gain power. When one lord struggled with another for territory, invariably their townsfolk would provide support, but only in return for various freedoms (an equation familiar to any player of sim games today), which were set down in charters. By the beginning of the 12th century, Dutch towns with sea access, such as Deventer and Zwolle, joined the Hanseatic League (a group of powerful trading cities in present-day Germany, including Hamburg and Rostock). Meanwhile,

Early residents of the soggy territory of Friesland built homes on mounds of mud (called *terpen*) to escape the frequent floods.

TIMELINE

3000–2000 BC	59 BC	800
People living in what is today's Drenthe province bury their dead under monolithic rocks called *hunebedden*. Long before Stonehenge, these people move enormous rocks and create structures.	The Romans extend their empire to what is today the Netherlands. Over the next four centuries, the Romans build advanced towns, farms and the roads that still shape the landscape.	Christianity arrives in the Low Countries by force. It replaces various Celtic belief systems – those who don't convert are killed. Charlemagne builds a church, parts of which survive in Nijmegen.

the many minor lords met their match in the dukes of Burgundy, who gradually took over the Low Countries.

Duke Philip the Good, who ruled from 1419 to 1467, showed the towns of the Low Countries who was boss by essentially telling them to stuff their charters. Although this limited the towns' freedom, it also brought a degree of stability to the region that had been missing during the era of squabbling lords. The 15th century ushered in great prosperity for the Low Countries, the first of many such periods. The Dutch became adept at shipbuilding in support of the Hanseatic trade, and merchants thrived by selling luxury items such as tapestries, fashionable clothing and paintings, as well as more mundane commodities such as salted herring and beer.

The Dutch National Archive (www.nationaalarchief.nl) has almost a thousand years of historical documents, maps, drawings and photos.

The Fight for Independence

Philip II of Spain was a staunch Catholic; he'd gained the Low Countries and Spain from his father in 1555 after a period in which control of large swaths of Europe shifted depending on who was marrying who. Conflict with the Low Countries was inevitable; the Protestant reformation had spread throughout the colony, fuelled by the ideas of Erasmus and the actions of Martin Luther. However, before the Spanish arrived, the religious landscape of the Low Countries was quite diverse: Lutherans wielded great influence, but smaller churches had their places too. For instance, the Anabaptists were polygamists and communists, and nudity was promoted as a means of equality among their masses (in the warmer seasons). In the end it was Calvinism that emerged in the Low Countries as the main challenger to the Roman Catholic Church, and to Philip's rule.

A big believer in the Inquisition, Philip went after the Protestants with a vengeance. Matters came to a head in 1566 when the puritanical Calvinists went on a rampage, destroying art and religious icons of Catholic churches. Evidence of this is still readily apparent in the barren interiors of Dutch churches today.

This sent Philip into action. The Duke of Alba was chosen to lead a 10,000-strong army in 1568 to quell the unruly serfs; as the Duke wasn't one to take prisoners, his forces slaughtered thousands, and so began the Dutch War of Independence, which lasted 80 years.

The Prince van Oranje, Willem the Silent (thus named for his refusal to argue over religious issues), was one of the few nobles not to side with Philip, and he led the Dutch revolt against Spanish rule. He was hampered by other Dutch nobles content to see which way the political winds blew. In 1572, Willem hired a bunch of English pirates to fight for his cause. Known as the Watergeuzen (Sea Beggars), they sailed up the

1150–1300	1200	1275	1287
Dams are built to retain the IJ River between the Zuiderzee and Haarlem, one of the first efforts in what becomes an ongoing tug-of-war with the sea.	The age of city states is in full bloom as lords rule in many riverside towns. Trading between the towns is the source of wealth and a powerful inducement against war.	Amsterdam is founded after the Count of Holland grants toll-free status to residents along the Amstel. The city gains its first direct access to the ocean via the Zuiderzee.	The Zuiderzee floods during a storm and upwards of 80,000 people die. Except in a few port cities around its periphery, the sea is widely regarded as a source of trouble.

myriad Dutch rivers and seized towns such as Leiden from the surprised and land-bound Spanish forces.

By 1579, the more Protestant and rebellious provinces in the north formed the Union of Utrecht. This explicitly anti-Spanish alliance became known as the United Provinces, the basis for the Netherlands as we know it today. The southern regions of the Low Countries had always remained Catholic and were much more open to compromise with Spain. They eventually became Belgium.

The battles continued nonetheless until the 1648 Treaty of Westphalia, which included the proviso that Spain recognise the independence of the United Provinces. This ended the Thirty Years' War.

The Golden Age

Throughout the turmoil of the 15th and 16th centuries, merchant cities, particularly Amsterdam, had managed to keep trade alive. Their skill at business and sailing was so great that, even at the peak of the rebellion, the Spanish had no choice but to use Dutch boats for transporting their grain. With the arrival of peace the cities began to boom. This era of economic prosperity and cultural fruition came to be known as the Golden Age, which produced artistic and architectural masterpieces still loved today.

The wealth of the merchant class supported numerous artists, including Jan Vermeer, Jan Steen, Frans Hals and Rembrandt. It allowed for excesses such as 'tulipmania', and the sciences were not forgotten: Dutch physicist and astronomer Christiaan Huygens discovered Saturn's rings and invented the pendulum clock; celebrated philosopher Benedict de Spinoza wrote a brilliant thesis saying that the universe was identical to God; and Frenchman René Descartes, known for his philosophy 'I think, therefore I am', found intellectual freedom in the Netherlands and stayed for two decades.

The Union of Utrecht's promise of religious tolerance led to an amount of religious diversity that was rare in Europe at the time. Calvinism was the official religion of the government, but various other Protestants, Jews and Catholics were allowed to practise their faith. However, in a legacy of the troubles with Spain, Catholics still had to worship in private, leading to the creation of clandestine churches. Many of these unusual buildings have survived to the present day.

Dutch Colonials

Wealth – and the need for more wealth – caused the Dutch to expand their horizons. The merchant fleet known as the Dutch East India Company was formed in 1602 and quickly monopolised key shipping and trade routes east of Africa's Cape of Good Hope and west of South Amer-

The Dutch 'bought' (a concept foreign to North American tribes at the time) the island of Manhattan from the Lenape in 1626 for the equivalent of US$24 worth of beads.

The *Flying Dutchman* is a mythical 17th-century ship cursed to sail the seas forever, unable to go home. The story has myriad variations, many embellished by grog-addled seamen.

1419	1452	1519	1555–66
The beginning of the end of the powerful city states. The dukes of Burgundy consolidate their power and unify rich trading towns under one geographic empire. Freedom suffers under central rule.	Fire devours wooden Amsterdam. New building laws decree that only brick and tile be used in future. Similar conflagrations in other towns lead to the 'Dutch' look prized today.	Spain's Charles V is crowned Holy Roman Emperor. Treaties and marriages make Amsterdam part of the Catholic Spanish empire. Protestants are tolerated in Holland and the northeast.	In the first major assault on Dutch tolerance, Philip II cracks down on Protestants. Religious wars follow and Calvinists pillage Catholic churches, stripping them of their decor and wealth.

TULIPMANIA

When it comes to investment frenzy, the Dutch tulip craze of 1636 to 1637 ranks alongside the greatest economic booms and busts in history.

Tulips originated as wildflowers in Central Asia and were first cultivated by the Turks, who filled their courts with these beautiful spring blooms ('tulip' derives from the Turkish word for turban). In the mid-1500s, the Habsburg ambassador to Istanbul brought some bulbs back to Vienna, where the imperial botanist, Carolus Clusius, learned how to propagate them. In 1590, Clusius became director of the Hortus Botanicus (p57) in Leiden – Europe's oldest botanical garden – and had great success growing and cross-breeding tulips in the cool, damp Dutch climate and fertile delta soil.

The more exotic specimens of tulip featured frilly petals and 'flamed' streaks of colour, which attracted the attention of wealthy merchants, who put them in their living rooms and hallways to impress visitors. Trickle-down wealth and savings stoked the taste for exotica in general, and tulip growers arose to service the demand.

A speculative frenzy ensued, and people paid top florin for the finest bulbs, many of which changed hands time and again before they sprouted. Vast profits were made and speculators fell over themselves to outbid each other.

Of course, this bonanza couldn't last, and when several bulb traders in Haarlem failed to fetch their expected prices in February 1637, the bottom fell out of the market. Within weeks many of the country's wealthiest merchants went bankrupt and many more people of humbler origins lost everything.

However, love of the unusual tulip endured. To this day, the Dutch continue to be the world leaders in tulip cultivation. They also excel in bulbs such as daffodils, hyacinths and crocuses.

So what happened to the flamed, frilly tulips of the past? They're still produced, though they have gone out of fashion, and are now known as Rembrandt tulips because of their depiction in so many 17th-century paintings.

For an explosion of modern-day blooms, visit Keukenhof Gardens (p200) near Leiden in season. To see wealth in bloom, visit the flower market (p121) at Aalsmeer. *Tulipomania: The Story of the World's Most Coveted Flower* (2001) by Mike Dash is an engaging look at the bizarre bulb fever that swept the nation in the 17th century.

ica's Strait of Magellan, making it the largest trading company of the 17th century. It became almost as powerful as a sovereign state, with the ability to raise its own armed forces and establish colonies.

Its sister, the Dutch West India Company, traded with Africa and the Americas and was at the very centre of the American slave trade. Seamen working for both companies 'discovered' (in a very Western sense of the word) or conquered lands including parts of Australia, New Zealand, Malaysia, Sri Lanka and Mauritius. While employed by the Dutch East India Company, English explorer Henry Hudson landed on the island of

1566–68	1579	1596	1600s
The Low Countries revolt against a lack of religious freedom, launching the Eighty Years' War. In Friesland the rebels win their first battle, immortalised in the Dutch national anthem.	With scores of Dutch towns captured by Calvinist brigands, known as Watergeuzen (Sea Beggars), a Dutch republic made up of seven provinces is declared by Willem the Silent.	A Dutch trade expedition to Indonesia loses half its crew but brings back cargo that's sold for a profit. The Dutch East India Company is formed and the archipelago colonised.	The Golden Age places Amsterdam firmly on the culture map. While Rembrandt paints in his atelier, the grand inner ring of canals is constructed. The city's population surges to 200,000.

Manhattan in 1609 as he searched for the Northwest Passage, and Dutch settlers named it New Amsterdam.

Not surprisingly, international conflict was never far away. In 1652 the United Provinces went to war with their old friend England, mainly over the increasing strength of the Dutch merchant fleet. Both countries entered a hotchpotch of alliances with Spain, France and Sweden in an effort to gain the upper hand. During one round of treaties, the Dutch agreed to give New Amsterdam to the English (who promptly renamed it New York) in return for Surinam in South America and full control of the Spice Islands in Indonesia.

This outward perspective coupled with the rich lives being enjoyed by the moneyed class at home caused a certain loss of focus. In 1672 the French army marched into the Netherlands and, as the Dutch had devoted most of their resources to the navy, found little resistance on land. During the decades of conflicts that followed, the Dutch could no longer afford their navy and foreign adventures. The English became the masters of the trade routes and keepers of the resulting wealth.

The Dutch managed to hold onto the Dutch East Indies (today's Indonesia) along with a smattering of spots in the Caribbean. The effectiveness of their rule in the East Indies ebbed and flowed depending on the situation at home. They never approached the intensive colonialism practised by the British. (In Indonesia today it takes real effort to find traces of the Dutch rule or its legacy in most of the country.)

The Dutch East Indies declared itself independent in 1945, and after four years of bitter fighting and negotiations, the independence of Indonesia was recognised at the end of 1949. Surinam also became independent in 1975. In the Caribbean, the Netherlands Antilles disbanded in 2010 but none of the islands severed ties completely.

The Foundation of Today's Netherlands

Wars with France proved the undoing of the Dutch in the 18th century. Shifting allegiances among the Dutch, English, Spanish and various German states did their best to keep the French contained. It was costly and the ties that bound the United Provinces together unravelled, beginning a spiral downwards. The population shrank due to falling fortunes and the dykes fell into a sorry state – there was little money to repair them, and widespread floods swept across the country. The Golden Age was long since over.

Politically, the United Provinces were as unstable as the dykes. A series of struggles between the House of Oranje and its democratic opponents led to a civil war in 1785. The situation reached a nadir when Napoleon renamed it the Kingdom of Holland and installed his brother, Louis Bonaparte, as king in 1806. Napoleon's failed Russian invasion allowed

In the early 1600s, the Dutch East India Company flooded the local market with cheap porcelain from China. The Dutch responded with what's known today as Delftware. Today, most 'Delftware' is a cheap import from China.

Hans Brinker, who supposedly stuck his finger in a dyke and saved the Netherlands from a flood, is an American invention and unknown in the Netherlands. He starred in a 19th-century children's book.

1602	1620	1642	1650s
Amsterdam becomes the site of the world's first stock exchange when the offices of the Dutch East India Company trade their own shares. Insider trading laws don't yet exist.	The pilgrims arrive in the New World aboard the Mayflower, a voyage that began with many fits and starts in the Dutch city of Leiden.	Rembrandt paints *The Night Watch*. Many of the men portrayed were unhappy as they'd paid to be in the lauded picture and didn't like being in the back rows.	Big mistake: the Dutch infamously trade away the colony of New Amsterdam (now New York) to the British.

the Dutch to establish a monarchy. Prince Willem VI landed at Scheveningen in 1813 and was named prince sovereign of the Netherlands; the following year he was crowned King Willem I, beginning a monarchy that continues to this day.

The Kingdom of the Netherlands – the Netherlands in the north and proto-Belgium in the south – was formed in 1815. However, the marriage was doomed from the start. The partners had little in common, including their dominant religions (Calvinist and Catholic), languages (Dutch and French) and favoured way of making money (trade and manufacturing). Matters weren't helped by Willem, who generally sided with his fellow northerners.

In 1830 the southern states revolted, and nine years later Willem was forced to let the south go. In return for recognition of Belgium, Willem secured the return of the eastern part of Limburg, ending Maastricht's nine years as a West Berlin–style isolated Dutch exclave. In a nice historical twist, Willem abdicated one year later so that he could marry – surprise! – a Belgian Catholic. It's not known if he ever spoke French at home.

His son, King Willem II, granted a new and more liberal constitution to the people of the Netherlands in 1848. This included a number of democratic ideals and even made the monarchy the servant of the elected government. This document remains the foundation of the Dutch government in the present day. Its role on the world stage long over, the Netherlands played only a small part in European affairs and concentrated on liberalism at home. It stayed out of WWI, but profited by trading with both sides.

In the 1920s, growing affluence of the middle class fuelled a desire for more liberalism. The Netherlands embarked on innovative social programs that targeted poverty, the rights of women and children, and education. Rotterdam became one of Europe's most important ports, and the massive scheme to reclaim the Zuiderzee was launched in 1932.

WWII

The Dutch tried to remain neutral during WWII, but in May 1940 the Germans invaded. The advancing Nazis levelled much of central Rotterdam in a raid designed to force the Dutch to surrender. They obliged.

Queen Wilhelmina issued a proclamation of 'flaming protest' to the nation and escaped with her family to England. The monarch, who had been key in maintaining Dutch neutrality in WWI, now found herself in a much different situation and made encouraging broadcasts to her subjects back home via the BBC and Radio Orange. The Germans put Dutch industry and farms to work for war purposes and there was much deprivation. Dutch resistance was primarily passive and only gained any

---

Jewish Historic Sites

••••••••••••••••••••••

Anne Frank Huis (Amsterdam)

Joods Historisch Museum (Amsterdam)

Kamp Westerbork (near Groningen)

Two films focus on the Dutch Resistance during WWI: in *Oorlogswinter* (Winter in Wartime; 2008), a boy's loyalty is tested when he helps the Resistance shelter a British pilot; while *Zwartboek* (Black Book; 2006) explores the Resistance's less heroic aspects.

1795	1813–14	1830	1865–76
French troops install the Batavian Republic, named after the Batavi tribe that rebelled against Roman rule. The fragmented United Provinces become a centralised state, with Amsterdam as its capital.	The French are overthrown, and Willem VI of Orange is crowned as Dutch king Willem I. The Protestant north and Catholic south combine as the United Kingdom of the Netherlands.	With help from the French, the southern provinces secede to form the Kingdom of Belgium. The remaining northern provinces form what continues to be the Netherlands of today.	A period of rapid economic and social change. The North Sea Canal is dug, the Dutch railway system expanded and socialist principles of government are established.

kind of momentum when thousands of Dutch men were taken to Germany and forced to work in Nazi factories. A far worse fate awaited the country's Jews.

The 'Winter of Hunger' of 1944–45 was a desperate time in the Netherlands. The British-led Operation Market Garden had been a huge disaster and the Allies abandoned all efforts to liberate the Dutch. The Germans stripped the country of much of its food and resources, and mass starvation ensued. Many people were reduced to eating tulip bulbs for subsistence. Canadian troops finally liberated the country in May 1945.

After the war, the Netherlands was shattered both economically and spiritually. War trials ensued in which 66,000 were convicted of collab-

DUTCH JEWS

The tale of Jews in Europe is often one of repression, persecution and division. In the Netherlands, it is more a tale of acceptance and prosperity, until the coming of the Nazis.

Amsterdam is the focus of Jewish history in the Netherlands, and Jews played a key role in the city's development over the centuries. The first documented evidence of Jewish presence in the city dates back to the 12th century, and numbers began to swell with the expulsion of Sephardic Jews from Spain and Portugal in the 1580s.

As was the case in much of Europe, guilds barred the newcomers from most trades. Some of the Sephardim were diamond cutters, however, for whom there was no guild. The majority eked out a living as labourers and small-time traders on the margins of society. Still, they weren't confined to a ghetto and, with some restrictions, could buy property and exercise their religion – freedoms unheard of elsewhere in Europe.

The 17th century saw another influx of Jewish refugees, this time Ashkenazim fleeing pogroms in Central and Eastern Europe. The two groups didn't always get on well and separate synagogues were established, helping Amsterdam to become one of Europe's major Jewish centres.

The guilds and all restrictions on Jews were abolished during the French occupation, and the Jewish community thrived in the 19th century. Poverty was still considerable, but the economic, social and political emancipation of the Jews helped their middle class move up in society.

All this came to an end with the German occupation of the Netherlands. The Nazis brought about the almost complete annihilation of the Dutch Jewish community. Before WWII, the Netherlands counted 140,000 Jews, of whom about two-thirds lived in Amsterdam. Fewer than 25,000 survived the war, and Amsterdam's Jewish quarter was left a ghost town. Many homes stood derelict until their demolition in the 1970s, and only a handful of synagogues throughout the country are once again operating as houses of worship.

Estimates put the current Jewish population of the Netherlands at around 50,000, with the largest community living in Amsterdam.

1914–20	1919	1932	1939
The Netherlands remains neutral in WWI while trading with both sides. Food shortages cripple the country, leading to strikes, unrest and growing support for the Dutch Communist Party.	KLM takes to the skies, with a flight from London to Amsterdam. The airline eventually becomes the world's oldest, still flying under its original name.	After centuries of schemes, dyke-building and floods, the Zuiderzee reclamation begins, spurred on by a deadly 1916 storm surge. The completion of the mammoth Afsluitdijk begins the process.	The Dutch government establishes Westerbork as an internment camp to house Jewish refugees. Eventually 107,000 Jews pass through this remote place in the east on their way to death camps.

orating with the Nazis (with 900 receiving the death penalty). Yet the number of collaborators was much higher, and scores – such as the party or parties who ratted out Anne Frank and her family – never saw justice. In contrast, many Dutch people risked everything to help Jews during the war.

Prosperity & Stability

The Dutch set about getting their house in order after the material and mental privations of WWII. During the 1950s a prosperous country began to re-emerge. After disastrous flooding in Zeeland and the south in 1953, a four-decades-long campaign began to literally reshape the land and keep the sea forever at bay.

The same social upheavals that swept the world in the 1960s were also felt in the Netherlands. Students, labour groups, hippies and more took to the streets in protest. Among the more colourful were a group that came to be known as the Provos. Amsterdam became the *magisch centrum* (magic centre) of Europe. Hippies flocked to Amsterdam during the 1960s and '70s; a housing shortage saw speculators leaving buildings empty and squatting became widespread. The Dutch authorities turned Vondelpark into a temporary open-air dormitory.

Tolerance towards drug use and gay rights also emerged at the time. The country's drug policy grew out of practical considerations, when Amsterdam's flower-power-era influx made the policing of drug laws impracticable. Official government policy became supportive of same-sex relationships and in 2001, the Netherlands became the first country in the world to introduce marriage equality.

Economically the Netherlands prospered more with each passing decade, allowing a largely drama-free middle-class society to be the norm by the late 1980s.

All governments since 1945 have been coalitions, with parties mainly differing over economic policies. However, coalitions shift constantly based on the political climate, and in recent years there have been winds of change. Tension between different political colours and creeds had never been a problem in the Netherlands, until the murders of Pim Fortuyn and Theo van Gogh stirred emotions and struck fear into the hearts of some.

The Provocative Provos

The 1960s were a breeding ground for discontent and anti-establishment activity, and in the Netherlands this underground movement led to the formation of the Provos. This small group of anarchic individuals staged street 'happenings' or creative, playful provocations (hence the name) around the Lieverdje (Little Darling) on Amsterdam's Spui.

> **WWII Museums**
>
> Museum Rotterdam: 1940-1945 NOW (Rotterdam)
>
> Airborne Museum Hartenstein (Oosterbeek)
>
> National Liberation Museum 1944–45 (Groesbeek)

> American expat Russell Shorto traces the evolution of his adopted city in the classic book, *Amsterdam: A History of the World's Most Liberal City* (2013).

HISTORY PROSPERITY & STABILITY

1940	1944–45	1946	1958
Germany invades the Netherlands. Rotterdam is destroyed by the Luftwaffe, but Amsterdam suffers only minor damage before capitulating. Queen Wilhelmina sets up a Dutch exile government in London.	The Allies liberate the southern Netherlands, but the north and west are cut off from supplies. The British Operation Market Garden fails and thousands perish in the 'Winter of Hunger'.	The UN-chartered International Court of Justice sets up shop in Den Haag, ensuring that the seat of Dutch government will grace the world's headlines for decades to come.	The Delta Project is launched following the great floods of Zeeland in 1953, which cause widespread destruction and death. Vast construction projects continue for four decades.

In 1962, an Amsterdam window cleaner and self-professed sorcerer, Robert Jasper Grootveld, began to deface cigarette billboards with a huge letter 'K' for *kanker* (cancer) to expose the role of advertising in addictive consumerism. Dressed as a medicine man, he held get-togethers in his garage and chanted mantras against cigarette smoking (all under the influence of pot). The movement grew.

The group gained international notoriety in March 1966 with its protests at the marriage of Princess (later Queen) Beatrix to German Claus von Amsberg. Protesters jeered the wedding couple as their procession rolled through Amsterdam.

In the same year the Provos gained enough support to win a seat on Amsterdam's city council. Environmental schemes and social schemes (such as giving everyone a free bike) proved unwieldy and the movement dissolved in the 1970s as some of its liberal policies became entrenched.

The Legacy of Fortuyn & Van Gogh

If the 2004 assassination of Theo van Gogh rocked the Netherlands, it was the assassination of Pim Fortuyn two years earlier that gave the initial push.

The political career of Fortuyn (pronounced fore-town) lasted a mere five months, yet his impact on the Netherlands has proved indelible. His campaign for parliament in 2002 is best remembered for his speeches on immigration: particularly that the Netherlands was 'full' and that immigrants should not be allowed to stay without learning the language or integrating.

Just days before the general election in May 2002, Fortuyn was assassinated by an animal-rights activist in Hilversum, some 20km from Amsterdam. Fortuyn's political party, the Lijst Pim Fortuyn (LPF), had a number of members elected to parliament and was included in the next coalition, but without the figurehead Fortuyn it faded away by 2007.

Enter Theo van Gogh, a film-maker and provocateur who made a short film claiming that Koranic verses could be interpreted as justifying violence against women. The film was a collaboration with Ayaan Hirsi Ali, a Muslim-born woman who had emigrated from Somalia to escape an arranged marriage and eventually became a member of parliament.

The film aired on Dutch TV in 2004, and Van Gogh was killed as he was cycling down an Amsterdam street. A letter threatening the nation, politicians and Hirsi Ali in particular, was impaled on a knife stuck in Van Gogh's chest. The killing was all the more shocking to locals because the 27-year-old killer, of Moroccan descent, was born and raised in Amsterdam. He proclaimed that he was acting in defence of Islam and would do the same thing again if given the chance (he was sentenced to life imprisonment).

John Lennon and Yoko Ono took to bed at the Amsterdam Hilton for a week in 1969 and invited the world's press to join them. Rather than salacious entertainment, however, they offered bromides about world peace.

1960s	1974	1980	2001
Social upheaval leads to the creation of the Provos, a provocative underground countercultural movement. Squatting in empty buildings is widespread. Conservative Dutch culture is challenged.	The Dutch soccer team finishes second in the World Cup. After doing so again in 1978 and 2010, they hold the record for the most second-place finishes without winning the final.	The investiture of Queen Beatrix is disrupted by a smoke bomb and riot on the Dam. The term 'proletarian shopping' (ie looting) enters the national lexicon as riotous behaviour becomes widespread.	Same-sex marriage is legalised in the Netherlands, the first country in the world to do so. In the next few years Belgium, Spain, Canada and South Africa follow suit.

CARIBBEAN NETHERLANDS
••

The Kingdom of the Netherlands shrunk even more with the end of the Netherlands Antilles. Effectively a grab-bag of Dutch holdings in the Caribbean, the country came into being in 1954 (as the autonomous successor of the Dutch colony of Curaçao and Dependencies), and islanders always saw themselves as residents of their island first.

Aruba flew the coop first, in 1986, and the Netherlands Antilles was disbanded altogether in 2010. All of the island territories that belonged to the Netherlands Antilles remain part of the Kingdom of the Netherlands today, although the legal status of each island varies. Following the dissolution, Curaçao and Sint Maarten became autonomous countries within the Kingdom, like Aruba, which saves a lot of money on operating embassies, having their own military and the like.

Bonaire, Sint Eustatius and Saba (known as the BES islands) became special municipalities of the Netherlands (nice warm ones popular with Dutch tourists).

Modern Politics

Among the qualities the Netherlands is best known for is its tolerance. Yet this idea of 'you don't bother me and I won't bother you' seemed under threat in 2010 when the Dutch demonstrated a clear shift to the right. The coalition government formed that year included Geert Wilders, leader of the Party for Freedom, a far-right movement with a tough stance on foreigners living in – or immigrating to – the Netherlands.

Prime Minister Mark Rutte made a number of proposals that were a sharp break from previous centrist Dutch policies. They weakened environmental regulations, slashed arts and culture funding, and passed what was thought to be a near-death sentence for the country's marijuana-selling *coffeeshops*. The formerly bedrock Dutch commitment to the European Union was openly debated.

> The official website of the Dutch royal family (www.koninklijkhuis.nl) features mini-biographies and virtual tours of the palaces, as well as news.

By the time an early election was called for September 2012, the Dutch political needle was heading back to the middle. Wilders' party won a reduced number of seats in the Dutch parliament and Rutte's centre-right Liberal Party had to break bread with the left-leaning Labour Party to form a coalition government. Rutte returned as prime minister.

The Netherlands assisted refugees from war-torn countries such as Syria. In 2015 the Dutch government pledged to receive 7000 of Europe's 120,000 asylum seekers over a two-year period, housing them in temporary tented refugee camps and former prisons.

In 2016 Wilders was convicted by a Dutch court for incitement against Moroccans, but received no sentence. The case arose from a pledge he'd made in 2014 to reduce the number of Moroccans in the Netherlands.

2002	2004	2008	2010
Leading politician Pim Fortuyn, a hardliner on immigration and integration, is assassinated. The ruling Dutch parties shift to the right after suffering major losses in the national election.	Activist film-maker Theo van Gogh, a critic of Islam, is assassinated, sparking debate over the limits of Dutch multiculturalism and the need for immigrants to adopt Dutch values.	Amsterdam announces plans to clean up the Red Light District and close *coffeeshops*. Other cities follow suit and the 'smart shops' selling mushrooms are closed.	Members of the Dutch government officially apologise to the Jewish community for failing to protect the Jewish population from genocide.

THE DUTCH ROYALS

In power now for 200 years, the House of Orange has roots back to the 16th century. Unlike a certain royal family to the west across the Channel, the Dutch royals have been of limited value to tabloid publishers or others hoping to profit from their exploits. The most notable was Queen Wilhelmina, who took a page from Britain's Queen Victoria and approached her job as if she were a general. Although some faulted her for fleeing the Germans in WWII, she ended up winning praise for her stalwart support of her people.

During the postwar years, the family were a mostly low-key and benign presence (they have no substantive power within the Dutch government) with the exception of Prince Bernhard, who was caught up in a bribery scandal in the 1970s with the US defence firm Lockheed. Queen Beatrix (b 1938) abdicated in 2013 in favour of her son, ending more than a century of female reign. King Willem-Alexander, father of three daughters, took the throne with his wife, Máxima Zorreguieta, a former banker he met at a party in Spain. Although her father's role in Argentina's Videla government raised a few eyebrows, Máxima has won praise for her work on immigrant issues and support of gay rights.

Despite being ranked among Europe's wealthiest royals, the family is considered by many as fairly modest. Beatrix was known for riding her bike in Den Haag. The one day the Dutch think of the House of Orange is on Koningsdag (King's Day).

The Dutch elections of March 2017 saw Rutte's party win a decisive victory, despite losing seats and Wilders' making gains to reach second place, which was welcomed by EU leaders as a victory over extremism.

When the Netherlands won the Eurovision Song Contest in 2019, the country looked forward to Rotterdam hosting the 2020 event. However, when the Covid-19 pandemic broke out in Europe early in 2020, leading to sweeping restrictions and lockdowns, it belatedly took place in 2021.

The revelation of the Dutch tax authorities' false allegations of child welfare fraud prompted Rutte and his cabinet to resign in January 2021. Rutte remained in power through to elections held in March 2021. An increased number of seats for his party (and decreased number for Wilders', which placed third) put Rutte in the position to form a new coalition government.

As leader, Rutte decried the July 2021 murder of crime reporter Peter R de Vries, an attack on free press that shocked the nation, and the role of climate change on the devastating 2021 European floods that affected the Netherlands.

Out of the Covid-19 pandemic has come an opportunity to reset and readdress tourism. Amsterdam mayor Femke Halsema has plans to ban foreign tourists from cannibals-selling coffeeshops, curb Airbnb-style holiday rentals, and relocate Red Light District sex businesses to the city's outskirts, while encouraging respectful cultural tourism instead.

King Willem-Alexander and his wife Queen Máxima have three daughters: Princess Catharina-Amalia (the Princess of Orange), Princess Alexia and Princess Ariane.

2013	2014	2018	2021
After a 33-year reign, Queen Beatrix abdicates in favour of her eldest son, Willem-Alexander, who becomes the Netherlands' first king in 123 years.	A flight travelling from Amsterdam to Kuala Lumpur crashes in Ukraine after being struck by a missile. The Dutch government holds Russian-backed rebels responsible; 298 people die, including 193 Dutch.	Left-wing, Haarlem-born Femke Halsema becomes Amsterdam's first female mayor.	Despite resigning over a childcare subsidies scandal, Prime Minister Mark Rutte's party places first in elections. Amsterdam officials redefine tourism policies following pandemic restrictions.

The Dutch Way of Life

The Netherlands has traditionally been a nation of entrepreneurs, from avid seafaring explorers, traders and ambitious engineers working to waterproof the country by building canals, *polders* and dykes, to artists, architects and designers, and a more recent start-up culture that is an increasingly key part of propelling the economy. But it's not all work, no play – the open-minded, free-spirited Dutch value conversation, camaraderie, socialising and getting out and about, more often than not by bike.

Tolerance

The Dutch flair for engineering extends to social engineering. The nation invented *verzuiling* (pillarisation), a social order in which each religion and political persuasion achieved the right to do its own thing, with its own institutions. This meant not only more churches, but also separate radio stations, newspapers, unions, political parties, sport clubs and so

Above Locals in a rooftop garden above a Rotterdam office building.

on. The idea got a bit out of hand with pillarised bakeries, but it did promote social harmony by giving everyone a voice.

While the pillars are less distinct today, they left a legacy of tolerance – a pivotal part of the Dutch psyche that's also good for business, including tourism and trade. They also fostered the easy intimacy of *gezelligheid* (cosiness, conviviality). The Dutch are irrepressibly voluble. Sit alone in a pub and you'll soon have a few merry friends. Don't be taken aback if the Dutch seem stunningly blunt – the impulse comes from the desire to be direct and honest.

Lifestyle

The wonderful Dutch verb *uitwaaien* (pronounced *out*-vwy-ehn) has no direct English translation, but essentially means 'to clear one's head by taking a walk outside in the windy fresh air'.

Many Dutch live independent, busy lives, divided into strict schedules. Notice is usually required for everything, including visits to your mother, and it's not done to just 'pop round' anywhere. Rural communities tend to be more relaxed, with *noabers* (neighbours) playing an important role in daily life. '*Noaberschap*', particular to Twente in rural Overijssel and Drenthe in the off-the-beaten-track northeast of the country, is the generous notion of happily helping one's neighbour with anything and everything.

Most Dutch families are small, with two or three children. Social housing is prevalent: some 31% of Dutch households live in rented accommodation, but few rent from private landlords. Rent for private rental-market properties is high and demand outstrips supply, so people might live with their parents well into their 20s, or share an apartment. Rental prices are naturally highest in Amsterdam, where a 65-sq-m flat costs around €1500 a month to rent – equivalent to €22.79 per sq metre, compared to €19.42 in Rotterdam, €15.82 in Den Haag and just under €9 in Friesland.

Dutch citizens earn an average monthly wage of €2816 (or €36,500 per annum) – more per capita than Germany. Consumer spending is healthy, especially for travel to warm climates.

Sex & Drugs

On sex and drugs, the ever-practical Dutch argue that vice is not going to go away, so you might as well control it. Sex is discussed openly but

---

DOUBLE DUTCH

For better or for worse, the Dutch have maintained close ties with the English for centuries, and this intimate relationship has led to a menagerie of 'Dutch' catchphrases in the English language. Here are some of the more well known.

➡ Double Dutch – nonsense or complete gibberish; a jump-rope game using two skipping ropes. 'Going double Dutch' refers to using two types of contraceptive at the same time.

➡ Dutch courage – strength or confidence gained from drinking alcohol.

➡ Dutch oven – large, thick-walled cooking pot with a tight-fitting lid; the act of breaking wind in bed, then trapping your partner – and the stench – under the covers.

➡ Dutch uncle – a person who sternly gives (often benevolent) advice.

➡ Dutch wife – pillow or frame used for resting the legs on in bed; a sex worker or sex doll.

➡ Going Dutch – splitting the bill at a restaurant. Also known as Dutch date or Dutch treat.

➡ Pass the dutchie – not a phrase as such, but the title of a top-10 hit by Musical Youth in 1982. 'Dutchie' refers to an aluminium cooking pot supposedly manufactured in the Netherlands and used throughout the West Indies.

promiscuity is the last thing on Dutch minds. Only about 5% of customers frequenting Amsterdam's Red Light District are Dutch.

By the same token, marijuana and hashish remain tolerated, yet only a fraction of the population partakes: studies show that only 8% of Dutch people had used any form of marijuana in the previous year, less than the average for France (11.1%), the USA (16.3%) and Australia (10.2%), where enforcement is much stricter. Harder drugs such as heroin, LSD, cocaine and ecstasy are outlawed, and dealers are prosecuted.

Population

The need to love thy neighbour is especially strong in the Netherlands, where the population density is the highest in Europe (507 per sq km). Nearly half of the country's 17 million residents live in the western hoop around Amsterdam, Den Haag and Rotterdam; the provinces of Drenthe, Overijssel and Zeeland in the southwest are sparsely settled, in Dutch terms at least.

Nearly 80% of the population is of Dutch stock; the rest is mainly made up of people from the former colonies of Indonesia, Surinam and the former Netherlands Antilles, plus more recent arrivals from Turkey, Morocco and countries throughout Africa.

Standing Tall

The Dutch are the world's tallest people, averaging 1.83m (6ft) for men and 1.71m (5ft 7in) for women. Copious intake of milk proteins, smaller families and superior prenatal care are cited as likely causes, but researchers also suspect there is some magic fertiliser in the Dutch gene pool. Whatever the reason, the Dutch keep growing, as do their doorways. Today, the minimum required height for doors in new homes and businesses is 2.315m (7ft 6in).

Religion

For centuries, religious preference was split between the two heavyweights of Western society, Catholicism and Protestantism, and if you were Dutch you were one or the other. Today, 67% of the population over the age of 18 claims to have no religious affiliation, and the number of former churches that house offices, art galleries and shops is evidence of those attitudes.

And faith is falling: 12% of the population follows Catholicism and 8% Protestantism, figures that decrease yearly. Vestiges exist of a religious border between Protestants and Catholics; the area north of a line running roughly from the province of Zeeland in the southwest to the province of Drenthe is home to the majority of Protestants, while anywhere to the south is predominantly Catholic.

The church has little or no influence on societal matters such as same-sex marriage, euthanasia and prescription of cannabis for medical purposes, all of which are legal in the Netherlands.

The latest religion to have any great impact on Dutch society is Islam. Today, 6% of the population classes itself as Muslim, and the number is steadily increasing, especially in multicultural Rotterdam.

Multiculturalism

The Netherlands has a long history of tolerance towards immigration and a reputation for welcoming immigrants with open arms. The largest wave of immigration occurred in the 1960s, when the government recruited migrant workers from Turkey and Morocco to bridge a labour gap. In the mid-1970s, the granting of independence to the Dutch colony of Surinam in South America saw an influx of Surinamese.

An increasing number of Dutch deaths each year result from euthanasia (some 7000 in 2017, compared to 4829 in 2014). The practice is tightly controlled and is administered by doctors at the request of patients.

Many Dutch houses have a flagpole in their front garden to fly the Dutch flag on national holidays and other celebratory days. On Uitslagdag in mid-June school bags are amusingly added to the flagpole to celebrate high-school students passing their exams and graduating.

THE DUTCH WAY OF LIFE POPULATION

MARC VENEMA/SHUTTERSTOCK ©

Top
Football fans supporting the national team.

Bottom
Ice-skating in Groningen (p227).

In the past few years, however, the country's loose immigration policy has been called into question. Politically, there has been a significant swing to the right and consequently a move towards shutting the door on immigration. The assassinations of Pim Fortuyn and Theo van Gogh caused tensions to rise between the native Dutch and Muslim immigrants, which also gave rise to far-right anti-Islam politicians such as Geert Wilders. However, when the former queen, Beatrix, wore a head scarf on a visit to a mosque in Oman and Wilders tried to make an issue out of it, she received overwhelming support from the population.

Still there is concern about immigrants not becoming 'Dutch'. Strongly urging people to take classes in the Dutch language and culture, where concepts such as tolerance are emphasised, is official government policy. How the paradoxical concept of forcing people to learn to be tolerant will play out remains to be seen.

Sport

The Netherlands is a seriously active country. Some 65% of all Dutch engage in some form of sporty activity, and the average person now spends 20 minutes longer doing some sort of exercise each week than in the 1970s. Sport is organised to a fault: about five million people belong to nearly 30,000 clubs and associations in the Netherlands.

Football (soccer), cycling and skating are the favourites.

Football

Football is the Dutch national game and passion for the game runs high. Clubs such as Ajax, Feyenoord and PSV enjoy international renown and the country has produced some world-class players (Ruud Gullit, Dennis Bergkamp and the legendary Johan Cruyff). The unique Dutch approach to the game – known as Total Football (in which all outfield positions are theoretically interchangeable) – fascinated viewers at its peak in the 1970s.

Despite an excellent recent track record – losing to Spain in the 2010 World Cup final and beating host country Brazil in 2014 to finish third – the national team did not qualify for the 2018 World Cup, much to the disappointment of fans everywhere. (Die-hard supporters sought solace in the fact that five of the players on Morocco's team, which qualified for the first time in 20 years, were born and raised in the Netherlands.) The World-Cup blow followed hot on the heels of the side's failure to make it into the UEFA European Championships in 2016, confirming fears that Dutch football had hit an all-time low on the international stage.

The national football association counts a million members, and weekends see professional and amateur teams hit pitches across the country. Many pro clubs play in modern, high-tech stadiums, such as Amsterdam's **Arena** (p77), assisted by a modern, high-tech police force to counteract hooligans.

Perhaps no household item represents Dutch thrift better than the popular *flessenlikker* (bottle-scraper). This miracle tool has a disk on the business end and can scrape the last elusive smears from a mayonnaise jar or salad-dressing bottle.

Learn about Amsterdam's evolution into the world's most bike-friendly city in the highly readable *In the City of Bikes: The Story of the Amsterdam Cyclist* (Pete Jordan; 2013).

THE DUTCH WAY OF LIFE SPORT

ORANGE FEVER

If you've ever attended a sporting event where the Dutch are playing, you'll already be familiar with *oranjegekte* (orange craze), also known as *oranjekoorts* (orange fever). The custom of wearing the traditional colour of the Dutch royal family, the House of Orange-Nassau, was originally limited to celebration days for the monarchy, such as Queen's Day *(Koninginnedag)*, now King's Day *(Koningsdag)*. But particularly since the 1974 football World Cup, when tens of thousands of orange-clad supporters cheered on every game involving the Netherlands, the ritual of wearing outlandish orange get-ups – clothes, scarves, wigs, fake-fur top hats, face paint, feather boas, you name it – has become a Dutch phenomenon. To really celebrate like a local, you know what colour to wear.

Cycling

You only have to spend five minutes in the Netherlands to realise that locals cycle everywhere. Literally everywhere. They bike to the dentist, to work, to the opera and to brunch; they bike in snow, rain, sunshine and fog. Dressing up to bike to dinner and a show, or to drinks and a club, is a typical Dutch activity. Pedal away: no matter what you wear or where you're going, you'll blend in (and have fun). Unsurprisingly, 84% of Dutch people own one or more bikes – a world-record-breaking 22.5 million or 1.3 per capita in total.

The nation's undisputed star of the 2016 Olympics was road cyclist Annemiek van Vleuten, who crashed spectacularly out of the Games, fracturing three vertebrae in the process, during the women's road race. Team-mate Anna van der Breggen went on to win gold, with another Dutch cyclist, 'the Cannibal' Marianne Vos – road-race gold medallist at the 2012 Games – finishing ninth.

Past Dutch cycling greats include Leontien van Moorsel (b 1970) who won scores of cycling championships in the 1990s, and, at the 2000 and 2004 Olympics, a combined total of four golds, one silver and one bronze. In the 1980 Tour de France, Joop Zoetemelk (b 1946) pedalled to victory after finishing second a record six times.

The biggest Dutch cycling race is the Amstel Gold Race around hilly Limburg in mid-April. It's about 260km in length and features dozens of steep climbs. It is considered one of the most demanding races on the professional circuit.

Skating

Thousands of Dutch people take to the ice when the country's lakes and ditches freeze over. When the lakes aren't frozen, the Netherlands has dozens of ice rinks, with Olympic-sized tracks and areas for hockey and figure skating. The most famous amateur event is Friesland's 200km-long **Elfstedentocht** (p212).

The Dutch perform exceptionally well in speed skating. At the 2018 Winter Olympics, the Dutch team scooped the gold, silver and bronze medals in the women's 3000m event, becoming the first country during those Games to achieve a podium sweep. The Netherlands returned home with 20 medals – all in skating and including gold in every speed-skating event bar one. Dutch star of the Games was 22-year-old Esmee Visser, who won the women's 5000m just months after doubting she would even qualify.

Dutch Design

The Dutch aren't just whizzes at engineering and sport; they also have a keen eye for aesthetics. Contemporary Dutch design has a reputation for minimalist, creative approaches to everyday furniture and homeware products, mixed with vintage twists and tongue-in-cheek humour to keep it fresh. Since the 1990s, what started out as a few innovators has accelerated to become a movement that has put the Netherlands at the forefront of the industry. Dutch fashion is also reaching far beyond the country's borders, with designs that are vibrant and imaginative, yet practical too.

Contemporary Dutch design has its roots in a handful of designers. Providing a key platform was Amsterdam-based Droog (www.droog.com), a design collective established in 1993 with its own concept store, cafe and even hotel in the city today. With signature surreal wit, it works with a community of designers to help them produce their works and sell them to the world, with partners to make it happen and the connections to facilitate collaborations with big brands.

Among the contemporary pioneers was design legend Marcel Wanders (b 1963), who first drew international acclaim for his iconic *Knotted Chair,* produced by Droog in 1996. Made from a knotted aramid and carbon-fibre thread and resin, Wanders' air-drying technique meant it

Best Design Online
....
Dezeen (www.dezeen.com/tag/netherlands) Dutch architecture, interiors and design.
....
Het Nieuwe Instituut (http://hetnieuweinstituut.nl) Architecture, design, fashion and e-culture.
....
Fashion Council NL (http://fashioncouncilnl.com) Design and fashion events Netherlands-wide.

was ultimately shaped by gravity. It's now in the permanent collection of the Museum of Modern Art in New York. In 2001, in Breda, Wanders founded world-leading design label Moooi (www.moooi.com) with design entrepreneur Casper Vissers: the eclectic brand's name was a play on the Dutch word for 'beautiful', with an additional 'o' symbolising extra beauty and uniqueness.

Wanders (www.marcelwanders.com) continues to design projects infused with his signature romantic, more humanistic touch at his studio in a former arts school in Amsterdam's artsy Jordaan 'hood. Vissers meanwhile went on to launch the new Rotterdam-based lighting and furniture brand, Revised, in 2018. Turning to the past for inspiration, its products by young Dutch designer Sjoerd Vroonland are named after English villages and feature traditional materials such as glass, wood, steel, marble and stone.

Maarten Baas (b 1978; http://maartenbaas.com) graduated from Eindhoven Design Academy in 2002 and won instant acclaim for his Smoke collection, a stash of secondhand furniture singed with a blowtorch to create a burnt effect. Risk-taking and a youthful flamboyance are the trademarks of this young designer, typical of a generation that is forever innovating.

Other revolutionary designers include Jurgen Bey (b 1965), who has strong architectural links, working with interior and public-space design; industrial designer Hella Jongerius (b 1963; www.jongeriuslab.com), whose designs include porcelain plates and tiles using new printing techniques; and Piet Hein Eek (b 1967; https://pietheineek.nl), who works with reclaimed wood. In Rotterdam, Lex Pott (b 1985; www.lexpott.nl) is a young designer working with wood, stone and metal in their most raw forms.

Scholten & Baijings (Stefan Scholten and Carole Baijings) produce colourful textiles and kitchenware. Ineke Hans (b 1966; www.inekehans.com) is best known for her celebrated recyclable plastic Ahrend 380 chair, which incorporates a table. Then there's furniture-, product- and interior designer Richard Hutten (www.richardhutten.com), famed for his 'no sign of design' humorous, functional furniture. His works are exhibited worldwide and held in the permanent collections of many museums, including Amsterdam's **Stedelijk Museum** (p69).

Eindhoven is an incubator of Dutch design. The Dutch Design Academy is in the ex-Philips lamp factory (along with a family-friendly, interactive museum showcasing the many products Philips has come up with over the years). Dutch Design Week (www.ddw.nl), climaxing with the annual Dutch Design Awards (www.dutchdesignawards.nl), is held in October at the former Philips industrial complex Strijp-S.

Futuristic Fashion

While the Netherlands' traditional fashion-design powerhouse Viktor & Rolf – aka duo Viktor Horsting and Rolf Snoeren – celebrate 25 years in the business with a dazzling all-white collection called Immaculate, millennial fashion designers are pioneering 3D-printed haute couture. Key protagonist is Iris van Herpen (b 1984; www.irisvanherpen.com), who launched her first 3D-printed dress during Paris Fashion Week in 2010 and has gone on to dress everyone from Björk to Lady Gaga. Eye-popping wearable sculptures rather than functional fashion, Van Herpen's pieces are designed very much for the catwalk – it's impossible to sit down in some of her dresses, crafted in transparent resin perhaps, or laser-cut mylar.

Traditional Dutch toilets come with a shelf where deposited goods sit until swept away by a flush of water. The reason is tied to health and the supposed benefit of carefully studying what comes out. Not, as some wags say, because the Dutch can't bear to see anything underwater.

Why the Dutch are Different: A Journey into the Hidden Heart of the Netherlands (Ben Coates; 2015), and brilliantly titled *The UnDutchables* (Colin White & Laurie Boucke; 1989) are indispensable, at times humorous reads on what makes the Dutch really tick.

Dutch Art

They don't call them the Dutch Masters for nothing. Rembrandt, Frans Hals and Jan Vermeer – these iconic artists are some of world's most revered and celebrated painters. And then, of course, there's Vincent van Gogh, the rock star of Impressionism who toiled in ignominy while supported by his loving brother, Theo; and 20th-century artists including De Stijl proponent Piet Mondrian, and graphic genius MC Escher. Understanding these quintessential Dutch painters requires a journey into history.

15th & 16th Century

Flemish School

Prior to the late 16th century, when Belgium was still part of the Low Countries, art focused on the Flemish cities of Ghent, Bruges and Antwerp. Paintings of the Flemish School featured biblical and allegorical subject matter popular with the Church, the court and to a lesser extent the nobility, who, after all, paid the bills and called the shots.

Among the most famous names of the era are Jan van Eyck (1390–1441), the founder of the Flemish School, who was the first to perfect the technique of oil painting; Rogier van der Weyden (1400–64), whose religious portraits showed the personalities of his subjects; and Pieter Bruegel the Elder (1525–69), who used Flemish landscapes and peasant life in his allegorical scenes.

Born Jheronimus van Aken, Hieronymous Bosch (c 1450–1516), who took his name from his home town of Den Bosch, created works for the ages with his macabre allegorical paintings full of religious topics. *The Prodigal Son,* which hangs in Rotterdam's Museum Boijmans Van Beuningen (currently closed for renovations; p157), is a study in motion and wit.

Dutch School

In the northern Low Countries, artists began to develop a style of their own. Although the artists of the day never achieved the level of recognition of their Flemish counterparts, the Dutch School, as it came to be called, was known for favouring realism over allegory. Haarlem was the centre of this movement, with artists such as Jan Mostaert (1475–1555), Lucas van Leyden (1494–1533) and Jan van Scorel (1495–1562). Painters in the city of Utrecht were famous for using chiaroscuro (deep contrast of light and shade), a technique associated with the Italian master Caravaggio.

Golden Age

When the Spanish were expelled from the Low Countries, the character of the art market changed. There was no longer the Church to buy artworks – most of its art had been burned by rampaging Calvinists in 1566 during the *Beeldenstorm* ('statue storm') – and no court to speak of, so art became a business. Fortunately the wealth pouring into the Dutch economy meant artists could survive in a free market. In place of Church and court emerged a new, bourgeois society of merchants, artisans and shopkeepers who didn't mind spending money to brighten

One-Artist Museums

....

Vermeer Centrum Delft (Delft)

....

Jheronimus Bosch Art Center (Den Bosch)

....

Museum het Rembrandthuis (Amsterdam)

....

Frans Hals Museum (Haarlem)

....

Mondriaanhuis (Amersfoort)

....

Escher in Het Paleis (Den Haag)

up their houses and workplaces. The key: they had to produce pictures the buyers could relate to.

Painters became entrepreneurs in their own right, churning out banal works, copies and masterpieces in factory-like studios. Paintings were mass-produced and sold at markets alongside furniture and chickens. Soon the wealthiest households were covered in paintings from top to bottom. Foreign visitors commented that even bakeries and butcher shops seemed to have a painting or two on the wall. Most painters specialised in one of the main genres of the day.

Rembrandt van Rijn

The 17th century's greatest artist, Rembrandt van Rijn (1606–69), grew up a miller's son in Leiden, but had become an accomplished painter by his early 20s.

In 1631 he came to Amsterdam to run the painting studio of wealthy art-dealer Hendrick van Uylenburgh. Portraits were the studio's cash cow, and Rembrandt and his staff (or 'pupils') churned out scores of them, including group portraits such as *The Anatomy Lesson of Dr Nicolaes Tulp*. In 1634 he married Van Uylenburgh's niece Saskia, who had travelled to Amsterdam with the Mennonite painters Govert Flinck and Jacob Backer, and often modelled for him.

Rembrandt fell out with his boss, but his wife's capital helped him buy the sumptuous house next door to Van Uylenburgh's studio (the current Museum het Rembrandthuis, p53). There Rembrandt set up his own studio, with staff who worked in a warehouse in the Jordaan. These were happy years: his paintings were a success and his studio became the largest in the country, though his gruff manner and open agnosticism didn't win him dinner-party invitations from the elite.

Rembrandt became one of the city's biggest art collectors. He was a master manipulator not only of images;he was known to have his own pictures' prices inflated at auctions by bidders he had planted there. He often sketched and painted for himself, urging his staff to do likewise. Residents of the surrounding Jewish quarter provided perfect material for his dramatic biblical scenes.

A new Rembrandt was 'discovered' in 2012 when leading expert Ernst van de Wetering verified its origin and claimed it was one of a pair from 1643. *The Old Man* (or *The Old Rabbi*) is in a private English collection and now thought to be a self-portrait.

DUTCH ART GOLDEN AGE

10 GREAT OLD DUTCH PAINTINGS (AND WHERE TO SEE THEM)

Amsterdam (Rijksmuseum; p70)

➡ *The Night Watch*, Rembrandt

➡ *Self Portrait*, Rembrandt

➡ *The Merry Drinker*, Frans Hals

➡ *The Merry Family*, Jan Steen

➡ *Woman in Blue Reading a Letter*, Vermeer

Den Haag (Mauritshuis; p181)

➡ *Girl with a Pearl Earring*, Vermeer

➡ *The Anatomy Lesson of Dr Nicolaes Tulp*, Rembrandt

Haarlem (Frans Hals Museum; p113)

➡ *Regents & the Regentesses of the Old Men's Almshouse*, Frans Hals

Rotterdam (Museum Boijmans Van Beuningen; p157)

➡ *Tower of Babel*, Bruegel the Elder

➡ *The Prodigal Son*, Hieronymus Bosch

The Night Watch

After losing three children in their infancy, in 1642, Rembrandt and Saskia's son Titus was born. A year later, Saskia died and business went downhill. Rembrandt's majestic group portrait *The Night Watch* (1642) was hailed by art critics (it's now a prize exhibit at Amsterdam's Rijksmuseum (p70); life-size bronze sculptures recreating the painting grace the Southern Canal Ring Square, **Rembrandtplein** (Map p62; 🚋4/14 Rembrandtplein)). However, some of the influential people Rembrandt depicted were not pleased. Each subject had paid 100 guilders, and some were unhappy at being shoved in the background. In response, Rembrandt told them where they could shove their complaints. Suddenly he received far fewer orders.

Rembrandt began an affair with his son's governess, Geertje Dircx, but kicked her out a few years later when he fell for the new maid, Hendrickje Stoffels, who bore him a daughter, Cornelia. The public didn't take kindly to the man's lifestyle and his spiralling debts, and in 1656 he applied for *cessio bonorum* (a respectable form of insolvency). His house and rich art collection were sold and he moved to the Rozengracht in the Jordaan.

Etchings

No longer the darling of the wealthy after his insolvency, Rembrandt continued to paint, draw and etch – his etchings on display in the Museum het Rembrandthuis (p53) are some of the finest ever produced. He also received the occasional commission, including the monumental *Conspiracy of Claudius Civilis* (1661) for Amsterdam's city hall (after Govert Flinck, who had originally been commissioned, died before beginning to paint). The authorities disliked Rembrandt's work and had it removed. In 1662 he completed the *Staalmeesters* (the 'Syndics') for the drapers' guild and ensured that everybody remained clearly visible (unlike in *Night Watch*), though it ended up being his last group portrait. It's now in Amsterdam's Rijksmuseum (p70).

Later Works

The works of his later period show that Rembrandt had lost none of his touch. No longer constrained by the wishes of clients, he enjoyed new-found freedom; his works became more unconventional yet showed an ever-stronger empathy with their subject matter, as in *The Jewish Bride* (c 1666), now in the Rijksmuseum (p70). The many portraits of his son Titus and lover Hendrickje, and his ever-gloomier self-portraits, are among the most stirring in the history of art.

A plague epidemic between 1663 and 1666 killed one in seven Amsterdammers, including Hendrickje in 1663. Titus died in 1668, aged 27 and just married, leaving behind a baby daughter, Titia, who was born six months after his death; Rembrandt died a year later, a broken man.

Frans Hals

A great painter of this period, Frans Hals (1583–1666) was born in Antwerp but lived in Haarlem. He devoted most of his career to portraits, dabbling in occasional genre scenes with dramatic chiaroscuro. His ability to capture his subjects' expressions was equal to Rembrandt's, though he didn't explore their characters as much. Both masters used the same expressive, unpolished brush strokes, and their styles went from bright exuberance in their early careers to dark and solemn later on. The 19th-century Impressionists also admired Hals' work. In fact, his *The Merry Drinker* (1628) in the Rijksmuseum (p70) collection, with its bold brush strokes, could almost have been painted by an Impressionist.

Carel Fabritius' exquisite masterpiece *The Goldfinch* (1654), today displayed in the Mauritshuis in Den Haag, is the focus of Donna Tartt's Pulitzer Prize–winning novel, *The Goldfinch* (2013). The titanic, 1000-plus-page book opens and closes in Amsterdam. The film adaptation, starring Ansel Elgort and Finn Wolfhard, premiered in 2019.

GROUP PORTRAITS BY HALS

Frans Hals specialised in beautiful group portraits in which the participants were depicted in almost natural poses, unlike the rigid line-ups produced by lesser contemporaries – though he wasn't as cavalier as Rembrandt in subordinating faces to the composition. A good example is the pair of paintings known collectively as the *Regents & the Regentesses of the Old Men's Almshouse* (1664) in the Frans Hals Museum (p113) in Haarlem. The museum occupies a space that Hals knew well; while he never lived in the almshouse (contrary to popular belief), in the 1630s he and his family lived in Groot Heiligland, the street where the Old Men's Almshouse stood.

Vermeer

The grand trio of 17th-century masters is completed by Johannes (also known as Jan) Vermeer (1632–75) of Delft. He produced only 34 (possibly 35) meticulously crafted paintings in his career that are attributed to him (although some estimates are as high as 66 works). Vermeer died poor with 11 children (four more had died in infancy); his baker accepted two paintings from his wife as payment for a debt of more than 600 guilders. Yet Vermeer mastered genre painting like no other artist. His paintings include historical and biblical scenes from his earlier career, his famous *View of Delft* (c 1660–61) in the Mauritshuis (p181) in Den Haag, and some tender portraits of unknown women, such as the stunningly beautiful *Girl with a Pearl Earring* (c 1665–67), also hanging in the Mauritshuis.

Famous Works

Vermeer's work is known for serene light pouring through tall windows. The calm, spiritual effect is enhanced by dark blues, deep reds, warm yellows and supremely balanced composition. Good examples include the Rijksmuseum's (p70) *Kitchen Maid* (also known as *The Milkmaid*, c 1660) and *Woman in Blue Reading a Letter* (c 1663), and, for his use of perspective, *The Love Letter* (c 1669–70).

The Little Street (c 1658), also known as *View of Houses in Delft,* in the Rijksmuseum's collection is Vermeer's only known street scene.

Other Golden Age Painters

Around the middle of the 17th century, the focus on mood and subtle play of light began to make way for the splendour of the baroque. Jacob van Ruisdael (c 1628–82) went for dramatic skies while Albert Cuyp (1620–91) painted Italianate landscapes. Van Ruisdael's pupil Meindert Hobbema (1638–1709) preferred less heroic, more playful scenes full of pretty bucolic detail. Note that Cuyp, Ruisdael and Hobbema all have main streets named after them in Amsterdam's Old South and De Pijp neighbourhoods, and many other streets here are named after other Dutch artists, including Frans Hals, Govert Flinck, Ferdinand Bol, Cornelis Troost and Jan Steen.

The genre paintings of Jan Steen (c 1625–79) show the almost frivolous aspect of baroque. Steen was also a tavern keeper, and his depictions of domestic chaos led to the Dutch expression 'a Jan Steen household'. A good example is the animated revelry of *The Merry Family* (1668) in the Rijksmuseum (p70); it shows adults having a good time around the dinner table, oblivious to the children in the foreground pouring themselves a drink.

The Girl with a Pearl Earring, a dramatised account of the painting of Vermeer's famous work, is a highly readable 1999 novel by Tracy Chevalier. It was made into a film in 2003, which was nominated for three Academy Awards.

18th Century

The Golden Age of Dutch painting ended almost as suddenly as it began when the French invaded the Low Countries in 1672. The economy collapsed and the market for paintings went south with it. Painters who stayed in business concentrated on 'safe' works that repeated earlier successes. In the 18th century they copied French styles, pandering to the fashion for anything French.

The results were competent but not ground-breaking. Cornelis Troost (1696–1750) was one of the best genre painters, and is sometimes compared to the British artist William Hogarth (1697–1764) for his satirical as well as sensitive portraits of ordinary people; Troost, too, introduced scenes of domestic revelry into his pastels.

Gerard de Lairesse (1641–1711) and Jacob de Wit (1695–1754) specialised in decorating the walls and ceilings of buildings – De Wit's trompe l'œil decorations (painted illusions that look real; French 'deceive the eye') in the Bijbels Museum (p60) are worth seeing.

Great Art Museums

Rijksmuseum (Amsterdam)

Van Gogh Museum (Amsterdam)

Mauritshuis (Den Haag)

Museum Boijmans Van Beuningen (Rotterdam)

Museum De Lakenhal (Leiden)

19th Century

The late 18th century and most of the 19th century produced little of note, save for the landscapes and seascapes of Johan Barthold Jongkind (1819–91) and the gritty, almost photographic Amsterdam scenes of George Hendrik Breitner (1857–1923). They appear to have inspired French Impressionists, many of whom visited Amsterdam.

Jongkind and Breitner reinvented 17th-century realism and influenced the Hague School of the last decades of the 19th century. Painters such as Hendrik Mesdag (1831–1915), Jozef Israëls (1824–1911) and the three Maris brothers, Jacob (1837–99), Matthijs (1839–1917) and Willem (1844–1910) created landscapes, seascapes and genre works, including Mesdag's impressive *Panorama Mesdag* (1881), a gigantic 14m-high, 120m-wide 360-degree cylindrical painting of the seaside town of Scheveningen viewed from a dune.

Without a doubt, the greatest 19th-century Dutch painter was Vincent van Gogh (1853–90), whose convulsive patterns and furious colours were in a world of their own and still defy comfortable categorisation. (A post-Impressionist? A forerunner of expressionism?)

Vincent Van Gogh

While the Dutch Masters were known for their dark, brooding paintings, it was Van Gogh who created an identity of suffering as an art form, with a morbid style all his own. Even today, he epitomises the epic struggle of the artist: the wrenching poverty; the lack of public acclaim; the reliance upon a patron – in this case his faithful brother, Theo; the mental instability; the untimely death by suicide. And of course, one of the most iconic images of an artist's self-destruction, the severed ear.

The Artist's Legend

Vincent van Gogh may have been poor – he sold only one painting in his lifetime – but he wasn't old. It's easy to forget from his self portraits, in which he appears much older (partly the effects of his poverty), that he was only 37 when he died. But his short life continues to influence art to this day.

Born in Zundert in 1853, he lived in Paris with his younger brother Theo, an art dealer, who financially supported him from his modest income. In Paris he became acquainted with seminal artists including Edgar Degas, Camille Pissarro, Henri de Toulouse-Lautrec and Paul Gauguin.

VAN GOGH IN WORDS & PICTURES

Few 20th-century artists inspired so many high-drama books and films as the emotionally ravished Vincent van Gogh. Even his rumoured last words ring with the kind of excruciating, melancholic beauty that his best paintings express. With Theo at his side, two days after he shot himself in the chest after a manic fit of painting, he is said to have uttered in French *'la tristesse durera toujours'* (the sadness will last forever).

Read

Vincent Van Gogh: The Letters contains all 902 letters to and from Van Gogh to his brother, friends, lovers, confidantes and fellow artists. It's a moving window into his inner life, plus a testimony to the extraordinary friendship and artistic connection he shared with his brother, Theo.

Watch

➡ *Lust for Life* (1956)

➡ *Vincent* (1987)

➡ *Vincent and Theo* (1990)

➡ *Loving Vincent* (2017)

Van Gogh moved south to Arles, Provence, in 1888. Revelling in its intense light and bright colours, he painted sunflowers, irises and other vivid subjects with a burning fervour. He sent paintings to Theo in Paris to sell, and dreamed of founding an artists' colony in Provence, but only Gauguin followed up his invitation. Their differing artistic approaches – Gauguin believed in painting from imagination; Van Gogh painting what he saw – and their artistic temperaments, fuelled by absinthe, came to a head with the argument that led to Van Gogh lopping his ear (which he gave to a sex-worker acquaintance) and his subsequent committal in Arles.

In May 1889, Van Gogh voluntarily entered an asylum in St-Rémy de Provence, where he painted prolifically during his one-year, one-week and one-day confinement, including masterpieces such as *Irises* and *Starry Night*. While there, Theo sent him a positive French newspaper critique of his work. The following month, Anna Boch, sister of his friend Eugène Boch, bought *The Red Vines* (or *The Red Vineyard;* 1888) for 400 francs (less than €100 today). It now hangs in Moscow's Pushkin Museum.

Legacy of a Tortured Genius

On 16 May 1890 Van Gogh moved to Auvers-sur-Oise, just outside Paris, to be closer to Theo, but on 27 July that year he shot himself, possibly to avoid further financial burden on his brother, whose wife had just had a baby son, named Vincent, and who was also supporting their ailing mother. Van Gogh died two days later with Theo at his side. Theo subsequently had a breakdown, was also committed, and succumbed to physical illness. He died, aged 33, just six months after Van Gogh.

It would be less than a decade before Van Gogh's talent would start to achieve wide recognition, and by the early 1950s, he had become a household name. In 1990 he broke the record for a single painting (*A Portrait of Doctor Gachet*) at Christie's – it fetched US$82.5 million. Accounting for inflation, it's still the highest price paid at a public auction for art to this day.

Van Gogh's Famous Five
....
Sunflowers (Van Gogh Museum)
....
Wheatfield with Crows (Van Gogh Museum)
....
Self Portrait with Felt Hat (Van Gogh Museum)
....
The Potato Eaters (Kröller-Müller Museum)
....
Weavers (Kröller-Müller Museum)

20th Century

De Stijl

De Stijl (The Style), also known as neoplasticism, was a Dutch design movement that aimed to harmonise all the arts by bringing artistic expressions back to their essence. Its advocate was the magazine of the same name, first published in 1917 by Theo van Doesburg (1883–1931). Van Doesburg produced similar rectangular patterns to Piet Mondrian's, though he dispensed with the thick, black lines and later tilted his rectangles at 45 degrees, departures serious enough for Mondrian to call off the friendship.

Throughout the 1920s and 1930s, De Stijl attracted sculptors, poets, architects and designers. One of these was Gerrit Rietveld (1888–1964), designer of the Van Gogh Museum (p74) and several other buildings, but best known internationally for his furniture, such as the *Red Blue Chair* (1918) and his range of uncomfortable zigzag seats, which, viewed side-on, formed a 'z' with a backrest.

Mondrian

A major proponent of De Stijl was Piet Mondrian (originally Mondriaan, 1872–1944), who initially painted in the Hague School tradition. After flirting with Cubism, he began working with bold rectangular patterns, using only the three primary colours (yellow, blue and red) set against the three neutrals (white, grey and black). He named this style neoplasticism and viewed it as an undistorted expression of reality in pure form and pure colour. His 1920 composition in red, black, blue, yellow and grey *(Composition No II)*, in Amsterdam's Stedelijk Museum (p69), is an elaborate example.

Mondrian's later works were more stark (or 'pure') and became dynamic again when he moved to New York in 1940. The world's largest collection of his paintings resides in the Gemeentemuseum (Municipal Museum; p183) in his native Den Haag.

MC Escher

One of the most remarkable graphic artists of the 20th century was Maurits Cornelis Escher (1898–1972). His drawings, lithos and woodcuts of blatantly impossible images continue to fascinate mathematicians: a waterfall feeds itself; people go up and down a staircase that ends where it starts; a pair of hands draw each other. You can see his work at Escher in Het Paleis (p183) in Den Haag. Admire Escher-inspired street art on paths and squares in Groningen, where he was born.

CoBrA

After WWII, artists rebelled against artistic conventions and vented their rage in abstract expressionism. In Amsterdam, Karel Appel (1921–2006) and Constant (Constant Nieuwenhuys; 1920–2005) drew on styles pioneered by Paul Klee and Joan Miró, and exploited bright colours and 'uncorrupted' children's art to produce lively works that leaped off the canvas. In Paris in 1945 they met up with the Danish Asger Jorn (1914–73) and the Belgian Corneille (Cornelis van Beverloo; 1922–2010), and together with several other artists and writers formed a group known as CoBrA (Copenhagen, Brussels, Amsterdam). It's been called the last great avant-garde movement.

Their first major exhibition, in the Stedelijk Museum in 1949, aroused a storm of protest (with comments such as 'my child paints like that too'). Still, the CoBrA artists exerted a strong influence in their respective countries, even after they disbanded in 1951. The CoBrA Museum (p83) in Amstelveen displays a good range of their works, including colourful ceramics.

Contemporary Scene

Modern Dutch artists are usually well represented at international events and are known for mixing mediums.

Artist duo Liet Heringa (b 1966) and Maarten van Kalsbeek (b 1962) are known for their moody, free-form sculptures, a couple of which can be admired in Otterlo's Kröller-Müller Museum (p258). Harma Heikens (b 1963; www.harmaheikens.nl) is another boundary-pushing sculptor, known for her bitter-sweet 'pop culture' figures loaded with innuendo and comment on controversial subjects such as violence, sexual abuse, war, religion and society.

Amsterdam-born Michael Raedecker (b 1963) creates dreamy, radiant still lifes at his UK-based studio, often incorporating embroidery in his textured paintings. In 2000 he was nominated for the prestigious Turner Prize.

Levi van Veluw (b 1985; https://levivanveluw.com) is a disciplinary Amsterdam artist who has been known to use his own body as a canvas – *Landscapes* (2004) sees him reinterpret traditional landscape painting as a series of four different landscapes, including a mossy heath specked with grazing white goats, wrapped around the 3D contours of his own face.

Anouk Kruithof (b 1981) works with photography to create social projects such as *Happy Birthday To You* (2011), a book featuring the birthday wishes – to smoke a birthday joint in Utrecht, to throw a big party with a live band and herring on toast for the guests – of 10 patients in a psychiatric hospital.

On the streets of Amsterdam, look out for the stunning tape art of urban street artist Max Zorn (b 1982; www.maxzorn.com), who, using nothing more than packing tape and a razor blade, works with shades of brown to create the most astonishing sepia-hued portraits of famous people, landscapes etc. Otherwise, hotfoot it to Amsterdam Noord to possibly the single-most fertile spot for street art in the entire country: the former shipyards-turned-alternative art collective NDSM-werf (p79), appropriately adorned with a dazzling, 24m-high portrait of Anne Frank by world-class Brazilian artist Eduardo Kobra on part of its gargantuan facade.

Dutch Graphic Arts

It's not all paint on canvas; modern Dutch graphic arts also win acclaim.

Dick Bruna (1927–2017) of Utrecht is famous for Miffy (Nijntje in Dutch), an adorable cartoon rabbit. He wrote and illustrated 124 children's books and designed thousands of book covers, as well as hundreds of other books, posters, postcards and prints. The Miffy Museum (p144) in Utrecht honours him.

The Dutch tradition of clear visual communications has developed since the start of the 20th century. You'll see examples every day, including on the national railway, which was an early trendsetter in graphic communication. Brilliant examples of Dutch graphic arts are displayed at the Stedelijk Museum Breda (p276).

Architecture

The Dutch are masters of architecture and use of space, but this is nothing new. Through the ages, few countries have exerted more influence on the discipline of art and construction than the Netherlands. From the original sober cathedrals to the sleek modern structures, their ideas and designs have spread throughout Europe and beyond. You may not find any bombastic statements such as St Peter's cathedral or the Louvre, but then again, ostentation was never in keeping with the Dutch character.

Romanesque

Above Noorderkerk (p65), Amsterdam

Romanesque architecture, which took Europe by storm between 900 and 1250, is the earliest architectural style remaining in the country, if you discount the *hunebedden* (chamber tombs). Its main characteristics are an uncomplicated form, thick walls, small windows and round arches.

The oldest church of this style in the Netherlands is Pieterskerk (p147) in Utrecht. Built in 1048, it's one of five churches that form a cross in the city, with the cathedral at its centre. Runner-up is Nijmegen's 16-sided Sint Nicolaaskapel (p252), which is basically a scaled-down copy of Charlemagne's chapel in Aachen, Germany. Another classic example of Romanesque is the Onze Lieve Vrouwebasiliek (p263) in Maastricht.

The Netherlands' countryside is also brimming with this style of architecture. The windy plains of the north are filled with examples of sturdy brick churches erected in the 12th and 13th centuries, such as the lonely church perched on a ma-made hill in Hegebeintum, Friesland.

The ultimate in early functionalism, windmills have a variety of distinctive designs and their characteristic look makes them national icons.

Gothic

By around 1250 the love affair with Romanesque was over, and the Gothic era was ushered in. Pointed arches, ribbed vaulting and dizzying heights were trademarks of this new architectural style, which was to last until 1600. Although the Dutch buildings didn't match the size of the French Gothic cathedrals, a rich style emerged in Catholic Brabant that could compete with anything abroad. Stone churches with soaring vaults and buttresses, such as St Janskathedraal (p269) in Den Bosch and Breda's Grote Kerk (p276), were erected. Both are good examples of the Brabant Gothic style, as it was later known.

You'll notice timber vaulting and the widespread use of brick among the stone. Stone is normally a constant fixture of Gothic buildings, but in the marshy lands of the western Netherlands it was too heavy (and too scarce) to use. The basic ingredients of bricks – clay and sand – were in abundance, however. Still, bricks are not exactly light material, and weight limits forced architects to build long or wide to compensate for the lack of height. The Sint Janskerk (p178) in Gouda is the longest church in the country, with a nave of 123m, and it has the delicate, stately feel of a variant called Flamboyant Gothic. Stone Gothic structures do exist in the western stretches of Holland, though: Haarlem's Grote Kerk van St Bavo (p113) is a wonderful example.

Mannerism

From the middle of the 16th century the Renaissance style that was sweeping through Italy steadily began to filter into the Netherlands. The Dutch naturally put their own spin on this new architectural design, which came to be known as mannerism (c 1550–1650). Also known as Dutch Renaissance, this unique style falls somewhere between Renaissance and baroque; it retained the bold curving forms and rich ornamentation of baroque but merged them with classical Greek and Roman and traditional Dutch styles. Building facades were accentuated with mock columns (pilasters) and the simple spout gables were replaced with step gables that were richly decorated with sculptures, columns and obelisks. The playful interaction of red brick and horizontal bands of white or yellow sandstone was based on mathematical formulas designed to please the eye.

Hendrik de Keyser (1565–1621) was the champion of mannerism. His Zuiderkerk (p55), Noorderkerk (p65) and Westerkerk (p57) in Amsterdam are standout examples; all three show a major break from the sober, stolid lines of brick churches located out in the sticks. Their steeples are ornate and built with a variety of contrasting materials, while the windows are framed in white stone set off by brown brick. Florid details enliven the walls and roof lines.

Golden Age

After the Netherlands became a world trading power in the 17th century, its rich merchants wanted to splash out on lavish buildings that proclaimed their status.

More than anything, the new architecture had to impress. The leading lights in the architectural field, such as Jacob van Campen (1595–1657) and the brothers Philips and Justus Vingboons, again turned to ancient Greek and Roman designs for ideas. To make buildings look taller, the step gable was replaced by a neck gable, and pilasters were built to look like imperial columns, complete with pedestals. Decorative scrolls were added as finishing flourishes, and the peak wore a triangle or globe to simulate a temple roof.

A wonderful example of this is the Koninklijk Paleis (Royal Palace; p43) in Amsterdam, originally built as the town hall in 1648. Van Campen, the architect, drew on classical designs and dropped many of De Keyser's playful decorations, and the resulting building exuded gravity with its solid lines and shape.

This new form of architecture suited the city's businessmen, who needed to let the world know that they were successful. As red sports cars were still centuries away, canal houses became showpieces. Despite the narrow plots, each building from this time makes a statement at gable level through sculpture and myriad shapes and forms. Philips and Justus Vingboons were specialists in these swanky residences; their most famous works include the Bijbels Museum (Biblical Museum; p60) and houses scattered throughout Amsterdam's western canal belt.

The capital is not the only city to display such grand architecture. Den Haag has 17th-century showpieces, including the **Paleis Noordeinde** (Map p182; Noordeinde; ⬚Kneuterdijk) and the Mauritshuis (p181), and scores of other examples line the picture-perfect canals of Leiden, Delft and Maastricht, to name but a few.

French Influence

By the 18th century the wealthy classes had turned their backs on trade for more staid lives in banking or finance, which meant a lot of time at home. Around the same time, Dutch architects began deferring to all things French (which reflected French domination of the country); dainty Louis XV furnishings and florid rococo facades became all the rage. It was then a perfect time for new French building trends to sweep the country. Daniel Marot (1661–1752), together with his assistants Jean and Anthony Coulon, was the first to introduce French interior design with matching exteriors. Good examples of their work can be found along the Lange Voorhout in Den Haag.

GABLES

Among the great treasures along the old canals in Amsterdam, Haarlem and elsewhere are the magnificent gables – the roof-level facades that adorn elegant houses. The gable hid the roof from public view, and helped to identify the house, until 1795, when the French occupiers introduced house numbers. Gables then became more of a fashion accessory.

There are four main types of gable: the simple spout gable, with diagonal outline and semicircular windows or shutters, that was used mainly for warehouses from the 1580s to the early 1700s; the step gable, a late-Gothic design favoured by Dutch Renaissance architects; the neck gable, also known as the bottle gable, a durable design introduced in the 1640s; and the bell gable, which appeared in the 1660s and became popular in the 18th century.

HOISTS & HOUSES THAT TIP

• •

Many old canal houses deliberately tip forward. Given the narrowness of staircases, owners needed an easy way to move large goods and furniture to the upper floors. The solution: a hoist built into the gable, to lift objects up and in through the windows. The tilt allowed loading without bumping into the house front. Some properties even have huge hoist-wheels in the attic with a rope and hook that run through the hoist beam.

The forward lean also makes the houses seem larger, which makes it easier to admire the facade and gable – a fortunate coincidence for everyone.

Neoclassicism

Architecture took a back seat during the Napoleonic Wars in the late 18th century. Buildings still needed to be built, of course, so designers dug deep into ancient Greek and Roman blueprints once more and eventually came up with neoclassicism (c 1790–1850). Known for its order, symmetry and simplicity, neoclassical design became the mainstay for houses of worship, courtyards and other official buildings. A shining example of neoclassicism is Groningen's town hall; of particular note are the classical pillars, although the use of brick walls is a purely Dutch accent. Many a church was subsidised by the government water ministry and so was named a Waterstaatkerk (state water church), such as the lonely house of worship in Schokland.

Late 19th Century

From the 1850s onwards, many of the country's large architectural projects siphoned as much as they could from the Gothic era, creating neo-Gothic. Soon afterwards, freedom of religion was declared and Catholics were allowed to build new churches in Protestant areas. Neo-Gothic suited the Catholics just fine as it recalled their own glory days, and a boom in church-building took place.

Nationwide, nostalgia for the perceived glory days of the Golden Age inspired neo-Renaissance, which drew heavily on De Keyser's earlier masterpieces. Neo-Renaissance buildings were erected throughout the country, made to look like well-polished veterans from three centuries earlier. For many observers, these stepped-gable edifices with alternating stone and brick are the epitome of classic Dutch architecture.

One of the leading architects of this period was Pierre Cuypers (1827–1921), who built several neo-Gothic churches but often merged the style with neo-Renaissance, as can be seen in Amsterdam's Centraal Station (p51) and Rijksmuseum (p70). These are predominantly Gothic structures but have touches of Dutch Renaissance brickwork.

Berlage & the Amsterdam School

As the 20th century approached, the neo styles and their reliance on the past were strongly criticised by Hendrik Petrus Berlage (1856–1934), the father of modern Dutch architecture. He favoured spartan, practical designs over frivolous ornamentation; Amsterdam's 1902 Beurs van Berlage (p53) displays these ideals to the full. Berlage cooperated with sculptors, painters and tilers to ensure that ornamentation was integrated into the overall design in a supportive role, rather than being tacked on as an embellishment to hide the structure. The Gemeentemuseum (p183) in Den Haag, Berlage's last major work, was an even more ambitious expression of his principles.

Berlage's residential designs approached a block of buildings as a whole, not as a collection of individual houses. In this he influenced the young architects of what became known as the Amsterdam School,

Rotterdam's 12-storey Witte Huis (built 1898) was Europe's first 'skyscraper'. Today it looks almost squat compared to its neighbours; it somehow survived the destruction of the city in 1940.

though they rejected his stark rationalism and preferred more creative designs. Leading exponents were Michel de Klerk (1884–1923), Piet Kramer (1881–1961) and Johan van der Mey (1878–1949); the latter ushered in the Amsterdam School (c 1916–30) with his extraordinary Scheepvaarthuis (p56), formerly the headquarters of several shipping firms, now a hotel.

Brick was the material of choice for such architects, and housing blocks were treated as sculptures, with curved corners, oddly placed windows and ornamental, rocket-shaped towers. Their Amsterdam housing estates, such as De Klerk's 'Ship' in the west, have been described as fairytale fortresses rendered in a Dutch version of art deco. Their preference for form over function meant their designs were great to look at but not always fantastic to live in, with small windows and inefficient use of space.

Housing subsidies sparked a frenzy of residential building activity in the 1920s. At the time, many architects of the Amsterdam School worked for the Amsterdam city council and designed the buildings for the Oud Zuid (Old South). This large-scale expansion – mapped out by Berlage – called for good-quality housing, wide boulevards and cosy squares.

> The website of who's who in Holland's architectural scene is www.architectenweb.nl. It also showcases newly commissioned projects and those underway.

Functionalism

While Amsterdam School–type buildings were being erected all over their namesake city, a new generation of architects began to rebel against the school's impractical (not to mention expensive) structures. Influenced by the Bauhaus school in Germany, Frank Lloyd Wright in the USA and Le Corbusier in France, they formed a group called 'the 8'. It was the first stirring of functionalism (1927–70).

Architects such as Ben Merkelbach (1901–61) and Gerrit Rietveld (1888–1965) believed that form should follow function and sang the praises of steel, glass and concrete. Their spacious designs were practical and allowed for plenty of sunlight; Utrecht's masterpiece Rietveld-Schröderhuis (p145) is the only house built completely along functionalist De Stijl lines.

After the war, functionalism came to the fore and stamped its authority on new suburbs to the west and south of Amsterdam, as well as war-damaged cities such as Rotterdam. High-rise suburbs were built on a large scale yet weren't sufficient to keep up with the population boom and urbanisation of Dutch life. But functionalism fell from favour as the smart design aspects were watered down in low-cost housing projects for the masses.

> The *Architectural Guide to the Netherlands* by Paul Groenendijk and Piet Vollaard is a comprehensive look at architecture since 1900, arranged by region, with short explanations and photos. It's in two volumes: *1900–2000* and *1980–Present*. The associated website, with a list of the Top 100 structures, is www.architectureguide.nl.

Modernism & Beyond

Construction has been booming in the Netherlands since the 1980s, and architects have had ample opportunity to flirt with numerous 'isms' such as structuralism, neorationalism, postmodernism and neomodernism.

Evidence of these styles can be found in Rotterdam, an architectural world hub where city planners have encouraged bold designs that range from Piet Blom's startling cube-shaped Boompjestorens to Ben van Berkel's graceful **Erasmusbrug** (Map p158; MWilheminaplein, Leuvehaven). In fact the whole city is a modern architectural showcase where new 'exhibits' are erected all the time. The former tallest building in the country, the MaasToren, which tops out at 165m, was dwarfed by the 215m-tall Zalmhaventoren in 2021. The residential tower, accompanied by two shorter towers, functions as a 'vertical city' with 492 homes and accompanying facilities.

A short distance away, a trio of transparent towers called De Rotterdam (2009; p166) were designed – ingeniously to be viewed in motion by passing cars – by Rotterdam's very own Rem Koolhaas (b 1944).

Top: Gabled facades (p308), Amsterdam

Bottom: Rietveld-Schröderhuis (p145), Utrecht City

One of the world's most influential architects, his firm, OMA, is a breeding ground for a whole new generation of architects. Its current work on the construction of a new stadium at Nieuwe Maas for the city's football team, to be built partly on water, is expected to kickstart the revitalisation of the entire Feyenoord City wedge of Rotterdam riverside.

Other striking examples of bold new architecture can be admired throughout the Netherlands, often combining symbolic references with a sense of play. Near Den Bosch, the Haverleij residential complex re-imagines a medieval landscape, with 10 moat-ringed communities, each with its own castle, sharing green pasturelands. In Breda, a surreal copper-plated blob forms an acoustically calibrated dome for the Mezz pop-music hall. In Zwolle, a UFO faced with reflective blue tiles appears to have landed on the rooftop of the stodgy neoclassical Museum De Fundatie (p245), shaking up the academy as it were.

At Utrecht's TivoliVredenburg (p152) music centre, four venues (each for a different musical style) hover around and above the original symphony hall like sections in a record store. The new Forum cultural centre of Groningen, which opened in 2019, rises like a great pyramid off the main square. And in Amsterdam, the NEMO Science Museum (p57) recalls a resurfacing submarine.

Much of the ground for experimentation is provided by zones or structures whose functions have changed, declined or been abandoned. Throughout the country are numerous fascinating examples of urban transformation and creative building reuse – a sustainable alternative to demolition. As their devotional function goes by the wayside, churches in Zwolle and Maastricht have been reborn as bookstores and a posh hotel. In Eindhoven, the sprawling industrial park of the Philips electronics firm has been retrofitted for creative talent, with an events centre, concert hall, hostel and skateboard park, collectively known as the Strijp-S.

On Maastricht's east riverbank, a residential district designed by an all-star team of international architects has sprung up on the site of an old ceramics factory, and is now suitably dubbed Céramique. At the NDSM (p79) shipyard in North Amsterdam, the former welding hangar now houses art and film studios, old shipping containers are student housing units and the crane track (Kranspoor) became the base for an elongated office building.

ART OR ARCHITECTURE?

For some contemporary Dutch artists, the line between art and architecture is very fine indeed. At his studio in Nieuwkoop in Zuid-Holland, Daan Roosegaarde (b 1979; www.studioroosegaarde.net) pushes the boundaries between art and urban technology, fusing innovative art installations with the environment to increase eco-awareness.

With *Icoon Afsluitdijk* (2017) the artist transformed part of Noord-Holland's 32km-long Afsluitdijk – a dyke built by hand, stone by stone – into a futuristic eco-landscape. Come dark, the headlights of passing cars reflect on 60 roadside floodgates wrapped in a luminous lining to create a sci-fi-like driving experience on an energy-neutral road. Roosegaarde's *Gates of Light* installation is part of a mammoth government project, starting in 2018, to renovate the 1930s dyke. By 2030 it will, like all national roads, be energy-neutral.

At first glance, John Körmeling's *Draaiend Huis* (2008) in Tilburg appears to be just another regular house, albeit one stuck all on its own in the middle of a 1950s, suburban-highway roundabout. But look closely and you'll notice that the house actually rotates around the roundabout.

Ben van Berkel's graceful Erasmusbrug (p157), Rotterdam

The Nederlands Architectuur Instituut (www.nai.nl) in Rotterdam is the top authority on the latest developments in Dutch buildings and design, and it has good retrospective shows on the trends that have shaped the nation's architecture.

ARCHITECTURE MODERNISM & BEYOND

The shores along Amsterdam's IJ River are a good place to see the vaunted Dutch traditions of urban design in action. Northwest of Centraal Station, there's a flurry of construction in the Houthaven ('lumber port') area, whose seven artificial islands are rising from the ashes as a new residential hub. One of the most striking sites in the area is the REM Eiland, a 22m-high former pirate-broadcasting rig now housing a restaurant and bar.

To the east, the burgeoning IJburg neighbourhood is slowly mushrooming on a string of artificial islands some 10km from the city centre. Some 45,000 residents are predicted to inhabit these islands by 2025. The curvaceous steel Enneüs Heerma Brug, dubbed Dolly Parton Bridge by locals, links it to the mainland. And so a new city rises where once there was marsh, the story of the Netherlands.

The Dutch Landscape

There's no arguing with the fact that the Netherlands is a product of human endeavour. Everywhere you look, from the neat rows of *polders* to the omnipresent dykes, everything looks planned and organised. 'God created the world, but the Dutch created the Netherlands', as the saying goes. Much of this nature tinkering has been out of necessity – it's hard to live underwater for any length of time. But all of the reorganisation has put a strain on the Dutch environment.

A Land Created

Above: Storm surge barrier, Delta Project (p205)

Flanked by Belgium, Germany and the choppy waters of the North Sea, the landmass of the Netherlands is to a great degree artificial, having been reclaimed from the sea over many centuries. Maps from the Middle Ages are a curious sight today, with large chunks of land 'missing' from North Holland and Zeeland. The country now encompasses over

41,500 sq km, making it roughly half the size of Scotland, or a touch bigger than the US state of Maryland.

Twelve provinces make up the Netherlands. Almost all of these are as flat as a *pannenkoek*; the only hills to speak of rise from its southern tip, near Maastricht. The soil in the west and north is relatively young and consists of peat and clay formed less than 10,000 years ago. Much of this area is below sea level, or reclaimed land.

Dykes

The efforts of the Dutch to create new land are almost superhuman. Over the past century alone three vast *polders* have been created through ingenious engineering: Wieringermeer in North Holland; the province-island of Flevoland; and the adjoining Noordoostpolder. Much of this, just over 1700 sq km, was drained after a barrier dyke closed off the North Sea in 1932. In total, an astounding 20% of the country is reclaimed land.

It's impossible to talk about the Dutch landscape without mentioning water, which covers 20% of the entire country. Most Dutch people shudder at the thought of a leak in the dykes. If the Netherlands were to lose its 2400km of mighty dykes and dunes – some of which are 25m high – the large cities would be inundated. Modern pumping stations (the replacements for windmills) run around the clock to drain off excess water.

The danger of floods is most acute in the southwestern province of Zeeland, a sprawling estuary for the rivers Schelde, Maas, Lek and Waal. The latter two are branches of the Rijn (Rhine), the endpoint of a journey that begins in the Swiss Alps. The Maas rises in France and travels through Belgium before draining into the North Sea in the Delta region.

The floods of 1953 devastated Zeeland and the surrounding region. The resulting Delta Project to prevent future flooding became one of the world's largest public works projects.

Myriad small roads run atop the old dykes and these can make great cycling routes, from which you can appreciate just how far the land lies below the water in the canals, and see the historic windmills once used to keep the water out.

Wildlife

Human encroachment has played a huge role in the wildlife of the Netherlands. Few habitats are left intact in the country, and more than 10% of species are imported. While the Netherlands' flora and fauna will always be in constant change, one fact remains – birds love the place.

In some cases, human activity works in favour of certain species. In Gelderland, the part of the Waal river flowing through the Geldersepoort – an area of lakes, ponds, marshes and willows – has been widened to accommodate increased flow volumes and so has become attractive to new types of birds such as avocets, which settle there. Similar cases of species returning include the great egret, which had inhabited the Austria-Hungary border region until 1988, showing up in Flevoland after establishment of new *polders* there, and the white-tailed eagle appearing in the Biesbosch National Park (p180). In other cases, species are introduced into nature reserves, such as the European bison, Highland cattle and Galloway cattle, which behave like extinct species, in a bid to return the landscape to its original state.

National Parks

With so few corners of the Netherlands left untouched, the Dutch cherish every bit of nature that's left, and that's doubly true for their national parks (www.nationaalpark.nl). But while the first designated natural reserve was born in 1930, it wasn't until 1984 that the first publicly funded park was established.

There's no denying the Netherlands is a low, flat country ('Nederlands' in Dutch means 'low land'). Its lowest point – the town of Nieuwerkerk aan den IJssel, near Rotterdam – is 6.74m below sea level, while its highest point – the Vaalserberg in Limburg – is a meagre 321m above.

THE DUTCH LANDSCAPE WILDLIFE

Larger mammals such as the fox, badger and fallow deer have retreated to the national parks and reserves. Some species such as boar, mouflon (wild sheep) and red deer have been reintroduced into controlled habitats.

NOTABLE NATIONAL PARKS & NATURE RESERVES

NAME	FEATURES	ACTIVITIES	BEST TIME TO VISIT
Biesbosch NP	Estuarine reed marsh, woodland	Canoeing, hiking, birdwatching, cycling	Mar–Sep
Duinen van Texel NP	Dunes, heath, forest	Hiking, cycling, birdwatching, swimming	Mar–Sep
Hoge Veluwe NP	Marsh, forests, dunes	Hiking, cycling, art-viewing	year-round
Oostvaardersplassen NR	Wild reed marsh, grassland	Hiking, cycling, birdwatching, fishing	year-round
Schiermonnikoog NP	Car-free island, dunes, mudflats	Hiking, mudflat-walking, birdwatching	Mar–Sep
Weerribben-Wieden NP	Peat marsh	Kayaking, canoeing, hiking, birdwatching	year-round
Zuid-Kennemerland NP	Dunes, heath, forest	Hiking, birdwatching, cycling	Mar–Sep

National parks in the Netherlands tend to be small affairs: for an area to become a park, it need only be bigger than 10 sq km and be important in environmental terms. Most of the 20 national parks in the country average a mere 64 sq km and are as likely to preserve a man-made environment as a wilderness area. A total of 1200 sq km (just over 3%) of the Netherlands is protected in the form of national parks; the most northerly is the island of Schiermonnikoog in Friesland, and the most southerly is the terraced landscape of De Meinweg in central Limburg.

Some national parks are heavily visited, not only because there's plenty of nature to see but also because of their well-developed visitor centres and excellent displays of contemporary flora and fauna. Hoge Veluwe, established in 1935, is a particular favourite with its sandy hills and forests that once were prevalent in this part of the Netherlands. It is the only park that charges admission.

Of the 19 remaining national parks, Weerribben-Wieden in Overijssel is one of the most important as it preserves a landscape once heavily scarred by the peat harvest. Here the modern objective is to allow the land to return to nature, as is the case on Schiermonnikoog, which occupies a good portion of land once used by a sect of monks and which was part of Unesco's 2009 recognition of the broader Waddenzee region.

Environmental Issues

As a society, the Dutch are more aware of environmental issues than most. But then again, with high population density, widespread car ownership, heavy industrialisation, extensive farming and more than a quarter of the country below sea level, they need to be.

As early as the 1980s a succession of Dutch governments began to put in motion plans to tighten standards to curb industrial and farm pollution. They also made recycling a part of everyday life, although this has become a subject of some debate. All agree on the need for recycling, but not on how it will be done or by whom. One plan for financing is to charge for waste that goes unsorted.

Drilling for natural gas in Groningen has been linked to increased earthquake activity in the area – a major quake measuring 3.4 on the Richter scale rocked towns in the northeastern Netherlands in early 2018 – prompting the Dutch government to impose severe caps on gas

In the coastal waters there are 12 crustacean species, including the invasive Chinese mitten crab. Further out, the stock of North Sea cod, shrimp and sole has suffered from chronic overfishing, and catches are now limited by EU quotas.

production in the Groningen field, with the aim to end drilling completely by 2022. Currently some 40% of the country's energy comes from gas.

Cars

While the Dutch are avid bike riders, they still like having a car at the ready. Despite good, reasonably cheap public transport, private car ownership has risen sharply over the past two decades. Use of vehicles is now about 50% above the levels of the late 1980s. Stiff parking fees, insufficient parking spaces, pedestrian spaces and outlandish fines have helped curb congestion in the inner cities.

Outside of town centres, minor roads are configured to put cyclists first, with drivers sharing single lanes. Such schemes, plus the aggressive building plan for separate cycling routes, have made some headway in slowing the growth in car use.

While elsewhere in the world environmentally concerned drivers are switching to hybrid vehicles, in the Netherlands the trend is toward electric bikes. Netherlanders now own 1.5 million of the battery-operated bicycles – ideal for commuting as they make it easier to cover long distances. Perhaps because of this, they're also pedalling nearly 30% more kilometres than five years previous, clocking up an average of 1018km per year.

Water

The effects of climate change are obvious in the Netherlands. Over the past century the winters have become shorter and milder. The long-distance ice-skating race known as the Elfstedentocht (p212) may die out because the waterways in the northern province of Friesland rarely freeze hard enough (the last race was in 1997). The Dutch national weather service KNMI predicts that only four to 10 races will be held this century. Although damp and cold, winter in the Netherlands today is not the ice-covered deep freeze you see in Renaissance paintings.

For a country with 26% of its land mass below sea level, a rise in sea levels could potentially constitute a disaster of epic proportions. If the sea level rises as forecast – by an estimated 20cm each century – the country could theoretically eventually sink beneath the waves, like Atlantis, or at least suffer annual flooding in centuries to come. Water-management is of

Freshwater species such as white bream, rudd, pike, perch, stickleback and carp enjoy the canal environment. You can admire them up close at Amsterdam's Artis Royal Zoo, in an aquarium that simulates an Amsterdam canal.

THE DUTCH LANDSCAPE ENVIRONMENTAL ISSUES

BIRDWATCHING FOR BEGINNERS

Seen through an amateur birdwatcher's eyes, some of the more interesting sightings might include the following:

Avocet – common on the Waddenzee and the Delta, with slender upturned bill, and black and white plumage.

Black woodpecker – drums seldom but loudly. To see it, try woodlands such as Hoge Veluwe National Park.

Bluethroat – song like a free-wheeling bicycle; seen in Biesbosch National Park, Flevoland and the Delta.

Great white egret – crane-like species common in marshlands. First bred in Flevoland in the early 1990s.

Marsh harrier – bird of prey; often hovers over reed beds and arable land.

Spoonbill – once scarce, this odd-looking fellow has proliferated on coasts in Zeeland and the Wadden Islands.

White stork – nearly extinct in the 1980s, numbers have since recovered. Enormous nests.

WINDMILLS

Central to the story of the Dutch and their struggles with water are windmills. These national icons were an ingenious development that harnessed the nearly constant winds off the North Sea to keep the waters at bay. First used in the 13th century, windmills pumped water up and over the dykes from land below sea level. Later their uses became myriad, and examples can be spotted among the 1200 windmills still standing.

Standerdmolen – Oldest type of windmill in the Netherlands. The wooden housing can be rotated. Used mostly for milling grain.

Wipmolen – Later variation on the *standerdmolen*; used to pump water out of *polders*. The smaller mill housing rotates on a fixed pyramidal base.

Stellingmolen – Raised atop a high platform so it can more easily catch the wind in urban areas, with a scaffold around the base, from which operators can rotate the mill and adjust the blades to take best advantage of the wind direction. Used for the production of paper and oil. A good example is **De Gooyer** (Funenkade 5; 🚇10 Hoogte Kadijk) beside the Brouwerij 't IJ in east Amsterdam.

Tjasker – Windmill blades placed at the top end of an angled shaft that operates as a pump; used by peat diggers to lower the water level to facilitate their work. Examples can be spotted in the Weerribben-Wieden National Park.

Rietmolen – Miniature windmill that looks like a weather vane; used by reed harvesters to keep the reeds wet.

By the mid-19th century there were more than 10,000 windmills operating in all parts of the Netherlands. But the invention of the steam engine made them obsolete. By the end of the 20th century there were only 950 operable windmills left, but this number has stabilised and there is great interest in preserving the survivors. The Dutch government runs a three-year school for prospective windmill operators, who must be licensed.

Running one of the mills on a windy day is as complex as being the skipper of a large sailing ship, and anyone who has been inside a mill and listened to the massive timbers creaking will be aware of the similarities. The greatest hazard is a runaway, when the sails begin turning so fast that they can't be slowed down. This frequently ends in catastrophe as the mill remorselessly tears itself apart.

These days you're more likely to encounter turbine-powered wind farms in the countryside than rows of windmills but there are still plenty of opportunities countrywide.

Kinderdijk, near Rotterdam, has oodles of windmills in a classic *polder* setting. To see mills operating and learn how they work, head to Zaanse Schans (p118) near Amsterdam.

Just about every operable windmill in the nation is open to visitors on National Mill Day, usually on the second Saturday of May. Look for windmills flying little blue flags.

paramount importance to the innovative Dutch who, over the years, have reshaped their landscape to safeguard against flooding.

As part of the ongoing Delta Works, recognised as one of the Seven Wonders of the Modern World by the American Society of Civil Engineers, dams and storm-surge barriers have been built as flood protection, while so-called 'water squares' in large towns and cities act as water containers during times of heavy rain if need be; Rotterdam's Benthemplein can hold a mind-boggling 1.7 million litres of water. Countrywide, green roofs, planted with water-absorbent foliage, are blooming.

Polders (areas of drained land to facilitate agriculture) form 60% of the Netherlands' landscape – by far the highest percentage of any country in the world.

Room for the River

As sea levels rise and the levels of water flowing down rivers increase, more space has to be made to handle the volume. A severe storm in 1995 raised fears that Holland's rivers might overflow and thousands of people had to be evacuated, particularly from the Waal River zone by Nijmegen.

Top: Black woodpecker (p317)

Bottom: Wind turbines, Flevoland (p141)

IURII BURIAK/SHUTTERSTOCK ©

Keeping It Green

Dutch Friends of the Earth (www. milieudefensie.nl)

Nature & Environment (www. natuurenmilieu.nl)

Holstein Friesian cow

This event was a catalyst for a nationwide project to widen the country's rivers and construct higher dykes at greater distances from the rivers, at a cost of €2.3 billion.

More than 30 separate cases of flood plain excavation, dyke relocation and removal of obstacles to water flows are under way along the Waal, Lek, Nederrijn and IJssel and all their tributaries. Besides widening the rivers, the project, called 'Room for the River', aims to create more space for nature and semi-natural environments. Species return not only due to the new habitat created but because the rivers are cleaner.

Agriculture

The Dutch chicken population hovers around 100 million, one of the largest concentrations in the industrialised world (six chickens for every citizen; pigs are close to a one-to-one ratio). Such industrialised farming has been the cornerstone of Dutch agriculture since WWII and has brought much wealth to the country. But with concerns about ground-water quality, intensive farming and all the artificial fertilisers, chemicals and animal waste that come with it is under scrutiny. The province of Noord-Brabant in the south was the first to limit farm size and ban antibiotics used in feed.

A third of the dairy cattle in the world are Holstein Friesian, the black-and-white variety from the north of the Netherlands that are often used as iconic cows in ads worldwide.

More attention is being paid to sustainable development. Organic *(biologische)* food is gaining in popularity,and the huge agriculture industry is realising that profits can be made from more sustainable practices and by going green. One approach is to make greenhouses more efficient by heating them from warm-air aquifers and having industrial outfits pump in the required carbon dioxide from the by-products of their own operations.

Survival Guide

Directory A-Z

Accessible Travel

The Netherlands' status as a relatively affluent country in the European Union guarantees a certain level of accessibility for people with disabilities, particularly when it comes to public buildings, spaces and transport. However, as in much of Europe, older buildings may not be wheelchair-accessible and cobblestoned streets may be an issue for the mobility- or vision-impaired.

➡ Most offices and larger museums have lifts and/or ramps, and toilets for people with a disability.

➡ Many budget and midrange hotels have limited accessibility, as they are in old buildings with steep stairs and no elevators.

➡ Cobblestone streets are rough for wheelchairs.

➡ Restaurants tend to be on ground floors, though 'ground' sometimes includes a few steps.

➡ Bathrooms in restaurants may not be wheelchair-accessible or fitted with rails.

➡ Train and other public-transport stations sometimes have lifts.

➡ Most train stations and public buildings have toilets for people with a disability.

➡ Trains usually have wheelchair access.

➡ The Dutch national organisation for people with a disability is ANGO (www.ango.nl).

Online Resources

Accessible Travel Netherlands (www.accessibletravelnl.com) Hotel bookings, transport, accessible tours, activities and tailored itineraries; rents mobility equipment too.

Ongehinderd (www.ongehinderd.nl) Detailed access reviews of thousands of points of interest across the country, organised city by city. Smartphone app too; Dutch only.

Museum4All (www.museum4all.eu) City-by-city listings of museums indicating their suitability for the vision-impaired and wheelchair users.

Lonely Planet (http://lptravel.to/AccessibleTravel) Download Lonely Planet's free Accessible Travel guides.

Public Transport

For information about using the national railway network, including requesting assistance, visit www.ns.nl/en/travel-information/traveling-with-a-functional-disability. Most buses and newer trams are wheelchair-accessible; not all tram stops have level entry with the trams. The wheelchair-accessible entrance is in the centre of the tram; if a platform doesn't align with the entrance, the conductor will put a ramp out for you – but be sure that they notice you before the tram pulls away.

When using the route planner for public transport in Amsterdam (http://maps.gvb.nl/en/lijnen), select a line and wheelchair-accessible stops are indicated by closed circles. On the public transport website www.connexxion.nl, wheelchair-accessible stops are indicated by a solid diamond.

Accommodation

The country's hotels, B&Bs and hostels provide any traveller – backpacker or five-star aficionado – with choice. If you're visiting in high season (especially August) or during a big event, reserve ahead

B&Bs

Bed-and-breakfasts are an excellent way to meet the friendly locals face to face, and to see the weird, the wacky and the wonderful interior designs of the Dutch first-hand. While they're not abundant in cities, the countryside is awash with them. Local tourist offices keep a list of B&Bs on file; count on between €70 and €100 for a double.

Camping

The Dutch are avid campers, even within their own country. Campgrounds range from wild and remote, often with stunning sea views, as is invariably the case on the Frisian Islands, to self-contained communities with shops, cafes, playgrounds and swimming pools. Lists of sites with ratings (one to five stars) are available from tourist offices.

A camp site, which costs from €10 to €20, covers two people and a small tent; a car is an extra €2 to €6. Caravans are popular and there are oodles of hook-ups.

Simple bungalows, wooden cabins or luxury tents with shared bathroom facilities are also an option at many campgrounds.

Hostels

Affiliated with Hostelling International (HI), the Dutch hostel association goes by the banner of Stayokay (www.stayokay.com). Most offer a good variety of rooms. Facilities tend to be impressive, with newly built hostels common. Some, such as Rotterdam's Stayokay, are in landmark buildings. Not all hostels offer guests use of a shared kitchen; if this is a priority, check before booking.

Almost all Stayokay hostels and most indie hostels have dorm rooms that sleep eight or more people, as well as private rooms for one to four people. Nightly

rates normally range from €20 to €30 per person for dorm beds and from €60 for private rooms. Book ahead, especially in high season.

Amsterdam has scores of indie hostels (some cutting-edge, some shambolic, some party central filled with high jinks and stoners), and there's an increasing number appearing around the rest of the country. In small towns and outside the main tourist areas, hostel accommodation is scarce.

Hotels

Any hotel with more than 20 rooms is considered large, and rooms tend to be on the snug side. You'll see a 'star' plaque on the front of every hotel, indicating its rating according to the Nederlandse Hotel Classificatie (NHC; national hotel classification system). The stars (from one to five) are awarded according to certain facilities, rather than quality. This means that a two-star hotel may be in better condition than a hotel of higher rank, albeit with fewer facilities.

AMENITIES

Wi-fi is nearly universal across the hotel spectrum, but air-conditioning and elevators are not. Be prepared for very steep stairs.

➡ **Top End** Expect elevators, minibars, Nespresso coffee machine and room service. At the top of top end, facilities such as air-conditioning and fitness centres are par for the course. Breakfast is often not included.

➡ **Midrange** Most hotels in this category are big on comfort, low on formality and small enough to offer

personal attention. Rooms usually have a toilet and shower, and a TV and phone. Not many hotels in this category over two storeys have lifts, and their narrow stairwells can take some getting used to, especially with luggage. Rates typically include breakfast.

➡ **Budget** Lodgings in the lowest price bracket, other than hostels, are thin on the ground. The better options tend to be spick and span with furnishings that are, at best, cheap and cheerful. Rates often include breakfast.

Rental Accommodation

Renting a property for a few days can be a fun part of a trip. In Amsterdam it gets you a kitchen and other amenities that make coming 'home' after a hard day having fun that much nicer, while out in the countryside it can provide your own retreat. Rentals are often priced competitively with hotels, which offer less in the way of facilities and space.

Bargaining

With the exception of the odd haggle at flea markets, little bargaining goes on in the Netherlands.

Customs Regulations

For visitors from EU countries, limits only apply for excessive amounts. See www.belastingdienst.nl for details.

Residents of non-EU countries are limited to goods

Climate

Amsterdam

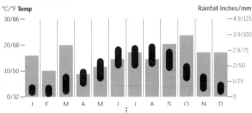

°C/°F Temp   Rainfall Inches/mm

worth a maximum value of €430, including:

➡ **Alcohol** 1L spirits, or 2L wine or 16L beer

➡ **Tobacco** 200 cigarettes, or 250g of tobacco (shag or pipe tobacco), or 100 cigarillos or 50 cigars

Discount Cards

Visitors of various professions, including artists and teachers, may get discounts at some venues if they show accreditation.

Students regularly get a few euro off museum admission; bring ID.

Seniors over 65, and with partners of 60 or older, benefit from reductions on public transport, museum admission, concerts and more. You may look younger, so bring your passport.

Many cities (eg Amsterdam, Den Haag and Rotterdam) offer discount-card schemes that are good for museums, attractions and local transport. Ask at tourist offices.

Cultureel Jongeren Paspoort (Cultural Youth Passport; www. cjp.nl; card €17.50) Big discounts to museums and cultural events nationwide for people under the age of 30.

Holland Pass (www.holland-pass.com; 3/4/6 attractions €40/55/75) You can visit sights over a month, valid from the date of your first visit. Prices are based on the number of admissions to attractions, which you pick from tiers (the most popular/expensive sights are gold-tier). Also includes discounted rates on bike tours, canal cruises and organised excursions. Buy it online, then you'll receive a confirmation email with barcode enabling you to pick up your pass at a designated point upon arrival in the Netherlands.

Museumkaart (Museum Card; www.museumkaart.nl; adult/child €59.90/32.45, plus registration fee €4.95) Free and discounted entry to some 400 museums all over the country, valid for one year. Strictly limited to five museum visits during the first 31 days; purchase a temporary card at participating museums and validate online prior to initial one-month expiry.

Electricity

Type C
230V/50Hz

Type F
230V/50Hz

Embassies & Consulates

Amsterdam is the country's capital but Den Haag is the seat of government. Many embassies (including those for Australia, Canada, New Zealand and Ireland) are in Den Haag, but Amsterdam has several consulates.

Amsterdam

French Consulate (☑020-530 69 69; www.consulfrance-amsterdam.org; De Boelelaan 7; ⊙9am-12.30pm Mon-Fri, 2-4pm Wed; Ⓜ50/51 RAI)

German Consulate (☑020-574 77 00; www.niederlande.diplo.de; Honthorststraat 36-38; ⊙8.30-11.30am & 1.30-3pm Mon-Thu, 8.30-11.30am Fri; ▣2/5 Hobbemastraat)

UK Consulate (☑070-427 04 27; www.gov.uk; Koningslaan 44; ⊙9.30am-12.30pm Mon, Tue, Thu & Fri; ▣2 Valeriusplein)

US Consulate (☑020-575 53 09; http://nl.usembassy.gov; Museumplein 19; ⊙8am-4pm by appointment, closed 1st Fri of the month; ▣3/5/12/16/24 Museumplein)

Food

Dining in the Netherlands is varied and wonderfully grown-up in its readiness to embrace the best of world cuisines alongside vegetarianism, vegan cuisine and a deep-rooted respect for local seasonal products and traditional Dutch cooking..

Health

It is unlikely that you will encounter unusual health problems in the Netherlands, and if you do, standards of care are world-class. It is still important to have health insurance for your trip.

A few travelling tips:

➡ Bring medications in their original, clearly labelled containers.

➡ Bring a list of your prescriptions (copies of the containers are good) including generic names, so you can get replacements if your bags get lost – carry this info separately.

➡ If you have health problems that may need treatment, bring a signed and dated letter from your physician describing your medical conditions and medications.

➡ If carrying syringes or needles, have a physician's letter documenting their medical necessity.

➡ If you need vision correction, carry a spare pair of contact lenses or glasses, and/or take your optical prescription with you.

Before You Go
HEALTH INSURANCE

If you're an EU citizen, a European Health Insurance Card (EHIC), usually available from health centres, covers you for most medical care. It will not cover you for non-emergencies or emergency repatriation. Citizens from other countries should find out if there is a reciprocal

arrangement for free medical care between their country and the Netherlands. If you do need health insurance, make sure you get a policy that covers you for the worst possible scenario, such as an accident requiring an emergency flight home. Find out in advance if your insurance plan will make payments directly to providers or reimburse you later for overseas health expenditures.

RECOMMENDED VACCINATIONS

No jabs are necessary for the Netherlands. However, the World Health Organization (WHO) recommends that all travellers should be covered for diphtheria, tetanus, measles, mumps, rubella and polio, regardless of their destination.

In the Netherlands
AVAILABILITY & COST OF HEALTH CARE

Good health care is readily available. For minor self-limiting illnesses an *apotheek* (pharmacy) can give valuable advice and sell over-the-counter medication. It can also advise when more specialised help is required and point you in the right direction. The standard of dental care is usually good; however, it is sensible to have a dental check-up before a long trip.

TAP WATER

Tap water country-wide is drinkable.

Insurance

Travel insurance is a good idea if your policies at home won't cover you in the Netherlands. Although medical or dental costs might already be

covered through reciprocal health-care arrangements, you'll still need cover for theft or loss, and for unexpected changes to travel arrangements (ticket cancellation etc). Check what's already covered by your local insurance policies or credit cards.

Internet Access

➡ Free wi-fi is widespread in hotels, restaurants, bars and *coffeeshops* (you may need to ask for the code), as well as many tourist offices and other public places.

➡ To search for free wi-fi hot spots in the Netherlands, visit www.hotspot-locations.com. In Amsterdam check www.wifi-amsterdam.nl.

➡ In Amsterdam rent a pocket-sized mobile wi-fi device to carry around with you, ensuring a fast wi-fi connection while roaming the city, from Pocket Wifi Amsterdam (www.pocketwifi-amsterdam.com); order online and arrange delivery to your hotel, apartment or Schiphol airport. Alternatively, try HipPocketWifi (http://hippocketwifi.com), Travel WiFi (http://travel-wifi.com) or My Webspot (http://my-webspot.com).

➡ Internet cafes are scarce. Some tourist offices, *coffeeshops* and hotels provide internet terminals (sometimes free).

➡ Co-working cafes providing unlimited, fast internet access are widespread in Amsterdam and increasingly common in other urban areas.

PRACTICALITIES

➡ **Newspapers** Dutch-language newspapers include *De Telegraaf* (www.telegraaf.nl), the Netherlands' biggest seller; and *Het Parool* (www.parool.nl), Amsterdam's paper, with the scoop on what's happening around town. Keep abreast of news back home via the *International Herald Tribune* or the *Guardian*, or weeklies such as the *Economist* or *Time*, all widely available on news-stands.

➡ **Smoking** The Netherlands bans cigarette smoking inside all bars and restaurants, but you're free to light up outdoors on terraces where they're completely open on one side.

➡ **Weights & Measures** The metric system is used.

Legal Matters

➡ Dutch *politie* (police) are pretty relaxed and helpful unless you do something clearly wrong, such as littering or smoking a joint right under their noses.

➡ Police can hold offenders for up to six hours for questioning (plus another six hours if they can't establish your identity, or 24 hours if they consider the matter serious). You won't have the right to a phone call, but they'll notify your consulate. You're presumed innocent until proven guilty.

LGBTIQ+ Travellers

The Netherlands was the first country to legalise same-sex marriage (in 2001), and Amsterdam is frequently cited as one of the world's most LGBTIQ+-friendly places.

➡ Amsterdam's gay and lesbian scene is huge, and there are smaller thriving scenes in Rotterdam, Den Haag, Utrecht and most university towns.

➡ Attitudes towards homosexuality tend to be more conservative in the countryside and villages, but remain refreshingly liberal nonetheless.

➡ **Pride Amsterdam** (www. pride.amsterdam; ⊙late

Jul–early Aug) features a traditional boat parade and march; it's celebrated over nine days in late July and early August.

Resources

COC Nederland (www.coc.nl) Government-subsidised and the best national source of information since 1946; branches throughout the country can offer advice.

Gay Amsterdam (www.gay-amsterdam.com) Lists hotels, shops and clubs, and provides maps.

PANN (https://pann.nl) Active in Utrecht since 1969 and host to a monthly 'straight-friendly' gay party, frequently voted the country's best gay party.

Maps

The best road maps of the Netherlands are those produced by Michelin and the Dutch automobile association ANWB (www.anwb. nl). The ANWB also puts out provincial maps detailing cycling paths and picturesque road routes. You'll find a wide variety of maps for sale at any tourist office, as well as at bookstores and news-stands.

Tourist offices sell all forms of maps, including local city-walk maps or brochures in English (€3.50).

Money

Cash is commonly used for everyday purchases throughout the Netherlands.

ATMs

ATMs, aka cash machines, can be found outside most banks and at airports and most train stations. Credit cards such as Visa and MasterCard/Eurocard are widely accepted, as well as cards from the Plus and Cirrus networks. Using an ATM can be the cheapest way to exchange your money from home, but check with your home bank for service charges before you leave.

You can use your ATM card to keep stocked up with euro throughout the Netherlands so there's no need for currency exchange. However, using your ATM card as a debit card, as opposed to a credit card, to pay for purchases won't always work, as an astonishing amount of businesses – including many restaurants, cafes and shops – only accept Dutch PIN cards.

Currency

The Netherlands uses the euro (€). Denominations of the currency are €5, €10, €20, €50, €100, €200 and €500 notes, and €0.05, €0.10, €0.20, €0.50, €1 and €2 coins (amounts under €1 are called cents).

Credit Cards

All the major international credit cards are recognised, and most hotels and large stores accept them. But many shops, restaurants and other businesses (including Dutch Railways and supermarket chains) do not accept credit cards, including European cards with security chips.

Some establishments levy a 5% surcharge (or more) on credit cards to offset the commissions charged by card providers. Always check first.

Pin Cards

In the Netherlands you'll notice people gleefully using 'PIN' cards everywhere, from shops to supermarkets and vending machines. These direct-debit cards look like credit or bank cards with little circuit chips on them, but they won't be of much use to visitors without a Dutch bank account.

Tipping

The Dutch do tip, but modestly.

➡ **Hotel porters** €1 to €2

➡ **Restaurants** round up, or 5% to 10%

➡ **Taxis** 5% to 10%

Opening Hours

Hours can vary by season and often decrease during the low season.

Banks 9am–4pm Monday to Friday, some Saturday morning

Cafes and Bars Open noon (exact hours vary); most close 1am Sunday to Thursday, 3am Friday and Saturday

General Office Hours 8.30am–5pm Monday to Friday

Museums 10am–5pm daily, some close Monday

Restaurants Lunch 11am–2.30pm, dinner 6–10pm

Shops 10am or noon to 6pm Tuesday to Friday, 10am–5pm Saturday and Sunday, noon or 1pm to 5pm or 6pm Monday (if at all)

Supermarkets 8am–8pm

Post

The national post office in the Netherlands is privatised and post offices are not always easy to find. To mail a letter or package, go to a PostNL (www.postnl.nl) postal service shop that may be a supermarket or tobacco shop or something else; use the website to find a location near you.

Public Holidays

Most museums adopt Sunday hours on public holidays (except Christmas and New Year, when they close) even if they fall on a day when the place would otherwise be closed, such as Monday. Many people treat Remembrance Day (4 May) as a day off.

Carnaval is celebrated with vigour in the Catholic south. Huge parties are thrown in the run-up to Shrove Tuesday and little work gets done.

Nieuwjaarsdag (New Year's Day) 1 January. Parties and fireworks galore.

Goede Vrijdag Good Friday

Eerste Paasdag Easter Sunday

Tweede Paasdag Easter Monday

Koningsdag (King's Day) 27 April (26 April if the 27th is a Sunday)

Bevrijdingsdag (Liberation Day) 5 May. Not a universal holiday: government workers have the day off, but almost everyone else has to work.

Hemelvaartsdag (Ascension Day) Fortieth day after Easter Sunday

Eerste Pinksterdag (Whit Sunday; Pentecost) Fiftieth day after Easter Sunday

Tweede Pinksterdag (Whit Monday) Fiftieth day after Easter Monday

Eerste Kerstdag (Christmas Day) 25 December

Tweede Kerstdag ('Second Christmas' aka Boxing Day) 26 December

Safe Travel

The Netherlands is one of the safest countries in Europe. Amsterdam and other larger Dutch cities require the same 'big-city street sense' as any other big European city.

➡ Bicycle theft is common; always use two locks (the standard bike lock with key built into most Dutch bikes plus a sturdy chain lock) and park in guarded bike parks when possible.

➡ Watch out for speeding bikes when crossing the road. Straying into a bike lane without looking both ways can cause serious accidents.

➡ In Amsterdam, pickpockets work tourist-heavy zones such as Centraal Station, the Bloemenmarkt and Red Light District. Stay alert.

Telephone

The Dutch phone network, KPN (www.kpn.com), is efficient. Prices are reasonable by European standards.

Collect Call (0800 01 01 for international, 0800 04 10 for domestic) Both numbers are free.

Phone Codes

To ring abroad, dial 00 followed by the country code for your target country, the area code (you usually drop the leading 0 if there is one) and the subscriber number.

Netherlands country code ☏31

Free calls ☏0800

Mobile numbers ☏06

Paid information calls ☏0900; cost varies between €0.10 and €1.30 per minute.

Drop the leading 0 on city codes if you're calling from outside the Netherlands (eg 20 for Amsterdam instead of 020). From a landline, don't dial the city code if you are in the area covered by it.

Mobile Phones

➡ The Netherlands uses GSM phones compatible with the rest of Europe and Australia but not with some North American GSM phones. The EU has abolished international roaming costs, but beware of high roaming charges from other countries.

➡ Alternatively, local prepaid SIM cards are widely available and can be used in most unlocked phones. Look for Phone House, Orange, T-Mobile and Vodafone shops in major shopping areas.

Time

➤ The Netherlands is in the Central European time zone (same as Berlin and Paris), GMT/UTC plus one hour. Noon in Amsterdam is 11am in London, 6am in New York, 3am in San Francisco and 9pm in Sydney.

➤ For daylight savings time, clocks are put forward one hour at 2am on the last Sunday in March and back again at 3am on the last Sunday in October.

➤ When telling the time, be aware that the Dutch use 'half' to indicate 'half before' the hour. If you say 'half eight' (8.30 in many forms of English), a Dutch person will take this to mean 7.30.

Toilets

➤ Public toilets are not a widespread facility on Dutch streets, apart from the free-standing public urinals for men in places such as Amsterdam's Red Light District.

➤ Most people duck into a *café* (pub) or department store.

➤ The app HogeNood (High Need; www.hogenood.nu) maps the nearest toilets based on your location; it covers some 4000 toilet locations countrywide.

Tourist Information

➤ For pre-trip planning, www.holland.com is a useful resource.

➤ Within the Netherlands, VVV (Vereniging voor Vreemdelingenverkeer, Netherlands Tourism Board; www.vvv.nl) is the official network of tourist offices around the country. Each tourist office is locally run and has local and regional info. Few VVV publications are free but tourist offices are a good place to buy maps and guides.

➤ ANWB (Dutch Automobile Association; www.anwb.nl) has maps and guidebooks for sale. It provides a wide range of useful information and assistance if you're travelling with any type of vehicle (car, bicycle, motorcycle, yacht etc). In some cities the VVV and ANWB share offices. You'll have to show proof of membership of your home automobile club to get free maps or discounts.

Visas

EU citizens and nationals of Liechtenstein, Norway, Iceland and Switzerland can enter indefinitely with a passport or national identity card; stays longer than four months need to be registered with your municipality's Personal Records Database (BRP).

Tourists from over 60 countries – including Australia, Canada, Israel, Japan, New Zealand, Singapore, South Korea, the UK and the USA – currently need only a valid passport to visit the Netherlands for up to three months. By the end of 2022 (dates to be finalised), citizens from countries who don't require a visa will need ETIAS (European Travel Information and Authorisation System) pre-travel authorisation. The cost for ages 18 to 70 will be €7 (older and younger travellers free), covering multiple entries for three years, and allowing travel in the Schengen area for up to 90 days in a 180-day period.

Nationals of most other countries need a Schengen visa, valid within the Schengen zone, for 90 days within a 180-day period. Schengen visas are issued by Dutch embassies or consulates overseas.

➤ **Government of the Netherlands** (www.government.nl) Lists consulates and embassies around the world.

➤ **Immigration & Naturalisation Service** (www.ind.nl) Handles visas and extensions. Study visas must be applied for through your college or university in the Netherlands.

Volunteering

➤ Check first with the Dutch embassy or consulate in your home country to find out whether volunteering affects your visa status.

➤ Online resources like Go Abroad (www.goabroad.com) and Transitions Abroad (www.transitionsabroad.com) throw up the occasional volunteering opportunities in the Netherlands.

➤ Volunteers For Peace (www.vfp.org) US-based nonprofit organisation. Can link you up with a voluntary service project dealing with social work, the environment, education or the arts.

➤ WWOOF Netherlands (World Wide Opportunities on Organic Farms; https://wwoofnetherlands.org) Work on a tulip farm, help with the blueberry harvest, help renovate an old farmhouse etc on a Dutch organic farm.

➤ Access (https://access-nl.org) Online resource covering everything internationals in the Netherlands need to know, with an excellent section on volunteering.

➤ I Amsterdam (www.iamsterdam.com) Volunteering organisations in Amsterdam.

Transport

GETTING THERE & AWAY

The Netherlands is an easy place to reach, with three major airports: Amsterdam's Schiphol International Airport, Rotterdam The Hague Airport and Eindhoven Airport.

High-speed trains are especially good from France, Belgium, Germany and the UK (London) aboard the Eurostar. Other land options are user-friendly and the border crossings are nearly invisible thanks to the EU. There are also ferry links with the UK.

What's more, once you get to the Netherlands the transport remains hassle-free. Most journeys by rail, car or bus are so short that you can reach most regional destinations before your next meal. And with its flat terrain, getting around by bicycle is a breeze.

Flights, cars and tours can be booked online at lonelyplanet.com/bookings.

Entering the Netherlands

Entering the Netherlands could not be more straightforward, providing your papers are in order.

Air

Amsterdam's huge and highly efficient Schiphol International Airport is the country's main air-travel hub, with numerous flights to/from cities all over the world – making flying an easy way of getting to/from the Netherlands. Within Europe, low-cost airlines use in Rotterdam and Eindhoven.

Airports

KLM Royal Dutch Airlines (www.klm.com) is the national carrier, with plenty of international flights. Departure tax is included in the price of a ticket.

There are no domestic flights within the Netherlands.

Schiphol International Airport (AMS; www.schiphol.nl) Conveniently near both Amsterdam and Rotterdam, this is the Netherlands' main international airport and the fourth busiest in Europe, serviced by most of the world's major airlines. The airport is like a small city, with a huge shopping mall filled with travellers' amenities and neighbouring airport hotels.

Rotterdam The Hague Airport (RTM; ✆010-446 34 44; www.rotterdamthehagueairport.nl; ☎) Serving more than 40 European destinations.

Eindhoven Airport (EIN; www.vliegeindhovenairport.nl; Luchthavenweg 25; ⊙4.30am-midnight) Budget-airline hub.

Land

High-speed trains and a plethora of international buses link the Netherlands with its neighbouring countries; advance ticket reservations

CLIMATE CHANGE & TRAVEL

Every form of transport that relies on carbon-based fuel generates CO_2, the main cause of human-induced climate change. Modern travel is dependent on aeroplanes, which might use less fuel per kilometre per person than most cars but travel much greater distances. The altitude at which aircraft emit gases (including CO_2) and particles also contributes to their climate change impact. Many websites offer 'carbon calculators' that allow people to estimate the carbon emissions generated by their journey and, for those who wish to do so, to offset the impact of the greenhouse gases emitted with contributions to portfolios of climate-friendly initiatives throughout the world. Lonely Planet offsets the carbon footprint of all staff and author travel.

HIDDEN SPEED CAMERAS

More than 1600 unmanned and hidden radar cameras (known as *flitspalen*) watch over Dutch motorways. Even if you are in a rental car, the rental company will track you down in your home country and levy a service charge, while the traffic authority also bills you for the fine.

are recommended, especially in high season, when some routes can fill up fast.

Arriving by car is straight-forward, with no border controls between the Netherlands and its Schengen neighbours. Car ferries link several ports in the UK with Dutch ports near Rotterdam or Amsterdam.

Bicycle

➡ Bringing your own bike into the Netherlands will cause no problems. Ask your carrier to see what you need to do to check it on a plane; by train you usually have to remove the front wheel and put it in a carrier bag.

➡ Long-distance bicycle paths are called *landelijke fietsroutes* (LF) and retain that label in northern Belgium.

BELGIUM

Long-distance cyclists can choose from a variety of safe, easy, specially designated routes to get to the Netherlands from Belgium. The LF2 route runs 350km from Brussels via Antwerp, Dordrecht and Rotterdam to Amsterdam.

GERMANY

Route LF4 stretches 300km from Enschede near the German border to Den Haag.

The fast German ICE trains from Cologne and Frankfurt are not bike-friendly; use regular trains instead.

UK

Most cross-Channel ferries only have a small bicycle surcharge, if any at all. You can also bring your two-wheeler on the connecting trains,

where it travels for free if it fits into a bike bag as hand luggage.

Bus

Check arrival and departure bus stops carefully; the following bus companies do not necessarily use stops at city bus stations, rather a stop on a main road into town:

Eurolines (www.eurolines.com) Consortium of coach operators running cheap international bus services to/from the Netherlands. Coaches have on-board toilets and reclining seats. Some services have on-board wi-fi.

Busabout (www.busabout.com) May to October, buses complete set circuits around Europe, stopping at major cities. Aimed at younger travellers; complex pricing.

Flixbus (www.flixbus.com) Low-cost, intercity bus travel between 27 European countries aboard comfy buses equipped with toilet, snacks, plug sockets and free wi-fi; night services too. Sample fares include from €32 for a one-way Amsterdam–Paris or from €23 for a Rotterdam–Cologne ticket.

IC Bus (www.dbicbus.com) Bus links between the Netherlands and Germany.

Car & Motorcycle

➡ Drivers need vehicle registration papers, third-party insurance and their domestic licence. Get a Green Card from your insurer to show you have coverage.

➡ ANWB (www.anwb.nl) provides information, maps, advice and services if you show a membership card from your own automobile association, such as the AA or AAA.

➡ Hitching is uncommon in the Netherlands. As with most destinations, it poses a small but potentially serious risk and is not recommended.

➡ Ferries take cars and motorcycles to the Netherlands from several ports in the UK including Harwich to Hoek van Holland, Hull to Europoort (both near Rotterdam) and Newcastle to IJmuiden (near Amsterdam).

Train

International train connections are good. All Eurail and Inter-Rail passes are valid on the Dutch national train service, NS (Nederlandse Spoorwegen; www.ns.nl). Many international services are operated by NS International (www.ns international.nl).

Reserve seats in advance during peak periods. Buy tickets online at SNCB Europe (www.b-europe.com).

Major Dutch train stations have international ticket offices; you can also buy tickets for local trains to Belgium and Germany at regular ticket counters.

The excellent website Seat 61 (www.seat61.com) has comprehensive information about train travel.

BELGIUM

Fast Thalys (www.thalys.com) trains serve Brussels (1hr 50mins from Amsterdam; at Brussels you can connect to the Eurostar) and Paris. The company has good advance fares and a range of discount schemes. In the south, an hourly service connects Maastricht and Liège (€5.80, 40 minutes).

GERMANY

German ICE high-speed trains run daily between Amsterdam and Cologne (from €35.90, three hours). Many continue to Frankfurt (from €45.90, four to 4¾ hours) via Frankfurt Airport. Buy tickets in advance at either www.b-europe.com or www.bahn.de.

With connections in Cologne or Frankfurt, you can reach any part of Germany easily. Other direct services include several regular trains a day between Amsterdam and Berlin (from €55.90, 6½ hours) and a local service from Groningen (€17.40, 55 minutes; actually covered by a bus) east across the border to tiny Leer, where you can get trains to Bremen and beyond.

From Maastricht you can reach Cologne via Liège in Belgium and Aachen in Germany (from €24.80, 1½ to two hours).

UK

Twice-daily direct Eurostar (www.eurostar.com) services link London St-Pancras with Rotterdam (three hours) and Amsterdam (3¾ hours). A standard single fare starts at UK£35/€40 but requires booking well in advance; the equivalent purchased a few days before can cost from £115/€132 to £185/€212.50.

Count on an hour longer for the return journey, which requires changing train in Brussels (high-speed Thalys train from Rotterdam/Amsterdam to Brussels, then a Eurostar to London). A Eurostar terminal, with passport-control facilities allowing direct UK-bound Eurostar trains to run, opened at Amsterdam Centraal (platform 15) and Rotterdam Centraal (platform 1) in 2019.

Dutch Flyer (www.stena-line.co.uk) 'rail and sail' services are one of the cheapest ways to reach the Netherlands from the UK. Trains from London (Liverpool St Station), Cambridge and Norwich connect with ferries sailing from Harwich to Hoek van Holland, where a further train travels on to Rotterdam and Amsterdam. The journey takes around nine hours and costs from £56 one way.

Sea

Several companies operate car/passenger ferries between the Netherlands and the UK; most offer frequent specials and also train–ferry–train packages.

Reservations are essential for cars in high season; motorcycles can often be squeezed in. Most ferries don't charge for a bike and have no shortage of storage space.

Stena Line (www.stena line.co.uk) sails between Harwich and Hoek van Holland, 31km northwest of Rotterdam, linked to central Rotterdam by train (30 minutes). The fast HSS ferries take 5½ hours and depart in each direction twice a day. Overnight ferries take 8½ hours (one daily), as do normal day ferries (one daily). Foot passengers pay from £39 one way. Fares for a car and driver range from £59 to £285 one way depending on the season and day of week. Options such as reclining chairs and cabins cost extra and are compulsory on night crossings.

P&O Ferries (www.po-ferries.com) operates an overnight ferry every evening (11¾ hours) between Hull and Europoort, 39km west of central Rotterdam. Book bus tickets (40 minutes) to/from Rotterdam when you reserve your berth. Single fares start at £108 for a foot passenger and £134 for a car with driver. Prices include berths in an inside cabin; luxury cabins are available. Prices are more than double in peak season.

DFDS Seaways (www.dfdsseaways.co.uk) sails between Newcastle and IJmuiden, 30km northwest of Amsterdam, linked to Amsterdam by bus; the 15-hour sailings depart daily. One-way fares start at £67 for a foot passenger in an economy berth, plus £148 for a car. Prices go up in peak season.

GETTING AROUND

The Netherlands' compact size makes it a breeze to get around.

Air

There are no domestic flights in the Netherlands.

Bicycle

The Netherlands is extremely bike-friendly and a *fiets* (bicycle) is the way to go. Many people have the trip of a lifetime using nothing but pedal power. Most modes of transport, such as trains and buses, are friendly to cyclists and their bikes. Dedicated bike routes go virtually everywhere.

Any Dutch town you visit is liable to be blanketed with bicycle paths. They're either on the streets or in the form of smooth off-road routes.

Boat

Year-round ferries connect the mainland with the Frisian Islands, and there are seasonal inte-risland ferry links between Texel, Vlieland and Terschelling.

Passenger ferries span the Westerschelde in the south of Zeeland, providing a link between the southwestern expanse of the country and Belgium. These are popular with people using the Zeebrugge ferry terminal and run frequently year-round.

The Waterbus (www.waterbus.nl) is an excellent fast ferry service linking Rotterdam with Dordrecht as well as the popular tourist destinations of Kinderdijk and Biesbosch National Park. Boats depart year-round, but some routes are seasonal.

Many more minor services provide links across the myriad Dutch canals and waterways.

ZONETAXI

Some 130 train stations countrywide offer the excellent NS Zonetaxi service, which takes you by taxi to/from the station within a 2km zone. Journeys are booked in advance, cutting out the hassle of finding a taxi. Highly competitive fares start at €6·and are fixed, meaning no nasty surprise upon arrival; up to three people can travel in one taxi. The service operates daily from when the first train leaves in the morning until the last train at night. Book in advance via the Reisplanner Xtra app or call 0900 679 82 94.

Hire

Renting a boat is a popular way to tour rivers, lakes and inland seas. Boats come in all shapes and sizes, from canoes to motor boats, small sailing boats, and large and historic former cargo sloops. Prices run the gamut and there are hundreds of rental firms throughout the country.

Bus

Buses are used for regional transport rather than for long distances, which are better travelled by train. They provide a vital service, especially in parts of the north and east, where trains are less frequent or nonexistent. The fares are zone-based. You can usually buy a ticket on board from the driver (aka a single-use, disposable OV-chipkaart; €2 to €5 for modest distances), but most people pay with a credit-loaded OV-chipkaart.

There is only one class of travel. Some regions have day passes good for all the buses; ask a driver – they are usually very helpful.

Car & Motorcycle

Dutch freeways are extensive but prone to congestion. Those around Amsterdam, the A4 south to Belgium and the A2 southeast to Maastricht are especially likely to be jammed at rush hour and during busy travel periods; traffic jams with a total length of 350km or more aren't unheard of during the holiday season.

Smaller roads are usually well maintained, but the campaign to discourage car use throws up numerous obstacles – two-lane roads are repainted to be one-lane with wide bike lanes or there are barriers, speed-bumps and other 'traffic-calming' schemes.

Parking a car in major cities can be a major headache and expensive. Cities purposely limit parking to discourage car use and rates are high: hotels boast about 'discount' parking rates for overnight guests of €30. Alternatively, consider a cheaper, fairly priced 'Park & Ride' car park, often located within a reasonable walking distance of the city centre.

Automobile Associations

ANWB (www.anwb.nl) is the automobile club in the Netherlands; most big towns and cities have an office. Members of auto associations in their home countries (the AA, AAA, CAA, NRMA etc) can get assistance, free maps, discounts and more.

Driving Licences

Visitors from outside the EU are entitled to drive in the Netherlands on their foreign licences for a period of up to 185 days per calendar year. EU licences are accepted year-round.

You'll need to show a valid driving licence when hiring a car in the Netherlands. An international driving permit (IDP) is not needed.

Fuel

As with much of Western Europe, petrol is very expensive and fluctuates on a regular basis. Prices are generally €1.76 per litre. Petrol (gasoline) is *benzine* in Dutch. Diesel (€1.45 per litre) is cheaper, making it worth renting a diesel car.

To check current fuel prices, visit www.fuel-prices-europe.info. For savvy motorists anywhere near the Belgian border, it is common to drive across the border to fill up (and, for smokers, to stock up on tobacco at the same time) for about €0.20 a litre less.

Car Hire

➡ The Netherlands is well covered for car hire; all major firms have numerous locations.

➡ Apart from in Amsterdam and at the airports, the car-hire companies can be in inconvenient locations if you're arriving by train.

➡ You must be at least 23 years of age to hire a car in the Netherlands. Some car-hire firms levy a small surcharge for drivers under 25.

➡ A credit card is required to rent.

➡ Less than 4% of European cars have automatic transmission; if you need this, you should reserve well ahead and be prepared to pay a huge surcharge for your rental.

Insurance

Collision damage waiver (CDW), an insurance policy that limits your financial liability for damage, is a costly add-on for rentals but may be worthwhile. Obviously, without insurance you'll be liable for damages up to the full value of the vehicle.

Many credit cards and home auto-insurance policies offer CDW-type coverage; make certain about this before you decline the costly (from €10 per day) CDW.

At most car-rental firms, CDW does not cover the first €500 to €1000 of damages incurred. Yet another add-on, an excess-cover package for around €10 to €20 per day, is normally available to cover this amount. See what your credit card and home auto insurance cover; you may not need anything extra.

Road Rules

Rules are similar to the rest of Continental Europe. Full concentration is required because you may need to yield to cars, bikes that appear out of nowhere and pedestrians in quick succession.

➡ Traffic travels on the right.

➡ The minimum driving age is 18 for vehicles and 16 for motorcycles.

➡ Seat belts are required for everyone in a vehicle, and children under 12 must ride in the back if there's room.

➡ Trams always have right of way.

➡ If you are trying to turn right, bikes have priority.

➡ At roundabouts yield to vehicles already travelling in the circle.

➡ Speed limits are 50km/h in built-up areas, 80km/h in the country, 100km/h on major through-roads and 120km/h on freeways (sometimes 100km/h, clearly marked). Speeding cameras are hidden everywhere.

Public Transport

Buses and trams operate in most cities; Amsterdam and Rotterdam have metro networks.

Taxi

Usually booked by phone – officially you're not supposed to wave them down on the street – taxis also wait outside train stations and hotels and cost roughly €12 to €15 for 5km. Even short trips in town can get expensive quickly.

Train

Dutch trains are efficient, fast and comfortable. Trains are frequent and serve domestic destinations at regular intervals, sometimes five or six times an hour. It's an excellent system and possibly all you'll need to get around the country, although there are a few caveats.

➡ National train company NS (Nederlandse Spoorwegen; www.ns.nl) operates all the major lines in the Netherlands. In the north

FARES, TICKETS & OV-CHIPKAARTS

The easiest and cheapest way to travel with a ticket on trains and public transport (buses, trams and metro) is with a credit-loaded, plastic smart-card known as an OV-chipkaart (www.ov-chipkaart.nl).

➡ Purchase an OV-chipkaart (€7.50), valid for five years, as soon as you arrive in the Netherlands at a train station, public-transport information office, supermarket or newsagent. Online, buy one in advance at www.public-transport-holland.com.

➡ Two types of OV-chipkaarts exist: 'anonymous' OV-chipkaarts are aimed at tourists and short-term visitors; 'personal' OV-chipkaarts require an address of residence in the Netherlands, Belgium, Germany or Luxembourg.

➡ To travel using your card, you must charge it with credit (minimum €10 on buses, or €20 to use it on NS trains) at any public-transport or station information counter or ticketing machine; the card must have sufficient credit to cover the cost of your journey.

➡ When you enter and exit a bus, tram or metro, hold the card against a reader at the doors or station gates. The system then calculates your fare and deducts it from the card. If you don't check out, the system will deduct the highest fare possible. At train stations, card readers are strategically placed at platform entrances/exits.

➡ Upon departure, you can retrieve any left-over credit from your card at any public-transport or station information counter; you'll pay a €1 fee to do this.

➡ For single journeys, if you don't have an OV-chipkaart, you can effectively purchase a more expensive, single-use, disposable OV-chipkaart each time you board a bus or tram, or buy a train ticket. On trains, this translates in reality as a €1 surcharge per transaction on top of the regular train fare.

➡ Some trams have conductors responsible for ticketing, while on others the drivers handle tickets. It is no longer possible to pay by cash on public transport in Amsterdam.

TIPS FOR BUYING TICKETS

Buying a train ticket is the hardest part of riding Dutch trains.

➡ Only some ticket machines accept cash, and those are coin-only, so you need a pocketful of change.

➡ Ticket machines that accept plastic will not work with most non-European credit and ATM cards. The exceptions are a limited number of machines at Schiphol and Amsterdam Centraal.

➡ Some machines only sell tickets for travellers with an OV-chipkaart.

➡ Ticket windows do not accept credit or ATM cards, although they will accept paper euro. Lines are often quite long and there is a surcharge for the often-unavoidable need to use a ticket machine.

➡ Discounted NS International tickets sold online require a Dutch credit card. The cheap fares can't be bought at ticket windows.

➡ The much-hyped *Voordeelurenabonnement* (Off-Peak Discount Pass) yields good discounts, but only if you have a Dutch bank account.

➡ To buy domestic and international train tickets online with an international credit card, visit SNCB Europe (www.b-europe.com). You may need to print a copy of the ticket.

and east minor lines have been hived off to private bus and train operators, but scheduling and fares remain part of the national system.

➡ Bikes are welcome on trains.

➡ Stations show departure information but the boards don't show trip duration or arrival times; check online or ask at the ticket or information window.

➡ The system shuts down roughly from midnight to 6am except in the Amsterdam–Schiphol–Rotterdam–Den Haag–Leiden circuit, where trains run hourly all night.

➡ High-speed NS trains operate between Amsterdam, Schiphol, Rotterdam and Breda.

Train Stations

Medium and large railways stations have a full range of services: currency exchange, ATMs, small groceries, food courts, FEBO-like coin-operated snack-food vending machines, flower shops and much more.

Smaller stations often have no services at all, not even a manned ticket window

(but tickets are available at vending machines); this is especially true on non-NS lines.

Left Luggage

Many train stations have automatic luggage lockers (*Bagagekluizen*) on one platform, operated using a credit card. The one-day fee at most stations is €3.85/5.70 per 24 hours for a small/large locker. If you return after more than 24 hours, you have to insert your credit card to pay €5.55/8.45 for each subsequent 24 hours.

Maximum rental is 72 hours, after which the station reserves the right to remove your goods, send them to the Central Found Items office in Utrecht (0900 321 2100) and fine you €70 on top of the higher 24-hour rate. Not recommended.

Lockers at train stations in Amsterdam (€7/10 per 24 hours), Rotterdam (€6/9), Den Haag (€6/9) and Utrecht (€6/9) are more expensive.

Some stations popular with day-trippers (eg Enkhuizen, Delft) do not have lockers.

Train Tickets

Train travel in the Netherlands is reasonably priced. We quote train fares using an OV-chipkaart (p333); add a €1 surcharge to the listed fare if you don't have an OV-chipkaart.

When buying tickets in the Netherlands, note that non-European credit and debit cards are almost impossible to use.

Ticket Machines Most only take Dutch bank cards. About 25% do take coins, none take notes (bills). All can be set for English.

Ticket windows Available at mid-sized to larger stations. Staff speak English and are super-helpful. Lines can be long and windows may be closed at night.

Online E-tickets are easy to buy using the NS website, but you do need to print out the ticket. Some routes, which can be displayed in the Reisplanner Xtra app, offer mobile tickets. Online fares are the same as tickets purchased with an OV-chip-kaart, ie you don't pay the €1 surcharge.

If you are at a station with a closed ticket window and don't have the coins for the machines, board the train and find the conductor. Explain your plight (they know where this applies so don't fib) and they will *usually* sell you a ticket without levying the fine (€50) for boarding without a ticket on top of the ticket price. If they do fine you, you can apply for a refund at a ticket window.

RESERVATIONS

For national trains, simply turn up at the station: you'll rarely have to wait more than 30 minutes for a train. Reservations are required for international trains.

TICKET TYPES

➡ *Enkele reis* (one way) – single one-way ticket; with a valid ticket you can break your journey along the direct route.

➡ *Dagretour* (day return) – normal day return; costs the same as two one-way tickets.

➡ *Dagkaart* (day pass) – €50.60/85 for 2nd/1st class and allows unlimited train travel throughout the country. Only good value if you're planning extensive train travel on any one day.

➡ Holland Travel Ticket – Unlimited, one-day travel on trains (2nd class), buses, trams and metro anywhere in the country (€55); the cheaper off-peak version (€39) means you can't use the pass between 6.30am and 9am on weekdays.

➡ Railrunner – €2.50; day pass for children aged four to 11 anywhere in the country. Note that for delays in excess of half an hour – irrespective of the cause – you're entitled to a refund. Delays of 30 to 60 minutes warrant a 50% refund and delays of an hour or more a 100% refund.

International trains require passengers to buy tickets in advance and carry surcharges, but also may have cheap fares available in advance.

RAIL PASSES

There are several train passes for people living both inside and outside the Netherlands. These should be purchased before you arrive in the country. However, the passes don't offer good value even if you plan on a lot of train travel.

Eurail (www.eurail.com) Non-Europeans resident outside of Europe are eligible for a Benelux pass, good for several days' travel in a month on all trains within the Netherlands, Belgium and Luxembourg. It costs US$158/190/221/297 for three/four/five/eight days in 2nd class.

InterRail (www.interrail.eu) For Europeans resident in Europe, a Benelux pass good for three/four/six/eight days in one month costs €226/272/354/427.

Train Classes

The longest train journey in the Netherlands (Maastricht –Groningen) takes about 4¼ hours, but most trips are far shorter. Trains have 1st-class sections, but these are often little different from the 2nd-class areas and, given the short journeys, not worth the extra cost.

That said, 1st class can be worth the extra money during busy periods when seats in 2nd class are oversubscribed.

Train Types

In descending order of speed:

Thalys (www.thalys.com) Operates French TGV-style high-speed trains from Amsterdam, Schiphol and Rotterdam south to Belgium and Paris. Trains are plush and have wi-fi. Dynamic pricing, making advance reservations essential to score the lowest fare.

ICE (Intercity Express; www.nsh ispeed.com) German fast trains from Amsterdam to Cologne and on to Frankfurt Airport and Frankfurt. Carries a surcharge for domestic riders; fares are likewise dynamic, ie a reflection of how far in advance you book.

Intercity The best non-high-speed domestic trains, with fixed fares. They run express past small stations on all major lines. Usually air-conditioned double-decker cars.

Sneltrain (Fast Train) Not an Intercity but not as slow as a *stoptrein*. May not be air-conditioned.

Stoptrein (Stop Train) Never misses a stop, never gets up to speed. Some have no toilets.

Language

Dutch has around 20 million speakers world-wide. As a member of the Germanic language family, Dutch has many similarities with English.

The pronunciation of Dutch is fairly straightforward. It distinguishes between long and short vowels, which can affect the meaning of words, for example, *man* (man) and *maan* (moon). Also note that aw is pronounced as in 'law', eu as the 'u' in 'nurse', ew as the 'ee' in 'see' (with rounded lips), oh as the 'o' in 'note', öy as the 'er y' (without the 'r') in 'her year', and uh as in 'ago'.

The consonants are pretty simple to pronounce too. Note that kh is a throaty sound, similar to the 'ch' in the Scottish *loch*, r is trilled and zh is pronounced as the 's' in 'pleasure'. This said, if you read our coloured pronunciation guides as if they were English, you'll be understood just fine. The stressed syllables are indicated with italics.

Where relevant, both polite and informal options in Dutch are included, indicated with 'pol' and 'inf' respectively.

BASICS

Hello.	*Dag./Hallo.*	dakh/ha·*loh*
Goodbye.	*Dag.*	dakh
Yes./No.	*Ja./Nee.*	yaa/ney
Please.	*Alstublieft.* (pol)	al·stew·*bleeft*
	Alsjeblieft. (inf)	a·shuh·*bleeft*
Thank you.	*Dank u/je.* (pol/inf)	dangk ew/yuh

WANT MORE?

For in-depth language information and handy phrases, check out Lonely Planet's *Dutch Phrasebook*. You'll find it at **shop.lonelyplanet.com**, or you can buy Lonely Planet's iPhone phrasebooks at the Apple App Store.

| You're welcome. | *Graag gedaan.* | khraakh khuh·*daan* |
| Excuse me. | *Excuseer mij.* | eks·kew·*zeyr* mey |

How are you?
Hoe gaat het met u/jou? (pol/inf) — hoo khaat huht met ew/yaw

Fine. And you?
Goed. — khoot
En met u/jou? (pol/inf) — en met ew/yaw

What's your name?
Hoe heet u/je? (pol/inf) — hoo heyt ew/yuh

My name is ...
Ik heet ... — ik heyt ...

Do you speak English?
Spreekt u Engels? — spreykt ew *eng*·uhls

I don't understand.
Ik begrijp het niet. — ik buh·*khreyp* huht neet

ACCOMMODATION

Do you have a ... room?	*Heeft u een ...?*	heyft ew uhn ...
single	*éénpersoons-kamer*	eyn·puhr·sohns·kaa·muhr
double	*tweepersoons-kamer met een dubbel bed*	twey·puhr·sohns·kaa·muhr met uhn du·buhl bet
twin	*tweepersoons-kamer met lits jumeaux*	twey·puhr·sohns·kaa·muhr met lee zhew·*moh*

How much is it per ...?	*Hoeveel kost het per ...?*	hoo·*veyl* kost huht puhr ...
night	*nacht*	nakht
person	*persoon*	puhr·*sohn*

Is breakfast included?
Is het ontbijt inbegrepen? — is huht ont·*beyt* in·buh·khrey·puhn

bathroom	badkamer	bat·kaa·muhr
bed and breakfast	gasten-kamer	khas·tuhn·kaa·muhr
campsite	camping	kem·ping
guesthouse	pension	pen·syon
hotel	hotel	hoh·tel
window	raam	raam
youth hostel	jeugdherberg	yeukht·her·berkh

DIRECTIONS

Where's the ...?
Waar is ...? — waar is ...

How far is it?
Hoe ver is het? — hoo ver is huht

What's the address?
Wat is het adres? — wat is huht a·dres

Can you please write it down?
Kunt u dat alstublieft opschrijven? — kunt ew dat al·stew·bleeft op·skhrey·vuhn

Can you show me (on the map)?
Kunt u het mij tonen (op de kaart)? — kunt ew huht mey toh·nuhn (op duh kaart)

at the corner	op de hoek	op duh hook
at the traffic lights	bij de verkeers-lichten	bey duh vuhr·keyrs·likh·tuhn
behind	achter	akh·tuhr
in front of	voor	vohr
left	links	lingks
near (to)	dicht bij	dikht bey
next to	naast	naast
opposite	tegenover	tey·khuhn·oh·vuhr
straight ahead	rechtdoor	rekh·dohr
right	rechts	rekhs

EATING & DRINKING

What would you recommend?
Wat kan u aanbevelen? — wat kan ew aan·buh·vey·luhn

What's in that dish?
Wat zit er in dat gerecht? — wat zit uhr in dat khuh·rekht

I'd like the menu, please.
Ik wil graag een menu. — ik wil khraakh uhn me·new

Delicious!
Heerlijk/Lekker! — heyr·luhk/le·kuhr

Cheers!
Proost! — prohst

Please bring the bill.
Mag ik de rekening alstublieft? — makh ik duh rey·kuh·ning al·stew·bleeft

KEY PATTERNS

To get by in Dutch, mix and match these simple patterns with words of your choice:

When's (the next bus)?
Hoe laat gaat (de volgende bus)? — hoo laat khaat (duh vol·khun·duh bus)

Where's (the station)?
Waar is (het station)? — waar is (huht sta·syon)

I'm looking for (a hotel).
Ik ben op zoek naar (een hotel). — ik ben op zook naar (uhn hoh·tel)

Do you have (a map)?
Heeft u (een kaart)? — heyft ew (uhn kaart)

Is there (a toilet)?
Is er (een toilet)? — is uhr (uhn twa·let)

I'd like (the menu).
Ik wil graag (een menu). — ik wil khraakh (uhn me·new)

I'd like to (hire a car).
Ik wil graag (een auto huren). — ik wil khraakh (uhn aw·toh hew·ruhn)

Can I (enter)?
Kan ik (binnengaan)? — kan ik (bi·nuhn·khaan)

Could you please (help me)?
Kunt u alstublieft (helpen)? — kunt ew al·stew·bleeft (hel·puhn)

Do I have to (get a visa)?
Moet ik (een visum hebben)? — moot ik (uhn vee·zum he·buhn)

I'd like to reserve a table for ...	Ik wil graag een tafel voor ... reserveren.	ik wil khraakh uhn taa·fuhl vohr ... rey·ser·vey·ruhn
(two) people	(twee) personen	(twey) puhr·soh·nuhn
(eight) o'clock	(acht) uur	(akht) ewr

I don't eat ...	Ik eet geen ...	ik eyt kheyn ...
eggs	eieren	ey·yuh·ruhn
fish	vis	vis
(red) meat	(rood) vlees	(roht) vleys
nuts	noten	noh·tuhn

Key Words

bar	bar	bar
bottle	fles	fles
breakfast	ontbijt	ont·beyt
cafe	café	ka·fey
cold	koud	kawt
dinner	avondmaal	aa·vont·maal

drink list	drankkaart	drang·kaart
fork	vork	vork
glass	glas	khlas
grocery store	kruidenier	kröy·duh·neer
hot	heet	heyt
knife	mes	mes
lunch	middagmaal	mi·dakh·maal
market	markt	markt
menu	menu	me·new
plate	bord	bort
pub	kroeg	krookh
restaurant	restaurant	res·toh·rant
spicy	pikant	pee·kant
spoon	lepel	ley·puhl
vegetarian (food)	vegetarisch	vey·khey·taa·ris
with/without	met/zonder	met/zon·duhr

Meat & Fish

beef	rundvlees	runt·vleys
chicken	kip	kip
duck	eend	eynt
fish	vis	vis
herring	haring	haa·ring
lamb	lamsvlees	lams·vleys
lobster	kreeft	kreyft
meat	vlees	vleys
mussels	mosselen	mo·suh·luhn
oysters	oester	oos·tuhr
pork	varkensvlees	var·kuhns·vleys
prawn	steurgarnaal	steur·khar·naal
salmon	zalm	zalm
scallops	kammosselen	ka·mo·suh·luhn
shrimps	garnalen	khar·naa·luhn
squid	inktvis	ingkt·vis
trout	forel	fo·rel
tuna	tonijn	toh·neyn
turkey	kalkoen	kal·koon
veal	kalfsvlees	kalfs·vleys

Question Words

How?	Hoe?	hoo
What?	Wat?	wat
When?	Wanneer?	wa·neyr
Where?	Waar?	waar
Who?	Wie?	wee
Why?	Waarom?	waa·rom

Fruit & Vegetables

apple	appel	a·puhl
banana	banaan	ba·naan
beans	bonen	boh·nuhm
berries	bessen	be·suhn
cabbage	kool	kohl
capsicum	paprika	pa·pree·ka
carrot	wortel	wor·tuhl
cauliflower	bloemkool	bloom·kohl
cucumber	komkommer	kom·ko·muhr
fruit	fruit	fröyt
grapes	druiven	dröy·vuhn
lemon	citroen	see·troon
lentils	linzen	lin·zuhn
mushrooms	paddestoelen	pa·duh·stoo·luhn
nuts	noten	noh·tuhn
onions	uien	öy·yuhn
orange	sinaasappel	see·naas·a·puhl
peach	perzik	per·zik
peas	erwtjes	erw·chus
pineapple	ananas	a·na·nas
plums	pruimen	pröy·muhn
potatoes	aardappels	aart·a·puhls
spinach	spinazie	spee·naa·zee
tomatoes	tomaten	toh·maa·tuhn
vegetables	groenten	khroon·tuhn

Other

bread	brood	broht
butter	boter	boh·tuhr
cheese	kaas	kaas
eggs	eieren	ey·yuh·ruhn
honey	honing	hoh·ning
ice	ijs	eys
jam	jam	zhem
noodles	noedels	noo·duhls
oil	olie	oh·lee
pastry	gebak	khuh·bak
pepper	peper	pey·puhr
rice	rijst	reyst
salt	zout	zawt
soup	soep	soop
soy sauce	sojasaus	soh·ya·saws
sugar	suiker	söy·kuhr
vinegar	azijn	a·zeyn

Drinks

beer	*bier*	beer
coffee	*koffie*	ko·fee
juice	*sap*	sap
milk	*melk*	melk
red wine	*rode wijn*	roh·duh weyn
soft drink	*frisdrank*	fris·drangk
tea	*thee*	tey
water	*water*	waa·tuhr
white wine	*witte wijn*	wi·tuh weyn

EMERGENCIES

Help!
Help!   help

Leave me alone!
Laat me met rust!   laat muh met rust

Call a doctor!
Bel een dokter!   bel uhn dok·tuhr

Call the police!
Bel de politie!   bel duh poh·leet·see

There's been an accident.
Er is een ongeluk gebeurd.   uhr is uhn on·khuh·luk khuh·beurt

I'm lost.
Ik ben verdwaald.   ik ben vuhr·dwaalt

I'm sick.
Ik ben ziek.   ik ben zeek

It hurts here.
Hier doet het pijn.   heer doot huht peyn

Where are the toilets?
Waar zijn de toiletten?   waar zeyn duh twa·le·tuhn

I'm allergic to (antibiotics).
Ik ben allergisch voor (antibiotica).   ik ben a·ler·khees vohr (an·tee·bee·yoh·tee·ka)

SHOPPING & SERVICES

I'd like to buy ...
Ik wil graag ... kopen.   ik wil khraakh ... koh·puhn

I'm just looking.
Ik kijk alleen maar.   ik keyk a·leyn maar

Can I look at it?
Kan ik het even zien?   kan ik huht ey·vuhn zeen

Do you have any others?
Heeft u nog andere?   heyft ew nokh an·duh·ruh

How much is it?
Hoeveel kost het?   hoo·veyl kost huht

That's too expensive.
Dat is te duur.   dat is tuh dewr

Can you lower the price?
Kunt u wat van de prijs afdoen?   kunt ew wat van duh preys af·doon

Signs

Ingang	Entrance
Uitgang	Exit
Open	Open
Gesloten	Closed
Inlichtingen	Information
Verboden	Prohibited
Toiletten	Toilets
Heren	Men
Dames	Women

There's a mistake in the bill.
Er zit een fout in de rekening.   uhr zit uhn fawt in duh rey·kuh·ning

ATM	*pin-automaat*	pin·aw·toh·maat
foreign exchange	*wisselkantoor*	wi·suhl·kan·tohr
post office	*postkantoor*	post·kan·tohr
shopping centre	*winkel-centrum*	wing·kuhl·sen·trum
tourist office	*VVV*	vey·vey·vey

TIME & DATES

What time is it?
Hoe laat is het?   hoo laat is huht

It's (10) o'clock.
Het is (tien) uur.   huht is (teen) ewr

Half past (10).
Half (elf).   half (elf)
(lit: half eleven)

am (morning)	*'s ochtends*	sokh·tuhns
pm (afternoon)	*'s middags*	smi·dakhs
pm (evening)	*'s avonds*	saa·vonts

yesterday	*gisteren*	khis·tuh·ruhn
today	*vandaag*	van·daakh
tomorrow	*morgen*	mor·khuhn

Monday	*maandag*	maan·dakh
Tuesday	*dinsdag*	dins·dakh
Wednesday	*woensdag*	woons·dakh
Thursday	*donderdag*	don·duhr·dakh
Friday	*vrijdag*	vrey·dakh
Saturday	*zaterdag*	zaa·tuhr·dakh
Sunday	*zondag*	zon·dakh
January	*januari*	ya·new·waa·ree
February	*februari*	fey·brew·waa·ree

March	maart	maart
April	april	a·pril
May	mei	mey
June	juni	yew·nee
July	juli	yew·lee
August	augustus	aw·khus·tus
September	september	sep·tem·buhr
October	oktober	ok·toh·buhr
November	november	noh·vem·buhr
December	december	dey·sem·buhr

TRANSPORT

Public Transport

Is this the ... to (the left bank)?	Is dit de ... naar (de linker-oever)?	is dit duh ... naar (duh ling·kuhr·oo·vuhr)
ferry	veerboot	veyr·boht
metro	metro	mey·troh
tram	tram	trem
platform	perron	pe·ron
timetable	dienst-regeling	deenst-rey·khuh·ling
When's the ... (bus)?	Hoe laat gaat de ... (bus)?	hoo laat khaat duh ... (bus)

Numbers		
1	één	eyn
2	twee	twey
3	drie	dree
4	vier	veer
5	vijf	veyf
6	zes	zes
7	zeven	zey·vuhn
8	acht	akht
9	negen	ney·khuhn
10	tien	teen
20	twintig	twin·tikh
30	dertig	der·tikh
40	veertig	feyr·tikh
50	vijftig	feyf·tikh
60	zestig	ses·tikh
70	zeventig	sey·vuhn·tikh
80	tachtig	takh·tikh
90	negentig	ney·khuhn·tikh
100	honderd	hon·duhrt
1000	duizend	döy·zuhnt

first	eerste	eyr·stuh
last	laatste	laat·stuh
next	volgende	vol·khun·duh

A ticket to ..., please.
Een kaartje naar ... graag. — uhn kaar·chuh naar ... khraakh

What time does it leave?
Hoe laat vertrekt het? — hoo laat vuhr·trekt huht

Does it stop at ...?
Stopt het in ...? — stopt huht in ...

What's the next stop?
Welk is de volgende halte? — welk is duh vol·khun·duh hal·tuh

I'd like to get off at ...
Ik wil graag in ... uitstappen. — ik wil khraak in ... öyt·sta·puhn

Is this taxi available?
Is deze taxi vrij? — is dey·zuh tak·see vrey

Please take me to ...
Breng me alstublieft naar ... — breng muh al·stew·bleeft naar ...

Cycling

I'd like ...	Ik wil graag ...	ik wil khraakh ...
my bicycle repaired	mijn fiets laten herstellen	meyn feets laa·tuhn her·ste·luhn
to hire a bicycle	een fiets huren	uhn feets hew·ruhn

I'd like to hire a ...	Ik wil graag een ... huren.	ik wil khraakh uhn ... hew·ruhn
basket	mandje	man·chuh
child seat	kinderzitje	kin·duhr·zi·chuh
helmet	helm	helm

Do you have bicycle parking?
Heeft u parking voor fietsen? — heyft ew par·king vohr feet·suhn

Can we get there by bike?
Kunnen we er met de fiets heen? — ku·nuhn wuh uhr met duh feets heyn

I have a puncture.
Ik heb een lekke band. — ik hep uhn le·kuh bant

bicycle path	fietspad	feets·pat
bicycle pump	fietspomp	feets·pomp
bicycle repairman	fietsenmaker	feet·suhn·maa·kuhr
bicycle stand	fietsenrek	feet·suhn·rek

GLOSSARY

abdij – abbey

ANWB – Dutch automobile association

apotheek – chemist/pharmacy

benzine – petrol/gasoline

bevrijding – liberation

bibliotheek – library

bos – woods or forest

botter – type of 19th-century fishing boat

broodje – bread roll (with filling)

bruin café – brown *café*; traditional drinking establishment

buurt – neighbourhood

café – pub, bar; also known as kroeg

coffeeshop – cafe authorised to sell cannabis

eetcafé cafes (pubs) serving meals

fiets – bicycle

fietsenstalling – secure bicycle storage

fietspad – bicycle path

gemeente – municipal, municipality

gezellig – convivial, cosy

GVB – Gemeentevervoerbedrijf; Amsterdam municipal transport authority

GWK – Grenswisselkantoren; official currency-exchange offices

haven – port

hof – courtyard

hofje – almshouse or series of buildings around a small courtyard, also known as begijnhof

hoofd – literally 'head', but in street names it often means 'main'

hunebedden – prehistoric rock masses purportedly used as burial chambers

jenever – Dutch gin; also genever

kaas – cheese

koffiehuis – espresso bar; cafe (as distinct from a coffeeshop)

klooster – cloister, religious house

koningin – queen

koninklijk – royal

kunst – art

kwartier – quarter

LF routes – landelijke fietsroutes; national (long-distance) bike routes

loodvrij – unleaded (petrol/gasoline)

markt – town square; market

meer – lake

molen – windmill; mill

NS – Nederlandse Spoorwegen; national railway company

OV-chipkaart – fare card for Dutch public transit

paleis – palace

polder – strips of farmland separated by canals

postbus – post office box

Randstad – literally 'rim-city'; the urban agglomeration including Amsterdam, Utrecht, Rotterdam and Den Haag

Rijk(s-) – the State

scheepvaart – shipping

schouwburg – theatre

sluis – lock (for boats/ships)

spoor – train platform

stadhuis – town hall

stedelijk – civic, municipal

stichting – foundation, institute

strand – beach

terp – mound of packed mud in Friesland that served as a refuge during floods

treintaxi – taxi for train passengers

tuin – garden

tulp – tulip

verzet – resistance

Vlaams – Flemish

VVV – tourist information office

waag – old weigh-house

wadlopen – mudflat-walking

weeshuis – orphanage

werf – wharf, shipyard

winkel – shop

zaal – room, hall

zee – sea

ziekenhuis – hospital

Behind the Scenes

SEND US YOUR FEEDBACK

We love to hear from travellers – your comments keep us on our toes and help make our books better. Our well-travelled team reads every word on what you loved or loathed about this book. Although we cannot reply individually to your submissions, we always guarantee that your feedback goes straight to the appropriate authors, in time for the next edition. Each person who sends us information is thanked in the next edition – the most useful submissions are rewarded with a selection of digital PDF chapters.

Visit **lonelyplanet.com/contact** to submit your updates and suggestions or to ask for help. Our award-winning website also features inspirational travel stories, news and discussions.

Note: We may edit, reproduce and incorporate your comments in Lonely Planet products such as guidebooks, websites and digital products, so let us know if you don't want your comments reproduced or your name acknowledged. For a copy of our privacy policy visit lonelyplanet.com/privacy.

WRITER THANKS

Nicola Williams

A huge thanks to so many friends and professionals including: in Groningen, Sara van Geloven (editor-in-chief *Lonely Planet Magazine* NL), Eeflie Smit and Annebel Nillessen Blaauw (Marketing Groningen) and Nick Nijboer (Mr Mofongo); in Arnhem, cycling queen Charlie Johnson, adopted local Louise Henstridge (and Sally Dibden for putting me in touch); in Nijmegen, Beppie (VVV) and Nico de Mol (Visit Holland); in Leeuwarden, Mariska and Eliszabeth for the lowdown on Frisian culture; in Sneek, Yorkshireman-turned-Frisian distiller Steve Sibson (Weduwe Joustra) and in Leeuwarden, Femke.

Abigail Blasi

A big thanks to Daniel Fahey for commissioning me, and Catherine Le Nevez for her support. A massive *dank je* to Jo Dufay for sharing her city knowledge and books, to Wouter Steenhuisen and Geerte Udo at iAmsterdam, to Esther Nelsey for local recommendations, and to Luca, Gabriel, Benjamin and Alessia for coming along for the ride.

Mark Elliott

A very special thank you to the wonderful Sally Cobham for love, company and so much human insight. En route, many thanks also to Lucile, Eveline and Niels in Utrecht; Jennick, Paul, Matt and family at Roermond; Hants van Gils in Breda; Robert Kingsbury in Maasbracht; Sam and Natalie at Koningshoeven; Aimée in Tilburg; Marie-Louise in Heusden; Hans, Anja and Olga at Philips (Eindhoven); Adrien, Joos, Alette, Lisette and 'Blackbird' in Den Bosch; and Simone, Karen and Jan.

Catherine Le Nevez

Hartelijk bedankt first and foremost to Julian, and to everyone in Amsterdam, Haarlem and North Holland and beyond who provided insights, inspiration and good times during this update and over the years. A huge thanks too to Destination Editor Daniel Fahey and my Netherlands co-authors, and everyone at LP. As ever, *merci encore* to my parents, brother, *belle-sœur*, *neveu* and *nièce*.

Virginia Maxwell

In the Netherlands, many thanks to Kim Heinen, Annemieke Loef, Renske Satijn, Nina Swaep and Eveline Zoutendijk. At LP's London office, thanks to Dan Fahey and Jennifer Carey. At home in Melbourne, thanks and much love to Peter and Max Handsaker.

ACKNOWLEDGEMENTS

Climate map data adapted from Peel MC, Finlayson BL & McMahon TA (2007) 'Updated World Map of the Köppen-Geiger Climate Classification', Hydrology and Earth System Sciences, 11, 1633-44.

Cover photograph: ZWooden Shoes wall in Zaanse Schans, North Holland, Sopotnicki/Shutterstock ©

THIS BOOK

This 8th edition of Lonely Planet's *The Netherlands* guidebook was curated by Nicola Williams, and researched and written by Nicola, Abigail Blasi, Mark Elliott, Catherine Le Nevez and Virginia Maxwell. Previous editions were written by Catherine and Daniel C Schechter, and Ryan Ver Berkmoes and Karla Zimmerman. This guidebook was produced by the following:

Destination Editor: Daniel Fahey

Senior Product Editors: Grace Dobell, Sandie Kestell, Genna Patterson

Product Editors: Ronan Abayawickrema, Lauren O'Connell

Regional Senior Cartographer: Mark Griffiths

Cartographers: James Leversha, Julie Sheridan

Cover Researcher: Brendan Dempsey-Spencer

Book Designer: Gwen Cotter, María Virginia Moreno

Assisting Editors: Michelle Bennett, Katie Connolly, Andrea Dobbin, Paul Harding, Kellie Langdon, Charlotte Orr, Fionnuala Twomey, Sam Wheeler

Thanks to Jennifer Carey, Hannah Cartmel, Melanie Dankel, Karen Henderson, Amy Lynch, Claire Rourke, James Smart, Angela Tinson

Index

Map Pages **000**
Photo Pages **000**

Map Legend

Sights
- Beach
- Bird Sanctuary
- Buddhist
- Castle/Palace
- Christian
- Confucian
- Hindu
- Islamic
- Jain
- Jewish
- Monument
- Museum/Gallery/Historic Building
- Ruin
- Shinto
- Sikh
- Taoist
- Winery/Vineyard
- Zoo/Wildlife Sanctuary
- Other Sight

Activities, Courses & Tours
- Bodysurfing
- Diving
- Canoeing/Kayaking
- Course/Tour
- Sento Hot Baths/Onsen
- Skiing
- Snorkelling
- Surfing
- Swimming/Pool
- Walking
- Windsurfing
- Other Activity

Sleeping
- Sleeping
- Camping
- Hut/Shelter

Eating
- Eating

Drinking & Nightlife
- Drinking & Nightlife
- Cafe

Entertainment
- Entertainment

Shopping
- Shopping

Information
- Bank
- Embassy/Consulate
- Hospital/Medical
- Internet
- Police
- Post Office
- Telephone
- Toilet
- Tourist Information
- Other Information

Geographic
- Beach
- Gate
- Hut/Shelter
- Lighthouse
- Lookout
- Mountain/Volcano
- Oasis
- Park
- Pass
- Picnic Area
- Waterfall

Population
- Capital (National)
- Capital (State/Province)
- City/Large Town
- Town/Village

Transport
- Airport
- Border crossing
- Bus
- Cable car/Funicular
- Cycling
- Ferry
- Metro station
- Monorail
- Parking
- Petrol station
- S-Bahn/Subway station
- Taxi
- T-bane/Tunnelbana station
- Train station/Railway
- Tram
- U-Bahn/Underground station
- Other Transport

Routes
- Tollway
- Freeway
- Primary
- Secondary
- Tertiary
- Lane
- Unsealed road
- Road under construction
- Plaza/Mall
- Steps
- Tunnel
- Pedestrian overpass
- Walking Tour
- Walking Tour detour
- Path/Walking Trail

Boundaries
- International
- State/Province
- Disputed
- Regional/Suburb
- Marine Park
- Cliff
- Wall

Hydrography
- River, Creek
- Intermittent River
- Canal
- Water
- Dry/Salt/Intermittent Lake
- Reef

Areas
- Airport/Runway
- Beach/Desert
- Cemetery (Christian)
- Cemetery (Other)
- Glacier
- Mudflat
- Park/Forest
- Sight (Building)
- Sportsground
- Swamp/Mangrove

Note: Not all symbols displayed above appear on the maps in this book

OUR STORY

A beat-up old car, a few dollars in the pocket and a sense of adventure. In 1972 that's all Tony and Maureen Wheeler needed for the trip of a lifetime – across Europe and Asia overland to Australia. It took several months, and at the end – broke but inspired – they sat at their kitchen table writing and stapling together their first travel guide, *Across Asia on the Cheap*. Within a week they'd sold 1500 copies. Lonely Planet was born.

Today, Lonely Planet has offices in the US, Ireland and China, with a network of over 2000 contributors in every corner of the globe. We share Tony's belief that 'a great guidebook should do three things: inform, educate and amuse'.

OUR WRITERS

Nicola Williams

Central Netherlands, Friesland (Fryslân), Northeastern Netherlands Border hopping is way of life for British writer, runner, foodie, art aficionado and mum-of-three Nicola, who has lived in a French village on the southern side of Lake Geneva for more than a decade. Nicola has authored more than 50 guidebooks for Lonely Planet, on destinations including Paris, Provence, Rome, Tuscany, France, Italy and Switzerland. Twitter/Instagram: @tripalong. Nicola also wrote the Plan Your Trip and Understand sections of this book.

Abigail Blasi

Amsterdam A freelance travel writer, Abigail has lived and worked in London, Rome, Hong Kong, and Copenhagen. Lonely Planet has sent her to India, Egypt, Tunisia, Mauritania, Mali, Italy, Portugal, Malta and around Britain. She writes regularly for newspapers and magazines, such as the *Independent*, the *Telegraph*, and *Lonely Planet Traveller*. She has three children and they often come along for the ride. Twitter/Instagram: @abiwhere

Mark Elliott

Maastricht & Southeastern Netherlands, Utrecht Mark had already lived and worked on five continents when, in the pre-internet dark ages, he started writing travel guides. He has since authored (or co-authored) around 60 books, including dozens for Lonely Planet. He also acts as a travel consultant, occasional tour leader, video presenter, speaker, interviewer and blues harmonica player.

Catherine Le Nevez

Amsterdam, Haarlem & North Holland Catherine's wanderlust kicked in when she roadtripped across Europe from her Parisian base aged four, and she's been hitting the road at every opportunity since, travelling to around 60 countries. Over the past dozen years she's written scores of Lonely Planet guides and articles, covering Paris, France, Europe and far beyond. Her work has also appeared in numerous online and print publications.

Virginia Maxwell

Rotterdam & South Holland Although based in Australia, Virginia spends at least half of her year updating Lonely Planet coverage across the globe, including destinations such as Spain, Italy, Turkey, Syria, Lebanon, Israel, Egypt, Morocco, Tunisia, Finland, Bali, Armenia and the Netherlands. Follow her: maxwellvirginia on Instagram and Twitter.

Published by Lonely Planet Global Limited
CRN 554153
8th edition – Jan 2022
ISBN 97 8 17886 80561
© Lonely Planet 2022   Photographs © as indicated 2022
10 9 8 7 6 5 4 3 2 1
Printed in China